Marriages of
GRANVILLE COUNTY, NORTH CAROLINA

1753–1868

Marriages of
GRANVILLE COUNTY, NORTH CAROLINA

1753-1868

Compiled by
BRENT H. HOLCOMB

Indexed by Patti Matulonis

CLEARFIELD

Reprinted for
Clearfield Company, Inc. by
Genealogical Publishing Co., Inc.
Baltimore, Maryland
1993, 1997, 2003

Copyright © 1981
Genealogical Publishing Co., Inc.
Baltimore, Maryland
All Rights Reserved
Library of Congress Catalogue Card Number 81-81769
International Standard Book Number 0-8063-0945-8
Made in the United States of America

INTRODUCTION

GRANVILLE COUNTY was formed in 1746 from Edgecombe County, but the first extant marriage bond dates from the year 1753. Orange County was formed in part from Granville County in 1752; Bute County (later Warren and Franklin counties) was formed from Granville in 1764. In the eighteenth century Granville County was a gateway for migration to the South and West, both for people coming from Pennsylvania and the Valley of Virginia and for people coming from southside and eastern Virginia.

This volume contains abstracts of all extant marriage bonds for Granville County. The original bonds are at the courthouse in Oxford, North Carolina, and these abstracts were made from microfilm copies of the bonds. There are within these bonds occasional lists of marriages performed by justices and ministers, and as some of these marriages have not been recorded elsewhere they are included here. In some cases both bonds and returns of officiants have survived, and in such cases the date of marriage indicated on the return is so noted after the abstract of the marriage bond. In some cases only a license is extant; therefore, no bondsman's name will appear in the abstract.

The marriage bond law was enacted in 1741 and remained in force until 1868. Inter-racial marriages were prohibited by law. In 1851 the clerk of the county court was required to keep a register of marriages performed by license (issued with the bond). The bonds alone are not proof that a marriage took place, only that a marriage was intended. Marriages could also be performed after publication of banns, and therefore no bond, license, or other official record of the marriage was kept.

BRENT H. HOLCOMB, C. A. L. S.
Columbia, South Carolina

Abbreviations

bm — bondsman
m — married
wit — witness

GRANVILLE MARRIAGES, 1753-1868

Abbet, Bennett & Sally Weaver, 16 Nov 1815; James Ball, bm; Richd. Sneed, wit.

Abbot, William & Martha Gill, 29 Dec 1834; L. Gilliam, bm.

Abbott, J. R. & Miss L. R. Edwards, 17 Dec 1866; m 20 Dec 1866 by Pro. A. Jones, J. P.

Abbott, Philip G. & Miss Laura Edwards, 22 Feb 1861; m 22 Feb 1861 by William B. Mann, J. P.

Adams, Benjamin & Frances Jones, 18 July 1814; Thornberry Green, bm; W. M. Sneed, wit.

Adams, Isaac & Wilmouth Lanier, 11 Feb 1824; Elijah Hester, bm; S. K. Sneed, wit.

Adams, John & Lucy Haladay, 3 Jan 1817; Wyatt Cannady, bm; Horace A. Burton, wit.

Adams, John P. & Sarah K. Forsythe, 26 June 1852; R. W. Lassiter, bm; m 28 June 1852 by Wm. H. Lyon, J. P.

Adams, Nathaniel, son of Edmond & Lucy Adams, & Mary Harris, daughter of Robt & Martha Harris, 28 Dec 1867; m 28 Dec 1867 by J. F. Harris, J. P.

Adams, Thomas F., son of William & Mary Adams, & Phoebe Ann Flinn, daughter of James M. & Margaret Flinn, 11 Aug 1868; m 18 Aug 1868 by J. W. Wellons, M. G.

Adcock, Abner & Rachael Gooch, 29 Dec 1811; John Hawkins, bm; Step. Sneed, wit.

Adcock, Absalem & Elizabeth Smith, 2 Oct 1846; James M. Land, bm; J. M. Wiggins, wit.

Adcock, Andrew & Mary Sutton, 21 May 1792; Beverly Harris, bm; W. Norris, wit.

Adcock, Barnett & Judith Dameron, 12 Jan 1805; Jno Watters, bm; Jun. Sneed, wit.

Adcock, Burgess & Catharine Wilkerson, 27 Dec 1825; Bowling Day, bm; A. M. Henderson, wit.

Adcock, Caleb & Louisa Moss, 4 March 1851; Elijah Fuller, bm; m 8 July 1852 by Wm. M. Blackwell, J. P.

Adcock, David & Salley Fraizer, 6 Sept 1815; Absolem D. Parrish, bm; W. M. Sneed, wit.

GRANVILLE MARRIAGES 1753-1868

Adcock, David & Synthia Elexson, 17 Jan 1839; L. Beasley Jr., bm.

Adcock, David & Martha Wooten (or Ooten), 19 Oct 1848; S. J. Jackson, bm.

Adcock, Edward & Tabitha White, 4 July 1780; Richard Brinkly, bm.

Adcock, Elvis H. & Sally H. Moss, 19 Aug 1843; Alex. Wood, bm; Wm. H. Whitfield, wit.

Adcock, Frederick & Fanny Foard, 17 Nov 1813; Arhey Partee, bm; J. P. Sneed, wit.

Adcock, George & Elizabeth Meadows, 27 Dec 1809; William Adcock, bm; Tho. Cooke, wit.

Adcock, Green & Lucy Ann Dickerson, 5 March 1846; Jos. McGehee, bm.

Adcock, Henderson & Lucy Edwards, 17 Dec 1838; William Mangum, bm.

Adcock, Henry C. & Sabriner Ellis, 6 May 1865; Miles S. Wall, bm.

Adcock, J. N. & Sarah J. Pucket, 4 Feb 1867; B. E. Humphris, bm; m 14 Feb 1867 by W. Overbey.

Adcock, James & Celia McFarling, 25 Aug 1837; Jno Jones, bm; Jas. M. Wiggins, wit.

Adcock, James W. & Julia Wall, 18 Oct 1856; Hugh A. M. Cadden, bm; m 19 Oct 1856 by J. M. Satterwhite, J. P.

Adcock, Jesse & Patsey Ross, 12 Jan 1799; Jacob Stem, bm; Step. Sneed, wit.

Adcock, John C. & Elizabeth Adcock, 20 Nov 1837; Jas. G. Lowrey, bm; S. G. Shearmon, wit.

Adcock, Joseph J. & Amanda P. Moss, 8 Sept 1853; A. Landis, bm; m 20 Oct 1853 by W. D. Allen, J. P.

Adcock, Linson & Sally Fletcher, 4 Dec 1794; David Parker, bm; H. Leawell, wit.

Adcock, Littleton & Lucretia Kimball, 28 Feb 1835; Elijah Meadors, bm; Benja. Kittrell, wit.

Adcock, Lovin & Ibby Russell, 13 Aug 1830; Willey Pollard, bm; David Laws, wit.

Adcock, Reaves & Martha Bynum, 26 Sept 1840; George Parrish, bm; J. M. Wiggins, wit.

Adcock, Stephen & Sarah Johnson, 5 Aug 1809; Wm. Adcock, bm; W. M. Sneed, wit.

Adcock, Thomas & Larceny M. Fowler, 24 Jan 1866; John G. Wheeler, bm; m 1 Feb 1866 by J. J. Lansdell, Min of the Gos.

Adcock, William & Polley Chadwick, 23 Aug 1813; Frederick Mason, bm; W. M. Sneed, wit.

GRANVILLE MARRIAGES 1753-1868

Adcock, William & Letha Harris, 23 Sept 1818; James Adcock, bm; S. K. Sneed, wit.

Adcock, Wm. & Elizabeth Johnston, 26 March 1803; Thos Henley, bm; Green Merritt, wit.

Adcock, William & Parthena Ann OBrien, 22 Aug 1854; Presley Williams, bm; A. Landis, wit; m 24 Aug 1854 by J. M. Satterwhite, J. P.

Adcock, William H. & Martha A. Bragg, 11 Jan 1856; James O. Mise(?), bm; m 17 Jan 1856 by W. D. Allen, J. P.

Add, Jacob & Leah Howard, 25 Dec 1866; m 27 Dec 1866 by B. D. Howard, J. P.

Adkinson, John & Betsey Smith, 8 May 1792; Benjamin Bradford, bm.

Ahem, Daniel J. & Mrs. Ellen R. Denman, 8 Dec 1865; Chs. L. Levett(?), bm; m 9 Dec 1865 by Joseph W. Murphy, Rector of Holy Innocents Church, Henderson.

Aikin, Joseph & Louisa Hobgood, 18 Nov 1859; W. T. Gooch, bm.

Akin, Benjamin F. & Mary E. Hester, m 2 April 1868 by John Tillett, minister of the Gospel.

Akin, Godfrey & Betsey Terry, 8 Jan 1793; William Terry, bm; W. Norwood, wit.

Akin, Isham & Zereviah Davis, 19 Jan 1789; Rowland Terry, bm; H. Potter, wit.

Akin, James & Ann Akin, 20 Aug 1783; John Brodie, bm; _____, wit.

Akin, James Jr. & Kissy Johnson, 8 Oct 1794; James Akin Sr., bm; H. Seawell, wit.

Akin, John & Phobe Norwood, 12 Sept 1817; Thomas Terry, bm; W. M. Sneed, wit.

Akin, John & Mary Coley, 25 Sept 1827; Isaac Adams, bm; S. K. Sneed, wit.

Akin, John & Mildred Burchett, 2 April 1857; John N. Gill, bm; m 22 April 1857 by R. B. Hester.

Akin, John A. & Ann M. Fleming, 16 Jan 1858; Robert H. Beck, bm; A. Landis, wit; m 24 Jan 1858 by T. D. Lyon, J. P.

Akin, Thomas & Betsey Tanner, 29 May 1827; Teakle Tanner, bm; Wm. H. Owen, wit.

Akin, Wm. & Mary Robertson, 10 Feb 1789; Robert Hargrove, bm; A. Henderson, wit.

Akin, William & Polley Nunn, 5 Aug 1797; Lewis Parrish, bm; Step. Sneed, wit.

Akin, William & Elizabeth Beck, 23 Oct 1821; John Landess, bm; S. K. Sneed, wit.

Akins, John & Susannah Frazer Davies, 8 Jan 1798; William Akin, bm; Step. Sneed, wit.

GRANVILLE MARRIAGES 1753-1868

Alexander, Charles & Sallie T. Latta, 22 Dec 1857; R. H. Kingsbury, bm; m 6 Jan 1858 by Wm. A. Smith, Minister of the Gospel M. E. Ch., South.

Alexander, Jacob & Milley Ridley, 3 Feb 1866; m 28 Feb 1866 by Maurice H. Vaughan, Rector St. Stephens Church, Oxford, N. C.; James Y. Landis, bm.

Alexander, John & Patsy Alexander, 15 Aug 1866.

Allen, Albert & Mary Perkinson, 11 Dec 1846; Wm. Paschall, bm; Jas. M. Wiggins, wit.

Allen, Ambrose & Rosa Gooch, 12 March 1867; Levi Gill, bm; A. Landis, wit; m 16 March 1867 by Benj. F. Jenkins.

Allen, Augustus A. & Mary H. Maben, 2 Nov 1854; J. C. Cooper, bm; m 2 Nov 1854 by Thos. U. Faucette.

Allen, Briant & Mary Ann Fouler, m 3 Jan 1860 by W. D. Allen, J. P.

Allen, Bryant & Susannah Allen, 14 Aug 1825; Archibald Huskey, bm; L. Gilliam, wit.

Allen, Bryant & Mary Ann Fowler, 3 Jan 1860; Johnathan Fuller, bm.

Allen, C. E. & Martha A. Royster, 25 June 1864; J. G. Jones, bm; m 29 June 1864 by J. W. Wellan, Min. of the Gospel.

Allen, Caswell & Frances Izzard, 4 Oct 1851; Wm. Champion, bm.

Allen, Charles & Fanny Garner, 8 Nov 1843; David Brogdon, bm; Wm. H. Whitfield, wit.

Allen, Charles & Panthea B. Boyd, 16 July 1855; A. Landis, bm.

Allen, Curtis & Susan Champion, 20 Oct 1842; Samuel Harris, bm; Wm. H. Whitfield, wit.

Allen, David & Sarah F. Webb, 25 Oct 1849; R. J. Mitchell, bm; A. Landis, wit.

Allen, David B. & Mary A. Montague, 17 Dec 1844; T. K. Hester, bm.

Allen, Drury & Rebecca Champion, 7 March 1809; Richard Champion, bm; W. M. Sneed, wit.

Allen, Elias, son of Zelpha Allen & Elizabeth A. Wilson, daughter of Sherard & Stacy Wilson, m 15 Jan 1868 by W. D. Allen, J. P.

Allen, Elijah & Susan Ross, 10 Oct 1863; Drury Estes, bm; m 11 Oct 1863 by W. D. Allen, J. P.

Allen, Erasmas & <u>P</u>issillar Allen, 5 Dec 1849; Jas. Blackly, bm.

Allen, Francis & Delphy Ann Adcock, 12 April 1847; William Paschell, bm; J. Brown Ferreby, wit.

Allen, Francis & Mary Ross, 2 Aug 1859; A. Davis, bm; m 13 Sept 1859 by Wm. D. Davis, J. P.

GRANVILLE MARRIAGES 1753-1868

Allen, Frank of color, son of Solomon & Phebe Allen, & Jane Smith, daughter of Vincent Smith, m 17 Dec 1867 by B. D. Howard, J. P.

Allen, Garland & Ruthy Bradford, 28 Nov 1806; William Jenkins, bm; W. M. Sneed, wit.

Allen, George & Abigail Johnston, 10 June 1786;. Cannon Cooper, bm.

Allen, Henderson & Harriet Mitchell, 18 Jan 1849; Wm. H. Short, bm; J. M. Wiggins, wit.

Allen, Henderson & Eveline Satterwhite, m 26 Aug 1866 by J. F. Harris, J. P.

Allen, Hinton J. & Harriet Weldon, 10 Feb 1841; Wm. J. Huskey, bm; J. M. Wiggins, wit.

Allen, Hoy & Susan Ann Overby, 10 Oct 1850; Thos. H. Rany, bm.

Allen, J. B. & Miss Julia Morgan, 25 Nov 1844; T. B. Baned(?), bm.

Allen, James & Elizabeth Brasfield, 23 Dec 1811; Garland Allen, bm; W. M. Sneed, wit.

Allen, James & Polly Stark, 11 July 1812; Nathaniel Williams, bm; Stephen D. Sneed, wit.

Allen, James & Elizabeth Jeter, 30 Dec 1814; Pascal Johnson, bm; W. M. Sneed, wit.

Allen, James & Barshabe Read, 22 May 1821; John Harris, bm; Jas. M. Wiggins, wit.

Allen, James & Dosha Clay, 24 April 1823; Allen Jeter, bm; Jas. M. Wiggins, wit.

Allen, James & Pully Hazwell, 21 Aug 1833; Stephen Harris, bm; S. Harris, wit.

Allen, James & Amarilla Morgan, 5 Sept 1837; A. Clements, bm; Jas. M. Wiggins, wit.

Allen, James & Priscillah Jackson, 19 Dec 1849; Allen Bridges, bm; A. Landis, wit; m by J. K. Cole, M. G.

Allen, James & Fannie Evans, of color, daughter of Malinda Evans, 9 July 1868; m 9 July 1868 by W. N. Harris, J. P.

Allen, James E. & Misanday D. Cannaday, 16 Dec 1835; Geo. Thompson Jr., bm; Benja. Kittrell, wit.

Allen, John & Gilley Medler, 26 March 1818; Major Jones, bm; W. M. Sneed, wit.

Allen, John & Lucy Preddy, 26 Jan 1824; William G. Bowen, bm; Wm. H. Owen, wit.

Allen, John & Isabella Green, 14 April 1865; Res. Russell, bm.

Allen, John & Cealy Perry (free people), 2 Aug 1866; m 4 Aug 1866 by M. J. Hunt.

GRANVILLE MARRIAGES 1753-1868

Allen, John of color, son of Miles White & Ann Allen & Margret Kerney of color, daughter of Adkin Qualls & Nancy Qualls, m 12 Oct 1867 by W. D. Allen, J. P.

Allen, Joseph & Frances Haswell, 5 Jan 1847; John T. Dew, bm; Jas. M. Wiggins, wit.

Allen, Josiah & Nancy White, 21 July 1794; Joshua White, bm; H. Seawell, wit.

Allen, Miles & Jinsey Bledsoe, 1 May 1810; Terrell B. Bledsoe, bm; W. M. Sneed, wit.

Allen, Nathan & Nancey Ratley, 16 Oct 1805; Joseph Bridges, bm; Jas. Sneed, wit.

Allen, Reddick & Emily Fuller, 9 Jan 1830; Allsey Fuller, bm; David Laws, wit.

Allen, Robert & Mary Garrett, freed people, 22 April 1867; m 22 April 1867 by J. P. Montague, M. G.

Allen, Robert, of color, son of Miles White & Ann Allen & Delila Rogers, daughter of Dessie Rogers & Charey Jenkins, m 29 March 1868 by W. D. Allen, J. P.

Allen, Robert B. & Caroline Mallory, 18 Feb 1851; D. L. Bullock, bm.

Allen, Samuel & Nilly Allen, 7 April 1845; Jas. F. Hicks, bm; Jesse Conyers(?), wit.

Allen, Solomon J. & Susan A. Downey, 13 Jan 1851; R. J. Devin, bm.

Allen, Squire & Nancy Slaughter, 15 Dec 1866; William Allen, bm; C. E. Landis, wit; m 15 Dec 1866 by B. D. Howard, J. P.

Allen, Thomas & Fanny Tayloe, 17 Jan 1816; James Lewis Jr., bm; Richd. Sneed, wit.

Allen, Thomas & Nancy Morris, 8 Feb 1831; Archd. Husky, bm; David Laws, wit.

Allen, Thos. A. & L. F. Allen, 15 Nov 1866; W. H. P. Jenkins, bm.

Allen, Thomas B. & Judith Bradford, 3 Dec 1821; James Thompson, bm; W. M. Sneed, wit.

Allen, Thomas B. & Emily N. Whitfield, 5 March 1860; Henry Hailey, bm; m 5 March 1860 by S. H. Cannady.

Allen, Turner & Tison Pearce, m 24 Sept 1866 by A. L. Davis, J. P.

Allen, William A. & Maria G. Hicks, 28 May 1849; Hy. Allen, bm; Jas. M. Wiggins, wit.

Allen, William D. & Emeline H. Allen, 22 March 1838; Jackson B. Bradford, wit.

Allen, William D. & Leveny Minnis, 5 Nov 1850; Henry Hailey, bm.

GRANVILLE MARRIAGES 1753-1868

Allen, William E., son of Chas. & Frances Allen, & Ann E. Byrd, daughter of Alex & Helen Byrd, m 9 Dec 1868 by B. B. Hester.

Allen, William H. & Frances Fuller, 2 Feb 1864; A. Landis, bm; m 2 Feb 1864 by Jas. J. Moore, J. P.

Allen, William N. & Frances E. Mayes, 18 March 1848; James J. Thomas, bm.

Allen, Willie & Jane Frazier, 17 Dec 1828; Archibald Huskey, bm; L. Gilliam, wit.

Allen, Woodson & Polley Ward, 11 Nov 1807; George Keith, bm; W. M. Sneed, wit.

Allen, Zachariah & Rebeccah Barnett, 21 Jan 1795; Step. Sneed, bm; Howel Morse, wit.

Alley, Albert H. & Martha Sarah Stanton, 28 Jan 1851; Jno. W. Edwards(?), bm; m 28 Jan 1851 by A. C. Harris, M. G.

Alley, Thomas J. & Mary B. Dent, 30 June 1865; W. H. Harris, bm; A. Landis, wit.

Allin, Champion & Lucy Roberts, 27 Dec 1784; John Champion, bm; Elisabeth Searcy, wit.

Allin, John & Bernulah Keeth, 12 ____ 1780; John Daniel, bm; Wm. Searcy, wit.

Allin, Reuben, of Wake County, & Elisabeth Jordan, 19 March 1775; Woodson Daniel, bm.

Allin, Robert & Armelia Howard, 26 Dec 1798; Smith Satterwhite, bm; M. Satterwhite, Jno. Taylor, wit.

Allin, William of Orange County, & Milley Morgan, 23 March 1778; Barnard Major of Wake County, bm; Bennet Searcy, wit.

Allison, James & Nansey Oglesey, 3 May 1796; John Allison, bm; Step. Sneed, wit.

Allison, James & Milly Whitfield, 16 Sept 1800; Richard Ogilvie, bm.

Allison, Robert & Elizabeth White, 29 July 1805; Leonard Cardwell, bm; Jas. Sneed, wit.

Alston, Absolem & Elizabeth Longmire, 2 Feb 1801; William Longmire, bm; P. Bullock, wit.

Alston, George & Elisabeth Mutter, 22 July 1806; Leonard Henderson, bm; Step. Sneed, wit.

Alston, John & Anne Hunt, 17 March 1760; Solomon Alston, bm; Jno. Bowie, wit.

Alston, Joseph R. & Susannah B. Hunt, 7 April 1858; Richard B. Hunt, bm; M. Bullock, wit; m 7 April 1858 by F. N. Shaley, Min. of the Gospel.

Alston, Richard & Margaret Stovall, freed people; m 22 April 1867 by John W. York.

GRANVILLE MARRIAGES 1753-1868

Amis, Alexander & Henrietta Lewis, 17 Feb 1840; William Royster Senr., bm; J. M. Wiggins, wit.

Amis, John & Polley Knight, 2 Oct 1797; Woodson Knight, bm; Step. Sneed, wit.

Amis, John & Mary Hunt, 21 July 1824; D. E. Young, bm.

Amis, John Junr. & Lucy Bryant, 3 March 1821; Asa Parham, bm; W. M. Sneed, wit.

Amis, Jonathan D. & Eliza Hill, 3 Sept 1820; Young Montague Junr., bm; Step. K. Sneed, wit.

Amis, Joseph & Elizabeth Downes, 3 March 1818; Rhodes N. Herndon, bm; A. Tomlinson, wit.

Amis, L. E. & Bettie R. Scott, 11 Feb 1867; m 12 Feb 1867 by E. Hines; J. S. Amis, bm.

Amis, Lewis & Elisabeth Knight, 25 Dec 1781; William Davis, bm; Bennet Searcy, wit.

Amis, Lewis & Elizabeth Amis, 19 Dec 1836; Howell G. Pittard, bm; J. M. Wiggins, wit.

Amis, Lewis & Marlta Amis, 8 Oct 1844; Joseph W. Barnett, bm; T. B. Barnett, wit.

Amis, Lewis & Martha I. Daniel, 1 June 1852; m by G. W. Ferrill, Minister of the Gospel.

Amis, Lewis E. & Rosa A. Amis, 29 Oct 1859; A. Landis, bm; m 31 Oct 1859 by E. Hines, M. G.

Amis, Madison J. & Candis H. Lumley, 25 Oct 1841; D. B. Hilliard, bm; Richd. Sneed, wit.

Amis, William & Judith Knight, 21 Jan 1789; John Raven, bm; A. Henderson, C. C., wit.

Amis, William & Elizabeth Puryear, 3 Dec 1804; John Amis, bm; E. W. Parham, wit.

Amis, William & Ann White, 28 Jan 1833; John Clarcke, bm; David Laws, wit.

Anderson, Abel & Susannah Evins, 23 May 1804; Benj. Mitchell, bm; E. W. Parham, wit.

Anderson, Abraham & Polley Bass, 24 April 1816; John Chavers, bm; W. M. Sneed, wit.

Anderson, Alexander & Adeline Anderson, 26 Nov 1859; Montgomery Trevan, bm; A. Landis, wit.

Anderson, Alexander & Nancy Winkfield, 1 Feb 1867; Tarry Petteford, bm; Jas. R. Duty, bm; m 6 Feb 1867 by Jas. R. Duty, J. P.

Anderson, Alfred, of color, son of Jerry Anderson & Sallie Anderson, & Nellie Tabon, daughter of Littleton & Lottie Tabon, m 21 July 1867 by B. F. Jenkins, J. P.

Anderson, Augustine & Patient Reaves, 19 Dec 1796; Abel Anderson, bm; Step. Sneed, wit.

GRANVILLE MARRIAGES 1753-1868

Anderson, Benjamin & Frankey Mitchell, 27 Aug 1816; Abel Anderson, bm; W. M. Sneed, wit.

Anderson, David R. & Abigail Lumpkin, 22 Feb 1825; D. E. Young, bm; D. J. Young, wit.

Anderson, Dennis & Eliza House, 24 Dec 1828; George Anderson, bm.

Anderson, Dennis & Linda Howell, 18 June 1852; Jacob Anderson, bm; A. Landis, wit.

Anderson, Dennis & Sallie Hedgpeth, 15 March 1855; James R. Duty, bm; m 15 March 1855 by Jas. R. Duty, J. P.

Anderson, Ferrington & Fanny Fuller, 10 April 1840; George Anderson, bm; J. M. Wiggins, wit.

Anderson, Frances & Annah Rustel, 7 May 1805; Thos. Y. Cooke, bm.

Anderson, George & Sarah Evans, 14 Oct 1800; William Petteford, bm; P. Bullock, wit.

Anderson, Henry & Nancy Mitchell, 9 July 1822; Thomas Anderson, bm; S. K. Sneed, wit.

Anderson, Henry & Nancy Richerson, 30 Oct 1823; Geo. Anderson, bm; Jas. M. Wiggins, wit.

Anderson, Horace & Polley Bass, 8 Aug 1815; Lemuel Tyler, bm; Step. Sneed, wit.

Anderson, Isaac & Melethan Hines, 28 Sept 1800; Peter Chaves, bm; P. Bullock, wit.

Anderson, Jacob Jr. & Nancy Bass, 24 Dec 1828; George Anderson, bm; L. Gilliam, wit.

Anderson, James & Mary Taylor, 23 Aug 1770; Joseph Taylor, bm; John Henderson, William Henderson, Zach Bullock, wit; consent from Thomas Anderson, 22 Aug 1770; wit by Thomas Banks(?), J. Taylor; consent also from Edmund Taylor, 22 Aug 1770, uncle of Mary, for who he was guardian, wit by Thomas Anderson, J. Taylor.

Anderson, James & Eliza Barton, 4 June 1829; Alexander Wilson, bm; Albert Sneed, wit.

Anderson, James & Aramitta Jackson, 5 Sept 1864; John Bass, bm; A. Landis, wit; m 6 Sept 1864 by L. M. VanHook, J. P.

Anderson, Jas. R. H. & Sarah O. Pettiford, 26 Feb 1853; William Anderson, bm; A. Landis, wit.

Anderson, Jerremier & Sary Hour, 26 Oct 1820; Lues Anderson, bm; Step. K. Sneed, wit.

Anderson, Jerry & Margaret An Jones, 7 Dec 1852; King D. Anderson, bm; A. Landis, wit.

Anderson, John & Charity Watson, daughter of John Watson, bm; Jno. Bowie, wit; consent from John Watson, 2 May 1761.

Anderson, John & Mourning Bass, 21 May 1812; Archibald H. Sneed, bm; W. M. Sneed, wit.

Anderson, John & Pricey Bass, 3 April 1821; George Anderson, S. K. Sneed, wit.

Anderson, John & Mary Mayho, 14 May 1851; Madison Jones, bm; A. Landis, wit; m 14 May 1851 by W. S. McClanahan, J. P.

Anderson, John & Margaret Parker, 27 Oct 1852; Henry Cousins, bm; L. B. Stone, J. P., wit; m 27 Oct 1857 by L. B. Stone, J. P.

Anderson, Joseph & Susan Ann Anderson, 31 Dec 1853; Thos. Jones, bm; A. Landis, wit.

Anderson, Joseph & Arena Mangum, 20 Jan 1859; Nash Hicks, bm; G. W. Landis, wit; m 20 Jan 1859 by H. Hester, J. P.

Anderson, Joseph & Mary Jane Berry, 24 March 1860; Nash Hicks, bm; A. Landis, wit; m 25 March 1860 by L. A. Paschall, J. P.

Anderson, Joseph L. R. & Mary Ann Anderson, 15 Dec 1849; Nelson Anderson, bm; A. Landis, wit.

Anderson, King D. & Emily Anderson, 6 Nov 1857; Jerry R. Anderson, bm; A. Landis, wit.

Anderson, Lewis & Mary Houze, 1 Jan 1822; George Anderson, bm; S. K. Sneed, wit.

Anderson, Louis Jr. & Ruthy Ann Boon, 13 June 1850; Iverson Mitchell, bm; B. C. Cooke, wit.

Anderson, Major & Betsey McGehe, 28 Aug 1830; Littleton Taborn, bm; David Laws, wit.

Anderson, Major & Nancy Pettiford, 24 Jan 1832; Lewis Curtis, bm; Step. K. Sneed, wit.

Anderson, Martin & Sally Kearsey, 21 Dec 1838; Thos. S. Hayes, bm.

Anderson, Pauller & Jane Craddock, 23 April 1799; Courtland Cabiniss, bm.

Anderson, Peter Jr. & Kissey Anderson, 5 Aug 1823; Leml. Tyler, bm; Jas. M. Wiggins, wit.

Anderson, Robert B. & Martha Chavis, 13 June 1854; T. W. McClanahan, bm; m 15 June 1854 by John Mallory.

Anderson, Royal & Maney Day, 25 April 1850; Robert Tabern, bm; A. Landis, wit.

Anderson, Royal & Minerva A. Curtis, 25 Dec 1858; John Norwood, bm; A. Landis, wit; m 25 Dec 1858 by W. R. Harris, J. P.

Anderson, Sandy F. & Mary Taburn, 24 Dec 1846; Geo. W. Anderson, bm; Jas. M. Wiggins, wit.

Anderson, Scarlet & Celia Oakley, 1 Oct 1805; Demarcus Oakley, bm; Jas. Sneed, wit.

GRANVILLE MARRIAGES 1753-1868

Anderson, Solomon & Sally Ann Mayho, 28 Jan 1859; Josiah Harris, bm; A. Landis, wit; m 30 Jan 1859 by W. R. Harris, J. P.

Anderson, Thomas & Elizabeth Owen, 2 March 1802; Thomas Owen, bm; W. M. Sneed, wit.

Anderson, Thomas & Salley Day, 16 Aug 1820; Anderson Petteford, bm; Jas. M. Wiggins, wit.

Anderson, Thomas & Elizabeth Meador, 30 March 1830; Wm. M. Meador, bm.

Anderson, Thomas & Beady Day, 28 Aug 1841; Wm. Taburn, bm; J. M. Wiggins, wit.

Anderson, Washington & Mary Tyler, 1 Jan 1829; Martin Anderson, bm; Wm. H. Owen, wit.

Anderson, William & Elizabeth Pettiford, 12 Nov 1808; Lewis Anderson, bm; W. M. Sneed, wit.

Anderson, William & Martha Butler, 19 Sept 1815; Wm. H. Gillian, bm; W. M. Sneed, wit.

Anderson, Wm. & Mary Ann Anderson, 17 Oct 1839; Barnett Bass, bm.

Anderson, William & Elizabeth Day, 25 Dec 1848; John Day, bm; J. M. Wiggins, wit.

Anderson, William & Sophiah Kearzey, 3 April 1850; Isaiah Harris, bm; A. Landis, wit.

Anderson, William & Isabella Jones, 3 Aug 1864; Saml. S. Williams, bm; m 3 Aug 1864 by Wm. Hicks, J. P.

Anderson, William & Ritter Anderson, 6 May 1866.

Anderson, William A. & Elizabeth A. Jones, _____ 18__; Dennis Anderson, bm; A. Landis, wit.

Anderson, Wm. J. & Anne Kearsey, 2 Aug 1852; William A. Anderson(?), bm.

Andrews, Bartlett & Mary Hunt, 22 Sept 1829; Augustine Landis, bm; David Laws, wit.

Andrews, Jesse P. & Nancy Brummit, 18 Oct 1836; Howell Gordun, bm; J. M. Wiggins, wit.

Angel, William J. & Mary Bragg, 23 March 1840; Ira E. Arnold, bm; J. M. Wiggins, wit.

Annat, Joseph & Elizabeth Atkins, 14 Feb 1816; James Harris, bm; H. Young, wit.

Apple, Scott, of color, son of Frem Puryear & Juda Apple, & Chana Watkins, daughter of William Watkins & Bettie Watkins, m 29 July 1868 by B. T. Winston, J. P.

Arendell, Benjamin & Emily Crews, 29 March 1830; Jos. B. Peace, bm; David Laws, wit.

Arington, Stephen & Aney Overby, 18 Jan 1838; Bedford Hite, bm; M. D. Royster, wit.

GRANVILLE MARRIAGES 1753-1868

Armistead, Stark & Harriot B. Tunstall, 28 June 1823; Joseph H. Bryan, bm; Jas. M. Wiggins, wit.

Arnold, Chesley & Sally Perry, 16 Jan 1826; Dorris Cannady, bm; Wm. H. Owen, wit.

Arnold, Daniel & Charlotte Wyche, freed people, D. A. Paschall, bm; m 27 Aug 1865 by Maurice H. Vaughan, Rector of St. Stephens Church.

Arnold, James & Polley Madison, 19 Sept 1815; James Bailey, bm; W. M. Sneed, wit.

Arnold, Jeremiah & Mary Hunt, 8 Dec 1789; Robert Burtch, bm; A. Henderson, Clk., wit.

Arnold, Job & Tabitha Cole, 4 Feb 1812; John Forsythe, bm; W. M. Sneed, wit.

Arnold (Ornel), John & Sarah Green, 29 Jan 1790; Edward Jones, bm; Henry Potter, wit.

Arnold, Richard & Betsey Wheeler, 4 Aug 1818; Henry Wheeler, bm; Step. K. Sneed, wit.

Arnold, Wm. & Mildred Waller, 27 Aug 1792; Zeph. Waller, bm; W. Norwood, wit.

Arrington, Caesar, of color, son of Jesse Beckwith & Ailsy Mann, & Susan Moss, daughter of Haly Moss & John Hobson, 19 Sept 1867; m 19 Sept 1867 by H. G. Hill, minister.

Arrington, Willis M. & Emily Weaver, 7 Jan 1846; Jas. R. Duty, bm.

Artis, Hardy & Elisabeth Howard, 25 June 1799; Leonard Cardwell, Benjamin Bullock, Franklin Satterwhite, bm; James Sneed, wit.

Ascue, Robert & Avin Matilda, 28 Oct 1819; Charles Duncan, bm; Jas. Wiggins, wit.

Ashley, Willie & Ann Bowles, 29 Oct 1858; C. Ashley, bm; A. Landis, wit.

Ashworth, Parker E. & Martha A. Wootten, 20 Dec 1852; William Ashworth, bm; Chs. R. Eaton, J. P., wit; m 20 Dec 1852 by C. R. Eaton, J. P.

Askew, Charles E. & Mary G. Pleasants, 5 Feb 1851; Thomas A. Stewart, bm.

Askew, William & Dicey Carden, 4 May 1789; James Carden, bm; A. Henderson, C. C., wit.

Askew, William & Amey Barns, 26 Jan 1816; Manus Weaver, bm; Step. Sneed, wit.

Askew, William S. & Elizabeth Slaughter, 3 Aug 1857; Howel Evans, bm; A. Landis, wit; m 4 Aug 1857 by Peterson Thorp, J. P.

Askue, John & Elisabeth Moore, 20 Feb 1786; Charles Moore, bm; Bennet Searcy, wit.

Asque, Soloman Greer & Elizabeth Slaughter, 12 Sept 1812; John Duncan, bm; W. M. Sneed, wit.

GRANVILLE MARRIAGES 1753-1868

Astrop, Henry & Pattsy Malone, 19 Sept 1809; William H. Lanier, bm; Saml. Hogg, wit.

Atkins, Allen & Ann Day, 19 Sept 1853; Anson Critcher, bm; m 2 Oct 1853 by _____, J. P.

Atkins, Henry & Elizabeth Mayho, 8 July 1863; John Harris, bm; A. Landis, wit.

Atkins, William S. & Virginia H. Homes, 9 Sept 1866; T. G. Burwell, Jno. P. Puryear, bm; m 9 Sept 1866 by W. M. Sneed, J. P.

Atkinson, Edward & Kissey Mitchel, 28 Jan 1819; John S. Glenn, bm; Step. K. Sneed, wit.

Atkinson, Roger & Margaret M. Littlejohn, 29 June 1826; Benson F. Jones, bm; Step. K. Sneed, wit.

Averett, Elijah & Rowan Garrett, 3 May 1853; m 8 May 1853 by Cam. W. Allen.

Averett, George W. R. & Roselia Williamson, 15 May 1862; Wm. C. Yancey, bm; m 25 May 1862 by L. B. Stone, J. P.

Averett, James Y. & Mary S. Wilkins, 8 Dec 1856; Henry M. Avrett, bm; m 8 Dec 1856 by Jno. W. Stovall, J. P.

Averett, Thomas R. & Martha Wright, 5 Oct 1850; Fielden Harris, bm.

Averett, Wyat & Dolly Puryear, 8 Nov 1848; L. B. Stem, bm.

Avery, Langston & Mary Loyd, 13 Jan 1790; John W. Hosbrey(?), bm; Step. Sneed, wit.

Avery, Wyatt, & Salley P. Pool, 6 Jan 1820; William Ladd, bm; Jno. P. Smith, wit.

Avory, Elijah & Rowan Garett, 3 May 1853; A. Landis, bm.

Avory, James T. & Margaret N. Carter, 9 Sept 1854; William T. Melton, bm; m 14 Sept 1854 by L. B. Stone, J. P.

Avory, Joel & Julia Ann Williams, 10 June 1852; William Longmire, bm; A. Landis, wit; m same day by Cam. W. Allen, J. P.

Babtist, Richard, of color, son of William Babtist and Henrietta Wimbish, and Sarah Bullock, daughter of Mordcai and Elizabeth Bullock, of color, 29 Dec 1807; m 29 Dec 1867 by Jas. R. Duty, J. P.

Bacon, Young F. & Martha Ann Scott, 11 March 1822; Peter W. Street, bm; Jas. M. Wiggins, wit.

Badger, George & Louisa Royster, 17 Nov 1865; Edward Hawkins, bm; J. P. Jordan, wit; m 25 Nov 1865 by Jos. W. Murphy, Rector, Holy Innocents Ch., Henderson.

Badget, James & Margaret Harrison, 30 March 1804; Andrew Badget, bm; Green Merritt, wit.

Badget, Peter & Rebecca Howard, __ Nov 1786; William Padgett, bm; Bennet Searcy, wit.

Badget, William & Betty Howard, 5 Dec 1788; Benton Badget, bm.

13

GRANVILLE MARRIAGES 1753-1868

Badgett, Andrew & Elizabeth Leavil, 26 Dec 1802; Jesse Johnston, bm; P. Bullock, wit.

Badgett, Benton & Leviney Partee, 23 Jan 1802; Abner Partee, bm; P. Bullock, wit.

Badgett, James & Rebecca OBrien, 15 March 1836; Thomas Badgett, bm; Benja. Kittrell, wit.

Badgett, James W. & Rhoda L. Adcock, 1 Dec 1866; C. E. Landis, bm; m 4 Dec 1866 by B. D. Howard, J. P.

Badgett, Jesse & Betsey Harrison, 7 Nov 1809; George Landis, bm; Jun. Sneed, wit.

Badgett, Samuel & Susan Curry, 4 April 1829; James Badgett, bm; Wm. H. Owen, wit.

Badgett, Samuel P. & Sarah Hobgood, 7 March 1840; Thomas E. Badgett, bm; J. M. Wiggins, wit.

Badgett, Thomas E. & Minerva Ann Mitchell, 26 Feb 1842; Weldon E. Hunt, bm; J. M. Wiggins, wit.

Badgett, William J., son of Samuel P. & Sarah Badgett, & Ellen Maria Currin, daughter of Fleming B. & Cornelia Currin, 24 Jan 1868; m 29 Jan 1868 by J. M. Satterwhite, J. P.

Bagley, Edward G. & Julia P. Trotter, 5 Aug 1845; Wm. T. Major, bm; Jas. M. Wiggins, wit.

Bailey, Alexander, son of Ransom & Frances Bailey & Eliza Ann Rust, daughter of Benjamin & Ann Rust, m 29 June 1867 by W. H. P. Jenkins, J. P.

Bailey, Alsey & Matilda Rhea, 2 Aug 1819; Samuel Bailey, bm; Step. K. Sneed, wit.

Bailey, Davis D. & Jacobina L. Grissom, 21 Dec 1848; Eaton Davis, bm; Jas. M. Wiggins, wit.

Bailey, Ephraim & Prescilla Bailey, 23 Nov 1838; William T. Laurence, bm.

Bailey, Gilchrist & Fanny Bragg, 15 Sept 1840; Hilsmon Dillard, bm; J. M. Wiggins, wit.

Bailey, Israel & Mary Harris, 14 June 1796; John Upchurch, bm; Step. Sneed, wit.

Bailey, John & Martha Bailey, 15 Feb 1841; Hilsmon Dillard, bm.

Bailey, John & Priscilla Ray, 28 May 1846; J. W. Estes, bm; J. M. Wiggins, wit.

Bailey, John H. & Nancy Adcock, 20 Nov 1865; Geo. Daniel, bm; A. Landis, wit; m 3 Dec 1865 by W. H. Puryear, J. P.

Bailey, Jonathan & Elizabeth Bailey, 21 Oct 1812; Wm. Estes, bm; W. M. Sneed, wit.

Bailey, Kennedy & Ellender Short, 21 Feb 1786; Harris Rice, bm; Bennet Searcy, wit.

GRANVILLE MARRIAGES 1753-1868

Bailey, Peleg & Mary Fuller, 3 May 1825; John Bailey, bm; Wm. Hayes Owen, wit.

Bailey, Randy & Isabella Lankford, 7 Feb 1843; Chs. Heflin, bm; Wm. H. Whitfield, wit.

Bailey, Ransom & Fanny Shaver, 31 Aug 1829; John Bailey(?), bm; S. K. Sneed, wit.

Bailey, Samuel & Judith Powell, 30 March 1803; Israel Bailey, bm; Green Merritt, wit.

Bailey, Samuel & Susan Hendley, 8 Dec 1820; Alsey Bailey, bm; Step. K. Sneed, wit.

Bailey, Solomon & Lucretia Eastridge, 15 Sept 1827; Jeremiah McGehee, bm; Wm. H. Owen, wit.

Bailey, Stephen & Alice Fleming, 6 Jan 1783; Daniel Fleming, bm; Reuben Searcy, wit.

Bailey, Thomas & Middy Bailey, 22 May 1833; Henry Loyd, bm; Step. K. Sneed, wit.

Bailey, William & Nancey Jarrott, 4 March 1793; Peyton Madison, bm; Step. Sneed, wit.

Bailey, William & Glafney Bailey, 30 Dec 1813; Peleg Bailey, bm; Jno. Cobbs, wit.

Bailey, William & Nancey Bailey, 4 Aug 1813; Israel Bailey, bm; W. M. Sneed, wit.

Bailey, William & Betsey Dutton, 27 April 1817; William Elliott, bm; Step. K. Sneed, wit.

Bailey, William & Martha Bailey, 30 Jan 1832; John W. McGhee, bm; David Laws, wit.

Bailey, William F. & Sarah Clay, 24 Jan 1848; William T. Laurence, bm; Jas. M. Wiggins, wit.

Bailey, William Y. & Sally P. Beasly, 5 Nov 1842; James T. Beasley, bm; J. M. Wiggins, wit.

Bailley, Flavius, J. & Lucy Moss, 29 June 1857; S. M. Cannady, bm; m 8 July 1857 by James S. Purify, Min. of the Gospel.

Baird, Dr. Wm. & Margaret L. Reece, (no date); consent only from Thomas F. & Nancy J. Read; L. Reed, wit.

Baity, John & Emily Blacknall, 25 Dec 1866; C. E. Landis, bm.

Baird, William & Margaret L. Reece, 7 Sept 1833; Jos. T. Hicks, bm; Benja. Kittrell, wit.

Baird, William G. & Bettie W. Morton, 8 Jan 1867; m 23 Jan 1867 by E. Hines; L. C. Edwards, bm.

Baker, Isaac & Mary A. Gilliam, 17 Jan 1827; Mark M. Henderson, bm; Wm. H. Owen, wit.

Baker, John & Owen Kittrell, 20 Dec 1866; m 20 Dec 1866 by L. K. Willie, M. G.; J. A. Peace, bm.

GRANVILLE MARRIAGES 1753-1868

Baker, Nathaniel & Pheba Freeman, 9 Aug 1810; Olive(r) Freeman, bm; A. H. Sneed, wit.

Baldwin, John W. & Catharine Wood, 27 Dec 1850; J. P. Hester, bm; A. Landis, wit.

Bale, Fields & Abigal Ascew, 9 Oct 183_; G. Stanton, bm.

Baley, Epharom & Marthey Harris, 24 Feb 1797; Jonathan Harris, bm; Richard Taylor, wit.

Ball, Anson & Polly Fuller, 29 Sept 1817; James Heflin, bm; R. N. Herndon, wit.

Ball, Chesley & Nancy Finch, 15 Dec 1834; James _____, bm; Tho. L. King, wit.

Ball, Edwin & Mary F. Grissom, 7 Jan 1867; W. Dement, bm; m 16 Jan 1867 by E. B. Lyon, J. P.

Ball, Elijah & Elizabeth Randsome, 5 May 1795; Richard Taylor, bm; L. Henderson, wit.

Ball, Elijah, son of Chesley Ball & Nancy Fynch, & Lucinda Catlett, daughter of Laborn Catlett & Lucy Crowder, m 12 March 1868 by W. H. P. Jenkins, J. P.

Ball, Erasmus & Ann Mitchell, 9 Oct 1850; George Catlett, bm.

Ball, Gilford & Elizabeth Fortner, 1 Nov 1819; Leonard Cardwell, bm; Albert Sneed, wit.

Ball, Harriss & Mary Fuller, 27 Dec 1828; Thos. Jackson, bm; Robt. B. Gilliam, wit.

Ball, Hinton & Susan Mayfield, 7 Oct 1836; Robert A. Long, bm; J. M. Wiggins, wit.

Ball, Isham & Betsey Clark, 13 July 1846; John Clark, bm.

Ball, Ivey & Lily Wren, 4 Aug 1849; Albert Ellington, bm; Jas. M. Wiggins, wit.

Ball, James & Jane Cooke, 25 Sept 1852; Young A. Minnis, bm.

Ball, John & Sary Wade, 7 May 1794; Saml. Bullock, bm; Ro. Harris, wit.

Ball, John & M---- Rodes(?), 28 Dec 1841.

Ball, Lemuel D. K. & Sally Ann McGehee, 12 Feb 1851; D. H. Whitfield, bm.

Ball, Orsborn & Molley Harp, 10 March 1803; John Harp, bm; Wm. Walker, wit.

Ball, Orsborn L. & Martha Ball, 16 Sept 1847; Jas. Ball, bm; Jas. M. Wiggins, wit.

Ball, Samuel & Tempey Collier, 6 Aug 1832; Dennis H. Ball, bm; Step. K. Sneed, wit.

Ball, Vincent & Tempey Priddy, 29 Dec 1808; Joseph Pridy, bm; Alfred Wilkins, wit.

GRANVILLE MARRIAGES 1753-1868

Ball, William & Helen Evans, 5 Dec 1856; Erasmus Ball, bm; A. Landis, wit; m 7 Dec 1856 by J. Y. McGehee, J. P.

Ball, William & Elizabeth Adams, 7 Dec 1858; William Dickerson, bm; A. Landis, wit; m 9 Dec 1858 by Elba L. Parrish, J. P.

Ball, William & Caroline Wrenn, 3 Nov 1865; Lewis Smith, bm; S. Landis, wit.

Ball, William D. & Milly Jane Falkner, 26 Dec 1843; Doctor Falconer, bm; J. M. Wiggins, wit.

Ballard, Lewis & Winney Barnes, 8 Jan 1787; John Weaver, bm; Robert Searcy, wit.

Ballard, Lewis & Nancy Wilson, 22 Dec 1789; William Harral(?), bm; Henry Potter, wit.

Banks, Richard & Ruthy Hooker, 11 Jan 1769; John Hooker, bm; Saml. Benton, C. C., wit.

Banks, Richard of Wake County, & Keronhappuck Hooker, 6 June 1774; Sherwood Harris of Granville Co., bm; Reuben Searcy, wit.

Banks, Thomas & Susanna Hurt, 11 March 1786; Henry White, bm; Bennet Searcy, wit.

Bard, William & Mary Knowland, 20 May 1769; Ephraim Hampton, bm; James Litton, wit.

Barham, Bailem & Elizabeth Elliott, 31 July 1812; John Hester, bm; W. M. Sneed, wit.

Barker, Ambrose & Mary Ann Ragland, 18 Nov 1773; Evan Ragland Jr., bm; Reuben Searcy, wit.

Barker, Ambrose & Jemima P. Wilson, 17 Dec 1830; Wm. S. McClanahan, bm; David Laws, wit.

Barker, David & Martha Allen, 2 Jan 1847; G. W. Hunt, bm.

Barker, Frank & Judy Turner, 11 Feb 1866; Armistead Wilson, bm; A. Landis, wit; m 13 Feb 1866 by J. F. Harris, J. P.

Barker, James & Martha Welsh, 20 Dec 1825; Jesse Rice, bm; Wm. H. Owen, wit.

Barker, John G. & Francis Saterwhite, 20 Dec 1837; Solomon G. Wilson, bm; S. G. Shearmon, wit.

Barker, John G. & Harriett E. Stone, 24 Nov 1854; Kyzer J. Stark, bm; m 30 Nov 1854 by S. G. Wilson, J. P.

Barker, Major & Isabella Lewis, 25 Nov 1865.

Barkeree, Jerry & Permelia Marrow, 17 Aug 1866.

Barlow, Simeon & Harriett Paschall, 9 Feb 1853; James Ross, bm; A. Landis, wit; m 10 Feb 1853 by B. B. Hester.

Barnard, John R. & Miss Margarett H. Jordan, 30 Oct 1867; m 30 Oct 1867 by P. H. Joyner.

GRANVILLE MARRIAGES 1753-1868

Barner, John & Nancy Perry, 15 Nov 1820; Samuel Keith, bm; Jas. M. Wiggins, wit.

Barnes, James B. & Leuvinia Weaver, 9 May 1859; W. T. Wier, bm; Jas. R. Duty, J. P., wit; m 12 May 1859 by Jas. R. Duty, J. P.

Barnes, John F. & Fanny R. Marshall, 26 June 1835; James M. Overbey, bm; Benja. Kittrell, wit.

Barnes, Hillman & Jane Cheatham, 8 May 1851; R. J. Mitchell, bm; m 15 May 1851 by Thos. N. Faucett, Minister of the Gospel.

Barnes, James B. & Mrs. Margaret Falkner, 11 Nov 1865; George W. Landis, bm.

Barnes, John M. & Parthenia J. Cheatham, 8 Sept 1848; George J. Kelly, bm.

Barnes, John W., son of William & Mildred Barnes, & Mrs. Elizabeth A. Brame, daughter of James Wortham & Martha Wortham, 29 Oct 1867; m 30 Oct 1867 by S. P. J. Harris.

Barnes, Merryman & Amey Rowland, 29 Jan 1798; Manus Weaver, bm; Step. Sneed, wit.

Barnes, Washington L. & Susan Ellis, 4 Dec 1828; Benjamin F. Crews, bm; David Laws, wit.

Barnet, John & Elisabeth Mitchel, 10 Dec 1781; Thos. Barnett, bm; Bennet Searcy, wit.

Barnet, John & Nancy Barnet, 29 Jan 1789; Jesse Barnett, bm; A. Henderson, wit.

Barnet, Thomas & Anne Stewert, 8 May 1824; John Anderson, bm.

Barnett, Elijah & Mary A. Hart, 21 Nov 1834; T. B. Barnett, bm; Benja. Kittrell, wit.

Barnett, James & Sarah Barnett, 25 Dec 1798; John Barnett, bm; Step. Sneed, wit.

Barnett, James & Spivey Wooton, 1 Oct 1821; William Clarke, bm; S. K. Sneed, wit.

Barnett, Jesse & Nancy D. Terry, 12 Jan 1829; Riley Suit, bm; Albert Sneed, wit.

Barnett, Jesse Senr. & Elizabeth Leny, 15 Sept 1823; Joseph Barnett, bm; W. M. Sneed, wit.

Barnett, Jessee Jr. & Frances Gregory, 20 Dec 1809; Thomas Terry, bm; A. N. Sneed, wit.

Barnett, John & Anny Sears, 27 March 1794; James Barnett, bm; L. Henderson, wit.

Barnett, John & Martha Beeks, 17 Jan 1809; John Moore, bm; Alfred Wilkins, wit.

Barnett, John, son of John, & Patsey Parham, 30 Sept 1809; Samuel Parham, bm; W. M. Sneed, wit.

Barnett, John D. & Rebecca G. Critcher, 18 June 1853; R. J. Mitchell, bm; m 18 June 1853 by W. S. McClanahan, J. P.

GRANVILLE MARRIAGES 1753-1868

Barnett, Joseph & Anne Sheppard, 21 May 1804; Wm. Barnett, bm; Step. Sneed, wit.

Barnett, Joseph & Lolly Williams, 11 May 1815; Joseph Harte, bm; Richd. Sneed, wit.

Barnett, Joseph & Drucilla Badgett, 21 Dec 1839; Jesse Barnett, bm; J. M. Wiggins, wit.

Barnett, Joseph G. & Mary Hart, 30 Sept 1829; Riley Suit, bm; Albert Sneed, wit.

Barnett, Robert & Louisa B. Neal, 28 Sept 1832; Sy. Terry, bm; David Laws, wit.

Barnett, Robert S. & Ann Satterwhite, 21 Jan 1838; T. B. Barnett, bm.

Barnett, Robert T. & Mary A. Davis, 1 Oct 1836; T. B. Barnett, bm.

Barnett, Thomas B. & Mary A. Norwood, 28 May 1825; Jabez Duty, bm; A. Sneed, wit.

Barnett, William & Lethy Hays, 9 Oct 1804; John A. Hutchins, bm; W. M. Sneed, wit.

Barnett, William & Emily Norwood, 10 Dec 1830; Thos. B. Barnett, bm; David Laws, wit.

Barnett, Willis & Frances Bullock, 26 Dec 1865; John Turner, bm; Jas. R. Duty, wit; m 25 Dec 1865 by H. H. Pewet.

Barnett, Woodson & Lizzie Marrow, freed people, m 16 May 1867 by A. C. Harris, M. G.

Barns, John & Sarah Mangrum, 16 July 1814; William Loyd, bm; Howel Moss, wit.

Barns, John W. & Malissa Cheatham, 2 Jan 1854; Stephen Burroughs, bm; m 4 Jan 1854 by R. J. Devin, V. M. D.

Barr, James & Sally Dickerson, 27 Jan 1787; John Peace, bm; Bennet Searcy, wit.

Bartholomew, Jacob & Elizabeth Atkerson, 8 Jan 1810; William M. Sneed, bm.

Bas, Benjamin & Milley Pettiford, 2 Jan 1781; Rubin Bass, bm; Denis Rawdin, wit.

Baskervill, William & Mary Eaton, 22 Jan 1786; H. E. Johnston, bm; G. H. Baskervill, wit.

Baskerville, Charles & Margaret H. Freear, 1 Nov 1841; Jas. W. Eaton, bm; J. M. Wiggins, wit.

Baskerville, Charles, of color, son of Charles & Faithy Baskerville & Melviney Brodie, daughter of George Higgs, & Agathey Davis, m 24 May 1868 by Jas. R. Duty, J. P.

Baskerville, H. E. C. & Isabella A. Hamilton, 9 Jan 1846; John Gilmour, bm; Jas. M. Wiggins, wit.

GRANVILLE MARRIAGES 1753-1868

Baskerville, John W. & Sally D. Young, 31 Oct 1843; James Turner, bm; Wm. H. Whitfield, wit.

Basnick, Joseph, of color, son of Clarasa, a slave & Lucy Davis, daughter of Esther Lewis, 25 Dec 1867; m 27 Dec 1867 by A. C. Harris, M. G.

Bass, Absolem & Patsey Hagues, 15 Jan 1794; Benjamin Bass, bm; W. Norwood, wit.

Bass, Arther, colored, son of Martha Bass, & Mary Taborn, daughter of Thomas & Till Taborn, 18 Dec 1868; m 18 Dec 1868 by Francis J. Tilley, J. P.

Bass, Boney, of color, son of William Bass & Patsy Bass, & Winney Anderson, of color, daughter of Henry Anderson & Nancy Anderson, m 16 June 1867 by B. F. Jenkins, J. P.

Bass, Chesley & Dicey Due, 11 April 1846; Bolling Anderson, bm; J. M. Wiggins, wit.

Bass, Darling & Rhody Anderson, 31 Jan 1796; Wm. Mitchell, bm; Wm. Robards, wit.

Bass, Demsey & Phereby Day, 4 Oct 1808; Reuben Day, bm; W. M. Sneed, wit.

Bass, George W. & Tabbitha Chavus, 24 Dec 1853; Dennis Anderson, bm; Jas. R. Duty, wit; m 14 Jan 1854 by Jas. R. Duty, J. P.

Bass, Hardey & Nancey Hines, 23 Dec 1788; Reubin Bass, bm. A. Henderson, wit.

Bass, Henry & Eliza Hart, 26 Feb 1824; Willis Bass, bm; S. K. Sneed, wit.

Bass, Henry & Selina Ann Valentine, 25 Oct 1838; Abram Plenty, bm; Jas. M. Wiggins, wit.

Bass, Jason & Sarah Taburn, 19 Jan 1807; George Pettiford, bm; W. M. Sneed, wit.

Bass, Jesse & Mary Blair, 11 Dec 1819; Claborn Cooke, bm; S. K. Sneed, wit.

Bass, Jetho & Polley Mitchell, 3 April 1809; Henry Anderson, bm; W. M. Sneed, wit.

Bass, John & Olive Richardson, 8 Dec 1798; Absalom Bass, bm; Ro. Harris, wit.

Bass, John & Nancy Harris, 21 Aug 1802; Peter Anderson, bm; Phil Bullock, wit.

Bass, John & Nancy Anderson, 27 Aug 1855; A. Landis, bm.

Bass, John W. & Abby Soloman, 6 July 1825; Wm. P. Volentine, bm; Wm. Hayes Owen, wit.

Bass, Mordicai & Nancy Chavers, 13 Dec 1803; George Pettiford, bm; A. H. Sneed, wit.

Bass, Moses & Betsey Pettiford, 28 Aug 1809; Thomas Anderson, bm; W. M. Sneed, wit.

Bass, Moses & Mason Evans, 31 Oct 1826; Jacob Anderson, bm; Wm.
H. Owen, wit.

Bass, Nathan & Sarah Bass, 2 Feb 1779; Thomas Critcher, bm;
_____ Potter, wit.

Bass, Nathan & Martha Bass, 19 June 1806; Jesse Bass, bm. W. M.
Sneed, wit.

Bass, Reuben & Polley Hines, 23 Dec 1788; Hardey Bass, bm; A.
Henderson, wit.

Bass, Right & Tabathy Snelling, 12 Nov 1781; Drury Pettiford,
bm.

Bass, Thomas & Phanney Parish, 9 Sept 1790; Drury Pettiford,
bm; Step. Sneed, wit.

Bass, Thomas & Charlott Wright, __ Sept 1801; Jesse Bass, bm.

Bass, William & Mary Harris, 9 Dec 1800; George Anderson, bm;
P. Bullock, wit.

Bass, William & Lucy Howard, 3 March 1836; Austin Valentine, bm;
Benja. Kittrell, wit.

Bass, William & Lucy Truman, 19 Dec 1861; Mat. Jones, bm; A.
Landis, wit; m 19 Dec 1861 by A. H. Cooke, J. P.

Bass, Willis & Olive Chavers, 14 Jan 1809; Charles Barnett, bm;
Step. Sneed, wit.

Bass, Willis & Julia A. Pettiford, 24 Dec 1847; Eldridge Mayho,
bm; J. M. Wiggins, wit.

Bass, Woodson & Frances Chavis, 24 Aug 1843; Thomas Anderson,
bm; Wm. H. Whitfield, wit.

Bassell, Alexander & Emily H. Russell, 20 Feb 1859; Rubin
Petteford, bm; m 20 Feb 1859 by A. Laurence, J. P.

Baswell, John, son of Jordan & Betsey Baswell, & Betsey Petterford, daughter of William & Averilla Petterford, 28 Dec 1868;
m 15 Jan 1869 by John W. Estes, J. P.

Bates, John & Susanna Huccabey, 20 Dec 1786; Claibourn Parish,
bm; Bennet Searcy, wit.

Bates, John & Elizabeth Hester, 22 June 1816; Willis L. Gorden,
bm; W. M. Sneed, wit.

Baxter, Reuben & Milly Bagly, 19 Feb 1800; Daniel Walker, bm.

Bayley, Wm. & Mary Stowvall, 22 July 1808; Thos. Faulkner, bm;
John Owen Jun., wit.

Bazill, Wright & Jane Jones, 17 Jan 1856; m 17 Jan 1856 by C.
E. Davis, J. P.; William S. Mitchell, bm.

Beal, Josiah W. & Elizabeth Jones, 16 Oct 1845; Edwin Beal, bm;
J. M. Wiggins, wit.

Beard, James & Mary Thacker, 12 April 1847; Jas. W. Eaton, bm;
Jas. R. Duty, wit.

GRANVILLE MARRIAGES 1753-1868

Bearden, Benjamin & Elizabeth Minor, 21 Nov 1814; Robert Longmire, bm; John C. Smith, wit.

Bearden, Charles & Fanny Parham, 14 Feb 1807; Thomas Parham, bm; W. M. Sneed, wit.

Bearden, William & Sarah Burton, 24 Aug 1803; Tyre Harris, Jr., bm; Step. Sneed, wit.

Beardin, Humphrey & Ann Filcher, 13 Aug 1768; James Jones, bm; Nathl. Henderson, wit.

Beardin John & Nancy Harris, 13 Dec 1804; William Beardin, bm; E. W. Parham, wit.

Beardin, Wm. & Nancey Fraizer, 4 Oct 1790; Jeremiah Fraizer, bm; Step. Sneed, wit.

Beasley, Almacus F., colored, son of Spence Green & Rebeca Brasley, & Mary Stewart, daughter of John & Mary Brewer, 8 Dec 1868; m 31 Dec 1868 by J. P. Montague, M. G.

Beasley, Fleming & Maria Thomas, 27 Oct 1824; Stephen Beasley, bm; Randal Puryear, wit.

Beasley, Fleming & Virginia Henry, 31 Aug 1849; Benj. C. Cooke, bm.

Beasley, Flemming & Polly T. Vass, 17 Jan 1818; Saml. S. Downing, bm; Rhodes N. Herndon, wit.

Beasley, James T. & Lethy Jane Royster, 31 Oct 1845; Fleming Beasley, bm.

Beasley, John F. & Alice C. Jones, 25 Nov 1847; George W. Hunt, bm. Jas. M. Wiggins, wit.

Beasley John P. & Eliza Ann Williams, 12 Nov 1816; Wm. Butler, bm; W. M. Sneed, wit.

Beasley, Maurice & Juda Couch, 13 Dec 1866; Robert Royster, bm; A. Landis, wit.; m 14 Dec 1866 by R. J. Devin.

Beasley, Robert & Stellah Royster, 5 Feb 1821; Alexr. Smith, bm.

Beasley, Stephen & Staley Pomfrett, 10 March 1787; John Wilkerson, bm; John Searcy, wit.

Beasley, Stephen & Judith Thomas, 22 Dec 1827; Wm. L. Owen, bm; Wm. H. Owen, wit.

Beasley, Stephen H. & Susan Ann Clark, 18 June 1868; m 21 June 1868 by W. H. Puryear, J. P.

Beasley, Thomas S. & Sarah A. M. Royster, 25 Nov 1840; J. M. Satterwhite, bm.

Beasley, William R. & Mollie T. Morris, 4 Dec 1862; J. A. Barnett, bm. m 4 Dec 1862 by W. M. Wingate, M. G.

Beasly, James & Mary Ann Green, 13 Oct 1840; W. B. Lormier, bm; Jas. M. Wiggins, wit.

Beavers, James & Cary Ann Pool, 20 Dec 1843; Bartlett Yancey, bm; Wm. T. Whitfield, wit.

Beck, David & Elizabeth Wheeler, 4 Dec 1855; W. E. Akin, bm;
A. Landis, wit; m 16 Dec 1855 by J. B. Lyon, J. P.

Beck, Fredrich (German signature) & Nancey Bailey, 8 March 1799;
John Huddleston, bm; Ro. Harris, wit.

Beck, Fredrick & Barbara Byars, 5 Dec 1788; Joseph Landis, bm;
A. Henderson, wit.

Beck, James & Mary Phillips, 1 Dec 1824; John Haley, bm; Step.
K. Sneed, wit.

Beck, James & Aily E. Garner, 16 July 1857; m 30 Aug 1857 by
T. B. Lyon, J. P.

Beck, John & Joannah Wood, 30 Jan 1809; Frederick Beck, bm; W.
M. Sneed, wit.

Beck, John W. & Mary Ann Clark, 20 Oct 1848; William E. Akin,
bm.

Beck, John W. & Mary Ann Clark, 18 Dec 1849; A. Landis, bm.

Beck, Michael & Angaline Nevels, 4 Oct 1835; R. N. Herndon, bm;
Benja. Kittrell, wit.

Beck, Robert & Adeline H. Aikin, 12 Dec 1859; Thos. B. Lyons,
bm; A. Landis, wit.

Beck, William & Christian Hoofman, _____ 178_; Joseph Landers, bm; A. Henderson, wit.

Beck, Wm. & Niah Davis, 8 May 1817; George Landis, bm.

Beck, William & Mary York, 29 Dec 1831; John Fowler, bm; Step.
K. Sneed, wit.

Beckham, John & Elizabeth Henderson, 12 Aug 1761; William Williams, bm; consent from Eliza. Henderson (apparently the bride);
12 Aug 1761.

Beckham, Joseph & Roxana Faulkner, 13 Dec 1856; Erasmus Wright,
bm; m 18 Dec 1856 by William B. Mann, J. P.

Beckham, Simon & Susanna McMillian, daughter of Alexander McMilian, 2 Jan 1759; Mathew McMillian, bm; Jno. Bowie, wit.

Beckum, John & Mary Denton, 17 Dec 1800; John Denton, bm; _____,
wit.

Beddingfield, William H. & Amanda F. Hunt, 28 Aug 1860; Dennis
Lynch, bm; m _____ 1860 by John F. Harris, J. P.

Bedford, William & Mayze Dance, 2 Nov 1813; W. M. Sneed, bm.

Bedingfield, Nedum & Mary Rogers, 23 Dec 1801; John Kelly, bm;
P. Bullock, wit.

Beech, Lodwick & Elizabeth Beech, 28 Aug 1811; James Middleton,
bm; J. Young, J. P., wit.

Beith, John & Mary P. Jones, 14 June 1825; R. N. Herndon, bm;
Wm. Hayes Owen, wit.

GRANVILLE MARRIAGES 1753-1868

Belbro, William T. & E. A. Read, 22 Dec 1847; S. S. Parrott(?), bm; J. M. Wiggins, wit.

Belcher, Francis & Phebe Caviness, 23 Dec 1771; Richard Hargroves, bm; Jesse Benton, wit.

Belcher, John W. & Susan Ann Newton, 20 Dec 1859; Joseph Noblin, bm.

Bell, Abraham & Elisabeth Ramey, 23 May 1797; John Earl, bm; Step. Sneed, wit.

Bell, Benjamin & Elisabeth Longmire, 9 Dec 1801; James Wall Ledbetter, bm; P. Bullock, wit.

Bell, James R. & Nancey Rowland, 7 Dec 1811; Presley Rowland, bm; Step. Sneed, wit.

Bell, John A. & Eliza J. Riggan, 25 April 1860; R. A. Heavlin, bm; m 2 May 1860 by B. F. Long, Minister.

Bell, Thomas & Sarah Hix, 7(?) Aug 1763; Benjamin Person, bm; consent from Robert Hicks, father of Sarah Hicks, 11 Aug 1763.

Bell, William, of color, son of Adam & Polly Eaton, & Patsy Miller, daughter of Ruffin & Sergina Miller, 31 July 1868; m 27 Sept 1868 by R. J. Horner, Minister.

Belt, Humphrey & Mildred C. Ford, 28 Nov 1798; Moses Tredway, bm; James Sneed, wit.

Belvin, James of Wake County, & Frances Brasfield, 31 Oct 1776; William Rochelle, bm, of Wake County.

Belvin, Wyatt A. & Sallie E. Wilkerson, m 8 Sept 1867 by Wm. H. Puryear, J. P.

Bennet, William & Clary Lyle, 23 Feb 1776; Wm. Liles, bm; John Dickerson, wit.

Bennett, Charles & Lucina Suit, m 10 Jan 1866 by Jas. W. Dalby, J. P.

Bennett, Charles L. & Martha Walker, 14 Aug 1805; John Wood, bm; Jas. Sneed, wit.

Bennett, Charles W. & Lucinda C. Suit, 10 Jan 1865; A. H. Cooke, bm.

Bennett, George & Martha Russell, 19 Feb 1829; Rupert Parham, bm; Step. K. Sneed, wit.

Bennett, Isham & Rose Lewis, 27 Aug 1866.

Bennett, Lewis & Ellender Bullock, 19 June 1816; W. M. Sneed, bm.

Bennett, Lewis W. & Margaret Lawson, 19 Sept 1864; A. Landis, bm; m 20 Sept 1864 by G. W. Ferrill, Minister.

Bennett, Thomas & Sarah W. Paschall, 27 July 1852; A. Landis, bm; m 28 July 1852 by L. K. Willie.

Benson, Francis L. & Mary A. Gold, 15 Nov 1840; Elijah Satterwhite, bm.

GRANVILLE MARRIAGES 1753-1868

Berkley, Henry W. & Louisa Linum, 2 Jan 1855; A. Landis, bm.

Berkley, John & Elizabeth Jane Puryear, 24 Feb 1858; John R. Griffin, bm; A. Landis, wit.

Berry, Thomas & Mildred Allin, 17 May 1781; Wm. Willis, bm; Vincent Vass Junr., wit.

Best, Henry & Maria L. Smith, 16 Feb 1848; Benj. C. Cooke, bm; Jas. M. Wiggins, wit.

Best, Henry & Mary Ann Jurphy(?), 8 Dec 1851; R. J. Mitchell, bm.

Best, John W. & Agness Burchett, 19 March 1849; R. Crabtree, bm.

Best, Kedar & Elisabeth Waddey, 7 Jan 1799; James Waddey, bm; Step. Sneed, wit.

Best, Thomas T. & Mary W. Finch, 9 Oct 1851; Geo. B. Reavis, bm.

Best, William M. & Louisiana Kittrell, 7 Feb 1840; John Blacknall, bm.

Beth, Saml. & Sabelia B. Moody, 9 May 1860; m 9 May 1860 by Wm. Holmes.

Betts, Henry J. & Jane Marable, freed people, 16 Feb 1867; m 16 Feb 1867 by W. Overbey, J. P.; Nathan Overbey, bm.

Bevill, William & Nancy Prewit, 30 Dec 1800; Benja. Prewett, bm.

Bevis, Stanford D. & Susan Morris, 27 Oct 1853; T. L. Hargrove, bm; m 27 Oct 1853 by L. K. Willie, M. G.

Biddy, Berry & Babarah Goodson, 9 March 1816; Wm. Priddy, bm; W. M. Sneed, wit.

Biggs, Elijah & Susan Mangum, 23 Oct 1858; A. Landis, bm; John W. Henry, wit; m 29 Oct 1858 by L. R. Parham, J. P.

Biggs, John L. & Martha Fuller, 15 Nov 1856; W. E. Coghill, bm.

Biggs, William & Lucy Coghill, 10 Jan 1857; George W. Brame, bm; A. C. Harris, wit; m 11 Jan 1857 by William B. Mann, J. P.

Biggs, Willis & Lucy Parrish, 27 Jan 1820; James J. Farrar, bm; Step. K. Sneed, wit.

Birch, Samuel & Elisabeth Holt, spinster, 1 May 1764; Robt. Cheek, bm; Jno. Bowie, wit.

Birchett, Green & Priscilla Bowers, 15 March 1828; Guy Smith, bm; S. K. Sneed, wit.

Birchett, James B. & Ann V. Walker, 19 May 1838; Thos. S. Ellington, Jos. C. Brem, M. M. Langwood(?), John R. Taylor, bm; Robert K. Clack, wit.

Bird, Burrel & Betsey Lawrance, 3 Jan 1805; Harris Perdue, bm; Step. Sneed, wit.

Bishop, Philip & Mary Wright, 20 Nov 1788; Harris Hicks, bm; A. Henderson, wit.

GRANVILLE MARRIAGES 1753-1868

Blackard, Charles & Betsey Henderson, 5 Aug 1783; Saml. Searcy, bm.

Blackley, Alexander, son of Thomson & Leathy Blackley, & Eliza Smith, daughter of Henry & Agness Smith, 15 Oct 1868; m 16 Oct 1868 by B. R. Hester.

Blackley, Armstead C. & Hicksey Fuller, 28 March 1861; John E. Freeman, bm; m 31 March 1861 by W. D. Allen, J. P.

Blackley, Charles & Milley Inscore, 12 July 1787; Reuben Inscoe Jr., bm; Reuben Searcy, wit.

Blackley, Charles R. & Bettie Hicks, 23 Jan 1867; m 24 Jan 1867 by W. H. P. Jenkins, J. P.; Alex Harris, bm; A. Landis, wit.

Blackley, Halyard & Beedy Smith, 1 Jan 1831; D. Winston, bm; David Laws, wit.

Blackley, Harvel & Letha Harris, 28 Dec 1833; Asa P. Harriss, bm.

Blackley, James & Phebe Smith, 20 Feb 1788; John Smith, bm; B. Searcy, wit.

Blackley, Thompson & Lethe Hayes, 8 April 1823; James Brummet, bm; Jas. M. Wiggins, wit.

Blackley, Thompson & Betsy A. Holden, 2 Aug 1867; m 2 Aug 1867 by D. H. D. Bullock, J. P.

Blackley, William & Levizah Hays, 25 Dec 1808; Thomas Dement, bm; Alfred Wilkins, wit.

Blackley, William T. & Emily S. Harris, 22 Dec 1845; M. Dement, bm; J. M. Wiggins, wit.

Blackley, Woodson B. & Elizabeth Jenkins, 24 Feb 1835; Anthony W. Cole, bm; Benja. Kittrell, wit.

Blackly, James & Elizabeth Cooke, 12 Dec 1833; S. Harris, bm; Benja. Kittrell, wit.

Blackman, James & Anne Highfield, 30 Dec 1782; William Ward, bm; Asa Searcy, wit.

Blacknall, Charles C. & Virginia B. Spencer, 13 Oct 1851; M. D. OBrien, bm; m 16 Oct 1851 by Jonah Crudup, Minister of the Gospel.

Blacknall, Charles H. & Martha Roberson, 22 Oct 1822; George Blacknall, bm; Jas. M. Wiggins, wit.

Blacknall, Gabriel & Sarah Fogg, 18 Oct 1856; Edward Mayo, bm.

Blacknall, John & Mary J. Nuttall, 11 April 1837; R. H. Kingsbury, bm.

Blacknall, John Jr. & Louisa McClanahan, 8 Jan 1847; J. H. Gooch, bm.

Blacknall, Jonathan T. & Martha Obriant, 2 Aug 1831; F. Kittrell, bm; David Laws, wit.

Blacknall, Nathan & Rachel Smith, 5 Oct 1865; Isaac Bell, bm; m 26 Aug 1866 by G. W. Blacknall, J. P.

GRANVILLE MARRIAGES 1753-1868

Blacknall, Richard & Harriet S. Russell, 9 March 1831; Wm. Mc-
   Clanahan, bm; David Laws, wit.

Blacknall, Thomas & Mary Kittrell, 11 Oct 1798; Zadoc Loyd, bm;
   P. Bullock, wit.

Blacknall, Thomas H. & Catharine McClanahan, 26 April 1854;
   Edward A. Crudup, bm; m 26 April 1854 by Thos. U. Faucette,
   M. G.

Blackwell, Fleming & Mary Edwards, 27 June 1822; Stephen Melton,
   bm; David J. Young, wit.

Blackwell, Hardy & Susan Royster, 25 Aug 1866.

Blackwell, James & Temperance Pope, 2 April 1772; Thos. Banks,
   bm; Reuben Searcy, wit.

Blackwell, James & Miss Polly Ann Vass, 1 June 1836; Edward
   Hunt Jr., bm; T. T. Wiggins, wit.

Blackwell, John & Levina Fraizer, 21 Dec 1819; Ephraim Fraizer,
   bm; S. K. Sneed, wit.

Blackwell, John, of color, son of John & Sarah Young, & Ann
   Lassiter, daughter of Richard Royster & Harriet Lassiter,
   4 July 1867; m 28 July 1867 by R. J. Devin.

Blackwell, Joseph & Salley Chandler Banks, 24 Dec 1771; Thomas
   Banks, bm; Reuben Searcy, wit.

Blackwell, Pomfrett & Rebecca Stovall, 16 Nov 1793; Thomas
   Appling, bm; W. Norwood, wit.

Blackwell, Pomphret & Martha G. Currin, 22 Dec 1857; Thomas B.
   Frazier, bm; m 23 Dec 1857 by F. B. Currin, J. P.

Blackwell, Stephen & Isabella Fraizer, 6 Nov 1827; Thomas Vass
   Jr., bm; S. K. Sneed, wit.

Blackwell, Steven & Mary Morrow, 25 Aug 1866.

Blackwell, W. M. & Mary E. Wortham, m 3 Oct 1866 by Edward Hines.

Blackwell, William & Elizabeth Marshall, 27 Nov 1804; Henry M.
   Kinchen, bm; Jas. Sneed, wit.

Blackwill, Lewis & Dianer Morrow, 17 Aug 1866.

Blackwood, William C. & Martha M. Minor, 17 Feb 1829; Wm. H.
   Minor, bm; Step. K. Sneed, wit.

Blake, William & Susanna Bell, 12 Feb 1781; Obedyah John, bm;
   John Henderson, wit.

Blalock, David & Frances Champion, 21 Dec 1782; Christopher
   Kitley, bm; Reuben Searcy, wit.

Blalock, Hubbard & Patsey Ward, 2 Sept 1808; Jesse Shering, bm;
   A. H. Sneed, wit.

Blalock, Jerimiah & Lucy Bradford, 18 Dec 1781; Jehu Hall, bm;
   Bennet Searcy, wit.

GRANVILLE MARRIAGES 1753-1868

Blalock, John P. & Elizabeth Booswell, 13 Jan 1835; J. D. Hobgood, bm; Benja. Kittrell, wit.

Blalock, Mathew & Martha Bowers, 8 Nov 1825; Elias Huskey, bm; Wm. Hays Owen, wit.

Blalock, Millington & Jane D. Gooch, 16 Dec 1865; A. Landis, bm; m __ Dec 1865 by T. J. Horner.

Blalock, Millonton & Rebecah Philpot, 9 Aug 1797; Thos. Philpott, bm; Step. Sneed, wit.

Blalock, Thomas & Rowan Shearmon, 29 July 1837; Saml. Philpott, bm.

Blankenship, Samuel & Harriot Perry, 24 Aug 1815; Samuel Greenhill, bm; H. Young, wit.

Blanks, James H. & Emily K. Wilkerson, 28 Sept 1860; Edward A. Jones, bm; m 28 Sept 1860 by L. B. Stone, J. P.

Blanks, Joel B. & Amanda F. Wilkins, 19 Feb 1863; James H. Blanks, bm; m 19 Feb 1863 by L. B. Stone, J. P.

Blanks, Lydall B. & Rebecca Owen, 3 Jan 1856; William H. Royster, bm.

Blanks, Vincent N. & Lucy A. Davis, 1 Aug 1864; James B. Blanks, bm; m 1 Aug 1864 by L. B. Stone, J. P.

Bledsoe, Barney L. & Polly Davis, 12 Nov 1805; Presly Rice, bm; Jas. Sneed, wit.

Bledsoe, James A. & Susan A. May, 30 Nov 1847; William H. White, bm; J. M. Wiggins, wit.

Bledsoe, Jordan & Martha Cogwell, 9 Dec 1843; D. A. Stone, bm; Jas. M. Wiggins, wit.

Bledsoe, Lewis & Mary Minor, 8 April 1816; James Bullock Jr., bm; W. M. Sneed, wit.

Blount, John B. & Margaret Mutter, 13 Feb 1801; Thomas B. Littlejohn, bm; Sterling Yancey, wit.

Blunt, Benjamin & Sally D. Ridley, 14 Dec 181_; Thos. L. Ridley, bm; Richd. Sneed, wit.

Bobbet, Wm. & Lively Hight, 18 June 1788; Wm. Bobbet, bm; John Searcy, wit.

Bobbett, David & Louisa Bullock, freed people, 25 Dec 1866; Daniel Hester, bm; m 27 Dec 1866 by W. E. Bullock, J. P.

Bobbett, William O. & Mary C. Yancey, 18 Nov 1851; m 25 Nov 1851 by L. K. Willie, M. G.

Bobbit, Archibald & Mary Due, 31 May 1828; Mead Smith, bm; David Laws, wit.

Bobbit, Green & Barbary Finch, 8 June 1813; William Bowers, bm; Tho. J. Hicks, wit.

Bobbitt, Arthur & Dicey Duke, 7 May 1811; John Hunt, bm.

GRANVILLE MARRIAGES 1753-1868

Bobbitt, Benjamin & Ellen Royster, freed people, 31 Aug 1866; m 1 Sept 1866 by W. Overbey, J. P.

Bobbitt, Clabon J. & Jacksy L. Higgs, 27 Sept 1859; A. H. Cooke, bm.

Bobbitt, George & Angie C. A. Jenkins, freed people, 20 Oct 1865; Rufus Bobbitt, bm.

Bobbitt, John H. & Sarah J. Ingram, m 9 Sept 1855 by A. C. Harris, M. G.; bond dates 9 Sept 1855.

Bobbitt, John J. & Polly A. Hunt, 3 May 1859; D. E. Bobbitt, bm; m 12 May 1859 by L. K. Willie, M. G.

Bobbitt, Lewis & Ann H. C. Walton, 2 Nov 1858; Samuel Edwards, bm; m 17 Nov 1858 by J. Tillett, Minister of the M. E. Church, South.

Bobbitt, Patrick H. & Lucy A. Cheatham, 3 Nov 1835; Samuel Edwards, bm; Tho. H. Willie, wit.

Bobbitt, Rufus & Elisabeth M. Compton, 14 June 1851; Wm. O. Bobbitt, A. Landis, bm.

Bobbitt, T. E., son of D. E. & Patsey Bobbitt, & Susan A. York, daughter of John W. & Sarah Jane York, 24 Dec 1868; m 24 Dec 1868 by John Tillett, M. G.

Bobbitt, Thomas V. & Nancy L. Parham, 8 March 1856; Eugene Grissom, bm; m 12 March 1856 by L. K. Willie, M. G.

Bobbitt, William & Mary C. Yancey, 18 Nov 1851; Benj. C. Cooke, bm.

Bobbitt, William A. & Jacksey E. Mitchell, 1 Feb 1842; Benj. C. Cooke, bm; J. M. Wiggins, wit.

Bobitt, Lewis & Frances Ivens, 6 July 1867; Robert White, bm.

Bobitt, Lewis & Francis Evans (colored), 2 Jan 1868; m by W. P. White, J. P.

Boling, Jessey & Jemima Keneday, 20 Aug 1819; James Cozart, bm; Step. K. Sneed, wit.

Boling, Riley & Fanny Glenn, 9 Aug 1820; Pleasant Glenn, bm; Jas. M. Wiggins, wit.

Bolling, Cephas & Betsey Davis, 21 May 1836; Abram Plenty, bm; J. M. Wiggins, wit.

Bolling, James Jr. & Christiana Moore, 24 July 1782; James Bolling, bm; _____ Cooke, wit.

Bolling, Richard P. & Ann G. Taylor, 22 Feb 1819; John L. Scott, bm; Step. K. Sneed, wit.

Bolling, William & Mary Ann White, 10 May 1787; Peyton Ward, bm; Reuben Searcy, wit.

Bonner, William & Elizabeth Veazey, 26 Sept 1800; Philip Bullock, bm; Nancy Bullock, James Critcher, wit.

GRANVILLE MARRIAGES 1753-1868

Bonner, Ezekiel & Jemimah Griggs, 19 Aug 1802; Philip Bullock, bm; Henry McCay, wit.

Bonner, Jesse & Elisabeth Hester, 7 Nov 1797; Alexander Sample, bm; Step. Sneed, wit.

Bonner, Neverson & Mary Carter, 7 Aug 1825; George Anderson, bm; L. Gilliam, wit.

Booker, Mercer M. & Ann Somerville, 31 July 1832; Josiah Moseley, bm.

Bookram, Alfred & Anna Peed, 10 Dec 1852; Jesse Headspeth, bm; A. Landis, wit.

Bookram, Gavin & Patsey Evans, 3 May 1842; Manson Stuart, bm; J. M. Wiggins, wit.

Bookram, Galvin & Polly Chavis, 13 Feb 1854; Moses Headspeth, bm; A. Landis, wit; m 19 Feb 1854 by Jno. Nance, J. P.

Bookram, Solomon & Sallie Ann Pettiford, 6 Sept 1859; Robt. Garner, bm; m 11 Sept 1859 by R. T. Heflin, Minister of the Gospel.

Boon, James & Martha Cartis, 5 Jan 1845; Thos. Evans, bm; Jas. M. Wiggins, wit.

Boon, James & Mary Drew, 22 July 1856; Robert Green, bm; R. S. Hughes, wit; m 22 July 1856 by Edmd. Townes.

Booth, William & Lavina Davis, 20 Sept 1833; D. Wright, bm; Benja. Kittrell, wit.

Boon, Willis & Isabella Mayho, 21 Jan 1850; John Kates, bm; A. Landis, wit.

Boorhess, Samuel & Amanda Neal, 24 Jan 1854; Woody Tilletson, bm; A. Landis, wit; m 25 Jan 1854 by L. B. Stone, J. P.

Booth, Harper & Nancey Norwood Jones, 1 Oct 1800; Francis Jones, bm; Step. Sneed, wit.

Booth, John W. & Martha A. O. Kittrell, 5 March 1852; D. J. Marron, bm; m 10 March 1852 by A. C. Harris, M. G.

Booth, William & Abigail S. Lamon, 13 Sept 1824; Thomas Booth, bm; Geo. G. Eldridge, wit.

Boothe, Abner & Frances Raggland, 27 Nov 1807; Lesly Gilliam, bm; Jun. Sneed, wit.

Boothe, John H. & Meriah Blackwell, 24 Oct 1818; Henry Trotter, bm; Thomas C. Foulker, wit.

Boothe, Joseph & Nancy K. Whitfield, 31 Dec 1814; Wesly Whitfield, bm; Leslie Gilliam, wit.

Boothe, Thomas & Mary Duke, 2 Sept 1808; John Jones, bm; Jas. Sneed, wit.

Boswell, George & Martha Ray, 8 Oct 1832; Joseph Howe, bm; David Laws, wit.

GRANVILLE MARRIAGES 1753-1868

Boswell, George F. W. & Ann Nuttall, 10 June 1807; Clairborne Cook, bm; W. M. Sneed, wit.

Boswell, James & Luetta Blalock, 25 Jan 1839; Joseph D. Hobgood, bm.

Boswell, John & Temperance Crudup, 10 Sept 1865; m by E. H. Overton, J. P.

Boswell, John M. & Polly Spears, 16 March 1819; James Clay or Jas. Nuttall, bm.

Boswell, Joseph & Lucey Griffin, 17 Jan 1809; John Stovall, bm; William Fraiser, wit.

Boswell, Joseph T. & Ann Jinkins, 24 April 1813; Geo. A. Nuttall, bm; Tho. J. Hicks, wit.

Boswell, Ransom & Elizabeth Moss, 15 Nov 1790; Richard Henderson, bm; H. Potter, wit.

Boswell, William R. & Mary F. Richards, 6 Aug 1844; John S. Overbey, bm; J. M. Wiggins, wit.

Bottom, William W. & Mrs. Nancy Pitchford, 3 Feb 1859; Mark C. Turner, bm; W. M. Sneed, J. P., wit; m 3 Feb 1859 by W. M. Sneed, J. P.

Bowden, James & Prissillah Williams, 29 Oct 1785; William Bowdon, bm; Bennet Searcy, wit.

Bowden, John Junr. & Mary Vaughan, 6 Sept 1807; John Wilson, bm; Step. Sneed, wit.

Bowden, Thomas & Betsey Turner, 28 Sept 1815; John Green, bm; W. A. Thorpe, wit.

Bowden, Thomas U., son of Wm. & Parthenia Bowden, & Esther Gooch, daughter of Wm. & Lucy Gooch, 11 Jan 1868; m 11 Jan 1868 by B. D. Howard, J. P.

Bowden, William & Nancey Wiggins, 23 Dec 1797; Thomas Jordan, bm; Step. Sneed, wit.

Bowden, William & Parthena Thomasson, 7 May 1839; G. C. Wiggins, bm; Jas. M. Wiggins, wit.

Bowen, Armstead, son of Salisbury Thomas & Minerva Bowen, & Minerva Daniel, daughter of Whitfield & Cloe Daniel, m 22 Dec 1868 by Andrew Williams, J. P.

Bowen, John & Charlotte Keyton, 26 Dec 1837; Alexander Puryear, bm; L. Beasley Jr., wit.

Bowen, John & Jane Vaughan, 23 Aug 1847; John Davis(?), bm; L. B. Stone, J. P., wit.

Bowen, John & Patience Dyer, 22 Sept 1854; Frances B. Hester, bm; A. Landis, wit; m 23 Sept 1854 by Thos. Hester.

Bowen, Sandy Lewis & Nancy Keen, 15 Jan 1856; James B. Elixson, bm; m 15 Jan 1856 by L. B. Stone, J. P.

Bowen, William E. & Mary Rittaylander, 3 July 1821; Rhodes N. Herndon, bm; S. K. Sneed, wit.

GRANVILLE MARRIAGES 1753-1868

Bowen, William F. & Mary J. Redd, 4 Dec 1862; William T. Bowen, bm; m 4 Dec 1862 by L. B. Stone, J. P.

Bowers, William G. & Nancy Williams, 26 Jan 1814; James Nuttall, bm.

Bowers, Young P. & Jane Williams, 15 Nov 1816; Wm. G. Bowers, bm; W. M. Sneed, wit.

Bowie, George W. & Ann Glasscock, 8 June 1856.

Bowles, Benjamin & Sally Kirkland, 5 May 1839; Albert D. Nance, bm.

Bowles, John & Salina Roberts, 10 Aug 1865; m 11 Aug 1865 by Robt. L. Heflin, J. P.

Bowles, John Jr. & Deborah Oakley, 21 Feb 1801; James Oakley, bm; P. Bullock, wit.

Bowles, Jordan & Polley Wood, 21 Feb 1804; John Bowles Jr., bm; E. W. Parham, wit.

Bowles, Samuel & Mary Wooten, 27 Dec 1841; Jas. T. Downey, bm; J. M. Wiggins, wit.

Bowles, Tarleton & Mary Peake, 12 June 1855; Squire Williford, bm; A. Landis, wit; m 14 June 1855 by Peterson Thorp, J. P.

Bowles, William H. & Elizabeth F. Hudgings, m 5 Dec 1867 by G. W. Ferrill, Minister.

Bowlin, Presley P. & Rebecca F. Aikin, 22 Dec 1858; W. W. Reavis, bm; m 23 Dec 1858 by G. W. Ferrill.

Bowling, James W. & Emily J. Cash, 8 Aug 1866; m by T. J. Horner, G. M.

Bowling, John & Martha Mangum, 12 Aug 1790; Arthur Frazer, bm; H. Potter, wit.

Bowling, John Chesley & Miss Sarah Morris, 23 Oct 1847; Jno. Jones, bm.

Bowling, Peter & Peggy Durham, 6 Sept 1832; Lewis Curtis, bm; David Laws, wit.

Bowling, Wesley & Sarah Mize, 14 Nov 1853; Presley Bowling, bm; m 14 Nov 1853 by Cam. W. Allen, J. P.

Bowling, William & Frances Edwards, 13 Dec 1852; Jas. C. Cozart, bm; m 16 Dec 1852 by Cam. W. Allen, J. P.

Bowling, Willis & Elizabeth Wilkerson, 4 ___ 181_; William Mangum, bm; W. M. Sneed, wit.

Boyd, Anderson & Mary Hester, 8 Dec 1806; Samuel Gorden, bm; W. M. Sneed, wit.

Boyd, Anderson & Mary Murrah, 26 Nov 1832; Thomas Hester, bm; Jno. P. Smith, wit.

Boyd, Anderson & Selina Hart, 15 Dec 1846; Geo. W. Daniel, bm; J. M. Wiggins, wit.

GRANVILLE MARRIAGES 1753-1868

Boyd, Bruce & Sally Hart, 10 Oct 1832; Robt. Boyd, bm; Jno. P. Smith, wit.

Boyd, Edward S. & Julia Ann Short, 6 Dec 1866; J. A. Boyd, bm; C. E. Landis, wit; m 9 Dec 1866 by Jas. R. Duty, J. P.

Boyd, George & Anne Fraizer, 1 Aug 1801; Sherwood Smith, bm; Step. Sneed, wit.

Boyd, James & Lethe Hester, 5 Dec 1832; Robt. Boyd, bm; Jno. P. Smith, wit.

Boyd, James H. & Harriet Daniel, 17 Dec 1860; William S. Eakes, bm; m 21 Dec 1860 by W. H. Currin, J. P.

Boyd, John & Mary Merrit, 30 Sept 1768; Robert Boyd, Joseph Langston, bm; Jesse Benton, wit.

Boyd, John & Sarah Hester, 15 Nov 1780; Robert Hester, bm; Bennet Searcy, wit.

Boyd, John A. & Elizabeth Frazier, 14 Dec 1865; Addison W. Gunn, bm; Jas. R. Duty, wit; m 21 Dec 1865 by W. H. Puryear, J. P.

Boyd, John Henry & Harriet Jane Moore, 10 Jan 1854; Bruce Boyd, bm; A. Landis, wit; m 12 Jan 1854 by Thos. Hester.

Boyd, P. A. & Adaline Wilkins, 13 Jan 1867; L. S. Wilkins, bm; m 13 Jan 1867 by L. B. Stone, J. P.

Boyd, Robert & Sarah Puryear, 11 Feb 1800; Peter Puryear, bm; Wm. Yancey Jr., wit.

Boyd, Robert J. & Mary G. Davis, 27 Oct 1833; Lewis D. Burnet(?), bm; James Twitty, wit.

Boyd, Thomas & Dolley Cox, 8 Feb 1780; James Yancey, bm; _____ Wade, wit.

Boyd, William & Frances Bullock, 28 April 1791; Lewis Potter, bm.

Boyd, William & Lidia Hart, 30 Nov 1842; Bartlet Knott, bm; Wm. H. Whitfield, wit.

Boyd, Wm. H. & Sarah V. Daniel, 13 April 1856; A. R. Burwell, bm; m 30 April 1856 by E. Hines.

Boyd, William T. & Jennie E. Speed, 14 Nov 1860; T. B. Lewis, bm; m 28 Nov 1860 by E. Hines.

Brach, Burwell & Nancy Brach, 26 Dec 1794; William Brach, bm; Step. Sneed, wit.

Brack, George & Nancy Griggs, 2 March 1790; Samuel Reeves, bm; A. Henderson, wit.

Brackett, Thomas H. & Martha P. Puryear, 13 March 1816; Jno. W. Nash, bm; H. Young, wit.

Bradford, Booker & Fanny Man, 5 Nov 1788; George Brasford, bm.

Bradford, David & Elisabeth Man, 6 Nov 1777; Benjamin Wright, bm; Pleasant Henderson, wit.

GRANVILLE MARRIAGES 1753-1868

Bradford, David Jr. & Mary Kerney, 2 Aug 1784; Arnold Harris(?), bm; Bennet Searcy, wit.

Bradford, Elijah & Nancy Welch, 14 March 1797; James Bradford, bm; Step. Sneed, wit.

Bradford, Harris & Mary Previt, 1 Feb 1790; Joseph Pewet, bm.

Bradford, Jackson R. & Ann E. Cannady, 10 Dec 1844; T. B. Moore, bm; J. M. Wiggins, wit.

Bradford, James & Lucy Paschall, 27 Sept 1839; John Smith, bm.

Bradford, John (of Elijah) & Nancy Smith, 1 Nov 1831; J. H. Cauthen, bm; Step. K. Sneed, wit.

Bradford, Kearney & Patsey Carrel, 27 Sept 1805; Isaac Husketh, bm; Jas. Sneed, wit.

Bradford, Robert & Nancy Karrel, 16 Dec 1809; Charles Moore (Moon?), bm; Richd. Sneed, wit.

Bradford, Thomas & Eve Kerney, 2 April 1782; Booker Bradford, bm; Bennet Searcy, wit.

Bradford, Thomas & Polley Hargraves, 12 Aug 1782; Nath. Hunt, bm; Bennet Searcy, wit.

Bradford, Wm. & Nancey Kittrell, 13 Feb 1808; Garland Allen, bm; W. M. Sneed, wit.

Bradford, William & Melvina Overton, 29 Aug 1857; D. E. Bobbitt, bm; m 30 Aug 1857 by Tho. L. Williams, J. P.

Bradley, Isaac & Rosey Knight, 1 Aug 1804; John Haskins, bm; E. Parham, wit.

Bradley, Isaac & Polley Cardwell, 6 Nov 1804; Aaron Farabough, bm; E. W. Parham, wit.

Bradshaw, Jesse & Martha C. Jones, 9 June 1821; Reuben Jones, bm; James M. Wiggins, wit.

Brady, Patrick & Molly Philpot, 18 July 1763; Henrey Fuller, bm; Jno. Bowie, wit.

Bragg, Alexander H. & Emah F. Meadows, 11 Feb 1861; John H. Bragg, bm; m 12 Feb 1861 by B. B. Hester.

Bragg, Alexander H. & Susan Meadows, 11 Jan 1865; W. W. Bragg, bm; m 15 Sept 1865 by B. B. Hester.

Bragg, Hugh & Molsey Priddy, 4 Sept 1812; Geo. Nuttall, bm.

Bragg, James F. & Margaret E. C. Brummett, 12 Dec 1856; John W. Mitchell, bm; m 23 Dec 1856 by J. H. Floyd, Minister.

Bragg, Joel & Sally Catlett, 20 Dec 1825; Laborn Catlett, bm; Wm. H. Owen, wit.

Bragg, Joel & Gilly Williams, 12 Dec 1829; William Cudden, bm; David Laws, wit.

Bragg, John W. & Sarah H. Rust, 6 Aug 1860; G. N. Hicks, bm; m 22 Aug 1860 by W. R. White, J. P.

GRANVILLE MARRIAGES 1753-1868

Bragg, Joseph & June Hunt, 15 Aug 1810; Benjamin Bragg, bm;
Step. Sneed, wit.

Bragg, Newman & Prudence Gooch, 9 March 1816; Hezekiah Strum,
bm.

Bragg, Newman N. & Nancey Mitchel, 26 Dec 1821; Richard Bullock,
bm; L. Gilliam, wit.

Bragg, Stephen & Susan Levister, 14 Dec 1824; Henry Hendly, bm;
Wm. H. Owen, wit.

Bragg, Thomas & Nancy Cokely, 5 March 1847; L. L. Philpott, bm;
J. M. Wiggins, wit.

Bragg, Thomas W. & Virginia A. Long, 7 Feb 1860; A. Landis, bm.

Bragg, Whittemore & Arabell Smith, 5 Jan 1842; Wm. M. Sykes, bm;
J. M. Wiggins, wit.

Braim, William R. & Elizabeth R. Pruit, 13 March 1841; Robert
Haris, bm; Jas. M. Wiggins, wit.

Bram, John J. & Lucretia R. Parham, 11 Nov 1860; William S.
Satterwhite, bm; m 11 Nov 1860 by John F. Harris, J. P.

Brame, Caleb & Rosa Reavis, 30 March 1866; m 31 March 1866 by
S. P. J. Harris, M. G.

Brame, George & Julia Harris, m 15 May 1866 by Jas. R. Duty,
J. P.

Brame, George W. & Lucy Stone, 16 Dec 1844; John W. Grissom,
bm; Wm. H. Whitfield, wit.

Brame, James & Amey Weaver, 6 Nov 1816; Meradith Ellington, bm;
Richd. Sneed, wit.

Brame, James A., son of James W. & Mary T. Brame, & Matilda
Debnam, daughter of John B. & Damsel R. Debnam, m 24 Dec
1868 by S. P. J. Harris, M. G.

Brame, James C. & Nancy Morgan, 10 May 1813; William H. Lanier,
bm; Richard Sneed, wit.

Brame, James W. & Mary T. Hester, 3 July 1839; Meredith Ellington, bm; J. M. Wiggins, wit.

Brame, John & Nancy Revis, 10 Dec 1792; Thos. H. Phillips, bm;
Step. Sneed, wit.

Brame, John T. M. & Mary E. Vaughan, 8 July 1851; John J. Vaughan, bm.

Brame, London & Catherine Durham, 23 July 1866; m by S. P. J.
Harris, M. G.

Brame, Peter & Martha Moss, 4 Sept 1827; Meredith Ellington,
bm; L. Gilliam, wit.

Brame, Robert P. & Martha A. E. Roberson, 2 Nov 1852; William
N. Robards, bm; A. Landis, wit; m 9 Nov 1852 by A. C. Harris,
M. G.

GRANVILLE MARRIAGES 1753-1868

Brame, Samuel & Nancy Revis, 17 Sept 1821; Thomas Brame, bm; Jas. M. Wiggins, wit.

Brame, T. H. & Martha E. Jones, 12 Dec 1854; A. H. Alley, bm; m 13 Dec 1854 by A. C. Harris, M. G.

Brame, Thomas & Elizabeth Roffe, 11 Feb 1778; James Brame, bm; Abner Tatom, wit.

Brame, Thomas & Nancey Royster, 15 Aug 1817; Absalom Yancey, bm; W. M. Sneed, wit.

Brame, Thomas & Julia Pinson, 18 Oct 1839; Littleton Ragland, bm; J. M. Wiggins, wit.

Brame, Tignal H. & Martha A. Burton, 25 Nov 1856; W. D. Hanon, bm; m 27 Nov 1856 by W. H. Jordan.

Brame, Warner & Sarah Paller, 24 March 1813; John Ellington, bm; Step. Sneed, wit.

Brame, William H. & Martha F. Dunn, 27 July 1857; Jas. R. Duty, bm; m 27 July 1857 by Jas. R. Dury, J. P.

Brame, William L. & Sarah E. Holmes, 21 Feb 1853; Asa C. Parham, bm; A. Landis, wit.

Brandam, Peter & Jane Brandam, 19 Dec 1833; Evans Chavis, bm; Benja. Kittrell, wit.

Brandon, Giles & Sally Ann Evans, 27 Nov 1846; Henry Parker, bm; Wm. H. Whitfield, wit.

Brandon, Jacob & Margaret Cousins, 25 Dec 1862; John Teal, bm; m 25 Dec 1862 by T. Hester, J. P.

Brandon, Oce, son of Hilliard & Betsey Brandon, & Panthea Eaton, daughter of Henry Peace and Mary Eaton, 23 Dec 1868; m 24 Dec 1868 by Jefferson Burll.

Brandum, Bivins & Gilly Ann Pettiford, 1 Dec 1857; m 3 Dec 1857 by George J. Rowland, J. P.

Brandum, Chesley & Susan Anderson, 8 Oct 1840; Collins Pettiford, bm; W. T. Hay---, wit.

Brandum, John & Mary Chavis, 20 Nov 1824; George Anderson, bm; Wm. H. Owen, wit.

Brantley, Abraham & Nancey Dickerson, 16 Oct 1807; Ransom Dickerson, bm; W. M. Sneed, wit.

Brasfield, Caleb & Lucy Peake, 2 Dec 1784; Bennet Searcy, bm; Reuben Searcy, wit.

Brassel, John & Louiza Petteford, 23 Feb 1858; Wright Brasel, bm; A. Laurence, wit; m 25 Feb 1858.

Brassfield, Caleb & Catharine Jeter, 18 Sept 1821; William Clement, bm; S. K. Sneed, wit.

Bray, Henry J. & Mary C. V. Tuck, 29 June 1864; G. W. Fletcher, bm; m 29 June 1864 by L. B. Stone, J. P.

GRANVILLE MARRIAGES 1753-1868

Bray, Obadiah & Sarah Ford, 25 June 1851; James Ford, bm; L. B. Stone, wit; statement from James Ford that Sarah Ford is over 21 years of age; m 25 June 1851 by Littlebury Stone, J. P.

Breedlove, David & Sippy Thomasson, 1 May 1862; A. Landis, bm; m 8 May 1862 by L. K. Willie, M. G.

Breedlove, Emanuel & Ellen Clarke, 22 May 1827; Bevil Ellington, bm; Wm. H. Owen, wit.

Breedlove, James W. & Martha R. Duke, 2 Nov 1863; T. A. Stewart, bm; m 18 Nov 1863 by T. A. Stewart, J. P.

Breedlove, John H., son of Manson H. & Martha P. Breedlove, & Susan C. Hunt, daughter of Joseph P. & Martha Hunt, 17 Dec 1868; m 24 Dec 1869 by L. K. Willie, M. G.

Breedlove, Manson H. & Martha P. Crews, 27 Dec 1832; Willis Daniel, bm; David Laws, wit.

Breedlove, Nathan H. & Ann Meriah Clark, 9 Sept 1854; A. Landis, bm; m 10 Sept 1854 by Lewis R. Parham, J. P.

Breedlove, Randal H. & Malissa Loyd, 21 Feb 1860; Wm. H. Kittrell, bm.

Breedlove, William & Euphemia C. Thomasson, 20 Nov 1860; L. K. Willie, bm; m 23 Nov 1860 by L. K. Willie, M. G.

Breedlove, William & Ann Eliza J. Woodliff, 1 Feb 1864; A. Landis, bm; m 3 Feb 1864 by E. H. Overton, J. P.

Breedlove, William A. & Fanny Rowland, 5 Jan 1838; Nelson Barns (?), bm.

Bressie, Francis & Mary Shearman, 2 Sept 1807; Robert Kinton, bm; W. M. Sneed, wit.

Bressie, Yerby & Susannah Frazer, 10 June 1802; Jeremiah Frazer, bm; Nancy Bullock, wit.

Brett, Obed & Polly Smith, 30 Oct 1782; Wiat Wilkerson, bm; Reuben Searcy, wit; consent from Anderson Smith, sister of Polly, 29 Oct 1782.

Briant, John C. & Edney Cash, 12 Oct 1861; Wiley L. G. Perry, bm; m 6 Nov 1861 by R. B. Hester.

Briant, William & Temperance Harris, 7 Jan 1800; Augustine Harris, bm; James Sneed, wit.

Bridgers, Samuel H. J. & E. Harriett Raney, 6 July 1865; A. Landis, bm.

Bridges, Allen & Harriet S. Sikes, 5 April 1838; Jos. B. Pean, bm; S. G. Shearmon, wit.

Bridges, Drury & Polley Cavender, 17 Jan 1786; Bryant Cavender, bm; Bennet Searcy, wit.

Bridges, Henry B. & Amanda M. Cannady, 4 Jan 1839; Fenner Tharrington, bm; J. M. Wiggins, wit.

GRANVILLE MARRIAGES 1753-1868

Bridges, John & Sarah Hendley, 24 Dec 1825; Maurice Byrum, bm; M. M. Henderson, wit.

Bridges, Stephen & Pheby Morriss, 19 Jan 1804; Bryant Cavendar, bm; Danl. Bridges, wit.

Bridges, Thomas & Anne Lashly, 10 Aug 1771; James Bridges, bm; Jesse Benton, wit.

Bridges, Thomas & Polly Bridges, 26 March 1803; Stephen Bridges, bm; Green Merritt, wit.

Bridges, Thomas & Mary Sykes, 8 Feb 1853; B. J. Blackley, bm.

Bridges, Wisemond(?) & Polley Bradford, 5 Dec 1784; Isaac Vincent, bm; Bennet Searcy, wit.

Briggs, Alexander & Betsy Arnold, 2 June 1845; Wilson Levington, bm.

Briggs, George & Frances Hunt, 11 Dec 1800; Jeremiah Fazrier Jr., bm; P. Bullock, wit.

Briggs, Henry & Elizabeth Huddleton, 30 Dec 181_; John Kinton, bm.

Briggs, Henry & Sarah West, 4 Feb 1840; Murry Wheeler, bm; J. M. Wiggins, wit.

Briggs, Henry & Rachel Strum, 8 Sept 1843; Wm. H. Wade, bm; Jas. M. Wiggins, wit.

Briggs, Howell & Lucey Parrish, 17 June 1812; John Duncan, bm; W. M. Sneed, wit.

Briggs, John & Frances Jackson, 26 March 1829; Wm. S. McClenahan, bm; Step. K. Sneed, wit.

Briggs, John S. & Ellen J. Kearney, 5 Dec 1850; Chesly Curren, bm.

Briggs, Joseph & Jemima Bradford, 7 Dec 1796; John Bradford Pruit, bm; Richard Taylor, wit.

Briggs, Richard & Alee West, 28 Dec 1784; Ephraim Fraizer, bm; Bennet Searcy, wit.

Brinkley, Alfred & Tyresa Roberts, 19 Nov 1831; Jas. Waller, bm; David Laws, wit.

Brinkley, Daniel & Jane Kernall, 13 Jan 1804; Locker Partee, bm; Step. Sneed, wit.

Brinkley, Henry A. & Mary R. White, 24 July 1819; George Parham, bm; Step. K. Sneed, wit.

Brinkley, Isham & Celey Cole, 6 Dec 1827; Henry Tilly, bm; David Laws, wit.

Brinkley, James & Martha Hester, 7 May 1833; John H. Brinkley, bm; David Laws, wit.

Brinkley, James C. & Frances Adcock, 9 March 1843; N. M. Carrington, bm; Wm. H. Whitfield, wit.

GRANVILLE MARRIAGES 1753-1868

Brinkley, James H. & Massay Fuller, 24 Nov 1824; James Parrott, bm; Wm. H. Owen, wit.

Brinkley, John & Edney Jenkins, 21 Feb 1838; William Jinkins, bm; J. M. Wiggins, wit.

Brinkley, John H. & Jane Parrish, 3 Dec 1832; Ralph Parish, bm; David Laws, wit.

Brinkley, Mark & Milley Johnson, 29 Dec 1829; Horace Sommerhill, bm; W. M. Sneed, wit.

Brinkley, Nelson & Sally Arnold, 8 May 1838; Wm. H. Jones, bm; Edward Jones, wit.

Brinkley, Richard & Elisabeth Turner, 1 April 1793; James Brinkley, bm; Step. Sneed, wit.

Brinkley, Robert & Frankey Griffin, 20 June 1809; James Spencer, bm; Jun. Sneed, wit.

Brinkley, Ruffin & Nancy OBriant, 9 Nov 1857; Macon Johnson, bm.

Brinkley, Walter J. & Brady Ann Oakley, 11 Nov 1865; H. Latta, bm; m 15 Nov 1865 by G. W. Ferrill, Minister of the Gospel.

Brinkley, Washington & Bettie Horner, 14 Sept 1860; Macon Johnson, bm.

Brinkley, William & Fortune Howell, 11 Sept 1793; John Lock, bm; Step. Sneed, wit.

Brinkley, William & Sarah Higgs, 8 March 1825; Henry A. Brinkley, bm; Wm. Hayes Owen, wit.

Brinkly, Stephen & Babby Goss, 21 Feb 1803; Benjamin Mise, bm; Green Merritt, wit.

Brintle, Jacob & Mary Parish, 28 Dec 1819(?); John Jinkins, bm; Jas. M. Wiggins, wit.

Bristow, George Jr. & Sarah Guest, 30 Nov 1782; Clabon Harris, bm; Sherwood Harris, wit.

Bristow, Phillip & Sarah Bell, 25 Jan 1779; Claborn Harris, bm; Edmond Smith, wit.

Dritton, Richard O. & Maria P. Kennon, 23 Oct 1846; R. H. Kingsbury, bm; J. M. Wiggins, wit.

Britton, Stephen W. & Susan C. Taylor, 7 Oct 1850; E. H. Hicks, bm.

Brock, James & Frankey Driskel, 9 Jan 1800; Burwell Brock, bm; James Sneed, wit.

Brodie, John & Mary Taylor, 3 Feb 1779; Joseph Taylor, bm; Reuben Searcy, wit; consent of Edmund Taylor, father of Mary, 3 Feb 1779; Elizabeth Hunter, wit.

Brodie, Thomas & Salley Kittrell, 26 Aug 1811; Henry Norman, bm; W. M. Sneed, wit.

Brodie, Thomas & Melvina Higgs (colored), 17 March 1866; m 17 March 1866 by Lewis H. Kittle, J. P.

GRANVILLE MARRIAGES 1753-1868

Brodie, Thomas L. & Elizabeth Thorp, 11 Jan 1840; Archibald Taylor, bm.

Brogden, David & Sarah Allen, 29 May 1852; D. C. Herndon, bm.

Brogden, Elias & Lucretia Cash, 28 May 1858; Kintchin Hathcock, bm; A. Landis, wit; m 28 May 1858 by J. H. Dalby, J. P.

Brogden, Elisha, son of James & Polly Brogden, & Elizabeth H. Vaughan, daughter of Jackson & Caroline Vaughan, 6 Oct 1868; m 9 Oct 1868 by R. B. Hester, M. G.

Brogden, George & Sarah Beck, 20 Dec 1821; Richard Ferguson, bm; Step. K. Sneed, wit.

Brogden, Isaiah & Susan Roberson, 8 Oct 1850; John Sherrin, bm; A. Landis, wit.

Brogden, James & Crissey Cash, 6 Nov 1811; William Cash, bm; W. M. Sneed, wit.

Brogden, James & Mary Cash, 19 Nov 1858; A. Landis, bm.

Brogdon, Benja. & Edy Wheler, 11 Oct 1822; William Suit, bm; Jas. M. Wiggins, wit.

Brogdon, David & Winneford Wheeler, 19 July 1822; Isaac Brogdon, bm; Jas. M. Wiggins, wit.

Brogdon, David & Susan Emory, 30 Sept 1840; Thos. Perry, bm; J. M. Wiggins, wit.

Brogdon, John & Susannah Hoofman, 22 Dec 1824; David Brogdon, bm; Step. K. Sneed, wit.

Brogdon, Washington & Jane A. Chappell, 17 June 1848; Thomas Pittard, bm; Jas. M. Wiggins, wit.

Brogdon, William & Anne Haley, 12 July 1838; Daniel Fowler, bm; S. G. Shearmon, wit.

Brogdon, William T. & Helon Jackson, 9 June 1862; Robert Garner, bm; m 11 June 1862 by W. D. Allen, J. P.

Brogdon, Willie & Betsey Hoofman, 24 Jan 1824; Moses H. Bonner, bm; Wm. H. Owen, wit.

Brook, Samuel P. & Stella Francis Pool, 9 Dec 1865; S. P. Pool, bm.

Brookbanks, William & Nancy Moss, 5 Jan 1841; George Parish, bm.

Brookhanks, William & Rhodey Harding, 15 Nov 1816; Absolam Parrish, bm; W. M. Sneed, wit.

Brooks, Gillis & Susan Card, 29 Aug 1861; Shemuel Cook, bm.

Brooks, Green & Elizabeth P. Smith, 7 Oct 1829; William P. Smith, bm; David Laws, wit.

Brooks, John Jr. & Levina Smith, 14 Sept 1834; William P. Smith, bm; S. Harris, wit.

GRANVILLE MARRIAGES 1753-1868

Brooks, Richard D. & Mrs. Elizabeth J. Sizemore, 6 Dec 1856; m 6 Dec 1866 by Samuel Hunt, J. P.; Geo. W. Dean, bm; A. Landis, wit.

Brooks, Silas H. & Addie Hambett, 18 June 1862; A. Landis, bm; m 19 June 1862 by W. H. Jordan.

Browden, James W. & Martha Ann Bowen, 7 Dec 1848; John Bowen, bm; L. B. Stone, J. P., wit.

Browden, Venus & Sarah Dunn, 31 Jan 1816; Larken White, bm; H. Young, wit.

Brown, Dempsey & Phereba Harden, 19 Jan 1811; Parmenus Johnson, bm; W. M. Sneed, wit.

Brown, Edmond & Rebecca Harris, 11 June 1859; L. J. Peoples, bm; m 11 June 1859 by W. M. Sneed, J. P.

Brown, Gaston E. & Louisa B. Cooke, 14 April 1835; J. W. Hancock(?), bm.

Brown, Isaac A. & Elizabeth Potter, 22 Sept 1819; Nathaniel Robards, bm; S. K. Sneed, wit.

Brown, James G. & Isabella Loyd, 25 March 1861; James Loyd, bm; m 28 March 1861 by Wm. M. Bennett, J. P.

Brown, John & Molley Hays, 6 Sept 1793; Benj. Hays, bm; Step. Sneed, wit.

Brown, John G. & Olivia(?) A. Brightwell, 17 Dec 1849; William Claiton, bm; Jas. N. Braly, wit.

Brown, John T. M. & Mary E. Vaughan, m 9 July 1851 by A. C. Harris, M. G.

Brown, Jonathan F. & Mary R. Parish, 14 May 1838; Peter Evans, bm; J. M. Wiggins, wit.

Brown, Josiah & Patsey Daniel, 6 June 1794; Thomas Daniel, bm; H. Seawell, wit.

Brown, Peyton J. & Sally W. Harris, __ Nov 1832; Thos. Coghill, bm; John B. Debnam, wit.

Brown, Richard H. & Fanney Honing, 1 Oct 1812; George W. Holloway, bm; Step. Sneed, wit.

Brown, Robert & Elisabeth Carter, 7 Sept 1792; William Collins, bm; Step. Sneed, wit.

Brown, Zadock & Susan Kimball, 10 Feb 1822; Joseph Harper, bm; S. K. Sneed, wit.

Bruce, Charles & Bettey Benton, 27 Oct 1768; Ben. Hardy, bm; Saml. Benton, wit.

Bruce, George & Amey Drewry, 7 Nov 1785; William Hester(?), bm; Wm. Searcy, wit.

Bruce, John N. & Mary S. Crymes, 4 Dec 1833; Philip P. Moore, bm; Benja. Kittrell, wit.

GRANVILLE MARRIAGES 1753-1868

Brummel, Henry & Emily Chavis, 3 Nov 1849; Frederick Ivy(?), bm; L. B. Stone, J. P., wit.

Brummett, John & Cassy Demont, 12 Oct 1805; Thomas Demont, bm; Jas. Sneed, wit.

Brummett, John H., son of Wesley & Martha Brummett & Lucy Frances Freeman, daughter of Calvin & Betsy Freeman, m 27 Feb 1868 by W. D. Allen, J. P.

Brummett, Nimrod & Nancy Fraizer, 28 Jan 1817; Daniel Fowler, bm; Rhodes N. Herndon, wit.

Brummett, Samuel & Mary Blackley, 29 Oct 1814; Garland Allen, bm; W. M. Sneed, wit.

Brummett, Wesley & Martha E. Bobbitt, 20 Dec 1837; W. D. Allen, bm; S. G. Shearman, wit.

Brummett, William & Mary Crews, 8 Jan 1800; Colbe Crews, bm; Step. Sneed, wit.

Brummett, William L. & Phebe Cawthorn, 6 March 1855; A. L. Dement, bm.

Brummitt, James R. & Elizabeth J. Grissom, 18 May 1858; L. K. Willie, bm; m 20 May 1858 by L. K. Willie.

Brummitt, John & Margaret B. Bobbitt, 13 June 1843; John J. Bobbitt, bm; Wm. H. Whitfield, wit.

Brummitt, Wm. C. & Ann E. Parish, 1 Jan 1846; Chas. Blackley, bm; J. M. Wiggins, wit.

Brundage, David & Elizabeth Baxter, 27 March 1786; Elijah Weazey, bm; John Searcy, wit.

Bryant, Edward & Nancy Parham, 14 Dec 1801; William Butler, bm; P. Bullock, wit.

Bryant, Edward & Elizabeth Amis, 17 Feb 1818; Rholles N. Herndon, bm; Saml. Montague, wit.

Bryant, Ferington & Harriot Amis, 23 Dec 1824; George Thomasson Jr., bm; Step. K. Sneed, wit.

Bryant, Ferrington & Martha Kittrell, 1 Jan 1837; James J. Bryant, bm; J. M. Wiggins, wit.

Bryant, James H. & Mary Boswell, 20 July 1822; Thomas Nuttall, bm; S. V. Sneed, wit.

Bryant, James J. & Rebecca J. Reavis, 14 Nov 1838; Jos. P. Hunt, bm.

Bryant, John & Nancey Hargrove, 4 Sept 1790; Robert Burton, bm; Henry Potter, wit.

Bryant, John & Anne Ruseteim, 3 Jan 1804; Joshua White, bm; A. H. Sneed, wit.

Bryant, John F. & Salley Amis, 3 Nov 1812; Lewis Parham Jr., bm; W. M. Sneed, wit.

GRANVILLE MARRIAGES 1753-1868

Bryant, Mathew (colored), son of Isaac & Rachiel Bryant, & Kevia Ann Grissom, daughter of Hod Pretty, 30 Dec 1868; m 31 Dec 1868 by C. M. Rogers, J. P.

Bryant, Robertson & Nancy Amis, 13 Feb 1818; Samuel Montague, bm; A. Tomlinson, wit.

Bryant, Rowland Junr. & Julia Ann Harris, 13 March 1820; James H. Bryant, bm; Step. K. Sneed, wit.

Bryant, Samuel & Mary Philpott, 20 Aug 1798; Thos. Philpott, bm; Step. Sneed, wit.

Buchanan, David & Elizabeth Johnson, 1 Feb 1810; John Buchanan, bm; W. M. Sneed, wit.

Buchanan, Davis & Caroline Elixson, 22 Jan 1833; Baldy Ramsey, bm; Jno. P. Smith, wit.

Buchanan, James & Elisabeth Weathers, 8 Nov 1796; James Paschal, bm; Step. Sneed, wit.

Buchanan, John & Amey Wilkerson, 1 Feb 1810; David Buchanan, bm; W. M. Sneed, wit.

Buchanan, John R. & Nancy A. Pittard, 8 Oct 1852; Alexander B. Montague, bm; A. Landis, wit; m 10 Oct 1852 by Jas. T. Montague, M. G.

Buchanan, Robert & Isabella Ellixson, 13 Nov 1844; Luther R. Jeffries, bm; Jas. M. Wiggins, wit.

Buchanan, Thomas F. & Mary F. Ford, 16 Dec 1854; Georg. W. Buchanan, bm; m 30 Dec 1854 by B. V. Hopkins.

Buchanan, William & Enicey Guy, 3 Jan 1806; John OBrien, bm; Jun. Sneed, wit.

Buckhannon, Hillard & Roza Clopton, 21 Aug 1833; Willis Hutchinson, bm; Benja. Kittrell, wit.

Buckhannon, William & Frances Hayes, 20 Dec 1837; H. E. Puryear, bm; L. Beasley Jr., wit.

Buckner, John & Susannah Caudle, 7 April 1813; John Jones, bm; Step. Sneed, wit.

Buckner, Paskel & Midda Bowers, 6 April 1816; Meredith Ellington, bm; Richard Sneed, wit.

Buffalo, Wm. & Susan Stroud, 7 Jan 1849; Green B. Elliot, bm; Jas. M. Wiggins, wit.

Bugg, Anselm & Lucy Morgan, 10 May 1791; John Allen, bm; W. Norwood, wit.

Bugg, John & Rebecka Mitchel, 24 Dec 1788; Henry Sandefer, bm.

Bugg, John J. & Martha J. Singleton, 15 Dec 1858; W. T. Rice, bm; m 15 Oct 1858 by James R. Duty, J. P.

Bugg, Napoleon C. & Eliza G. Harris, 22 Dec 1856; Watkins M. Bugg, bm; J. R. Duty, wit; m 30 Dec 1856 by Jas. R. Duty, J. P.

GRANVILLE MARRIAGES 1753-1868

Bugg, Saml. & Frances Lewis, 25 Nov 1788; Henry Pattillo, bm; A. Henderson, C. C., wit.

Bugg, Watkins M. & Mary J. Simmons, 8 Dec 1859; Thomas E. Rucks, bm; Jas. R. Duty, wit; m 8 Dec 1859 by Jas. R. Duty, J. P.

Bull, William C. & Maranda A. Collier, 26 Jan 1830; M. J. Whitacer, bm; David Laws, wit.

Bullock, Albert & Harriett Wright, 2 March 1867; John T. Jenkins, bm; m 3 March 1867 by Benj. F. Jenkins.

Bullock, Alex & Celia Daniel, freed people, 25 Dec 1866; m by A. C. Harris, M. G.

Bullock, Benjamin F. & Martha A. Smith, 20 Jan 1859; D. A. Paschall, bm; m 25 Jan 1859 by B. B. Hester.

Bullock, Benjamin F. Jr. & Henrietta E. Fleming, 3 May 1864; E. Dalby, bm.

Bullock, Doctor C. & Martha H. Whitfield, 27 May 1846; Jas. B. Webster, bm.

Bullock, Durant & Mary J. Green, 27 Jan 1852; W. D. Allen, bm; m 29 Jan 1852.

Bullock, Edmund & Frances Venable, freed people, 8 Oct 1865; Peter Hunt, bm; m 8 Oct 1865 by Maurice H. Vaughan, Rector of St. Stephens Church.

Bullock, Edward & Catharine White, 16 Dec 1865; David Bobbitt, bm; A. Landis, wit; m 22 Dec 1865 by E. Dalby, J. P.

Bullock, George & Mary Freeman, 25 Oct 1796; Peter Mann, bm; _____ Sneed, wit.

Bullock, George & Malinda Green, 24 April 1833; Tarlton Johnson, bm; David Laws, wit.

Bullock, Gideon F. & Susan Haskins, 5 Sept 1853; Jas. S. Finch, bm; m 6 Sept 1853 by Jeff Horner, J. P.

Bullock, Henry A. & Nancy F. Goss, 25 Jan 1847; Young Jones, bm; J. M. Wiggins, wit.

Bullock, James & Mary Phillips, 30 Sept 1792; William Phillips, bm; W. Norwood, wit.

Bullock, James & Martha Webb, 21 Aug 1833; Eaton H. Kittrell, bm; Benja. Kittrell, wit.

Bullock, James A. & Agness B. Taylor, 6 June 1853; H. T. Watkins, bm; James R. Duty, wit; m 8 June 1853 by Thos. F. Davis.

Bullock, James Jr. & Ruth Adcock, 20 Dec 1815; Samuel Bullock, bm; Leslie Gilliam, wit.

Bullock, James M. & Sarah A. Lewis, 4 Nov 1835; Will. H. Bullock, bm.

Bullock, James T. & Uphemia E. Ferabow, 21 Dec 1852; H. F. Moore, bm.

GRANVILLE MARRIAGES 1753-1868

Bullock, John & Susan Cobb, 23 Aug 1824; John T. Hunt, bm; Wm. H. Owen, wit.

Bullock, John & Mary Mitchell, daughter of James Mitchell, 12 Nov 1759; John Williams Jr., bm; consent from James Mitchell, father of Mary, 12 Nov 1759; Zac. Bullock, Richd. Satterwhite, wit.

Bullock, John & Susan Wilkerson, 29 Dec 1866; m 29 Dec 1866 by Wm. H. Puryear, Esq.

Bullock, John Jr. & Catherine Lewis, 11 March 1771; William Bullock, bm; William Kennon, wit.

Bullock, John H. & Mary H. Burns, 8 Oct 1834; Theo(?), L. Huey, bm.

Bullock, Joseph & Tealey Mitchell, 17 March 1866; A. R. Chappell, bm; m 13 May 1866 by B. B. Hester.

Bullock, Joshua & Ann Cook, 21 Jan 1781; James Hawkins, bm; Avary Parham, wit.

Bullock, Joshua & Milly Richard, 7 Nov 1825; Henry Chambliss, bm; Wm. Hayes Owen, wit.

Bullock, Joshua A. & Frances Coley, 16 June 1836; Wm. M. Bullock, bm; J. M. Wiggins, wit.

Bullock, Leonard & Permelia Dalbey, 16 Dec 1802; Edward Bullock, bm; Step. Sneed, wit.

Bullock, Leonard H. & Caroline S. Crews, 1 Dec 1854; Augustin Landis, bm; m 13 Dec 1854 by R. B. Hester.

Bullock, Leonard Henley & Fanny Hawkins, 7 Nov 1760; Thos. Lowe, bm; Jno. Bowie, wit; request for license from Will. Hurst, 7 Nov 1760, for Capt. Phillemon Hawkins.

Bullock, Leonard Henley & Susannah Goodloe, 6 Aug 1766; John Hamilton, Robert Goodloe, bm; Stephen Jett, wit.

Bullock, Micajah & Francis Pryor, 21 June 1769; John Chiles, bm; James Litterel, Sml. Benton, C. C., wit; consent from Ann Pryor, 19 June 1769.

Bullock, Nathaniel & Mary Hawkins, 12 Aug 1760; Leonard Henley Bullock, bm; Jn. Bowie, wit; consent from John Hawkins, father of Mary, 3 Aug 1760, she being under age.

Bullock, Olive & Rebecca Lile, 23 Oct 1821; Aaron Haskins, bm; Jas. M. Wiggins, wit.

Bullock, Philip & Anne Butler, 31 Oct 1797; Wm. Walker, bm; John Mitchel, wit.

Bullock, Philip P. & Nancy Green, 27 July 1830; Tarlton Johnson, bm; Step. K. Sneed, wit.

Bullock, Ramson & Palla Royster, 31 July 1866.

Bullock, Richard & Betsey Chambless, 16 May 1803; John Jinkins, bm; Green Merritt, wit.

GRANVILLE MARRIAGES 1753-1868

Bullock, Richard & Milly Walker, 19 Oct 1803; John Wood, bm; Green Merritt, wit.

Bullock, Richard H. & Martha Freeman, 30 March 1822; William Flemming, bm; Jas. M. Wiggins, wit.

Bullock, Ruffin & Sarah Hays, freed people, m 26 Jan 1867 by J. O. Montague.

Bullock, Rufus & Louisa Royster, 1 Aug 1866.

Bullock, Samuel & Sarah Bullock, 20 Jan 1817; Jordan Ball, bm; W. M. Sneed, wit.

Bullock, Walter & Judith C. Watkins, 7 Dec 1865; m 13 Dec 1865 by H. H. Prout.

Bullock, Walter A. & Sarah T. Gill, 28 Nov 1846; J. P. Hester, bm; J. M. Wiggins, wit.

Bullock, Welden & Sarah A. Lyon, 19 Jan 1864; R. H. D. Bullock, bm; m 28 Jan 1864 by R. B. Hester.

Bullock, William & Anny Bullock, 3 Jan 1815; Samuel Bullock, bm; Leslie Gilliam, wit.

Bullock, William C. & Francis C. Daniel, 10 April 1852; James R. Duty, bm; m 14 April 1852 by E. Hines.

Bullock, Wm. C. & Sallie S. Henderson, 10 Oct 1861; Jno. Bullock, bm; m 15 Oct 1861 by F. N. Whaley.

Bullock, William E. & Ann H. Mitchell, 7 Oct 1857; A. Landis, bm; m 25 Oct 1857 by B. B. Hester.

Bullock, William G. & Frances Jenkins, 24 Oct 1854; P. A. T. Farabow, bm; m 24 Oct 1854 by Geo. J. Rowland, J. P.

Bullock, Wm. M. & Malinda Brinkley, 12 May 1836; Young Jones, bm; J. M. Wiggins, wit.

Bumpass, James C. & Emily R. Norwood, 2 March 1857; Lemuel C. Smith, bm; m 18 March 1857 by R. J. Devin.

Bumpass, John K. & Elisabeth Thomas, 29 Oct 1850; J. H. Gooch, bm.

Bumpass, Jesse & Anna Clement, 3 Feb 1812; Thomas Pool, bm; A. H. Sneed, wit.

Bumpass, M. D. C. & Nancy Ann Carnal, 10 Jan 1854; John Duncan, bm; A. Landis, wit; m 11 Jan 1854 by Peterson Thorp, J. P.

Bumpass, Robert D. & Nancy M. Thomas, 20 May 1858; Robert W. Thomas, bm.

Bumpass, Samuel & Martha Clement, 3 Jan 1807; John Clement, bm; W. M. Sneed, wit.

Bumpass, William T. & Maria Thomas, 15 Dec 1854; Robert D. Bumpass Jr., bm; m 20 Dec 1854 by G. W. Ferrill.

Bunton, Irby & Ann Dueberry, 5 Dec 1826; Prior Scot, bm; Jno. P. Smith, wit.

GRANVILLE MARRIAGES 1753-1868

Burch, Henry & Agness Hester, 12 Feb 1781; Robert Hester, bm; Reuben Searcy, wit.

Burchet, Green & Mary Holeby, 20 Sept 1825; Samuel Nance, bm; L. Gilliam, wit.

Burchet, Isaac & Eliza Adcock, 22 Jan 1866; Davy Burchet, bm.

Burchett, Frank & Nancy Kittle, 7 Jan 1852; Elias Hesketh, bm.

Burchett, Isaac & Ruth Nance, 6 Nov 1799; Wm. H. Searcy, bm; Step. Sneed, wit.

Burchett, J. F., son of Green & Prissy Burchett & Indianna Hedgespeth, daughter of James & Patsy Hedgespeth, 24 Dec 1867; m 26 Dec 1867 by T. J. Horner.

Burchett, Joseph & Mary Mitchel, 24 Aug 1860; Nathaniel Freeman, bm; A. Landis, wit.

Burchett, Richard & Jane Fuller, 22 Dec 1834; Josephus Moss, bm; Benja. Kittrell, wit.

Burford, Daniel & Margaret Beaver, 21 Feb 1779; John Searcy Senior, bm; Reuben Searcy, wit.

Burge, William & Fanny A. Robards, 20 March 1820; Wm. Barnes, bm; Step. K. Sneed, wit.

Burkley, Henry W. & Louisa Leneve, m 3 Jan 1855 by E. Hines, Minister of the Gospel.

Burkley, John Bunion & Mary J. Clark, 18 Jan 1849; Hamon Newton, bm; L. B. Stone, J. P., wit.

Burnett, Addison R. & Mildred A. F. Philpott, 12 July 1843; L. S. Philpott, bm; Wm. H. Whitfield, wit.

Burnett, John J. & Susan Cardwell, 2 Jan 1828; Leonard Cardwell, bm; A. Sneed, wit.

Burnett, Zach H. & Martha Jane Garrett, 11 March 1845; Jno. R. Herndon, wit.

Burns, Crafford & Nancey Smith, 7 June 1802; Green Merritt, bm; Step. Sneed, wit.

Burrough, James W. & Rowan E. Bobbitt, 30 June 1852; S. G. Hayes, bm.

Burroughs, George W. & Faney Norwood, 9 Feb 1841; Stephen Satterwhite, bm; T. B. Barnett, wit.

Burroughs, George W. & Nancey Norwood, 6 Sept 1853; James R. Duty, bm; Jas. S. Norwood, wit; m 8 Nov 1853 by Jas. R. Duty, J. P.

Burroughs, John & Sary Strum, 6 Dec 1803; Hezekiah Strum, bm; A. H. Sneed, wit.

Burroughs, John E. & Mary J. Glover, 1 July 1864; m 6 July 1864 by L. K. Wille, M. G.

Burroughs, Stephen & Sarah Ann Wilkerson, 21 Oct 1855; John Fleming, bm.

GRANVILLE MARRIAGES 1753-1868

Burroughs, William L. & Mrs. Rebecca W. Turner, 20 Nov 1865; Wm. C. Gannon, bm; m 22 Nov 1865 by W. Gannon, M. G.

Burrow, Tazwell & Caroline Taylor, freed people, 23 Dec 1865; m 23 Dec 1865 by Thomas U. Faucette.

Burrows, James W. & Miss Rowan E. Bobbitt, 1 July 1852; m by A. C. Harris, M. G.

Burrows, Washington & Sarah Satterwhite, 25 Oct 1830; Joseph Hart, bm.

Burt, John & Suckey Bridges, 22 Aug 1789; M. Hunt, bm;

Burtin, Dicks, son of Edmund & Sarah Burton, & Ann Rebecca Chavis, parents unknown, 11 May 1868; m 11 May 1868 by Jas. R. Duty, J. P.

Burton, Austin & June Mayho, 1 Sept 1866; m by Robt. L. Heflin, J. P.

Burton, Edmond, colored, son of Henry Yancey & Mary Burton, & Rowena Thorp, daughter of Thos. Thorp, 31 Oct 1868; m 3 Nov 1868 by E. T. Lamberton, J. P.

Burton, Jas. M. & Elizabeth Ridley, 14 May 1789; S. Sneed, bm; A. Henderson, wit.

Burton, James M. Jr. & Prudence W. Robards, 2 July 1809; Junius Sneed, bm.

Burton, Jesse & Mariah Madison, 13 June 1849; J. M. Ashley, bm; J. M. Wiggins, wit.

Burton, John & Margaret Madison, 18 Oct 1845; Philip Forsythe, bm; Jas. M. Wiggins, wit.

Burton, John Wms. & Susan P. Lyne, 21 Sept 1819; A. E. Henderson, bm; Albert Sneed, wit.

Burton, Larry & Patsey Madison, 23 April 1839; James Forker, bm; J. M. Wiggins, wit.

Burton, Robert & Agatha Williams, 12 Oct 1775; Thomas Satterwhite, bm.

Burton, Robert, of Bedford County, Va., & Mary Lewis, spinster, of Grenville Co., 14 July 1781; John Lewis, bm; John Taylor, John Taylor Jr., wit.

Burton, William & Catharine Levingston, 10 Dec 1850; Jas. Ooten, bm; A. Landis, wit.

Burwell, Armistead R. & Bettie K. Norman, 26 March 1852; A. Landis, bm; m 7 April 1852 by W. K. Willie.

Burwell, Benjamin & Mary Seats, freed people, 30 June 1866; m by L. K. Willie, M. G.

Burwell, Edmund & Mary Homer, freed people, 7 April 1866; m 21 April 1866 by James S. Purifoy, Baptist Minister.

Burwell, Harry & Mary Pratcher, m 15 Sept 1866 by Joseph W. Murphy, Rector of the Church of the Holy Innocents, Henderson, N. C.

GRANVILLE MARRIAGES 1753-1868

Burwell, Henry H. & Susan C. Hargrove, 12 Aug 1851; Benj. C. Cooke, bm.

Burwell, John & Mary Burwell, 25 Dec 1865; m 25 Dec 1865 by T. M. Lynch, J. P.

Burwell, John & Isabella Blackwell (colored), 22 Dec 1866; m 23 Dec 1866 by F. N. Whaley, Minister of the Gospel.

Burwell, John A. & Lucy P. Guy, 19 June 1833; William T. Hargrove, bm; Albert Sneed, wit.

Burwell, Lewis D. & Matilda B. Burwell, 20 Aug 1842; Wm. A. ___, bm; Blair Burwell, wit.

Burwell, Nelson & Lucy Hargrove, 20 Feb 1866; John S. Hargrove, bm; A. Landis, wit; (freed people), m 4 March 1866 by W. C. Gannon, M. G.

Burwell, Ottoway & Nancy Gregory, m 25 Dec 1865 by T. M. Lynch, J. P.

Burwell, Robert R. & Jessie A. Dawson, 2 Nov 1858; Wm. M. Blackwell, bm; m 9 Nov 1858 by F. N. Wahley, Minister of the Gospel.

Burwell, Spotswood & Mary Marshall, 6 Oct 1808; Alexr. Closwell, bm; A. H. Sneed, wit.

Burwell, Stephen & Jane Fain, 25 Dec 1865; m 10 Jan 1866 by A. Landis.

Busbee, Charles M., son of Perrin & Anne Busbee, & Lillie L. Littlejohn, daughter of James F. & Phoebe D. Littlejohn, 30 July 1868; m 30 July 1868 by M. H. Vaughan, Rector of St. Stephen's Church.

Busbey, William & Nancey Mitchell, 9 Dec 1803; John Dunn, bm; Step. Sneed, wit.

Butler, Alexander & Mary W. Reavis, 10 Oct 1832; John Vandyck, bm; David Laws, wit.

Butler, James H. & Mary J. Pulliam, 1 Oct 1806; Tho. Cook, bm; W. M. Sneed, wit.

Butler, John & Polley Hunt, 24 Dec 1797; William Butler, bm; W. M. Sneed, wit.

Butler, John P. & Elizabeth W. Puryear, 18 May 1837; F. B. Hester, bm; Jas. M. Wiggins, wit.

Butler, Samuel & Martha Spears, 22 Oct 1811; Thomas Creedle, bm; W. M. Sneed, wit.

Butler, William & Martha Crenshaw, 6 Dec 1803; Thomas Crenshaw, bm; Jun. Sneed, wit.

Butler, William C. & Coateny J. OBrien, 15 June 1835; J. Johnson, bm; Benja. Kittrell, wit.

Butte, William & Martha Sturdavent, 8 May 1816; Richard Inge, bm; Richard Sneed, wit.

Byars, David & Sally Haley, 20 Dec 1826; John Haley, bm; Wm. H. Owen, wit.

GRANVILLE MARRIAGES 1753-1868

Byars, George & Sally Flemming, 8 Dec 1813; Cyrus Davis, bm; J. P. Sneed, wit.

Byars, George & Frances Joplin, 4 May 1819; Edward Chappel, bm; S. K. Sneed, wit.

Byars, Henry & Martha Byars, 5 Nov 1822; Cyrus Davis Jr., bm.

Byars, William & Lucey Nunn, 26 July 1790; Jas. Vaughan, bm; H. Potter, wit.

Byers, Alexander & Elizabeth Byers, 16 Feb 1813; William Beck, bm; Thos. Hicks, wit.

Byers, James & Serah Campbell, 3 Feb 1789; Stephen Terry, bm; A. Henderson, wit.

Bynum, James & Mary Hutchinson, 19 Feb 1832; Wm. F. Kittrell, bm; Step. K. Sneed, wit.

Bynum, Morris & Movey Morris, 21 Oct 1826; John McFarling, bm; S. K. Sneed, wit.

Byram, Doctor W. & Rebecca Allen, 29 Nov 1852; Jas. L. Strother, bm.

Byram, Jacob & Lucy Winningham, 3 Nov 1783; Christopher Hoover(?), bm; William Bowdon, wit.

Byrd, Alexander & Helen Mangum, 3 Jan 1850; Josiah C. Rogers, bm.

Byrd, Frank & Caroline Hicks, 13 June 1867; Adkin Jenkins, bm.

Byrd, Wiley, of color, son of Jim & Marullus Byrd & Penny Daniel, daughter of Jerry & Ailcy Daniel, m 11 Sept 1868 by R. H. Kingsbury, J. P.

Byrom, Alexander J. & Mary E. Grissom, 2 Aug 1858; J. C. Hester, bm; m 3 Aug 1858 by L. K. Willie.

Byrum, Archibald & Susannah Banks, 4 Nov 1799; Kinchen Byrum, bm; Step. Sneed, wit.

Byrum, Doctor, son of Kinchen & Cynthia Byrum, & Jane Freeman, parents unknown, 14 April 1868; m 14 April 1868 by E. B. Lyon, J. P.

Byrum, Doctor W. & Priscilla Howard, 5 Sept 1843; Hilman Dement, bm; Jas. M. Wiggins, wit.

Byrum, Henry K. & Elizabeth A. Gresham, 13 Dec 1834; W. D. Jinkins, bm.

Byrum, John & Milley Morris, 4 Oct 1785; Jacob Byrum, bm; Bennet Searcy, wit.

Byrum, John R. & Atha Ann Ross, 14 Dec 1835; Anthony W. Cole, bm; Benja. Kittrell, wit.

Byrum, Kinchen & Cinthy Ross, 23 Dec 1801; Archibald Byrum, bm; P. Bullock, wit.

Byrum, William & Mary Sanders, 4 July 1795; John Byrum, bm; Step. Sneed, wit.

GRANVILLE MARRIAGES 1753-1868

Cadden, Hugh A. M. & Virginia Wall, 24 May 1856; Jas. W. Adcock, bm; A. Landis, wit.

Calaham, James R. & Virginia A. Buchanan, 27 March 1867; J. H. Chandler, bm; m 28 March 1867 by A. Apple, M. G.

Calaham, John R. & Louisa Wilkerson, 13 June 1861; Howel S. Nelson, bm; m 13 June 1861 by L. B. Stone, J. P.

Califer, W. H. & Alice Bennett, 31 Oct 1864; Joseph L. Smith, bm; m 4 Nov 1864.

Callahan, Edward & Ann Hunt Ellixson, 30 May 1833; Thos. G. Blackwell, bm; Jno. P. Smith, wit.

Callis, Charles W. & Sarah Alice Wagstaff, 7 Jan 1867; C. E. Landis, bm.

Callis, Richard R. & Sophia H. Wright, 11 Dec 1865; James L. Hobgood, bm; m 13 Dec 1865 by E. F. Beachum, a regular G. M.

Cammel, John & Susanna Eperson, 21 April 1785; Robert Hargrove, bm; Reuben Searcy, wit.

Campbell, John & Elizabeth Adcock, 10 Dec 1853; m 12 Dec 1853; Wm. A. Wirt, bm; A. Landis, wit.

Canaday, Andrew & Mary Nipper, 24 Nov 1801; Wm. Canaday, bm; Danl. Bridges, wit.

Canaday, A. J. M. & Nancy R. Garner, 6 May 1856; Robert Garner, bm; m 14 May 1856 by T. B. Lyon, J. P.

Canaday, Wyatt M. & Martha Morris, 30 Sept 1852; James P. Paschall, bm; m 30 Sept 1852 by W. K. Willie, M. G.

Cannaday, Nathaniel E. & Nancy P. Gooch, 17 Dec 1832; William Burge, bm; Step. K. Sneed, wit.

Cannaday, Wm. & Dosha _____, 5 Nov 1793; Ransom Cooper, bm; W. Norwood, D. C., wit.

Cannaday, Wm. & Rebekah Brasfield, 19 Jan 1799; Archd. Betterson, bm; Geo. Brasfield, wit.

Cannaday, Wm. H. & Elizabeth J. H. Williams, 8 Aug 1859; Jas. M. Wiggins, wit.

Cannady, Major (colored) & Frances Gill, 2 Nov 1866; Jonathan Jenkins, bm; m 3 Nov 1866 by W. H. P. Jenkins, J. P.

Cannady, William E. & Lucy A. Satterwhite, 8 Dec 1860; W. R. Beasley, bm; m 9 Dec 1860 by M. Baldwin, Minister.

Cannon, William, son of Ned & Linda Cannon, & Sallie Fain, daughter of Alfred & Caroline Fain, 23 Dec 1868; m 24 Dec 1868 by W. A. Belvin, J. P.

Card, Azariah & Nancy Barley, 25 Dec 1838; Jos. B. Peace, bm.

Card, Azariah & Lucy Sanderford, 2 Sept 1845; Jas. Heflin, bm.

Card, Samuel L. & Susan Fuller, 16 May 1853; Addison Okley, bm; m "at or near the dwelling house of John H. Webb" by Jeff Horner, J. P., 16 May 1853.

GRANVILLE MARRIAGES 1753-1868

Carden, George & Lucy Garratt, 21 April 1795; Robert Cardin, bm; L. Henderson, wit.

Carden, James & Susannah Floyd, 8 Oct 1810; Henry Floyd, bm; W. M. Sneed, wit.

Cardin, James & Elisabeth Fuller, 20 Jan 1784; Stephen Fuller, bm; Bennet Searcy, wit.

Cardwell, Fendal & Eveline D. Freeman, 18 March 1826; Christian A. Mitchell, bm; Wm. H. Owen, wit.

Cardwell, Leonard & Lucy Strum, 18 Nov 1802; Elijah Longmire, bm; A. H. Sneed, wit.

Cardwell, Richard Wilson & Peggy Loyd, 2 Dec 1806; Isaac Bradley, bm; A. H. Sneed, wit.

Cardwell, Thomas & Nancy Loyd, 24 Dec 1801; T. Satterwhite, bm; Junius Sneed, wit.

Cardwell, William N. & Anne Laurence, 4 Nov 1806; Wm. T. Laurence, bm; Jun. Sneed, wit.

Carey, Henry & Matilda A. E. Crutchen, 7 Nov 1839; William C. Brooks, bm; Henry Carey & William B. Brook swear before Richd. Sneed, J. P. that Matilda A. E. Crutchin of Charlotte County, Va. is 21 years of age, 7 Nov 1839.

Carey, Moses & Britty Ann Duke, 30 Sept 1845; Fielding Mangum, bm.

Carey, Thomas & Celia Oakly, 1 Feb 1823; Thos. Waller, bm; Jas. M. Wiggins, wit.

Carnal, Elijah & Sally Wood, 7 Nov 1815; Anthony B. Wood, bm; Step. K. Sneed, wit.

Carnal. James & Lucy Wood, 11 Jan 1818; William Terry, bm; W. M. Sneed, wit.

Carnal, Jesse & Polley Oakley, 2 Nov 1813; William Oakley, bm; W. M. Sneed, wit.

Carnal, John W. & Elizabeth Dean, 16 Feb 1839; Moses Carnal(?), bm.

Carneal, Moses & Margaret Dean, 9 March 1835; Samuel A. Dixon, bm; Benja. Kittrell, wit.

Carnel, Moses & Sarah Meadows, 21 Aug 1804; William Carnel, bm; E. Parham, wit.

Carrel, John & Rebeckah Huskey, 17 Sept 1781; Bird Driver, bm; Bennet Searcy, wit.

Carrel, Spencer & Sarah Huskey, 28 April 1785; John Carrel, bm; Bennet Searcy, wit.

Carrin, William R. & Lucy Arrington, 3 Jan 1860; R. W. Fitts, bm; A. Landis, wit.

Carrington, A. S. & Mary A. Cozort, m 3 Oct 1867 by G. W. Ferrill, Minister.

GRANVILLE MARRIAGES 1753-1868

Carrington, Chesley & Ellen Baptist, freed people, 4 May 1867; m 4 May 1867 by Joseph H. Riddick.

Carrington, William D. & Fanny Cozort, 6 Sept 1813; John J. Carrington, bm; Thos. J. Hicks, wit.

Carrison, Sidney & Mary Lovett, 29 Aug 1866; m 29 Aug 1866 by Maurice H. Vaughan, Rector St. Stephen's Church.

Carrol, Benjamin & Charity Bonner, 27 Dec 1770; Moses Bonner, Robert Harris, bm; Jesse Benton, wit.

Carson, Archabald & Mary Ligon, 14 Nov 1862; John Thomas, bm; m 14 Nov 1862 by L. B. Stone, J. P.

Carson, Charles R. & Lucy Ann Falkner, 18 May 1852; James Gooch, bm; Jas. K. Duty, wit; m 18 May 1852 by James Gooch, J. P.

Carson, Richard R. & Milly B. Young, 25 Nov 1824; Henry W. Ransom, bm; Step. K. Sneed, wit.

Carter, Charles & Susanna Roberson, 19 Aug 1782; Wm. Skelton, bm; Bennet Searcy, wit.

Carter, Frederick J. & Lucy Bullock, 28 Oct 1836; Jas. Nuttall, bm; Jas. M. Wiggins, wit.

Carter, Jesse & Deborah Stephens, 20 Nov 1798; Wm. Marshall, bm.

Carter, John & Patsey Mayfield, 12 Dec 1796; Jesse Carter, bm; John Taylor, wit.

Carter, Joseph Y. & Emaly Loftin, m 20 Oct 1867 by L. B. Stone, J. P.

Carter, Thomas J. & Abbigal K. Spears, 24 Nov 1826; Riley Penny, bm; Wm. H. Owen, wit.

Carter, William H. & Emaly J. Murry, 2 Dec 1850; Rufus Hendrick, bm; L. B. Stone, J. P., wit.

Carver, Asa & Oney Bouls, 5 March 1833; Yancy Oakly, bm; S. K. Sneed, wit.

Carver, Henry & Arianna Norwood, 6 Jan 1853; Jno. L. Harris, bm; m 6 Jan 1853 by G. W. Ferrill, Minister.

Cash, Bryant, son of Joseph & Polly Cash, & Nancy Adeline Walker, daughter of Willis & Betsy Walker, m 22 Oct 1867 by T. B. Lyon Jr.

Cash, Bryon & Creassey Garner, 8 Feb 1800; Peter Cash, bm; William Byars, wit.

Cash, Dennis & Susan Haley, 30 March 1844; Wm. H. Haley, bm; Jas. M. Wiggins, wit.

Cash, Edward & Sarah Ann Goss, 2 Aug 1855; Calvin Thomasson, bm; A. Landis, wit; m 5 Aug 1855 by A. M. Veasey, J. P.

Cash, Elijah & Fanny Lewis, 27 Oct 1826; James Brogdon, bm; Wm. H. Owen, wit.

Cash, Elisha & Sallie Davis, 29 Sept 1864; S. B. Can----, bm.

GRANVILLE MARRIAGES 1753-1868

Cash, Elkins & Mary Garner, 1 Sept 1792; Robert Griggs, bm; Step. Sneed, wit.

Cash, Elkins & Frances Phips, 29 March 1856; James Cash, bm; A. Landis, wit; m 30 March 1856 by A. M. Veazey, J. P.

Cash, Hinton & Eliza Robertson, 10 Nov 1852; T. W. Hicks, bm; A. Landis, wit; m 16 Dec 1852 by E. Hester, Minister of the Gospel.

Cash, Howard & Linney Dyer, 21 Aug 1779; Thomas Wilmon Culverhouse, bm; Sherwood Harris, wit.

Cash, Isham & Nancy Haley, 21 Oct 1835; T. Giffers, bm.

Cash, Jacob & Polley Haley, 2 Aug 1836; Dorris Cannady, bm.

Cash, James & Anney Thurm, 7 Oct 1783; Peter Cash, bm; Bennet Searcy, wit.

Cash, James & Nelley Walker, 27 Nov 1807; John Walker, bm; W. M. Sneed, wit.

Cash, James & Delila Pettigure, 2 May 1843; James T. Gill, bm; Wm. H. Whitfield, wit.

Cash, James & Sallie Walker, 9 Sept 1857; John J. Walker, bm; m 13 Sept 1857 by E. Hester.

Cash, James & Polly Walker, 16 Sept 1863; Lorenzo Walker, bm; A. Landis, wit.

Cash, James & Hasseltine Coley, 27 April 1867; m 9 July 1867 by R. H. Hobgood, J. P.

Cash, James Junr. & Amanda Bledsoe, 24 Jan 1826; John Cash, bm; Wm. H. Owen, wit.

Cash, James R. & Jemima Philpott, 18 Dec 1850; James Philpott, bm.

Cash, James W. & Adeline Allen, 1 Jan 1853; Moses Tanner, bm; A. Landis, wit; m 1 Feb 1857 by Wm. H. Lyon, J. P.

Cash, Joe & Mary Pettegrue, 19 Jan 1824; William Walker, bm; Wm. H. Owen, wit.

Cash, John & Mary Calvert, 5 May 1795; Richard Taylor, bm; L. Henderson, wit.

Cash, John & Palley Brogdon, 11 Aug 1821; Jechonias Bledsoe, bm; Jas. M. Wiggins, wit.

Cash, John & Nancy Yokely, 2 Jan 1830; William Suit, bm.

Cash, Josias & Rebeccah Garner, 6 Nov 1798; Richard Omerry, bm.

Cash, Michael & Salley Yoakley, 2 Feb 1808; Mark Yokely, bm; W. M. Sneed, wit.

Cash, Moses & Frances Coley, 15 Dec 1846; Jno. B. Green, bm; Jas. M. Wiggins, wit.

Cash, Moses & Sarah Coley, 20 Aug 1866; m by T. B. Lyon Jr., J. P.

GRANVILLE MARRIAGES 1753-1868

Cash, Peter & Cressey Hoofman, 3 May 1803; Nicholas Byars, bm; Step. Sneed, wit.

Cash, Ransom & Rebecca Oakley, 24 Aug 1841; George Oakly, bm; J. M. Wiggins, wit.

Cash, Richard N. & Jerusha Jackson, 26 Aug 1859; James Beck, bm; A. Landis, wit.

Cash, Riley & Demeris Washington, 3 Aug 1841; Alexander Washington, bm; J. M. Wiggins, wit.

Cash, Thomas & Fanny Denny, 27 Sept 1802; Frederick Beck, bm; Nancy Bullock, wit.

Cash, Thomas J. & Emily J. Moize, 8 Jan 1861; Thos. A. Obrian, bm; m 10 Jan 1861 by M. Baldwin, Minister.

Cash, Valentine, son of Valentine & Prudence Cash, & Henriettae Chappell, daughter of Jack & Betsy Ann Chappell, 22 Oct 1867; m 4 Nov 1867 by T. B. Lyon.

Cash, Volentine & Prudence Yokely, 2 Feb 1830; Henry Wheeler, bm; David Laws, wit.

Cash, William & Lucey Lanier, 28 Nov 1806; Peter Cash, bm; W. M. Sneed, wit.

Cash, William & Phillipina Hoofman, 7 Aug 1827; John Beck, bm; Step. K. Sneed, wit.

Cash, Willie & Barbara Ann Washington, 15 Oct 1841; John Coley, bm.

Cate, John & Elizabeth Day, 8 April 1847; Henry Best, bm.

Cates, William H. & Nancy F. Moton, 30 March 1864; J. G. Staunton, bm; m 30 March 1864 by Jas. J. Moore, J. P.

Catlet, Clark & Martha Williams, 18 Feb 1800; Henry Hendley, bm; P. Bullock, wit.

Catlett, George & Amanda C. Cook, 7 Nov 1850; A. Landis, bm.

Catlett, George & Martha House, 23 Nov 1865; Elijah Ball, bm; A. Landis, wit; m 28 Nov 1865 by E. B. Lyon, J. P.

Catlett, John & Prissilla Wethers, 23 April 1862; Benjamin Mason, bm.

Catlett, Labon & Mary Ward, 4 Sept 1855; Wm. J. Loyd, bm; A. Landis, wit; m 17 Sept 1855 by E. Davis, J. P.

Catlett, William & Sicily Bragg, 21 Dec 1831; Samuel Mason, bm; David Laws, wit.

Catlett, William & Mary E. Williams, 7 April 1854; Samuel Catlett, bm; m 9 April 1854 by Jas. J. Moore, J. P.

Cattel, George & Caroline Cooke, 1 April 1843; George T. Leavin, bm; Jas. M. Wiggins, wit.

Cattlet, Labourn & Emily Rudd, 6 Feb 1827; Wm. Catlet, bm; Wm. H. Owen, wit.

GRANVILLE MARRIAGES 1753-1868

Caudle, Richard, son of Jas. & Dolly Caudle, & Jane Keter, daughter of Joseph & Elizabeth Keter, 5 Sept 1867; m 5 Sept 1867 by E. L. Parrish, J. P.

Caudle, William & Grassie Bradiway (Brodiway?), 29 June 1813; John Buckner, bm; Step. Sneed, wit.

Causley, William & Tabitha H. Farrar, 24 Jan 1833; _____, bm.

Cauthen, John C. & Nancy E. Bragg, 28 Dec 1865; G. W. Harrison, bm; m 18 Jan 1866 by R. B. Hiet.

Cavaness, George & Tabby Griffin, 18 Nov 1813; Thornton Yancy, bm; H. Young, wit.

Cavenar, Bryant & Frances Bridges, 8 Feb 1792; Drury Bridges, bm; W. Norwood, wit.

Cavenar, Thos. & Nanncy Griggis, 13 Jan 1801; Wm. Williams, bm; Danl. Bridges, wit.

Cavender, John & Lucy Owens, 23 July 1807; Stark Daniel, bm; Jas. Sneed, wit.

Cavender, John & Lucy Champion, 7 Oct 1831; Allen Clarke, bm; S. K. Sneed, wit.

Cavendish, John H. & Eliza Clark, 29 Oct 1838; Elijah Daniel, bm; L. Beasly, wit.

Caviners, John H. & Henrietta Royster, 4 Sept 1832; Thomas Mathews, bm; David Laws, wit.

Cavenish, Mathew & Jenny Freeman, 5 Dec 1798; Anderson Taylor, bm; James Sneed, wit.

Cawthon, Henry & Happy Rowland, 14 Oct 1842; George J. Rowland, bm; Wm. H. Whitfield, wit.

Cawthon, James H. & Phebe Heflin, 11 March 1817; Saml. Harris, bm; Rhodes N. Herndon, wit.

Cawthon, Lemuel & Elisabeth Smith, 11 Jan 1801; Ezekiel Huddleton, bm; Philip Bullock, wit.

Cawthon, Nathan & Ava Bradford, 30 Oct 1792; Richd. Hudspeth, bm; W. Norwood, wit.

Cawthorn, John W., son of A. L. & Elizabeth Cawthorn, & Cornelia Allen, daughter of David B. & Polly Ann Allen, m 25 Oct 1868 by J. L. Purefoy, Minister of the Gospel.

Cerns, Joseph & Comfert Cash, 12 Nov 1783; Charles Bullock, bm; Bennet Searcy, wit.

Chadwick, Samuel & Nancey Blalock, 20 Dec 1807; Henry H. Vincent, bm; W. M. Sneed, wit.

Chalkley, Erastus & Fannie A. Knott, 16 April 1866; m 19 April 1866 by W. H. Puryear.

Chambers, Aza & Mary A. Barnett, 3 Dec 1856; R. S. Hunt, bm; m 4 Dec 1856 by W. H. Jordan.

GRANVILLE MARRIGES 1753-1868

Chambers, Josiah & Martha Mottaugh(?), 27 Dec 1817; Fleming Duff, bm.

Chambless, Henry & Sally Huckeby, 7 Dec 1817; Robert Chambless, bm; Rhodes N. Herndon, wit.

Chamblis, William O. & Martha A. Jones, 23 Nov 1836; Tingnal Jones, bm.

Champen, Benjamin & Piety Harris, 28 Dec 1833; John Champen, bm; Benja. Kittrell, wit.

Champion, Alexander M. & Areline E. Falkner, 2 March 1863; Leander R. Edwards, bm; m 4 March 1863 by T. A. Stewart, J. P.

Champion, Bennett & Charlotte Fuller, 18 Jan 1829; A. Huskey, bm; L. Gilliam, wit.

Champion, James & India Roberson, 6 Aug 1863; A. M. Champion, bm; A. Landis, wit; m 6 Aug 1863 by William B. Mann, J. P.

Champion, Josep & Elizabeth Cook, 6 Oct 1813; Joseph Priddy, bm; T. J. Hicks, wit.

Champion, Merritt & Elisabeth Robertson, 20 July 1813; Richard Champion, bm; Tho. J. Hicks, wit.

Champion, Richard & Barbara Allen, 20 Feb 1809; William Huskey, bm; W. N. Sneed, wit.

Champion, Richard & Mary Moore, 11 Sept 1813; Charly Moore, bm; J. T. Hicks, wit.

Champion, Robert T. & Bettie Holmes, 4 April 1864; A. Landis, bm; m 6 April 1864 by P. H. Joyner.

Champion, William & Alice Izzard, 5 Jan 1847; Bailey Winters, bm; Jas. M. Wiggins, wit.

Chandler, Alexander & Mary Ann Stone, 9 July 1857; George W. James, bm; m 9 July 1857 by L. B. Stone, J. P.

Chandler, Daniel & Martha Jones, 18 Aug 1828; Henry Obriant, bm; D. J. Young, wit.

Chandler, David K. & Ann Eliza Weaver, 5 Sept 1848; Wm. C. Chandler, bm; Jno. M. Wiggins, wit.

Chandler, David K. & Mary Jane Cox, 26 Oct 1853; William H. Weaver, bm; Jas. R. Duty, wit; m 25 Oct 1853 by Jas. R. Duty, J. P.

Chandler, Jackson & Lucy Underwood, 19 July 1836; William P. Smith, bm; J. M. Wiggins, wit.

Chandler, John Y. & Susan Stovall, 27 Nov 1836; Benj. Stone, bm; Robert K. Clack, wit.

Chandler, Littleberry & Panthea B. Royster, 27 Jan 1831; M. D. Royster, bm.

Chandler, Mathew Jr. & Emily White, 25 Jan 1846; James Hester, bm; L. B. Stone, wit.

GRANVILLE MARRIAGES 1753-1868

Chandler, Matthew & Polly Crenshaw, 23 Dec 1802; Sterling Yancey, bm; Step. Sneed, wit.

Chandler, Matthew L. & Mollie H. Throckmorton, 18 Feb 1863; L. B. Stone, bm; m 19 Feb 1863 by L. B. Stone, J. P.

Chandler, McVay & Margaret J. Fillpott, 19 Nov 1833; Sol. Philpott, bm; Benja. Kittrell, wit.

Chandler, Spotswood & Fortune Overbey, freed people, m 28 Aug 1867 by W. Overbey, J. P.

Chandler, Thomas & Sarah An Puryear, 8 Nov 1837; David Overbey, bm.

Chandler, William & Mealy Ann Overbey, freed people, 28 Dec 1866; m by W. Overbey, J. P.

Chandler, William & Ann Blackwell, freed people, 26 July 1867; Wm. Chandler, son of Stephen Amis & Winny Betts, & Ann Blackwell, daughter of David & Sarah Currin, m 28 July 1867 by R. J. Devin.

Chandler, William C. & Rhoda Ann Knott, 3 Sept 1844; James M. OBriant, bm; J. M. Wiggins, wit.

Chapel, Reddin & Louisa Garner, 7 Nov 1849; Robert H. Brogdon, bm.

Chapell, Darlin A. & Lucinda Tanner, 14 March 1860; Joseph Self, Ephraim E. Emery, bm; m 18 March 1860 by W. D. Allen, J. P.

Chapman, Isaac & Elizabeth Floid, 11 Oct 1788; Seamore Duncan, bm; A. Henderson, C. C., wit.

Chapman, Thomas & Mary G. Smith, 4 Jan 1815; Thos. Worrel, bm; Richard Sneed, wit.

Chapman, Thomas & Mary A. Short, 2 Jan 1856; Jas. O. K. Paschal, bm; m 2 Jan 1856 by Jas. R. Duty, J. P.

Chapman, William A. & Caroline J. Newman, 6 Dec 1849; James R. Duty, bm.

Chappell, Alfred R., son of Richard and Anna Chappell, & Mrs. Elitha T. Emory, daughter of Thomas & Reney Perry, 17 Nov 1868; m 17 Nov 1868 by L. K. Willie, M. G.

Chappell, Andrew J. & Mary E. Perry, 16 Dec 1864; A. Landis, bm.

Chappell, John H. & Mary E. Davis, 18 Sept 1865; Willie L. Perry, bm; m 20 Sept 1865 by R. B. Hester.

Chappell, John W. & Elizabeth A. Guarner, 24 April 1846; George Omry, bm; Clement Wilkins, wit.

Chappell, Major & Susan Emery, 8 March 1841; Fielding A. ____, Thos. S. Morris, bm; J. M. Wiggins, wit.

Chappell, Minton & Amanda O. Wilson, 31 Dec 1853; Wm. H. Wilson, bm; A. Landis, wit; m 5 Jan 1854 by A. Laurence, J. P.

Chappell, Samuel & Cynthia Pollard, 27 Aug 1823; Willie Pollard, bm; Jas. M. Wiggins, wit.

Chappell, Wm. H. & Susan J. Sherrin, 26 May 1852; W. W. Lyon, bm;
A. Landis, wit; m 28 June 1852 by Wm. Lyon, J. P.

Chavers, Charles & Nancy Tabern(?), 4 Nov 1795; Ben. Bass Jr.,
bm.

Chavers, Evin & Ciller Smith, 29 July 1805; H. Hutchings, bm;
Step. Sneed, wit.

Chavers, Henry & Luiza Day, free persons of color, 18 Aug 1866;
F. J. Tilley, bm; m 19 Aug 1866 by D. Tilley, J. P.

Chavers, John & Sarah Anderson, 8 June 1815; Abraham Anderson,
bm; W. M. Sneed, wit.

Chavers, John & Nancey Cozins, 13 June 1828; Step. K. Sneed, bm;
David Laws, wit.

Chavers, Thomas & Lucy Chavas, 15 Feb 1804; Pearson Hawley, bm;
E. W. Parham, wit.

Chavers, William & Sarah Kersey, 13 March 1790; John Johnson,
bm; Henry Potter, wit.

Chaves, William & Delila Guy, 16 Oct 1834; L. A. Paschall, bm;
Benja. Kittrell, wit.

Chavis, Alexander, of color, son of Harry Satterwhite & Ritter
Chavis, & Eliza Hunt, daughter of Harriet Hunt, 15 Nov 1867;
m 16 Nov 1867 by Wm. R. Hicks, J. P.

Chavis, Allen & Susannah Chavis, 9 May 1816; Samuel S. Downey,
bm; Step. K. Sneed, wit.

Chavis, Anderson & Harriet Turner, 21 Nov 1842; J. C. Cooper,
bm; Wm. H. Whitfield, wit.

Chavis, Anderson & Caroline Jones, 11 Jan 1859; Jno. Nance, bm.

Chavis, Bennett & Rebecca Ann Pettiford, 4 Sept 1860; E. Dallyr,
bm.

Chavis, Evin & Lucy Smith, 21 April 1802; Charles Chavis, bm;
Green Merritt, wit.

Chavis, George & Eliza Freeman, 16 May 1864; m 16 May 1864 by
J. H. Wheeler, M. M. E. C. South.

Chavis, George A. & Eliza Trumore(?), 16 May 1864; Jas. Chavers,
bm; Jas. R. Duty, wit.

Chavis, Gipson & Tabby Stuart, 19 July 1825; Joins Chavis, bm.

Chavis, Howell & Harriet Jones, 19 July 1844; Mins Guy, bm; J.
M. Wiggins, wit.

Chavis, Isaac & Elizabeth Evans, 6 Sept 1800; Peter Chaves, bm;
Philip Bullock, wit.

Chavis, James & Angeline Chavis, 29 Nov 1853; James Byrd, bm;
A. Landis, wit.

Chavis, James Jun. & Betsey Smith, 4 July 1799; Thos. Wilson,
bm; Jas. Edwards, wit.

GRANVILLE MARRIAGES 1753-1868

Chavis, Jefferson & Sarah Amis, freed woman, 13 April 1867; m 22 April 1867 by A. C. Harris, M. G.

Chavis, Jesse & Nancey Mitchel, 2 May 1812; Darling Bass, bm; W. M. Sneed, wit.

Chavis, John & Nancy Harding, 19 July 1820; Jesse Bass, bm; Step. K. Sneed, wit.

Chavis, Levi & Frances Kearzey, 24 April 1865; James Anderson, bm; A. Landis, wit.

Chavis, Peter & Maron(?) Bird, 4 Nov 1800; Charles Evans, bm; Green Merritt, wit.

Chavis, Philip & Caroline Proctor, 21 Sept 1861; A. Landis, bm; Jas. Y. Landis, wit; m 22 Sept 1861 by A. H. Cooke, J. P.

Chavis, Samuel & Sallie Tabern, 26 May 1860; Baldy Kearzey, bm; A. Landis, wit.

Chavis, Starling & Martha Evans, 6 Nov 1843; William Chavis, bm; Wm. H. Whitfield, wit.

Chavis, Thomas & Nancy Harris, 14 Nov 1828; Martin Anderson, bm; Wm. H. Owen, wit.

Chavis, William & Ann Eliza Harris, 21 Jan 1845; Jas. Weaver, bm; Jas. M. Wiggins, wit.

Chavis, William & Isabella Howell, 18 July 1849; Thos. Curtis, bm; J. M. Wiggins, wit.

Chavis, William & Mary Day, 3 Oct 1857; Moody Mangum, bm; A. Landis, wit; m 8 Oct 1857 by Geo. J. Rowland, J. P.

Chavis, William & Mary Bookram, 19 Dec 1862; Robt. W. Minor, bm.

Chavis, Willie & Lethe Harris, 9 Sept 1830; James Evans, bm; S. K. Sneed, wit.

Cheatham, David T. & Ann E. Reavis, 17 Dec 1866; Charles E. Landis, bm; m 19 Dec 1866 by Lewis K. Willie, M. G.

Cheatham, Edward & Nancy Davis, 20 Feb 1792; Henry Townes, bm; W. Norwood, wit; consent from Baxter Davis, father of Nancy, 21 Feb 1791.

Cheatham, Isham & Jane Wood, 16 Jan 1816; John Moore, bm; Leslie Gilliam, wit.

Cheatham, Isham J. & Miss Mary E. Hunt, 4 Nov 1858; W. T. Estes, bm; W. M. Sneed, wit; m 9 Nov 1858 by R. N. Whaley, Minister of the Gospel.

Cheatham, Jack & Anna Hunt, freed people, 9 July 1865; Richard Burwell, bm; A. Landis, wit.

Cheatham, James & Sally Norwood, 26 Nov 1829; Henry Norman, bm; David Laws, wit.

Cheatham, James Jr. & Rebecca A. Crews, 18 June 1834; D. T. Paschall, bm.

GRANVILLE MARRIAGES 1753-1868

Cheatham, Thomas & Martha H. Amis, 29 Oct 1830; A. Higgs, bm; David Lawes, wit.

Cheatham, Thomas G. & Mary J. Davis, 31 Dec 1859; A. Landis, bm; m 4 Jan 1860 by L. K. Willie, M. G.

Cheatham, William A. & Asenath F. Parham, 5 Oct 1856; Jas. A. Turner, bm; m 9 Oct 1856 by L. K. Willie, M. G.

Cheatham, William H. H., son of Isaac & Cynthia A. Cheatham, & Sallie H. Gooch, daughter of Daniel T. & Nancy Gooch, 10 April 1868; m 22 April 1868 by T. J. Horner.

Cheatham, Dr. Wm. S. & Miss Martha G. Davis, 4 Oct 1859; Danl. Harvey Christie, bm; m 5 Oct 1859 by Ira T. Wyche, Minister of the Gospel.

Child, Nathan & Betsey Terry, 12 Sept 1778; Stephen Terry, bm; Solomon Walker, wit.

Childry, Henry & Eliza Thomas, 11 Oct 1834; William Collar, bm.

Childs, Hezekiah & Sarah Bevell, 20 Sept 1785; John Downy, bm; Bennet Searcy, wit.

Choley, David & Beckey Garner, 19 March 1800; Jehu Sherin, bm; William Byars, wit.

Chovis, John & Rebecca Anderson, 26 Dec 1835; Benjamin Curtis(?), bm; Benjn. Kittrell, wit.

Christian, Gedion & Sarah Morse(?), 6 Dec 1785; Wm. Walker, bm; Reuben Searcy, wit.

Christian, Michael & Polley Green, 30 May 1814; Abner Jones, bm; W. M. Sneed, wit.

Christmas, Edmund, son of Willis & Rose Green, & Mary A. Glover, daughter of Wallace Glover, 24 Dec 1868; m 29 Dec 1868 by E. Hines.

Christmas, William & Jinsey Yancey, 28 July 1790; Anderson Pattillo, bm; H. Potter, wit.

Christopher, John & Catharine Moss, 18 Aug 1798; James Christopher, bm; James Sneed, wit.

Chumbly, Edward & Nancy L. Waddle, 19 Aug 1816; James Chumbly, bm; Richd. Sneed, wit.

Clack, James & Salley Dickins, 26 Nov 1804; Wm. Dickins, bm; M. Parham, wit.

Clack, Robert K. & Sarah Lewis, 10 Dec 1822; James Lewis, bm; Jas. M. Wiggins, wit.

Clardy, Benjamin & Elisabeth Collins, 26 Dec 1796; William Collins, bm; Step. Sneed, wit.

Clardy, John & Elizabeth Johnston, 30 Jan 1798; John Mitchell, bm; W. Smith, wit.

Clardy, John & Peggy Morse, 5 April 1810; William Collens, bm; Jun. Sneed, wit.

GRANVILLE MARRIAGES 1753-1868

Clark, Alexander & Mary Hester, 3 March 1824; Bevelle Ellington, bm; S. K. Sneed, wit; consent from Elisabeth Hester, mother of Mary, 3 March 1824; A. Paschall, wit.

Clark, Alexr. & Martha Tally, 5 Nov 1856; Thomas J. Pittard, bm; m 11 Nov 1856 by Thos. Hester, J. P.

Clark, Andrew J. & Eaton Clark, 1 Jan 1867; E. Clark, bm.

Clark, Andrew J. & Julia Williamson, m 1 Jan 1867 by E. L. Parrish, J. P.

Clark, Benjamin & Ann Eliza Aikin, 2 Dec 1853; Wm. D. Goss, bm; A. Landis, wit; m 18 Dec 1853 by Thos. B. Lyon, J. P.

Clark, Brumfield & Ann May, 16 Sept 1856; H. W. Stone, bm; m 17 Sept 1856 by L. R. Parham, J. P.

Clark, David & Elizabeth Falkner, 6 Nov 1839; John Powell, bm.

Clark, Drury & Flora McDonald, 12 Dec 1784; John Downey, bm; John Tuder, wit.

Clark, Edward, son of Jas. & Nancy Clark, & Mary A. Vaughn, daughter of David & Lettie Vaughn, m 12 March 1868 by E. L. Parrish, J. P.

Clark, Francis & Nancy Suit, 11 Jan 1817; John Clark, bm; Rhodes N. Herndon, wit.

Clark, Henry & Nancey Philpot, 7 Jan 1808; Mark White, bm; W. M. Sneed, wit.

Clark, James & Jane Weaver, 13 Jan 1795; William Weaver, bm; Step. Sneed, wit.

Clark, James & Celia Smith, 29 Oct 1839; Nelson Brame, bm.

Clark, James & Sally W. Faulkner, 14 Aug 1853; Randal A. Grisham, bm.

Clark, James G. & Martha J. Bray, 22 Dec 1854; Richard A. Morris, bm; T. B. Wilkerson, wit; m 22 Dec 1854 by D. S. Wilkerson, J. P.

Clark, Jesse & Betsey Smith, 25 May 1831; Abel Landis, bm.

Clark, John E. & Emma Red, 6 Sept 1860; A. Landis, bm; m 6 Sept 1860 by T. M. Lynch, J. P.

Clark, John G. & Elizabeth Noblin, 17 Dec 1840; Saml. Daniel, bm; J. M. Wiggins, wit.

Clark, John J. & Sarah C. Clarke, 29 Dec 1838; Robert Fuller, bm; S. G. Shermon, wit.

Clark, John L. & Eliza Eaks, 2 Oct 1865; L. H. Beasley, bm; m 4 Oct 1865 by B. T. Winston, J. P.

Clark, Joseph & Mary Jane Mangum, 6 Aug 1849; Hilman Barnes, bm; Jas. M. Wiggins, wit.

Clark, Joseph & Rebecca Roberts, 3 Dec 1857; J. R. Fuller, bm; m 9 Dec 1857 by T. B. Lyon, J. P.

GRANVILLE MARRIAGES 1753-1868

Clark, Joseph & Emily Mangum, 24 Dec 1861; Lunsford Loyd, bm; m 24 Dec 1861 by E. L. Parrish, J. P.

Clark, Michael & Rebeccah Farmer, 26 Dec 1803; Thomas Farmer, bm; Step. Sneed, wit.

Clark, Reuben & Nancy Ball, 19 Nov 1852; Isaac Loyd, bm; A. Landis, wit.

Clark, Rufus, son of William & Nancy Clark, & Ruth Ann Allen, daughter of Wm. D. & Emeline H. Allen, m 24 Dec 1868 by M. H. Vaughan, Rector of St. Stephen's Church.

Clark, Samuel & Stellarah Hester, 13 Dec 1837; Robt. Fuller, bm; Jas. M. Wiggins, wit.

Clark, Samuel & Louisa J. Wheeler, 3 Dec 1857; Joseph Clark, bm; m 6 Dec 1857 by T. B. Lyon, J. P.

Clark, Solomon & Rebecca Hester, 29 March 1841; William Clark, bm; Jas. M. Wiggins, wit.

Clark, William D. & Emma Watkins, 9 Nov 1868; m 11 Nov 1868 by R. J. Devin, M. G.

Clarke, Adam & Susan Thomasson, 27 Sept 1842; J. S. Ellis, bm; Wm. H. Whitfield, wit.

Clarke, Benjamin & Mary Fleming, 28 Dec 1782; William Clark, bm; Wm. Lassiter, wit.

Clarke, James & Mrs. Sally W. Faulkner, m 14 Aug 1853 by A. C. Harris, M. G.

Clarke, James K. & Fanny Wilson, 30 March 1810; Bartholomew Falkner, bm; Jun. Sneed, wit.

Clarke, John & Salley Suit, 8 Feb 1814; James H. Bryant, bm; W. M. Sneed, wit.

Clarke, Joseph & Sarah Campbell, 6 Dec 1774; James Johns(t)on, John Searcy, bm; Sherwood Harris, wit.

Clarke, Levi & Jane Byars, 6 Nov 1827; William Reynolds, bm; S. K. Sneed, wit.

Clarke, William F. & Catharine Haylander, 12 July 1825, Mark M. Henderson, bm; S. K. Sneed, wit.

Clay, Allen & Elizabeth Lawrence, 2 Oct 1827; Allen Higgs, bm; Wm. H. Owen, wit.

Clay, Archibald M. & Catharine Y. Montague, 26 Jan 1846; Thomas Pittard, bm; Jas. M. Wiggins, wit.

Clay, Archibald M. & Francis L. Montague, 6 Oct 1855; m 7 Oct 1855 by Saml. Wait, Minister of the Gospel.

Clay, Charles & Pamale T. Mitchel, 16 Dec 1815; Matthew Mitchel, bm; Rhodes Herndon, wit.

Clay, Charles W. & Rebecca S. Pittard, 5 April 1849; John E. Mitchell, bm; Jas. M. Wiggins, wit.

GRANVILLE MARRIAGES 1753-1868

Clay, Charles W. & Susan F. Stirk, 14 Jan 1856; Eugene Grissom, bm; m 15 Jan 1856 by R. J. Devin.

Clay, Doctor & Betsey Hill, 10 Nov 1807; Nelson Thomasson, bm; W. M. Sneed, wit.

Clay, Henry M. & Sophia Clay, 1 Jan 1803; Green Merritt, bm; Step. Sneed, wit.

Clay, James G. & Victoria C. Byrd, _____ 1866; James M. Davis, bm.

Clay, John & Hannah Crawley, 26 Aug 1797; Robert Crawley, bm; Step. Sneed, wit.

Clay, John M. & Eliza F. Henning, 8 Sept 1812; Robert C. Adams, bm; Stephen K. Sneed, wit.

Clay, William & Eliza Longmire, 8 March 1831; Asbury Dement, bm; David Laws, wit.

Clay, William & Emily Freeman, 24 April 1866; m 28 April 1866 by George J. Rowland, J. P.

Clay, William H. & Frances J. Critcher, 1 April 1856; Denis Lynch, bm.

Clayton, Benjn. & Sarah Cozort (no date, during admn. of Gov. D. L. Swain); Danl. Clayton, bm; Jno. P. Smith, wit.

Clayton, David, son of William & Liza Clayton, & Panola White, daughter of Buck & Tobitha White, 15 Nov 1868; m 15 Nov 1868 by Robert T. Overton, J. P.

Clayton, James C. & Mary Hampton, 24 June 1865; D. C. Cozart, bm; m 9 July 1865 by Robt. S. Heflin, J. P.

Clayton, Munroe & Edna Brinkley, 19 June 1861; Dolphin Oakley, bm; m 23 June 1861 by G. W. Freeill.

Clayton, Reuben R. & Amelia R. Jones, 24 Nov 1848; Wm. H. Royster, bm; Jas. M. Wiggins, wit.

Clayton, Thomas & Elizabeth Ragland, 29 Oct 1810; Alexander Elixson, bm; Oba. Ferrar, wit.

Clayton, William B. & Mary Heggie, 15 Aug 1843; Wm. Satterfield, bm; J. M. Wiggins, wit.

Cleaton, George, of color, & Sally Roberts, 2 July 1868; m 4 July 1868 by Edward Hines, M. G.

Clegg, George W. & Amie M. Moore, 20 Nov 1852; Thos. C. Moses, bm; m 14 Dec 1852 by Thos. C. Moses, Minister of the Gospel.

Clement, Anderson, of color, son of Jim Jones & Maria Clement, & Malina Jones, daughter of Henry Wortham & Jenny Jones, 27 Dec 1867; m 28 Dec 1867 by B. D. Howard, J. P.

Clement, Elijah & Anna Jenkins, 29 Dec 1865; m 29 Dec 1865 by W. A. Currin, J. P.

Clement, Henry & Elisabeth West, 5 March 1782; James Comer, bm.

GRANVILLE MARRIAGES 1753-1868

Clement, John T. & Nancy Brasfield, 1 June 1816; George Landers, bm; R. N. Herndon, wit.

Clement, Samuel & Judah Knight, 13 Dec 1788; David Gooch, bm.

Clement, Simon & Mary Pirdon Wright, 24 Oct 1783; William Henlig, bm; Bennet Searcy, wit.

Clement, Simon & Nancy Cozort, 22 Oct 1822; Wm. Morriss, bm; Jas. M. Wiggins, wit.

Clement, Stephen & Nancy Eastes, 26 Sept 1785; Zephaniah Clement, bm; Bennet Searcy, wit.

Clement, Stephen & Elizabeth Terry, 15 Oct 1803; John Thorp Jr., bm; Green Merritt, wit.

Clement, William & Mary Brasfield, 2 May 1809; John Terrell, bm; Step. Sneed, wit.

Clement, William & Jane Gooch, 5 April 1826; Wm. Terry, bm; Wm. H. Owen, wit.

Clement, William A., son of Simon & Nancy Clement, & Rachael Jenkins, daughter of Wm. & Charity Jenkins, 4 Feb 1868; m 1 March 1868 by Thos. B. Lyon, J. P.

Clements, Anderson & Catharine L. Russell, 5 July 1838; Jno. Russell, bm.

Clements, Elijah, (colored), son of Cuffee Jones & Easter Jenkins, & Adeline Gregory, daughter of Johnson Gregory, 28 Oct 1868; m 30 _____ 1868 by Palmer Jenkins, M. G.

Clements, William & Elisabeth Daniel, 15 March 1779; Wm. Burford, Jr., bm; Reuben Searcy, wit.

Clerk, James & Margaret Vincent, 15 Jan 1782; Nathaniel Clerk, bm; Bennet Searcy, wit.

Clerk, Young & Elisabeth Willis, 30 March 1785; George Wharf, bm; Reuben Searcy, wit.

Cliborne, Nathaniel T. & Lucy Ussery, 3 June 1837; Jas. M. Wiggins, bm.

Cliborne, Robert F. & Eugenia F. Barker, 3 Oct 1865; William H. Crews, bm; m 8 Oct 1865 by John F. Harris, J. P.

Clifton, Dr. James B., parents unknown, & Ann R. Smith, daughter of Samuel W. & Isabella Smith, m 6 Nov 1867 by M. H. Vaughan, Rector of St. Stephen's Church.

Climen, Thos. & Edith R. Suit, 16 Dec 1834; Jas. P. Tayloe, bm; Tho. S. Mauvin, wit.

Clopton, Archibald & Sary Blackwell, 7 March 1797; Richd. Taylor, bm.

Clopton, Devereaux & Nancey Dickerson, 20 Nov 1809; Jonathan Davis, bm; W. M. Sneed, wit.

Clopton, George W. & Amelia Ann Robertson, 16 Sept 1856; Peter Robertson, bm.

GRANVILLE MARRIAGES 1753-1868

Clopton, Guy & Polley Bryant, 21 Nov 1803; Jno. Walker, bm.

Clopton, James D. & Lucretia Bailey, 11 Jan 1843; S. H. Harrington, bm; Wm. H. Whitfield, wit.

Clopton, William & Rose Blackwell, 11 March 1814; William Heflin, bm; J. P. Sneed, wit.

Clopton, Willie & Lacy Ann Huskey, 3 Feb 1846; John J. Harget, bm.

Cloy, Archibald M. & Francis L. Montague, 6 Oct 1855; A. Landis, bm.

Cobb, Richard & Harriett Davis, 16 Sept 1865; A. Landis, wit.

Cobb, William & Roxanna Malone, freed people, m 5 May 1866 by W. P. White, J. P.

Cobbs, John & Mildred Lewis, 6 Sept 1769; Howell Lewis, John Bell, bm.

Cobbs, John & Anne Lewis, 22 Feb 1786; Charles Lewis, bm; Bennet Searcy, wit.

Coe, Amos & Bitsey Harris, 1 March 1812; Thomas Harris, bm; W. M. Sneed, wit.

Coffey, Peter & Sarah Smith, 14 Nov 1773; James Alston, bm.

Cofield, Warren, of color, son of Warren & Dilsey McCarter & Mary Sandford, of color, daughter of William Green & Lucy Sandford, m 5 Nov 1867 by L. M. Vanhook, J. P.

Coghill, Gideon & Judith Fuller, 28 Dec 1814; Samuel Edwards, bm; Step. Sneed, wit.

Coghill, Henderson & Adeline Duty, 14 Nov 1866; C. E. Landis, bm; A. Landis, wit; m 18 Nov 1866 by Maurice H. Vaughan, Rector of St. Stephen's Church.

Coghill, Jonathan F. & Zuluka K. Fuller, 10 Dec 1866; E. M. Hunt, bm; m 19 Dec 1866 by S. K. Willie, M. G.

Coghill, Kinchen & Fannie C. Lassiter, 15 July 1865; W. K. Brosius, bm.

Coghill, Kinchen W. & Fannie C. Lassiter, 15 July 1865; m ___ Aug 1865 by P. H. Joyner.

Coghill, Kinchin & Martha E. Hunt, 20 Dec 1858; William N. Fuller, bm; m 23 Dec 1858 by L. K. Willie, M. G.

Cokly, John & Hawkins Haswell, 30 Feb 1848; Isom Smith, bm; Benj. C. Cooke, wit.

Colclough, Alexander & Mary Haswell, 16 Aug 1819; James J. Farrar, bm; Step. K. Sneed, wit.

Cole, B. L. & Margaret C. Webb, 29 June 1846; H. J. Robards, bm.

Cole, Charles T. & Pamelia P. Hutchison, 9 Nov 1837; Elias S. Jinkins, bm.

Cole, Doctor & Mary A. Jones, 20 Dec 1841; Jas. Blackly, bm.

GRANVILLE MARRIAGES 1753-1868

Cole, Duke & Lucy Stephenson, 4 Feb 1817; Joseph Arnold, bm; Step. Sneed, wit.

Cole, J. H. & S. A. M. Tuck, m 18 Oct 1865 by A. Apple, M. G.

Cole, Jesse K. & Electra Grissom, 9 March 1843; W. D. Allen, bm; J. M. Wiggins, wit.

Cole, John J. & Pattie E. Lipford, 28 Feb 1864; P. H. Worsham, bm; m 28 Feb 1864 by L. B. Stone.

Cole, Nelson & Martha Cooke, 23 Dec 1817; James Blackley, bm; Rhodes N. Herndon, wit.

Cole, Rhodam & Hannah Fleming, 16 April 1780; William Fleming, bm; Winfred Jett, wit.

Cole, William & Eliza Richerson, 28 July 1858; Fama Hayes, bm; A. Landis, wit; m 29 July 1858 by Jas. R. Duty, J. P.

Coleman, Charles B. & Sarah A. Eaton, 13 Feb 1836; Robert V. Eaton, bm; Benja. Kittrell, wit.

Coleman, Daniel R. & Nancy Blackwell, 21 Nov 1826; James Overbey, bm.

Coleman, Littleton & Lucy Ann Hawkins, 17 Feb 1823; Rhodes N. Herndon, bm; L. Gilliam, wit.

Coleman, Oliver & Nancey Robertson, freed people, 16 March 1867; m 16 March 1867 by W. Overbey, J. P., Ruffin Yancey, bm; R. Amis, wit.

Coley, Edmund & Rosa B. Buchanan, 22 Aug 1843; Richard H. Coley, bm; J. M. Wiggins, wit.

Coley, James M. & Nancy Phillips, 22 Dec 1822; William Phillips, bm; (uncertain as to which is groom and which is bm); James M. Wiggins, wit.

Coley, James M. & Rebecca Clark, 16 Dec 1858; Edmund Coley, bm; m 22 Dec 1858 by Jas. H. Dalby, J. P.

Coley, Richard & Barshaba Cash, 11 Jan 1833; John Beck, bm; David Laws, wit.

Coley, Richard & Arrena Dalby, 27 Nov 1830; William Coley, bm.

Coley, Simeon D. & Frances C. Cash, 11 Jan 1867; J. W. Ferrell, bm; m 22 Jan 1867 by T. B. Lyon Jr., J. P.

Coley, Thomas & Rowan Bullock, 18 Dec 1837; Jno. C. Taylor, bm; Jas. M. Wiggins, wit.

Coley, William & Lucy Cooley, 6 Nov 1827; Mark Veazy, bm; Step. K. Sneed, wit.

Coley, William & Amelia Hicks, 3 April 1845; Seth J. Garrett, bm.

Coley, William D. & Angeline Cash, 24 Nov 1860; Edmund Coley, bm.

Collier, Archelaus & Polly Hight, 30 Dec 1812; Thomas Collier, bm; Thos. J. Hicks, wit.

GRANVILLE MARRIAGES 1753-1868

Collier, Herbert & Mahala Fuller, 20 Oct 1792; Jno. McAden, bm; W. Norwood, wit.

Collier, Thomas & Rhoda Ball, 11 Jan 1805; Cole Collier, bm; J. Sneed, wit.

Collins, Jas. A. & Susan Barnes, 9 Nov 1844; B. J. Mitchell, bm.

Collins, John & Nancey Hartgrove, 23 Oct 1790; John Brodie, bm; H. Potter, wit.

Collins, John & Henrietta Wilson, 24 April 1849; L. W. Jones, bm; J. M. Wiggins, wit.

Collins, Mark & Harriet Bobbitt, 22 Oct 1865; Daniel Hester, bm; A. Landis, wit; m 22 Oct 1865 by W. M. Wingate, M. G.

Collins, Thomas & Peggy Wyars, 29 Sept 1788; Thos. Kelley, bm; A. Henderson, C. C., wit.

Collins, William & Polley Clardey, 13 Dec 1791; Thomas Collins, bm; A. Henderson, wit.

Collins, William C., son of Isham & Permelia Collins, & Martha Ann Floyd, daughter of William & Mary Floyd, 15 Feb 1868; m 20 February 1868 by E. F. Beachum, M. G.

Colman, Charles(?) & Mary Cook, 17 Sept 1781; Robert Harris Sr., bm; James Claxton, wit.

Comer, James & Elisabeth Clements, 4 Oct 1779; William Clements, bm; Sherwood Harris, wit.

Compton, Edward C. & Emily C. Throckmorton, 1 Jan 1862; John To---, bm; m 1 Jan 1862 by L. B. Stone, J. P.

Connell, John & Eliza Cottrel, 22 Oct 1839; William Strum, bm; T. B. Barnett, wit.

Connell, Wyat G., son of G. C. & Usley Connell, & Lucy Briggs, daughter of Henry Briggs, 11 April 1868; m 12 April 1868 by B. F. Jinkins, J. P.

Cook, Blanton & Mary Hunt, 17 Jan 1786; William Cook, bm.

Cook, James & Elisabeth Johnson, 28 Dec 1792; Benjamin Johnson, bm; Step. Sneed, wit.

Cook, James & Haskey Cole, 5 Dec 1818; James Nuttall, bm; W. M. Sneed, wit.

Cook, James R. & Margaret Hicks, 12 July 1837; Hardy Patterson, bm; G. C. Wiggins, wit.

Cook, John D. & Mary Landers, 20 Jan 1794; George Bullock, bm; W. Norwood, wit.

Cook, John M. & Nancey McGehee, 26 Dec 1825; William Holmes, bm; Halyard Blackley, bm; A. M. Henderson, wit.

Cook, Joseph & Tamor Nothern, 31 Aug 1803; David T. Cook, bm.

Cook, Rollin & _____, 18 July 1812; Knight Dolby, bm; W. M. Sneed, wit.

GRANVILLE MARRIAGES 1753-1868

Cook, Shem & Temprance Blackwell, 17 Sept 1800; Jeremiah Rust, bm; Wm. Walker, wit.

Cook, Shem & Myrick Gilliam, 7 Dec 1826; Hallyard Blackley, bm; Wm. H. Owen, wit.

Cook, Thos. & Abigale Jones, widow, 10 Aug 1763; Benjamin Person, bm.

Cook, Wm. & Mary McGee, 22 Aug 1789; John Rust, bm.

Cook, William & Betsey Freeman, 7 Feb 1821; Thomas Cole, bm; Jas. M. Wiggins, wit.

Cook, William L. & Ann Blackley, 22 Oct 1856; Willis H. Jeffreys, bm; A. Landis, wit; m 30 Oct 1856 by W. D. Allen.

Cooke, Augustus H. & Sarah M. McCadden, 7 Nov 1848; W. A. Philpott, bm.

Cooke, Benjamin C. & Petronella C. Griffin, 26 Nov 1849; F. B. Hester, bm; A. Landis, wit.

Cooke, James & Harriet Overton, 28 Jan 1846; Isaac Cheatham, bm; J. M. Wiggins, wit.

Cooke, James R. & Sarah E. Sandlen, 20 Sept 1847; S. S. Parrott, bm.

Cooke, Lemuel & Lotty Dickerson, 19 Aug 1829; Willie Grisham, bm; David Laws, wit.

Cooke, Mark & Nancy Hill, 7 Feb 1806; Green Hill, bm; A. H. Sneed, wit.

Cooke, Richard & Mary Blacknall, 3 Nov 1808; Thomas Cooke, bm; J-- Hawkins, wit.

Cooke, Richd. H. & Mary Dickerson, 27 Jan 1842; Jonathan Jones, bm; Jas. M. Wiggins, wit.

Cooke, Richard Henry & Elizabeth Blacknall, 21 Dec 1809; John Hawkins, bm; W. M. Sneed, wit.

Cooke, Step. & Fanny Cole, 3 Oct 1822; Benja. Knight, bm; Jas. M. Wiggins, wit.

Cooke, Thomas & Sarah G. Clay, 15 Dec 1802; Wm. Butler, bm; W. M. Sneed, wit.

Cooke, William Junr. & Elisabeth Bedford, 24 May 1784; Peyton Wood, bm; Bennet Searcy, wit.

Cooper, Alexander & Harriet J. Young, 12 Nov 1840; D. O. Herndon, bm; J. M. Wiggins, wit.

Cooper, Benjamin & Temperance Simon, 4 Nov 1794; John Harris, bm; L. Henderson, wit.

Cooper, Collins & Luvenia Lewis, 20 Oct 1866; m 20 Oct 1866 by L. A. Paschall, J. P.; A. Landis, bm.

Cooper, Cornelius & Jane Wood, 20 Feb 1796; Solomon McGehee, bm; Step. Sneed, wit.

GRANVILLE MARRIAGES 1753-1868

Cooper, Harry & Emily Lewis, 4 Aug 1866; m 4 Aug 1866 by T. M. Lynch, J. P.

Cooper, Henderson & Maria Hunt, freed people, 26 March 1867; m by John Tillett, 26 March 1868.

Cooper, James & Martha Harrisson, 19 Jan 1780; Cannon Cooper, bm; Asa Searcy, wit.

Cooper, James & Anna Downey, 29 Dec 1815; Anson Mitchel, bm; Jno. Cobbs, bm.

Cooper, John & Abigal White, 1 Dec 1784; William Prittey(?), bm; John Searcy Jr., wit.

Cooper, Oliver & Sallie Worthington, 26 Aug 1865; J. Waldo, bm; A. Landis, wit; m 27 Aug 1865 by Maurice H. Vaughan, Rector of St. Stephen's Church.

Cooper, P. A. & Susan Ann Tillottson, 4 Jan 1860; L. A. Blankenship, bm; m 4 Jan 1860 by L. B. Stone, J. P.

Cooper, Robert & Mary Rice, 26 Dec 1866; Joseph Hunt, bm; Jas. R. Duty, wit; colored; m 26 Dec 1866 by Jas. R. Duty, J. P.

Cooper, Russell & Eliza Hunt, freed people, m 20 Dec 1866 by Thomas U. Faucette.

Cooper, William & Mary Mangrom, 29 Aug 1799; Matthew Allen, bm; W. M. Sneed, wit.

Cord, Abraham & Temperance Levester, 14 Dec 1799; Josiah Megehe, bm; Step. Sneed, wit.

Cornel, William & Catharine Slaughter, 24 July 1800; William Fowler, bm; Philip Bullock, wit.

Cotton, William & Eveline Ridley, 24 Jan 1867; Richard Hicks, bm; C. E. Landis, wit; m 24 Jan 1867 by John L. Carroll, Minister.

Cottrell, Armstead & Caroline Marable, m 15 Dec 1866 by R. L. Hunt, J. P.; E. G. Butler, bm; C. E. Landis, wit.

Cottrell, James & Lucy Sears, 25 Nov 1836; Thomas Rice, bm; J. M. Wiggins, wit.

Cottrell, Mark & Betsey Strung, 21 Nov 1799; Nathaniel Thomasson, bm; Ro. Harris, wit.

Cottrell, Mathew & Happy Loyd, 4 Dec 1841; Willis Hicks, bm; J. M. Wiggins, wit.

Cottrell, Samuel & Frances Satterwhite, 19 June 1811; David Rice, bm; Step. Sneed, wit.

Cottrell, Samuel & Catharine Hicks, 10 March 1840; Thos. Rice, bm; J. M. Wiggins, wit.

Cottrell, Solomon & Lucy Ann Crews, 26 Oct 1841; Manson Breedlove, bm.

Courtney, John & Frances Bedford, 25 Dec 1805; Maurice Smith, bm; Step. Sneed, wit.

GRANVILLE MARRIAGES 1753-1868

Cousin, James Henry & Sally Day, 31 March 1866; m 1 April 1866 by W. H. Jordan, M. G.

Cousin, John Joseph & Martha Ann Cousin, 19 Dec 1840; William Trowler, bm.

Cousins--see also Cozens.

Cousins, Benton & Elizabeth Mayhoe, 21 March 1835; Willie Chavis, bm; Benja. Kittrell, wit.

Cousins, Elijah, of color, son of Martin & Nancy Cousins, & Susan Winfield, daughter of Henderson & Susan Winfield, m 12 Sept 1867 by Jas. R. Duty, J. P.

Cousins, Frederick J. & Elizabeth Day, 6 Jan 1843; Alexander Howel, bm; Wm. H. Whitfield, wit.

Cousins, Henry & Martha Howell, 16 April 1840; Evan Petteford, bm; J. M. Wiggins, wit.

Cousins, Larkin & Polly Peel, 13 Oct 1849; John Kates, bm; A. Landis, wit.

Cousins, Martin & Jane Brandom, 26 March 1845; Evans Pettiferd, bm.

Cousins, Richard & Phillis Maynard, m 14 April 1866 by G. N. Hicks, J. P.

Cousins, William A. & Matilda B. Duty, 7 Dec 1832; John B. Hicks, bm; Step. K. Sneed, wit.

Coward, Col. D. Y. & Miss Jane J. Jones, m 4 April 1866 by Joseph W. Murphy, Rector of Holy Innocents Ch., Henderson.

Cox, Eli & Martha Wilborn, 1 Sept 1857; Henry Newton, bm; A. Landis, wit; m 4 Sept 1857 by L. B. Stone, J. P.

Cox, George Jr. & Polley Cox, 29 Oct 1799; Benjamin E. Person, bm; Step. Sneed, wit.

Cox, James & Elizabeth Matthews, m 20 Dec 1866 by Warren Overbey, J. P.

Cox, Thomas & Elizabeth Philips, 9 June 1858; Henry Newton, bm; A. Landis, wit; m 11 June 1858 by L. B. Stone, J. P.

Cox, William & Polley Daniel, 11 Dec 1799; Samuel F. Williams, bm; Step. Sneed, wit.

Cox, William & Julia Ann Ramsay, 29 Nov 1853; Miles Cox, bm; m 30 Nov 1853 by M. D. Royster, J. P.

Coy, Pleasant & Mary G. Mallory, 23 Feb 1830; A. H. Higgs, bm; David Laws, wit.

Cozart, Benjamin & Salley Reeves, 7 Oct 1786; Joseph Mangham, bm; Reuben Searcy, wit.

Cozart, Benjamin H. & Rebecca F. Rogers, 29 Feb 1864; John H. Webb, bm; m 2 March 1864 by G. W. Ferrill, Minister.

GRANVILLE MARRIAGES 1753-1868

Cozart, Carrington & Ailcy Parrish, 15 Oct 1851; J. P. Hester, bm; m 15 Oct 1851 by Jno. Nance, J. P.

Cozart, Hubbard & Mary Howard, 23 Aug 1802; Brodie Howard, bm; Phil. Bullock, wit.

Cozart, James & Frances Howard, 19 Oct 1797; Hubbard Cozart, bm; Step. Sneed, wit.

Cozart, Jesse & Elisabeth Walker, 14 May 1786; Sherwood Harris, Edward Jones, bm; Reuben Searcy, wit.

Cozart, Person & Wilmuth Wilkerson, 6 Sept 1820; William M. Cassady, bm; S. K. Sneed, wit.

Cozart, Pinkney & Eliza Omerry, 9 April 1858; S. W. Mitchell, bm; A. Landis, wit; m 11 April 1858 by Jeff Horner, J. P.

Cozart, Reuben & Elisabeth Weaver, 10 Aug 1798; Jno. Philpott, bm; Step. Sneed, wit.

Cozart, Thomas & Mary Goss, 9 Feb 1791; Solo. Williams, bm; A. Potter, wit.

Cozart, Thomas & Nancy Clayton, 23 Aug 1865; D. C. Cozort, bm; m 27 Aug 1865 by Robt. L. Heflin, J. P.

Cozart, W. W. & Mary E. Jones, 2 Feb 1857; James T. Hunt, bm.

Cozart, Wiatt & Polley Whitlow, 14 Nov 1815; Wm. Mangrum, bm; W. M. Sneed, wit.

Cozens, Allen & Elizabeth Parker, 7 Sept 1825; Wiley Cozens, bm; L. Gilliam, wit.

Crabtree, Edward R. & Rowan P. Williams, 23 June 1836; Edward D. Hard, bm.

Crabtree, James W. & Sarah Ann D. Moss, 12 March 1856; Joseph Hobgood, bm; m 13 March 1856 by B. B. Hester.

Crabtree, William C. & Mary R. McCraw, 10 Dec 1848; Benj. C. Cook, bm.

Craddock, Edward A. & Mrs. L. Hutcherson, 29 Nov 1849; James J. Thomas, bm.

Craft, John & Polley Daniel, 28 Feb 1842; Wm. H. Prather, bm; J. M. Wiggins, wit.

Craft, John B. & Seney Harris, 10 Dec 1835; William Parish, bm; Benja. Kittrell, wit.

Craft, Presley & Polley Warf, 7 June 1806; John Brame, bm; Step. Sneed, wit.

Craft, Samuel & Polley Williams, 21 Dec 1796; Charles Williams, bm; Step. Sneed, wit.

Craft, Samuel & Mary Morris, 18 Dec 1847; W. A. Parish, bm; Jas. M. Wiggins, wit.

Craft, Thomas & Amey Majors, 3 March 1796; Benjamin Denton, bm; Step. Sneed, wit.

GRANVILLE MARRIAGES 1753-1868

Craft, William & Pattey Morse, 17 Dec 1791; Jacob Watters, bm; Step. Sneed, wit.

Craft, Willis & Amy Vincent, 18 March 1834; Tho. T. Hester, bm; Benja. Kittrell, wit.

Crafts, John & Pattey Morse, 24 May 1791; Benjn. Denton, bm; Step. Sneed, wit.

Cragg, Richard & Francis Glamp, 28 Dec 1795; Stephen Oakley, bm; Step. Sneed, wit.

Craig, John & Mary D. Wood, 9 Nov 1805; Robt. M. Ridley, bm; Jas. Sneed, wit.

Crainshaw, Absalom & Mary Dodson, 12 Dec 1792; Samuel Smith, bm.

Crawford, Thomas D. & Edla L. Grandy, 15 Oct 1866; Jas. Y. Landis, bm; C. E. Landis, wit; m 16 Oct 1866 by W. M. Wingate, M. G.

Crawley, Robert & Mary Taylor, 15 July 1767; Joseph Davenport, Charles Gillam, b; _____ Pryor, Jesse Benton, wit.

Creath, Irby & Caroline Wake Norris, 17 Nov 1832; Moses Neal, bm.

Creath, John & Mary Irby, 1 Jan 1794; William Irby, bm; W. Norwood, D. C., wit.

Creath, John & Elizabeth Irby, 20 July 1816; Melus Broom, bm; Richard Sneed, wit.

Creath, John & Mary Elexon, _____ 184_; David A. Dock, bm; J. M. Wiggins, wit.

Creath, Samuel & Nancey Ragland, 14 Feb 1795; Reubin Ragland, bm; Step. Sneed, wit.

Crenshaw, Benjamin & Frances Owen, 11 Dec 1778; Charles Edwards, bm.

Crenshaw, Charles & Elizabeth Vass, 11 July 1791; Edward Hunt, bm; Step. Sneed, wit.

Crenshaw, Henry P. & Millissia A. Bacon, 15 June 1815; Wright Ellington, bm; Richd. Sneed, wit.

Crenshaw, Mabin & Sarah Goss, 12 Dec 1784; William Puryear, bm; Bennet Searcy, wit.

Crenshaw, Robert & Fanney Hester, 30 Oct 1798; William Graves, bm; W. M. Sneed, wit.

Crenshaw, Thomas & Rebeccah Knott, 22 Sept 1803; Sterling Yancey, bm; Jun. Sneed, wit.

Crenshaw, William & Elisabeth Hart, 23 Feb 1793; Shadrick Frainer, bm; W. Norwood, wit.

Crews, Ashley & Kittey Lemay, 5 Dec 1826; Gideon Crews, bm. Wm. H. Owen, wit.

Crews, Benjamin F. & Fanny Elliss, 18 July 1829; Willis Daniel, bm; David Laws, wit.

Crews, Benj. F. & Hannah Hunt, 15 Aug 1845; Mansom Breedlove, bm.

GRANVILLE MARRIAGES 1753-1868

Crews, David G. & Louisa J. Fleming, 9 June 1866; m 10 June 1866 by W. C. Gannon, M. G.

Crews, Doctor & Mary E. Taylor, freed people, m 30 June 1866 by L. K. Willie, M. G.

Crews, Edward N. & Martha G. Parham, 11 Dec 1847; Wm. B. Crews, bm; J. M. Wiggins, wit.

Crews, Elijah T. & Mary J. Parham, 10 April 1847; Wm. B. Crews, bm; Jas. M. Wiggins, wit.

Crews, Gideon & Temperance Lemay, 19 Dec 1805; John Johnson, bm; Jun. Sneed, wit.

Crews, Gideon & Parthena Glover, 23 May 1853; A. Landis, bm; m 25 Aug 1853 by Richd. H. Gregory, J. P.

Crews, Hardamond & Pheby J. Merimond, 23 June 1821; William A. Taylor, bm; A. Sneed, wit.

Crews, Harrod & Nutty Blackwell (freed people), 5 Aug 1865, m 5 Aug 1865 by Wm. M. Blackwell, J. P.

Crews, Herod & Nutty Blackwell, 27 Aug 1866; m 27 Aug 1866 by H. C. Herndon, J. P.

Crews, Horace, of color, son of Anderson & Frances Crews, & Priscilla Henderson, daughter of Peter & Phebe Henderson, 13 Dec 1867; m 14 Dec 1867 by J. F. Harris, J. P.

Crews, Isaac, of color, son of Abram & Emily Crews, & Luvenia Taylor, daughter of Peter & Ava Taylor, m 26 Dec 1867 by Wm. R. Hicks, J. P.

Crews, James & Sally Earl, 2 Feb 1808; David Rice, bm; A. H. Sneed, wit.

Crews, James Senr. & Sarah Currin, 12 March 1867; m 14 March 1867 by W. S. Hester, M. G.

Crews, James B. & Sallie F. Hunt, 26 April 1861; W. R. Beasley, bm.

Crews, John & Susan Rice, 18 May 1820; Nathl. Roberson, bm; Jas. M. Wiggins, wit.

Crews, John & Sarah E. Hight, 6 Feb 1837; D. A. Paschall, bm; G. C. Wiggins, wit.

Crews, Littlebery & Elisabeth Earl, 21 Sept 1807; Joseph Cruce, bm; John H. Farra, wit.

Crews, Littlebury & Nancy Cheatham, 18 Dec 1824; Parker A. Stone, bm; Step. K. Sneed, wit.

Crews, Meredith & Nancy Wade, 16 Dec 1815; Thomas Hunt, bm; Wm. Thomasson, wit.

Crews, Meredith & Mary D. Thomasson, 21 Dec 1829; Geo. Thomasson, bm; Step. K. Sneed, wit.

Crews, Robert D. & Sarah E. Royster, 13 June 1851; R. W. Lassiter, bm; m 25 June 1851 by G. W. Ferrill, M. G.

GRANVILLE MARRIAGES 1753-1868

Crews, Samuel, colored, son of Andrew Fleming & Hannah Crews, & Indiana Horner, daughter of David ____ & Rily Horner, 14 Nov 1868; m 14 Nov 1868 by John Tillett.

Crews, Sim & Lucy Crews, m 30 Aug 1866 by John W. York.

Crews, Solomon & Mary Ann Taylor, 18 Dec 1865; A. Landis, wit.

Crews, Thomas & Mary Wicker, 23 May 1789; Mathew Snipes, bm; A. Henderson, C. C., wit.

Crews, Thomas & Lucinda Gilliam, 24 Nov 1864; Solomon B. Crews, bm; m 24 Nov 1864 by Robt. S. Hunt, J. P.

Crews, William A. & Mary A. Parrish, 26 Jan 1828; James Cheatham Junr., bm; David Laws, wit.

Crews, William B. & Rebecca A. H. Burge, 27 Oct 1851; John H. Webb, bm.

Crews, William H. & Sarah W. Ussery, 23 March 1840; George W. Lumpkin, bm; J. M. Wiggins, wit.

Critcher, Albert J. & Martha Ann Morris, 21 Oct 1854; A. Landis, bm; m 24 Oct 1854 by H. Hester, J. P.

Critcher, Anson & Phebe Mallory, 25 Nov 1831; Jas. Russell, bm; David Laws, wit.

Critcher, Anson & Tabitha Barnett, 25 Oct 1851; R. J. Mitchell, bm; m 29 Oct 1851 by R. J. Devin.

Critcher, Guilford & Rebecca Satterwhite, 28 Dec 1852; Wm. Critcher, bm; A. Landis, wit; m 29 Dec 1852 by S. G. Wilson, J. P.

Critcher, James T. & Hannah Wheeler, 3 July 1858; A. Landis, bm; m 4 July 1858 by W. R. Harris, J. P.

Critcher, John & Sarah Marshal, 14 Jan 1794; John Craft Jr., bm; Step. Sneed, wit.

Critcher, Joseph A. & Lucy C. Barnett, 5 Nov 1862; R. G. Barnett, bm; m 5 Nov 1862 by Thomas U. Faucette.

Critcher, Mastin & Martha Longmire, 18 Jan 1826; Thos. Critcher, bm; Wm. H. Owen, wit.

Critcher, William & Elizabeth Satterwhite, 11 July 1839; Anson Critcher, bm.

Critcher, William H. & Eliza Norwood, 24 Feb 1854; Detrion T. Rowland, bm; A. Landis, wit; m 24 Feb 1854 by Jas. M. Heggie, J. P.

Crook, John & Bulky White, 2 Nov 1819; Clement Wilkins, bm; W. E. Hargis, wit.

Crosby, James N. & Emily J. Reavis, 21 Nov 1838; John C. Poe, bm.

Cross, Isaac, colored, son of Jack & Cherry Cross, & Angeline Bullock, daughter of Buck Bullock & Sally Richards, m 7 Nov 1868 by John W. Estes, J. P.

GRANVILLE MARRIAGES 1753-1868

Cross, Samuel G., of color, son of Amos G. & Eliza Cross, & Rebecca Marrow, daughter of Anderson & Lucy Marrow, 6 Oct 1867; m 10 Oct 1867 by Wyatt Walker, M. G.

Crowder, Hilkiah & Lydda Harding, 16 Sept 1786; William Cook, bm; Bennet Searcy, wit.

Crowder, Isaac & Betsey Loyd, 5 May 1818; Jonathan Lankford, bm; W. Sneed, wit.

Crowder, Isaac T. & Agnes Loyd, 25 Sept 1858; Robert Bragg, bm; m 30 Oct 1858 by W. D. Allen, J. P.

Crowder, Jacob & Susannah Magehee, 5 March 1821; Johnathan Langford, bm; Richd. Sneed, wit.

Crowder, James M. & Mary R. Sandys, 1 March 1837; Spencer C. Griffin, bm.

Crowder, John & Lacy Jackson, 25 Nov 1844; Jonan. Jenkins, bm; J. M. Wiggins, wit.

Crowder, Uel & Molley Harding, 3 June 1789; Wm. Cook, bm; A. Henderson, wit.

Crowder, William & Sarah Ann Catlett, 11 Dec 1852; Wm. J. Loyd, bm; A. Landis, wit.

Crump, O. C., son of Genl. John C. Crump & Emeline Crump, & Mattie S. Lassiter, daughter of Riddick & Lovea Lassiter, 20 June 1867; m _____ by P. H. Joyner.

Crutchfield, S. C. & Mary A. Puryear, 12 July 1848; Warren Amis, bm; Wm. H. Whitfield, wit.

Culbreath, Green & Nancy W. Heflin, 6 Feb 1840; Elijah Satterwhite, bm; W. T. Hayne, wit.

Culbreath, James & Anne Philips, 7 Jan 1836; John Philips, bm; Robert K. Clack, wit.

Culbreath, Lewis & Agness Pruit, 4 July 1810; John Caveness, bm; Junius Sneed, wit.

Culbreath, William & Elizabeth Hughes, 29 Jan 1830; James Vaughan, bm; Step. K. Sneed.

Culbreath, William & Tabitha Overbey, 27 Nov 1855; Francis Wilson, bm; A. Landis, wit.

Culbreth, John & Mary Farrar (Farmer?), 10 Nov 1830; O. W. Turner, bm; _____ Sneed, wit.

Culverhouse, Jeremiah & Chloe Tanner, 4 Feb 178_; Futrall Hall, bm; A. Henderson, wit.

Culverhouse, Moses & Parthena Roberson, 11 Feb 1835; L. Gilliam, bm; Benja. Kittrell, wit.

Culverhouse, Thos. & Rhodey Turner, 6 May 1795; Briant Cash, bm; Step. Sneed, wit.

Culverhouse, Thomas Jr. & Franky Primrose, 21 Aug 1822; Thomas Haskins, bm; Step. K. Sneed, wit.

GRANVILLE MARRIAGES 1753-1868

Cumby, J. J. & Camella F. Bowers, m 20 Oct 1867 by L. B. Stone, J. P.

Cunningham, Ransom & Sarah W. Peace, 28 Feb 1821; James Hart Jr., bm; Jas. M. Wiggins, wit.

Currin, Abner & Phoebe Blackwell, 24 Jan 1831; Stephen Blackwell, bm; Step. K. Sneed, wit.

Currin, Ansel & Lethe Ann Hester, 25 June 1836; Thos. Vass Jr., bm.

Currin, Benjamin & Charity Knoll, 29 Nov 1824; Larkin Currin, bm; Wm. H. Owen, wit.

Currin, Benjamin & Miss Annah(?) Knott, 28 March 1834; J. Harris, bm; Benja. Kittrell, wit.

Currin, Chas. F., son of Stephen & Sallie P. Currin, & Martha A. Elam, daughter of Richard & Harriet Elam, 6 Oct 1868; m 22 Oct 1868 by E. Hines, M. G.

Currin, Chesley & Nicey Guy, 2 Dec 1851; L. Latham, bm; m 9 Dec 1851 by J. M. Satterwhite, J. P.

Currin, David & Salinea Wagstaff, 15 Oct 1833; L. Gilliam, bm; Benja. Kittrell, wit.

Currin, Doctor, son of David Currin & Sarah Blacknell, & Fanny Ferrill, daughter of _____ & Leza _____; 25 Sept 1868; m 27 Sept 1868 by R. J. Devin, M. G.

Currin, Edward L. & Radaan Smith, 8 Nov 1849; J. B. Currin, bm.

Currin, Elijah & Sally Blackwell, 2 Nov 1824; Flemming Beasley, bm; Wm. H. Owen, wit.

Currin, Elijah T. & Mary Eliza Wiggins, 24 Nov 1858; Stephen Satterwhite, bm; m 24 Nov 1858 by J. F. Harris, J. P.

Currin, Fleming B. & Sarah C. M. Laughter, 14 Oct 1850; E. L. Currin, bm.

Currin, Hugh & Mildred Gorden, 24 Nov 1847; Wm. H. Gorden, bm; Jas. M. Wiggins, wit.

Currin, J. & _____ Harris, 29 July 1865; A. Landis, bm, m 2 Aug 1865 by E. Hines.

Currin, Jacob & Sally Curren, 19 Oct 1842; Hamilton Hester, bm; J. M. Wiggins, wit.

Currin, James & Lucey Fraizer, 11 Oct 1808; John Hester, bm; W. M. Sneed, wit.

Currin, James & Elizabeth Blackwell, 22 Sept 1846; Thos. West, bm; Jas. M. Wiggins, wit.

Currin, James & Lucy Ann Hobgood, 1 Jan 1858; Lotan G. W. Currin, bm; m 5 Jan 1858 by Peterson Thorp, J. P.

Currin, James F. & Susan Jones, 23 April 1844; George W. Hunt, bm; Wm. H. Whitfield, wit.

GRANVILLE MARRIAGES 1753-1868

Currin, Jeremiah & Sally Hobgood, 1 July 1857; A. Landis, bm;
m 10 July 1857 by R. J. Devin.

Currin, John & Mary Rice; Joseph Crews, bm; Spence Hinton, wit.

Currin, John B. & Sophronia Hunt, 12 April 1864; A. A. Gresham,
bm; m 13 April 1864 by Richd. H. Gregory, J. P.

Currin, John W. & Malissa Stone, 24 Sept 1852; Henry Hobgood, bm;
m 30 Sept by J. E. Montague, Young X Roads, N. C.

Currin, John W. & Ann E. Hobgood, 24 Feb 1855; W. A. Currin, bm;
m 4 March 1855 by R. J. Devin.

Currin, Larkin & Rebecca Badgett, 27 June 1826; Samuel Badgett,
bm; W. Hayes Owen, wit.

Currin, Lemmuel & Elizabeth Crews, 4 March 1802; Joseph Crews,
bm.

Currin, Lemuel & Emily Catharine Chandler, 28 Aug 1841; James
Hester, bm; Jas. M. Wiggins, wit.

Currin, Lotan G. W. & Jane Knott, 20 Nov 1857; J. H. Currin,
bm; m 24 Nov 1857 by Peterson Thorp, J. P.

Currin, Mitchel & Mary Ann Frazier, 15 Feb 1839; William A.
Currin, bm.

Currin, Robert S. & Mary Jane Elliott, 2 Feb 1864; John E.
Greenway, bm; A. Landis, wit.

Currin, Samuel J. & Bettie Ragland, 21 Dec 1858; J. B. Crews, bm.

Currin, Stephen & Sarah P. Barker, 20 Sept 1834; Mitchel Satterwhite, bm.

Currin, Stephen & Mary Currin, 6 Feb 1866; Abner Cworn(?), bm;
m 8 Feb 1866 by John F. Harris, J. P.

Currin, Thomas H. & Rebecca Blackwell, 19 Dec 1859; Robt. H.
Hobgood, bm; m by F. B. Currin, J. P.

Currin, Wiatt & Jemima Crews, 16 Oct 1810; William Gorden, bm;
W. M. Sneed, wit.

Currin, William & Elizabeth Mangum, 15 Dec 1852; Hampleton
Currin, bm; A. Landis, wit; m 15 Dec 1852 by H. Hester, J. P.

Currin, William A. & Lucy H. Hobgood, 19 July 1843; James House,
bm; J. M. Wiggins, wit.

Currin, Willie & Nancy Hester, 21 Feb 1806; Joel Boothe, bm; W.
M. Sneed, wit.

Currin, Wyatt & Frances A. Blackwell, 23 July 1851; Thomas F.
Pear(?), bm.

Curry, Wiatt & Elizabeth Hester, 9 March 1824; D. E. Young, bm.

Curtice, Abram & Molly Hicks, 3 March 1865; L. B. Stone, wit;
m 5 March 1865 by R. H. Marsh, Minister of the Gospel.

Curtice, Isham & Eliza Ann Curtice, 5 Sept 1838; Denis Grenaway,
bm; S. G. Shearnon, wit.

GRANVILLE MARRIAGES 1753-1868

Curtice, Peter & Elizabeth Wells, 1 Nov 1830; John S. Jones, bm; David Laws, wit.

Curtis, Aaron & Fanny Tyler, 4. Sept 1823; Littleton Taborm, bm; Jas. M. Wiggins, wit.

Curtis, Aaron & Polly Ann Howell, 13 March 1866; m 21 March 1866 by E. F. Beachum; a regular G. M.; Terrell Curtis, bm; John C. Russell, wit.

Curtis, Abel & Rebecca Chavis, 26 Jan 1856; Jerry Anderson, bm.

Curtis, Alexander & Frances Tyler, 26 Aug 1865; A. Landis, bm; m 27 Aug 1865 by A. H. Cooke, J. P.

Curtis, Anderson & Elizabeth Tally, 28 Dec 1834.

Curtis, Chas. & Mariah Bass, 8 May 1848; Bob Valentine, bm; Jas. M. Wiggins, wit.

Curtis, Charles & Nancy Curtis, 28 Jan 1859; Lewis Evans, bm; A. Landis, wit; m 30 Jan 1859 by H. R. Harris, J. P.

Curtis, Henry & Ellen Lemay, 24 Dec 1866; Lunsford Willeford, bm; m 25 Dec 1866 by James Howell.

Curtis, John Ruffin & Susan Hailstock, 30 Nov 1866; m by W. Overbey, J. P.

Curtis, Joseph & Wealthy Wright, 8 March 1842; Moses Curtis, bm; J. M. Wiggins, wit.

Curtis, Joseph & Jane Gordun, 2 Jan 1847; James R. Duty, bm; Jabez Duty, wit.

Curtis, Joseph & Nancey Lyne, 24 July 1854; Jas. R. Duty, bm.

Curtis, Joseph & Nancy Lyne (free persons of color); m 30 Oct 1854 by James R. Duty, J. P.

Curtis, Joseph & Elizabeth Royster, m 12 May 1867 by James Howell; Tony Petteford, bm; Jas. R. Duty, wit.

Curtis, Lewis & Fanny Due, 2 Sept 1830; Moses Curtis, bm; David Laws, wit.

Curtis, Moses & Elizabeth Grinneway, 31 May 1832; Henderson Hawley, bm; David Laws, wit.

Curtis, Paul & Eliza Jane Curtis, 6 June 1864; Alexr. Curtis, bm; A. Landis, wit; m 8 June 1864 by H. W. Jones, J. P.

Curtis, Robert & Margaret Pettiford, m 12 April 1866 by L. B. Stone, J. P.

Curtis, Simeon & Margaret Tyler, 10 June 1865; Silas Curtis, bm; A. Landis, wit; m 1 Nov 1866 by B. T. Winston, J. P.

Curtis, Terrell & Elizabeth Evans, 24 Feb 1858; Lewis Evans, bm; m 24 Feb 1858 by J. C. Cooper, J. P.

Curtis, Thadeus H. & Mary Jane Tyler, 6 Dec 1862; Elijah Howell, bm; A. Landis, wit.

Curtis, Thomas & Arabella Anderson, 23 Oct 1841; James Day, bm.

GRANVILLE MARRIAGES 1753-1868

Curtis, William & Polly Ann Day, 24 Feb 1848; Jas. Curtis, bm; Jas. M. Wiggins, wit.

Curtis, William & Becky Jane McGehee, 24 Dec 1859; Wm. Day, bm; George Landis, wit.

Curtis, William & Hicksy Pettiford, 8 July 1861; A. Landis, bm; m 10 July 1861 by D. J. Paschall, J. P.

Curtis, William & Frances Mitchell, 1 Jan 1864; Presley Day, bm; m 3 Jan 1864 by Geo. J. Rowland, J. P.

Cusens, Wiley & Ann Norwood, m 7 Nov 1862 by Wm. M. Bennett, J. P.

Cuts, William & Mary Ann Pittard, 8 Sept 1845; Archibald W. Clay, bm; Jas. M. Wiggins, wit.

Cutts, James & Lucinda Knott, 17 June 1843; William A. Currin, bm; Jas. M. Wiggins, wit.

Cuzort, William & Lidia Culverhouse, 23 Aug 1793; Moses Jones, bm; W. Norwood, wit.

Dalby, Deck H. & Prudence Weather, 26 Dec 1815; Allen Clay, bm; Wm. Thomasson, wit.

Dalby, Edward & Mariah F. Fleming, 8 Nov 1864; B. F. Bullock, bm; m 15 Nov 1864 by Jas. W. Dalby, J. P.

Dalby, John A. & Louisa W. Davis, 5 Feb 1839; John Flemming, bm.

Daman, David P. & _____, 1 June 1826; Jas. M. Wiggins, bm; Wm. H. Owen, wit.

Dance, Stephen M. & Sarah Smith, 27 Dec 1813; James Smith, bm; Jno. Cobbs, wit.

Daniel, Beverly & Eliza Jane Daniel, 21 Jan 1840; Thos. Mathews, bm; J. M. Wiggins, wit.

Daniel, Beverly & Sarah Gregory, freed people, 22 Sept 1866; m 29 Sept 1866 by A. C. Harris, M. G.

Daniel, Cephus & Arrene Harris, 27 Feb 1821; Wm. W. Reavis, bm; A. Sneed, wit.

Daniel, Chesley & Agness Williams, 2 Nov 1807; Willie Williams, bm; W. M. Sneed, wit.

Daniel, Chesley & Lucy Noblen, 5 July 1826; Nimrod Tuck, bm; David J. Young, wit.

Daniel, David & Marget Linch, 13 Feb 1781; John Allin, bm; Samuel Searcy, wit.

Daniel, David, of color, son of William & Lucy Palmer, & Charlotte Thorp, daughter of James & Peggy Thorp, m 16 May 1868 by W. H. Puryear, J. P.

Daniel, Elijah & Lucy Cavendish, 1 Dec 1829; D. E. Young, bm.

Daniel, George & Martha Daniel, 13 March 1786; John Daniel, bm; Thomas Ligon, wit.

Daniel, George S. & Mildred Land, 1 Feb 1866; James A. Blackwell, bm; m 7 Feb 1866 by Wm. H. Puryear, J. P.

Daniel, George W. & Caroline Blackwell, 15 Dec 1846; Anderson Boyd, bm; J. M. Wiggins, wit.

Daniel, Henry & Jane Hester, 29 Dec 1865.

Daniel, Henry M. & Sarah L. Blount, 16 Oct 1827; Isaac N. Jones, bm; Wm. H. Owen, wit.

Daniel, James & Salley Cooke, 30 Nov 1772; Wm. Cooke, bm; William Rardon, wit.

Daniel, James & Nancy Macklin, 12 Sept 1809; Samuel Hogg, bm.

Daniel, James & Asjain(?) Wiggins, 4 May 1835; Jno. Wiggins, bm; Benja. Kittrell, wit.

Daniel, James & Sarah Turner, 23 Feb 1867; Beverly Edwards, bm; W. M. Sneed Jr., wit; (freed people), m 23 Feb 1867 by E. Hines.

Daniel, James B. & Jane E. Read, 10 Dec 1832; Danl. A. Penick, bm.

Daniel, James T. & Mima Puryear, 3 July 1858; Z. Daniel, bm; A. Landis, wit.

Daniel, Jesse & Elija Somerhill, 18 Nov 1833; Peyton West, bm; S. Harris, wit.

Daniel, Jessee & Raney Boswell, 22 March 1855; Asa Vaughn, bm; L. B. Stone, J. P., wit.

Daniel, John & Elisabeth Jordan, 1 May 1786; Joseph Daniel, bm; Bennet Searcy, wit.

Daniel, John & Elizabeth Jenkins, 22 Sept 1791; Elias Jinkins, bm; W. Norwood, wit.

Daniel, John & Latha Haven(?), 11 Dec 1815; Bannister Parish, bm; Step. Sneed, wit.

Daniel, Jordan, of color, parents unknown, & Mary Jane Gillis, daughter of Mary Gillis, 9 Dec 1867; m 9 Dec 1867 by J. M. Satterwhite, J. P.

Daniel, Josiah & Martha Jane Royster, 7 Nov 1842; Thomas S. Beasley, wit; J. M. Wiggins, wit.

Daniel, Leonard & Anne Graves, 21 Dec 1789; Joseph Smith, bm; Henry Potter, wit.

Daniel, Lewis & Martha D. Lanier, 21 Jan 1812; Benjamin H. Wortham, bm; W. M. Sneed, wit.

Daniel, Lewis C. & Mary F. Adcock, 21 Jan 1867; R. S. Philpott, bm; m 24 Jan 1867 by W. Overbey, J. P.

Daniel, Martin & Elisabeth Briggs, 22 Dec 1801; George Boyd, bm; Step. Sneed, wit.

Daniel, Maurice S. & Emily Watkins, 17 Dec 1853; Stephen H. Beasley, bm; m 22 Dec 1853 by Lewis Amis, J. P.

GRANVILLE MARRIAGES 1753-1868

Daniel, Mitchell & Sarah C. Lemay, 12 April 1826; John H. Ragsdale, bm; Wm. H. Owen, wit.

Daniel, Reuben & Elisabeth Harrisson, 12 Dec 1786; Isham Harrison, bm; William Skelton, wit.

Daniel, Ruben, colored, son of Joseph & Daphney Daniel, & Susan Daniel, daughter of Armstead & Tamer Daniel, m 2 Jan 1869 by E. Hines, M. G.

Daniel, Richard A. & Louisa Land, 21 Dec 1852; Mauris S. Daniel, bm; A. Landis, wit.

Daniel, Richard V. & Mary G. Venable, 9 Jan 1847; Archd. Taylor, bm; Benj. C. Cooke, wit.

Daniel, Robert M. & Ellen Daniel, 22 Dec 1855; Jos. L. Shuno, bm; A. Landis, wit; m 26 Dec 1855 by J. M. Satterwhite, J. P.

Daniel, Rufus & Susan J. Overbey, 22 Dec 1847; Stephen Chandler, bm; J. M. Wiggins, wit.

Daniel, Samuel & Lucy A. Wilkerson, 2 June 1852; A. J. Wilkinson, bm; L. B. Stone, J. P., wit; m 2 June 1852 by L. B. Stone, J. P.

Daniel, Stith G. & Sarah F. Wilkerson, 7 Sept 1849; Joseph A. Wilkerson, bm; L. B. Stone, J. P., wit.

Daniel, Thomas & Elisabeth Satterwhite, 29 Jan 1793; Robert Elliott, bm; W. Norwood, wit.

Daniel, Thomas & Eliza Daniel, 10 Nov 1813; William H. Gilliam, bm; Step. Sneed, wit.

Daniel, Thos. B. & Martha Jane Pucket, 15 June 1858; David Ford, bm; m 15 June 1858 by D. S. Wilkerson, J. P.

Daniel, Walter & Milley Overbey, 28 June 1809; Zachariah Glasscock, bm; H. Young, wit.

Daniel, Walter & Roda P. Pool, 13 July 1833; John F. Mealer, bm.

Daniel, Wilie & Sarah Wilkerson, 1 Jan 1811; James Tillison, bm; Wm. Farrar, wit.

Daniel, William & Martha Jones, 18 Aug 1832; William Worham, bm; Jno. P. Smith, wit.

Daniel, William H. & Martha Ann Currin, 26 April 1852; Thos. F. Pease, bm; m 27 April 1852 by J. E. Montague.

Daniel, Willis & Elizabeth Ellis, 27 Nov 1822; Gideon Crews, bm; Jas. M. Wiggins, wit.

Daniel, Woodson & Mary Mealor, 18 Dec 1832; Matthew Chandler, bm; Jno. P. Smith, wit.

Daniel, Zachariah & Martha Jane Critcher, 28 March 1860; John T. Jenkins, bm.

Daniel, Zachariah & Emily A. Calleham, 30 Jan 1866; Jose Noblin, bm; m 1 Feb 1866 by R. J. Devin.

GRANVILLE MARRIAGES 1753-1868

Daniel, Zadok & Elizabeth Lewis, 24 July 1792; Step. Sneed, bm; W. Norwood, wit.

Darnel, John & Mary Brack, 30 Aug 1786; George Worp, bm; John Searcy Jr.; wit.

Davey, William & Peggy Jones, 14 Feb 1783; Benjamin Hawkins, bm; Bennet Searcy, wit.

Davidson, William & Rhoda T. Ragsdale, 9 Oct 1815; Thos. D. Ridley, bm.

Davie, Robert & Rebecca Cozort, 29 Jan 1824; McVay Chandler, bm; Step. K. Sneed, wit.

Davis, Absalom & Nancy Ramey, 22 Feb 1797; Thomas H. Phillips, bm; Samuel Phillips, wit.

Davis, Albert & Caroline Howard, m 17 Oct 1866 by M. H. Vaughan, Rector of St. Stephen's Church; Moses Owen, bm.

Davis, Alexander C. & Joanah Clark, 19 Oct 1866; m 21 Oct 1866 by R. B. Hester; Richd. S. Wood, bm.

Davis, Alfred & Frances Landis, 25 Dec 1837; Daniel Fowler, bm.

Davis, Allen & Louisa H. Loyd, 15 Dec 1828; Joseph Loyd, bm; David Laws, wit.

Davis, Archd. & Rebecca Higgs, 11 May 1836; James H. Davis, bm; J. M. Wiggins, wit.

Davis, Archibald & Mary E. J. Harris, 8 Dec 1846; John Powell, bm; J. M. Wiggins, wit.

Davis, Archibald & Lucy Debman, 29 Nov 1852; Eugene Grissom, bm.

Davis, Augustin & Mary Jeetor, 2 Sept 177_; Saml. Jeter, bm; Reuben Searcy, wit.

Davis, Baxter Jr. & Mary Webb, 28 Sept 1801; Alexander Smith, bm; H. Satterwhite, wit.

Davis, Benjamin & Barbara Bobbit, 24 Aug 1818; Chesley Davis, bm; Step. K. Sneed, wit.

Davis, Chesley & Charity Hopkins, 3 Feb 1818; William Thomasson, bm; A. Tomlinson, wit.

Davis, Cyrus & Sally Guy, 28 Dec 1805; Leonard Branson, bm; Jun. Sneed, wit.

Davis, Cyrus & Mahala Fowler, 16 Feb 1835; R. Bullock, bm.

Davis, Cyrus Junr. & Salley Byars, 11 Sept 1813; Edward Chappel, bm; W. M. Sneed, wit.

Davis, Dewit & Helen F. Forsythe, 13 June 1866; Thomas C. Oakley, bm; T. J. Tilley, J. P., wit; m 13 June 1866 by D. Tilley, J. P.

Davis, Duncan & Elizabeth Fletcher, 4 Sept 1832; J. Davis, bm; David Laws, wit.

GRANVILLE MARRIAGES 1753-1868

Davis, Eaton & Candis Bailey, 12 Jan 1839; William T. Laurence(?), bm; Jas. M. Wiggins, wit.

Davis, Frank & Lynda Davis, 5 Sept 1865; Jas. Davis, bm; A. Landis, wit; m 28 Oct 1865 by Wm. M. Blackwell, J. P.

Davis, George R. & Leah E. Floyd, 26 Jan 1867; Thos. G. Cheatham, bm.

Davis, Gideon & Babby Fleming, 28 Nov 1818; Major Pollard, bm; Step. K. Sneed, wit.

Davis, Gideon & Mary Ferebough, 3 Nov 1835; Ezekiel Wheeler, bm; Benja. Kittrell, wit.

Davis, Hugh & Nancy Jenkins, 21 June 1811; John Thompson, bm; Step. Sneed, wit.

Davis, Humphrey & Elisabeth Comer, 23 Feb 1775; John Searcy, bm; Wm. Reardon, wit; consent from Samuel Pittard, 23 Feb 1775.

Davis, Isaac H. & Ann A. Downey, 29 Sept 1853; R. W. Lassiter, bm; m 1 Oct 1853 by G. W. Ferrill.

Davis, Isham & Ann Eliza Mason, freed people, 9 May 1866; m 12 May 1866 by Lewis H. Kittle, J. P.

Davis, Jackson & Elizabeth Landis, 9 March 1837; Daniel Fowler, bm.

Davis, James & Mary Jordan, 31 Dec 1803; Lesly Gilliam, bm; Js. Sneed, wit.

Davis, James & Lucy Chavis, 8 April 1830; Willie Chavis, bm; Step. K. Sneed, wit.

Davis, James & Mary Ann Curtis, 1 Dec 1857; A. Landis, bm; H. Hester, wit; m 3 Dec 1857 by T. Hester, J. P.

Davis, James H. & Francis May, 16 May 1835; Anthony W. Cole, bm.

Davis, James M., son of Dolphin & Frances Davis, & Jackobina L. Bailey, daughter of Davis D. & Jackobina Bailey, 8 April 1868; m 9 April 1868 by J. W. Wellons.

Davis James Robin & Virginia V. Debnam, m 15 Oct 1863 by H. H. Prout.

Davis, James W. & Mary A. Duty, 3 Dec 1846; Geo. Wortham, bm; J. M. Wiggins, wit.

Davis, Jessee & Mary Knott, 3 Jan 1792; Willis Roberts, bm; W. Norwood, wit.

Davis, John & Sally Jenkins, 19 May 1808; John Norwood, bm; A. H. Sneed, wit.

Davis, John & Liddy Lyon, 28 Dec 1812; Zachariah Lyon, bm; Thos. J. Hicks, wit.

Davis, John & Tildathe Bayley, 17 Nov 1822; William Bayley, bm; Wm. H. Owen, wit.

Davis, John & Frances Cousin, 20 Oct 1848; Geo. Wortham, bm; J. R. Wiggins, wit.

GRANVILLE MARRIAGES 1753-1868

Davis, John Jr. & Elizabeth Estridge, 22 Nov 1824; Israel Bailey Jr., bm; Step. K. Sneed, wit.

Davis, John R. & Lucinda Davis, 4 Jan 1859; A. S. Davis, bm; m 5 Jan 1859 by Jas. J. Moore, J. P.

Davis, Jonathan & Milly Johnston, 3 Nov 1801; Joshua Johnston, bm; Phil. Bullock, wit.

Davis, Jonathan & Polley Butler, 20 Nov 1809; Devereaux Clopton, bm; W. M. Sneed, wit.

Davis, Jonathan & Susannah Wortham, 28 Dec 1811; Thomas Taylor, bm; Step. Sneed, wit.

Davis, Jonathan & Cornelia Dillard, 23 Jan 1861; Alexander L. Davis, bm; m 24 Jan 1861 by Wm. D. Davis, J. P.

Davis, Joseph C. & Mary Eliza Perry, 2 Aug 1859; A. E. Davis, bm; m 4 Aug 1859 by B. B. Hester, M. G.

Davis, Joseph Pomfret & Frances Satterwhite, 22 Dec 1774; Henry Melton, bm; Sherwood Harris, wit.

Davis, Joshua & Nancy Sturdavant, 21 Nov 1823; William R. Hargrove, bm; Wm. H. Owen, wit.

Davis, Lewis G. & Jane Arnold, 21 Jan 1856; Joseph S. Loyd, bm; A. Landis, wit; m 25 Jan 1856 by T. B. Lyen(?), J. P.

Davis, Lewis J. & Martha T. Chesley, 17 June 1850; A. Landis, bm.

Davis, Nicholas & Amanda _____, 3 April 1819; Leslie Gilliam, bm.

Davis, Nomed & Elisabeth Daniel, 10 Sept 1818; Samuel D. Daniels, bm.

Davis, Owen & Sarah W. Smith, 23 Jan 1833; Jas. M. Wiggins, bm; David Laws, wit.

Davis, Robert & Emily F. M. Lyon, 3 July 1843; R. A. Jenkins, bm; T. B. Barnett, wit.

Davis, Sirous & Ann Semple, 27 Dec 1781; Thomas Williams, bm; Bennet Soarcy, wit.

Davis, Thomas J. & Jane Lyon, 22 Nov 1847; Y. Montague, bm; J. M. Wiggins, wit.

Davis, Venable J. & Sally Grissom, 2 Dec 1863; C. Hudson, bm; A. Landis, wit; m 5 Dec 1863 by E. F. Beachum, M. G.

Davis, William & Martha J. Hicks, 29 June 1846; William Hunter, bm; Jas. M. Wiggins, wit.

Davis, William & Margaret Short, freed people, 5 Dec 1866; m by B. T. Winston, J. P.

Davis, William D. & Caroline H. Estes, 4 Sept 1862; W. D. Allen, bm; m 4 Sept 1862 by W. D. Allen, J. P.

Davis, William H., son of Joseph P. & Mary A. Davis, & Julia H. Knott, daughter of David W. & Lundy Knott, 20 Nov 1867; m 24 Nov 1867 by J. L. Caudle(?), M. G.

GRANVILLE MARRIAGES 1753-1868

Davis, William S. & Susannah Bullock, 12 Aug 1811; John Davis, bm; Stephen Sneed, wit.

Davy, William & Nancy M. Gill, 8 July 1818; Thomas Pool, bm.

Daws, George & Lucy Raney, 8 Dec 1866; A. Landis, bm; m 8 Dec 1866 by L. K. Willie, M. G.

Daws, Richard, colored, son of Green Jones & Matilda Daws, & Louisa Parham, daughter of James Parham, 19 Dec 1868; m 19 Dec 1868 by B. Smith, J. P.

Day, Benjamin & Henrietta Mitchell, 8 Feb 1856; Allen Adkins, bm; Eugene Grissom, wit.

Day, Bolling & Martha Ford, 26 July 1820; Fleming Lumpkin, bm; W. M. Sneed, wit.

Day, David & Nancy Bass, 16 Jan 1862; Moses Chavis, bm; m 16 Jan 1862 by Peterson Thorp, J. P.

Day, Doctor & Sallie Chavis, 3 Jan 1860; William Chavis, bm; m 6 Jan 1860 by Geo. J. Rowland, J. P.

Day, Goodman & Candis Roberts, free persons of color, 2 Oct 1865; m 8 Oct 1865 by Dennis Tilley, J. P.

Day, Henornon & Happy Cousins, 9 July 1823; Jesse Day, bm; Jas. M. Wiggins Jr., wit.

Day, Isaac Newton & Mary T. Blalock, 4 April 1861; Jn. G. Jones, bm; m 4 April 1861 by E. F. Beachum.

Day, James & Sarah L. McGhee, 15 March 1824; Stephen Petteford, bm; Wm. H. Owen, wit.

Day, Jesse & Prissey Bass, 6 Nov 1782; Solo. Walker, bm; Thornton Yancey, wit.

Day, Jno. & Lottie Anderson, 28 Dec 1848; William Anderson, bm.

Day, Kindle & Nancy Brown, 22 May 1860; Wm. Mitchell, bm; A. Landis, wit.

Day, Kindle & Francis Curtis, 29 Oct 1860; Moses Chavis, bm; m 1 Nov 1860 by Peterson Thorp, J. P.

Day, Samuel W. & Adeline Adcock, 31 Aug 1855; John B. Houler, bm; A. Landis, wit; m 2 Sept 1855 by James King.

Day, Thomas & Jane Tabern, 31 May 1856; Rufus Bobbitt, bm.

Day, Vincent & Elley Louisa Huddleston, 3 Jan 1809; Reuben Day, bm; W. M. Sneed, wit.

Day, Vincent & Nancy Owen, 12 Oct 1832; George Anderson, bm; Step. K. Sneed, wit.

Day, Vincent & Elizabeth Hawley, 4 Jan 1856; John H. Chavis, bm; A. Landis, wit.

Day, William & Lucy Day, 5 Dec 1854; Saml. Day, bm; m 5 Dec 1854 by Cam. W. Allen, J. P.

GRANVILLE MARRIAGES 1753-1868

Day, William & Armenta Tabourn, people of color, 5 Nov 1865;
Rufus Tabour, bm; F. J. Tilley, J. P., wit; m 19 Nov 1865 by
Francis J. Tilley, J. P.

Day, William, colored, son of Julius Jorden & Betsey Day, &
Jemima Curtis, daughter of Henry Ragsdale & Lucinda Curtis,
m 12 Nov 1868 by James Puryear, J. P.

Day, Willis & Charlotte Allen, freed people, 20 April 1867; m
by J. L. Carroll, Minister.

Dean, Jesse & Sarah Carnel, 20 July 1806; William Carnel, bm;
W. M. Sneed, wit.

Dean, Jesse C. & Jane Soakeley(?), 26 Sept 1835; William Deas,
bm; Benja. Kittrell, wit.

Dean, Jesse Thomas & Ann Eliza Owen, 15 June 1858; Squire Willeford, bm; A. Landis, wit; m 16 June 1858 by Peterson Thorp,
J. P.

Dean, John H. & Affie L. Slaughter, 17 Feb 1862; J. C. Howard,
bm; m 18 Feb 1862 by Peterson Thorp, J. P.

Dean, Lorenzo Dow, son of Wm. & Sarah Dean, & Nancy Evans, daughter of Coleman & Babby Evans, 21 Nov 1867; m 2 Jan 1868 by
B. T. _____, J. P.

Dean, Moses C. & Lucinda R. Sherman, 23 Oct 1835; Wm. Terry, bm;
Benja. Kittrell, wit.

Dean, Rowland C. & Eady E. Brinkley, 17 July 1860; A. D. Freezar,
bm; m 19 July 1860 by A. H. Cooke, J. P.

Dean, William W. & Candis Landis, 15 Dec 1846; ____ Terry, bm;
J. M. Wiggins, wit.

Debnam, Thos. C. & Elisabeth A. Davis, 27 Jan 1857; Saml. J.
Parham, bm; m 28 Jan 1857 by A. C. Harris, M. G.

Debram, John B. & Mary A. Raney, 8 Oct 1855; William J. Cobb,
bm; m 8 Oct 1855 by Wm. Holmes.

Debrans, John B. & Damsel V. Coghill, 17 July 1826; William P.
Forrest, bm; Wm. H. Owen, wit.

Debuler, Micajah & Mary Hicks, 11 Oct 178_; John Tatum, bm;
Asa Searcy, wit.

Deckker, Henry & Patsey Talley, 6 Jan 1792; John Whobery, bm; W.
Norwood, wit.

Deen, Daniel & Elizabeth Carnel, 9 Nov 1807; William Carnel,
bm; W. M. Sneed, John H. Farmer, wit.

Deer, Isaac & Polley Wilkins, 14 Oct 1823; Jacob Robinson, bm;
Jas. M. Wiggins, wit.

Delenback, Christian & Cargelia Mason, 2 Oct 1865; W. H. H.
Moore, bm; m 18 Feb 1866 by W. D. Allen, J. P.

Dement, Asbury & Susan Hester, 22 Dec 1836; Henderson Dement,
bm; J. M. Wiggins, wit.

GRANVILLE MARRIAGES 1753-1868

Dement, Henderson & Mary Ann Hedspeth, 3 Jan 1832; Wesley Brummit, bm; David Laws, wit.

Dement, James D. & Priscilla Woodliff, 27 Jan 1847; William T. Grisham, bm.

Dement, Matthew & Lottey Cawthor, 15 Nov 1816; John Brummit, bm; W. M. Sneed, wit.

Dement, Peter G. & Susan G. Floyd, 5 Nov 1839; Wilson W. Dement, bm.

Dement, Robert & Priscilla Harden, 6 July 1816; Garland Allen, bm; W. M. Sneed, wit.

Dement, Stephen E. & Ann Maria Floyd, 12 Dec 1837; D. A. Paschall, bm; J. M. Wiggins, wit.

Dement, Thomas & Lucey Hays, 7 Jan 1807; John Brummet, bm; W. M. Sneed, wit.

Dement, Thomas J. & Harriet Pitchford, 11 May 1842; John Brummett, bm.

Dement, William & Lucy Blackley, 19 March 1811; John Boummitt, bm; W. M. Sneed, wit.

Dement, William & Josephine Russell, m 7 Jan 1867 by B. D. Howard, J. P.

Dement, Willis & Dilly Longmire, 1 Jan 1855; Alexander Sutton, bm; Thos. W. McClanahan, wit; m 4 Jan 1855 by J. W. Floyd, Minister.

Dennis, John & Patsey Maddocks, 26 Aug 1799; Jesse Snipes, bm; Ro. Harris, wit.

Dennis, John & Sarah Hobgood, 13 May 1807; Hezekiah Hobgood, bm; W. M. Sneed, wit.

Denny, Henry A. & Mary J. Edwards, 7 Oct 1848; Alfred Williams, bm.

Denson, Evans & Harriet Jones, 15 May 1839; Benjamin Mitchell, bm.

Denton, Benjamin & Sealah Wiggins, 18 Nov 1772; Miles Williams, bm; Reuben Searcy, wit.

Denton, John & Sarah Starks, 24 Feb 1797; Howel Morse, bm; Sterling Yancey, wit.

Denton, Reubin & Eliner Harrison, 14 Jan 1804; John Denton, bm; A. H. Sneed, wit.

Denton, Samuel & Elisabeth Mitchell, 3 May 1798; Howel Morse, bm; Step. Sneed, wit.

Derham, Isaaih & Polly George, 27 March 1821; Thomas Chotman, bm.

Desarn, Nathaniel & Ellendar Cozort, 15 April 1786; Henry Tudar, bm; John Searcy, wit.

Deshazo, William & Nancey Parish, 16 March 1779; William Parish, bm; M. Bullock, wit.

GRANVILLE MARRIAGES 1753-1868

Deson, Frederick & Nancy Hanes, 21 Jan 1808; Aaron Pinson, bm; A. H. Sneed, wit.

Devin, Robert J. & Cynthia R. Herndon, 26 Jan 1848; Asa C. Parham, bm; Jas. M. Wiggins, wit.

Dew, Franklin & Frances Evans, 29 Jan 1856; John Harris, bm; Jas. R. Duty, wit; m 31 Jan 1856 by Jas. R. Duty, J. P.

Dew, Wallace & Lucey Anderson, 2 June 1811; Abel Anderson, bm; W. M. Sneed, wit.

Dewberry, Thomas R. & Susanner Pool, 9 Jan 1833; Irby G. Bunten, bm; Willie Royster, J. P., wit.

Diall, James & Susannah Little, 1 March 1804; Burrel Kemp, bm; Danl. Bridges, wit.

Dicken, Uriah & Susanna May, 19 Jan 1826; Thos. May, bm; Wm. H. Owen, wit.

Dickens, William & Nancy W. Pulliam, 17 May 1810; Thomas Webb, bm; W. M. Sneed, wit.

Dickerson, Duke & Elizabeth Mitchell, 15 March 1832; Patrick Ross bm; David Laws, wit.

Dickerson, Edward V. & Louisa J. Fuller, 2 Feb 1864; James P. Kess, bm.

Dickerson, Edward W. & Louisa P. Fuller, 2 Feb 1864.

Dickerson, Edwin & Ardelia Aregon Overton, 13 Feb 1867; W. D. Pleasants, bm.

Dickerson, Epaphroditus & Chastool Moore, 5 May 1789; William Dickerson, bm.

Dickerson, Epaphroditus & Dicey Moore, 7 May 1811; Wm. Dickerson, bm; Junius Sneed, wit.

Dickerson, Isham & Elizabeth Shadwick, 5 Jan 1837; Moses Tanner, bm; J. M. Wiggins, wit.

Dickerson, James & Polly Dickerson, 14 Nov 1833; Duke Dickerson, bm; Benja. Kittrell, wit.

Dickerson, James & Dansel Ball, 12 Feb 1844; John Crowder, bm; Wm. H. Whitfield, wit.

Dickerson, James & Mary Ann Wrenn, 3 Dec 1850; Thos. Dickerson, bm; A. Landis, wit.

Dickerson, Jas. & Sally Roberson, m 20 April 1866 by J. F. Harris J. P.

Dickerson, Joel & Agley(?) Grissam, 1 Jan 1824; Willie Grissam, bm; Wm. H. Owen, wit.

Dickerson, John & Rebecca W. Qualls, 28 July 1849; James Ross, bm; J. M. Wiggins, wit.

Dickerson, John Jr. & Sarah C. Hayes, 22 July 1838; Samuel L. Hayes, bm; Jas. M. Wiggins, wit.

GRANVILLE MARRIAGES 1753-1868

Dickerson, Leonidas & Mary E. Harris, 15 Dec 1855; James Mitchel, bm; A. Landis, wit; m 17 Dec 1855 by D. P. Paschall, J. P.

Dickerson, Martin & Catey Pendergrass, 25 May 1778; Richd. Nants, bm; Ralph Banks, wit.

Dickerson, Mastin & Sally Ball, 22 Nov 1857; Reuben Clark, bm; A. Landis, wit.

Dickerson, Ransom & Rody Stanton, 18 Sept 1800; Wm. Garrott, bm; Wm. Walker, wit.

Dickerson, Ransom & Rowan Qualls, 5 Jan 1841; Patrick Ross, bm; J. M. Wiggins, wit.

Dickerson, Samuel W. & Jane Dement, 22 Dec 1835; Hartwell Overton, bm; Benja. Kittrell, wit.

Dickerson, Samuel W. & Sarah J. Tippett, 13 April 1867; m 15 April 1867 by E. F. Beachum, R. G. Minister.

Dickerson, Whitmell & Catharine Fowler, 22 Nov 1857; John C. Hester, bm; m 22 Nov 1857 by J. Y. McGehee, J. P.

Dickerson, William & Rhody Patience, 3 Oct 1810; William Harris, bm; W. M. Sneed, wit.

Dickerson, William & Milley Inschere, 19 Dec 1810; Jonathan Inschore, bm; W. M. Sneed, wit.

Dickerson, Wylie & Molley Simmons, 19 Dec 1794; Ben. Coop, bm; Step. Sneed, wit.

Dickins, Robert & Martha Y. Webb, 26 Nov 1821; Isaac Webb, bm; Richd. B. Thompson, wit.

Dickins, Samuel & Fanny Henderson Burton, 1 Aug 1831; James Ridley, bm; David Laws, wit.

Dickinson, Zachariah & Jane Finch, 3 Nov 1837.

Dickson, Edmund & Permelia C. Puryear, 22 Aug 1850; Daniel T. Gillis, bm; L. B. Stone, J. P., wit.

Dickson, John & Roan Adcock, 24 Dec 1838; Edward D. Callaham, bm; M. D. Royste, wit.

Dickson, Joseph & Phebey Linsey, 17 Dec 1795; Benjamin Denton, bm; Step. Sneed, wit.

Dickson, Samuel & Mary A. E. Dunkin, 20 Jan 1834; Alfred Dunkin, bm; Benja. Kittrell, wit.

Dillard, Hillsman & Candis Bailey, 20 Aug 1838; Gilcrease Bailey, bm; S. G. Shearman, wit.

Dillard, Israel F. & Mahala Bailey, 4 Feb 1833; J. Davis, bm; David Laws, wit.

Dillard, William & Clay Bailey, 14 Sept 1810; Israel Bailey, bm; W. M. Sneed, wit.

Diment, John & Salley Brummett, 24 Dec 1804; John Brummett, bm; E. W. Parham, wit.

GRANVILLE MARRIAGES 1753-1868

Dinny, Benjamin & Keronhappuck Taylor, 19 Dec 1798; John Taylor, bm; Geo. Brasfield, wit.

Dispain, Benjamin & Delilah Winningham, 18 Oct 1780; Nathan Harris, bm; Richard Searcy, wit.

Dixon, George W. & Frances Duncan, 5 April 1833; John B. Slaughter, bm; Step. K. Sneed, wit.

Dixon, Marion & Nancy Duncan, 1 Dec 1854; Alfred Gorden, bm; A. Landis, wit; m 1 Dec 1854 by Peterson Thorp, J. P.

Dixon, Nelson & Emily C. L. Oakly, 23 Oct 1847; R. C. Dean, bm; J. M. Wiggins, wit.

Dixon, Young P. & Catharine Cozort, 29 June 1854; Edwd. W. Garrett, bm; A. Landis, wit; m 2 July 1854 by Allen Cozort, J. P.

Doake, Daniel G. & Mary Patillo, 7 Sept 1837; Hugh McCadden, bm.

Docrey, George & Pattey Emery, 9 Aug 1797; Robert Docry, bm; Step. Sneed, wit.

Docrey, Robert & Polley Emery, 9 Aug 1797; John Emery, bm; Step. Sneed, wit.

Dodson, Charles & Lucy Dodson, 15 Aug 1801; Wm. Hargrove, bm; Archibald Sneed, wit.

Downey, James & Elizabeth Butler, 7 Dec 1808; Solomon Hunt, bm; W. M. Sneed, wit.

Dodson, Martin & Catherine Edwards, 23 Oct 1809; Major Wall, bm; W. M. Sneed, wit.

Dodson, Rubin, of color, son of Brister & Susan Dodson, & Eliza Amis, of color, daughter of unknown, 26 Dec 1867; m 29 Dec 1867 by B. T. Winston, J. P.

Dodson, Stephen & Polly Smith, 8 Nov 1803; William Dodson, bm; A. H. Sneed, wit.

Dodson, William & Frances Gillam, 26 June 1763; John Gillam, Francis Gillam, bm; Peter Gillam, Edward Roberson, wit.

Dodson, William & Francis Gillam, 28 June 1763; Charles Gillam, bm.

Dodson, William & Sally Cunningame, 20 Nov 1806; Thomas Williams, bm; Jas. Sneed, wit.

Dolby, Richard & Fanny Mitchell, 12 Nov 1807; Macajah B. Dolby, bm; W. M. Sneed, John H. Farrar, wit.

Donohoe, Edwd. & Parthenia Dickens, 6 April 1811; William Dickins, bm; W. M. Sneed, wit.

Dorman, Jesse & Polley Loyd, 15 Aug 1810; Willie Loyd, bm; Step. Sneed, wit.

Dorsey, Edward Rutland & Edna Bailey Denson, 14 June 1862; Robert B. Peebles, bm; m 17 June 1862 by Jos. Jas. Ridley, D. D.

GRANVILLE MARRIAGES 1753-1868

Dortch, Noah & Elisabeth Eaton, 27 July 1801; Hutchins Burton, bm; Step. Sneed, wit.

Doub, William C. & Susan Duty, 29 Nov 1864; John W. Hays, bm; m 30 Nov 1864 by L. M. Jones.

Douglas, Joseph & Dorcas Eastland, 7 Aug 1787; Leavis Ashman, bm.

Dowdy, John A. & Mary Booker, 15 Aug 1829; Samuel A. Tally, bm.

Dowling, John & Norsisa G. Satterwhite, 18 Dec 1865; A. A. Walker, bm; Jas. R. Duty, wit.

Downey, Dudley & Nancy Wood, m 23 Sept 1866 by James E. Pattillo, J. P.

Downey, James & Elizabeth Smith, 23 Aug 1791; Jas. W. Smith, bm; Will. H. Haywood, wit.

Downey, James Jr. & Jane Mitchell, 4 Sept 1806; Thomas Potter, bm; W. M. Sneed, wit.

Downey, Jim & Catharine Venable, freed people, 7 Jan 1867; m 4 March 1867 by B. T. Winston, J. P.

Downey, John & Margaret Wade, 6 Dec 1784; Arthur Frazer, bm; Bennet Searcy, wit.

Downey, John & Mary Gooch, 11 Sept 1813; Ishman Vincent, bm; W. M. Sneed, wit.

Downey, Matthew H. & Priscilla Holcomb, 27 Dec 1820; Zachr. Herndon, bm; Jas. M. Wiggins, wit.

Downey, Samuel Smith & Jane Harrison, 1 Oct 1812; John P. Smith, bm; W. M. Sneed, wit.

Downey, Sandy, of color, son of Reuben and July Overby, & Betty Butler, daughter of Solomon & Nancy Butler, 21 Dec 1867; m 21 Dec 1867 by E. L. Parrish, J. P.

Downey, Wm. J., son of Thomas & Mary Downey, & Frances P. Knott, daughter of John & Polly Knott, 22 Nov 1867; m 23 Nov 1867 by B. T. Winston, J. P.

Downey, Zebulon M. P. & Susan R. Royster, 3 Oct 1863; Robt. Elliott, bm; A. Landis, wit; m 4 Oct 1863 by Thomas U. Faucette.

Downing, Saml. S. & Sally P. Smith, 17 June 1829; Step. K. Sneed, wit.

Doyle, Adam & Mary Norwood, 10 Aug 1801; John Dunn, bm; Step. Sneed, wit.

Drake, Merritt & Elizabeth Grisham, 8 Aug 1839; P. D. Reavis, bm.

Drake, William C. & Olivia D. Fitts, 23 Jan 1863; m 29 Jan 1863 by Jas. A. Duncan, Minister of the M. E. Church, South; A. Landis, bm.

Drake, Wm. J. & Joanna Blackwell, 8 Oct 1856; B. F. Hancock, bm; m 15 Oct 1856 by Gaston Farrar.

GRANVILLE MARRIAGES 1753-1868

Draughan, William & Eunice Latham, daughter of Lyman & Francis Latham, 10 Nov 1868; m 11 Nov 1868 by Maurice H. Vaughan, Rector of St. Stephen's Church.

Drewry, Ellis & Amey Rose, 6 Aug 1771; Geo. Alston, bm; Jesse Benton, wit.

Driver, Bird & Elizabeth Levister, 17 Sept 1781; John Carrel, bm; Bennet Searcy, wit.

Due, John & Nancy Loyd, 3 Aug 1824; Reddin Haswell, bm; Wm. H. Owen, wit.

Due, John T. & Tison Ann Bailey, 2 Nov 1852; George W. Lynam, bm.

Due, Jorden & Betsy Ann Pettiford, 21 Aug 1849; Cuffee Mayho, bm; A. Landis, wit.

Due, Thomas & Penny Haswell, 27 July 1829; William Y. Bailey, bm; David Laws, wit.

Due, Thomas & Elizabeth Williams, 14 May 1832; Anderson Bailey, bm; David Laws, wit.

Duff, Robert & Caroline Walker, 29 April 1830; Hugh Duff, bm; Robert K. Clack, wit.

Duffey, Patrick & Salley Brightwell, 2 Aug 1779; Runnold Brightwell, bm; Reuben Searcy, wit.

Duggen, Thomas C. & Matilda Waldon, 2 Oct 1837; James Royster, bm.

Duke, Bennet & Lucey Johnson, 15 Sept 1803; Claborn Cook, bm; Shem. Cook, wit.

Duke, Britain & Sarah Dickerson, 29 April 1811; James Smith, bm; W. M. Sneed, wit.

Duke, Clevious & Rebecca Dickerson, 20 Nov 1818; Jonathan Inscore, bm; W. M. Sneed, wit.

Duke, Dabney & Abbey Howze, 15 April 1816; Merrit Champain, bm; Leslie Gilliam, wit.

Duke, Daniel B. & Victoria E. Cargill, 1 Jan 1866.

Duke, Gilford & Frances Vaughan, 29 March 1809; Hardy Harris, bm; Step. Sneed, Clk., wit.

Duke, Haldelony & Mahala Wagoner, 10 Oct 1848; Henry W. Gates, bm; J. M. Wiggins, wit.

Duke, Hardimon & Mary Wallace, 11 March 1784; Thomas King, bm; Sam Walker, wit.

Duke, Harell & Susannah Dickerson, 23 Sept 1818; Eppy Dickerson, bm; W. M. Sneed, wit.

Duke, James B. & Lucy M. Hight, 13 Dec 1866; T. A. Stewart, bm; m 18 Dec 1866 by Lafayette W. Martin, M. G.

Duke, John W. & Arabelah Brume, 1 Feb 1852; James R. Duty, bm.

GRANVILLE MARRIAGES 1753-1868

Duke, Nelson N. & Ann Hunt, 9 May 1809; John Landis, bm; W. M. Sneed, wit.

Duke, Noah & Ann Duke, 23 Dec 1859; A. F. Wood, bm; m by Peterson Thorp, J. P.

Duke, Peyton V. & Milly B. Paschall, 11 Feb 1835; Thomas Duke, bm.

Duke, Peyton V. & Lucy R. Turner, 4 Jan 1848; D. J. Paschall, bm.

Duke, Thomas & Lucy Paschall, 27 April 1833; John S. Murray, bm; David Laws, wit.

Duke, William & Patsey Vaughan, 16 May 1803; Thomas Coghill, bm; Step. Sneed, wit.

Duke, Young & Elizabeth Weaver, 9 Jan 1830; Woodrow Knight, bm; David Laws, wit.

Duke, Young & Nancy Mangum, 9 Dec 1835; Green A. Mangum, bm; Benja. Kittrell, wit.

Duncan, Abraham S. & Adeline Stroud, 16 Oct 1853; A. Gorden, bm; A. Landis, wit.

Duncan, Alfred & Franky Slaughter, 19 Aug 1820; Anderson Duncan (Dunkin), bm; Step. K. Sneed, wit.

Duncan, Anderson & Elizabeth Slaughter, 18 Dec 1814; Elijah Carnal, bm.

Duncan, Charles & Henney W. Wilkerson, 17 June 1820; Isaac Duncan, bm; Step. K. Sneed, wit.

Duncan, Charles H. & Ailey G. OBriant, 4 Nov 1851; Howel Duncan, bm.

Duncan, Charles H. & Joanah Dixon, 15 Feb 1866; S. D. Duncan, bm; A. Landis, wit; m 16 Feb 1866 by W. H. Puryear, J. P.

Duncan, David & Joannah Duncan, 29 May 1850; Charles K. Duncan, bm.

Duncan, George W. & Margaret Meadows, 16 Dec 1846; W. P. B. Slaughter, bm; J. M. Wiggins, wit.

Duncan, Giles R. & Rebecca Duncan, 24 Jan 1854; Robt. L. Bumpass Jr., bm; m 25 Jan 1854 by Peterson Thorp, J. P.

Duncan, Isaac & Affey Hester, 19 June 1821; Paschall Hudson, bm; S. K. Sneed, wit.

Duncan, Isaac & Louisa E. A. Carnal, 3 Feb 1862; James H. Duncan, bm; m 4 Feb 1862 by Peterson Thorp, J. P.

Duncan, James R. & Rebecca J. Duncan, 30 Sept 1857; Howell Duncan, bm; m 6 Oct 1857 by Peterson Thorp, J. P.

Duncan, John & Frances Robertson, 3 Oct 1792; Field Rudd, bm; W. Norwood, wit.

Duncan, John & Chloe Moore, 2 Nov 1793; Zachariah Shamwell, bm; W. Norwood, wit.

GRANVILLE MARRIAGES 1753-1868

Duncan, John & Susey Clardy, 23 Jan 1798; William Collins, bm; Step. Sneed, wit.

Duncan, John & Elizabeth Duncan, 24 Feb 1806; William Fowler, bm; Jun. Sneed, wit.

Duncan, John & Elizabeth Hayes, 12 May 1810; James Hayes, bm; W. M. Sneed, wit.

Duncan, John & Lethe Briggs, 28 Dec 1839; Henry Briggs, bm; J. M. Wiggins, wit.

Duncan, John Junr. & Elisabeth Peyton, 3 Dec 1782; John Bristow, bm; Asa Searcy, wit.

Duncan, John B. & Susan Slaughter, 5 March 1830; James T. Terry, bm; David Laws, wit.

Duncan, John H. & Luetta Clark, 19 Oct 1866; J. N. Dunn(?), bm; m __ Oct 1866 by T. J. Homer, G. M.

Duncan, Seamore & Priscilla Hicks, 26 Nov 1792; John Morris, bm; W. Norwood, wit.

Duncan, Simeon & Sarah Jones, 21 Feb 1860; David Duncan, bm; m 22 Feb 1860 by Peterson Thorp, J. P.

Duncan, Simeon & Sally F. Carnell, 10 April 1866; m 11 April 1866 by Benj. D. Howard, J. P.

Duncan, Standford H. & Frances Myze, 26 Feb 1850; John B. Duncan, bm.

Duncan, Sterling H. & Mary Slaughter, 9 March 1854; Abram Evans, bm; m 13 March 1854 by Peterson Thorp, J. P.

Duncan, Thomas & Elizabeth Malone, 12 April 1860; Major A. Nelson, bm; m 12 April 1860 by L. B. Stone, J. P.

Duncan, Zachariah H. & Charity Caroline Frazier, 18 Oct 1856; James M. Beasly, bm; m 21 Oct 1856 by Peterson Thorp, J. P.

Dunevant, Walter & Jane Glasscock, 10 June 1815; Zacheriah Glasscock Jr., bm; H. Young, wit.

Duncvin, Werter & Martha T. Daniel, 13 July 1833; Bartlet Elliott, bm; Willie Royster, J. P., wit.

Dunham, David M. & Louisa Owen, 20 Jan 1858; Wm. K. Brosius, bm.

Dunken, George & Miss Polly Slaughter, request for license 14 May 1781; consent from Mary Slaughter, "her parents having given their consent" 14 May 1781.

Dunlop, Donald M., son of James & Isabella L. Dunlop, & Mildred C. Lewis, daughter of Dr. Willis & Rosa A. Lewis, 2 April 1868; m 2 April 1868 by H. G. Hill, Minister.

Dunn, Henry & Frances Fuller, 18 Feb 1854; John F. Cannady, bm; m 30 March 1854 by W. D. Allen, J. P.

Dunn, Junious H., son of William & Sarah Dunn, & Laura A. Southerland, 25 Nov 1868; m 9 Dec 1868 by W. T. Brooks, Min.

Dunn, Thomas & Nancy Harkney, 16 March 1813; __ Young, bm.

GRANVILLE MARRIAGES 1753-1868

Dunn, William & Sarah Duncan, 20 Dec 1831; Alfred Duncan, bm; David Laws, wit.

Dunstan, Henderson & Martha Ann Mitchell, 23 Dec 1865; m by S. P. J. Currin(?), M. G.

Dunston, Henry, of color, son of Charles & Mary Dunston, & Francis Glasgow, daughter of Harriett Glasgow, 25 Dec 1867; m 25 Dec 1867 by Wyatt Walker, M. G.

Dunston, John & Martha Ann Dunston, 15 Jan 1866; Bivens Brandum, bm; A. Landis, wit; m 16 Dec 1866 by S. P. J. Harris, M. G.

Dunston, Richard & Mary L. Mitchell, 19 Dec 1859; J. A. Pardue, bm; m 24 Dec 1859 by Wm. B. Mann, J. P.

DuPre, Warren & Mary A. Sydner, 19 March 1845; Robt. H. Read, bm.

Duren, John & Nancy Coward, 9 Aug 1768; Michl. Whatley, Stephen Gupton, bm.

Duren, John & Nancy Coward, 9 Aug 1763; Michl. Whatley, Stephen Gupton, bm; Benjamin Person, wit.

Durham, Charles, of color, son of Charles Evans & Nanney Durham, & Mary Bullock of color, daughter of Robert Collins & Rhoda Bullock, 24 Aug 1867; m 24 Aug 1867 by Jas. R. Duty, J. P.

Durham, Henry & Anne Steward, 16 Sept 1826; John Wiggins, bm; Jas. Sneed, wit.

Durham, Henry & Nancy Harris, 19 Sept 1853; James R. Duty, Nelson Brame, bm.

Durham, Isham, of color, son of Samuel Bruno & Frances Durham, & Mary Daniel, daughter of Hester Daniel, m 12 April 1868 by S. P. J. Harris, M. G.

Durham, John & Fanny Pettiford, 30 Dec 1822; William Pettiford, bm; S. K. Sneed, wit.

Durham, John & Fanny Harris (free persons of color), 22 March 1852; Wm. Green, bm; m 14 May 1852 by James R. Duty, J. P.

Durham, Stephen & Prudence Trevan(?), 28 Dec 1814; Frederick Hammond, bm; Step. Sneed, wit.

Durham, William & Sally Peel, 15 Oct 1845; Jas. Brandum, bm; Jas. M. Wiggins, wit.

Durram, James & Mary Petteford, 31 Dec 1814; Austin Petteford, bm; Step. Sneed, wit.

Dutton, John & Omey Parish, 14 Jan 1806; Zachariah Dutton, bm; W. M. Sneed, wit.

Dutton, Stephen & Sally OBrient, 23 Sept 1818; Howell Briggs, bm; W. Sneed, wit.

Dutton, Zachariah & Judith Parish, 23 Nov 1798; Leonard Henderson, bm; James Sneed, wit.

Duty, George & Eliza Thomas, 28 Sept 1798; Wm. Lanier, bm; J. Vaughan, wit.

GRANVILLE MARRIAGES 1753-1868

Duty, George L. & Eliza G. Barrett, 4 Feb 1835; Jas. M. Heggie, bm; Benja. Kittrell, wit.

Duty, Jabez & Frances Kimbrall, 20 Oct 1804; Pleasant Kimbal, bm; A. H. Sneed, wit.

Duty, James K. P., son of George L. Duty & Eliza Duty, & Martha A. Arrington, daughter of Willis Arrington & Emily Arrington; m 1 Aug 1867 by S. P. J. Harris.

Duty, Littleton & Mildred Owen, 8 Dec 1797; Sihon Smith, bm; Step. Sneed, wit.

Duty, Samuel & Fanny H. Harris, 13 Feb 1812; Abner Hicks, bm; W. M. Sneed, wit.

Dyar, William & Sarah Wheelar, 2 Jan 1787; Benjamin Wheler, bm; B. Searcy, wit.

Dyer, James H. & Frances Morgan, 26 Nov 1860; F. J. Hester, bm; m 20 Dec 1860 by Thos. Hester.

Eakes, Barnard & Leathey Tucker, 29 March 1818; Robert Kinton, bm; A. Tomlinson, wit.

Eaks, Beverly & Isabella West, 16 March 1830; Thomas S. Frazer, bm; David Laws, wit.

Eaks, Edmund & Mary Tucker, 16 Dec 1820; William Hester, bm; Step. K. Sneed, wit.

Eaks, Iverson H. & Ann Eliza Daniel, 4 Sept 1860; m 10 Sept 1860 by L. B. Stone, J. P.

Eaks, James & Mary A. West, 23 Dec 1835; Hardemon West, bm; Benja. Kittrell, wit.

Eaks, John S., son of Zachariah & Jane Eaks, & Alley G. Moore, parents not known, 14 Dec 1867; m 19 Dec 1867 by R. J. Devin.

Eaks, Madison & Elizabeth Swain, 8 March 1864; m 8 March 1864 by L. B. Stone, J. P.

Eaks, Timothy & Susanna Parish, 8 Aug 1786; William Parish, bm; Reuben Searcy, wit.

Eaks, William S. & Susan Morgan, 21 Sept 1865; W. D. Clark, bm; m 24 Sept 1865 by B. T. Winston.

Eaks, William S. & Mary Jane Fraizer, 25 Sept 1866; Robt. S. Eaks, bm; m 28 Sept 1866 by B. T. Winston, J. P.

Eaks, Woodson & Jane Wilkerson, 20 Dec 1831; Willis West, bm; David Laws, wit.

Eaks, Zachariah & Salley Traylor, 8 Nov 1788; John Traylor, bm; A. Henderson, C. C., wit.

Eaks, Zachariah & Jane Tuck, 10 May 1831; Woodson Eaks, bm; David Laws, wit.

Earl, John & Fanny Allen, 28 July 1807; George Boothe, bm; A. H. Sneed, wit.

GRANVILLE MARRIAGES 1753-1868

Earles, Reuben & Nancy Glasgow, 14 May 1840; James Neal, bm; Jas. M. Wiggins, wit.

Earls, Reuben & Nancy Glasgow, 23 Aug 1840; William Tillison, bm; William T. Hayne, wit.

Easters, Daniel & Salley Smith, 6 Dec 1808; Wiatt Smith, bm; Alfred Wilkins, wit.

Easton, Henry P. & Sallie S. Herndon, 20 July 1854; Jas. Y. Hunt, bm; m 20 July 1854 by R. J. Devin, Minister of the Gospel.

Eastridge, Henry & Elisabeth Floyd, 29 July 1799; George Floyd, bm; R. Satterwhite, wit.

Eastwood, Charles L. & L. Mitchell, 28 March 1866; m by G. W. Ferrill, Minister of the Gospel.

Eastwood, Elijah H. & Martha G. Lawson, 3 June 1837; W. F. Russell, bm; J. M. Wiggins, wit.

Eastwood, Israel & Rhoda Wilkerson, 9 Oct 1819; Hardy Hayes, bm; S. K. Sneed, wit.

Eastwood, James & Nancy Morris, 23 Sept 1818; Henry W. Jones, bm; S. K. Sneed, wit.

Eastwood, John & Salley Wilkerson, 9 April 1792; James Patterson, bm; Step. Sneed, wit.

Eastwood, John & Mary Wright, 10 Dec 1834; R. N. Herndon, bm; Benja. Kittrell, wit.

Eaton, Allen P. & Eliza Williams, colored, m 26 Dec 1866 by Joseph W. Murphy, Rector of Holy Innocents, Henderson.

Eaton, Charles R. & Martha Ann Landis, 15 Oct 1862; Saml. A. Williams, bm; m 15 Oct 1862 by W. M. Wingate, M. G.

Eaton, James of Orange County, & Anne Sythe, 5 July 1773; James Foeest, of Orange County, bm.

Eaton, James & Latitia Williams, colored, m 8 July 1866 by Jos. Jas. Ridley, D. D.

Eaton, John & Martha Morrow, 19 Aug 1866.

Eaton, John R. & Susannah Somervill, 15 Sept 1801; George Brasfield, bm; Step. Sneed, wit.

Eaton, John S. & Sally T. Burwell, 6 Aug 1827; Moses Neal, bm; A. Sneed, wit.

Eaton, Richard & Sallie Winfield, colored, 26 Dec 1866; m 28 Dec 1866 by Jun. Sneed, J. P.

Eaton, William A. & Christian B. Burwell, 7 Dec 1834; Isham Cheatham, bm; Benja. Kittrell, wit.

Eavins, Burrell & Mary Michell, 22 Feb 1796; William Roberson, bm; Richard Taylor, wit.

Edwards, Charles & Peggey Smith, 15 Jan 1799; Thomas Mimms, bm; Step. Sneed, wit.

GRANVILLE MARRIAGES 1753-1868

Edwards, Charles & Lucy Wright, 25 Dec 1826; Thomas S. Edwards, bm; Wm. H. Owen, wit.

Edwards, Charles B. & Delia Ann Longmire, 10 May 1866; m 10 May 1866 by Robt. L. Heflin, J. P.

Edwards, Daniel & Jaqulin Peace, 6 Nov 1838; Benjamin Thomasson, bm; S. G. Shearmon, wit.

Edwards, Devereaux & Martha Ann Watkins, 27 Aug 1853; G. C. Farrar, bm; m 17 Sept 1853 by A. C. Harris, M. G.

Edwards, Francis & Isabella Glen, 19 Dec 1866; Souless Hamilton, bm; Jas. R. Duty, wit; m 23 Dec 1866 by F. N. Whaley, Minister of the Gospel.

Edwards, Henry A. & Harriett Hester, 8 March 1850; Samuel Edwards, bm; A. Landis, wit.

Edwards, James & Prudence Norman, 10 Dec 1802; Joshua Wynne, bm; Step. Sneed, wit.

Edwards, James & Mary A. Powel, 17 March 1829; William B. Mann, bm; David Laws, wit.

Edwards, James & Rebecca McFarling, 5 Aug 1835; James Madderson, bm; Benja. Kittrell, wit.

Edwards, John & Patsey Thornton, 31 Aug 1795; George R. Edwards, bm; Step. Sneed, wit.

Edwards, John & Fanny Vaughan, 17 Feb 1821; Woodard Vaughan, bm; A. Sneed, wit.

Edwards, John Washington & Ann Hunt, 25 April 1825; Joseph T. Jinkins, bm; S. K. Sneed, wit.

Edwards, L. C. & Frances G. Cooper, 24 Feb 1852; Thos. J. Reid, bm; A. Landis, wit.

Edwards, Lee & Hannah Crews, freed people, m 25 Jan 1866 by William S. Hester, M. G.

Edwards, Leonidas R. J. & Sefroney E. J. Edwards, 18 Sept 1852; Devreaux Edwards, bm; m 23 Sept 1852 by A. C. Harris, M. G.

Edwards, Liles & Martha Vaughan, 26 Feb 1812; John Vaughan, bm.

Edwards, Lucius & Sallie A. Watkins, 4 Jan 1858; W. K. Brosius, bm; m 17 Feb 1858 by Wm. N. Bragg, Minister.

Edwards, McDonald & Arreny N. Watkins, 13 March 1857; George K. Parham, bm; m 24 March 1857 by Wm. B. Mann, J. P.

Edwards, Pomphret & Elizabeth Minor, 17 Jan 1810; James Ball, bm; W. M. Robards, wit.

Edwards, Richard & Martha Johnston, 28 Sept 1778; James Cooke, bm; James Jett, wit.

Edwards, Samuel & Nancy Purdue, 16 Dec 1810; Noel Johnston, bm; Step. Sneed, wit.

Edwards, Samuel & Ann H. Bobbitt, 18 Dec 1865; Robt. B. Gilliam, bm; m 27 Dec 1865 by P. H. Joyner.

GRANVILLE MARRIAGES 1753-1868

Edwards, Thomas & Nancy Steward, 23 Nov 1835; William Breadlove, bm; Benja. Kittrell, wit.

Edwards, Thomas J. & Sally Nelms, 24 Dec 1821; Jordan Right, bm; S. K. Sneed, wit.

Edwards, Walter & Kizziah Hampton, 9 Oct 1857; James Crabtree, bm; A. Landis, wit; m 14 Oct 1857 by Allen Cozart, J. P.

Edwards, William & Polley Mosely, 3 Feb 1797; James Wilkerson, bm; Jn. Satterwhite, Mitchel Satterwhite, wit.

Edwins, Albert & Sarah Short, 23 Aug 1855; Benj. Stone, bm; m 24 Aug 1855 by A. C. Harris, M. G.

Egerton, Joseph J. & Virginia C. Landis, 6 Dec 1865; Saml. A. Williams, bm; m 6 Dec 1865 by W. C. Gannon, M. G.

Elam, George & Leathy Burwell, 23 Dec 1865; G. A. Reams, bm; m 23 Dec 1865 by T. M. Lynch, J. P.

Elexson, John A. & Mary Chandler, 11 Sept 1864; Samuel F. Whitt, bm; m 11 Sept 1864 by L. B. Stone, J. P.

Elexon, Jos. J. & Jno. A. Elexson (sic), 30 April 1849; John D. Elexson, bm; J. M. Wiggins, wit.

Elington, Albert & Mary Wright, m 2 Oct 1851 by W. S. McClcnahan, J. P.; John Barnes, bm.

Eliot, Robert & Nancey Turner, 6 Feb 1828; James Fraizer, bm; David Laws, wit.

Elis, Philemon & Elizabeth Haskins, 10 Dec 1840; E. M. Hargrove, bm.

Elixson, William & Mary Hencock, 2 Nov 1782; Gilliam Norwood, bm; Bennet Searcy, wit.

Elixson, William & Sarah Wilkerson, 18 Dec 1833; David R. Buckhana, bm; Willie Royster, J. P., wit.

Ellickson, William & Mary Blackwell, 17 May 1811; Pleasant Kimbal, bm; Richd. Sneed, wit.

Ellington, Archibald & Elizabeth Hayes, 3 Oct 1834; Isaac(?) Cheatham, bm.

Ellington, Benjamin & Nancy Johnson, 5 Nov 1860; Shelton Hobgood, bm; m 8 Nov 1860 by Jeff Horner, J. P.

Ellington, Bevel & Anneney Barns, 9 Dec 1809; John Ellington, bm; Step. Sneed, wit.

Ellington, Charles B. & Martha F. Barnett, 11 Dec 1865; James S. Hobgood, bm; m 13 Dec 1865 by T. J. Horner, G. M.

Ellington, George W. & Mary M. Parrish, 10 Dec 1866; Jas. M. Ellington, bm; A. Landis, wit; m 10 Jan 1867 by L. B. Stone, J. P.

Ellington, Guilford & Pamelia Perkinson, 31 Jan 1838; John Barnes, bm.

GRANVILLE MARRIAGES 1753-1868

Ellington, Horace & Frances L. Parrish, 29 Dec 1860; John M. Parrish, bm; A. Landis, wit; m 2 Jan 1861 by Wm. Holmes.

Ellington, James B. & Judith McClanahan, 27 Jan 1818; Eaton H. Kittrell, bm; David Laws, wit.

Ellington, James M. & Sarah F. Fleming, 22 Feb 1867; John Smith, bm; m 24 Feb 1867 by J. F. Harris, J. P.

Ellington, John & Elisabeth Barns, 18 June 1800; James Ellis, bm; Step. Sneed, wit.

Ellington, John & Elizabeth Barnes, 29 June 1801; Henry Rowland, bm; A. Sneed, wit.

Ellington, John M. & Ann W. Hicks, 7 Dec 1857; W. A. Johnston, bm; m 8 Dec 1857 by Robt. B. Sutton, Rector of St. Stephen's Church, Oxford.

Ellington, Jordan & Betsey Cox, 1 Dec 1806; Jones Ellington, bm; Junius Sneed, wit.

Ellington, Meredith & Mary Brome, 23 Oct 1816; John Ellington, bm; Richard Sneed, wit.

Ellington, Meredith & Louisa Ellington, 12 Dec 1853; Jas. R. Duty, bm; m 14 Dec 1853 by Jas. R. Duty, J. P.

Ellington, Patrick & Lucy Ann Thomasson, 2 Jan 1850; A. Landis, bm.

Ellington, Richard & Ann S. Jenkins, m 26 Dec 1866 by Jas. R. Duty, J. P.

Ellington, S. J. & Lucy A. Wiggins, m 9 Oct 1860 by Wm. Holmes.

Ellington, Samuel D. A. H. & Mary Ann Perkerson, 10 Jan 1828; David Ellington, bm; Albert Sneed, wit.

Ellington, Thomas & Fannie Ellington, 19 Oct 1854; A. Landis, bm.

Ellington, William B. & Priscilla Kittrell, 24 Aug 1840; Wm. D. Hicks, bm; Jas. M. Wiggins, wit.

Ellington, William L. & Louisa Ella Thompson, 15 Oct 1852; Richard H. Turner, bm; m 15 Oct 1852 by A. C. Harris.

Ellington, William N. & Mary Ellington, 14 Dec 1852; James R. Duty, bm; Jabez Duty, wit.

Elliott, Alexander & Frances Fraizer, 25 March 1822; John West, bm; David J. Young, wit.

Elliott, Auguston & Sally Glasscock, 2 Nov 1814; Thomas Philips, bm; H. Young, wit.

Elliott, Charles & Nancy Browder, 23 July 1853; Alexander G. Land, bm; m 24 July 1854 by M. D. Royster.

Elliott, Charles G. & Jeannette T. Cooper, 28 March 1867; m 28 March 1867 by H. G. Hill, Minister.

Elliott, Edward M., son of Marshall & Louiza Jane Elliott, & Rebecca M. Tally, daughter of Beverly B. & Emaly Tally, m 22 Dec 1867 by L. B. Stone, J. P.

GRANVILLE MARRIAGES 1753-1868

Elliott, George A., son of Ruben & Elizabeth J. Elliott, & Izabella J. Seat, daughter of Drury & Martha Seat, m 19 Dec 1867 by L. B. Stone, J. P.

Elliott, Green B. & Susan R. Land, 1 April 1850; William F. Hester, bm.

Elliott, James & Mary Eliott, 20 July 1837; Alexander Puryear, bm.

Elliott, James & Lucy A. Currin, 20 Dec 1841; James T. Beasley, bm.

Elliott, John & Peggie Haley, 10 Aug 1826; Wm. H. Carter, bm; Jno. P. Smith, wit.

Elliott, John & Nancey E. Murray, 16 Dec 1851; John H. Murry, bm; L. B. Stone, J. P., wit; m 31 Dec 1851 by L. B. Stone, J. P.

Elliott, L. S. & Laura Elliott, 31 Jan 1867; L. F. Elliott, bm; C. E. Landis, wit; m 3 Feb 1867 by B. T. Winston, J. P.

Elliott, Robert & Charity Trairer, 3 Sept 1791; Archd. Gordon, bm; W. Norwood, D. C., wit.

Elliott, Robert & Mary Ann Downey, 8 Jan 1849; Green Elliott, bm; J. M. Wiggins, wit.

Elliott, Robert, son of Wm. & Martha Elliott, & Rebecca Hunt, daughter of William & Isabella Hunt, 8 Dec 1868; m 15 Dec 1868 by R. J. Devin, M. G.

Elliott, William & Martha Hester, 28 Nov 1813; Benjamin Bearden, bm; W. M. Sneed, wit.

Elliott, William A. & Jane Watkins, 9 March 1858; John B. Land, bm.

Elliott, William A. & Martha A. Glasscock, 20 Dec 1860; E. B. Yancey, bm; m 20 Dec 1860 by L. B. Stone, J. P.

Ellis, Andrew J. & Temperance W. Barker, 17 Nov 1857; James R. Duty, bm; m 18 Nov 1857 by James R. Duty, J. P.

Ellis, Calloway & Oaly Cash, 5 Jan 1835; Isaac Hester, bm; Benja. Kittrell, wit.

Ellis, Ezekiel & Lindy Worrell, 15 April 1815; Reubin Smith, bm; Richd. Sneed, wit.

Ellis, Fenwick & Lucinda Tilley, 26 Dec 1844; D. B. Johnson, bm; Jas. M. Wiggins, wit.

Ellis, Granville (colored), son of Windsor & Lillie Rowland, & Dolly Gilliam, daughter of John Gilliam, 22 Oct 1868; m 22 Oct 1868 by M. H. Vaughan.

Ellis, James & Mary Hester, 29 Dec 1842; Samuel Hunt Jr., bm; J. M. Wiggins, wit.

Ellis, John S. & Fanny Moss, 13 Oct 1830; Thos. A. Langly, bm; David Laws, wit.

GRANVILLE MARRIAGES 1753-1868

Ellis, Joseph & Frances Tatum, 10 Aug 1792; Anderson Hunt, bm; W. Norwood, wit.

Ellis, Joseph & Betsey Horton, 20 Sept 1796; Smullen Lafield, bm; M. Bullock, wit.

Ellis, Levin & Dilley Cole, 21 May 1814; George Robards, bm; W. M. Sneed, wit.

Ellis, Michael & Peggey McClove, 26 Sept 1810; Wm. Murphey, bm; Step. Sneed, wit.

Ellis, Moses & Mary Mangum, 1 Jan 1862; Emmett Gooch, bm; A. Landis, wit; m 2 Jan 1862 by Rob. A. Heflin, J. P.

Ellis, Robert M. & Virginia H. Wilson, 17 Oct 1861; m 20 Oct 1861 by J. H. Harris, J. P.

Ellis, Sidney & Viney Wagoner, 9 Aug 1851; D. H. Whitfield, bm.

Ellis, Stephen & Polly Matison, 6 Oct 1820; Robert F. P. Jones, bm; Step. K. Sneed, wit.

Ellis, Stephen J. & Parthenia F. Duty, 10 Dec 1847; Benj. C. Cooke, bm.

Ellis, William H. & Vandelia V. Baker, 22 Jan 1859; James R. Duty, bm; m 26 Jan 1859 by James R. Duty, J. P.

Ellis, William W. & Martha S. Mann, 22 Nov 1864; James P. Hunger, bm; m 24 Nov 1864 by Rev. P. H. Gilbreath.

Ellis, Wilson & Sally Loyd, 15 April 1815; William Loyd, bm; Richd. Sneed, wit.

Ellixson, James & Elizabeth OBriant, 2 Dec 1845; Mathew Chandler Jr., bm; Jas. M. Wiggins, wit.

Emery, Aron & Ann Eliza Hughs, 9 Nov 1864; S. H. Ferrell, bm; W. D. Allen, wit.

Emery, Aron & Ann Eliza Hughs, 15 Sept 1864; Wiley L. Emery, bm.

Emery, Edmund & Elizabeth Gains, 23 Feb 1807; Brian Cash, bm; Howell Loyd, John H. _____, wit.

Emery, Gideon & Sally Shearin, 30 May 1831; Henry Emery, bm; David Laws, wit.

Emery, Green & Elizabeth Ladd, 31 Oct 1825; John Emery, bm; Step. K. Sneed, wit.

Emery, Henry & Mary Shearin, 22 Oct 1830; John Beck, bm; David Laws, wit.

Emery, James & Francis Beck, 14 Oct 1864; Lewis Emery, bm.

Emery, James A. & Frances Perry, 6 Feb 1867; W. L. Emery, bm; m 14 Feb 1867 by William E. Bullock, J. P.

Emery, Jasper & Telitha T. Perry, 25 Jan 1861; A. J. Chappell, bm.

Emery, John & Cary Heflen, 9 Aug 1797; George Dorcy, bm; Step. Sneed, wit.

GRANVILLE MARRIAGES 1753-1868

Emery, John & Elizabeth Perry, 14 Feb 1818; Green Spain, bm; Step. K. Sneed, wit.

Emery, Lewis & Phanney Garner, 9 Nov 1798; David Beck, bm; Step. Sneed, wit.

Emery, Lewis & Elizabeth Keith, 28 Sept 1812; Lemuel Keith, bm; W. M. Sneed, wit.

Emery, Wiley L. & Rebecca Tucker, m 13 May 1866 by W. D. Allen, J. P.

Emery, Willis & Martha York, 22 Dec 1824; John Garner, bm; Step. K. Sneed, wit.

Emory, George & Frances Harris, 11 Feb 1835; S. Harris, bm.

Emory, Hinton & Frances Mangum, 29 Dec 1851; Darling A. Chappell, bm.

Emory, Hinton & Francis Mangum, 29 Dec 1851; m 30 Dec (1851) by Wm. P. Lyon, J. P.

Emory, Wm. & Emily Allen, 3 Feb 1849; John W. By---, bm.

Emory, Wyatt & Eliza Sykes, 7 Nov 1843; Allen Bridges, bm; Wm. H. Whitfield, wit.

Englebright, B. F. & Melly Jones, 20 Oct 1867; m 27 Oct 1867 by L. B. Stone, J. P.

Epenbeck, Frederick & Minerva Nanny, 23 Aug 1843; Charles Nanny, bm; Wm. H. Whitfield, wit.

Epps, Joel & Polley Bass, 31 Dec 1804; John Johnson, bm; Step. Sneed, wit.

Estes, Erasmus & Elizabeth Clary, 15 Jan 1856; Romulus Estes, bm.

Estes, Henry B. & Anna Marrow, 16 June 1865; A. Landis, bm; m 21 June 1865 by E. Hines.

Estes, James B. & Lucy Fuller, 26 Oct 1813; Hardy Smith, bm; T. J. Hicks, wit.

Estes, John & Elisabeth Nevel, 6 March 1815; John Nevel, bm; Step. Sneed, wit.

Estes, John & Patsey Peace, 28 Nov 1817; Anderson Smith, bm; Step. K. Sneed, wit.

Estes, John W. & Cassanda Hicks, 13 Oct 1842; G. C. Wiggins, bm; Wm. H. Whitfield, wit.

Estes, John W. & Patsy Estes, 28 Oct 1865; m 29 Oct 1865 by Wm. Hockaday, J. P.; W. D. Allen, bm.

Estes, Lucas & Nancy Hawkins Arnold, 18 April 1857; Jesse Headspeth, bm; A. Landis, wit; m 30 April 1857 by T. B. Lyon, J. P.

Estes, Lyddal & Martha Thomason, 7 April 1789; Chs. Long, bm; A. Henderson, C. C., wit.

GRANVILLE MARRIAGES 1753-1868

Estes, Nathaniel H. & Margaret Aiken, 5 Dec 1845; Jubilee Jones, bm; Jas. M. Wiggins, wit.

Estes, Samuel P. & Amanda Mangum, 18 Oct 1845; James B. Peace, bm; J. M. Wiggins, wit.

Estes, Thomas & Rosey Smith, 8 March 1804; Nathl. Estes, bm; Danl. Bridges, wit.

Estes, Triplett T. & Elizabeth Jones, 21 June 1841; Robert Kyle, bm; J. M. Wiggins, wit.

Estis, James & Charlott Mangrum, 11 Sept 1813; Hardy Smith, bm; J. T. Hicks, wit.

Estis, Jeremiah & Sarah Davis, 26 Jan 1828; Ancell Prewit, bm; David Laws, wit.

Evans, Abram & Jane Melton, 30 Jan 1854; Isaac Evans, bm; m 31 Jan 1854 by Peterson Thorp, J. P.

Evans, Alexander & Rebecca Ann Prewitt, 17 Dec 1859; J. R. Reams, bm; A. Landis, wit; m 22 Dec 1859 by J. Y. McGehee, J. P.

Evans, Bartlett & Jincy Cole, 28 July 1836; Wm. Arrington, bm; Wm. T. Hargrove, wit.

Evans, Bartlett & Martha Richerson, 28 July 1858; Fern Hayes, bm; A. Landis, wit; m 29 July 1858 by Jas. R. Duty, J. P.

Evans, Benjamin & Lucey Mitchell, 1 Aug 1811; George Anderson, bm; W. M. Sneed, wit.

Evans, Chas. & Sally Thomas, 14 Nov 1854; John Harris, bm; C. R. Eaton, wit; m 14 Nov 1854 by C. R. Eaton, J. P.

Evans, Coleman & Jane Bowles, 1 May 1855; A. Slaughter, bm.

Evans, Daniel & Phereby Jones, 10 Sept 1800; Amenuel Scott Jones, bm.

Evans, David & Susan Truman, 14 Aug 1844; Wm. Tergury(?), bm; Jas. M. Wiggins, wit.

Evans, George & Lucy Tyler, 13 Jan 1842; Geo. Anderson, bm; J. M. Wiggins, wit.

Evans, Griffin & Sally Mayson, 9 Nov 1819; Richard Evans, bm; A. Sneed, wit.

Evans, Griffin & Elizabeth Green, 20 Oct 1851; Joshua Mason, bm; free persons of color, m 22 Oct 1851 by James R. Duty, J. P.

Evans, James & Martha Taborn, 23 Dec 1829; George Anderson, bm; David Laws, wit.

Evans, James O. & Joanna Duncan, 10 Aug 1847; Moses Carnal(?), bm; Jas. M. Wiggins, wit.

Evans, John & Lucy Taylor, 6 Oct 1800; James Taylor, bm; _____ Bullock, wit.

Evans, John & Hannah Anderson, 22 Feb 1806; Abel Anderson, bm; W. M. Sneed, wit.

GRANVILLE MARRIAGES 1753-1868

Evans, John & Martha Harris, 23 Dec 1853; Hilliard Evans, bm; A. Landis, wit.

Evans, Major & Mary Jane Evans, 22 Jan 1845; Benj. C. Cook, bm; Jas. M. Wiggins, wit.

Evans, Marcellus & Amelia F. Headspeth, 6 Feb 1866; S. W. Mitchell, bm; m 17 Feb 1866 by W. P. White, J. P.

Evans, Morris & Lidda Anderson, 3 Dec 1784; Burwell Evans, bm; Bennet Searcy, wit.

Evans, Morris & Sally Chavis, 18 March 1835; Harrel G. Pittard, bm; Benja. Kittrell, wit.

Evans, Peter & Elizabeth Mitchell, 7 Oct 1821; Lemuel McGehee, bm; Jas. M. Wiggins, wit.

Evans, Richard A. & Ann Moss, 10 Dec 1845; Neill S. Grisham, bm; Jas. M. Wiggins, wit.

Evans, Saml. & Martha Catlett, 21 Sept 1860; Thomas Evans, bm; A. Landis, wit; m 23 Sept 1860.

Evans, Thomas & Salley Bass, 30 Feb 1812; Moses Bass, bm; W. M. Sneed, wit.

Evans, Thomas & _____, 20 Nov 1818; John Y. Parker, bm; W. M. Sneed, wit.

Evans, Thomas & Mary Volentine, 1 June 1843; Jas. B. Peace, bm; Wm. H. Whitfield, wit.

Evans, Thomas & Polly Read, 28 March 1845; William H. Harris, bm.

Evans, Thomas & Elizabeth Barnett, 30 Oct 1854; Griffin Evans, bm; Jas. T. Duty, wit; m 30 Oct 1854 by James R. Duty, J. P.

Evans, Thomas S. & Emily Ann Harris, 16 Dec 1850; William Evans, bm; A. Landis, wit; m by J. K. Cole, M. G.

Evans, William & Frankey Anderson, 27 Sept 1812; Abel Anderson, bm; W. M. Sneed, wit.

Evans, Wm. B. & Rebecca Ann E. Hart, 10 Jan 1860; E. W. Harris, bm; m 11 Jan 1860 by A. C. Harris, M. G.

Evans, William T. G. W. & Emily Scott, 13 June 1855; Eugene Grissom, bm; Thos. W. McClanahan, wit.

Evans, Willie & Parthena Mayho, 27 Dec 1856; Elbert Finch, bm; A. Landis, wit.

Evans, Willis & Mana Copeland, 12 March 1846; Sterling Chavis, bm; Jas. M. Wiggins, wit.

Evans, William & Elizabeth Anderson, 6 Nov 1854; Augustine Landis, bm; Thos. W. McClanahan, wit; m 9 Nov 1854 by H. Hester, J. P.

Evins, Archibald & Anna Mason, 13 Jan 1814; Lewis Anderson, bm.

Evins, Charles & Betsey Norman, 31 Dec 1803; James Hargrove, bm; Step. Sneed, wit.

GRANVILLE MARRIAGES 1753-1868

Evins, Jorge W. & Mary Loging, 26 Sept 1833; Seth White, bm; Willie Royster, J. P., wit.

Ezell, Hartwell F. & Frances H. Royster, 19 Nov 1849; John H. Royster, bm.

Ezell, Wm. T. & Susan A. Lewis, 18 Nov 1855; Jas. S. Lewis, bm; Wm. T. Haynie, wit.

Fain, Grandison & Martha Reavis, colored, 23 Feb 1867; m by Wyatt Walker, M. Gospel.

Fain, Wm. & Isabella Wilkerson, 8 Nov 1848; Alexr. Howell, bm.

Fairbank, William S. & Nancy R. Mallory, 27 Sept 1822; James Hunt, bm; Jas. M. Wiggins, wit.

Faison, Oshen & Amanda Kingsbury, 26 Dec 1865; A. Landis, wit; m 28 Dec 1865 by L. K. Willie, M. G.

Falconer, Joseph & Lucy Mangum, 12 Oct 1837; David Clark, bm; J. M. Wiggins, wit.

Falconer, Robert & Feraby Roberson, 10 Feb 1810; William Clarke, bm; Saml. Hogg, wit.

Falconer, Thomas & Betsey Hunt, 25 Dec 1802; W. M. Sneed, bm; Step. Sneed, wit.

Falconer, William & Sally T. Roberson, 13 March 1826; Mills Tayloe, bm; Albert Sneed, wit.

Falconer, William & Frances Ball, 5 June 1843; James Short, bm; J. M. Wiggins, wit.

Falkner, Butler & Frances N. Hoyle(?), 1 April 1858; Geo. K. Parham, bm; m 4 April 1858 by T. A. Stewart, J. P.

Falkner, Champion & Elizabeth Powell, 29 Nov 1859; Thos. Short, bm; A. Landis, wit.

Falkner, Francis & Nancy Robertson, 13 April 1831; John W. Weaver, bm; Albert Sneed, wit.

Falkner, George W. & Tabitha A. Mangum, 2 Feb 1867; m 6 Feb 1867 by Saml. K. Hunt, J. P.; Alfred Hobgood, bm; C. E. Landis, wit.

Falkner, James & Martha Hicks, 7 Feb 1861; B. Cook, bm.

Falkner, James W. & Tabbitha Roberson, 22 Sept 1857; Wm. A. J. Falkner, bm; Jas. R. Duty, wit; m by Jas. R. Duty, J. P.; 23 Sept 1857.

Falkner, Jefferson & Margaret Griffin, 5 Aug 1851; L. H. Howe, bm; m 6 Aug 1851 by James Gooch, J. P.

Falkner, John & Sealey Johnson, 26 Dec 1810; Phileman Perdue, bm; Step. Sneed, wit.

Falkner, John & Sally Stewart, 7 Jan 1837; James Stewart, bm; J. M. Wiggins, wit.

Falkner, Neverson & Martha Edwards, 1 March 1843; Isham Ball, bm; J. M. Wiggins, wit.

GRANVILLE MARRIAGES 1753-1868

Falkner, Terence & Elizabeth Tucker, 24 Jan 1848; Jas. R. Duty, bm; Jabez Duty, wit.

Falkner, Thomas N. & Amanda E. Champion, 19 Oct 1865; A. M. Champion, bm.

Falkner, William & Nelly Faukner, 18 Dec 1851; Littleton Falkner, bm; B. C. Cooke, wit.

Falkner, William R. & Harriett Wilkerson, 22 June 1850; Jesse J. Burton, bm; Benj. C. Cooke, wit.

Farabough, James & Dorthey Cooper, 16 Jan 1815; Aaron Farabough, bm; W. M. Sneed, wit.

Farabow, D. B. D. & Eliza C. Green, 1 Oct 1856; A. N. Jones, bm; m 1 Oct 1856 by Geo. J. Rowland, J. P.

Farabow, W. S., son of William Farabow decd., & Susan Farabow, & Susan M. Green, daughter of Thomas & Susan Green, 3 Sept 1867; m 4 Sept 1867 by F. J. Tilley, J. P.

Fargoson, Richard & Elizabeth Brogdon, 26 Dec 1814; David Brogdon, bm; Leslie Gilliam, wit.

Farmer, James H. & Mary T. Knight, 8 March 1828; Lodowick Farmer, bm.

Farrabough, William & Susan Bullock, 4 Aug 1831; Robert Maben, bm; David Laws, wit.

Farrar, Alexr. J. & Pamelia S. Walton, 3 Jan 1828; James Hunt, bm; Jno. P. Smith, wit.

Farrar, George & Delilah Hays, 1 Dec 1819; William Farrar, bm; R. N. Herndon, J. P., wit.

Farrar, Jefferson W. E. & Elizabeth M. Paschall, 11 Aug 1847; Henry C. Herndon, bm; Benj. C. Cooke, wit.

Farrar, Obadiah & Betsey Newberry Graves, 3 June 1799; David Graves, bm; James Sneed, wit.

Farrar, Peter F. & Tempey Hays, 2 Sept 1795; Jesse Hayes, bm; Step. Sneed, wit.

Farrow, Thomas & Anne Daws(?), 25 Oct 1803; Daniel Tucker, bm; Step. Sneed, wit.

Faucet, William & Mary Matthews, 7 July 1858; Cephus Hudson, bm; A. Landis, wit; m 7 July 1858 by Jno. W. Stovall, J. P.

Faucett, John H. & Mary Beal, 24 April 1865; Jos. Matthews, bm.

Faulkner, Henry, son of Wm. & Sallie Faulkner, & Mary Barr, daughter of Jno. & Mildred Barr, 13 May 1868; m 13 May 1868 by Wm. Holmes, Minister.

Faulkner, Jacob & Martha Clay, 9 April 1810; Peyton Wood, bm; Jun. Sneed, wit.

Faulkner, John K. & L. V. Chandler, 14 Dec 1861; W. Overby, bm; m 15 Dec 1861 by Wm. Slate, M. G.

GRANVILLE MARRIAGES 1753-1868

Faulkner, Moses & Susanna Saulter, 1 Oct 1782; Asa Faulkner, bm; Elisabeth Searcy, wit.

Fautner, Ford & Tabatha Roberson, 25 Nov 1815; Wiley Loyd, bm; Richd. Sneed, wit.

Fennett, William C., son of Nancy Fannett & Delila J. Fleming, daughter of Rowan & Elizabeth Fleming, 4 Nov 1867; m 5 Nov 1867 by John L. Michaux.

Ferabow, Preston A. T. & Jane Wheeler, 18 Jan 1858; Arthur Stevens, bm; A. Landis, wit; m 19 Jan 1858 by Jeff Horner, J. P.

Ferebee, Enoch D. & Hester C. Bell, 10 Jan 1860; E. F. Beachum, bm; m 10 Jan 1860 by E. F. Beachum, a regular Minister of the Gospel.

Ferges, Saml. P. & _____, 4 Aug 1835; Elis Walker, bm; Howel G. Pittard, wit.

Ferguson--see also Fargoson

Ferguson, James T. & Ann Wynn, 20 Dec 1853; Willis R. Phillips, bm; m 20 Dec 1853 by A. C. Harris, M. G.

Ferguson, Joel & Mary Gwin Laurence, 17 March 1808; William Laurence, bm; W. M. Sneed, wit.

Ferrel, James & Tabitha Hayes, 15 June 1784; Wm. Burford Jr., bm; Bennet Searcy, wit.

Ferrel, Micajah & Tabitha Jordan, 27 April 1778; Wm. Reeves, bm; Sherwood White, wit.

Ferrel, Samuel H. & Mary Eliza Davis, 17 Nov 1864; John M. Ellington, bm.

Ferrell, Samuel H., son of William & Eliza Ferrill, & Margaret Isabella Perry, daughter of Thomas & Maria Perry, m 1 March 1868 by B. B. Hester.

Ferrell, William & Eliza Garner, 30 Nov 1839; Wm. S. Hayes, bm.

Ferrill, Samuel D. & Martha A. Paschall, 26 Feb 1850; Benj. C. Cooke, bm; A. Landis, wit.

Ferry, John & Mary Gomer, 19 April 1784; William Gomer, bm; John Morris, wit.

Field, George & Frances B. Littlejohn(?), 24 Feb 1841; Alexr. S. Jones, bm; G. C. Wiggins, wit.

Field, Hume R. & Millicent(?) Young, 18 Dec 1797; Anderson Taylor, bm; Step. Sneed, wit.

Field, John & Allce Dufoy, 9 Nov 1767; Jno. Southerland, bm; Jesse Benton, wit.

Fiffer, Henry & Anne Cole, 22 Nov 1786; Henry Gilpin, bm; Thomas Ligon, wit.

Field, Solomon & Martha Proctor, m 24 Oct 1866 by M. H. Vaughan, Rector of St. Stephen's Church; Henry Morton, bm.

GRANVILLE MARRIAGES 1753-1868

Finch, Claburn & Sarah Hunt, 26 Jan 1790; John Finch, bm; A. Henderson, wit.

Finch, Elbert & Ann Petteford, 1 June 1854; Norrell W. Mayho, bm; m 1 June 1854 by John Mallory.

Finch, Elijah & Martha Mann, 2 Feb 1842; John Brummett, Jr., bm; J. M. Wiggins, wit.

Finch, Farrar & Sarah Heap, 4 Dec 1839; Zachr. Dickinson, bm; J. M. Wiggins, wit.

Finch, George R. & Caroline Bratcher, 5 Dec 1847; Samuel D. Edwards, bm.

Finch, James & Mary Floyd, 5 Jan 1807; Hezekiah Lock, bm; W. M. Sneed, wit.

Finch, James, son of William Finch & Eliza Finch, daughter of Elijah & Patsy Finch, 28 Dec 1867; m 1 Jan 1868 by J. F. Harris, J. P.

Finch, John & Elizabeth Haynes, 9 April 1789; Charnell Hight, bm; H. Potter, wit.

Finch, John & Judith Hockady, 8 July 1815; James Jinkins, bm; John Hicks, wit.

Finch, John & Polly Bradford, 24 Oct 1815; Britain Bobbitt, bm; Stephen Sneed, wit.

Finch, John & Julia Mann, 12 Oct 1852; Thos. W. Hicks, bm; Eugene Grissom, wit.

Finch, Lewis W. & Luvisa Moore, 1 March 1862; Cephas Hudson, bm; m 5 March 1862 by Richard W. Harris, J. P.

Finch, Richard & Julia Ann Chavis, 16 May 1862; A. Landis, bm.

Finch, Wm. & Elizabeth Hedspeth, 3 April 1834; James Sims, bm; Tho. L. King, wit.

Finch, Wm. & Sarah Mangum, 2 Feb 1847; Arch Ell--, bm; D. A. Paschall, wit.

Finley, Thomas & Martha Strum, 25 Dec 1820; Leonard Cardwell, bm; A. Sneed, wit.

Fitch, Thomas & Dulcena Aubrey, 10 May 1838; Peter G. Vaughan, bm.

Fitcher, Thomas & Sarah Wright, 13 Dec 1800; Abner Jones, bm; W. M. Sneed, wit.

Fitsgerell, John & Nancy Rabon, 3 Feb 1864; Merit Champion, bm; m 3 Feb 1864 by Jas. J. Moore, J. P.

Fitts, Henry & Winney P. H. Hayes, 20 Dec 1845; Will _____, bm; J. M. Wiggins, wit.

Fitts, Robert W. & Mary Eliza Arrington, 4 Dec 1849; R. H. Walker, bm; L. B. Stone, J. P., wit.

Fitts, Thomas & Francis Edwards, 23 Oct 1845; Wm. R. Hicks, bm; Jno. J. Eaton, wit.

GRANVILLE MARRIAGES 1753-1868

Fitz, William & Frances Johnston, 11 Nov 1801; Gideon Mitchell, bm; Phil. Bullock, wit.

Fleeman, Henry & Ellendar Hargroves, 6 May 1786; Tho. Rice, bm; John Keeling, wit.

Flemin, Thomas & Mary Flemin, 28 Dec 1783; William Flemin, bm; Bennet Searcy, wit.

Fleming, Alexander & Elizabeth A. McCadden, 2 April 1853; J. G. Hester, bm;

Fleming, Benjamin, colored, son of Benj. Daniel & Nancy Jones, & Pattie Hester, daughter of Charles Bullock & Lishia Fleming, 12 Dec 1868; m 25 Dec 1868 by J. P. Montague, M. G.

Fleming, Charles & Nicholas Stanback (sic), 17 Feb 1798; W. Moore, bm; Step. Sneed, wit.

Fleming, Daniel & Anne Farrar, 6 Jan 1783; Stephen Bailey, bm; Reuben Searcy, wit.

Fleming, Edward L. & Frances L. Hester, 19 Dec 1866; J. W. Fleming, bm; m 25 Dec 1866 by William S. Hester.

Fleming, Geo. H. & Sallie A. Stewart, m 23 Oct 1867 by J. H. Riddick.

Fleming, James & Elizabeth Wilkerson, 24 Dec 1842; D. A. Paschall, bm.

Fleming, John & Delila M. Murphey, 8 July 1861; m 10 July 1861 by John W. Kelly, J. P.

Fleming, John W., son of Thos. Beverly & Frances Fleming, & Martha A. C. Heflin, daughter of James & Martha Heflin, 1 Oct 1867; m 3 Oct 1867 by Robt. L. Heflin, J. P.

Fleming, Middleton & Nancy Kimbral, 20 Aug 1825; Peter F. Regans, bm; A. Sneed, wit.

Fleming, Robert & Polley Dodson, 27 Feb 1794; John Hargrove, bm; Step. Sneed, wit.

Fleming, William & Frances Bullock, 24 Dec 1810; William Dalbey, bm; W. M. Sneed, wit.

Flemming, John & Nancy W. Lyon, 3 March 1835; Benjamin F. Bullock, bm; Benja. Kittrell, wit.

Flemming, Thomas B. & Frankey Akins, 7 Jan 1824; Clement B. Lyon, bm; Wm. H. Owen, wit.

Fletcher, Abner & Lucy Estes, 20 May 1815; Anderson Smith, bm; W. M. Sneed, wit.

Fletcher, Abner & Precilah Rochel, 3 Dec 1834; Abner Peace, bm; Jno. White, wit.

Fletcher, Joseph & Polley Searcey, 25 July 1816; B. H. Wortham, wit.

Fletcher, Patrick Henry & Martha Ann Arnold, 16 Oct 1832; William C. York, bm; David Laws, wit.

GRANVILLE MARRIAGES 1753-1868

Fletcher, William & Leanna Jones, 20 Dec 1803; Martin Wheeler, bm; A. H. Sneed, wit.

Fletcher, William E. & Narcissa H. York, 30 July 1856; Thos. J. Horner, bm.

Fletcher, William P. J. & Mary Ann Wilkerson, 9 Oct 1860; William Rice, bm; m 9 Oct 1860 by L. B. Stone, J. P.

Fletcher, Willie & Martha Lawrence, 15 Dec 1829; Benjamin Hester, bm; David Laws, wit.

Floyd, Bartholomew & Elizabeth Wrothill, (no date, during admn. of Gov. Samuel Johnston); John H---, bm; A. Henderson, C. C., wit.

Floyd, Charles & Louisa A. Moss, 19 Feb 1834; Thos. B. Taylor, bm; Benja. Kittrell, wit.

Floyd, Charles & Frances Waller, 26 Aug 1867; m by Jas. B. Floyd, J. P.; Henry Fuller, bm.

Floyd, George & Keziah Parish, 19 Dec 1786; Hesekiah Hefil(?), bm; B. Searcy, wit.

Floyd, George & Martha Lock, 4 April 1795; Hezekiah Highfill, bm; Step. Sneed, wit.

Floyd, George & Obedience Mann, 15 Nov 1823; John Glasgow, bm; Step. Sneed, wit.

Floyd, George & Rosey Denton, 27 Aug 1835; Wm. Floyd, bm; Thos. H. Read(?), J. P., wit.

Floyd, Henry & Susan Rogers, 1 Dec 1812; John Parrish, bm; Step. K. Sneed, wit.

Floyd, Henry & Sarah Parham, 3 Aug 1830; Lewis Parham, bm; David Laws, wit.

Floyd, Hichman & Selea Hayes, 27 Dec 1799; John Hayes, bm; James Sneed, wit.

Floyd, James B. & Mary S. White, 23 Oct 1852; Eugene Grissom, bm; A. Landis, wit.

Floyd, James W. & Eliza Howell, 6 Sept 1845; Richd. Mayhoe, bm; Jas. M. Wiggins, wit.

Floyd, James W. & Mary Ann Maynard, 15 Nov 1853; James P. Maynard, bm; A. Landis, wit.

Floyd, James Y. & Elisabeth Daws, 12 Aug 1850; Zachariah Higgs, bm.

Floyd, Lewis & Martha Rogers, 15 Dec 1821; Spence McClennahan, bm; S. K. Sneed, wit.

Floyd, Pleasant & Martha _____, 1 Jan 1821; Caleb Lindsey, bm; W. M. Sneed, wit.

Floyd, Presly & Winifred K. Hodges, 13 Aug 1831; James Fuller, bm; David Laws, wit.

GRANVILLE MARRIAGES 1753-1868

Floyd, Rufus, of color, son of Thomas & Reaney Floyd, & Cary Ann
Hicks, daughter of Cherry Hicks, 20 Sept 1867; m 15 Sept 1867
by W. P. White, J. P.

Floyd, Stephen & Rachel Rogers, 17 Dec 1825; William McClenahan,
bm; Wm. H. Owen, wit.

Floyd, Thos. & Betsy Fowler, 26 Oct 1803; Hickman Floyd, bm;
Green Merritt, wit.

Floyd, William & Patsey Hendisy, 23 May 1789; Hezekiah Highfill,
bm; A. Henderson, C. C., wit.

Floyd, William & Martha Parham, 17 Dec 1823; Samuel Fuller, bm;
Wm. H. Owen, wit.

Floyd, William Jr. & Mary Parham, 5 Jan 1830; George P. Thomasson, bm; S. K. Sneed, wit.

Floyd, William J. & Eliza M. Duke, m 9 Sept 1857 by L. K. Willie;
A. E. Fuller, bm.

Foard, James & Elizabeth McClarin, 17 May 1816; John Robertson,
bm; H. Young, wit.

Foard, John & Mary Jones, 6 Jan 1810; Robert Lewis, bm; J.
Sneed, wit.

Foard, John & Patsey Meadows, 14 Dec 1813; James Mangum, bm;
J. P. Sneed, wit.

Ford, Absalom & Frances Justice, 6 Aug 1799; William Philpott,
bm; Step. Sneed, wit.

Ford, John & Francis Bowdon, 9 Nov 1814; Elias Bowdon, bm; Roling Cook, wit.

Ford, Thornton & Jane Henning, 4 May 1807; Stephen Motlow, bm;
Step. Sneed, wit.

Ford, William & Judith Williams, of the age of 21 years, spinster,
daughter of John Williams, 27 Dec 1760; John Renals, bm; Jno.
Bowie, wit.

Forde, William F. & Nancy Tuck, 4 Feb 1833; William A. Laws, bm.

Forker, Anderson & Lucy Forker, 17 June 1828; Vines Short, bm;
Richd. Sneed, wit.

Forker, James & Bedey Matterson, 25 Aug 1829; Lang King, bm;
B. Bullock, wit.

Forkner, Frank & Nancey Rogers, 22 Aug 1804; James Babb(?), bm;
_____ Cash, wit.

Forkner, Littleton & Dilly Edwards, 1 June 1831; Warren Duty,
bm; David Laws, wit.

Forrest, James & Elisa W. Russell, 21 July 1813; Ezekiel B.
Currin, bm; Tho. J. Hicks, wit.

Forsyth, Duncan H. & Margaret F. Nance, 6 Feb 1856; Thomas
Green, bm.

GRANVILLE MARRIAGES 1753-1868

Forsyth, James & Nancy Waller, 28 Feb 1802; Samuel Bradley, bm; John H. Farrar, wit.

Forsyth, William P. & Sarah M. Ihappell, 31 March 1860; Terrel Loyd, bm; m 26 May 1860 by B. B. Hester.

Forsythe, John & Mary Thomas Goss, 6 Feb 1852; Woodson Washington, bm; m 9 Feb 1852 by Jno. Nance, J. P.

Forsythe, Lawson & Rebecca Ann Peed, m 26 May 1867 by Robt. L. Heflin, J. P.

Forsythe, Philip & Betsey Green, 14 Dec 1811; Cader Parker, bm; Stephen K. Sneed, wit.

Forsythe, Redmon & Elizabeth Freeman, 2 July 1837; Henry McFarling, bm; David Laws, wit.

Forsythe, Samuel & Lucy Jones, 20 Dec 1828; Henry Wheeler, bm; David Laws, wit.

Forsythe, Simpson & Catharine Bledsoe, 11 Feb 1846; James T. Bullock, bm; Jas. M. Wiggins, wit.

Forsythe, Smith & Nancy Waller, 5 Sept 1840; William Forsythe, bm; Jas. M. Wiggins, wit.

Forsythe, William & Benjamin (sic) Adams, 8 April 1809; Benjamin Adams, bm; W. M. Sneed, wit.

Forsythe, Willie & Caroline Laws, 8 June 1865; H. A. Bullock, bm.

Fort, William & Charlotte Lile, 24 Nov 1792; Isaac Jackson, bm; W. Norwood, wit.

Foster, Alexander, of color, son of Lily Foster & Mollie Haskins, daughter of Lettie Haskins & Henry Sands, 26 Dec 1867; m 26 Dec 1867 by Warren Overbey, J. P.

Foster, O. H. & Miss Mary F. Jones, 27 Sept 1859; R. J. Shaw, bm; D. E. Young, wit; m 28 Sept 1859 by H. H. Prout, Rector of Church of Holy Innocents, Henderson, N. C.

Foster, Richard Donalson & Henrietta Hunter, freed people, 3 Nov 1866; m by Lewis H. Keith, J. P.

Foster, William & Tabitha Moore, 2 Oct 1792; George Moore, bm; W. Norwood, wit.

Fowler, Alexander & _____, 2 Sept 1789; Stephen Lock, bm; A. Henderson, wit.

Fowler, Bennett & Mary Ann Qualls, 15 Dec 1839; Albert An----, bm; J. M. Wiggins, wit.

Fowler, Bumpass & Indiana Hunt, 26 March 1853; Levi Wilkerson, bm; m 29 March 1853 by Peterson Thorp, J. P.

Fowler, Daniel & Betsey Mize, 2 Sept 1803; Obadiah Mize, bm; Jun. Sneed, wit.

Fowler, Daniel & Polley Fraizer, 7 May 1816; Archibald Cawthon, bm; W. M. Sneed, wit.

GRANVILLE MARRIAGES 1753-1868

Fowler, Gabriel & Pheebey Oakley, 13 Aug 1797; Abraham Slaughter, bm; M. Satterwhite, Smith Satterwhite, wit.

Fowler, Henry & Nancy Mabery, 5 May 1841; Jas. W. Heggie, bm; G. C. Wiggins, wit.

Fowler, John & Bethiah Tippet, 23 Jan 1811; James Spencer, bm; W. M. Sneed, wit.

Fowler, John & Nancy Sims, 7 Oct 1812; Mills Tayloe, bm; Stephen Sneed Junior, wit.

Fowler, John & Elizabeth Fowler, 26 March 1844; Stephen Cook, bm; Wm. H. Whitfield, wit.

Fowler, John & Martha Dement, 2 Jan 1854; Sandy Sutton, bm; A. Landis, bm; m 3 Jan 1854 by D. P. Paschall, J. P.

Fowler, Killman & Eliza Booth, 7 Sept 1841; Peter Drury(?), bm.

Fowler, Malachi & Fanney Priddy, 3 Nov 1840; G. C. Wiggins, bm.

Fowler, Moody & Polly Harris, 7 Sept 1830; J. Shearman, bm; S. K. Sneed, wit.

Fowler, Richd. T. & Charity W. Roberts, 23 June 1848; William S. Parrish, bm.

Fowler, Ruffin & Nancy Shadrick, 1 Dec 1859; William Wadford, bm; A. Landis, wit; m 1 Dec 1859 by W. D. Allen, J. P.

Fowler, Sterling & Patsey Barnett, 22 Dec 1817; Richd. Sneed, bm.

Fowler, Thomas & Jane Jones, 1 Jan 1841; James Cottrell, bm.

Fowler, Thomas & Lucy Fuller, 4 Sept 1864; Shemwell MeGehee, bm; m 4 Sept 1864 by J. Y. McGehee, J. P.

Fowler, Washington & Elizabeth Sanderford, 17 Feb 1849; James Fowler, bm; Jas. M. Wiggins, wit.

Fowler, William & Lucy Hudspeth, 2 Jan 1786; William Farrar, bm; Bennet Searcy, wit.

Fowler, William & Ann Byars, 7 Dec 1816; John Fowler, R. N. Herndon, wit.

Fraiser, Thomas & Jane Jones, 19 May 1825; Thomas J. Landford, bm; Jno. P. Smith, wit.

Fraizer, Arthur & Polly Goodrum, 6 Feb 1799; Rowland Bryant, bm; Step. Sneed, wit.

Fraizer, Barnett & Mary Potter, 17 March 1798; Robert Potter, bm; Step. Sneed, wit.

Fraizer, Charles & Elizabeth Currin, 5 Jan 1831; Abner Currin, bm; David Laws, wit.

Fraizer, Charles & Louisa Grandy, 3 Nov 1866; David Magby, bm; A. Landis, wit.

Fraizer, Ephraim & Elizabeth Blackwell, 12 Dec 1820; Ransom Frazer, bm; Step. K. Sneed, wit.

GRANVILLE MARRIAGES 1753-1868

Fraizer, James & Mary Hunt, 8 July 1828; Allen Gordan, bm; David Laws, wit.

Fraizer, James & Minerva W. Neal, 21 Dec 1839; Jas. M. Satterwhite, bm; Step. K. Sneed, wit.

Fraizer, Jeremiah & Betsey Milton, 19 Oct 1789; Henry Melton, bm; Henry Potter, wit.

Fraizer, John & Nancy Barton, 7 March 1803; William Barton, bm; Green Merritt, wit.

Fraizer, Lewis & Salley Hart, 28 Dec 1795; William Fraizer, bm; Step. Sneed, wit.

Fraizer, Robert & Miss Susannah West, 16 Dec 1822; Masten Fraizer, bm; D. J. Young, wit.

Fraizer, Stephen & Jincey Goodrum, 18 Sept 1804; Howel Fraizer, bm; Step. Sneed, wit.

Fraizer, Thomas F. & Jane Fraizer, 11 Feb 1831; W. Frazar, bm; David Laws, wit.

Fraizer, William & Sarah Potter, 17 Aug 1797; Robert Potter, bm; Jas. W. Smith, wit.

Fraizer, William & Patsey Beardon, 20 Nov 1804; Nathaniel Snipes, bm; E. W. Parham, wit.

Frazer, John & Sarah Hawkins, 4 April 1805; Robert Potter, bm; Jas. Sneed, wit.

Frazer, Stephen & Mary Vass, 4 June 1798; Thos. Vass, bm; Step. Sneed, wit.

Frazier, Abraham & Polley Hedspeth, 5 Aug 1819; Peleg Bailey, bm; Jas. Wiggins, wit.

Frazier, Arthur & Eliza Petty, 7 Dec 1817; Ephraim Fraizer, bm; Rhodes N. Herndon, wit.

Frazier, Augustine D. & Frances Dean, 8 Oct 1856; J. H. Currin, bm; m 12 Oct 1856 by Peterson Thorp, J. P.

Frazier, Charles H. & Isabella Hunt, 29 Aug 1854; Wm. G. Washington, bm; R. W. Lasseter, bm; m 29 Aug 1854 by Peterson Thorp, J. P.

Frazier, Dennis O. & Mary Ann Blackwell, 18 Dec 1838; Charles F. Frazier, bm.

Frazier, Elijah & Susan Tucker, 19 Aug 1850; Samuel A. Hunt, bm.

Frazier, Elijah C. & Mary Jane Hobgood, 25 Nov 1856; J. H. Currin, bm; m 27 Nov 1856 by Jno. R. Hicks, J. P.

Frazier, Elisha T., son of William B. Frazier & Margaret A. Frazier, & Margaret A. Boyd, daughter of Bruce Boyd & Sarah Boyd, 21 Nov 1867; m 27 Nov 1867 by Jas. R. Duty, J. P.

Frazier, James & Rowan Chandler, 1 Jan 1852; John W. Currin, bm; m 5 Jan 1852 by L. B. Stone, J. P.

GRANVILLE MARRIAGES 1753-1868

Frazier, James H. & Elizabeth J. Hester, 17 Nov 1859; E. R. Frazier, bm; m 22 Nov 1859 by F. B. Currin, J. P.

Frazier, Mastin & Elizabeth D. Caniel, 14 Dec 1822; Robert Fraizer, bm.

Frazier, Ransom & Milley OBriant, 2 Sept 1808; Howel Frazer, bm.

Frazier, Robert & Elisabeth Graves, 8 Aug 1786; Ephraim Frazier, bm.

Frazier, Robert H. & Ann E. Chandler, 3 Dec 1847; F. B. Curring, bm; Jas. M. Wiggins, wit.

Frazier, Robert H. & Almira Chandler, 6 June 1850; James M. Frazier, bm.

Frazier, Shadric & Jane Granger, 20 Dec 1790; Thomas Daniel, bm; Saml. Griffin, wit.

Frazier, Thomas B. & Jane Ann Knott, 19 Dec 1859; Robt. H. Hobgood, bm.

Frazier, William & Nancey Jones, 19 March 1822; Robert Blackwell, bm; Jno. P. Smith, wit.

Frazier, William B. & Margaret Vass, 8 Nov 1838; Howel T. Wilkerson, bm.

Frear, Joseph M. & Martha M. Allgood, 26 Sept 1866; m by James R. Duty, J. P.

Freeman, Charles A. & Rutha Hooker, 11 Dec 1822; Daniel Mitchell, bm; Jas. M. Wiggins, wit.

Freeman, Charles B. & Lucretia Weldon Freeman, 31 Dec 1865; m 31 Dec 1865.

Freeman, Charles H. & Alice OBriant, m 5 Nov 1851 by William E. Oakley.

Freeman, Edmond & Judia Johnston, 21 Sept 1789; James Allen, bm; Richard Grubb, Henry Potter, wit.

Freeman, Edward E., son of Evan E. & Francis C. Freeman, & Katharine A. Hester, daughter of John G. & Frances Hester, 8 Sept 1868; m 16 Sept 1868 by John J. Lanodell, Min. Gos.

Freeman, Evan & Sarah Hooker, 18 Feb 1802; Beverley Harris, bm; Step. Sneed, wit.

Freeman, Evan E. & Frances C. Lyon, 20 Dec 1845; R. B. Hester, bm; J. M. Wiggins, wit.

Freeman, Evans & Dosia Clay, 28 May 1866; m 30 May 1866 by George J. Rowland, J. P.

Freeman, George & Ellender Brummet, 24 Jan 1804; Leroy Brummet, bm; Step. Sneed, wit.

Freeman, Gideon Jr. & Isabella Clemment, 23 June 1801; Claborn A. Freeman, bm; Phil. Bullock, wit.

Freeman, Hatsville & Lucy Weathers, 15 Nov 1823; James A. Freeman, bm; S. K. Sneed, wit.

GRANVILLE MARRIAGES 1753-1868

Freeman, Henry & Molly Carter, 28 Dec 1791; Saml. Smith, bm; W. Norwood, wit.

Freeman, James A. & Malissa L. Moss, 11 Dec 1860; Robt. S. Hunt, bm; m 13 Dec 1860 by W. D. Allen, J. P.

Freeman, James W. & Emeline Mitchell, 5 Dec 1848; Benj. C. Cooke, bm; J. M. Wiggins, wit.

Freeman, John & Massey Hooker, 19 Dec 1820; James A. Freeman, bm; Step. K. Sneed, wit.

Freeman, John & Nancy Mitchell, 9 Jan 1833; Robert Freeman, bm; David Laws, wit.

Freeman, John & Elizabeth Steward, 16 March 1840; Burwell Brandon, bm; T. B. Barnett, wit.

Freeman, John E., son of Hatchwell & Lucy Freeman, & Octavia Hays, daughter of T. P. & Mariah Hays, 23 Sept 1868; m 24 Sept 1868 by B. R. Hester, M. G.

Freeman, Julius & Mary Carter, 20 Dec 1791; Saml. Smith, bm; A. Henderson, wit.

Freeman, Mastain & Penney Weathers, 15 Oct 1816; Pascal Johnson, bm; Wm. Thomasson, wit.

Freeman, Oliver & Agness Mitchel, 29 Aug 1801; Gideon Freeman Jnr., bm; Phil. Bullock, wit.

Freeman, Richardson & Sarah Beardin, 12 Sept 1789; Beverly Harris, bm; A. Henderson, C. C., wit.

Freeman, Robert & Haley Freeman, 2 Sept 1823; Willis B. Mitchell, bm; Jas. M. Wiggins, wit.

Freeman, Rufus C. & Elizabeth Adams, 10 Nov 1845; Charles H. Weak, bm; J. M. Wiggins, wit.

Freeman, William & Phoebe Ann Baker, 2 Feb 1820; Masten Freeman, bm; Step. K. Sneed, wit.

Freeman, William & Rebecca Mangum, 9 Feb 1848; James Peace, bm.

Freman, Henry T. & Susan A. Moss, m 10 Oct 1867 by W. D. Allen, J. P.

French, Charles C. & Eliza Lewis, 18 March 1842; Thos. S. Jones, bm.

Frost, Benjamin D. & Martha Duty, 4 Dec 1859; John W. Hayes, bm; m 5 Dec 1859 by T. W. Moore.

Fulcher, George G. & Susan A. Clarke, 9 Oct 1856; William Dickerson, bm; m 9 Oct 1856 by Lewis H. Kittle, J. P.

Fulford, Benjamin & Frances Furgerson, 24 Feb 1836; Edwd. Burton, bm; Benja. Kittrell, wit.

Fuller, Archabald T. & Mary M. Pittard, 6 May 1823; Sol. Mangum, bm; Jas. M. Wiggins, wit.

Fuller, Arthur & Selah Fuller, 15 Jan 1782; Isom Fuller, bm; Bennet Searcy, wit.

GRANVILLE MARRIAGES 1753-1868

Fuller, Arthur & Mary Hendley, 22 April 1799; Henry Hendly, bm; Step. Sneed, wit.

Fuller, Arthur & Betsey Fuller, 7 Nov 1812; Daniel Fuller, bm; W. M. Sneed, wit.

Fuller, Arthur & Martha West, 13 Sept 1863; W. D. Fuller, bm; A. Landis, wit; m 13 Sept 1863 by W. D. Allen, J. P.

Fuller, Benjamin & Polley York, 18 July 1787; Richd. Thomasson, bm; B. Searcy, wit.

Fuller, Brittain & Mary Ward, 20 Dec 1786; Wiley Kittral, bm; H--- Ligon, wit.

Fuller, Crofford & Elisabeth Cavennah, 9 Jan 1798; Bryan Cavenah, bm; Step. Sneed, wit.

Fuller, Daniel & Martha McGehe, 9 Feb 1802; Stephen Garrett, bm; P. Bullock, wit.

Fuller, David & Martha Cole, 10 Oct 1828; Stephen Cook, bm; David Laws, wit.

Fuller, David & Mary A. Hendley, m 5 Sept 1861 by W. D. Allen, J. P.

Fuller, David W. & Virginia C. Grissom, 10 June 1865; Joseph Fuller, bm.

Fuller, Demcy & Nancey Harris, 27 June 1797; Samuel Bailey, bm; Richard Taylor, wit.

Fuller, Dempsey H. & Sarah Ward, 24 Sept 1835; William _____, bm; H. W. Peace, wit.

Fuller, Elijah & Mildred Powel, 18 Oct 1806; (groom signed as Joseph Fuller); George Harris, bm; Thos. D. Burch, wit.

Fuller, Elijah & Nancy M. Adcock, 7 Sept 1841; John E. Peace, bm; J. M. Wiggins, wit.

Fuller, Ezekiel & Fanny Moody, 22 Sept 1762; Henry Fuller, John Bowie, bm; Anne Spivey, wit.

Fuller, Ezekiel & Sarah Martin, 2 Sept 1803; Green Merritt, bm; Jun. Sneed, wit.

Fuller, Green & Nancy Heflin, 6 Dec 1816; Joseph Bradford, bm; R. N. Herndon, wit.

Fuller, Hampton & Unity May, 14 Dec 1836; William May, bm; J. M. Wiggins, wit.

Fuller, Harris & Martha Williams, 5 Sept 1822; Robert Weathers, bm; S. Sneed, wit.

Fuller, Henry, the younger, & Mary Earl, 5 Feb 1768; Joseph McDaniel, bm; Saml. Benton, C. C., wit.

Fuller, Isaiah R. & Rebecca W. Hicks, 30 May 1864; A. Landis, bm; m 31 May 1864 by M. H. Vaughan, Rector of St. Stephen's Parish.

Fuller, Isham & Sally Harris, 4 Nov 1834; Peleg Bailey, bm; Tho. H. Willie, wit.

GRANVILLE MARRIAGES 1753-1868

Fuller, Isiah R. & Mary H. Clark, 14 April 1842; Sam. Clark, bm; Jas. M. Wiggins, wit.

Fuller, James & Sally Carol(?), 20 July 1830; Thomas Leavister, bm; David Laws, wit.

Fuller, James & Martha A. Taylor, 29 Aug 1833; Charles Floyd, bm; Benja. Kittrell, wit.

Fuller, James W. & Nancy W. Tharington, 14 Jan 1852; Samuel H. Tharington, bm; m ____ by Jesse K. Cole, M. G.

Fuller, John & Rebecca G. Munn, 26 Jan 1830; Charles Floyd, bm; David Laws, wit.

Fuller, John & Nancy Ussery, 10 July 1833; W. S. McClanahan, bm; David Laws, wit.

Fuller, John & Ellen Bass, 4 March 1851; Allen Bridges, bm; A. Landis, wit.

Fuller, John A. & Mary A. R. Creth, 17 Dec 1850; E. H. Overton, bm.

Fuller, John W. & Indianah H. Bragg, 21 Jan 1862; John E. Freeman, bm; m 23 Jan 1862 by W. D. Allen, J. P.

Fuller, Jonathan & Celia Carden, 19 April 1790; James Cardin, bm; H. Potter, wit.

Fuller, Jonathan & Elizabeth J. May, 28 Aug 1861; R. C. Qualls, bm; A. Landis, wit; m 28 Aug 1861 by H. B. Bridges.

Fuller, Jones & Sarah Bradford, 13 May 1786; Reuben Searcy, bm; Bennet Searcy, wit.

Fuller, Jones S. & Nancey Mann, 21 Dec 1799; Samuel Fuller, bm; ____ Sneed, wit.

Fuller, Joseph & Nancy Hooker, 6 Oct 1818; James Hefflin, bm.

Fuller, Joseph & Isabella R. Hayes, 28 July 1860; Henry A. Fuller, bm; A. Landis, wit; m 1 Aug 1860 by W. D. Allen, J. P.

Fuller, Joseph L. & Mary Hillman Adcock, 3 Jan 1857; Rufus C. Freeman, bm; m 21 Jan 1857 by Geo. J. Rowland, J. P.

Fuller, Milton B. & Anna Nuttall, 8 Feb 1865; Jas. P. Hunt, bm; m 8 Feb 1865 by E. H. Overton, J. P.

Fuller, Robert & Milley Parham, 18 March 1824; John Moore, bm; S. K. Sneed, wit.

Fuller, Robert & Eliza Parham, 30 July 1831; George P. Thomasson, bm; David Laws, wit.

Fuller, Robert & Emila Clark, 8 Jan 1834; James Cheatham Jr., bm; D. T. Paschall, wit.

Fuller, Samuel & Nancy Bryant, 24 Feb 1830; Presly Floyd, bm; David Lawson, wit.

Fuller, Washington, colored, son of Tom Burns, & Senia Southerland, m 10 Aug 1867 by Lewis H. Kittle, J. P.

GRANVILLE MARRIAGES 1753-1868

Fuller, Wesley & Charity Adcock, 11 Sept 1846; A. T. Jinkins(?), bm; Jas. M. Wiggins, wit.

Fuller, William & Mary F. Taylor, 7 Dec 1835; Jas. E. Allen, bm; Benja. Kittrell, wit.

Fuller, William & Mary Jane Parham, 14 Jan 1851; Wm. Clark, bm; A. Landis, wit.

Fuller, William S. & Mary Stone, 2 Nov 1858; J. R. Fuller, bm; m 10 Nov 1858 by L. K. Willie, M. G.

Fuller, Young & Elinor Rogers, 7 Aug 1792; Benjamin Bradford, bm; W. Norwood, wit.

Fullerton, John & Laura N. Norman, 9 May 1854; H. C. Herndon, bm; m 11 May 1854 by Thos. U. Faucette, Preacher of the Gospel.

Fuqua, Benjamin L. & Mary Ann R. Watson, 15 Dec 1829; Ro. B. Warrick, wit.

Gaines, Francis & Anne Collier, 21 Sept 1798; John Brodie, bm; Elijah Mitchel, wit.

Gales, Mason, of color, son of Ned Gales & Caty Gates, & Susan Amis, of color, daughter of Sam Amis, m 25 March 1868 by Saml. P. Hunt, J. P.

Garland, Cornelias S. & Martha Robey, 13 Oct 1850; John E. Montague, bm; L. B. Stone, J. P., wit.

Garner, John C. & Rebeca Susan Overbey, 24 Nov 1852; John E. Montague, bm; L. B. Stone, J. P., wit; m 25 Nov 1852 by John E. Montague, M. G.

Garland, Thos., colored, son of Ned Garland, & Martha Burwell, formerly M. Nuttall, 2 Nov 1867; m 7 Nov 1867 by Wyatt Walker, M. G.

Garner, John & Susannah Hall, 7 May 1794; Thomas Culverhouse, bm; Ro. Harris, wit.

Garner, John T. & Ann E. Garner, 30 Jan 1866; F. J. Bailey, bm; m 1 Feb 1866 by W. D. Allen, J. P.

Garner, Robert & Martha Williams, 4 Nov 1841; John Byrd, bm; W. H. Whitfield, wit.

Garner, Thomas & Margaret Lawrence, 6 Aug 1828; John Beck, bm; David Laws, wit.

Garratt, William & Mary Walker, 5 April 1801; Robert Potter, bm; Philip Bullock, wit.

Garrett, Jesse & Elisabeth Dickerson, 13 Dec 1782; John Dickerson Jr., bm; Reuben Searcy, wit.

Garrett, Stephen & Ann McGehee, 19 March 1781; Joseph McGehee, bm; Philip Vass, wit.

Garrett, Willis Lewis & Susan M. Hutson, 2 Sept 1857; David A. Hunt, bm.

Garrot, William & Fanney York, 18 Jan 1791; Benjamin Fuller, bm; A. Henderson, wit.

GRANVILLE MARRIAGES 1753-1868

Garrott, Stephen & Elizabeth P------, ___ Aug 1815; W. M. Sneed, wit.

Garrott, Wm. G. & Mary J. Edwards, 20 Nov 1866; m 22 Nov 1866 by Pro. A. Jones, J. P.

Gatch, Thos. A., son of Benj. W. & Martha R. Gatch, & Amanda J. Hicks, daughter of Thomas C. & Susan T. Hicks, 22 Dec 1868; m 23 Dec 1868 by M. H. Vaughan, Rector of St. Stephen's Church.

Gatland, Noah, colored, & Bettie Kittle, 14 Aug 1867; m 14 Aug 1867 by Lewis H. Kittle.

Gay, Abner W. & Ann H. Crews, 14 June 1848; Jno. R. Herndon, bm.

Gayden, George & Lois Collins, 4 Dec 1782; Edward Collins, bm; Reuben Searcy, wit.

Geer, David & Susannah Matterson, 16 Jan 1770; Peyton Clements, Peyton Matterson, bm; Jesse Benton, wit.

Gelipee (Gilespie?), Robert & Elizabeth Hunter, 12 July 1779; David Mason, wit; (only expression of intent from Elizabeth Hunter).

George, Beverly & Jane Sigue(?), 23 May 1847; Jas. R. Duty, bm; Jabez Duty, wit.

George, Ephraim & Nancey Bruce, 10 Sept 1806; Joseph White, bm; W. M. Sneed, wit.

George, Forney & Mary J. Wortham, 30 Nov 1858; Wm. D. E. Vane(?), bm; m 30 Nov 1858 by G. W. Ferrill.

Gholson, Benjamin & Sarah Andrews, 15 Oct 1810; Charles A. Hill, bm; W. N. Sneed, wit.

Gibbs, Richard & Elizabeth Brome, 21 Dec 1832; Henry Rowland, bm; Albert Sneed, wit.

Gilbreath, James H. & Amy J. Hunt, 13 May 1864; W. C. Kennett, bm; m 18 May 1864 by T. H. Pegram, Elder.

Gilchrist, James & Rebeccah Eastwood, ___ April 1792; John Eastwood, bm; Step. Sneed, wit.

Gill, Gideon G. & Sallie A. Johnson, 22 Dec 1860; W. P. White, bm; m 24 Dec 1860 by Wm. N. Bragg, Minister.

Gill, Henry F. & Isabella F. Currin, 13 March 1848; John H. Owen, bm; Jas. M. Wiggins, wit.

Gill, Hilliard & Jane Bracy, 3 Sept 1865; Ransom Gill, bm.

Gill, James O. & Mary E. Wortham, 3 Nov 1846; Wm. B. Crews, bm.

Gill, James S. & Elvira H. Blanks, 19 Feb 1856; S. O. Pardue, bm.

Gill, John N. & Elizabeth J. Taylor, 26 Nov 1839; Jas. M. Wiggins, bm.

Gill, John R. & Mary Jane Morgan, 12 Oct 1859; Jas. W. H. Edmonds, bm; Jas. R. Duty, wit.

GRANVILLE MARRIAGES 1753-1868

Gill, Levi, of color, son of Pleasant Gill & Lutitia Gill, & Queen Allen, daughter of Malinda Allen, 30 Dec 1867; m by B. D. Howard, J. P.

Gill, Peter & Sarah E. E. Jones, 20 May 1830; D. A. Paschall, bm; David Laws, wit.

Gill, Robert & Emily Crews, 21 Nov 1830; Part. F. Stone, bm; David Laws, wit.

Gill, Robert & Rebecca A. Jones, 30 Nov 1841; Jas. M. Wiggins, wit.

Gill, William & Emmit Washington, 8 April 1841; Samuel Bowls, Macon Bledsoe, bm; J. M. Wiggins, wit.

Gill, William A. & Salley Hicks, 7 March 1816; James Nuttall, bm; Wm. Tomasson, wit.

Gillam, Harbert & Mary Nevels, 22 Dec 1786; Joshua Gillam, bm; Bennet Searcy, wit.

Gillam, Jordan & Mary McLemore, 16 Oct 1779; Harris Gillam bm; John Heflin Cooper, wit.

Gillespie, Robert & Elisabeth Hunter, 8 July 1779; David Mason, bm; Reuben Searcy, wit.

Gilliam, Charles & Jemima Harris, 27(?) July 1762; Robert Gillam, bm; Jno. Bowie, wit.

Gilliam, Edmund & Polly Jefferson, 15 March 1817; John Jeffers, bm; R. N. Herndon, wit.

Gilliam, Henry & Frances Ridley, freed people, 30 Sept 1865; Jo. Walsh, bm; m 1 Oct 1865 by Maurice H. Vaughan, Rector of St. Stephen's Church.

Gilliam, John & Priscilla Hart, 8 July 1783; Jariot Loyed, bm; Reuben Searcy, wit.

Gilliam, John & Leathy Barker (freed people), 2 April 1866; m 7 April 1866 by Maurice H. Vaughan, Rector of St. Stephen's.

Gilliam, Lesley & Elisabeth Ballard, 8 June 1801; William H. Lanier, bm; Step. Sneed, wit.

Gilliam, Leslie & Frances Sandford, 16 April 1845; Charles H. Weathers, bm.

Gilliam, Peter, son of Daniel McClanhan & Ann Gilliam, & Clora Edwards, daughter of William & Dicey Palmer, 10 Dec 1868; m 10 Dec 1868 by L, K. Willie, M. G.

Gilliam, William & Fanny Hooker, 11 Aug 1818; James Cooke, bm; Step. K. Sneed, wit.

Gilmore, Jackson C. & Annie E. Dalby, 26 Oct 1866; Saml. A. Williams, bm.

Gilmore, John J. & Phebe Chandler, 21 April 1840; B. Burns, bm; Jas. M. Wiggins, wit.

Glascock, E. B. & Sylvania Glasscock, 25 Aug 1864; Jos. P. Tuck, bm; m 25 Aug 1864 by L. B. Stone, J. P.

GRANVILLE MARRIAGES 1753-1868

Glasgow, Allen & Chamsy Fuller, 13 Nov 1850; Jas. M. Wiggins, bm.

Glasgow, John & Peggy McClenachan, 4 Jan 1816; George Floyd, bm; W. M. Sneed, wit.

Glasgow, John & Isabella Taylor, 16 Feb 1828; James Fuller, bm; Step. K. Sneed, wit.

Glasgow, John & Jane Mitchell, 28 June 1858; John B. Woodleff, bm; A. Landis, wit; m 29 June 1858 by William B. Mann, J. P.

Glasgow, Martin & Harriet Mitchell, 15 April 1843; Jno. Pruitt, bm; Jas. M. Wiggins, wit.

Glasgow, Martin & Priscilla Figg, 5 Aug 1857; David Stover, James P. Hunt, bm; m 20 Aug 1857 by Wm. B. Mann, J. P.

Glass, William & Amey Ragland, 21 Nov 1774; Ambrose Barker, bm; Wm. Reardon, wit.

Glasscock, Anderson & Lenny Lisemore, 10 Aug 1815; Benjamin Wood, bm; H. Young, wit.

Glasscock, James & Locky Ann Neel, 3 Sept 1862; C. A. Yancy, bm; m 3 Sept 1862 by L. B. Stone.

Glasscock, Nathaniel S., son of Sandford & Sarah Glasscock, & Sarah F. Shotwell, daughter of Alfred & Julia Shotwell, m 13 Feb 1868 by W. Overby, J. P.

Glasscock, R. B. & Sarah Elliott, 25 Dec 1860; E. B. Glasscock, bm; m 25 Dec 1860 by L. B. Stone, J. P.

Glasscock, Thomas & Jane Lunsford, 20 Nov 1850; Ceb Newton, bm; L. B. Stone, J. P., wit.

Glasscock, Thomas & Caroline McCartey, 18 Dec 1856; Isham H. Warren, bm; m 18 Dec 1856 by L. B. Stone, J. P.

Glasscock, Thomas G., son of Thomas & Elizabeth Glasscock, & Mrs. Rebecca Ann Lowery, daughter of Wm. & Elizabeth Bowen, 6 Feb 1868; m 6 Feb 1868 by L. B. Stone, J. P.

Glasscow, Sanford & Sarah Tuck, 16 May 1833; Reuben H. Newton, bm; Willie Royster, J. P., wit.

Glaze, Samuel & Mary Knight, 30 Oct 1782; Thos. Pool, bm; Reuben Searcy, wit.

Glen(?), Etham C. & Mary S. Mayes, m 15 Feb 1868 by John Tillett.

Glendenning, William & Salley Lile, 20 Oct 1796; Step. Sneed, bm; Wm. Robards, wit.

Glenn, George & Pheriba Brinkley, 10 Feb 1836; William Weaver, bm; Benja. Kittrell, wit.

Glenn, Patrick & Francis Taylor, 26 Nov 1865; Geo. W. Landis, bm.

Glenn, Robert J. & Elizabeth C. Marshall, 29 Oct 1829; Geo. Thomasson, bm; Step. K. Sneed, wit.

Glidewell, Barnnister & Nancy Hayley, 4 Sept 1819; Lemuel Keith, bm; Step. K. Sneed, wit.

GRANVILLE MARRIAGES 1753-1868

Glimph, George & Milly Wheeler, 6 Aug 1799; Abraham Landers, bm; W. M. Sneed, wit.

Glover, Daniel & Mary Ann Mitchel, 18 Jan 1794; Joshua Bell, bm; W. Norwood, D. C., wit.

Glover, Daniel R. & Parthenia H. Heggie, 22 Feb 1839; Richard H. Hunt, bm.

Glover, David K. & Julia E. Kittrell, 9 Nov 1843; Jas. W. Heggie, bm; Wm. H. Whitfield, wit.

Glover, Jas. & Mary Chevers (fee colored), 22 Feb 1867; m 22 Feb 1867 by Lewis H. Kittle, J. P.

Glover, Joab & Sarrah Gomah, 13 Jan 1784; Charles Long, bm; Bennet Searcy, wit.

Glover, Lowry & Margaret McMillian, spinster, 3 Nov 1761; Robert Robinson, bm; Jno. Bowie, wit.

Glover, Ransom & Mary Barnett, 21 Nov 1792; Daniel Glover, bm; W. Norwood, wit.

Glover, Wallace & Phoebe Davis, 26 May 1866; m 3 June 1866 by J. J. Speed, J. P.

Glover, William & Martha Attwood, 17 March 1778; Reuben Searcy, bm; consent from Jos. Glover, father of William & from Elisabeth Attwood, mother of Martha G. Attwood, 14 March 1778.

Glover, William B. & Martha Lewis, 23 Oct 1829; Drury Satterwhite, bm; Step. K. Sneed, wit.

Gober, George & Nancey Gober, 5 Oct 1796; W. Moore, bm.

Gober, John & Margeret Suit, 12 Dec 1792; William Gober, bm; Step. Sneed, wit.

Gober, Lewis & Mary Gober, 8 Sept 1801; Evan Ragland, bm; A. Sneed, wit.

Gober, William & Frances Scurry, 7 Oct 1795; John Gober, bm; S. Worthington, wit.

Godfrey, James & Jomima Weaver, 9 Sept 1777; William Fleming, bm.

Godsey, Henry & Mary E. Freeman, 11 July 1844; Robt. H. Read, bm; Wm. T. Hargrove, wit.

Godwin, James Verling & Mary Scott, 30 Nov 1791; Theodorick Scott, bm; W. Norwood, wit.

Going, Edward & Rebecca Anderson, 31 Oct 1807; George Anderson, bm; W. M. Sneed, wit.

Gold, John & Sarah Collins, 16 Nov 181_; Samuel Tarry Jr., bm; Jas. Wiggins, wit.

Gold, Pleasant & Sarah Wilson, 19 Nov 1800; Robert Wilson, bm; W. M. Sneed, wit.

Gomer, William & Amey Floyd, 19 April 1784; John Long, bm; John Morris, wit.

GRANVILLE MARRIAGES 1753-1868

Gooch, Alonzo & Susan Jones, 4 April 1855; Wm. H. Whitaker, bm; m 8 April 1855 by Jno. Nance, J. P.

Gooch, Amos & Martha Knight, 1 March 1824; Thomas House, bm; Wm. H. Owen, wit.

Gooch, Calvin & Mary Latta, 22 Dec 1865; Isaac Latta, bm; A. Landis, wit; m 22 Dec 1865 by Wm. B. Hicks, J. P.

Gooch, Daniel & Nancey Sneed, 6 Oct 1789; William Gooch, bm; Henry Potter, wit.

Gooch, Daniel C. & Mary Tillerson, 12 Sept 1832.

Gooch, Daniel T. & Nancy Hester, 20 Dec 1831; Lewis Bennett, bm; David Laws, wit.

Gooch, Dudley & Mary F. Jones, 30 Dec 1850; L. A. Paschall, bm; Jas. M. Wiggins, wit.

Gooch, Dudly S. & Mary J. Bennett, 26 Jan 1836; W. S. McClanahan, bm; Benja. Kittrell, wit.

Gooch, Emmett & Fanny Roberts, 7 Sept 1840; Wm. Jones, bm; Jas. M. Wiggins, wit.

Gooch, George & Matilda Herndon, 3 Jan 1867; m 4 Jan 1867 by Benjamin F. Jenkins.

Gooch, George, son of Emmit & Frances Gooch, & Susan A. Bullock, daughter of George Bullock decd., & Malinda Bullock, 9 Aug 1867; m 11 Aug 1867 by Francis J. Tilley, J. P.

Gooch, Gideon & Nancy Leavel, 18 Oct 1796(?); James Terry, bm; Wm. Robards, wit.

Gooch, Henry, of color, son of Currell Downey & Patsy Gooch, & Sinia Cooper, daughter of Bob Marable & Clarias Cooper, 3 Feb 1868; m 8 Feb 1868 by William S. Hester.

Gooch, Huel R. & Sallie J. Walker, 17 Jan 1860; Robert T. Sten, bm; m 19 Jan 1860.

Gooch, James & Sally W. Harris, 9 Oct 1854; W. H. Rowland, bm; m 17 Oct 1854 by R. J. Devin.

Gooch, James T. & Susannah Chambless, 6 July 1816; Jeremiah Bullock, bm; W. M. Sneed, wit.

Gooch, Jerry & Polly Ann Cooper, 25 Dec 1866; Wesley Cooper, bm; m 25 Dec 1866 by L. A. Paschall, J. P.

Gooch, Joel & Lucinda Draper, 9 July 1841; Jas. OBriant, bm; Jas. M. Wiggins, wit.

Gooch, John & Sarah Terry, 8 March 1790; Rowland Terry, bm; Henry Potter, wit.

Gooch, John & Elisabeth Gooch, 30 Jan 1817; John Downey, bm.

Gooch, Johnson & Harriet Sherrin, 27 July 1844; L. Gilliam, bm; J. M. Wiggins, wit.

Gooch, Joseph & Sarah Hawkins, 12 Aug 1806; Rowland Gooch, bm; W. M. Sneed, wit.

GRANVILLE MARRIAGES 1753-1868

Gooch, Joseph & Louisa M. Philpott, 2 Jan 1837; Oxford Moize, bm; J. M. Wiggins, wit.

Gooch, Littleton & Lucy Waller, 20 Sept 1826; Tarlton Johnson, bm; Wm. H. Owen, wit.

Gooch, Paul & Margaret Tilley, 17 Dec 1844; M. P. Roberts, bm.

Gooch, Pomphret & Rebecah Williams, 29 Sept 1800; William Goss, bm; _____ Bullock, wit.

Gooch, Radford & Martha Cole, 31 July 1861; m 1 Aug 1861 by Wm. H. Jones, J. P.

Gooch, Redford & Elizabeth Wheeler, 11 May 1816; Robert F. P. Jones, bm; Rhodes N. Herndon, wit.

Gooch, Robert & Agnes Bullock, 22 Dec 1865; C. Winston, bm; m 23 Dec 1865 by E. Dalby, J. P.

Gooch, Rowland & Mary Walker, 2 Nov 1790; William Jones Jr., bm; H. Potter, wit.

Gooch, Rowling & Hannah Cozort, 27 Dec 1817; John Cozort, bm; A. Henderson, wit.

Gooch, Saml. J., son of Dudley S. & Polly Gooch, & Sallie F. Thomas, daughter of William G. & Susan Thomas, 24 Dec 1868; m 24 Dec 1868 by W. Webb, J. P.

Gooch, Sproggin & Mrs. Jane R. Roberts, 23 Oct 1860; J. S. Meadows, bm; m 24 Nov 1860 by B. B. Hester.

Gooch, Thomas & Jamima Hester, 22 Jan 1803; Wm. Sample, bm; Green Merritt, wit.

Gooch, W. M., son of D. T. & Nancy Gooch, & C. A. Cheatham, daughter of Isaac & Cynthia R. Cheatham, m 2 Dec 1868 by W. P. J. Harris, M. G.

Gooch, William & Elizabeth Gooch, 16 March 1790; Daniel Gooch, bm; Henry Potter, wit.

Gooch, William & Phanney Bailey, 18 Nov 1796; James Sampel, bm; Step. Sneed, wit.

Gooch, William & Sarah Gooch, 4 Oct 1808; Peyton Wood, bm; W. M. Sneed, wit.

Gooch, William & Lucy Ann Mitchel, 5 Aug 1851; Joh. C. R. Howard, bm.

Gooch, Wm. & Lucy Ann Mitchell, m 7 Aug 1851 by James King.

Gooch, William Redford & Martha Stem, 23 Sept 1829; Thomas Goss(?) bm; Step. K. Sneed, wit.

Gooch, Wm. S. & Ailsey Jones, 6 Sept 1822; Joshua Bullock, bm; Jas. M. Wiggins, wit.

Gooch, William T. & Caroline F. Waller, 18 Jan 1858; R. L. Heflin, bm.

Good, Daniel C. & Mary Ullerson(?), 12 Sept 1832; Haley Cole, bm; William Royster, J. P.

GRANVILLE MARRIAGES 1753-1868

Good, J. H. & Louisa Hite, 31 March 1864; George H. Wells, bm; m 31 March 1864 by L. B. Stone, J. P.

Good, William & Elizabeth J. Gold, 9 Jan 1862; Marshal Overby, bm; m 9 Jan 1862 by L. B. Stone, J. P.

Good, William C. & Mary Ullerson(?), 12 Sept 1832; Haley Cole, bm; William Royster, J. P.

Goode, Edward B. & Lucy Watkins, 16 Jan 1865; Saml. L. Graham, bm.

Goode, Hillery & Sallie Watkins, freed people, 1 Sept 1865; Richd. Scott, bm; A. Landis, wit.

Goodloe, James K. & Mary R. Jones, 20 Jan 1811; Isaac Houze, bm; Jun. Sneed, wit.

Goodrum, Sterling & Polley Fraizer, 27 Oct 1804; Stephen Hester, bm; Step. Sneed, wit.

Goodwin, Beal & Morning Hutson, 26 Nov 1827; Caleb A. Hudson, bm.

Goodwin, Samuel & Jusiah Tatom, 29 March 1773; Robt. Bell, bm; William Rardon, wit.

Goodwyn, Stephen A. & Sallie R. Hicks, 28 May 1861; M. V. Lanier, bm; m 12 June 1861 by Jacob Doll, Pastor of Presby. Ch., Yanceyville, N. C.

Gordan, James H. & Nancy Twisdale, 22 Dec 1830; Archabald Gordon, bm; S. K. Sneed, wit.

Gorden, Allen & Sarah Duty, 9 Sept 1821; William H. Strum, bm; S. K. Sneed, wit.

Gorden, Allen & Susan Shanks, 16 Dec 1828; Ira E. Arnold, bm; David Laws, wit.

Gorden, Archibald & Rhoda Landrum, 4 Nov 1817; William Gorden, bm; W. Sneed, wit.

Gorden, James R. & Sabilla Wilson, 4 Sept 1845; Stephen Satterwhite, bm; J. M. Wiggins, wit.

Gorden, John & Polly Hester, 2 Nov 1813; Thomas Hunt, bm; W. M. Sneed, wit.

Gorden, Robert & Elizabeth Howell, 21 Oct 1811; Thomas Taylor, bm; W. M. Sneed, wit.

Gorden, Samuel & Loney Wilkerson, 3 Aug 1866; m 13 Aug 1866 by R. J. Devin.

Gorden, William H. & Sally Jane Dean, 20 Nov 1844; Wm. W. Dean, bm; Jas. M. Wiggins, wit.

Gorden, Willis & Ann Twisdal, 23 Dec 1818; John Howel, bm; Z. Herndon, wit.

Gorden, Willis L. & <u>C</u>atarine Warren, 19 Feb 1846; John Paulk, bm.

Gorden, Willis & Valleria Chandler, 5 Dec 1849; ____ Duncan, bm; A. Landis, wit.

GRANVILLE MARRIAGES 1753-1868

Gordng, Aarcher & Sarah Frashier, 18 Jan 1787; George Gresham, bm; Robt. Searcy, wit.

Gordon, Calvin & Rowan Frazier, 5 Oct 1842; Lewis Parham, bm; Wm. H. Whitfield, wit.

Gordon, Henry & Lucy Carson, 7 March 1865; H. H. Rowland, bm; m 9 March 1865 by H. H. Rowland.

Gordon, John & Nancey Hack, 23 July 1771; Robert Reid, bm; Jesse Benton, wit.

Gordon, William & Nancy Hester, 25 Feb 1818; William B. Hare, bm

Gordun, Howell & Patsey Brummett, 28 July 1836; William Hester, bm.

Goss, Elijah & Nancy Minor, 4 May 1812; William Forsythe, bm; A. H. Sneed, wit.

Goss, Elijah & Eliza Jones, 17 Sept 1868; m 17 Sept 1868 by G. W. Ferrill, Minister.

Goss, John & Rehab Crenshaw, 8 Nov 1785; R. Crenshaw, bm; Bennet Searcy, wit.

Goss, John & Rebecca Washington, 27 Dec 1853; Robert Goss, bm; m 28 Dec 1853 by Jno. Nance, J. P.

Goss, Robert & Malinda Gooch, 9 Sept 1853; Benjamin Clark, bm; m 10 Sept 1853 by Jno. Nance, J. P.

Goss, Rowland & Barbary Waller, 19 Nov 1829; Allen Waller, bm; David Laws, wit.

Goss, Rowland Jr. & Frances Cash, 15 July 1865; John Forsythe, bm.

Goss, Sherman & Lively Goss, 26 Dec 1825; Thomas Goss, bm; A. M. Henderson, wit.

Goss, Sherman & Rebecca Goss, 10 Aug 1832; John Williams, bm; Benja. Kittrell, wit.

Goss, William & Sarah Gooch, 29 Sept 1800; Pumphrett Gooch, bm; Step. Snood, wit.

Goss, William & Martha Fleming, 22 May 1855; Robert Goss, bm; m 12 Dec 1855 by T. B. Lyon, J. P.

Goss, William & Rebecca Green, 17 Aug 1866; m 24 Aug 1866 by D. Tilley, J. P.

Graham, Jordan & Eliza Ann Gregory, freed people, 24 Aug 1866; m 24 Aug 1866 by Robt. L. Hunt, J. P.

Grandy, Miles, of color, son of Isaac Bell & Sarah Grandy, & Lizzie Ann Miller, daughter of Sally Miller, 19 Nov 1867; m 23 Nov 1867 by Henry Cruse, Minister of the Gospel.

Grans, Henry & Eliza J. Toter, 3 Dec 1835; James Howel, bm; Benja. Kittrell, wit.

Graves, David & Nancy Hunt, 19 Dec 1796; Thos. Hunt, bm; Wm. Robards, wit.

GRANVILLE MARRIAGES 1753-1868

Graves, Henry & Nancy Daniel, 2 Dec 1789; Joseph Smith, bm.

Graves, John & Penolepee _____, 17 Sept 1796; Edmund Hunt, bm; Wm. Robards, wit.

Graves, Nathaniel & Frances Montague, 20 Aug 1798; William Montague, bm; James Sneed, wit.

Graves, Ralph & Elisabeth Hart, 20 July 1795; Robert Elliott, bm; Step. Sneed, wit.

Graves, Sterling & Nancy Amis, 26 Dec 1817; James Pittard, bm.

Graves, William & Polley Hester, 21 Dec 1798; Graves Hester, bm; Step. Sneed, wit.

Graves, William C. & Elizabeth Amis, 10 Sept 1811; Joseph Amis, bm; Oba. Farrar, wit.

Gray, Henry & Virginia F. Speed, 2 Sept 1856; Tho. Speed, bm; m 3 Sept 1856 by Robt. O. Burton, Minister of the Gospel.

Gray, Molton & Kattey Snelling, 6 April 1786; Hugh Snelling, bm; A. Barker, wit.

Gray, Thompson & Lucey Snelling, 2 March 1813; Charles Blackley, bm; W. M. Sneed, wit.

Green, Asa & Pricilla Wheeler, 9 April 1803; Abner Jones, bm; Green Merritt, wit.

Green, Clayborne & Amy F. Beasley, 18 May 1867; m 19 May 1867 by R. B. Lyon; (colored).

Green, Daniel & Mary Umphstead, 17 Feb 1787; Job Green, bm; Bennet Searcy, wit.

Green, Elijah & Elisabeth Culverhouse, 10 Aug 1792; Nicholas Green, bm; D. Norwood, wit.

Green, Evan & Anne Green, 12 Nov 1806; Lain Moore, bm; W. M. Sneed, wit.

Green, Ezekiel & Chancy Perkerson, (no date, during admn. of Gov. Saml. Ash); John McLemore, bm; Step. Sneed, wit.

Green, Franklin, colored, son of Frank & Anna Green, & Lucy Harris, daughter of Henry & Matilda Harris, 27 Nov 1868; m 26 Dec 1868 by James Puryear, J. P.

Green, Greenbury & Lotty Wheeler, 17 June 1809; Nicholas Green, bm; W. M. Sneed, wit.

Green, Henry & Ann Moore, 27 April 1867; H. C. McCadden, bm; Robt. L. Heflin, wit; m 27 April 1867 by Robt. L. Heflin; (colored people).

Green, Henry, colored, & Bettie Harris, m 20 Sept 1868 by G. W. Ferrill, Minister.

Green, James W. & Rebecca Morris, 11 Jan 1804; William Solomon, bm; Wm. Walker, wit.

Green, John & Mimy Mangrum, 3 Dec 1799; John Kennedy, bm; Roberg Harris, Willm. Henry Clay, wit.

GRANVILLE MARRIAGES 1753-1868

Green, John & Betsey Butler, 1 Jan 1807; Jno. Hawkins, bm; Jun. Sneed, wit.

Green, John & Elizabeth Griggs, 17 Jan 1807; Nicholas Green, bm; W. M. Sneed, wit.

Green, John & Sandal Lile, 19 Jan 1829; Low Jackson, bm; David Laws, wit.

Green, Jno. B. & Aramanta P. Hester, 14 Dec 1848; Jas. M. Wiggins, bm.

Green, Joseph & Mary Anderson, 21 Nov 1835; Jas. C. Cooper, bm; Benja. Kittrell, wit.

Green, Joseph & Harriet Perry, 23 Feb 1867; m 23 Feb 1867 by W. H. P. Jenkins, J. P.; M. G. May, bm.

Green, Lewis & Nancy Thorp, 6 Oct 1820; Jno. Bullock, bm; Step. K. Sneed, wit.

Green, Nathan & Mary Field, 23 July 1813; James Daniel, bm; Richd. Sneed, wit.

Green, Nicholas & Hannah Arnold, 23 Jan 1790; William Jones, bm; A. Henderson, C. C., wit.

Green, Nicholas F. & Nancy Jones, m 2 Sept 1868 by G. W. Ferrill, Minister.

Green, Obed & Elisabeth Green, 25 Aug 1774; Arthur Lord, bm; William R----, wit.

Green, Richd. & Julea J. Sneed, 27 Aug 1835; R. H. Kingsbury, bm; Benja. Kittrell, wit.

Green, Rufus, of color, son of Osborn & Catharine Green, & Margaret Mitchell, daughter of Ned & Sophia Mitchell, 28 Feb 1868; m 1 March 1868 by W. P. White, J. P.

Green, Simeon, son of Thomas & Susan Green, & Ellen Walker, daughter of William Walker, m 22 March 1868 by F. J. Tilley, J. P.

Green, Soloman, of color, son of Jacob & Lilia Green, & Penny Harris, daughter of Thomas & Hannah Harris, m 23 Dec 1867 by W. H. P. Jenkins, J. P.

Green, Thomas & Susan Freeman, 5 March 1830; William F----, bm; David Laws, wit.

Green, Thornbury & Celia Jones, 26 Jan 1811; Benjamin Adams, bm; Jun. Sneed, wit.

Green, William & Mary Vandyke, 15 Oct 1798; Jno. Vandyck, bm; Daniel J. Manire, wit.

Green, William & Rachel Haskins, 4 Feb 1812; Samuel Forsythe, bm; W. M. Sneed, wit.

Green, William & Charity Eastwood, 5 Dec 1812; Henry Jones, bm; Stephen K. Sneed, wit.

Green, William & Emily B. Longmire, 2 Dec 1845; G. W. Hunt, bm; Jas. M. Wiggins, wit.

GRANVILLE MARRIAGES 1753-1868

Green, William A. & Desdimonia Allen, 3 Oct 1853; Robert J. Devin, bm; m 6 Oct 1853 by R. J. Devin, V. D. M.

Green, William H. & Lucy M. Currin, 4 Nov 1856; P. A. T. Farabow, bm; m 12 Nov 1856 by Jno. R. Hicks, J. P.

Green, Wm. M. & Sally W. Sneed, 22 Dec 1818; E. D. Sneed, bm; Sam Sneed, wit.

Green, Willis & Rose Christmas, 6 Aug 1866.

Greenway, John E. & Selona Currin, 27 June 1865; Geo. Watkins, bm; A. Landis, wit.

Greenwood, Yancey & Polley Blackwell, 5 March 1806; William Pool, bm; W. M. Sneed, wit.

Gregory, A. V. & Miss L. J. Brodie, 6 Feb 1866; m 13 Feb 1866 by Joseph W. Murphy, Rector of the Church of the Holy Innocents, Henderson.

Gregory, Abraham & Nancy West, 18 Sept 1866; m 29 Dec 1866 by Wm. H. Puryear, Esq.

Gregory, Bedford & Patsy Jones, 1 March 1814; James H. Newton, bm; H. Young, wit.

Gregory, Herbert & Ella A. Thorp, m 2 Oct 1866 by Maurice H. Vaughan, Rector of St. Stephen's Church, Oxford, N. C.

Gregory, James & Mary Montigue, 17 May 1790; Young Montague, bm; H. Potter, wit.

Gregory, James H. & Martha Puryear, 5 Aug 1844; M. D. Royster, bm.

Gregory, John C. & Martha Jane McCargo, 24 Sept 1846; Thomas B. Moseley(?), bm; Jas. M. Wiggins, wit.

Gregory, Johnson & Joanna Graham, freed people, 1 Feb 1867; m 1 Feb 1867 by B. T. Winston, J. P.

Gregory, Kinton, colored, son of George Cragett & Diner Cragett, & Letha Downey, parents unknown, m 28 Dec 1868 by Alexander Satterwhite, J. P.

Gregory, Squire & Martha Knott, 25 Dec 1866; m 25 Dec 1866 by J. E. Pattillo, J. P.

Gregory, T. J. & Lucy O. Bullock, m 5 Jan 1853 by E. Hines.

Gregory, Thos. & Pheby Hawkins, 18 Oct 1787; Gabriel Jones, bm; John Searcy, wit.

Gregory, Thomas J. & Lucy O. Bullock, 1 Jan 1853; T. Brown Venable, bm.

Gregory, William & Jane Lewis, freed people, 26 Aug 1865; J. Waldo, bm; A. Landis, wit.

Grenaway, Alexander & Caroline West, 9 Jan 1854; John E. Grenaway, bm; m 11 Jan 1854 by Lewis Amis, J. P.

Grenaway, Dennis & Mary Fuller, 7 July 1837; H. Williams, bm; J. M. Wiggins, wit.

GRANVILLE MARRIAGES 1753-1868

Grenaway, Henry G. & Raney Brinkley, 18 June 1823; Martin Anderson, bm; Step. K. Sneed, wit.

Grenaway, Samuel & Mary Jane Parrot, 30 Sept 1847; W. T. Hunt, bm; Jas. M. Wiggins, wit.

Grenaway, Thomas & Sarah Craft, 4 Aug 1798; James Cocke, bm; James Sneed, wit.

Gresham, Alexander & Francis Wiggins, 13 Oct 1800; John Gresham, bm; Step. Sneed, wit.

Gresham, Benjamin & Lucinda Davis, 1 Oct 1818; Wheeler Gresham, bm.

Gresham, Craven & Lucy Hester, 3 March 1818; Bevelle Ellington, bm; Step. K. Sneed, wit.

Gresham, John & Sally Grisham, 16 Nov 1818; Absalom Hicks, bm; Rich. Sneed, wit.

Gresham, Labon & Mary Gresham, 10 Sept 1805; William Boothe, bm; Step. Sneed, wit.

Gresham, Richd. & Nancey Spear, 24 June 1805; Jas. Hamilton, bm; Step. Sneed, wit.

Gresham, Willie & Elizabeth Dickerson, 24 Dec 1818; Daniel Gresham, bm; Herndon, wit.

Gresham, Willie & Sally Davis, 20 Dec 1834; Anderson Grisham, bm; Benja. Kittrell, wit.

Grice, Stephen B. & Margaret Hayes, 19 June 1844; Geo. L. Gould, bm.

Griffin, Abslom & Elizabeth Susan Whitler, 25 April 1850; Cams. Wortham, bm; L. B. Stone, J. P., wit.

Griffin, Alexander & Eliza Elliott, 29 Nov 1831; Henry H. Dedman, bm; Jno. P. Smith, wit.

Griffin, Hardy & Winnefred Jones, 23 March 1818; Absalom Yancey, bm; W. M. Sneed, wit.

Griffin, John R. & Permelia J. Wall, 18 Sept 1850; Ezekiel B. Perkins, bm; L. B. Stone, J. P., wit.

Griffin, Lawrence & Massey Winningham, 28 Dec 1781; Sherwood Winningham, bm; Tho. Henderson, wit.

Griffin, Saml. & Mary Pattillo, 9 Jan 1794; W. Norwood, bm; Anderson Pattillo, wit.

Griffin, Samuel T. & Frances Forlines, 18 Aug 1842; Andrew J. Chandler, bm; J. M. Wiggins, wit.

Griffin, T. H. & C. A. Bragg, 11 Dec 1854; T. H. Blacknall, bm; m 21 Dec 1854 by B. N. Hopkins.

Griffin, William & Phebe M. Glover, 4 Oct 1813; Richard Taylor, bm.

Griffin, William D. & Sarah C. Eppes, 12 Feb 1840; Thos. A. Tate, bm.

Griffin, Zachariah & Martha P. Nash, 5 March 1859; Wm. S. White, bm; L. B. Stone, J. P., wit; m 5 March 1859 by L. B. Stone, J. P.

Griggs, John & Jane Byars, 20 March 1811; John Green, bm; W. M. Sneed, wit.

Griggs, Robert & Susannah Cash, 16 Aug 1781; Fruitrel Hall, bm; Bennet Searcy, wit.

Griggs, William & Mary Walker, 23 Dec 1802; Josias Cash, bm.

Grinnage, Aaron & Ruth Stroud, 24 July 1790; Joseph Akin, bm; H. Potter, wit.

Grisham, Albert C. & Lucy W. Brummett, 30 Sept 1841; Hillyard J. Parish, bm; T. A. Wiggins, wit.

Grisham, Anderson & Mary Stone, 2 Sept 1837; Henry K. Byrum, bm; Jas. M. Wiggins, wit.

Grisham, Archabald & Amy Wilson, 25 Dec 1838; Benja. Howell, bm.

Grisham, Archd. A. & Elizabeth Wilson, 24 Oct 1846; Elijah Satterwhite, bm.

Grisham, Benjamin & Fanny Davis, 28 April 1813; Wheler Grisham, bm; Richd. Sneed, wit.

Grisham, Benjamin Jr. & Mary Seats, 28 Feb 1799; James Grisham, bm; Step. Sneed, wit.

Grisham, Burges N. & Elizabeth J. Grisham, 10 June 1843; Hillyard J. Parish, bm; Jas. M. Wiggins, wit.

Grisham, Daniel & Julia Ann Parham, 14 Feb 1826; Thomas Grissom, bm; Wm. H. Owen, wit.

Grisham, Daniel & Mary M. Grisham, 10 Aug 1847; Edwin W. Kittrell, bm.

Grisham, Elvis & Mary Perkinson, 26 Dec 1836; Kennan Parham, bm; J. M. Wiggins, wit.

Grisham, Eppy & Peggy Mitchell, 4 Jan 1843; Hilliard J. Grisham, bm; J. M. Wiggins, wit.

Grisham, Granville & Masey Wilson, 30 Dec 1840; John Hargrove, bm.

Grisham, James & Jane Clerk, 1 Aug 1782; Drury Kimball, bm; Bennet Searcy, wit.

Grisham, James D. & Martha Upchurch, 17 Jan 1846; W. W. Dement, bm; Jas. M. Wiggins, wit.

Grisham, James Henry & Polly Clarke, 8 April 1857; Randolph Hilliard Grisham, bm; A. C. Harris, wit; m 9 April 1857 by Elba L. Parrish, J. P.

Grisham, John & Pattey Hill, 11 Jan 1802; Pleasant Peace or Parish, bm; Step. Sneed, wit.

Grisham, John & Polley Floyd, 12 July 1820; David Rice, bm; Jas. M. Wiggins, wit.

GRANVILLE MARRIAGES 1753-1868

Grisham, Lesley & Nancy Taylor, 20 April 1820; Reuben Clark, bm; Jas. M. Wiggins, wit.

Grisham, Stephen & Temperance Gallohoon, 9 Aug 1787; Abner Sears, bm.

Grisham, Thomas & Elizabeth Blackley, 21 Dec 1829; Thompson Blackley, bm; W. M. Sneed, wit.

Grisham, Thomas & Fanny J. Clay, 5 Jan 1837; D. A. Paschall, bm.

Grisham, Wheeler & Elizabeth Hester, 29 Dec 1818; Thomas P. Grisham, bm; Sam. Sneed, wit.

Grisham, William T. & Martha House(?), 11 Dec 1847; Edwin W. Kittrell, bm; Jas. M. Wiggins, wit.

Grisham, Willie & Frankey Grisham, 7 Jan 1812; Hezekiah Plummer, bm; W. M. Sneed, wit.

Grisham, Willis & Sabrina H. Coghill, 2 March 1847; Jesse Pendergrass, bm; Jas. M. Wiggins, wit.

Grisham, Willis & Martha Evans, 12 April 1847; Jno. Falkner, bm; Jas. M. Wiggins, wit.

Grissam, Eppy & Ann Eliza Davis, 9 Jan 1858; Thos. W. Pool, bm; m 12 Jan 1858 by D. P. Paschall, J. P.

Grissam, James A. & Martha Cliborn, 10 Oct 1857; G. N. Hicks, bm; m 15 Oct 1857 by S. G. Wilson, J. P.

Grissam, Richard W. & Mary E. Critcher, 23 July 1853; James R. Brummett, bm; A. Landis, wit; m 7 Aug 1853 by Cam. Waller, J. P.

Grissom, Charles & Mary F. Tippett, 18 April 1864; T. J. Brummitt, bm.

Grissom, Elijah & Penelope P. Weather, 22 Nov 1851; James A. White, bm; m 1851 by J. K. Cole, M. G.

Grissom, Hilliard & Mary Mitchell, 8 May 1838; Peter Evans, bm.

Grissom, James & Elizabeth Hester, 2 Oct 1771; William Huckabay, Bonjamin Whicker Junr., bm; Jesse Benton, wit.

Grissom, James T., son of Thomas Grissom & Susan Grissom, & Susan Artelia Jeffreys, daughter of Charles & Tison Jeffreys, m 17 Dec 1867 by W. D. Allen, J. P.

Grissom, Jerone & Hariot Bridges, 12 Jan 1855; Lewis T. Grissom, bm; A. Laurence, wit; m 14 Jan 1855 by A. Laurence, J. P.

Grissom, John & Julia Ann Brame, 4 April 1840; William J. Angel, bm; J. M. Wiggins, wit.

Grissom, Thomas & Elisabeth Johnson, 30 Jan 1866; Simeon Tippett, bm.

Grissom, Turner & Lucy Laurence, 11 Nov 1826; Richard Allen, bm; Wm. H. Owen, wit.

Grissom, Willie & Mary M. Fuller, 27 Nov 1838; Thomas V. Duke, bm.

GRANVILLE MARRIAGES 1753-1868

Grisson, Thomas & Elizabeth Johnson, m 1 Feb 1866 by W. D. Allen, J. P.

Gunn, James H. & Mary A. Boyd, 4 April 1862; James C. Knott, bm; m 6 April 1862 by Jas. R. Duty, J. P.

Gunn, Jesse & Eleanor Hudson, 2 Nov 1802; John Leach, bm; Step. Sneed, wit.

Gunn, John & Anne Weaver, 24 Nov 1802; Reuben Denton, bm; Leod. Cardwell, wit.

Guy, Benjamin & Elizabeth Parrot, 18 April 1844; Thomas T. Guy, bm; Wm. H. Whitfield, wit.

Guy, Clack & Polley Jones, 1 July 1820; John Henson, bm; Jas. M. Wiggins, wit.

Guy, Hansel & Polley Harris, 15 Aug 1818; William Butler, bm; W. M. Sneed, wit.

Guy, Joseph & Sally Stephens, 24 Dec 1815; Thomas Nunn, bm; Richard Sneed, wit.

Guy, Miles & Betsey Bonner, 22 May 1817; Nevison Bonner, bm; R. N. Herndon, wit.

Guy, Miles & Henrietta Dunstan, 19 Oct 1854; Admiral G. Dunstan, bm; m 19 Oct 1854 by C. R. Eaton, J. P.

Guy, Miles & Susan Tabern, 2 Sept 1865; Saml. A. Williams, bm; m 13 Sept 1865 by W. R. Harris, J. P.

Guy, Minnis & Polly Jones, 28 July 1843; Thomas Evans, bm; Wm. H. Whitfield, wit.

Guy, Sandy, of color, son of Mins & Polly Guy, & Millie Ann Thorp, parents unknown, 8 Nov 1868; m 28 Nov 1868 by B. Smith, J. P.

Guy, Thomas & Lucy P. Hunt, 27 May 1813; Henry Tompkins Jr., bm; Step. Sneed, wit.

Guy, Thomas & Mary Easter, 10 April 1840; Elijah Satterwhite, bm; W. Haynie, wit.

Hackney, Robert & Lucy Weaver, 30 Sept 1791; George Perdue, bm; W. Norwood, D. C. C., wit.

Hagin, William & Martha Curtis, 27 June 1855; Geo. Thomasson, bm; A. Landis, wit; m 28 June 1855 by Robt. B. Sutton, Rector of St. Stephen's Church, Oxford.

Hagood, Wm. R. & Martha A. Peoples, m 23 Dec 1852 by E. Hines.

Hagner, J. W. & Mrs. Mary J. Moore, 12 July 1866; John T. Richardson, bm; L. B. Stone, wit; m 12 July 1866 by L. B. Stone, J. P.

Hailey, John & Josey Adcock, 1 Oct 1827; Paschall Shadrach, bm; David Laws, wit.

Hailey, John H. & Rebecca Lad, 21 July 1828; Parker Brogdon, bm; David Laws, wit.

GRANVILLE MARRIAGES 1753-1868

Hailey, Thomas W. & Agitha Shearing, 25 Jan 1825; Stephen Inscore, bm; Step. K. Sneed, wit.

Hailey, William & Sarah Shadrach, 18 Aug 1843; William Jinkins, bm; Wm. H. Whitfield, wit.

Hair, James W. & Tabitha Harp, 22 Aug 1834; John C. Long, bm.

Haislep, Laban & Elleanor Williams, 23 Feb 1779; Stephen Jett, bm; Winnefred Jett, wit.

Haislip, Laban & Rebecca Welch, 8 Nov 1785; William Williams, bm; Reuben Searcy, wit.

Haithcock, Eaton & Caroline H. Lemay, 24 Dec 1847; W. B. Evans, bm; Jas. R. Duty, wit.

Haley, Gideon & Betsey More, 10 Oct 1823; Moses H. Bonner, bm; Wm. H. Owen, wit.

Haley, Henry & Mary Winston, 20 Dec 1845; Alfred Davis, bm; Jas. M. Wiggins, wit.

Haley, Joseph & Elisabeth Crowder, 11 March 1851; Willie J. Loyd, bm; A. Landis, wit.

Haley, Thomas & Catharine Haley, 27 Feb 1828; John Hailey, bm; S. K. Sneed, wit.

Hall, Futral & Edy Morgain, 23 Oct 1782; Joseph Cash Hall, bm; Bennet Searcy, wit.

Hall, Henry & Jane Stacey, 30 March 1783; James Claxton, bm; Reuben Searcy, wit.

Hall, Joel & Elizabeth Fuller, 20 Dec 1802; Arthur Fuller, bm; P. Bullock, wit.

Hall, John & Martha Leathers, 14 April 1781; Steaven Hicks, bm; Asa Searcy, wit.

Hall, John & Polly Hewit, 24 Sept 1784; Joseph Hall, bm; Dennis Reardon, wit.

Hall, John & Charity Harris, 8 May 1787; Len. Hayes, bm.

Hall, John & Caty Strater, 23 Oct 1804; Evan Mitchell, bm; E. W. Parham, wit.

Hall, John L. & Henrietta A. Coley, 6 Feb 1866; R. N. Minor, bm.

Hall, John T. & Mollie E. Yance, 2 Jan 1866; James E. Yancey, bm.

Hall, Joshua, of color, son of Henry Hall & Rebecca Hall, & Jemima Hunt, 19 Dec 1867; m 19 Dec 1867 by M. H. Vaughan, Rector of St. Stephen's Church.

Hall, Theodrick & Frances Jones, 28 Nov 1797; Sterling Yancey, bm; Step. Sneed, wit.

Hall, Thomas R. & Rowan Lyon, 8 Jan 1842; John F. Lyon, bm; J. M. Wiggins, wit.

Halliburton, David & Sarah T. Williams, 12 Nov 1816; Wm. Butler, bm; W. M. Sneed, wit.

GRANVILLE MARRIAGES 1753-1868

Halliburton, John & Lydia Puryear, 2 Dec 1816; Stephen Melton, bm; Step. K. Sneed, wit.

Ham, Beremon & Elisabeth Henson, 29 Dec 1797; Uel Crowder, bm; H. Williams, wit.

Hamilton, Anthoney Jr., son of Anthoney Sr. & Sarah Hamilton, & Lucey Taylor, daughter of Manuel Johnson & Sarah Taylor, 26 Dec 1868; m 26 Dec 1868 by Saml. G. Cross, J. P.

Hamilton, James & Polly Ridley, 27 Sept 1803; James Ridley, bm; Ro. M. Ridley, wit.

Hamilton, James, colored, son of Lawson & Hanah Watkins, & Alice Jordan, daughter of Harrison & Sarah Jordan, 31 Oct 1868; m 5 Nov 1868 by W. A. Belvin, J. P.

Hamilton, John & Sarah Brach, 5 Jan 1793; Thomas Phillips, bm; W. Norwood, wit.

Hamilton, Oscar B. & Elizabeth Mayho, 4 Jan 1864; L. A. Blankenship, bm.

Hamilton, Robert A. & Mrs. Martha E. Morton, 6 April 1865; m 8 April 1865 by E. Hines.

Hamilton, Samuel & Isabella Fain, 18 Jan 1866; Harrison Bullock, bm; Jas. R. Duty, wit; m 20 Jan 1866 by H. H. Prout.

Hamilton, Thomas & Martha Murry, 23 Jan 1827; Edward T. Marable, bm; A. Sneed, wit.

Hamilton, Valentine & Eliza Hays, freed people, 12 Aug 1865; A. Landis, bm.

Hamilton, William, of color, son of James & Temperance Hamilton, & Frances Thomas, father unknown, mother Caroline Wimbish, 24 Feb 1868; m 26 Feb 1868 by Rev. Wyatt Walker, M. G.

Hamilton, William B. & Mary P. Turner, 29 Feb 1836; M. Neal, bm; Benja. Kittrell, wit.

Hamlett, William J. & Lucy R. Chambers, 30 June 1837; E. A. Williams, bm; Robert K. Clack, wit.

Hammic, William & Elizabeth Taylor, freed people, 16 Sept 1865; m 22 Oct 1865.

Hammie, William & Elizabeth Taylor, 16 Sept 1865; A. Landis, wit.

Hammond, Rawley & Sarah Daniel, 6 June 1780; John Rooker, bm; Edmond Smith, wit.

Hammonds, Willie & Eliz. Linn(?), 9 Feb 1793; Leonard Smith, Thomas Collens, bm; Step. Sneed, wit.

Hammons, Federick & Nancy Pettiford, 19 May 1802; George Anderson, bm; P. Bullock, wit.

Hampton, John & Kesiah Howell, 8 Sept 1794; William Landiss, bm; Step. Sneed, wit.

Hampton, Zachariah H. & Sally Rust, 27 Dec 1826; Wilburn L. Hampton, bm.

GRANVILLE MARRIAGES 1753-1868

Hancock, Benjamin F. & Virginia E. Tunstall, 5 May 1858; Benja. J. Paschall, bm; m 5 May 1858 by L. K. Willie, M. G.

Hancock, Benoni & Susanna Tuen(?), 18 Aug 1785; Howel Morn, bm.

Hancock, John W. & Cynthia M. Cooke, 8 Sept 1831; R. B. Laurence, bm; David Laws, wit.

Hancock, Johnson M. & Sarah Ann Chandler, 3 Sept 1846; Wm. C. Chandler, bm; J. M. Wiggins, wit.

Hancock, Robert & Lucy Granger, 15 Oct 1792; Benone Hancock, bm; W. Norwood, wit.

Hanks, Argil & Frances Hargraves, 20 June 1783; Richard Hargraves, bm; Reuben Searcy, wit.

Hanks, Argill & Million Hargraves, 28 Dec 1773; William Hanks, Elijah Hanks, bm.

Hanks, Jacob & Rhoda Wright, 9 June 1867; Solomon Pettiford, bm; Jas. R. Duty, wit; m 10 June 1867 by Jas. R. Duty, J. P.

Hanmer(?), Richard H. & Elizabeth H. Davis, 9 Dec 1839; H. H. Burwell, bm; Wm. T. Hargrove, wit.

Hard, Edward D. & Sally Ann Mallory, 9 Jan 1838; Thos. S. Hayes, bm.

Harden, Jesse, of color, parents unknown, & Agnes Burwell, parents unknown, m 24 Nov 1867 by J. D. C. Pool, J. P.

Harden, Starling & Sally Worls, 7 Aug 1816; John Brummett, bm; Rhodes Herndon, wit.

Harden, Thornton & Elizabeth Harrison, 18 Feb 1801; Uel Crowder, bm; Wm. Walker, wit.

Hardin, James & Betsey Fowler, 14 Oct 1842; Charles Allen, bm; Wm. H. Whitfield, wit.

Hardin, John & Mariah Haley, 5 Jan 1840; Danl. Fowler, _____ Watson, bm.

Harding, Solomon & Louisa Merrit, 1 Nov 1833; Iverson Mitchell, bm; Benja. Kittrell, wit.

Hardy, Sterling & Lotty Inscore, 3 Jan 1816; A. D. Parrish, bm; Horace A. Hester, wit.

Hargrave, Stephen, request for license for (?) John Bryon, 4 Sept 1790.

Hargrove, Gideon & Martha McGwin, 11 Jan 1867; T. L. Hargrove, bm; m 18 Jan 1867 by W. M. Sneed Jr., J. P.

Hargrove, Granderson & Betsey Ann Burwell, m 19 June 1867 by Jas. R. Duty, J. P.

Hargrove, Israel & Polley Hargrove, 4 March 1796; John Hargrove, bm; W. Robards, wit.

Hargrove, Israel W. & Nancy J. Hargrove, 11 Dec 1827; John D. Hanks, bm; Alfred Sneed, wit.

GRANVILLE MARRIAGES 1753-1868

Hargrove, James & Amey Hargrove, (no date, during admn. of Richard D. Spaight); George Chapman, bm; Step. Sneed, wit.

Hargrove, John & Charlott Estis, 16 Jan 1845; Samuel W. Smith, bm; Wm. T. Hargrove, wit.

Hargrove, Lewis & Kizziah Hargrove, 26 Dec 1865; G. Hargrove, bm; A. Landis, wit.

Hargrove, Richard & Betsey Dodson, 28 Dec 1799; Charles Dodson, bm; Step. Sneed, wit.

Hargrove, Robert & Mary Norwood, 9 Feb 1796; Israel Hargrove, bm; Step. Sneed, wit.

Hargrove, Thomas & Amy Hargrove, (freed people), 9 Nov 1865; Burwell Hargrove, bm; G. W. Landis, wit.

Hargroves, Shephard & Rebecca Hargrove, 27 Nov 1798; John Jones, bm; James Sneed, wit.

Haris, Habon & Parthena Stovall, 14 Aug 1846; John L. Day, bm; L. B. Stone, wit.

Harley, David & Mary Madison, 4 Jan 1816; John Giles, bm; W. M. Sneed, wit.

Harley, David & Sarah Ann Edwards, 16 Dec 1829; John McFarling, bm; David Laws, wit.

Harlow, Thomas & Jane Downey, 13 Oct 1855; William Hinton, bm; m 14 Oct 1855 by A. Barker, J. P.

Harp, Benjamin & Sally Moss, 25 Dec 1839; Ransom Bailey, bm.

Harp, Beverly & Sarah Dickerson, 30 Sept 1805; John Haynes, bm; Step. Sneed, wit.

Harp, John & Mary Lewis, 3 June 1778; Benjamin Cash, bm; Sherwood Harris, wit.

Harp, Samson & Sarah Tudor, 19 Oct 1779; John Harp, bm; John Pulliam, wit.

Harp, Simon & Lucy Ham, 3 Dec 1788; John Harp, bm; A. Henderson, wit.

Harp, Thomas Jr. & Elisabeth Lewis, 3 Nov 1778; William Roberts, bm.

Harp, Thompson & Delaney McGehee, 4 April 1853; Willis Roe, bm; A. Landis, wit.

Harp, Wiley & Catherine Fuller, 19 Jan 1865; William Harp, bm.

Harp, William & Salley Stanton, 24 May 1787; John Harp, bm; Bennet Searcy, wit.

Harp, William & Lotty Harrison, 5 Nov 180_; Thomas King, bm.

Harp, William & Tabitha Johnson, 30 May 1804; Samson Harp, bm; W. M. Sneed, wit.

Harp, William & Winney Ball, 2 July 1833; Stephen Harris, bm; David Laws, wit.

GRANVILLE MARRIAGES 1753-1868

Harper, Joseph & Mary A. C. Hays, 30 Dec 1834; C. Gupton, bm.

Harper, Wyatt W. & Martha J. May, 25 Sept 1844; Willie T. Jordan, bm; J. M. Wiggins, wit.

Harrals, Harmon & Rachael Brown, 23 Sept 1793; Elijah Bradford, bm; W. Norwood, wit.

Harril, William & Ann Mearemon, 14 Aug 1780; Drury Purkins, bm; John Searcy Jr., wit.

Harring, Sterling & Lucy Farrar, 17 Nov 1866; Osborn Harris, bm; W. L. H. Thomas, J. P., wit; m 17 Nov 1866 by W. L. H. Thomas, J. P.

Harris, A. L. & Kate Mangum, 16 March 1866; m 18 March 1866 by Francis J. Tilley, J. P.

Harris, Abner & Salley Moore, 8 Nov 1814; Needham Cavender, bm; W. M. Sneed, wit.

Harris, Abner & Elizabeth Allen, 30 Oct 1833; Willie Allen, bm; Benja. Kittrell, wit.

Harris, Alexander & Mary A. Weaver, 19 Dec 1857; Jesse Hayes, bm; m 20 Dec 1857 by D. P. Paschall, J. P.

Harris, Alexander, of color, son of Susan Harris, & Lucy Amy Tabern, daughter of Littleton & Lotty Tabern, m 24 July 1867 by T. M. Lynch, J. P.

Harris, Anderson & Elizabeth H. Collier, 6 Jan 1832; Willie Grisham, bm; Step. K. Sneed, wit.

Harris, Anderson & Nancy Jones, 26 Jan 1842; William Mills, bm; Jas. M. Wiggins, wit.

Harris, Anderson G. & Lucy A. R. Rivers, 23 July 1827; Robt. Vaughan, bm.

Harris, Andrew J. & Martha A. B. G. Farrar, 7 June 1854; E. W. Wortham, bm; m 7 June 1854 by A. C. Harris, M. G.

Harris, Arthur & Rebeccah Reavis, 24 June 1800; Samuel J. Reavis, bm; Step. Sneed, wit.

Harris, Asa P. & Mary H. Blackley, 15 Dec 1832; Howel Blackley, bm. Step. K. Sneed, wit.

Harris, Augustine & Elizabeth Cocke, 2 Dec 1826; Thomas Hunt, bm; Step. K. Sneed, wit.

Harris, Augustus & Barbary Harris, 31 March 185_; Joseph Harris, bm.

Harris, Augustus & Barbary Harris, 31 March 1856; m 1 April 1856 by Jas. J. Moore, J. P.

Harris, Austin & Tabitha Kittrell, 24 Jan 1804; Robert Potter, bm; E. Parham, wit.

Harris, Benja. F. & Ann Eliza Rogers, 10 Feb 1849; Archibald Davis, bm; Jas. M. Wiggins, wit.

GRANVILLE MARRIAGES 1753-1868

Harris, Bethel & Sally G. Freeman, 13 April 1840; Jno. W. Hunt, bm; Jas. M. Wiggins, wit.

Harris, Bezelee & Ann Red, 14 Oct 1842; Jas. R. Duty, bm; Wm. H. Whitfield, wit.

Harris, Britton & Mary Andrews, 11 Jan 1848; J. H. Gooch, bm; Jas. M. Wiggins, wit.

Harris, Burgess & Susan Mangum, 15 Dec 1832; Allen Mangum, bm; Step. K. Sneed, wit.

Harris, Calvin & Lucy Green, freed people, m 17 Feb 1866 by Wm. E. Bullock, J. P.; Wm. H. Adcock, bm.

Harris, Charles & Sarah Allen, 12 Aug 1760; Larkin Johnston, bm; Jno. Bowie, wit.

Harris, Charles & Sally L. Roffe, 13 Oct 1825; Woodson Roffe, bm; Step. K. Sneed, wit.

Harris, Charles & Isabella Moss, 13 Nov 1865; A. F. Spencer, bm; m 25 Nov 1865 by Joseph W. Murphy, Rector Ch. of Holy Innocents, Henderson, N. C.

Harris, Charles, son of Thomas & O. Harris, & Elizabeth Roberts, daughter of M. P. & Rebecca Roberts, 14 April 1868; m 14 April 1868 by F. J. Tilley, J. P.

Harris, Charles, of color, son of Allen & Mourning Harris, & Ritter Moss, daughter of George Garrett & Franky Moss, 1 June 1868; m 6 June 1868 by E. J. Montague, M. G.

Harris, Charley & Martha Gooch, 7 Dec 1827; Willis Gooch, bm; Step. K. Sneed, wit.

Harris, Claborn & Mary Champion, 27 Sept 1792; John Champion, bm; Step. Sneed, wit.

Harris, Darvin & Elisabeth Wilkins, 2 Jan 1782; Wm. Currin, bm; William Skelton, wit.

Harris, David & Lemender Harris, 28 Dec 1783; John Hawkins, bm; Bennet Searcy, wit.

Harris, David & Sarah Milton, 5 Dec 1802; Stephen Milton, bm; P. Bullock, wit.

Harris, David & Betsey Evans, 4 Aug 1834; Willis Emery, bm; Benja. Kittrell, wit.

Harris, David & Mary Jane Stovall, 26 Oct 1850; John E. Montague, bm; L. B. Stone, J. P., wit.

Harris, Dennis & Ellen Short, 30 Dec 1865; m 30 Dec 1865 by L. K. Willie, M. G.

Harris, Dennis, of color, son of Rachel Mangum & Mary Gilliam, daughter of John Gilliam, 11 June 1868; m 11 June 1868 by M. H. Vaughan, Rector of St. Stephen's Church.

Harris, Dennis & Mary J. Royster, 15 Dec 1866; Thomas Cheatham, bm; C. E. Landis, wit; m 15 Dec 1866 by W. H. Puryear, J. P.

GRANVILLE MARRIAGES 1753-1868

Harris, Drury & Elisabeth Butler, 15 Sept 1811; Habun Wiles, bm; H. Young, wit.

Harris, Edward W. & Susan L. Allen, 18 Feb 1837; D. A. Paschall, bm; J. M. Wiggins, wit.

Harris, Fielding & Lucina Kenaday, 27 Jan 1828; William Hobgood, bm; David Laws, wit.

Harris, Fielding & Mary J. Barnett, 15 Nov 1850; John H. Tippit, bm.

Harris, Frederick & Lucy Williams, 24 Feb 1867; John Young, bm; Jas. R. Duty, wit; m 24 Feb 1867 by Jas. R. Duty, J. P.

Harris, George, colored, son of Abram & Fanny Harris, & Martha Catlett, daughter of Boson Levister & Rachel Catlett, m 7 Nov 1868 by John W. Estes, J. P.

Harris, George A. & Mary E. Webb, 4 Feb 1833; Ira E. Arnold, bm; David Laws, wit.

Harris, George B. & Anadella Reavis, 3 Nov 1863; m 13 Nov 1863 by Wm. Holmes; John Wiggins, bm.

Harris, Gideon & Anney Gresham, 23 Feb 1796; John Gresham, bm; Step. Sneed, wit.

Harris, Gideon & Agnes Grisham, 3 May 1837; Rowland Bryant Jr., bm; G. C. Wiggins, wit.

Harris, Goldmon & Elisabeth Bell, 26 Aug 1781; Blake Mauldin, bm; Wm. Searcy, wit.

Harris, Hardy & Rebecah Vaughan, 17 June 1806; Thomas Coghill, bm; Thos. Reavis, wit.

Harris, Hardy & Emily H. Stone, 25 Sept 1839; Samuel J. Reavis Jr., bm; Jas. M. Wiggins, wit.

Harris, Harison & Marina Ann Cole, 22 Dec 1830; John Byrum, bm; David Laws, wit.

Harris, Harrison & Edney Roberts, 19 Oct 1833; Squire Drew(?), bm.

Harris, Harvey & Ann Blackley, 3 Feb 1846; Benj. F. Bullock, bm; J. M. Wiggins, wit.

Harris, Col. Harvill & Miss Joanna R. Lassiter, 2 March 1866; m 6 March 1866 by Joseph W. Murphy, Rector of Holy Innocents, Henderson; James H. Lassiter, bm.

Harris, Henry & Salley Ussery, 1 Nov 1822; Thos. Hutcherson, bm; Jas. M. Wiggins, wit.

Harris, Henry & Mary Cooper, 5 Feb 1859; Jerry Champion, bm; m 5 Feb 1859 by Jas. J. Moore, J. P.

Harris, Henry & Mary Brame, 30 March 1866; Terry Pettiford, bm; Jas. R. Duty, bm; m 31 March 1866 by S. P. J. Harris, M. G.

Harris, Henry & Fannie Howard, 27 Dec 1866; m 27 Dec 1866 by B. D. Howard, J. P.

GRANVILLE MARRIAGES 1753-1868

Harris, Hinton, of color, son of Bed & Phebe Harris, & Dolly Evans, daughter of Thos. Jordan & Mary Simpson, m 24 Dec 1867 by Wyatt Walker, Minister of the Gospel.

Harris, Isaiah & _____ Guy, 13 Nov 1850; R. Herndon, bm.

Harris, Isaih T. & Martha Dickerson, 15 Oct 1866; C. R. Blackly, bm; C. E. Landis, wit; m 18 Oct 1866 by E. F. Beachum, R. G. Minister.

Harris, Isham & _____, 12 April 1806; Samuel Mangrum, bm; N. Satterwhite, wit.

Harris, James & Priscilla Gillam, 20 June 1783; Isham Harrison, bm; Reuben Searcy, wit.

Harris, James & Nancey Dailey, 1 Dec 1809; William N. Cardwell, bm; W. M. Sneed, wit.

Harris, James & Jincy Roberson, 12 Dec 1812; Thomas Puet, bm; Stephen K. Sneed, wit.

Harris, James & Harriott Blackly, 18 Nov 1834; Howel Blackley, bm; Benja. Kittrell, wit.

Harris, James & Mary Ann Allen, 12 Jan 1852; Bennett Champion, bm; m 13 Jan 1852 by Saml. S. Hicks, J. P.

Harris, James & Eliza Tabern, 21 Jan 1864; Hunley Mitchell, bm; A. Landis, wit.

Harris, James A. & Fanny Jones, freed people of color, 18 Oct 1866; Alex. Harris, bm; F. J. Tilley, wit; m 18 Oct 1866 by D. Tilley, J. P.

Harris, James H. & Elizabeth Blackwell, 24 Aug 1829; Ira E. Arnold, bm; David Laws, wit.

Harris, James H. & Elizabeth Norman, 7 Nov 1831; Tho. H. Willie, bm; David Laws, wit.

Harris, James H. & Mary L. Clark, 11 Sept 1843; John H. Boswell, bm; Wm. H. Whitfield, wit.

Harris, James H. Jr. & Elizabeth H. Allen, 24 Oct 1836; Ira C. Arnold, bm; J. M. Wiggins, wit.

Harris, James Harvey & Elizabeth P. Glover, 29 Sept 1801; Jno. Hicks, bm; P. Bullock, wit.

Harris, John & Mary Atwood, 5 Jan 1793; Richd. Grissum, bm; W. Norwood, wit.

Harris, John & Mary Brinkley, 5 Aug 1835; George Emrey, bm; Thos. H. Willie, wit.

Harris, John & Martha Welch, 29 Oct 1835; L. Gilliam, bm; Benja. Kittrell, wit.

Harris, John & Lucy C. Blackley, 18 Dec 1839; John C. Peace, bm.

Harris, John & Cary McGehee, 27 Nov 1841; Shem McGehee, bm; J. M. Wiggins, wit.

GRANVILLE MARRIAGES 1753-1868

Harris, John & Mahala Evans, 17 April 1847; John Fuller, bm; J. M. Wiggins, wit.

Harris, John & Lydia Ann Allen, 15 March 1850; Bennett Chappell, bm; A. Landis, wit.

Harris, John & Maria Hicks, 25 April 1866; m 29 April 1866 by W. C. Gannon, M. G.

Harris, John & Minerva Harris, freed persons, 8 Jan 1867; m 8 Jan 1867 by F. J. Tilley, J. P.; Henry Day, bm.

Harris, John, of color, son of Edmer Burton & _____, & Margarett Chebers, daughter of Caswell & Elisa Cheves, m 18 Dec 1868 by Braxton Hunt.

Harris, John F. & Mary A. E. Drumright, 29 Oct 1862; N. C. Bugg, bm; m 29 Oct 1862 by Jas. R. Duty, J. P.

Harris, John G. & Minerva Maham, 14 Dec 1832; Thos. T. Hester, bm; David Laws, wit.

Harris, John P. & Caroline Loyd, 19 May 1867; M. H. Strum, bm; Jas. R. Duty, wit; m 19 May 1867 by Jas. R. Duty, J. P.

Harris, Jorden & Delilah Guy, 24 April 1810; Sanders Harris, bm; Step. Sneed, wit.

Harris, Jordon & Manery Pedeford, 19 Sept 1860; George Richerson, bm.

Harris, Joseph & Isabella Clay, 6 Oct 1866; Francis J. Tilley, bm.

Harris, Joseph D. & Amy Hays, 24 Dec 1866; Isham Cheatham, bm; m 24 Dec 1866 by A. C. Parham, J. P.

Harris, Kinchin & Cynthia Allen, 17 July 1845; Burwell Henley, bm; D. A. Paschall, wit.

Harris, Lenard C. & Martha Blackley, m 14 Feb 1866 by W. D. Allen, J. P.

Harris, Leonard C. & Martha Blackley, 12 Feb 1866; G. T. Harris, bm; A. Landis, wit.

Harris, Lewis & Piety Adcock, 8 Sept 1846; H. Reeves(?), bm.

Harris, Lunsford & Keziah Evans, 16 March 1865; Lewis Evans, bm, A. Landis, wit.

Harris, Micajah & Ann Parrish, 2 Feb 1808; Hezekiah Plummer, bm; A. H. Sneed, wit.

Harris, Mosbey & Judith Peace, 7 Oct 1793; Tyre Harris, bm; Step. Sneed, wit.

Harris, Moses (colored) & Isabella Webb, 15 May 1866; John C. Cauthon, bm; Robt. L. Heflin, J. P., wit; m 20 May 1866 by Wm. H. Puryear, J. P.

Harris, Newsom & Mary Neale, 13 May 1782; Nimrod Jordan(?), bm; Reuben Searcy, wit.

Harris, Orsburn & Isabella Beasley, m 17 Nov 1866 by W. S. H. Thomas, J. P.; Sterling Harris, bm.

GRANVILLE MARRIAGES 1753-1868

Harris, Peter, of color, son of Isah & Ann Harris, & Judy Bullock, daughter of Jesse & Mary Bullock, m 25 July 1868 by S. P. J. Harris, M. G.

Harris, Philip W. F. & Amanda M. Harris, 12 July 1842; Ira E. Arnold, bm; Wm. H. Whitfield, wit.

Harris, Ransom & Elizabeth Gilliam, 20 Aug 1785; Jno. Daniel, bm; James Ferrell, wit.

Harris, Ransom & Sucky Highfield, 30 Dec 1805; Tiery Harris, bm; A. H. Sneed, wit.

Harris, Ransom & Sallie Mayfield, 4 Jan 1859; A. Landis, bm; John G. Watson, wit; m 6 Jan 1859 by S. H. Cannady, J. P.

Harris, Richard, of color, son of Henry & Tildy Harris, & Sylvia Sandford, daughter of Ellen & Epps Sandford, 14 Sept 1867; m 14 Sept 1867 by W. H. Puryear, J. P.

Harris, Richard Jr. & Mary Gwin, 17 April 1777; Richard Harris, Wm. Jones, bm; Reuben Searcy, wit.

Harris, Richard J. & Bettie Jones, 26 Jan 1863; Saml. A. Williams, bm; m 12 Feb 1863 by H. H. Prout.

Harris, Ro. & Mary Jones, 19 Sept 1794; Robt. Hyde, bm; Step. Sneed, wit.

Harris, Robert & Sarah Philpot, 23 Oct 1826; Jno. P. Smith, bm.

Harris, Robert & Elizabeth Davis, 24 Feb 1853; James Loyd, bm; A. Landis, wit; m 25 Feb 1853 by Lewis Amis, J. P.

Harris, Robert & Martha Adams, 21 Dec 1859; John J. Brame, bm; m 22 Dec 1859 by E. L. Parrish, J. P.

Harris, Robt. & Catherine Bullock, 13 Jan 1836; S. Harris, bm.

Harris, Robert, of color, parents unknown, & Rhody White, daughter of Frank White & Gracy Cannady, 4 June 1868; m 7 June 1868 by E. B. Lyon, J. P.

Harris, Robert Junr. & Elisabeth Phillips, 21 Sept 1775; Thos. Harris, bm; William Reardon, wit.

Harris, Robert C. & Emily F. Royster, 6 Nov 1854; W. A. Gillis, bm; m 21 Dec 1854 by James King.

Harris, Robert G. & Jane Strowd, 8 Feb 1853; Wm. Longmire, bm.

Harris, Robin Hood & Mima Harris, 9 Aug 1793; William Ogilvie, bm; W. Norwood, wit.

Harris, Rowland & Sarah Daniel, 21 Aug 1783; D. Royster, bm; Richd. Henderson, wit.

Harris, Rowland & Betsy Reavis, 9 Nov 1794; Reuben Moss (Morse?), bm; H. Seawell, wit.

Harris, S. P. J. & Hixie B. Baskett, 5 Dec 1857; H. H. Rowland, bm; m 20 Dec 1857 by N. J. Barham.

Harris, Samuel & Fanney Biggs, 3 March 1817; James H. Cawhon, bm; Rhodes N. Herndon, wit.

GRANVILLE MARRIAGES 1753-1868

Harris, Samuel & Riney Harris, 9 Feb 1828; Absalom Harris, bm;
David Laws, wit.

Harris, Samuel & Nettie Brandum, 17 Sept 1864; J. T. Poll, bm;
m 18 Sept 1864 by Jno. S. Burwell, J. P.

Harris, Saml. C. & Sally A. Dickerson, m 18 Nov 1866 by W. P. J.
Harris, M. G.

Harris, Sherwood & Rebecca Wilkins, 12 April 1778; Thos. Harris,
bm; P. Henderson, wit.

Harris, Sherwood & Judith Woodall, 27 Nov 1787; Absalom Woodall,
bm; Reuben Searcy, C. C., wit.

Harris, Spears & Elisabeth Bearden, 5 Oct 1795; John Bearden,
bm; Step. Sneed, wit.

Harris, Spears & Polly Hobkins, 4 Feb 1815; Thomas Potter, bm;
John C. Smith, wit.

Harris, Stephen & Mary Stanton, 14 Aug 1827; George P. Thomasson,
bm; David Laws, wit.

Harris, Stephen & Parthenia Omary, 9 May 1845; Benj. C. Cook,
bm.

Harris, Sterling & Jane Daniel, 13 Dec 1810; Alexander Elixson,
bm; H. Young, wit.

Harris, Thomas & Mary Kittle, 11 Feb 1805; Barnett Adcock, bm;
Jas. Sneed, wit.

Harris, Thomas & Elizabeth Seats, 8 Jan 1810; Gideon Harris, bm;
W. M. Sneed, wit.

Harris, Thomas & Prudence Winston, 27 Oct 1848; R. J. Mitchell,
bm; Jas. M. Wiggins, wit.

Harris, Thomas & Airy Ann Williams, 30 Jan 1863; Lemuel Moore,
bm; m 30 Jan 1863 by Moses J. Hunt.

Harris, Thomas B. & Sarah Buchanan, 2 July 1834; Jas. L. Webb,
bm; Wm. L. Owen, wit.

Harris, Thomas B. & Rebecca Perry, 7 Nov 1836; G. C. Wiggins,
bm; J. M. Wiggins, wit.

Harris, Thomas D. & Harriett F. Harris, 6 Dec 1850; Richd. W.
Harris, bm.

Harris, Thomas H. & Elizabeth Mayo, 4 Aug 1840; Cuffee Mayo, bm.

Harris, Thomas H. & Bettie T. Shotwell, 9 Jan 1866; James D.
Elam, bm; m 17 Jan 1866 by R. J. Devin.

Harris, Tiry & Polly Gooch, 2 Aug 1790; Benjamin Fowler, bm;
H. Potter, wit.

Harris, Tyre & Betsey Hawkins, 21 Jan 1796; John Hawkins, bm;
Step. Sneed, wit.

Harris, Tyre & Nancey Higgs, 8 Aug 1807; John Moore, bm; W. M.
Sneed, wit.

GRANVILLE MARRIAGES 1753-1868

Harris, Washington & June Graham, 9 Nov 1866; F. B. Hester, bm; C. E. Landis, wit; m 15 Nov 1866 by R. J. Devin.

Harris, Wilie & Jiney Cozart, 24 Feb 1819; Isaac Weaver, bm; Step. K. Sneed, wit.

Harris, William & Catharine Grisham, (date missing); George King, bm; A. Henderson, wit.

Harris, William & Hennessee Riggs, 2 March 1819; James H. Cauthen, bm.

Harris, William & Fanny McGehee, 5 Sept 1842; Jerh. Rust, bm; J. M. Wiggins, wit.

Harris, William & Eliza Corn, 19 Nov 1846; Sterling Chavis, bm; Jas. M. Wiggins, wit.

Harris, William & Miranda Champion, 22 March 1854; James Harris, bm; A. Landis, wit.

Harris, William & Fanny Burwell, 19 May 1866; m by Jas. R. Duty, J. P.

Harris, William A. & Lucy A. G. Harris, 7 Sept 1841; G. C. Wiggins, bm; J. M. Wiggins, wit.

Harris, William A. & Amanda M. Harris, 19 May 1849; Benj. C. Cooke, bm; J. M. Wiggins, wit.

Harris, William H. & Miss Nancy A. Sanford, 13 Oct 1858; Wm. S. Norwood, bm; m 27 Oct 1858 by Eld. B. N. Hopkins.

Harris, William R. & Eliza J. Allen, 12 Sept 1848; J. H. Webb, bm; Jas. M. Wiggins, wit.

Harris, William R. & Sarah E. Allen, 24 Nov 1860; J. W. Curring, bm; m 28 Nov 1860 by G. W. Ferrill.

Harris, Willis & Sarah Duty, 24 May 1808; Ivey Harris, bm; Step. Sneed, wit.

Harris, Willis N. & Susan B. Smith, 29 Dec 1854; D. C. White, bm; m 19 Jan 1855 by J. W. Floyd, Minister.

Harrison, Alexander & Elizabeth Bowls, 30 April 1834; John Baily, bm; Benja. Kittrell, wit.

Harrison, Elious & Patey Moon (Moore?), 25 May 1798; William Harp, bm; H. Williams, wit.

Harrison, George & Martha Wood, 22 June 1818; Robert T. Wood, bm; Zacha. Herndon Jr., wit.

Harrison, George A. & Susan Knight, 16 Feb 1857; L. K. Willie, bm; m 23 Feb 1857 by L. K. Willie, M. G.

Harrison, Grandison G. & Elender Lunsford, 3 Jan 1843; Valen. V. Lunsford, father of Elender, bm; J. M. Wiggins, wit.

Harrison, Isham & Amey Gillam, 20 June 1783; James Harris, bm; Reuben Searcy, wit.

Harrison, Kinchen & Mary G. Harris, 13 Feb 1830; A. H. Heggs, bm; David Laws, wit.

GRANVILLE MARRIAGES 1753-1868

Harrison, Thomas & Bettie J. Hester, 31 Dec 1862; Z. M. P. Dordeg(?), bm; m 4 Jan 1863 by B. T. Winston, J. P.

Harrison, Thomas Y. & Anna Y. Beasly, 25 Dec 1866; C. E. Landis, bm; m 1 Jan 1867 by R. J. Devin.

Harriss, Henry & Bitha Ann Tabon, 2 Jan 1838; George Anderson, bm; S. G. Shearmon, wit.

Harriss, Jonathan & Barbara Bradford, 20 Sept 1811; Stephen Bridges, bm; W. M. Sneed, wit.

Harriss, Richard J., son of Henry & Martha A. Harriss, & Lucy H. Jones, daughter of Prof. E. A. & Mary Jones, 14 Nov 1868; m 25 Nov 1868 by Matthias M. Marshall, M. G.

Harriss, Wiley & Mary Holeby, 21 Sept 1825; James Brinkley, bm; L. Gilliam, wit.

Harrisson, William & Elvice Cooper, 31 Jan 1786; Kannon Cooper, bm; Bennet Searcy, wit.

Hart, Asa & Betsey Cousins, 27 Nov 1823; Howell Briggs, bm; Jas. M. Wiggins, wit.

Hart, George W. & Parthena Newton, 4 Dec 1866; James S. Hobgood, bm; m 13 Dec 1866 by R. J. Devin.

Hart, James & Rebecka Graves, _____ 1789; Samuel Pittard, bm.

Hart, James W. & Rebecca Frances Currin, 6 Nov 1859; M. S. Hart, bm; m 8 Dec 1859 by F. B. Currin, J. P.

Hart, James Jr. & Hannah Amis, 16 Oct 1821; Ransom Cunningham, bm; Jas. M. Wiggins, wit.

Hart, John & Nancy Vass, 8 Nov 1803; Thomas Crenshaw, bm; Green Merritt, wit.

Hart, John G. & Amey P. Kindrach, 24 Oct 1815; David Tilman, bm; Step. Sneed, wit.

Hart, Joseph & Mary A. Jinkins, 7 Oct 1831; Willie Smith, bm; David Laws, wit.

Hart, Joseph & Frances Hudson, 12 Jan 1842; Bruce Boyd, bm; J. M. Wiggins, wit.

Hart, Joseph & Mary A. Watkins, 6 April 1854; Gardner OBriant, bm; m 12 April 1854 by Lewis Amis.

Hart, Joseph Jr. & Nancy Hester, 9 Nov 1820; Thomas Hester, bm; Step. K. Sneed, wit.

Hart, Joseph B. & Sarah D. Stevens, 20 Dec 1831; Riley Smith, bm; Albert Sneed, wit.

Hart, Lawson & Sarah Hart, freed people, 11 Aug 1865; Madison Young, bm; A. Landis, wit; m 12 Aug 1865 by H. H. Prout.

Hart, Lewis & Mary Currin, 20 Dec 1865; James Y. Landis, bm; freed people.

Hart, Owen & Mary Ann Howell, 18 Sept 1832; Lambert Hudleston, bm; David Laws, wit.

GRANVILLE MARRIAGES 1753-1868

Hart, Pleasant & Eliza Covington, 1 June 1833; David L. Williams, bm; Albert Sneed, wit.

Hart, Pleasant & Elizabeth Ann Bass, 29 Dec 1834; James Royster, bm; Wm. L. Owen, wit.

Hart, Pomfrett & Elizabeth P. Hunt, 21 June 1820; James Hart Jr., bm; Jas. M. Wiggins, wit.

Hart, Robert & Susan Bass, 29 July 1848; William Ker(?), bm.

Hart, Shepard, son of Osborn & Lizza Hart, & Lucy Parham, daughter of William & Eveline Parham, 16 Nov 1868; m 21 Nov 1868 by E. Hines.

Hart, Stephen & Julia Barker, m 12 May 1866 by Jas. R. Duty, J. P.

Hart, William H. & Sarah A. Wilson, 14 Jan 1867; A. Landis, bm; m 23 Jan 1867 by J. F. Harris, J. P.

Hart, William W. & Sallie J. Knott, 20 May 1865; Robert Hester, bm.

Harton, Jehu & Mourning Harp, 12 May 1789; John Harp, bm; A. Henderson, C. C., wit.

Harvey, William W. & Mary D. Anderson, 5 June 1856; Wm. O. Manning, bm; J. J. Cheatham, wit; m 5 June 1856 by Edwd. Townes, J. P.

Haskins, Cruel & Mary Scott, 18 Dec 1861; Allen Haskins, bm; Jas. R. Duty, wit; m 25 Dec 1861 by Jas. R. Duty, J. P.

Haskins, George & Jane Johnston, 14 Nov 1827; William Farabough, bm; David Laws, wit.

Haskins, Isaac & Nancy Moore, 22 Dec 1840; Tallon Johnson, bm; J. M. Wiggins, wit.

Haskins, Isaac & Susan Wheeler, 17 Jan 1848; Jas. B. Webster, bm; Jas. M. Wiggins, wit.

Haskins, John R. & Ann S. Norwood, 6 Sept 1852; N. M. Norwood, bm; Jno. Bullock, wit.

Haskins, Thomas & Jane Culverhouse, 22 Oct 1823; George Haskins, bm; Jas. M. Wiggins, wit.

Haskins, William C. & Emeline Wheeler, 20 Aug 1850; James S. Finch, bm.

Haswell, Henry M. & Mary R. Jackson, 27 Sept 1852; M. D. Huskath, bm; m 28 Sept 1852 by J. M. Stone, J. P.

Haswell, John R. & Mary Bridges, 5 Feb 1821; John B. Estes, bm; Jas. M. Wiggins, wit.

Haswell, Nathan & Nancey Jackson, 23 Dec 1823; Jno. R. Haswell, bm; Wm. H. Owen, wit.

Haswell, Redding & Penelope Balely, 28 Dec 1824; Stephen Bridges, bm; R. N. Herndon, wit.

GRANVILLE MARRIAGES 1753-1868

Haswell, William A., son of Nathan & Nancy Haswell, & Martha A. Haswell, daughter of Edward & Jane Haswell, m 12 Jan 1868 by W. D. Allen, J. P.

Haswill, Jordan & Mary Jackson, 31 Oct 1818; Thos. G. Morris, bm; R. W. Herndon, wit.

Hatchet, Elisha & Sally Myars, 11 July 181_; Samuel Forsyth, bm; Step. K. Sneed, wit.

Hathcock, Kinchen & Mary R. Scot(?), 8 Feb 1848; Josiah C. Royal, bm.

Hatt, Charles & Jane Pound, 11 Sept 1799; John Collins, bm; Step. K. Sneed, wit.

Hawkins, Benjamin F. & Sarah B. Person, 30 Aug 1807; William Hawkins, bm.

Hawkins, Edmond & Sabrina Ricards, 21 Nov 1865; George Badger, bm; m 25 Nov 1865 by Joseph Murphy, Rector of Holy Innocents, Henderson, N. C.

Hawkins, George & Lucy Reavis, daughter of Saml. & Nancy Reavis, of color, m 12 Dec 1867 by Aaron Pratcher, Minister of the Gospel.

Hawkins, John & Sarah (Salley) Harris, 26 July 1780; Norwood Harris, bm; David Harris, wit.

Hawkins, Reuben & Polly Bryant, 8 Sept 1810; John Newton, bm; Junius Sneed, wit.

Hawkins, Sampson, of color, son of Sallie Hawkins, & Delsey Wright, 7 March 1868; m 7 March 1868 by Aaron Pratcher, M. G.

Hawley, George & Julia Ann Pettiford, 27 June 1840; Geo. Anderson, bm; Jas. M. Wiggins, wit.

Hawley, Henderson & Kisiah Anderson, 8 Feb 1842; George Anderson, bm; Wm. H. Whitfield, wit.

Hawley, Jacob & Liddy _____, 9 July 1804; Burton Tabern, bm.

Hawley, Joseph & Eliza Tabern, 16 Nov 1865; Terrel Curtis, bm; A. Landis, wit; m 17 Nov 1865 by T. M. Lynch, J. P.

Hawley, Nathan & Susan Day, 12 July 1851; Samuel Hawley, bm; m 13 July 1851 by Jno. Nance, J. P.

Hawley, Samuel & Mary Jane Anderson, 31 May 1841; Cuffee Mayo, bm; J. M. Wiggins, wit.

Hawley, Samuel & Emeline J. Boon, 25 May 1855; A. Landis, bm; Thos. W. McClanahan, wit; m 27 May 1855 by John Mallory.

Hawley, William & Dicey Day, 2 June 1854; James L. Jenkins, bm.

Hayes, Alfred & Emily Smith, 6 Sept 1831; Wilson W. Dement, bm; David Laws, wit.

Hayes, Allen & Brety Smith, 9 Dec 1815; Hezekiah Plumer, bm; W. M. Sneed, wit.

GRANVILLE MARRIAGES 1753-1868

Hayes, Benjamon & Tilda G. Spencer, 11 Sept 1866; m 15 Sept 1866 by W. P. White, J. P.

Hayes, Brodie & Nancy Jeffers, 11 Jan 1842; John Bookram, bm; J. M. Wiggins, wit.

Hayes, David A. H. & Martha W. Smith, 3 Feb 1851; Charles Moss, bm; A. Landis, wit.

Hayes, George R. & Rowan Culbreath, 8 July 1850; John H. Royster, bm.

Hayes, Hardeman & Mary Wilkerson, 8 Dec 1819; John Duncan, bm; S. K. Sneed, wit.

Hayes, James & Piety Hayes, 23 Dec 1824; Danl. Grisham, bm; Wm. H. Owen, wit.

Hayes, James & Beady Pettiford, 2 June 1860; F. M. Meadors, bm.

Hayes, James G. & Mary Jane Parham, 15 Nov 1851; A. Landis, bm.

Hayes, James H. & E. A. T. Jenkins, 14 Jan 1851; John Powell, bm.

Hayes, John & Elisabeth Rogers, 5 April 1791; William Moore Johnston, bm; Henry Potter, wit.

Hayes, John W. & Sallie Duty, 22 March 1859; A. Landis Jr., bm; m 23 March 1859 by L. K. Willie, M. G.

Hayes, Joseph D. & Anna T. Forrest, 24 May 1856; Eugene Grissom, bm.

Hayes, Joseph M. S. & Catharine Clay, 2 Jan 1854; F. T. Fuller, bm.

Hayes, Joshua Jr. & Martha Loyd, 18 March 1783; Henry Hayes, bm; Reuben Searcy, wit.

Hayes, Josiah & Mary Laurence, 6 March 1792; Ezekiel Hays, bm; Step. Sneed, wit.

Hayes, Junius & Candis Quarles, 12 April 1852; John Dickerson, bm; A. Landis, wit; m 21 April 1852 by Wm. M. Blackwell, J. P.

Hayes, Lenard & Sarah Bradford, 14 Jan 1786; John Searcy Jr., bm.

Hayes, Peter & Elizabeth Buckhanon, 17 Dec 1835; George J. Morris, bm; Benja. Kittrell, wit.

Hayes, Peyton & Salley P. Richardson, 4 April 1813; James Hayes, bm; W. M. Sneed, wit.

Hayes, Presley & Polley Smith, 9 Nov 1815; Samuel Butler, bm; W. M. Sneed, wit.

Hayes, Samuel & Elizabeth Parham, 8 Nov 1837; W. Paschall, bm.

Hayes, Samuel L. & Elizabeth Dickerson, 28 Feb 1839; Jno. Dickerson, bm.

Hayes, Samuel Jr. & Sally Murray, 1 Dec 1821; Aroma Clark, bm; Step. K. Sneed, wit.

GRANVILLE MARRIAGES 1753-1868

Hayes, Silas & Sally Ann Tabern, 16 Oct 1858; Nash Hicks, bm; A. Landis, wit.

Hayes, Simeon & Polly Hester, 5 Oct 1803; Garland Hester, bm; Green Merritt, wit.

Hayes, Simeon & Elizabeth Morris, 30 Nov 1822; William H. Hunt, bm; Jas. M. Wiggins, wit.

Hayes, Solomon & Milley Hester, 9 Nov 1814; William Hester, bm; W. M. Sneed, wit.

Hayes, Simon & Sarah Floyd, 1 April 1838; John Dickerson, bm; Jas. M. Wiggins, wit.

Hayes, Simon & Jane Tippett, 18 Dec 1856; James A. Parham, bm.

Hayes, Thomas & Martha Adcock, 6 April 1844; M. A. Smith, bm; Wm. H. Whitfield, wit.

Hayes, Thos. & Huldy Falkner, 6 Dec 1820; Vines Short, bm; J. M. Wiggins, wit.

Hayes, Thomas P. & Maria Blackley, 17 Dec 1824; Archabald Jordan Jr., bm; Wm. H. Owen, wit.

Hayes, Thomas Peyton & Jane Blackley, 26 Oct 1821; Thomas Hutchinson, bm; Step. K. Sneed, wit.

Hayes, Thomas S. & Eliza Ann Williams, 4 April 1839; M. S. Smith, bm.

Hayes, Whitmel & Martha Smith, 11 April 1827; Lyman Latham, bm; Wm. H. Owen, wit.

Hayes, William A. & Damsel Robertson, 14 Aug 1843; James A. Shert, bm; J. M. Wiggins, wit.

Hayes, William F. & Elizabeth Jordan, 22 Sept 1829; Archibald Turner, bm; A. Sneed, wit.

Hayes, Thomas & Judith Valentine, 5 Sept 1781; Henry Fuller, bm; A--- Fuller, wit.

Hayes, Thomas & Nancy Smith, 7 Jan 1816; John Duncan, bm; Step. K. Sneed, wit.

Hayly, James & Elizabeth B. Thompson, 20 Sept 1818; Henry R. Jones, bm; Zacha. Herndon, Jr., wit.

Haynes, John & Lydda Eastridge, 6 Aug 1782; Thomas _____, bm; Ben Wade, wit.

Hays, Ezekiel & Rhoda Lock, 9 Nov 1789; Willis Cooper, bm; H. Potter, wit.

Hays, George R. & Barbary L. Daniel, 26 May 1847; William _____, bm; D. S. Wilkerson, wit.

Hays, Hardy & India Pendergrass, 23 March 1863; Samuel F. Edwards, bm; A. Landis, wit; m 5 April 1863 by William B. Mann, J. P.

Hays, Henery & Mary Paton, 1 Oct 1783; Rowland Bryant, bm; Bennet Searcy, wit.

GRANVILLE MARRIAGES 1753-1868

Hays, James & Abbie Parham, 1 Feb 1867; m 2 Feb 1867 by A. C. Parham, J. P.

Hays, James H. & Martha Ellington, 10 Sept 1838; Tho. L. King, bm; Elizabeth Ann King, wit.

Hays, James M., son of Peter & Betsy Hays, & Carlina Bullock, daughter of John D. & Sophia Bullock, m 28 Jan 1869 by B. B. Hester.

Hays, Jesse & Judith Farrar, 4 Aug 1795; Peter Farrar, bm; Step. Sneed, wit.

Hays, Jesse & Patsy Johnston, 1 July 1817; John M. Peace, bm.

Hays, Jesse & Celestia May, 22 March 1859; Thos. W. Pool, bm; m 24 March 1859 by M. H. Hight.

Hays, Joel & Rebecah Crutcher, 15 Oct 1815; Martin Srutcher, bm; Leslie Gilliam, wit.

Hays, John Junr. & Ann Blackwell, 14 Oct 1806; William Kittrell, bm; W. M. Sneed, wit.

Hays, Joseph S. & Caroline Morris, 7 April 1862; Arch. Mangum, bm; A. Landis, wit.

Hays, Joseph S. & Caroline Morris, 7 April 1862; m 8 April 1862 by L. K. Willie, M. G.

Hays, M. S. & Catharine Clay, m 11 Jan 1854 by W. D. Allen, J. P.

Hays, Samuel & Penny Spears, 2 Feb 1790; James McDaniel, bm; Henry Potter, wit.

Hays, Samuel & Lucey Parham, 28 Dec 1791; Frederick Parham, bm; W. Norwood, wit.

Hays, Thomas D. & Macen Pendergras, 4 Sept 1857; A. C. Harris, bm; m 4 Sept 1857 by A. C. Harris, M. G.

Hays, Weldon, son of Jessey & Patsey Hays, & Nancy Weathers, daughter of Edward & Polly Weathers, 7 May 1868; m 7 May 1868 by William E. Bullock, J. P.

Hays, William & Marenah Hays, 28 Dec 1811; William Bowers, bm; Step. Sneed, wit.

Head, Carter & Elisabeth Clardy, 23 Dec 1797; William Collens, bm; Step. Sneed, wit.

Headen, Pulaski & Teressey E. Daniel, 19 Sept 1865; W. B. Routon, bm; A. Landis, wit; m 21 Sept 1865 by B. T. Winston, J. P.

Headspeth, Richard & Fanny Smith, 8 Feb 1825; James Finch, bm; S. K. Sneed, wit.

Headspeth, William & Cornelia Ann Clark, 29 April 1863; m 1 May 1863 by Wm. Parham, J. P.; Geo. Roberson, bm.

Heavlin, Robert A. & Lizzie Strong, 7 Nov 1860; Will. R. Hughes, bm; m 14 Nov 1860 by T. G. Lowe.

GRANVILLE MARRIAGES 1753-1868

Hedgepath, Moses & Sally Pookrum, 4 Sept 1845; J. Walker, bm;
J. M. Wiggins, wit.

Hedgepeth, Gaston & Sarah Teasley, free persons of color, 26
Dec 1866; Henry Jones, bm; m 28 Dec 1866 by D. Tilley, J. P.

Hedgepeth, James & Martha Avery, 1 Nov 1843; J. H. Gooch, bm;
Wm. H. Whitfield, wit.

Hedgepeth, Jesse & Emiline Bookram, 10 May 1845; J. Walker, bm.

Hedgpeth, William H. & Mary Boswell, 29 Nov 1836; W. S. McClenahan, bm; J. M. Wiggins, wit.

Hedspath, James & Elilia Taybourn, 15 Feb 1797; William Mitchel, bm; Jno. Hall, wit.

Heffernon, Fielding & Frances Snelling, 16 Dec 1779; John Williamson Cape, bm; Charles Mitchel, wit.

Heffernon, William & Elisabeth Cooke, (no date, during admn. of Richd. Caswell); William Heffernon, bm; James Jett, wit.

Heffernun, Jonathan & Elizabeth Champion, 4 Jan 1791; David Blalock, bm; Saml. Griffin, wit.

Heffler, James & Elisabeth Davis, 6 Sept 1802; Jno. D. Cooke, bm.

Hefflin, James & Patsey Hester, 6 Oct 1818; Joseph Fuller, bm.

Heflen, John & Molley Kittle, 9 Aug 1797; Evan Freeman, bm; Wm. Norwood, wit.

Heflin, Benjemin & Mary Hanks, 3 Dec 1816; Israel Hargrove, bm; A. Sneed, wit.

Heflin, Henry H., son of Lewis & Harriet Heflin, & Narcissa C. Morton, daughter of Joseph & Betsy Morton, 19 Feb 1868; m 20 Feb 1868 by W. H. P. Jenkins, J. P.

Heflin, James & Elisabeth Pain(?), 12 May 1800; Charles Heflin, bm; _____ Bullock, wit.

Heflin, James & Mary H. Akin, 16 Jan 1848; W. E. Bullock, bm; Jas. M. Wiggins, wit.

Heflin, Robt. S. & Laura A. Johnson, 9 June 1859; S. D. Ferrill, bm; m 12 June 1859 by J. P. Moore.

Heflin, Rufus & Martha C. Whitfield, 23 Oct 1841; J. A. Stone, bm; Wm. H. Whitfield, wit.

Heflin, Rufus T. & Lucy Ann Steed, 13 June 1846; Wm. D. Heflin, bm.

Heflin, William & Susanna Heflin, 6 Nov 1799; John Heflin, bm; James Sneed, wit.

Hegge, Thomas & Dianna Hide, 14 Feb 1802; John Taylor, bm; Step. Sneed, wit.

Heggie, James & Frances Blackwel, 24 Nov 1800; James Royster, bm; Step. Sneed, wit.

GRANVILLE MARRIAGES 1753-1868

Heggie, James M. & Mary Ann Hunt, 22 Nov 1838; Eaton H. Kittrell, bm; Jas. M. Wiggins, wit.

Heggie, William & Mary Parkman, 10 April 1774; Henry Parkman, bm; Reuben Searcy, wit.

Henderson, James A. & Jennie Maynard, 9 May 1863; Alexander Colclough, bm.

Henderson, James A. & Jennie Maynard, 9 May 1863; Ira E. Arnold, bm; m 12 May 1863 by A. W. Mangum, M. G.

Henderson, James L. & Sarah E. Nethery, 10 June 1865; Henry H. Sethey(?), bm; m 14 June 1865 by F. N. Whaley, Minister.

Henderson, John & Sarah Alston, 4 June 1772; Saml. Henderson, Reuben Searcy, bm; Richard Searcy, wit.

Henderson, Leonard & Frances Farrar, 3 Nov 1795; John Hare, bm; Thomas Falconer, wit.

Henderson, Leonard & Miss Nancy B. Turner, 1 Nov 1851; E. Satterwhite, bm; m 12 Nov 1851 by Thos. F. Davis, Minister of the Episcopal Church.

Henderson, Nathaniel & Sarah Jones, 31 Oct 1763; Reuben Searcy, bm; Joseph Williams, wit.

Henderson, Nathaniel & Charlotte Morgan, 29 Aug 1781; Reuben Searcy, wit.

Henderson, Richard & Elizabeth Keeling, 28 Dec 1763; John Williams, Reuben Searcy, bm; John Williams, wit.

Hendley, Burrell & Pheby Morris, 9 Sept 1825; Stephen Bridges, bm; Wm. Hayes Owen, wit.

Hendley, Henry & Martha Allen, 20 Sept 1838; Philip Moore, bm.

Hendley, Hudson & Helly Stone, 26 Aug 1829; William Levister, bm; David Laws, wit.

Hendley, William & Charlotte Wood, 7 Aug 1855; J. M. Beck, bm; m 1 Oct 1855 by Jas. J. Moore, J. P.

Hendrick, John & Lucy R. Turner, 21 March 1825; Moses Neal, bm; A. Sneed, wit.

Hendrick, Thomas & Jacky Fowler, 28 Nov 1815; Mills Tayloe, bm; Richd. Sneed, wit.

Henerick, George & Eddy Sisemore, 25 March 1815; Newton Wright, bm; H. Young, wit.

Henley, Henry & Martha Finch, 11 May 1858; W. J. Mitchell, bm; m 11 May 1858 by W. Parham(?), J. P.

Henley, Stephen & Ellen H. Brame, 20 Dec 1854; A. Landis, bm.

Henly, James D. & Nancy Overbey, 13 Nov 1860; Jas. T. Hunt, bm; m 13 Nov 1860 by Eld. S. Gilmore.

Hennon, William & Betsey Bullock, 11 March 1771; William Bullock, bm.

GRANVILLE MARRIAGES 1753-1868

Hendry, Henry & Martha Bragg, 20 Dec 1821; Halyard Blackley, bm; S. V. Sneed, wit.

Henslee, Richard & Salley Johnson, 30 May 1808; Isaac Johnson, bm; W. M. Sneed, wit.

Herring, William & Jane Culverhouse, 28 Sept 1785; Joseph Culverhouse(?), bm; John Searcy, wit.

Hester, Alfred & Mary Smith, 31 May 1816; Robert Hester, bm; W. M. Sneed, wit.

Hester, Benjamin & Molley Dyer, 23 Dec 1778; Reuben Talley, bm; Reuben Searcy, wit.

Hester, Benjamin & Nancey Harris, 6 Sept 1814; William Hester, bm; W. M. Sneed, wit.

Hester, Benjamin & Patsey Burnett, 15 Nov 1818; Jessee Huddleston, bm; Step. K. Sneed, wit.

Hester, Benjamin & Martha Howell, 28 Dec 1825; John J. Williams, bm; M. M. Henderson, wit.

Hester, Benjamin & Charity Laurence, 23 Oct 1829; Israel Estes, bm; S. K. Sneed, wit.

Hester, Bennett & Isabella Howard, 6 Feb 1810; David Hunt, bm; W. M. Sneed, wit.

Hester, Charles & Elisabeth King, 28 May 1800; Samuel Creath Jr., bm; Step. Sneed, wit.

Hester, Daniel & Alice Burwell (colored), 23 Sept 1865; Benj. Davis, bm; m 23 Sept 1865 by E. H. Overton, J. P.

Hester, E. J. & Virginia Hobgood, 6 Dec 1859; Z. M. P. Lowry, bm; m 10 Dec 1859 by R. J. Devin.

Hester, Elijah & Mary U. P. William Giles, 23 Sept 1818; William Veasey, bm; S. K. Sneed, wit.

Hester, Edward & Pattie Ann Hicks, 25 Dec 1865.

Hester, Francis & Elizabeth Blanks, 29 Sept 1795; Francis Royster, bm; Step. Sneed, wit.

Hester, Francis & Polly Hester, 18 Oct 1816; William Hester, bm; Stephen Koutousoff Sneed, wit.

Hester, Francis & Rebecca Stovall, 25 Feb 1840; James Hester, bm; J. M. Wiggins, wit.

Hester, Francis G. & Mary Ann Currin, 31 Oct 1838; Gardner OBriant, bm; J. M. Wiggins, wit.

Hester, Francis G. & Frances Currin, 8 March 1842; Samuel Hunt Jr., bm; J. M. Wiggins, wit.

Hester, Francis K. & Mary C. Allen, 23 Jan 1851; Jas. P. Paschall, bm.

Hester, Garland & Charlotte Parker, 11 Dec 1799; John Parrish, bm; James Sneed, wit.

GRANVILLE MARRIAGES 1753-1868

Hester, George & Elizabeth Hester, 2 Jan 1833; Benjamin Wilson, bm; S. K. Sneed, wit.

Hester, Graves & Mary Graves, 4 Sept 1802; Overton Wiles, bm; Step. Sneed, wit.

Hester, Green & Mary Ann Crews, 11 Jan 1866.

Hester, Hambleton & Frances Hunt, 24 Oct 1820; Patrick OBriant, bm; Step. K. Sneed, wit.

Hester, Henry & Mary Graves, 8 Nov 1774; Robert Hester, bm; Wm. Reardon, wit.

Hester, Henry & Mary Wilson, 20 Dec 1825; Henry Wilson, bm; Wm. Hayes Owen, wit.

Hester, Henry J. & Martha Elliott, 29 Sept 1858; Elijah J. Hester, bm; m 30 Sept 1858 by F. B. Currin, J. P.

Hester, Henry J., son of Francis & Mary Hester, & Susan A. Elliott, daughter of James & Lucy Ann Elliott, 30 May 1867; m 2 June 1867 by Robert J. Devin.

Hester, Hinton G. & Martha A. Jones, 9 June 1829; James Cheatham, bm; David Laws, wit.

Hester, Isaac & Lydia Starke, 31 May 1811; Presley Rowland, bm; Jun. Sneed, wit.

Hester, Isaac & Pathenia R. Hester, 23 Aug 1838; Wm. C. Macem(?), bm.

Hester, James & Tabitha Stovall, 5 Oct 1803; Francis Hester, bm; Green Merritt, wit.

Hester, James & Patsey Whitefeild, 12 Nov 1805; Saml. Young, bm; Jas. Sneed, wit.

Hester, James & Patsey Whitfield, 20 Jan 1808; Thos. Yarbrough, bm; W. M. Sneed, wit.

Hester, James & Salome H. Chandler, 3 Dec 1847; Thomas Hester, bm; Jas. M. Wiggins, wit.

Hester, Jeremiah & Polley Maynor, 24 May 1815; Benjamin Hester, bm; W. M. Sneed, wit.

Hester, Jeremiah & Harriot Harris, 7 Jan 1816; William Hester, bm; Step. N. Sneed, wit.

Hester, John & Margaret Frazier, 18 Dec 1783; Aaron Springfield (?), bm; Reuben Searcy, wit.

Hester, John & Milley Crews, 23 Dec 1793; Daniel Owens, bm; W. Norwood, D. C., wit.

Hester, John & Mary Whitfield, 29 Dec 1796; Stephen Hester, bm; Step. Sneed, wit.

Hester, John & Margaret Highfield, 15 Jan 1807; Robert Hester, bm; W. M. Sneed, wit.

Hester, John & Frankey Bates, 6 June 1812; Patrick OBriant, bm; W. M. Sneed, wit.

GRANVILLE MARRIAGES 1753-1868

Hester, John & _____, 5 Nov 1816; William Hester, bm; W. M. Sneed, wit.

Hester, John C. & Lucy A. Hamlett, 20 Jan 1864; A. Landis, bm; m 20 Jan 1864 by T. W. Moore, Minister of the Gospel.

Hester, John G. & Susan A. F. Fleming, 22 March 1847; Jno. B. Green, bm; J. M. Wiggins, wit.

Hester, John G. & Sallie P. Crews, 8 Oct 1859; John Fleming, bm; m 11 Oct 1859 by B. B. Hester.

Hester, John H. & Sally Newton, 11 May 1849; Jno. Noblin, bm; J. M. Wiggins, wit.

Hester, John H. & Lucy T. Overby, 20 June 1855; John W. Rice, bm; Jas. R. Duty, wit; m 20 June 1855 by Jas. R. Duty, J. P.

Hester, Joseph & Elisabeth Parker, 4 July 1781; Barnet Pulliam, bm.

Hester, Joseph & Elizabeth Lewis Epps, 10 Oct 1817; L. Gilliam, bm; Step. K. Sneed, wit.

Hester, Joseph & Robena Burrows, 19 Dec 1826; Wm. Norman, bm; Wm. H. Owen, wit.

Hester, Joseph P. & Sarah Bullock, 3 Nov 1840; B. A. Mitchel, bm.

Hester, Joseph P. & Hicksey Bradford, 18 Jan 1859; Wm. L. Mitchell, bm; m 20 Jan 1859 by B. B. Hester.

Hester, Joseph Reed & Patsey Johnston, 21 Dec 1806; Stephen Johnson, bm; W. M. Sneed, wit.

Hester, Kinchen Y. & Penny Morgan, 6 Nov 1827; James Heflin, bm; S. K. Sneed, wit.

Hester, Knapper & Mary Hester (freed people), 27 Dec 1865; Geo. W. Landis, wit; m 31 Dec 1865 by L. K. Willie, M. G.

Hester, Matthew & Margaret Loyd, 28 March 1838; Archabal A. Gresham, bm; S. G. Shearmon, wit.

Hester, Memucan H. & Mary A. Cooper, 24 May 1847; Alex Fleming, bm; J. M. Wiggins, wit.

Hester, Michael & Joanney Melton, 9 Feb 1789; Wm. Moore, bm; A. Henderson, wit.

Hester, Randal & Clarissa Wren, 22 Sept 1829; John Gum, bm; Step. K. Sneed, wit.

Hester, Randolph & Sarah Fleming, 15 March 1849; Jno. H. Wright, bm; Jas. M. Wiggins, wit.

Hester, Ro. & Barbara Smith, 5 Nov 1788; Jo. Smith, bm; A. Henderson, wit.

Hester, Robert & Seley Daniel, 29 April 1785.

Hester, Robert & Elisabeth Norman, 17 Oct 1804; Henry Norman, bm; Step. Sneed, wit.

GRANVILLE MARRIAGES 1753-1868

Hester, Robert (of F) & Salley Vass, 14 May 1812; Robert Hester (of Wm), bm; W. M. Sneed, wit.

Hester, Robert & Nancy Hart, 28 Feb 1824; Thomas Hester, bm; David J. Young, wit.

Hester, Robert & Nancy Evans, 5 Feb 1839; Howel G. Pittard, bm.

Hester, Robert & Rebecca Brinkley, 28 Dec 1831; James Briky, bm; David Laws, wit.

Hester, Robert & Mollie Knott, 14 Dec 1865; H. J. Hester, bm; m 17 Dec 1865 by B. T. Winston, J. P.

Hester, Robert, of color, son of Green Hester & Mary A. Hester, & Martha Hare, daughter of Sally Bullock, 12 Dec 1867; m 26 Dec 1867 by H. G. Hill, Minister.

Hester, Solomon & Laura Hester (freed people), 25 July 1865; Lawrence Hester, bm; A. Landis, wit; m 27 July 1865 by L. A. Paschall, J. P.

Hester, Stephen & Elizabeth Smith, 19 Dec 1791; Thomas Daniel, bm; W. Norwood, wit.

Hester, Stephen & Sarah Sears, 20 Nov 1806; George Thomas, bm.

Hester, Thomas & Elizabeth Stovall, 8 May 1798; Francis Royster, bm; Step. Sneed, wit.

Hester, Thomas & Faithy Fraizer, 13 Oct 1818; Robert Hester, bm; Step. K. Sneed, wit.

Hester, Thomas & Liddey Hunt, 8 May 1821; James Hart Jr., bm; Jas. M. Wiggins, wit.

Hester, Thomas & Frances Y. Ragsdale, 30 Oct 1841; Part--- Knott, bm; J. M. Wiggins, wit.

Hester, Thomas B. & Catharine Satterwhite, 7 May 1850; Robert H. Frazier, bm.

Hester, Thomas D. & Narcissa J. B. Mann; 24 June 1841; L. L. Kimbal, bm.

Hester, Thomas D. & Ann E. G. Moss, 17 May 1853; James R. Duty, bm; m 18 May 1853 by Jas. R. Duty, J. P.

Hester, William & Mary Frazier, 27 Dec 1780; Frederick Reeves, bm; Bartlet Wright, wit.

Hester, William & Bearsha Norman, 27 Nov 1799; Henry Norman, bm; Step. Sneed, wit.

Hester, William & Judah Hester, 21 Dec 1808; Francis Hester, bm; Alf. Wilkins, wit.

Hester, William & Lizy Hester, 4 Sept 1810; Lazarus Minor, bm; W. M. Sneed, wit.

Hester, William & Martha Fowler, 27 Oct 1825; Almond Tuck, bm.

Hester, William & Frances Mayho, 18 Jan 1866; m 20 Jan 1867 by M. H. Vaughan, Rector of St. Stephen's Church.

GRANVILLE MARRIAGES 1753-1868

Hester, William F. & Rebecca Harbauk, 8 May 1850; Wm. Strum, bm.

Hester, William H. & Aremisa Mann, 17 Feb 1846; William Hunter, bm; Jas. M. Wiggins, wit.

Hester, William H. & Emily Vaughan, 4 July 1850; J. P. Hester, bm.

Hester, William S. & Malissa F. Crews, 3 March 1856; Eugene Grissom, bm; m 19 March 1856 by L. K. Willie, M. G.

Hester, Winfree & Rebecca Ann Parrish, 2 Aug 1848; Richard T. Fowler, bm.

Hester, Zachariah & Elisabeth Frazier, 11 Sept 1782; Joseph Hester, bm; Asa Searcy, wit.

Hester, Zachariah & Nancey Rice, 9 Feb 1809; John Earle, bm; Jas. Sneed, wit.

Hester, Zachariah & Drucilla Badgett, 1 June 1814; Jesse Badgett, bm; W. M. Sneed, wit.

Hevlin, John & Lethy Kimball, 16 Dec 1834; Robt. J. Yancey Jr., bm; Benja. Kittrell, wit.

Hews, David & Judah Daniel, 24 Jan 1786; J. Bedford, bm; Bennet Searcy, wit.

Heydon, David & Sarah J. Linum, 16 April 1838; Wm. M. Hight, bm; _____ King, wit.

Hickman, William & Nancy Floyd, 12 Dec 1800; Wiatt Hickman, bm; W. M. Sneed, wit.

Hickmon, Corbin & Charrity Parrish, 5 June 1783; Sherwed Parrish, bm; Reuben Searcy, wit.

Hicks, Abner & Elizabeth Harris, 27 Aug 1800; Thomas Ricks, bm; Philip Bullock, wit.

Hicks, Abaslom & Dorcas Strum, 9 Oct 1825; Lyman Latham, bm; Jas. W. Wiggins, wit.

Hicks, Absalom & Mary Wall, 29 June 1832; William Parrish, bm; Step. K. Sneed, wit.

Hicks, Alexander, of color, son of William Hicks & Mary Shanks, & Amy Mitchell, saughter of _____ Satterwhite & Dolly Mitchell Satterwhite, 6 Sept 1867; m _____ by A. C. Harris, M. G.

Hicks, Alfred & Lucy Blacknall, 30 Nov 1818; William A. Gill, bm; John J. Strum, wit.

Hicks, Archibald & Mary Norman, 3 Aug 1839; John Ellington, bm.

Hicks, Benjamin W. & Susan A. Hester, 2 Dec 1851; Benj. C. Cooke, bm; m 23 Dec 1851 by L. K. Willie, Minister of the Gospel.

Hicks, Benjamin W. & Isabella J. Crews, 17 Oct 1854; Albert C. Parham, bm; m 19 Oct 1854 by L. K. Willie, M. G.

Hicks, Charles & Philis Taylor, 25 Dec 1865; m 31 Dec 1865 by _____ Hester.

GRANVILLE MARRIAGES 1753-1868

Hicks, Daniel & Rebecca Walker, 29 May 1826; Edmund A. Freeman, bm; Wm. Hayes Owen, wit.

Hicks, Henry & Ellen Slaughter, 2 Nov 1853; John D. Tingen, bm; m 2 Nov 1853 by Peterson Thorp, J. P.

Hicks, Henry C. & Catharine E. Bobbitt, 22 Nov 1858; A. Landis, bm; m 24 Nov 1858 by L. K. Willie, M. G.

Hicks, James & Sarah Jordan, 18 Sept 1798; Abel Farrall, bm; Step. Sneed, wit.

Hicks, James & Delia Hester, 25 Dec 1865.

Hicks, Jasper & Mary Hicks, 22 Feb 1810; A. Mitchel, bm; W. M. Sneed, wit.

Hicks, John & Susanah P. Jones, 16 July 1800; John Hutchings, bm; Step. Sneed, wit.

Hicks, John & Polly Lamay, 23 Oct 1816; David Satterwhite, bm; Richd. Sneed, wit.

Hicks, John B. & Sarah A. Mallory, 8 Jan 1842; Samuel S. Hicks, bm; J. M. Wiggins, wit.

Hicks, John F. & Martha Y. Montague, 14 Dec 1841; Solomon Cottrell, bm; W. R. Wiggins, wit.

Hicks, John R. & Rebecca B. Wood, 23 Sept 1823; Spence McClenahan, bm; Jas. M. Wiggins, wit.

Hicks, John R. & Jane S. Downey, 25 Dec 1828; James Cooper, bm; David Laws, wit.

Hicks, Joseph & Indiana Hester, freed people, 27 Dec 1865; Geo. W. Landis, wit; m 31 Dec 1865 by L. K. Willie, M. G.

Hicks, Joseph M. & Evelina Horner, 15 July 1846; S. J. Jackson, bm; J. M. Wiggins, wit.

Hicks, Leonidas & Amy Ann Ellington, 10 Sept 1852; m by S. G. Wilson, J. P.

Hicks, Leonidas H. & Amey Ann Ellington, 28 Aug 1852; James R. Duty, bm.

Hicks, Leonidas H. & Miranda S. Blackley, 24 Nov 1858; A. Landis, bm; m 25 Nov 1858 by D. P. Paschall, J. P.

Hicks, Levi & Sarah Oakley, 20 Dec 1840; Ransom Cash, bm; Jas. M. Wiggins, wit.

Hicks, Nash & Susan J. Anderson, free persons of color, 1 March 1855; William Evans, bm; Jas. R. Duty, bm; m 7 April 1855 by Jas. R. Duty, J. P.

Hicks, Nathaniel & Elisabeth Jackson, 14 April 1781; Steaven Hicks, bm; Asa Searcy, wit.

Hicks, Nelson & Lucy Ellington, 2 Dec 1836; Samuel Pittar, bm; J. M. Wiggins, wit.

Hicks, Robert & Sarah Ravens, 10 Sept 1793; Thomas Hicks, bm; Step. Sneed, wit.

GRANVILLE MARRIAGES 1753-1868

Hicks, Robert & Sarah Grisham, 3 Dec 1821; <u>Kinelm</u> White, bm; W. M. Sneed, wit.

Hicks, Samuel S. & Nancy E. Cannaday, 1 Nov 1843; Saml. Duty, bm; Wm. H. Whitfield, wit.

Hicks, Thomas A., son of Nelson N. Hicks & Lucy Ellington, & Martha A. Morton, daughter of Joseph H. Morton & Betsy A. Ball, 12 Jan 1868; m 12 Jan 1868 by W. H. P. Jenkins, J. P.

Hicks, Thomas W. & Elizabeth H. Johnson, 2 Nov 1857; George L. Daly, bm; m 2 Nov 1857 by J. F. Harris, J. P.

Hicks, William & Elisabeth Ann Tatum, 24 March 1778; John Potter, bm; Edward Bullock, wit.

Hicks, William & Mourning Hunt, 27 May 1778; John Searcy Senr., bm.

Hicks, William & Jane Creth, 17 May 1825; Washington Sears, bm; L. Gilliam, wit.

Hicks, William & Martha C. Slaughter, 31 Aug 1848; Jacob S. Tingel, bm; Jas. M. Wiggins, wit.

Hicks, William R. & Mary Cheatham, 26 Nov 1821; Bartholomew Kimbell, bm; Jas. M. Wiggins, wit.

Hicks, William R. & Ann N. Kittrell, 23 April 1847; J. C. Cooper, bm; Jas. M. Wiggins, wit.

Hicks, Willis & Polly Harris, 10 Sept 1817; Anderson Sears, bm; R. N. Herndon, wit.

Hicks, Willis & Nancy Sears, 2 March 1826; Jno. H. Ragsdale, bm; Wm. H. Owen, wit.

Higgs, John & Nancey Dickerson, 20 May 1792; James Bedford, bm; Step. Sneed, wit.

Higgs, John & Mary Johnson, 20 March 1813; Richard Wood, bm; Thos. Hicks, wit.

Higgs, John & Martha Harrison, 31 March 1821; James Nuttall, bm; J. J. Farrar, Step. K. Sneed, wit.

Higgs, Jonathan & Polley Langford, 5 Aug 1799; John Fuller, bm; Step. Sneed, wit.

Higgs, Jonathan & Mary Wood, 18 Dec 1802; Levi Higgs, bm; Spencer Hinton, wit.

Higgs, Kinelm & Susanah Johnston, 9 Feb 1801; John Mirchel, bm; P. Bullock, wit.

Higgs, Leonard & Sarah Kittrell, 14 May 1777; Jonathan Kittrell, bm; Thos. Bradford, wit.

Higgs, Levi & Nancy Bradford, 20 May 1813; Richard Wood, bm; Thos. Hicks, wit.

Higgs, Southern & Selina T. Harris, 17 Nov 1827; Willis Johnson, bm; Wm. H. Owen, wit.

GRANVILLE MARRIAGES 1753-1868

Higgs, Southern & Rebecca Harrison, 11 Jan 1830; Levi Higgs, bm; David Laws, wit.

Higgs, Thompson & Sally Johnson, 2 Nov 1819; Jonathan Amis, bm; S. K. Sneed, wit.

Higgs, Zachariah & Elizabeth G. Hamson, 24 Dec 1852; Alfred Knight, bm; m 6 Jan 1853 by D. J. Paschall, J. P.

High, Robert & Sarah Winston, 6 March 1778; James Blackwell, bm; Reuben Searcy, wit.

Highfill, Hezekiah & Delila Floyd, 5 Oct 1784; John Laurance, bm; Bennet Searcy, wit.

Hight, Charnal & Sucey Finch, 24 Oct 1786; Richard Hight, bm; Bennet Searcy, wit.

Hight, Herbert H. & Caroline Kittrell, 4 Jan 1864; Wm. Breedlove, bm; A. Landis, wit; m 8 Jan 1864 by W. K. Willie, M. G.

Hight, Herbert Thomas & Helen Haswell, 15 Dec 1853; Wm. Moss, bm; A. Landis, wit.

Hight, Howard & Peggie Powel, 25 Dec 1821; William Carr, bm; L. Gilliam, wit.

Hight, James Y. & Mary Ann Powell, 15 Dec 1845; William J. Hunt, bm; Jas. M. Wiggins, wit.

Hight, Jno. S. & Abigail Merritt, 5 Jan 1849; John M. Ellington, bm; J. M. Wiggins, wit.

Hight, Medius H. & Mary E. Nuttall, 9 Dec 1857; L. K. Willie, bm; m 10 Dec 1857 by L. K. Willie, M. G.

Hight, Ridick & Mary Jane Duke, 3 Feb 1857; Robert T. Overton, bm; m 5 Feb 1857 by D. P. Paschall, J. P.

Hight, Robert & Beady Bragg, 6 Sept 1852; Thos. Woodliff, bm; A. Landis, wit; m 7 April 1852 by J. M. Stone, J. P.

Hight, Thomas D. & Sallie Stone, 24 Oct 1859; Festus M. Fuller, bm; m 25 Oct 1859 by C. F. Harris.

Hight, William & Averellah Bobbet, 3 Oct 1785; Shaw Johnson, bm; Bennet Searcy, wit.

Hight, William J. & Fanny Overton, 2 Nov 1850; Thos. D. Hight, bm.

Hightower, William & Susannah Dicker, 24 July 1789; Henry Dicker, bm; A. Henderson, wit.

Hill, Burrell & Sally Harris, 26 Dec 1866; m 28 Dec 1866 by Aaron Pratcher(?), Minister of the Gospel.

Hill, Ellis & Nancy Night, 1 Aug 1801; James Forsyth, bm; Philip Bullock, wit.

Hill, James & Prescilla Hifield, 20 Dec 1794; John Morris Jr., bm; Step. Sneed, wit.

Hill, James & Precilla Hiefield, 24 Aug 1805; John Gresham, bm; A. H. Sneed, wit.

GRANVILLE MARRIAGES 1753-1868

Hill, John Y. & Salina Clark, 6 June 1850; J. J. Hill, bm; L. B. Stone, J. P., wit.

Hill, Nicholas L. & Nancy Jones, 26 Nov 1842; W. A. Bullock, bm.

Hill, Philip M. & Malinda L. Apperson, 16 Feb 1836; F. A. Brightwell, bm; Benja. Kittrell, wit; statement that Malinda L. Apperson is over 15 years of age.

Hill, Thomas & Nelley Highfield, 24 Dec 1799; Thomas Forsythe, bm; Step. Sneed, wit.

Hill, William & Milley Knight, 22 July 1795; John Hill, bm; Step. Sneed, wit.

Hill, William W. & Mary A. Ramsay, 5 April 1858; J. J. Hill, bm; m 8 April 1858 by B. N. Hopkins, a Minister of the Gospel.

Hilliard, Dandridge & Elizabeth A. Strong, 22 July 1836; Jeremy Hilliard, bm; W. S. Hayne, bm.

Hilliard, Jeremy & Amelia M. Ridley, 21 June 1841; Jno. R. Herndon, bm; J. M. Wiggins, wit.

Hilliard, Micajah & Unis R. Strong, 28 Dec 1843; Robt. H. Read, bm; Wm. S. Hargrove, wit.

Hillyard, Benjamin & Betsey Potter, 21 Nov 1790; Lewis Potter, bm; H. Potter, wit.

Hillyard, William & Lucy Walker, 29 Oct 1797; Washington Norwood, bm; Step. Sneed, wit.

Hines, Julien C. & Anne E. Rainey, 17 Feb 1866; C. W. Rainey, bm.

Hines, Thomas, of Wake County, & Mary Hardy, of Granville County, 14 Nov 1777; James Alston, bm; Saml. Henderson Jur., wit.

Hines, Thomas & Frances Lewis, 6 May 1790; Thomas Person, bm; A. Henderson, wit.

Hinton, David & Jane Lewis, 13 Nov 1790; Thos. Hines, bm.

Hinton, Kimborough & Lottey Harper, 25 Nov 1791; Wm. Pattillo, bm; W. Norwood, wit.

Hite, E. S. & Bettie A. Owen, 26 Nov 1866; Edward Jones, bm; m 26 Nov 1866 by L. B. Stone, J. P.

Hite, James & Elizabeth J. Bowen, 15 June 1862; J. R. Blanks, bm; m 15 June 1862 by L. B. Stone, J. P.

Hite, Standley & Matilda Talley, 5 Jan 1820; Stephen Tally, bm; Jno. P. Smith, wit.

Hobgood, Alfred & Sophia J. Hunt, 2 Feb 1867; m 7 Feb 1867 by T. J. Horner, G. M.; H. F. Holeman, bm.

Hobgood, Barnett & Nancy Wood, 28 Sept 1825; Thomas Hobgood, bm; Wm. H. Owen, wit.

Hobgood, Daniel G. & Sophia Jane Hester, 18 Nov 1863; J. D. Knott, bm.

GRANVILLE MARRIAGES 1753-1868

Hobgood, Fowler & Elisabeth Goss, 10 May 1799; Solomon Williams, bm; Step. Sneed, wit.

Hobgood, H. & N. A. S. Anthony, 6 Feb 1834; S. Harris, bm; M. Hunt, wit.

Hobgood, Henry & Mildred Hayes, 29 Oct 1833; James Gooch, bm; Benja. Kittrell, wit.

Hobgood, Henry & Harriet Frazier, 20 Jan 1853; Hamilton Currin, bm; A. Landis, wit; m 20 Jan 1853 by R. J. Devin.

Hobgood, Hesekiah & Elizabeth Walker, 26 Jan 1817; Lemuel Hobgood, bm; Rhodes N. Herndon, wit.

Hobgood, Hezekiah & Sarah Mangum, 21 April 1830; Henry House, bm; David Laws, wit.

Hobgood, James & Elizabeth House, 8 Oct 1828; Henry House, bm; Wm. H. Owen, wit.

Hobgood, James S. & Rebecca Frazier, 28 Jan 1858; John C. Hester, bm; m 28 Jan 1858 by Peterson Thorp, J. P.

Hobgood, John R. & Mary Adcock, 23 Sept 1818; Hezekiah Hobgood, bm; Zacha. Herndon, J. P., wit.

Hobgood, Joseph D. & Nancy Blalock, 13 Jan 1835; Jn. P. Blalock, bm; Benja. Kittrell, wit.

Hobgood, Legan & Elizabeth Davis, 5 Oct 1853; James M. Pittard, bm; m 5 Oct 1853 by R. J. Devin, V. D. M.

Hobgood, Lemuel & Ruthy Tippet, 17 Nov 1821; James Meadows, bm; S. K. Sneed, wit.

Hobgood, Lemuel & Julia Ann Harris, 16 Jan 1849; Thos. Tippett, bm; J. M. Wiggins, wit.

Hobgood, Presley B. & Sarah E. Terry, 18 Jan 1861; George W. Hobgood, bm; m 23 Jan 1861 by Peterson Thorp, J. P.

Hobgood, Reuben & Mary Ann Hester, freed people, 9 Dec 1865; A. Landis, wit; m 9 Dec 1865 by E. F. Beachum, a regular G. M.

Hobgood, Roberson B. & James Catharine Lyon, 13 Oct 1856; George W. Hobgood, bm; m 16 Oct 1856 by Peterson Thorp, J. P.

Hobgood, Robert H. & Sarah A. Hester, 13 Dec 1860; m 20 Dec 1860 by Heff Horner, J. P.

Hobgood, Robert W. & Mary A. Hunt, 4 Nov 1856; Wm. G. Washington, bm; m 6 Nov 1856 by Peterson Thorp, J, P.

Hobgood, Samuel & Rebecca Blalock, 3 May 1856; W. A. Currin, bm.

Hobgood, Simpson, son of Rowland & Perthena Hobgood, & Maz Newton, daughter of John & Mary Newton, 13 Nov 1867; m 14 Nov 1867 by L. C. Ragland.

Hobgood, Thomas & Sarah Russell, 8 Feb 1790; Howel Rose, bm; Henry Potter, wit.

Hobgood, Thomas & Emily Hayes, 5 May 1840; Thos. Tippett, bm; Jas. M. Wiggins, wit.

GRANVILLE MARRIAGES 1753-1868

Hobgood, Thomas & Martha L. Morris, 4 Nov 1856; Zachariah OBriant, bm; m 6 Nov 1856 by Peterson Thorp, J. P.

Hobgood, Thomas & Martha L. Morris, 4 Nov 1856; Chesley L. Jackson, bm.

Hobgood, Thomas & Lucy Thomasson, 31 May 1859; Wm. McFarling, bm; m 1 June 1859 by L. K. Willie, M. G.

Hobgood, Thomas & Mrs. Parthena A. Adcock, 17 April 1865; m 26 April 1865 by Samuel Hunt, J. P.

Hobgood, William & Sarah Goss, 16 Dec 1822; Thomas Goss, bm; S. K. Sneed, wit.

Hobgood, William & Lucinda Harris, 4 Dec 1839; Person Williams, bm.

Hobgood, William S. & Mary E. Wright, 8 Feb 1850; Logan Hobgood, bm; A. Landis, wit.

Hobgood, Willie P. & Sally A. Mangum, 24 Oct 1851.

Hockaday, James & Delila Bailey, 6 Sept 1836; W. Rogers, bm; J. M. Wiggins, wit.

Hockaday, William & Margarett J. Garner, 13 Feb 1855; Eugene Grissom, bm; m 15 March 1855 by W. D. Allen, J. P.

Hockady, Jas. M. & Elizabeth W. Morgan, 20 Jan 1849; W. D. Allen, bm; J. M. Wiggins, wit.

Hodge, Franklin & Ann Curtis, freed people, m 23 June 1867 by B. F. Winston, J. P.

Hodge, James B., son of Wm. H. Hodge & Fannie Hodge, & Frances Wilson, daughter of Frank & Martha Wilson, 16 Nov 1868; m 16 Nov 1868 by C. Allen.

Hodges, Philemon & Winnefred Kittrell, 18 Sept 1783; Jos. McDaniel, bm.

Hofman, James & Mary Clarke, 25 Sept 1827; Henry Byars, bm; S. K. Sneed, wit.

Hogan, Thomas & Jane O. Southerland, 1 April 1844; William Coley, bm; Wm. H. Whitfield, wit.

Hogge, Saml. & Sarah Williams, 14 May 1792; W. Norwood, bm; Saml. Worthington, wit.

Holden, Isaiah & Leah Kittrell, 11 May 1814; F. N. W. Benton, Wm. V. Taylor, Richard Sneed, W. M. Sneed, bm.

Holden, Jeremiah & Jane Farrar, 8 Aug 1797; Levi Whitted (Whithead), bm; Step. Sneed, wit.

Holden, Jessie, colored, son of Lewis & Silvia Holden, & Judy Kearney, daughter of Woodson Alston & Patience Kearney, 21 Dec 1868; m 28 Dec 1868 by John W. Estes, J. P.

Holder, William & Mourning Duggar, 7 Sept 1787; Willison Loyd, bm; B. Searcy, wit.

GRANVILLE MARRIAGES 1753-1868

Holeman, John & Sarah Lyon, 9 June 1867; Allen Green, bm; F. J. Tilley, wit; m 10 June 1867 by D. L. Bullock, J. P.

Holloway, George F. & Elizabeth P. Hamlet, 30 Nov 1859; J. T. Hunt, bm; m 1 Dec 1859 by E. F. Beacham, a regular Minister of the Gospel.

Holloway, John & Martha R. Neal, 2 Oct 1835; John F. Neal, bm; Tho. H. Willie, wit.

Holloway, Robert & Mrs. Pattie Reade, 23 Nov 1865; L. C. Smith, bm.

Holmes, Henry B. & Arena Hendley, 7 Nov 1850; Thos. H. Usry, bm; A. Landis, wit.

Holmes, John & Elizabeth Ann Nance, 11 Jan 1849; John May, bm; Benj. C. Clark, wit.

Holmes, Richard R. & Amanda Bridges, 4 Nov 1857; J. C. Hester, bm.

Holmes, Saml. & Kitty Ussery, 22 Dec 1821; Archer Mitchell, bm; Jas. M. Wiggins, wit.

Holmes, Thomas & Rebecca Izzard, 13 Feb 1834; John Pierce, bm.

Holmes, William, son of William & Nancy Holmes, & Ceney Pool, daughter of Francis & Eliza Dent, 31 Aug 1867; m 4 Sept 1867 by J. S. Purifoy, Bap. Minister.

Holmes, Willie & Martha McGehee, 24 March 1831; William R. Leavister, bm; David Laws, wit.

Holstein, Jacob & Catherine Kraider, 19 Feb 1780; Wm. Ogilvie, bm; Sherwood Harris, wit.

Holt, John & Sarah Fuller, 8 Feb 1791; James Holt, bm; A. Potter, wit.

Homes, James & Sally Harris, 17 Feb 1829; Samuel Harris, bm; David Laws, wit.

Hood, Charles & Elisabeth Peace, 2 Jan 1804; Joshua White, bm; A. H. Sneed, wit.

Hooffman, George & Susan McFarland, 16 April 1829; John McFarland (McFarling), bm; David Laws, wit.

Hoofman, Jacob & Nancey Stephenson, 9 March 1814; George Byard, bm; W. M. Sneed, wit.

Hooker, Wily & Polly Quarles, 21 Oct 1801; Peter Mann, bm; Nancy Bullock, wit.

Hopkin, William T. & Martha A. Hart, 27 Jan 1863; Jas. J. Landis, bm; m 29 Jan 1864 by Thomas U. Faucette.

Hopkins, Alexander & Nancey Mallory, 30 Sept 1811; Meredith Crews, bm; W. M. Sneed, wit.

Hopkins, Cannon & Mary Bullock, 8 Sept 1845; G. F. Bullock, bm; Jas. M. Wiggins, wit.

GRANVILLE MARRIAGES 1753-1868

Hopkins, Cannon & Nancy Jane Bullock, 3 Oct 1863; A. Landis, bm; m 15 Oct 1863 by Jeff Horner, J. P.

Hopkins, Charles & Sarah Linsey, (no date, during admn. of Gov. Samuel Johnston); Hardy Reaves, bm; Henry Potter, wit.

Hopkins, George & Janet Semple, 13 Dec 1784; Thomas Williams, bm; Matthew Snipes, wit.

Hopkins, Henry & Frances Parrish, 26 May 1840; Thomas Fowler, bm.

Hopkins, John & Pheba Walters, 30 Dec 1805; Abner Searcy, bm; A. H. Sneed, wit.

Hopkins, Nathaniel & Sophia Longmire, 13 Sept 1839; Ira E. Arnold, bm.

Hopkins, Samuel & Elizabeth Daniel, 1 Dec 1797; Stephen Satterwhite, bm; m. Satterwhite, Woodson Daniel, wit.

Hopkins, Wait & Harriett Arnold, 12 Dec 1856; Dudley Peed, bm; A. Landis, wit.

Hopkins, William R. & Mary Ann Boothe, 1 Nov 1843; Cannon Hopkins, G. F. Bullock, bm; Wm. H. Whitfield, wit.

Horn, William N. & Lucy A. E. Atkins, 15 Dec 1813; Mills Tayloe, bm; Step. Sneed, wit.

Horne, James L. & Margaret Sam, 18 March 1839; Leroy Smith, bm.

Horner, Anderson, of color, son of parantage unknown, & Cornela Smith, daughter of Hawkins & Charity Smith, 3 Aug 1867; m 20 Oct 1867 by W. P. White, J. P.

Horner, Horriss, of color, son of Samuel & Billy Horner, & Caroline Jones, daughter of Edmon Powel & Tiley Jones, 3 Nov 1867; m 3 Nov 1867 by D. Tilley, J. P.

Horner, Jefferson & Elizabeth W. Rowland, 12 Sept 1840; George J. Reeves(?), bm; Jas. M. Wiggins, wit.

Horner, Thomas J. & Isabella Norwood, 12 March 1846; James T. Gill, bm; Jas. M. Wiggins, wit.

Horner, William J. & Nancy Forsythe, 11 Feb 1854; D. B. Johnson, bm; m 23 Feb 1854 by Wm. H. Jones, J. P.

Hornes, Richard & Sarah Langford, 4 Jan 1794; Nelson Nailing, bm; Step. Sneed, wit.

Hornsby, James & Elisabeth Hancock, 8 Sept 1778; Patrick Duffy, bm; James Jett, wit.

Horton, Daniel & Armon Stovall, 20 Dec 1833; J. Harris, bm.

Horton, Daniel & Lucinda Hughs, 21 May 1864; Jerry Estes, bm; m 21 May 1864 by B. R. Hester, M. G.

Horton, Doctor B. & Susan Mangum, 5 June 1866; m 5 June 1866 by R. B. Hester.

Horton, Hardy & Malinda Arnold, 4 July 1842; John Garner, bm; J. M. Wiggins, wit.

GRANVILLE MARRIAGES 1753-1868

Horton, John & Deritha Harris, 25 Nov 1843; William Edwards, bm; Wm. H. Whitfield, wit.

Horton, John, son of Presley & Elizabeth Norton, & Elizabeth OBrien, daughter of Zachariah & Elizabeth OBrien, 3 Sept 1867; m 8 Sept 1867 by F. J. Tilley, J. P.

Horton, Priestly & Elizabeth Jenkins, 19 Dec 1843; Priestly Jenkins, bm; Wm. H. Whitfield, wit.

Horton, Wm. P. & Emeline R. White, 14 March 1848; P. R. Merryman, bm; Jas. M. Wiggins, wit.

Hoskins, John & Elizabeth Bullock, 1 Aug 1804; Isaac Bradley, bm; E. Parham, wit.

Hostein, Niclauss (German signature) & Catherine Hostein, 31 May 1773; Henry Straider, bm.

Hough, J. G. & Christianna Watkins, 1 Jan 1867; m 3 Jan 1867 by Lewis H. Kittle, J. P.

House, Benjamin & Sally Hair, 10 Oct 1812; John Rust, bm; Richd. Sneed, wit.

House, Bolden & Eliza Jones, 4 April 1838; Henderson Hailly(?), bm; S. G. Shearmon, wit.

House, Dudly P. T. & Keziah Dickson, 23 Dec 1814; Thos. House, bm; Leslie Gillam, wit.

House, Edmund & Salley Finch, 20 Feb 1812; Samuel Lockhart, bm; Step. Sneed, wit.

House, Henry & Martha Goss, 12 Feb 1833; David Laws, wit.

House, Henry A. & Mary J. Burge, 1 Nov 1853; A. A. Allen, bm.

House, Isham & Fanny Williams, 18 Nov 1802; Thomas Jordan, bm; W. M. Sneed, wit.

House, Jno. & Martha Stone, 8 Feb 1842; _____ Cheatham, bm; D. A. Paschall, wit.

House, John W. & Mary M. Jeffreys, 8 Dec 1866; m by W. H. P. Jenkins, J. P., 12 Dec 1866; J. W. Bynum, bm.

House, Robt. & Mary Shackelford, 16 May 1838; Enid Rainey, bm; M. A. Burnett, wit.

House, Thomas & Rachael D. Roffe, 5 Sept 1817; Absalom D. Parrish, bm; Richd. Sneed, wit.

Howard, Allen & Phebe Marshall, 17 Sept 1787; John Longmire, bm; B. Searcy, wit.

Howard, Allen & Susanna Howard, 6 April 1832; Thomas Howard, bm; David Laws, wit.

Howard, Barnard & Jane Hunt, 11 March 1794; Thomas Potter, bm; Leonard Henderson, wit.

Howard, Elijah & Harriet Harris, freed people, 25 Dec 1865; Geo. W. Landis, bm; m 26 Dec 1865 by Samuel Hunt, J. P.

GRANVILLE MARRIAGES 1753-1868

Howard, Elijah, of color, son of James & Pidy Howard, & Harriett Reavis, daughter of Jack & Nancy Reavis, 27 June 1868; m 28 June 1868 by Aaron Prather.

Howard, Groves & Catharine Grave, 12 Feb 1792; Thomas Owen, bm; W. Norwood, wit.

Howard, Henry & Adeline Jones, 26 Dec 1866; m 28 Dec 1866 by B. D. Howard, J. P.

Howard, James H. & Jackey Bowden, 30 Aug 1820; James Hunt, bm; Step. K. Sneed, wit.

Howard, James W. & Delia Ann Frazier, 23 Nov 1842; John Johnson, bm; Wm. H. Whitfield, wit.

Howard, John C. R. & Rebecca Gorden, 17 Nov 1853; John T. Howard, bm; m 17 Nov 1853 by Peterson Thorp, J. P.

Howard, Joseph & Mary A. D. Parham, 25 Jan 1830; Wm. T. McClanahan, bm; Step. K. Sneed, wit.

Howard, Joseph & Mrs. Lucy E. Hunt. 25 Dec 1844; Hamilton Hunt (?), bm.

Howard, Joseph T. & Susan Morris, 11 Jan 1859; James A. Howard, bm; m 13 Jan 1859 by Peterson Thorp, J. P.

Howard, Littleton & Patsey Tharp, 10 Jan 1789; Thomas Owen Jr., bm; A. Henderson, wit.

Howard, Lucius P. & Elvira A. Piper, 4 Jan 1860; W. B. Routon, bm; m 4 Jan 1860 by Wms. Harris.

Howard, Mark & Rachael Webb, 22 Nov 1792; Barnard Howard, bm; W. Norwood, wit.

Howard, Solomon & Mary House, 4 July 1835; Will M. S. Ridley, bm; Benja. Kittrell, wit.

Howard, Solomon, son of Allen & Phebe Howard, & Martha A. Morris, daughter of Blunt & Patty Morris, 18 May 1868; m 21 May 1868 by R. S. Hunt, J. P.

Howard, Thomas & Rachel Gooch, 22 May 1816; James Howard, bm; Step. K. Sneed, wit.

Howard, William & Winney Cozort, 9 Feb 1824; John Amis, bm.

Howard, William H. & Judith Gorden, 20 Dec 1847; R. W. Dunn, bm; Jno. M. Wiggins, wit.

Howel, Allen & Malinda Parish, 12 March 1847; Henderson Floyd, bm; N. H. Wiggins, wit.

Howel, Benjamin & Mary Bailey, 31 May 1830; Thomas Tucker, bm; David Laws, wit.

Howel, James & Ann Troler, 14 Aug 1834; Edwd. Burton, bm; Benja. Kittrell, wit.

Howel, John & Elizabeth Voluntine, 3 June 1822; Noel Johnson, bm; L. Gilliam, wit.

Howel, John & Jane Harris, 5 Aug 1836; Abram Plenty, bm; Jas. M. Wiggins, wit.

Howel, Joseph & Elizabeth Hicks, 26 Nov 1819; Ransom Smith, bm; Jas. M. Wiggins, wit.

Howel, Mack & Ann Harris, 1 June 1844; John D. Rudd, bm; J. M. Wiggins, wit.

Howel, Robards & Rebecah Hunt, 26 Oct 1802; John Hanton, bm.

Howel, Thomas & Susannah Baits, 22 Sept 1799; Robert Brinkly, bm; R. Harris, wit.

Howell, Doctor A. & Betsey Ann Anderson, 4 July 1839; Wm. Howell, bm; J. M. Wiggins, wit.

Howell, Elijah & Harriett Evans, 19 April 1862; Royal Anderson, bm; A. Landis, wit; m 20 April 1862 by L. M. Van Hook, J. P.

Howell, Eppes & Elisabeth Sercey, 18 Nov 1800; Hardy Falkner, bm; Step. Sneed, wit.

Howell, James & Frances Rowland, 22 March 1843; D. P. Paschall, bm; Jas. M. Wiggins, wit.

Howell, James & Betsy Ann Tyler, 26 March 1867; m by William R. Hicks, J. P., 6 April 1867.

Howell, James M. & Emily Ragland, 2 April 1828; Woodson Knight, bm; S. K. Sneed, wit.

Howell, John F. & Elisabeth Jackson, 11 Nov 1851; John Kates, bm; A. Landis, wit; m by Lewis Amis, J. P.

Howell, John T. & Lucy T. Duke, 13 Dec 1852; Alexander Reames, bm; m 23 Dec 1852 by R. J. Devin, V. D. M.

Howell, John T. & Sarah E. Parham, 28 Sept 1859; C. W. Clay Jr., bm; m 29 Sept 1859 by E. F. Beachum, a Minister of the Gospel.

Howell, Junius, of color, son of Alex & Betsy Ann Howell, & Panthea Brandon, daughter of Betsy Brandon, m 5 Aug 1867 by J. D. C. Pool, J. P.

Howell, Mathew & Mary Pettiford, 29 March 1831; Robert Kirton, bm; David Laws, wit.

Howell, William & Peggy Pettiford, 22 March ____; Burton Cousins, bm; Wm. H. Owen, wit.

Howington, Willis & Caty Johnson, 1 June 1804; Thomas Parham, bm; E. W. Parham, wit.

Howse, Samuel H. & Sarah Hedgepeth, 14 March 1838; James Hobgood, bm.

Howson, John of Amelia County, Virginia, & Sarah Jones, 25 July 1762; John Williams, bm; Jn. Bowie, wit.

Hoyle, William & Mary E. Stewart, 2 Jan 1841; M. A. Smith, bm; J. M. Wiggins, wit.

Huddleston, Benjamin & Franky Parham, 18 Feb 1828; Wyatt Canady, bm; David Laws, wit.

GRANVILLE MARRIAGES 1753-1868

Huddleston, Ezekiel & Betsey Lock, 17 Feb 1811; Jesse Huddleston, bm; Jun. Sneed, wit.

Huddleston, Ezekiel & Agga Eaks, 28 Aug 1816; Robert Kenton, bm; Rhodes N. Herndon, wit.

Huddleston, Henry & Margaret Hellier, 30 Feb 1815; David Jones, bm; Henry E. Smith, wit.

Huddleston, Jesse & Catey Upchurch, 23 May 1799; Ezekiel Huddleston, bm; Ro. Harris, wit.

Huddleston, Jesse & Matilda Morris, 28 May 1832; Chapman Hester, bm; David Laws, wit.

Huddleston, Jessee & Betsey Jones, 21 May 1807; James Badgett, bm; W. M. Sneed, wit.

Huddleston, John & Lueilla Collinsworth, 23 Dec 1783.

Huddleston, John & Elisabeth Curtis, 28 Jan 1786; Henry Smith, bm; Bennet Searcy, wit.

Huddleston, John & Susey Grenaway, 3 Feb 1807; Squire Shearman, bm; W. M. Sneed, wit.

Huddleston, John W. & Sarah O. Mize, 8 Sept 1864; Howel L. Mize, bm; A. Landis, wit; m 14 Sept 1864 by W. D. Allen, J. P.

Huddleston, Lambert & Nancy Currin, 6 April 1825; Larkin Currin, bm; Step. K. Sneed, wit.

Huddleston, Samuel & Dinna Wooten, 26 July 1855; Samuel H. Jeffreys, bm.

Huddleston, William & Dicey Grenaway, 8 Nov 1831; Samuel Hunt, bm; Jas. M. Wiggins, wit.

Hudgins, James F. & Lethy Balton, 7 Jan 1845; Hezekiah Pitchford, bm; Jas. M. Wiggins, wit.

Hudson, Cephus & Martha Newton, 23 Jan 1856; A. Landis, bm; m 27 Jan 1856 by Thos. Hester, J. P.

Hudson, Cephus & Sallie Averett, 31 Oct 1860; Jno. M. Ellington, bm; m 1 Nov 1860 by G. W. Ferrill.

Hudson, Cephus & Nancy E. Pulley, 1 Feb 1866; A. Landis, bm; m 1 Feb 1866 by E. F. Beachum, a regular G. M.

Hudson, Charles W. & Mary J. Cargill, 6 Dec 1865; R. P. Blacknall, bm.

Hudson, Creed & Critia Notgrass, 26 June 1818; Joseph Taylor, bm; Step. N. Sneed, wit.

Hudson (Hutson), John & Elisabeth Burnett, 29 Aug 1804; Joseph Hamilton, bm; Step. Sneed, wit.

Hudson, John & Ann Lumpkin, 31 Oct 1815; George Lumpkin, bm; Jno. Cobbs, wit.

Hudson, John J. & Virginia Hutcherson, 7 Nov 1863; W. J. Pitchford, bm; m 8 Nov 1863 by Geo. J. Rowland, J. P.

Hudson, Mastin & Mary Matthews, 9 Dec 1858; Rufus Tilletson, bm; A. Landis, wit.

Hudson, Wm. & Frances Magee, 6 Aug 1789; Jas. Johnson, bm; A. Henderson, C. C., wit.

Hudspeth, Carter & Sarah Ann Stovall, 23 Jan 1843; John W. Hunt, bm; Wm. H. Whitfield, wit.

Hudspeth, Richard & Rosa Finch, 11 May 1838; G. Stanton, bm.

Hudspeth, Richd. & Salley Searcy, 12 Jan 1808; William Bradford, bm; W. M. Sneed, wit.

Hudspeth, Solomon & Anne Thomason, 22 Aug 1792; Thomson Harris, bm; W. Norwood, wit.

Hudspeth, Thompson & Massy Briggs, 21 Dec 1812; Saml. Montague, bm; Thos. J. Hicks, wit.

Huffman, Benjamin & Elisabeth Nunn, 2 Feb 1802; William Akin, bm; Step. Sneed, wit.

Hufman, Jacob & Mildred Turner, 22 Jan 1780; James MaL----, bm; John Taylor, wit.

Hughes, Richard & Mary Kearsey, 13 Feb 1841; Thomas Pettiford, bm; J. M. Wiggins, wit.

Hughes, Robert P. & Lucy W. Coghill, 13 Dec 1829; Thos. Turner, bm; Albert Sneed, wit.

Hughes, Rutledge, son of Samuel M. & Louise Hughes, & Willie Worthington, daughter of William Worthington & Margaret M. Worthington, 20 Nov 1867; m 20 Nov 1867 by H. G. Hill, Min.

Hughes, Washington & Frances Eaks, 29 Sept 1865; S. H. Beasly, bm; m 29 Sept 1865 by B. T. Winston, J. P.

Hughes, William H. & Mary F. Coghill, 4 Oct 1847; A. H. Alley, bm.

Hughs, Henry & Winney Smith, 25 June 1829; James Vaughan, bm; Robert K. Clack, wit.

Hughs, Jacob Y. & Louisa Jeffreys, 10 June 1863; John E. Freeman, bm; m 14 June 1863 by W. D. Allen, J. P.

Hull, John & Sophia Derieux, 22 April 1811; Francis Derieus, bm; Wm. M. Sneed, wit.

Humphreys, Benjamin R. & Bettie Williams, 12 Nov 1863; Henry Tilletson, bm; m 12 Nov 1863 by Peterson Thorp, J. P.

Humphreys, Levi C. & Elizabeth Burkley, 20 Sept 1865; H. Tilletson, bm; m 26 Sept 1865 by B. T. Winston, J. P.

Humphries, James M. & Elizabeth Daniel, 11 July 1857; Sept. P. Pool, bm; R. W. Lassiter, wit.

Humphries, Levi C. & Eliza Puryear, 19 Dec 1859; Adonirim Humphries, bm.

Humstead, Richard & Elizabeth Veazy, 6 Aug 1824; Jeremiah Bullock, bm.

GRANVILLE MARRIAGES 1753-1868

Hunnicut, Joshua P. & Mary E. Southall, 7 Feb 1851; B. C. Cooke, bm; m 9 Feb 1851 by A. C. Harris, M. G.

Hunt, Absalom & Retis(?) Hester, 3 Jan 1810; Chisem Hester, bm; Richard Sneed, wit.

Hunt, Absolum & Amey M. Saterwhite, 5 Sept 1839; Jos. M. Heggie, bm; John T. Hunt, J. P., wit.

Hunt, Bird & Lucy Ann Duty, m 25 May 1867 by Robt. L. Hunt, J. P.

Hunt, David A. & Elizabeth Herndon, 18 May 1852; Jos. F. Hobgood, bm.

Hunt, David Y. & Caroline V. Hobgood, 19 Nov 1866; J. M. Currin, bm; C. E. Landis, wit; m 22 Nov 1866 by E. F. Beacham, R. G. Minister.

Hunt, Edward & Lucey Howard, 4 Nov 1806; Broady Hoard, bm; W. M. Sneed, wit.

Hunt, Elijah & Kitty Hicks, 15 Nov 1865; George W. Landis, bm; m 25 Dec 1865 by L. K. Willie, M. G.

Hunt, Elijah M. & Ann Elizabeth Coghill, 10 Dec 1866; P. F. Coghill, bm; m 19 Dec 1866 by L. K. Willie, M. G.

Hunt, George & Elleanor Harrison, 24 Jan 1778; Abner Tatom, bm; Reuben Searcy, wit.

Hunt, George & Lucy Woodfork, 15 Jan 1780; Samuel Hunt, bm; Thomas Searcy, wit.

Hunt, George W. & Susan C. Crews, 23 Oct 1848; R. L. Hunt, bm; Jas. M. Wiggins, wit.

Hunt, George Washington & Caroline Hester, 6 Jan 1838; L. Beasley Jr., bm.

Hunt, Granville, of color, son of Stephen Hunt & Elvira McKeever, & Viney Chambers, daughter of Charles Dunigan & Betsy Chambers, m 11 July 1867 by Maurice H. Vaughan, Rector of St. Stephen's Church.

Hunt, Henderson & Mary Burwell, 26 Dec 1865; m 31 Dec 1865 by L. K. Willie, M. G.

Hunt, James & Ann Saterwhite, 24 July 1785; George Hunt, bm; Dennis _____, wit.

Hunt, James & Amey Jones, 30 Aug 180_; Goodman Smith, bm; Jun. Sneed, wit.

Hunt, James & Ann Thomson, 21 Dec 1814; Michael Hunt, bm.

Hunt, James & Lucinda Butler, 4 Dec 1824; Thomas Hunt, bm; Wm. H. Owen, wit.

Hunt, James H. & Martha Ann Kittrell, 18 Dec 1865; A. Landis, bm.

Hunt, James M. B. & Sarah Ellen Lewis, 30 July 1863; J. M. Bullock, bm; m 30 July 1863 by F. N. Whaley.

Hunt, James P. H. & Ann Eliza Hicks, 23 Oct 1858; Thos. W. McClanahan, bm; m 24 Oct 1858 by James L. Purifoy, M. G.

GRANVILLE MARRIAGES 1753-1868

Hunt, James T. & Helen George, 22 May 1861; W. R. Beasley, bm; m 22 May 1861 by R. J. Devin.

Hunt, John & Frances Penn, 5 Aug 1771; James Hunt, bm; Jesse Benton, wit.

Hunt, John & Betsey Taylor, 17 Sept 1804; John Vaughan, bm; E. W. Parham, wit.

Hunt, John Jr. & Appha Hester, 14 Dec 1802; Tarlton Johnson, bm; P. Bullock, wit.

Hunt, John P. & Salley Longmire, 19 Dec 1811; James Cooper, bm; W. M. Sneed, wit.

Hunt, John R. & Agnes P. Hudson, 23 July 1849; James McLan---, bm.

Hunt, Jonathan & Dicey Smith, 6 Dec 1792; William Finch, bm; Step. Sneed, wit.

Hunt, Joseph P. & Martha M. Crews, 28 Oct 1839; George W. Hunt, bm.

Hunt, Leonidas & Mary Borough, 13 Sept 1865.

Hunt, Lewis, of color, son of Anderson & Ann Hunt, & Mary Susan Venable, daughter of Jane Venable, 5 July 1867; m 5 July 1867 by M. H. Vaughan.

Hunt, M. S. & Parthenia P. Vass, 16 April 1831; Pleasant Hart, bm; Step. K. Sneed, wit.

Hunt, Michael & Frankey Hunt, 5 Feb 1812; J. Edwards, bm; W. M. Sneed, wit.

Hunt, Peter & Alice Baskerville, freed people, 8 Oct 1865; Edmund Hunt, bm; m 8 Oct 1865 by Maurice H. Vaughan, Rector of St. Stephen's Church.

Hunt, Peter & Sallie Hester, 25 Dec 1865, (no bond or return).

Hunt, Presley & Mary Thweat, 21 Aug 1780; Abner Tatom, bm; John Searcy Jr., wit.

Hunt, Richard B. & Mrs. Marina Lewis, 12 March 1860.

Hunt, Richard H. & Elizabeth A. Puryear, 16 Nov 1840; Elisha B. Parham, bm; Jas. M. Wiggins, wit.

Hunt, Richard H. & Mary Heggie, 3 March 1863; W. A. Philpott, bm; m 3 March 1863 by W. S. Hester, M. G.

Hunt, Robert & Cornelia Taylor, 25 Aug 1866; m 25 Aug 1866 by J. L. Caudle, Minister.

Hunt, Robert L. & Caroline N. White, 2 Dec 1856; A. Landis Jr., bm; m 3 Dec 1856 by L. K. Willie, M. G.

Hunt, Samuel & Sarah Howard, 20 May 1780; James Hunt, bm; Reuben Searcy, wit.

Hunt, Samuel & Mary Ransom, 10 Oct 1788; Wm. Hanes, bm; A. Henderson, C. C., wit.

GRANVILLE MARRIAGES 1753-1868

Hunt, Samuel, son of Michael & Frances Hunt, & Elizabeth P. Poole, daughter of John E. & Frances B. Poole, 2 July 1867; m 3 July 1867 by J. A. Stradley, M. G.

Hunt, Samuel & Sarah Hester, 18 Jan 1834; Stephen Currins, bm.

Hunt, Samuel G. & Mary Young, 5 Jan 1855; A. Landis, bm; m 6 Jan 1855 by Jas. J. Moore, J. P.

Hunt, Solomon & Elizabeth Sneed, 20 Dec 1817; David Owen, bm; Step. K. Sneed, wit.

Hunt, Thomas T. & Mary S. Taylor, 15 April 1828; W. H. Hodge, bm; A. Sneed, wit.

Hunt, William & Elisabeth Taylor, 25 Oct 1792; Thos. Satterwhite, bm; Step. Sneed, wit.

Hunt, William & Patsey Knott, 22 Dec 1801; John Petteway, bm; James Sneed, wit.

Hunt, William & Isabella Downey, 9 Sept 1842; Jos. H. Gooch, bm; Wm. H. Whitfield, wit.

Hunt, William Junr. & Nanney Kittrell, 24 Jan 1780; Rowland Bryant, bm; Charles Mitchel, wit.

Hunt, William B. & Agnes B. Hare, 2 March 1852; C. R. Lewis, bm; A. Landis, wit; m 8 March 1852 by N. L. Graves.

Hunt, William J. & Delilah Fuller, 21 Dec 1829; William B. Ellington, bm; Step. K. Sneed, wit.

Hunt, William T. & Isabella Garrat, 7 Oct 1847; Robert Fr---, bm; J. M. Wiggins, wit.

Hunter, Isaac & Martha Alston, spinster, 18 April 1760; Jos. Johnson, bm; Jno. Bowie, wit; consent of Solomon Alston, father of Martha, 15 April 1760.

Hunter, J. Beverly & Martha Burwell, 15 June 1857; H. C. Herndon, bm; m 16 June 1857 by L. K. Willie.

Hunter, Jesse & Anne Alston, 20 June 1758; Jonathan Parker, bm; _____ Weldon, wit.

Hunter, William & Minerva Strother, 24 Feb 1842; John W. Hunter, bm; J. M. Wiggins, wit.

Hurst, John Smith & Sarah Parker, 2 Nov 1773; Micajah Bullock, bm; Chas. Partee, wit.

Hurt, John & Susan Land, 23 Oct 1820; Braxton Land, bm; Jas. M. Wiggins, wit.

Husketh, Archibald & Elizabeth Hooker, 31 Dec 1821; Isham Husketh, bm; S. K. Sneed, wit.

Husketh, Archibald & Louisa Allen, 3 July 1854; Jas. J. Peace, bm; m 4 July 1854 by Jas. J. Moore, J. P.

Husketh, Elias & Arabella C. Usry, 13 Jan 1857; John Y. Smith, bm; m 16 Jan 1857 by J. W. Floyd, Pastor.

GRANVILLE MARRIAGES 1753-1868

Husketh, Isaac & Gilley McGehe, (no date, during admn. of Gov. Alexander Martin); John Carrel, bm; Step. Sneed, wit.

Husketh, Thomas & Anne Champion, 25 June 1791; John Husketh, bm; Wm. Norwood, D. C. C., wit.

Husketh, William & Linsey M. Wilson, 18 Nov 1836; Henry B. Wilson, bm; Jas. M. Wiggins, wit.

Huskey, Archelaus & Clara Bailey, 1 Aug 1815; William Estes, bm; Step. Sneed Jr., wit.

Huskey, Elias & Jincy Blalock, 15 Jan 1814; William Blalock, bm; J. P. Sneed, wit.

Huskey, John & Sarah Allin, 13 Sept 1781; William Husky, bm; Reuben Searcy, wit.

Huskey, William D. & Julia A. Haswell, 29 Nov 1842; Chesly Quols, bm; Wm. H. Whitfield, wit.

Hutcherson, John B. & _____ R. Kittrell, 14 Dec 1819; George Farrar, bm.

Hutcherson, John S. & Elizabeth Smith, 27 Nov 1815; Joel Smith, bm; Richd. Sneed, wit.

Hutcherson, William T. & Elizabeth Hudson, 4 Dec 1855; A. N. Gibbs, bm; m 20 Dec 1855 by J. W. Floyd, Minister.

Hutchings, John A. & Frances Strum, 18 May 1803; Jno. Wilson, bm.

Hutchinson, Charles & Rebecah Glasgow, 17 Nov 1812; Richard H. Brown, bm.

Hutchinson, John C. & Martha Hester, 7 Jan 1831; Edwin G. Read, bm; A. Sneed, wit.

Hutchinson, Joshua & Susannah Hays, 4 Oct 1788; Sothoron Higgs, bm; A. Henderson, C. C., wit.

Hutchinson, Willie & Agness Buchanan, 21 Dec 1829; Doctor Cole, bm; S. K. Sneed, wit.

Hutson, Drury & Nancy Weaver, 25 April 1786; William Weaver, bm; Bennet Searcy, wit.

Hutson, Mastin & Elizabeth Sadler, 27 Dec 1854; Alexander Matthews, bm.

Hyde, Irwin & Mary Clark, 8 Jan 1793; Robert Burton, bm; W. Norwood, wit.

Hyde, Robert & Elisabeth Harper, 22 Oct 1781; Thos. Lanier, bm; Reuben Searcy, wit; consent from Jesse Harper, father of Elizabeth, 22 Oct 1781.

Inge, Richd. & Mary Sturdivant, 28 Aug 1806; Wm. Marshal, bm; Lewis Nicholson, wit.

Inge, Richard Jr. & Elisabeth Bullock, 16 Dec 1812; Nathan Patterson, bm.

GRANVILLE MARRIAGES 1753-1868

Inscoe, Stephen & Tabitha Lankford, 23 June 1786; Charles Blackley, bm; Bennet Searcy, wit.

Inscor, Anderson & Elizabeth C. Allen, 1 Jan 1861; John C. Hudgins, bm; m 13 Jan 1861 by T. B. Lyon, J. P.

Inscore, Abner & Susan Ann Brogden, 14 Oct 1842; Charles Allen, bm; Wm. H. Whitfield, wit.

Inscore, Benjamin & Sally Walls, 19 Feb 1830; William Blackley, bm; Step. K. Sneed, wit.

Inscore, Jonathan & Tabithey Duke, 19 May 1798; William Inscore, bm; H. Williams, wit.

Inscore, Jonathan & Ruthy Stroud, 13 March 1830; Ransom Harris, bm; Step. K. Sneed, wit.

Inscore, Jordan & Salley Johnson, 25 Sept 1812; Charles Blackley, bm; W. M. Sneed, wit.

Inscore, Joseph & Lucy Inscore, 1 Oct 1861; Benjamin Inscore, bm.

Inscore, Joshua & Frances Allen, 7 Feb 1859; David Beck, bm.

Inscore, Pleasant & Harriet Mason, 19 May 1842; Benj. C. Cook, bm.

Inscore, Thomas & Priscilla Weldon, 9 May 1836; James Paschall, bm; J. M. Wiggins, wit.

Inscow(?), Joshuaway & Fanny Allen, 21 Feb 1859; Moses Gaven(?), bm.

Inscow, Reuben & Mary Hays, 25 Oct 1792; Charles Black, bm; Step. Sneed, wit.

Isbell, Daniel & Nelley Hunt, 14 Jan 1797; Samuel Hunt, bm; Step. Sneed, wit.

Isler, Jesse & Mary E. Bryan, 26 Dec 1820; Henry L. Plummer, bm; Jas. M. Wiggins, wit.

Ivens, Coleman & Barbara Slaughter, 1 Jan 1824; Robert Elliott, bm; D. J. Young, wit.

Ivens, William & Emily Scot, 19 April 1859; m by W. D. Allen, J. P.

Ivins, Lewis & Ann Eliza Curtis, 2 May 1850; George Anderson, bm; Benja. C. Cooke, wit.

Jackson, Berry, of color, son of Arter & Susan Jackson, & Dicy Estes, daughter of Rebecca Estes, m 8 April 1868 by W. D. Allen, J. P.

Jackson, Cavel & Petsey Jackson, 13 March 1801; Wm. Moore, Hutchins _____, Leonard Williams, bm; Step. Sneed, wit.

Jackson, Chesley D. & Sally Morris, 20 May 1849; Tho. Tucker, bm; Jas. M. Wiggins, wit.

Jackson, David T. & Mary A. Bragg, 30 Dec 1859; Wesley Keith, bm; m 4 Jan 1860 by W. D. Allen, J. P.

GRANVILLE MARRIAGES 1753-1868

Jackson, Ezekiel & Ferebey Oakley, 6 March 1810; Elless Walker, bm; Stephen Sneed, Jr., wit.

Jackson, Ezekiel & Susan Milton, 1 Dec 1816; D. J. Young, bm; Steo. K. Sneed, wit.

Jackson, George W. & Susanna Afscue, 2 Aug 1836; Jacob L. Slaughter, bm; G. C. Wiggins, wit.

Jackson, Henry & Mary Winfield, 11 Aug 1853; Henderson Winfield, bm; Jas. R. Duty, wit.

Jackson, Herbert & Milly Marrow, freed people, 14 Aug 1867; m 18 Aug 1867 by Edward Hines.

Jackson, Isaac & Susanna A. Wortham, 10 May 1851; J. J. Wortham, H. A. Taylor, bm; m 30 May 1851 by E. Hines.

Jackson, Jonathan & Rebecca Morgan, 28 Dec 1830; Allen Clark, bm; Wm. H. Owen, wit.

Jackson, Jonathan & Delphia Watkins, 28 July 1845; Tho. W. Howen, bm; J. M. Wiggins, wit.

Jackson, Lemlen & Nancy Haskins, 16 April 1855; Henry Haskins, bm; Jas. R. Duty, wit; m 19 April 1855 by Jas. R. Duty, J. P.

Jackson, Loe & Frances Harris, 5 Oct 1792; Jonothan Thompson, bm; W. Norwood, wit.

Jackson, Lorenzo D. & Ann Winston, 12 Dec 1833; Nathaniel H. Weathers, bm; Benja. Kittrell, wit.

Jackson, Marion & Lucy Jackson, 13 Nov 1844; Wm. W. Worworth, bm; J. M. Wiggins, wit.

Jackson, Nathaniel & Milley Holmes, 6 Nov 1806; Francis Jackson, bm; Jas. Sneed, wit.

Jackson, Nathon & Nansey Loyls, 18 May 1780; Alsey High, bm; Asa Searcy, wit.

Jackson, Ransom & Caroline Crowder, 21 Feb 1844; William Warmuth, bm; Wm. H. Whitfield, wit.

Jackson, Ransom H. & Priety Winston, 7 Nov 1821; Lowe Jackson, bm; Jas. M. Wiggins, wit.

Jackson, Rice & Clary Furgerson, 1 Nov 1827; George Brogdon, bm; David Laws, wit.

Jackson, Samuel & Judah Hunt, 20 March 1780; Wm. Hicks, bm; Bennet Searcy, wit.

Jackson, Samuel J. & Emily S. Parham, 31 Dec 1838; R. H. Hunt, bm.

Jackson, Thomas H. & Christiana B. Eaton, 21 April 1857; Wm. A. Eaton, bm; m 5 May 1857 by Robt. B. Sutton, Record of St. James Church, Granville Co., N. C.

Jackson, William & Frances Reeks(?), 22 Feb 1808; David Hunt, bm; W. M. Sneed, wit.

GRANVILLE MARRIAGES 1753-1868

Jackson, William G. & Sallie T. Eaton, 26 Nov 1856; William H. Wade, bm; m 27 Nov 1856 by Rich Hines.

Jackson, Willis & Patsey Finch, 5 Feb 1818; Jesse Jenkins, bm; W. Sneed, wit.

Jackwell, Levan & Nancy Chain, 18 Sept 1797; Joseph Waller Jr., bm; P. Bullock, wit.

James, Thomas & Nancy Cuzzort, 13 June 1792; Aron Jones, bm; Step. Sneed, wit.

James, Wm. & Mary Ann Overbey, 22 Dec 1831; Wm. B. Holloway, bm; Jno. P. Smith, wit.

Jarratt, John & Milly Veazey, 2 Nov 1833; Standfield H. Sitgraves, bm; Benja. Kittrell, wit.

Jeffers, David & Mary Holmes, 30 Dec 1820; Stephen Cook, bm; Z. Herndon, wit.

Jeffers, Green & _____, 6 May 1806; Claiborn Cooke, bm; Jun. Sneed, wit.

Jeffers, Robert & Elizabeth Johnson, 8 May 1816; William P. Sample, bm; W. M. Sneed, wit.

Jeffers, Thomas & Jane Oaky, 21 April 1830; William Daniel, bm; David Laws, wit.

Jeffers, William & Aletha Cox, 9 Nov 181_; Wm. Trailor, bm; R. N. Herndon, wit.

Jefferson, John & Sarah Hester, 26 Dec 1865.

Jeffreys, Charles & Martha Wilson, 4 Nov 1845; Caswel H. Sandling, bm; J. M. Wiggins, wit.

Jeffreys, Cornelius, colored, son of Green & Eliza Jeffreys, & Emily Jane Thomas, daughter of Lucinda Thomas, 2 Nov 1868; m 14 Nov 1868 by Richard D. Jones, J. P.

Jeffreys, John & Elizabeth Homes, 9 April 1818; Wm. Nailing, bm; A. Tomlinson, wit.

Jeffreys, Littleton & Lucy Pruitt, 1 Jan 1847; William Leavister, bm; J. M. Wiggins, wit.

Jeffreys, Samuel & Martha Kearney, 1 Jan 1855; William Sandlin, bm; A. Landis, wit.

Jeffreys, Samuel & Frances May, 7 Nov 1859; m 22 Dec 1859 by E. B. Lyon, J. P.

Jeffreys, Thomas & Milley Mitchel, 18 Sept 1792; Step. Sneed, bm; M. Bullock, wit.

Jeffreys, William & Nancy Gilliam, 22 April 1823; Stephen Jeffreys, bm; Step. K. Sneed, wit.

Jeffreys, William & Polly Weathers, 29 June 1858; Rufus Bobbitt, bm; m 11 July 1858 by W. D. Allen, J. P.

Jeffreys, William & Sally Harris, m 29 July 1860 by Geo. J. Rowland, J. P.

GRANVILLE MARRIAGES 1753-1868

Jeffreys, William B. & Mary E. Bragg, 1 Dec 1854; Leonard H. Bullock, bm; m 3 Dec 1854 by B. B. Hester.

Jeffreys, Thomas & Harriett Bowles, 20 Feb 1858; J. C. Cloyer, bm; m 28 Feb 1858 by A. H. Cooke, J. P.

Jeffrys, Willis & Martha Ann Adcock, 26 March 1849; James Ross, bm; J. M. Wiggins, wit.

Jenkins, Benjamin F. & Nancy Jones, 3 Nov 1845; L. S. Philpott, bm; Jas. M. Wiggins, wit.

Jenkins, Elias & Patsey Morse, 22 Sept 1800; Wilson Jenkins, bm; P. Bullock, wit.

Jenkins, George, colored, son of Adkin Qualls & Nancy Qualls, & Nancy Bullock, daughter of Buck Bullock & Sally Hockerday, m 7 Dec 1868 by John W. Estes.

Jenkins, James & Nancey Finch, 6 Dec 1816; Jesse Jenkins, bm.

Jenkins, John & Agness Brinkley, 27 April 1821; Noland Hampton, bm; Step. K. Sneed, wit.

Jenkins, John & Lundy W. Lemay, m 22 Feb 1853 by James R. Duty, J. P.; Richard H. Turner, bm.

Jenkins, John Sanforde & Molley Thomas, 19 Dec 1789; Jessee Jenkins, bm; A. Henderson, wit.

Jenkins, John W. & Frances Peace, 16 Dec 1821; Lemuel McGehee, bm; Jas. M. Wiggins, wit.

Jenkins, Richard, colored, son of Raymond Norwood & Hannah Jenkins, & Milfred Barnett, parents unknown, m 19 Dec 1868 by B. Smith, J. P.

Jenkins, Robert A. & Elizabeth T. Hicks, 25 Oct 1845; J. C. Cooper, bm; J. M. Wiggins, wit.

Jenkins, Samuel & Julia Davis, 24 Dec 1844; John W. Rogers, bm; Jas. M. Wiggins, wit.

Jenkins, Silas D. & Selina H. Kirkland, 10 Jan 1853; Wm. Jenkins, bm; A. Landis, wit.

Jenkins, Thomas & Martha L. Creekmore, 6 Oct 1857; N. P. Copeland, bm; m 6 Oct 1857 by J. W. Floyd, Minister of the Gospel.

Jenkins, Thomas Junr. & Sarah Lyon, 13 July 1803; Thos. Jenkins Senr., bm; Green Merritt, wit.

Jenkins, W. H. P. & P. W. Allen, 12 Nov 1866, m by Lewis K. Willie, M. G.; Jonathan Jenkins, bm.

Jenkins, Walter & Dolley Mann, 10 Oct 1807; Wm. Hillyard, bm; Step. Sneed, wit.

Jenkins, William & Elizabeth Finch, 28 Nov 1806; Garland Allen, bm; W. M. Sneed, wit.

Jenkins, William K. & Ann Eliza Mallory, 24 Dec 1851; John T. Jenkins, bm.

Jenkins, Wm. T. & Lucy A. Royster, ___ Jan 1806; Alex Crews, bm.

GRANVILLE MARRIAGES 1753-1868

Jennings, Alexander W. & Polley Tisdale, 3 April 1809; Daniel Crenshaw, bm; Step. Sneed, wit.

Jentry, Bedney F. & Mary F. Martin, 23 Dec 1855; _____ Gentry, bm; L. B. Stone, J. P., wit.

Jerand(?), Phillip H. & Marinda Wilson, m 2 May 1861 by Jas. R. Duty, J. P.

Jeter, Samuel & Ann Brassfield, 16 Aug 1818; Rhodes N. Herndon, bm; Zacha. Herndon, J. P., wit.

Jewel, James & Faithy Cox, 21 Nov 1830; William Philips, bm; Robert Kollack(?), wit.

Jiner, Moses & Nancy Kersey, 30 June 1827; William Robertson, bm; A. Sneed, wit.

Jinkins, Atha T. & Emeline Huskey, 1 Sept 1848; Benj. C. Cooke, bm.

Jinkins, Cibble & Jane Madison, 9 June 1818; Nathl. M. Taylor, Esqr., bm; Rhodes N. Herndon, wit.

Jinkins, Elias & Salley Taylor, 19 Dec 1789; Jessee Jenkins, bm; A. Henderson, wit.

Jinkins, Elias & Hasky Ann White, 26 Nov 1830; A. H. Walker, bm; Step. K. Sneed, wit.

Jinkins, Henry & Lethe Craft, 13 Oct 1821; Richard H. Alexander, bm; S. K. Sneed, wit.

Jinkins, James & Mariah Cook, 6 April 1818; William Montague, bm; A. Tomlinson, wit.

Jinkins, James F. & Ann Davis, 3 Nov 1840; Elijah Barnett, bm; G. C. Wiggins, wit.

Jinkins, John & Winney Allen, 30 Oct 1809; Jesse Jenkins, bm; W. M. Sneed, wit.

Jinkins, John & Mary Caskey, 22 Dec 1815; David Satterwhite, bm; Step. Sneed, wit.

Jinkins, John L. & Elizabeth Haskins, 11 Nov 1824; George Haskins, bm; Wm. H. Owen, wit.

Jinkins, Jonathan & Mary M. May, 16 Feb 1826; Joseph G. Williams, bm; Step. K. Sneed, wit.

Jinkins, Jonathan & Juliann Loyd, 3 Jan 1829; Isaac Crowder, bm; S. K. Sneed, wit.

Jinkins, Joseph & Rosa Peace, 15 Oct 1824; James Nuttall, bm; S. K. Sneed, wit.

Jinkins, Robert & Polley Howard, 24 July 1810; Bennet W. Beville, bm; Step. Sneed, wit.

Jinkins, Robert Junr. & Ann B. Smith, 6 Feb 1833; Riley Suit, bm.

Jinkins, Thomas & Ann Stem, 18 Oct 1827; George Haskins, bm; David Laws, wit.

GRANVILLE MARRIAGES 1753-1868

Jinkins, W. & Lucey Peace, 27 Jan 1801; C. Cook, bm.

Jinkins, Walter & Nancy B. Lyon, 18 Nov 1823; William Russell, bm; Jas. M. Wiggins, wit.

Jinkins, William & Martha Mangum, 5 Sept 1842; Allin Cozart, bm; J. M. Wiggins, wit.

Jinkins, William P. & Nancy Blacknall, 11 Dec 1826; Thomas Hicks, bm; Wm. H. Owen, wit.

Jinkins, Willis D. & Dorey N. Cardwell, 7 Sept 1830; Thomas Bullock, bm; David Laws, wit.

Johnson, Absolem & Peggy Saunders, 5 April 1790; Saml. Clay, bm; J. Vaughan, wit.

Johnson, Allen & Elmira Parrish, 17 Feb 1831; Maredeth Peace, bm; David Laws, wit.

Johnson, Anderson & Polley Talley, _____ 1799; John Morris, bm; R. Harris, wit.

Johnson, Anderson & Delia Curtis (freed people), 4 May 1867; m 4 May 1867 by W. E. Bullock, J. P.

Johnson, Archer & Mildred Johnston, 19 March 1791; Thos. Snipes, bm; A. Potter, wit.

Johnson, Benjamin & Elizabeth Walker, 5 Sept 1812; James Walker, bm; W. M. Sneed, wit.

Johnson, Benjamin & Leanah Walker, 8 Feb 1844; Jas. Forker, bm; Wm. H. Whitfield, wit.

Johnson, Benjamin & Mary Ann Wright, 5 Feb 1864; James Anderson, bm; A. Landis, wit.

Johnson, Dempsy & Martha J. Winston, 14 July 1856; L. C. Edwards, bm; m 15 July 1856 by E. Davis, J. P.

Johnson, Drury & Nancey Eastridge, 22 May 1818; Henry Johnson, bm; Zacha. Herndon Jr., wit.

Johnson, Dudley B. & Mary Tilley, 1 Jan 1844; M. P. Roberts, bm; Jas. M. Wiggins, wit.

Johnson, Isham & Polley Harp, 1 April 1806; Samson Harp, bm; W. M. Sneed, wit.

Johnson, James & Nancy Howard, 3 Dec 1800; Brodie Howard, bm; P. Bullock, wit.

Johnson, James & Elisabeth Edwards, 7 Nov 1804; Joshua Johnston, bm; Step. Sneed, wit.

Johnson, James N. & Mary Lawson, 24 April 1828; Willie Royster, bm; Jnp. P. Smith, wit.

Johnson, James T. & Nancy E. Keeton, 9 Oct 1861; John W. Davis, bm; m 9 Oct 1861 by L. B. Stone, J. P.

Johnson, Kemp & Polly Roberts, 24 Oct 1844; Geo. Thomasson, bm; J. M. Wiggins, wit.

GRANVILLE MARRIAGES 1753-1868

Johnson, Leonard Henry & Mary Kindrick, 20 March 1821; Willie Smith Jr., bm; Jas. M. Wiggins, wit.

Johnson, Meacons & Rebecca Brinkley, 3 Sept 1855; Wm. H. Jones, bm; m 8 Sept 1855 by Wm. H. Jones, J. P.

Johnson, Michael & Milley Clardy, 28 Dec 1793; Daniel Johnson, bm; Step. Sneed, wit.

Johnson, Moses & Nancy Mayfield, 6 May 181_; Anson Ball, bm; Step. K. Sneed, wit.

Johnson, Philip & Elisabeth Thomerson, 7 Nov 1797; Thomas Thomasson, bm; Step. Sneed, wit.

Johnson, Richard & Betty Russell, 16 Nov 1860; Archibald Kearzey, bm; m 19 Nov 1860 by L. M. VanHook, J. P.

Johnson, Samuel & Polly Stark, 18 Sept 1804; Jno. Somerville Jr., bm; Jun. Sneed, wit.

Johnson, Samuel H. & Susan Kearney, 1 Feb 1848; Wm. Tyler, bm; J. M. Wiggins, wit.

Johnson, Stephen & Sally T. Gill, 13 Dec 1820; Miles S. Lemay, bm; Step. K. Sneed, wit.

Johnson, Talton & Mary Green, 23 Dec 1833; Hester Moore, bm; Benja. Kittrell, wit.

Johnson, Tatton & Milly Walker, 4 July 1803; Robert Potter, bm; Green Merritt, wit.

Johnson, Thomas & Jinny Nance, 6 May 1808; W. M. Sneed, bm; A. H. Sneed, wit.

Johnson, Thomas & Jane Moss, 8 Jan 1819; Jno. C. Johnson, bm; Saml. Sneed, wit.

Johnson, William & Sary Hudspeath, 29 Dec 1798; William Fowler, bm; Ro. Harris, wit.

Johnson, William & Anna M. V. Ross, 15 June 1816; Wm. F. Barritt, bm; H. Young, wit.

Johnson, William & Lucy Farror, 9 Nov 1820; James Heflin, bm; Jas. M. Wiggins, wit.

Johnson, William & Elizabeth Upchurch, 20 March 1838; Lewis Heflin, bm; S. G. Shearmon, wit.

Johnson, William & Sallie Ann Norwood, 29 June 1858; Wm. Copeland, bm; A. Landis, wit; m 1 July 1858 by Jno. W. Stovall, J. P.

Johnson, William A. & Permelia W. Allen, 27 Oct 1825; Isaac Cheatham, bm; Step. K. Sneed, wit.

Johnson, William D. & Mary K. Hart, daughter of Robert D. & Martha A. Hart, 21 Nov 1867; m 21 Nov 1867 by M. H. Vaughan, Rector of St. Stephen's Church.

Johnson, William H. & Mary Jane Strum, 22 Dec 1858; Jas. R. Duty, bm; m 22 Dec 1858 by James R. Duty, J. P.

GRANVILLE MARRIAGES 1753-1868

Johnson, William K. & Mary Abbott, 21 May 1855; L. Gilliam, bm; Benja. Kittrell, wit.

Johnson, Willis & Mary Higgs, 12 June 1826; Step. K. Sneed, bm.

Johnston, Benjamin & Charity Bobbet, 29 Jan 1781; William Bobbet, bm; Moses Potter, wit.

Johnston, Daniel & Elisabeth Higgs, 20 Jan 1789; John Higgs, bm; A. Henderson, C. C., wit.

Johnston, George & Clary Minor, 19 April 1813; R. Minor, bm; Zach. Herndon, wit.

Johnston, Henry & Mary Terry, 12 April 1785; Bartholomew Sturm, bm; Bennet Searcy, wit.

Johnston, James & Delila Benont, 23 Jan 1781; William Brown, bm; James Langston, wit.

Johnston, Jehu & Otamour Dew, 14 Aug 1805; Anderson Smith, bm; Jas. Sneed, wit.

Johnston, Jesse & Elisabeth Dickerson, 22 Jan 1802; William Dickerson, bm; P. Bullock, wit.

Johnston, Jonathan & Rebecah Moore, 2 June 1800; James Glasgow, bm; P. Bullock, wit.

Johnston, Joseph & Susannah Ward, 23 Dec 1790; Saml. Fuller, bm.

Johnston, Joshua & Frances Burnett, 3 Nov 1801; Frederick Parham, bm; Phil. Bullock, wit.

Johnston, Leroy & Polley Brummit, 25 Sept 1811; Samuel Brummit, bm; W. M. Sneed, wit.

Johnston, Littleton & Lusey Chiles, 2 Jan 1781; Nathan Childs, bm; Asa Searcy, wit.

Johnston, Parmenas & Pryey Brummett, 9 Aug 1805; John Brummett, bm; Jas. Sneed, wit.

Johnston, Robert & Mary Pickrel, 11 March 1784; Frances Bressie(?), bm; Chas. Partee, wit.

Johnston, Tarlton & Alcey Qualls, 9 Nov 1805; John Hawkins, bm; Jas. Sneed, wit.

Johnston, Turner & Elizabeth Woodley, 19 Oct 1805; Benjamin Johnston, bm; Jas. Sneed, wit.

Johnston, William & Mary Isbell, 29 Oct 1787; George Hunt, bm; Reuben Searcy, wit.

Johnston, William & Ann Johnston, 21 Feb 1806; Thomas Potter, bm; W. M. Sneed, wit.

Johnston, William & Elisabeth Smith, 20 Aug 1811; John N. Johnson, bm; Step. Sneed, wit.

Johnston, Wm. T. & Lucy Crabtree, 19 Dec 1848; R. J. Mitchell, bm; Jas. M. Wiggins, wit.

GRANVILLE MARRIAGES 1753-1868

Joiner, Austin & Margaret Evans, 29 Oct 186_; Allen Haskins, bm; W. M. Sneed, wit.

Joiner, Austin & Margaret Evans, 26 Oct 1863; m 26 Oct 1863 by W. M. Sneed, J. P.

Joiner, Isham & Sarah Smith, 6 Sept 1800; James Chavis, bm; Step. Sneed, wit.

Jollee, Wm. J. & Joella Strand(?), 4 June 1839; L. D. Burwell, bm.

Jones, Aaron & Silvia Wheeler, 27 Dec 1792; Luke Tippit, bm; W. Norwood, wit.

Jones, Abner & Dicey Eastwood, 9 May 1811; Ralph Jones, bm; W. M. Sneed, wit.

Jones, Abner N. & Emily W. Philpott, 18 March 1841; W. J. McClanahan, bm; Jas. M. Wiggins, wit.

Jones, Achillis & Rachal Pool, 7 Dec 1866; m 7 Dec 1866 by L. B. Stone, J. P.; Edd Jones, bm.

Jones, Alexander & Nelly Ann Chavis, 8 Nov 1855; William Jones, bm; A. Landis, wit.

Jones, Alexander C. & Bettie A. Rogers, 3 Oct 1853; Rufus P. Jones, bm.

Jones, Alexander S. & Lucinda J. Littlejohn, 3 April 1839; John J. Speed, bm.

Jones, Alfred & Eady Parrish, 6 Feb 1824; Jeremiah Bullock, bm; Wm. H. Owen, wit.

Jones, Americay & Line Wheeler, 24 July 1798; Moses Jones, bm; Step. Sneed, wit.

Jones, Amos T. T. & Luetta Blalock, 8 Jan 1838; Jas. A. Russell, bm; S. G. Shearmon, wit.

Jones, Amos T. T. & Harriet A. Duty, 20 July 1839; Thos. V. Duke, bm.

Jones, Archer & Rebecca Jones, 15 Oct 1824; Mathew J. Morris, bm.

Jones, Barnett & Peggy Laurence, 10 Sept 1822; James Brinkley, bm; S. K. Sneed, wit.

Jones, Benjamin & Mary Baynes, 5 Feb 1770; Thornton Yancey, James Yancey, bm.

Jones, Benson F. & Anne W. Littlejohn, 12 June 1827; Roger P. Atkinson, bm; Wm. H. Owen, wit.

Jones, Benton & Temperancy Weathers, 29 Oct 1860; J. R. Jones, bm.

Jones, Brerton & Martha Dianne Brisse, 11 Oct 1779; William Palmer, bm; Reuben Searcy, wit.

Jones, Charles & Sarah Clement, 4 March 178_; Samuel Clement, bm; Stephen Jett, wit.

GRANVILLE MARRIAGES 1753-1868

Jones, Charles & Delia Mayho, 20 April 1867; m 21 April 1867 by L. M. VanHook, J. P.

Jones, Charles, colored, son of Tom Jones & Harriett Meadows, & Miss Lucey Thompson, daughter of Peter & Francis Thompson, 26 Dec 1868; m 28 Dec 1868 by B. O. Howard, J. P.

Jones, Chesley & Betsey Waller, 10 Aug 1804; Martin Wheeler, bm; E. R. Parham, wit.

Jones, Daniel & Jenny Robards, 9 April 1794; L. Henderson, bm; Wm. Lanier, wit.

Jones, Daniel & Ann Hawkins, 4 Nov 1823; William M. Sneed, bm.

Jones, Daniel & Mary Ann Cooper, 2 March 1867; m 2 March 1867 by B. F. Jenkins.

Jones, David & Jemima Hobgood, 29 March 1825; James B. Kilzer, bm; Step. K. Sneed, wit.

Jones, David & Ann Wilkins, 18 March 1867; Ryley H. Hite, bm; (colored), m 18 March 1867 by L. B. Stone, J. P.

Jones, Edd, freed man & Anna Jones, 20 Dec 1866; Chaves Overbey, bm; m 20 Dec 1866 by L. B. Stone, J. P.

Jones, Edward & Rebecha Green, 1 Feb 1780; Henry Green, bm; Bennet Searcy, wit.

Jones, Edward & Mary Murphey, 3 Nov 1813; Abraham Landers, bm; T. J. Hicks, wit.

Jones, Edward Jr. & Nancy Greer, 3 Aug 1813; William P. Sample, bm; W. M. Sneed, wit.

Jones, Edward E. & Nancy Roberts, 29 Nov 1834; Henry Lilly, bm; Benja. Kittrell, wit.

Jones, Edward Hawkins & Indiana Currin, 28 Oct 1852; Jos. J. W. Jones, bm; m 28 Oct 1852 by Cam. Allen, J. P.

Jones, Elijah & Elizabeth Moore, 4 May 1841; Joseph R. Moore, bm.

Jones, Fowler & Elisabeth Tatom, 17 Nov 1779; John Tatom, bm.

Jones, Fowler & Sally Mires, 4 July 1803; Abner Jones, bm; Mary Green, Edward Jones, wit.

Jones, Frank & Christian Patterson, 16 Feb 1785; Morris Evans, bm; Bennet Searcy, wit.

Jones, Gabriel & Polley Allison, 6 Aug 1806; Maurace Smith, bm; Step. Sneed, wit.

Jones, Gabriel & Nancy R. Amis, 23 July 1842; John S. Wilkes, bm; Wm. H. Whitfield, wit.

Jones, Hardy & Jennet Allison, 18 Oct 1805; Saml. Harris, bm; Jas. Sneed, wit.

Jones, Henrey & Winney Dinkins, 24 June 1809; Benjamin Harris, bm; W. M. Sneed, wit.

GRANVILLE MARRIAGES 1753-1868

Jones, Henry & Elisabeth Jones, 13 June 1799; Francis Jones, bm; Step. Sneed, wit.

Jones, Henry W. & Sarah Parker, 2 Nov 1813; Abner Jones, bm; D. Hicks, wit.

Jones, Henry W., son of Littleton Z. & Edney Jones & Virginia Nance, daughter of John & Fannie Nance, 26 Oct 1867; m 14 Nov 1867 by F. J. Tilley, J. P.

Jones, Isaac N. & Ann Eliza Booth, 19 Dec 1821; Jno. Henry Hawkins, bm; S. K. Sneed, wit.

Jones, Isaac N. & Elizabeth W. Littlejohn, 13 March 1828; David Rogers, bm; Step. K. Sneed, wit.

Jones, James & Charity Alston, 12 Aug 1761; Solo. Alston, Junr., bm.

Jones, James A. & Nanny R. Amis, 14 Dec 1866; Joseph Hobgood, bm; m 18 Dec 1866 by R. J. Devin.

Jones, Jeremiah, son of Edward & Nancy Jones, & Elizabeth Briggs, daughter of James & Polly Arnold, 27 Oct 1867; m 27 Oct 1867 by F. J. Tilley, J. P.

Jones, Jerry & Rebecca Jones, freed people, 31 July 1866; m 5 Aug 1866 by T. J. Horner, M. G.

Jones, Jobe, son of William Jones, & Eliza Harris, daughter of Oxford Harris, freed people of color, 26 Dec 1867; m 26 Dec 1867 by W. H. Puryear, J. P.

Jones, John & Mary Boswell, 30 Sept 1828; James Cheatham, bm; David R. Laws, wit.

Jones, John B. & Sarah Yancy, 15 Aug 1850; Hamon W. Newton, bm; L. B. Stone, J. P., wit.

Jones, John G. & Cornelia F. Puryear, 5 Jan 1857; Elbert S. P. Pool, bm; m 6 Jan 1851 by J. E. Montague.

Jones, John G. & Mary H. Rogers, 5 June 1865; Wm. Hunter, bm.

Jones, John L. & McCaraga(?), 27 Dec 1833; J. Harris, bm.

Jones, John S. & Harriot Taborn, 16 Feb 1829; George Anderson, bm; L. Gilliam, wit.

Jones, John W., son of Robert A. & Mary Ann Jones, & Prudence Hailey, daughter of Henry Hailey, 28 Oct 1868; m by B. R. Hester, M. G., 5 Nov 1868.

Jones, Jonathan & Lucy Harris, 5 May 1794; John Eastwood, bm; W. Norwood, wit.

Jones, Jonathan & Ellenor Heflin, 3 Nov 1795; John Hefflen, bm; Step. Sneed, wit.

Jones, Jubille & Lucy Ann York, m 19 July 1857 by W. D. Allen, J. P.

Jones, Jubille R. & Cinthy York, 27 Oct 1849; Peter Perry, bm; A. Landis, wit.

GRANVILLE MARRIAGES 1753-1868

Jones, Jubilee R. & Arryann Loyd, 18 Feb 1861; Jno. J. Bobbitt, bm; m 10 Feb 1861 by W. D. Allen, J. P.

Jones, Lewellin & Ann A. Kittrall, 10 Sept 1814; John Hicks, bm; Richard Sneed, wit.

Jones, Lewis, of color, son of Henry Oakley & Jenny Jones, & Harriett Cooper, daughter of Moses & Caty Cooper, 27 Dec 1867; m 27 Dec 1867 by B. F. Jenkins, J. P.

Jones, Lewis J., cold., son of Isaac & Bettie Jones, & Ella Hicks, 27 Nov 1868; m 5 Dec 1868 by Bourbon Smith, J. P.

Jones, Littleton & Edna Wheeler, 1 Oct 1840; Canon Johnson, bm; Jas. M. Wiggins, wit.

Jones, Mager & Honor Bass, 25 Aug 1814; Elijah Valentine, bm; W. M. Sneed, wit.

Jones, Marcus L. & Martha Thomasson, 18 May 1861; M. H. Jones, bm.

Jones, Martin & Sally Adcock, 8 June 1838; John McFarling, bm.

Jones, Moses (of America) & Melana H. Clay, 12 June 1832; Hester Moore, bm; Step. K. Sneed, wit.

Jones, Moses & Mary Roberts, 10 Nov 1784; Francis Roberts, bm; Bennet Searcy, wit.

Jones, Moses & Dicey Wheeler, 5 Nov 1799; Aaron Jones, bm; Step. Sneed, wit.

Jones, Moses & Eleany Dunston, 4 Aug 1859; John J. Bobbitt, bm; m 7 Aug 1859 by W. D. Davis, J. P.

Jones, Nicholas & Martha Moore, 6 Aug 1782; Arthur Moore, bm; Thornton Yancey, wit.

Jones, Nicholas & Nancey Parker, 21 Sept 1811; John Eastwood, bm; W. M. Sneed, wit.

Jones, Pearce & Sarah Graves, 24 Dec 1780; Robert Graves, bm; Sherwood Harris, wit.

Jones, Ralph & Sarah Nance, 22 Oct 1805; James Sockwell, bm; Jas. Sneed, wit.

Jones, Richard D. & Susan J. Smith, 5 Feb 1844; James A. King, bm.

Jones, Richard H. & Lethy Newton, 19 April 1849; Stephen Wilkinson, bm; L. B. Stone, J. P., wit.

Jones, Robert & Mary Jordan, 2 Feb 1756; John Jones, bm; D. S. Weldon, wit.

Jones, Robert & Polley Earl, 17 June 1805; Richard Sparks, bm; Step. Sneed, wit.

Jones, Robert & Nancy Kittrell, 15 Dec 1812; Thomas Brodie, bm; Stephen Sneed Jr., wit.

Jones, Robert A. & Mary Ann Mayes, 7 May 1838; A. N. Walker, bm; S. G. Shearmon, wit.

GRANVILLE MARRIAGES 1753-1868

Jones, Robert B. & Virginia C. Mayes, 5 Oct 1859; T. L. Hargrove, bm; m 27 Oct 1859 by L. K. Willie, M. G.

Jones, Robert S. & Elizabeth Pettiford, 14 March 1827; William Chavis, bm; Wm. H. Owen, wit.

Jones, Robert T. P. & Ailsey Jones, 10 May 181_; Redford Gooch, bm; Rt. Herndon, wit.

Jones, Samuel & Ann Harris, 24 Nov 1780; Edward Harris, bm; John Peace Jr., wit.

Jones, Samuel & Elizabeth Goodloe, 27 Sept 1790; Henry Potter, bm; William Goodloe, wit.

Jones, Shugars & Sarah Allen, 12 May 1836; George W. Loyd, bm; J. M. Wiggins, wit.

Jones, Solomon W. & Mary Gooch, 17 Dec 1838; T. O. McClanahan, bm.

Jones, Sterling & Harriet Chavis, 31 Nov 1854; Alex Jones, bm; A. Landis, wit; m 1 Nov 1854 by R. J. Devin.

Jones, Sterling & Joycy Mayho, 14 Feb 1867; m 16 Feb 1867 by E. F. Beachum, R. G. Minister.

Jones, Thomas & Elizabeth Gooch, 8 Dec 1819; Samuel Forsythe, bm; Step. K. Sneed, wit.

Jones, Thomas & Viney Jones, 17 Sept 1839; Allen Jones, bm.

Jones, Thomas & Elizabeth Currin, 23 May 1848; William King, bm.

Jones, Thomas & Permilia J. Anderson, 9 March 1850; Sterling Jones, bm; A. Landis, wit.

Jones, Thomas & Jane Wilson, 20 Oct 1853; Conrad Garner, bm; m 20 Oct 1853 by Jno. W. Stovall, J. P.

Jones, Thomas & Stella West, m 13 Feb 1866 by Wm. H. Puryear, J. P.; Thos. B. Daniel, bm.

Jones, Trim & Milly Hodge (freed people), 12 May 1866; Mathew Watson, bm; m 12 May 1866 by Joseph W. Murphy, Rector of the Church of the Holy Innocents, Henderson.

Jones, Washington & Jane Stephenson, 17 April 1833; Ezekiel Wheeler, bm; Step. K. Sneed, wit.

Jones, Wiley & Joanna (Leanna?) Garner, 21 Sept 1816; David Beck, bm; Leslie Gilliam, wit.

Jones, William & Elizabeth Norman, 8 April 1808; Harbert C. Loften, bm; A. H. Sneed, wit.

Jones, William & Elizabeth Blacknall, 25 April 1809; Wm. Blacknall, bm; W. M. Sneed, wit.

Jones, William & Eliza Waller, 5 Sept 1826; Moses Jones Jr., bm; S. K. Sneed, wit.

Jones, William & Martha Chandler, 23 Aug 1849; Stephen Vaughan, bm; L. B. Stone, J. P., wit.

GRANVILLE MARRIAGES 1753-1868

Jones, William, son of William & Matella Jones, & Roxa M. Berkly, daughter of B. & Mary Berkly, m 25 Sept 1868 by R. J. Devin.

Jones, William E. & Aramanta B. Champion, 2 Oct 1858; P. R. Merryman, bm; m 6 Oct 1858 by Wm. T. Brooks.

Jones, William H. & Rosa C. Clopton, 15 Oct 1845; John G. Thompson, bm; J. M. Wiggins, wit.

Jones, William R. & Polly T. Chane, 13 Dec 1800; Martin Wheeler, bm; P. Bullock, wit.

Jones, Williard & Salley Smith, 27 April 1809; John Hawkins, bm; W. M. Sneed, wit.

Jones, William & Nancey Ragland, 22 April 1826; D. J. Young, bm.

Jones, William & Martha Washington, 7 May 1850; Thomas Latta, bm; A. Landis, wit.

Jones, William D. & Lucinda A. Johnson, 2 Nov 1852; A. Landis, bm.

Jones, William Watts & Elizabeth Littlejohn, __ May 1822; Richard H. Alexander, bm.

Jones, Willie & Judith Wright, 7 Nov 1799; Allen Jones, bm; Step. Sneed, wit.

Jones, Young & Mary Jane OBryant, 6 Nov 1866; Millington Washington, bm; C. E. Landis, wit; m 18 Nov 1866 by J. P. Montague.

Joplin, James & Ledy Mobly, 1 April 1780; John Baly, bm; Asa Searcy, wit.

Jordan, Archibald W. & Mary H. Reavis, 18 Dec 1843; Jno. Bullock, bm; J. M. Wiggins, wit.

Jordan, Benjamin & Betsey Stemper, 22 Jan 1808; Wm. Parnell, bm; Step. Sneed, wit.

Jordan, Turner & Nancey Smith, 14 Dec 1772; Reuben Morse, bm; William Rardon, wit.

Jordan, Willie T. & Mary Jane White, 30 July 1846; Jas. Steagall, bm; Jas. M. Wiggins, wit.

Jorden, George & Salley Crews, 10 Dec 1793; Samuel Allen Junr., bm.

Joyner, Daniel & Jane Mitchel, 29 July 1860; Eldridge Mayho, bm; A. Landis, wit.

Joyner, Joseph & Rebecah Scott, 23 Dec 1862; Creed Haskins, bm; Jas. R. Duty, wit; m 25 Dec 1862 by Jas. R. Duty, J. P.

Judge, James & Martha Jenkins, 22 Feb 1811; Fletcher Taylor, bm; W. M. Sneed, wit.

Justice, Garrison & Teresa Perdue, 4 Feb 1808; Abner Jones, bm; W. M. Sneed, wit.

Justice, William & Mary Cole, 10 May 1805; Brerton Jones, bm; Jas. Sneed, wit.

GRANVILLE MARRIAGES 1753-1868

Justus, William & Eliza Harris, 15 Aug 1833; Saml. B. Meachum, bm; Benja. Kittrell, wit.

Kay, Daniel & Salley Daniel, 28 Nov 1796; Ransome Smith, bm; Step. Sneed, wit.

Keangey, William J. & Indiana Howell, 30 Oct 1866; Thos. A. James, bm.

Kearney, Henry & Nancy Adcock, 31 May 1844; Stephen Cooke, bm; Wm. H. Whitfield, wit.

Kearney, Lewis Crawford, son of Henry & Nancy Kearney, & Mary Frances Priddy, daughter of George & Eliza Priddy, 17 Dec 1868; m 20 Dec 1868 by B. Walker, J. P.

Kearney, Shem H. & Mary Ann Fuller, 23 Sept 1865; Shem McGehee, bm; A. Landis, wit.

Kearney, George, son of John Kearney & Sallie McGehee, & Lavina Leavister, daughter of W. R. Leavister & Martha Gilliam, m 24 Sept 1867 by W. H. P. Jenkins, J. P.

Kearsey, Baldy & Frances Tyler, 11 March 1841; John Stuart, bm; J. M. Wiggins, wit.

Kearsey, Weldon & Betsey Hawley, 13 June 1817; William Kearsey, bm.

Kearsey, William Jr. & Elizabeth McGehee, 26 Dec 1832; Austin Voluntine, bm; Step. K. Sneed, wit.

Kearzy, William J. & Indiana Howell, 30 Oct 1866; m 2 Nov 1866 by E. F. Beachum, R. G. Minister.

Keath, Isaac, son of Wesley & Geloann Keath, & Louisa Smith, daughter of Henery & Agness Smith, m 16 July 1868 by B. B. Hester.

Keath, Wesley & Polly Ann Sherrin, 7 Feb 1860; A. Landis, bm; S. J. Parham, wit.

Keen, L. O. & Ann Arrington, 9 June 1864; Wm. E. Wilkinson, bm; L. B. Stone, J. P., wit; m 9 June 1864 by L. B. Stone, J. P.

Keeton, William H. & Mary White, 11 Dec 1843; B. D. Oaks, bm; Wm. H. Whitfield, wit.

Keith, Wesley & Gilley Ann Jackson, 5 Dec 1839; George Ward, Saml. Keith, bm; Jas. M. Wiggins, wit.

Keith, William & Mary Tippett, 8 Sept 1831; John Beck, bm; David Laws, wit.

Kelley, John & Frances Rogers, 19 Feb 1800; John Rogers, bm; W. M. Sneed, wit.

Kelley, Thomas & Elisabeth Wyers, 4 May 1785; John Wadkins, bm; Bennet Searcy, wit.

Kelly, George J. & Mrs. Ann H. Owen, 23 Sept 1857; Richard H. Hunt, bm; m 23 Sept 1857 by A. C. Harris, M. G.

Kelly, Henry & Frances Alston, freed people, 3 Aug 1867, m by N. C. Harris, M. G.

GRANVILLE MARRIAGES 1753-1868

Kelly, Jesse J. & Susan Brame, 17 June 1823; John B. Manier, bm; Step. K. Sneed, wit.

Kelly, John W. & Adelia Hunt, 30 Nov 1846; D. T. Barker, bm; Jas. M. Wiggins, wit.

Kelly, Joseph, son of Henry Sneed & Lucy Sneed, & Maria Fain, daughter of _____ & Delphia Fain, 30 Dec 1868; m 31 Dec 1868 by W. A. Belvin, J. P.

Kelly, Martin & Elizabeth Akin, 22 Dec 1801; Joseph Akin Junr., bm; James Sneed, wit.

Kemp. John & Viney Peace, 5 Jan 1840; Wm. Mangum, bm.

Kemp, Richard & Sarah Reece, 4 Nov 1799; Fielden Neele, bm; Geo. Brasfield, wit.

Kemp, Solomon & Judah Langford, 7 Feb 1801; Murphey Kemp, bm; Danl. Bridges, wit.

Kenday, James & Jemima Goss, 6 Jan 1807; Caswell Vaughan, bm; W. M. Sneed, wit.

Kendrick, Dennis L. & Nancy Duncan, 13 Oct 1819; Leonard Cardwell, bm; Jas. M. Wiggins, wit.

Kennedy, John & Elisabeth Mangrum, 8 Jan 1795; John Johnson, bm; Step. Sneed, wit.

Kennedy, John G. & Roxanna Wise, 14 Jan 1829; Mont. S. Bacon, bm; A. Sneed, wit.

Kennon, Charles & Mary Lewis, 19 April 1770; Joseph Taylor, Thomas Person, bm.

Kenton, Robert & Mary Eaks, 6 May 1820; John White, bm; Step. K. Sneed, wit.

Kenton, Robert E. & Delia Ann Duncan, 5 Jan 1847; John Kinton, bm; Jas. M. Wiggins, wit.

Kern, David & Mary Ann Robards, 19 Feb 1829; Gibs W. Pearson, bm; L. Gilliam, wit.

Kerney, Samuel & Catharine Farmer, 30 March 1786; Wm. Bettes, bm; Thomas Ligon, wit.

Kerr, Duncan M. & Mary Ann Cox, 27 Feb 1839; Willis Loyd, bm.

Kerson, Charles R. & Elizabeth Murray, 20 Jan 1843; John Culbreath, bm; J. M. Wiggins, wit.

Key, James & Mary Daniel, 21 Nov 1792; James Bedford, bm; W. Norwood, wit.

Key, Martin & Elenor Daniel, 7 Aug 1804; Lesly Gilliam, bm; Jas. Sneed, wit.

Kidmon, James A. S. & Jane Taylor, freed people, 15 Sept 1865; m 27 Oct 1865 by Wm. R. Hicks, J. P.

Kilzer, James B. & Jincey Adcock, 28 Dec 1825; Shelton Hobgood, bm; A. M. Henderson, wit.

GRANVILLE MARRIAGES 1753-1868

Kimbal, Duke J. & Susan A. Cliborn, 15 Feb 1855; James R. Duty, bm; m 15 Feb 1855 by James R. Duty, J. P.

Kimball, Abington & Nancey Hunt, 27 Aug 1812; Michael Hunt, bm; W. M. Sneed, wit.

Kimball, Abington & Patsey Rice, 5 Dec 1829; Step. K. Sneed, bm.

Kimball, Drury & Susanna Grisham, 13 Oct 1783; Dennis Driskel, bm; Drury Kimbell Jr., wit.

Kimball, Drury Jr. & Polly Riggins, 11 May 1805; Leonard Cardwell, bm; Jas. Sneed, wit.

Kimball, Duke & Betsey Christopher, 22 June 1803; Willie Williams, bm; Step. Sneed, wit.

Kimball, Jackson & Molley Loyd, 2 Jan 1794; William Loyd, bm; Step. Sneed, wit.

Kimball, Pleasant & Nanny Cuty, 13 April 1802; Leonard Williams, bm; Step. Sneed, wit.

Kimball, Sion & Susannah Bennet, 27 Jan 1800; Thomas Ricks Junr., bm.

Kimball, William D., son of Edward & Mary A. Kimball, & Susan F. Stark, daughter of Kyzer J. & Dionetia S. Stark, m 16 June 1867 by S. P. J. Harris.

Kimbral, Bartholomew & Emily J. Brame, 26 May 1842; James Fleming, bm; J. M. Wiggins, wit.

Kimbrough, Ormon & Milley Pattillo, 29 April 1802; John F. Pattillo, bm; Green Merritt, wit.

King, Brewer (alias Brewer Vaughan) & Sarah Ashley, 4 April 1811; Thomas King, bm; _____ Sneed, wit.

King, George & Susanna Linear, 30 Dec 1781; Lewis Lanier, bm; Bennet Searcy, wit.

King, Henry & Charity Wade, 27 March 1807; Green Berry Green, bm; T. D. Burch, wit.

King, Henry & Susannah Turner, 5 Nov 1810; Thomas Culverhouse, bm; W. M. Sneed, wit.

King, James & Peggey Ellixson, 2 Nov 1802; Ephm or Barnett Frazier, bm; Step. Sneed, wit.

King, James & Parthena Stokes, 26 Dec 1838; David D. Campbell(?), bm.

King, James D. & Susan Ann King, 3 July 1866; m 4 July 1866 by A. C. Harris, M. G.

King, John & Elizabeth Hester, 4 Oct 1792; Harbert Sims, bm; W. Norwood, wit.

King, John & Sally Madison, 25 Jan 1837; Jas. Falkner, bm.

King, John & Elizabeth C. Bowen, 14 Nov 1850; Benj. C. Cooke, bm; A. Landis, wit.

GRANVILLE MARRIAGES 1753-1868

King, Joseph & Lucy Williams, widow, 11 Aug 1762; Daniel Harris, bm.

King, Joseph & Narcissa Mitchell, 5 Nov 1845; A. H. Venable, bm; J. M. Wiggins, wit.

King, Myles & Elisabeth Potter, 11 Sept 1779; Arthur Jordan, bm; Asa Searcy, wit; consent from Elizabeth Potter "Doctor M. King has my leave to take out his license" 11 Sept 1779.

King, Spencer & Nancy Wilkerson, colored, 7 July 1867; William Royster, bm; m __ July 1867 by W. Overbey, J. P.

King, Thomas & Catharine Vaughan, 4 April 1811; Brewer Vaughan alias Brewer King, bm; Jun. Sneed, wit.

King, Thomas & Polley Robards, 24 March 1815; John Wood, bm; W. M. Sneed, wit.

King, Thomas L. & Catharine Hayes, 26 March 1822; Saml. P. Butler, bm; Jas. M. Wiggins, wit.

King, Tilghman E. & Sarah J. Read, 31 March 1852; Jas. R. Duty, bm; m 14 May 1852 by Jas. R. Duty, J. P.

King, Tilghman E. & Sarah Claiborne, 20 Dec 1859; M. Baldwin, bm; m 21 Dec 1859 by M. Baldwin.

King, William & Dolley Gilliam, 21 Sept 1790; Arthur Jordan, bm; H. Potter, wit.

King, William & Mary Jane Currins, 21 Dec 1844; Chas. Elliott, bm; J. M. Wiggins, wit.

Kingsburg, Haywood & Anna Blacknall (freed people), 18 Aug 1865; Saml. A. Williams, bm; m 20 Aug 1865 by Maurice H. Vaughan, Rector of St. Stephen's Church.

Kingsbury, Russell A. & Elizabeth L. Gilliam, 12 June 1848; Jas. M. Wiggins, bm.

Kingsbury, Theodore B. & Sallie J. Atkinson, 1 May 1851; Jas. J. Davis, bm.

Kingsbury, Thomas D. & Mary Ann Bryant, 16 Aug 1851; Benj. C. Cooke, bm.

Kinnamon, John & Dize Parish, 8 Oct 1793; Joseph Booker, bm; Step. Sneed, wit.

Kinneman, James & Susannah Weaver, 23 Sept 1799; Green Merritt, bm; Step. Sneed, wit.

Kinsey, Justus & Indiana Duty, 29 May 1856; Thomas U. Faucette, bm; m 29 May 1856 by Thos. U. Faucette, Minister of the Gospel.

Kinton, Chapman & Margaret House, 14 May 1826; Thomas Tucker, bm; Wm. H. Owen, wit.

Kinton, Littlejohn & Lucy A. J. Chandler, 23 July 1861; Wm. T. Clayton, bm; m 23 July 1861 by L. B. Stone, J. P.

Kinton, Robert E. & Lucinda West, 21 Dec 1857; Bartlett Knott, bm; A. Landis, wit; m 23 Dec 1857 by Thos. Hester, J. P.

GRANVILLE MARRIAGES 1753-1868

Kinton, Tony & Mary Pettiford, 20 July 1861; A. C. Harris, bm.

Kinton, William T. & Susan Wilson, 6 Feb 1847; Bartlett Knott, bm; Jas. M. Wiggins, wit.

Kirkland, Shadrack & _____, 20 Aug 1799; Samuel Shemwell, bm; W. M. Sneed, wit.

Kirkland, Wm. D. & Ann Cawthorn, 9 Dec 1848; T. W. Hicks, bm.

Kitrell, Samuel & Nelley Shamwell, 30 Dec 1800; Samuel Shemwell, bm; Henry Yarbrough, wit.

Kitrell, Jonathan & Tabbie Bryant, 17 Nov 1772; William Bryant, bm; Reuben Searcy, wit.

Kittle, Isham M. & Frances A. Hayes, 30 May 1856; Philoe White, bm.

Kittle, Jaret & Sally Adcock, 14 Dec 1805; John Miers, bm; _____ Caldwell, wit.

Kittle, Jerry B. & Celestia R. Johnson, 7 Aug 1855; Lewis H. Kittle, bm; m 17 Sept 1855 by J. W. Floyd, Minister of the Gospel.

Kittle, Joel & Katharine Hotsteen, 24 Oct 1796; James Claxton, bm; Micajah Bullock, wit.

Kittle, Lewis H. & Elizabeth J. Reavis, 28 Oct 1842; H. J. Robards, wit.

Kittle, William & Elizabeth Huskey, 2 July 1814; Stephen Garrott, bm; W. M. Sneed, wit.

Kittrel, Isaac & Polley Peace, 30 May 1786; Jas. Barr, bm; Bennet Searcy, wit.

Kittrel, Joshua & Ruth Kittrel, 19 May 1784; William Hunt, bm; Dennis Reardon, wit.

Kittrell, Bryant & Mary Normion, 16 Jan 1798; William Hunt, bm; Richard Taylor, wit.

Kittrell, Edward W. & Lucy A. D. Harrison, 14 Feb 1857; L. K. Willie, bm; m 23 Feb 1857 by L. K. Willie, M. G.

Kittrell, Egbort B. & Elizabeth J. Evans, 25 July 1835; H. G. Hester, bm; Benja. Kittrell, wit.

Kittrell, George & Elizabeth Booswell, 8 Aug 1827; John Glasgow, bm.

Kittrell, Geo. W. & Lucy Crudup, 27 Aug 1862; P. Hinneberry, bm; m 28 Aug 1862 by W. M. Wingate, M. G.

Kittrell, Isaac & Frances Snipes, 14 Nov 1813; Ephraim Fraizer, bm; J. C. Hicks, wit.

Kittrell, James H. & Lucy Paschall, 4 May 1847; E. P. Paschall, bm; Jas. M. Wiggins, wit.

Kittrell, John & Elizabeth Smith, 19 Oct 1772; Samuel Smith, bm; William Rardon, wit.

GRANVILLE MARRIAGES 1753-1868

Knight, John & Martha Montague, 29 March 1788; William Knight, bm; R. Searcy, wit.

Kittrell, John & Orpha Harrison, 18 Dec 1797; John Kittrell, bm; Step. Sneed, wit.

Kittrell, John & Rosey Bryant, 13 Jan 1801; Benjamin Barton, bm; Wm. Walker, wit.

Kittrell, Jonathan & Lucy Farrar, 20 April 1804; William Kittrell, bm; E. W. Parham, wit.

Kittrell, Pleasant & Nancey Atkins, 5 Feb 1812; Levi Heggs, bm; W. M. Sneed, wit.

Kittrell, Simon W. & Dolly Debnam, 15 March 1849; A. H. Cooke, bm; J. M. Wiggins, wit.

Kittrell, Soloman & Ann T. Brodie, 23 April 1813; William M. Sneed, bm; Thos. Hicks, wit.

Kittrell, Thomas & Catharine Floyd, 21 April 1849; Henry Best, bm; J. M. Wiggins, wit.

Kittrell, William & Tabitha Wood, 3 Nov 1812; Jonathan Kittrell, bm; W. M. Sneed, wit.

Kittrell, William & Martha B. Earl, 29 July 1816; Littleberry Crews, bm; W. M. Sneed, wit.

Knight, Alfred & Francis Amis, 16 Dec 1829; H--- Harrison, bm; Step. K. Sneed, wit.

Knight, Andrew & Sarah Bedwile, 9 April 1782; Jno(?) Davis, bm; Ben Wade, wit.

Knight, Benjamin & Nancy Cooke, 8 Oct 1822; William G. Bowers, bm; Step. K. Sneed, wit.

Knight, Benjamin & Jane Parrett, 5 Oct 1850; W. Dement, bm; A. Landis, wit.

Knight, Charles & Lucy Evans, 28 Aug 1822; John R. Nailing, bm; S. K. Sneed, wit.

Knight, John & Letty Bearden, 27 Dec 1799; Spears Harris, bm; Step. Sneed, wit.

Knight, John R. & Charlotte Peace, 5 Jan 1847; S. S. Parrott, bm; J. M. Wiggins, wit.

Knight, John W. & Mary Ann Elizabeth Jeter, 2 Feb 1820; Henry Thompson, bm.

Knight, Jonathan & Christian U. Bennett, 5 Feb 1793; Mark Howard, bm; W. Norwood, wit.

Knight, Lewis & Sallie M. Duke, 16 Jan 1855; Robert W. Kittrell, bm; m 7 Feb 1855 by L. K. Willie, M. G.

Knight, William & Martha Hayes, 24 March 1854; David A. Stone, bm.

Knipper, Solomon & Elizabeth Hailey, 24 Jan 1810; Richard Hailly, bm; W. M. Sneed, wit.

GRANVILLE MARRIAGES 1753-1868

Knotgrass, Thomas & Mary Hudson, 19 June 1818; Creed Hudson, bm; Step. K. Sneed, wit.

Knott, Bartlett & Jane Hester, 5 Feb 1811; Robert Hester, bm; W. M. Sneed, wit.

Knott, Bartlett & Martha Eaks, 2 Feb 1857; M. S. Hart, bm; m 3 Feb 1857 by L. B. Stone, J. P.

Knott, Bartlett, son of Frances Knott, & Elizabeth <u>Strange</u>, daughter of James & Milly <u>Knott</u>, m 18 Feb 1868 by W. H. Puryear, J. P.

Knott, Caleb & Elizabeth Tucker, 21 Jan 1823; Edmund Eakes, bm; J. M. Wiggins, wit.

Knott, David A. & Nancy Downy, 26 Jan 1814; William Mallory Junr., bm; J. C. Sneed, wit.

Knott, David W. & Lindy B. Wilson, 3 May 1836; James R. Duty, bm; J. M. Wiggins, wit.

Knott, Fielding & Mildred Knott, 5 Dec 1848; George W. Knott, bm; W. P. Wiggins, wit.

Knott, George W. & Rebecca Hobgood, 19 Dec 1857; T. L. Hargrove, bm; m 5 Jan 1858 by Peterson Thorp, J. P.

Knott, Henry T. & Elizabeth Knott, 18 Sept 1852; William Currin, bm.

Knott, James & Sally Brasfield, 26 Jan 1784; David Knott, bm; Elisabeth Searcy, wit.

Knott, James & Rebekah Hart, 30 Dec 1799; John Knott, bm; Ro. Harris, wit.

Knott, James & Patsey Salter, 9 June 1804; Beverley Daniel, bm; E. W. Parham, wit.

Knott, James Jr. & Sarah Eaks, 26 Aug 1813; Timothy Clark, bm; W. M. Sneed, wit.

Knott, James C. & Mary Jane Currin, 8 Nov 1853; Geo. Thomasson, bm; m 24 Nov 1853 by H. Hester, J. P.

Knott, James D. & Jerusha E. Farbanks, 28 June 1851; J. P. Hester, bm; m 9 July 1851 by J. M. Satterwhite, J. P.

Knott, John & Amelia Roberts, 3 Jan 1792; Willis Roberts, bm; W. Norwood, wit.

Knott, John & Charlotte Daniel, 20 Oct 1810; James Edwards, bm; Step. Sneed, wit.

Knott, John & Polly Fraizer, 27 Nov 1828; Franklin Fraizer, bm.

Knott, Joseph & Sarah Smith, 22 June 1820; Willis A. Royster, bm; Jno. P. Smith, wit.

Knott, Risdon & Mary Curne, 11 Jan 1827; George Knott, bm; Wm. H. Owen, wit.

Knott, Robert & Mary L. Graves, 24 Dec 1814; Wm. Thomasson, bm; Leslie Gilliam, wit.

GRANVILLE MARRIAGES 1753-1868

Knott, Robert & Mary C. Hester, 18 Dec 1843; James Hester, bm; J. M. Wiggins, wit.

Knott, Robt. & Jane Hazzard, 15 Feb 1837; Thos. S. Hayes, bm.

Knott, Robert, son of David W. & Lundy Knott, & Mrs. Harriett S. Norwood, daughter of John C. & Mildred Lemay, 12 May 1868; m 13 May 1868 by James E. Pattillo, J. P.

Knott, Stephen G. & Elija J. Wilson, 3 May 1862; John R. Wilson, bm; m 4 May 1862 by Jas. R. Duty, J. P.

Knott, Thomas & Barbary Walton, 6 Oct 1810; Josiah Daniel Jr., bm; W. M. Sneed, wit.

Knott, Thomas & Elizabeth Hester, 6 Feb 1849; Barrott Goode(?), bm.

Knott, Thomas W. & Harriett Downey, 17 Oct 1859; Robert Elliott, bm; A. Landis, wit; m 18 Oct 1859 by Willis Lewis, J. P.

Knott, Thomas H., son of Robert & Mary C. Knott, & Mildred F. Currin, daughter of Hugh & Mildred Currin, 17 Dec 1867; m by B. F. Winston, 18 Dec 1867.

Kyle, Neverson & Jane Lassiter, m 1 Jan 1867 by L. K. Willie.

Laboun, Littleton & Polly Anderson, m on (or about) the 10th of Dec 1859 by Jas. P. Montague.

Ladd, Absalom, son of ____ & Martha G. Ladd, & Fannie E. Elliott, daughter of John & Elizabeth N. Elliott, 19 Aug 1868; m 19 Aug 1868 by Warren Overby, J. P.

Ladd, James T. & Louisa Perry, 12 March 1866; W. P. Forsythe, bm; m 14 March 1866 by B. B. Hester.

Ladd, John & Elizabeth Inscore, 16 July 1832; Saml. Chappell Jr., bm; David Laws, wit.

Ladd, R. T. & Magga Roberts, m 29 Dec 1866; L. B. Stone, J. P.; Powel Tuck, bm.

Ladd, Wm. & Francis Stegall, daughter of Dury & Martha Seat, 23 Dec 1868; m 24 Dec 1868 by Richard D. Jones, J. P.

Laffon, Nathaniel & Angelina Bowen, 11 Nov 1835; Allen Smith, bm; Benja. Kittrell, wit.

Lain, Alfred & Martha Puliam, 10 Dec 1816; James Nuttall, bm; R. N. Herndon, wit.

Lamkin, Samson & Martha Wood, 13 Sept 1762; Penuel Wood, bm.

Lamont, James F. A. & Cornelia A. Harris, 3 Dec 1863; m by Wm. Holmes, 3 Dec 1863.

Lancaster, James & Sarah Y. Luveesey(?), 27 Jan 1859; D. E. Young, J. P., wit; Thos. Sevesey, bm; m 27 Feb 1859 by D. E. Young, J. P.

Lancaster, Washington & Mrs. Emily Clark, 20 Dec 1865; Joseph Basket, bm; m 21 Dec 1865 by S. C. J. Harris, M. G.

GRANVILLE MARRIAGES 1753-1868

Land, Alexander G. & Mildred T. Beasley, 13 June 1854; Charles Elliott, bm; A. Landis, wit.

Land, Braxton & Elizabeth Strum, 25 July 1820; James Land, bm; A. Sneed, wit.

Land, James M. & Elizabeth Beasly, 10 Dec 1846; James H. Struno, bm; J. M. Wiggins, wit.

Land, John & Lucy Satterwhite, 28 June 1819; Joseph P. Sneed, bm; Step. K. Sneed, wit.

Landers, Abraham & Precilla Cooke, 2 Aug 1796; George Bullock, bm; Step. Sneed, wit.

Landers, Abraham & Susannah Gooch, 16 Dec 1816; Wm. Thomasson, bm; Step. K. Sneed, wit.

Landers, David & Elizabeth Harris, 17 Dec 1806; Sherwood Harris, bm; W. M. Sneed, wit.

Landers, George & Nancey OBriant, 2 Feb 1802; Robert OBrien, John Landers, bm; Step. Sneed, wit.

Landers, George & Rebecah Wade, 24 Aug 1803; Abraham Landers, bm; Step. Sneed, wit.

Landers, John & Mary Paris, 1 Nov 1768; Jacob Slaughter, bm; Sml. Benton, Heinrich B--- (German signature), wit.

Landers, John & Lucey Johnston, 29 Nov 1783; John Dowdy(?), bm; Sol. Walker, wit.

Landers, John & Biddy Brinkley, 1 Sept 1795; William Landers, bm; Step. Sneed, wit.

Landers, Tyree & Francis Davis, 17 Sept 1787; Joseph Smith, bm; B. Searcy, wit.

Landess, John & Elizabeth Lanier, 23 Jan 1808; George Landus, bm; W. M. Sneed, wit.

Landford, Stephen & Catharine Melton, 4 Feb 1805; Logustin P. Pool, bm; Jas. Sneed, wit.

Landis, Augustin & Frances OBrient, 13 Nov 1832; Tryon Tancey, bm; David Laws, wit.

Landis, Augustus & Mary Tazwell, 30 Nov 1859; L. A. Paschall Jr., bm; m 2 Dec 1859 by T. U. Faucette.

Landis, Smith & Mary Wilkins, m 24 March 1866 by B. B. Hester.

Landis, Willis & Agnes Herndon, freed people, m 26 May 1867 by M. H. Vaughan.

Lanford, Parrish & Sarah Larrane, 7 Jan 1783; Elijah Parrish, bm; Sherwood Harris, wit.

Langford, John A. B. & Lucy P. Russell, m 27 Aug 1866 by L. M. VanHook, J. P.

Langford, Robert & Ann Eliza Mullen, 19 Sept 1844; C. M. Hargrove, bm; Wm. T. Hargrove, wit.

GRANVILLE MARRIAGES 1753-1868

Lanhorn, William & Elizabeth Busbey, 16 Nov 1801; James Busbey, bm; Step. Sneed, wit.

Lanier, Benjamin Allen & Dolley Nance, 2 April 1804; John Nance, bm; E. W. Parham, wit.

Lanier, Lewis G. & Sarah Jane Caster Fleming, 2 June 1819; Albert G. Tomlinson, bm; Step. K. Sneed, wit.

Lanier, Marcellus & Lucretia R. Hicks, 11 May 1847; Benj. C. Cooke, bm; Jas. M. Wiggins, wit.

Lanier, Marcellus V. & Bettie Hicks, 13 May 1867; m 16 May 1867 by H. G. Hill, Minister.

Lanier, Robert & Elizabeth Phillips, 18 Dec 1828; John Landers, bm; Wm. H. Owen, wit.

Lanier, William L. & Emma C. Booker, 20 April 1831; Jos. McKenzie, bm.

Lankford, Jesse & Betty Johnston Parish, 30 Dec 1779; Elijah Parish, bm; Reuben Searcy, wit.

Lankford, Jonathan & Kessiah Crouder, 4 Nov 1817; Willis Parish, bm; W. Sneed, wit.

Lankford, Joseph & Sarah E. Holloway, 12 Jan 1857; Ephraim D. Johnson, bm; James R. Duty, wit; m 13 Jan 1857 by Jas. R. Duty, J. P.

Lashley, James & Nancy Shearin, 2 Nov 1824; Samuel Chappell, bm; Wm. H. Owen, wit.

Latham, Lyman & Frances Barnes, 14 Aug 1833; James C. Harris, bm; Benja. Kittrell, wit.

Lathram, Wm. & Agness Trusty, 25 Aug 1782; Wm. Jones, bm; Chas. Partee, wit.

Latta, Granderson & Caroline Reaves, 10 Dec 1845; R. J. Mitchell, bm; Jas. M. Wiggins, wit.

Latta, Isaac & Martha Minor, freed people, 22 Dec 1865; C. Gooch, bm; A. Landis, wit; m 22 Dec 1865 by Wm. R. Hicks, J. P.

Latta, Thomas & Luetta Barnett, 7 Oct 1847; Jos. D. Hobgood, bm; J. M. Wiggins, wit.

Latta, William L. & Sarah C. Ridly, 9 Nov 1835; R. H. Kingsbury, bm.

Latta, William S. & Mary M. Pickett, 11 Nov 1845; R. H. Kingsbury, bm; Jas. M. Wiggins, wit.

Laughhorn, James & Betsey Grenaway, 16 June 1809; Junius Sneed, bm; James M. Yancey, wit.

Laughter, John L. & Ann Hunt, 8 Aug 1809; Michael Hunt, bm; W. M. Sneed, wit.

Laughter, William & Franky Hunt, 4 May 1807; John L. Laughter, bm; Richd. Sneed, wit.

GRANVILLE MARRIAGES 1753-1868

Laurance, Henry B. & Elisabeth Prewett, 2 Sept 1808; Wm. T. Laurence, bm; Step. Sneed, wit.

Laurance, John & Engelina Mary Hornsby, 31 June 1786; Parish Lankford, bm; Bennet Searcy, wit.

Laurence, Abraham & Margret York, 8 March 1860; W. D. Allen, bm.

Laurence, Abraham Jr. & Lucy Chambliss, 4 Feb 1818; Willie Grissom, bm.

Laurence, James E. & Martha E. Johnson, 15 March 1855; John W. Hicks, bm; m 15 March 1855 by A. C. Harris.

Laurence, Samuel & Elizah Bass, 21 Dec 1802; William Lanier, bm; A. H---, wit.

Laurence, Turner & Priscilla M. Upchurch, 14 Feb 1835; Allen Clay, bm; Benja. Kittrell, wit.

Laurence, William & Marget T. Jones, 21 Jan 1783; William Jones, bm; Bennet Searcy, wit.

Laurence, William & Pamelia Barnes, 22 Dec 1822; Robt. Lawrence, bm; Jas. M. Wiggins, wit.

Laurence, Wm. T. & Lyddy Pewett, 11 Oct 1805; John Smith, bm; Step. Sneed, wit.

Lawrence, James & Elizabeth Bailey, 22 Jan 1793; Mark White, bm; W. Norwood, wit.

Lawrence, Abraham & Leonnera Jones, 17 April 1781; John Gwin, bm; John Henderson, wit.

Lawrence, Abraham & Margret York, m 8 March 1860 by W. D. Allen, J. P.

Lawrence, B. F., son of J. P. & Francis C. Lawrence, & Mary A. Winston, daughter of Elijah & Candis Winston, 19 Dec 1868; m 23 Dec 1868 by R. B. Hester.

Lawrence, Edward B. & Mary E. Allen, 26 Oct 1850; N. M. Laurence, bm.

Lawrence, John E. & Fanny W. Debnam, 17 Nov 1863; m by Wm. Holmes.

Lawrence, John P. & Francis C. Bullock, 23 April 1828; Nathaniel Dabney, bm; David Laws, wit.

Lawrence, John W. & Mary Eliza Clay, 22 July 1865; A. Landis, bm; m 26 July 1865 by R. B. Hester.

Lawrence, Nathaniel M. & Mary A. Lawrence, 18 April 1853; David A. Hunt, bm.

Lawrence, William & Susan Ford, 16 May 1828; William Johnston, bm; A. Sneed, wit.

Lawrence, William T. & Clarey Bailey, 4 Oct 1838; Benjamin B. Hester, bm.

Laws, George & Francis Waller, 3 Feb 1830; Richd. Humsted, bm; David Laws, wit.

GRANVILLE MARRIAGES 1753-1868

Laws, George & Lucy Walker, 26 Dec 1859; A. Landis, bm.

Laws, James & Susan Bullock, 30 July 1827; Abraham Umstead, bm; Wm. H. Owen, wit.

Laws, James G. & Elizabeth Madison, 31 Jan 1843; John King, bm; Jas. M. Wiggins, wit.

Laws, John & Susan McFarlin, 4 Aug 1824; Moses Jones, Jr., bm.

Laws, Jonathan & Sarah Bullock, 30 Dec 1823; John Waller, bm; S. K. Sneed, wit.

Laws, Leonard & Polly Chambliss, 26 June 1820; John T. Gooch, bm; M. Jones Jun., wit.

Laws, Washington & Harriet Waller, 24 April 1841; Jos. H. Gooch, bm; J. M. Wiggins, wit.

Laws, William & Darka Bailey, 15 Dec 1788; John Knight, bm; Henry Potter, wit.

Lawson, Green, of color, son of Gabe & Polly Lawson, & Mary Thornton, daughter of Harry & Anna Thornton, m 25 Dec 1867 by L. B. Stone, J. P.

Laws, Jonathan & Elizabeth Haley, 19 Feb 1842; Willie Mangum, bm.

Laws, Spencer & Mary Mitchell, 1 Oct 1818; David Mitchell, bm; R. N. Herndon, wit.

Lawson, Francis & Cathorine Kimbal, 29 Dec 1829; J. H. Bobbitt, bm.

Leak, James H. & Sarah J. Dixon, 1 Oct 1856; R. J. Mitchell, bm.

Leatherman, Daniel & Nancy Partee, 4 Nov 1794; Abner Partee, bm; L. Henderson, wit.

Leathers, James & Mary Vincent, 12 Oct 1799; Adam Strator, bm; James Sneed, wit.

Leathers, William & Piety Adcock, 15 May 1812; Frederick W. Nance, bm; Richd. Sneed, wit.

Leavester, Davis & Jean Hendley, 15 Oct 1799; Henry Hendley, bm; W. M. Sneed, wit.

Leavister, George T. & Louisa Strother, 16 Dec 1843; Wm. Hunter, bm; Jas. M. Wiggins, wit.

Leavister, Jas. J. & Susan McGehee, 19 Nov 1829; Thomas Cole, bm; David Laws, wit.

Lee, Isham & Martha Scott, 8 Aug 1866.

Leeman, William & Sally Steward, 3 Nov 1830; James Steward, bm; David Laws, wit.

Lemay, Herbert P., son of John C. & Mildred H. Lemay, & Frances A. Currin, daughter of Stephen & Sarah Currin, 22 Oct 1867; m 24 Oct 1867 by Jas. R. Duty, J. P.

GRANVILLE MARRIAGES 1753-1868

Lemay, John C. & Mildred Wilson, 30 Dec 1828; Samuel Lemay, bm; Step. K. Sneed, wit.

Lemay, John P. & Anne Parker, 24 Dec 1813; John M. Peace, bm; Jno. Cobbs, wit.

Lemay, Lewis & Lucy Peace, 19 Dec 1791; Thomas Daniel, bm; W. Norwood, wit.

Lemay, Richard U. & Easter Stovall, 26 Feb 1828; Saml. Lemay, bm; S. K. Sneed, wit.

Lemay, Samuel & Temperance Ussery, 11 Sept 1843; Ambrose Barker, bm; Wm. H. Whitfield, wit.

Lemon, John & Susey Levester, 16 Nov 1820; William Carr, bm; Step. K. Sneed, wit.

Leneau, William & Dolley Yancey, 6 Feb 1839; Robert A. Phillips, bm.

Lester (Luster?), John & Lucy An Holt, 19 Dec 1837; Jas. H. Wells, bm.

Levington, Cornelius R. & Viney Gooch, 20 Dec 1845; W. A. Parish, bm.

Levister, John & Patsey Hendley, 20 Dec 1799; James Levister, bm; James Sneed, wit.

Leviston, Robert & Jane Hopkins, 18 Jan 1821; William Reynolds, bm; W. M. Sneed, wit.

Lewesey, James & Lucy Ann Short, 19 Feb 1827; Leonard H. Cardwell, bm; Wm. H. Owen, wit; consent from Wyatt Short, father of Lucey Ann, who is under age.

Lewis, Abraham & A---- Sadler, 19 Nov 1814; Absalom Yancey, bm; Step. Sneed, wit.

Lewis, Burrell & Nancy Harris, 16 Sept 1865; m 15 Oct 1865 by R. W. Harris, J. P.

Lewis, Charles & Nancy Smith, 15 April 1793; Thomas Hines, bm; W. Norwood, wit.

Lewis, Charles W. & Anne C. Lightfoot, 4 Feb 1810; Fras. Lewis, bm; John Price, wit.

Lewis, David & Ann Eliza Howard, 15 Feb 1867; m 16 Feb 1867 by S. P. J. Harris, M. G.

Lewis, Frank & Julia Barnett (freed people), 29 Oct 1865; m 20 Oct 1865 by T. M. Lynch, J. P.

Lewis, Granderson & Permelia Lewis, 26 Nov 1865; Geo. W. Landis, bm; m 26 Nov 1865 by T. U. Faucette.

Lewis, Horatio, colored, son of Saml. & Dolly Lewis, & Jane Crews, daughter of Alfred Wooding & Crity Crews, m 9 Jan 1869 by A. C. Harris, M. G.

Lewis, James S. & Amanda M. Berkley, 22 Nov 1853; G. W. Pittand, bm; John E. Montague, wit; m 9 Dec 1853 by E. Hines, Minister.

GRANVILLE MARRIAGES 1753-1868

Lewis, John & Ann Chisum, 23 Dec 1844; M. S. Hart, bm; J. M. Wiggins, wit.

Lewis, John Junr. & Sally S. Taylor, 15 Dec 1827; Jno. Bullock, bm; Albert Sneed, wit.

Lewis, Joseph & Elizabeth Walker, 27 Oct 1800; Benja. Hillyard, bm.

Lewis, Joseph & Nancey Marrow, 8 Dec 1828; D. E. Young, bm.

Lewis, Nathaniel & Salley Harris, 29 Nov 1790; Thomas Owen, bm; A. Henderson, wit.

Lewis, Nicholas M. & Lucy Bullock, 4 June 1823; James H. Cobbs, bm; Jas. M. Wiggins, wit.

Lewis, Richard & Leviney Cooper, 22 Dec 1866; Harisson Bullock, bm; Jas. R. Duty, wit; m 22 Dec 1866 by Jas. R. Duty, J. P.

Lewis, Rufus & Amanda Sneed, 25 Oct 1866; Lewis Sneed, bm; C. E. Landis, wit; m 2 Dec 1866 by J. J. Speed, J. P.

Lewis, Thomas B. & Eliza Cobbs, 9 June 1809; Willis Ridley, bm; W. M. Sneed, wit.

Lewis, Warner M. & Elizabeth A. Hinton, 28 Oct 1823; James H. Cobbs, bm; Jas. M. Wiggins, wit.

Lewis, William & Elisabeth Howard, 21 Oct 1773; Groves Howard, bm; Reuben Searcy, wit.

Lewis, Willis & Mary Anne Taylor, 10 Oct 1790; Chas. Lewis, bm; Henry Potter, wit.

Ligon, Charles & Martha E. Yancy, 26 Feb 1866; Chas. Pruit, bm; Jas. R. Duty, wit; m 27 Feb 1866 by Jas. R. Duty, J. P.

Ligon, Thomas & Michal S. Moody, 7 Jan 1788; John Searcy, bm; Asa Searcy, wit.

Ligon, Thomas & Rebeccah Puryer, 4 Nov 1805; William Puryear, bm; Step. Sneed, wit.

Ligon, William P. & Irena P. Puryear, 12 Aug 1831; Jno. P. Smith, bm.

Lile, Benjamin & Drusilla Gill, 20 Jan 1821; William Lile, bm; Step. K. Sneed, wit.

Lile, Benjamin & Catharine Weathers, 3 Sept 1822; James H. Lile, bm; Jas. M. Wiggins, wit.

Lile, James H. & Lucy P. Nance, 2 Nov 1816; Joseph Hester, bm; Step. K. Sneed, wit.

Lile, William & Mary Wilson, 8 Aug 1820; James H. Lile, bm; Jas. M. Wiggins, wit.

Link, Moses & Martha Thorp, m 27 Dec 1866 by Wm. H. Puryear, J. P.

Linsey, Elisha & Elisabeth Loyd, 25 Dec 1779; Jarrett Loyd, bm; Asa Searcy, wit.

GRANVILLE MARRIAGES 1753-1868

Linsey, Labon & Susanna Johnston, 14 April 1782; Wm. Searcy, bm.

Lipscomb, Parsha L. & Mary M. Watson, 31 May 1850; William A. Lipscomb, bm; L. B. Stone, J. P., wit.

Little, George & Mary Person, (no date, during reign of George III, 1760-1776); Danl. Weldon, bm; Isaac Edwards, wit.

Littlejohn, James T. & Sophie M. Micheau, 25 Feb 1856; R. W. Lassiter, bm; m 25 Feb 1856 by Robt. B. Sutton, Rector of St. Stephen's Church, Oxford.

Littlejohn, Thomas Blount & Elisabeth Mutter, 5 Dec 1798; Thomas Mutter Junr., bm; Thomas Brown, wit.

Livingston, James & Nansey Hendley, 19 April 1797; Leonard Card, bm; Step. Sneed, wit.

Lloyd, Joseph R. & Maria A. Pugh, 19 July 1827; Henry L. Plummer, bm.

Loafman, Reuben A. & Mary S. Puryear, 2 Jan 1851; R. O. Gillespie, bm; L. B. Stone, J. P., wit.

Lock, George A. & Mary J. Peoples, 5 July 1851; W. Woodward, bm; m 16 July 1851 by Edmd. Townes, J. P.

Lock, Hesekiah & Sarah Floyd, 20 Aug 1790(?); George Floyd, bm; W. M. Sneed, wit.

Locke, Jonathan & Elisabeth Suit, 1 June 1782; John Sute, bm; Philip Vass, wit.

Lockett, Henry E. & Catharine J. Johnson, 2 Sept 1840; G. Y. Robards, bm; Jas. M. Wiggins, wit.

Locklayer, Caswell & Mary Brandon, 12 April 1861; W. K. Brosius, bm.

Lockwell, James & Rachel Green, 22 Oct 1805; Ralph Jones, bm; Jas. Sneed, wit.

Locust, Henry & Martha Evans, 25 Sept 1842; William Mayo, bm; Wm. H. Whitfield, wit.

Loftis, Byrd & Catron Jones, 21 March 1801; Wm. Jones, bm; Wm. Robards, wit.

Loftis, Stanly & Jane Wilbourn, 26 Sept 1821; John Hutson, bm; Jno. P. Smith, wit.

Loftis, William & Ann Jones, 16 June 1817; Reuben Jones, bm; R. N. Herndon, wit.

Loftis, William D. & Nancy A. Carter, 20 Dec 1848; William Reavis, bm; L. B. Stone, J. P., wit.

Logan, Peter Jr., of color, son of Peter Logan Sen. & Betsey Wembish, & Susan Richmond, saughter of Peter & Obra Richmond, 23 Sept 1868; m 24 Sept 1868 by Rev. Saml. G. Cross.

Long, Charles & Mary Thomasson, 10 March 1784; Richd. Long, bm; Rowland Gooch, wit.

GRANVILLE MARRIAGES 1753-1868

Long, George W. & Sarah C. Lewis, 12 May 1802; Step. Sneed, bm; J. Brodie Junr., wit.

Long, Henry & Frances Ivens, 29 Nov 1864; James Merit, bm; m 29 Nov 1864 by Jas. J. Moore, J. P.

Long, James Columbus & Docia Ann Clay, 11 Dec 1865; D. L. Mangum, bm; m 17 Dec 1865 by R. B. Hester.

Long, P. T. & Eliza Frances Cooke, 16 Dec 1839; G. T. Leavister, bm; J. M. Wiggins, wit.

Long, Robert, of color, son of Franklin Barnett & Elizabeth Long, & Clora Yearborough, daughter of Jacob & Nellie Yearborough, 26 Dec 1867; m 26 Dec 1867 by James J. Moore, J. P.

Longmen, William & Delia Ann Avorett, 16 May 1853; John L. Stroud, bm; A. Landis, wit.

Longmire, Allen & Elizabeth Stroud, 23 Dec 1851; William Longmire, bm; A. Landis, wit; m 23 Dec 1851 by W. S. McClanahan, J. P.

Longmire, Burwell & Deana Hamilton, 11 Aug 1865; A. Landis, bm.

Longmire, Burwell, colored, son of Saml. & Millie Hunt, & Dinah Webb, daughter of Mimcock & Jinnie Webb, 7 Nov 1868; m 18 Dec 1868 by A. Satterwhite, J. P.

Longmire, Elijah & Nancey Norwood, 7 Aug 1799; John Knight, bm; W. M. Sneed, wit.

Longmire, Elijah & Polly Moss, 25 May 1803; Archibald H. Sneed, James M. Burton, bm; Step. Sneed, wit.

Longmire, Elijah & Minta Hayes, 5 Nov 1822; James Hunt, bm; Jas. M. Wiggins, wit.

Longmire, Iverson & Milchisa Harris, 19 Sept 1856; Edward B. Lyon, bm; m 30 Sept 1856 by J. W. Floyd, Minister.

Longmire, James & Melvina Bradford, 17 Nov 1865; G. A. Dement, bm; m 21 Nov 1865 by G. B. Lyon, J. P.

Longmire, John & Nancy Marshal, 24 Dec 1788; Sineth Ogilby, bm; A. Henderson, wit.

Longmire, Robert & Elizabeth Hunt, 15 Nov 1810; Jonathan Knight, bm; W. M. Sneed, wit.

Longmire, Robert B. & Emma R. Burnett, 20 Jan 1865; ____ Montague, bm; m 25 July 1865 by Jas. P. Montague, Minister.

Longmire, Samuel & Eliza Dement, 24 Nov 1854; John C. Cawthon, bm; A. Landis, wit.

Longmire, Samuel H. & Martha A. Burnett, 17 June 1842; Jas. C. Cooper, bm.

Lorton, John & Frankey Floyd, 29 July 1802; Thomas Williams, bm; Jun. Sneed, wit.

Lovliss, Joseph & Susanna Woodmon, 10 Sept 1800; George Pullin, bm; Wm. Walker, wit.

GRANVILLE MARRIAGES 1753-1868

Lowe, Thomas & Mrs. Mary Eaton, relict of Willm. Eaton Esqr., late decd., 10 Nov 1760; Joshua Moss, bm; Jno. Bowie, wit.

Lowe, Thomas & Sary Williams, 14 Aug 1770; James McCartney, Nathaniel Williams, bm; Jesse Benton, wit.

Lowery, James & Peggy Mangum, 2 March 1835; ____ Mangum, bm.

Lowery, William T., son of Henry & Mary Ann Lowery, & Margaret F. Gravett, daughter of Wm. & Elizabeth Gravett, 30 July 1868; m 30 July 1868 by Warren Overby, J. P.

Lowry, Joseph N. & Emeline Bailey, 27 June 1866; m 11 June 1866 by J. W. Wellons.

Lowry, Newton & Elizabeth Bailey, 28 Oct 1852; Israel F. Dilliard, bm; m ____ 1852 by Jonathan M. Stone, J. P.

Loyd, David & Sarah Jane Hester, 15 April 1838; Samuel P. Wilson, bm.

Loyd, David & Frances Taylor, 9 Oct 1844; J. H. Gooch, bm; J. M. Wiggins, wit.

Loyd, Eaton & Sally Wilson, 4 May 1833; James Irby, bm; David Laws, wit.

Loyd, Edward & Jane Hart, 25 March 1802; West Lindsey, bm; P. Bullock, wit.

Loyd, G. T. & Carolina Eaks, 26 Jan 1862; m by Thos. Hester.

Loyd, Horace D. & Mary Yancey, 14 Jan 1863; James Loyd, bm; m 30 Jan 1863 by Thos. Hester, J. P.

Loyd, Isham & Ann Estridge, 15 Dec 1836; George W. Loyd, bm; J. M. Wiggins, wit.

Loyd, James & Mary Noblen, 2 Jan 1837; Thomas Keaton, bm.

Loyd, James & Sarah Ann Hicks, 19 Nov 1848; Elijah R. Frazier, bm; J. M. Wiggins, wit.

Loyd, James W. & Mary A. C. Merritt, 5 Jan 1852; John F. Bullock, bm; m ____ 1852 by J. K. Cole, M. G.

Loyd, Jarret & Salley Hart, 23 March 1785; Joshua Hayes, bm; Robert Reid, wit.

Loyd, John & Rachel Wilson, 22 Feb 1803; Thomas Taylor, bm; Green Merritt, wit.

Loyd, John & Rebecca Linster, 11 Aug 1824; Richd. Allen, bm; Wm. H. Owen, wit.

Loyd, Joseph & Mary Ann Sowell, 2 Sept 1839; Thomas Wright, bm; G. C. Wiggins, wit.

Loyd, Joshua & Susannah Johnson, 6 March 1804; Benjamin Thomasson, bm; E. W. Parham, wit.

Loyd, Lemmuel & Lively Rogers, 23 Dec 1809; John Loyd, bm; W. M. Sneed, wit.

Loyd, Lewis & Frances Buchanan, 13 Feb 1837; Joseph Hart, bm.

GRANVILLE MARRIAGES 1753-1868

Loyd, Lunsford & Nanvy Clark, 7 Dec 1858; William Dickerson(?), bm; m 7 Dec 1858 by Elba L. Parrish, J. P.

Loyd, Nathaniel & Martha Mangum, 5 Jan 1854; Wm: Ball, bm; A. Landis, wit.

Loyd, Nicholas & Martha West, 28 Dec 1828; Daniel Delap, bm.

Loyd, Pomfrett & Jane Hart, 27 Oct 1829; Edward Hunt, bm.

Loyd, Pomfrett & Dolly Moody, 4 April 1832; Edward Hunt, bm.

Loyd, Robert & Fannie Short, 3 Dec 1851; William Ball, bm; A. Landis, wit.

Loyd, Thomas & Rhoda Clarke, 17 Sept 1822; Berelle Ellington, bm; S. K. Sneed, wit.

Loyd, Thomas Jr. & Cordelia Ann Clark, 18 Dec 1856; William Dickerson, bm; m 18 Dec 1856 by L. R. Parham, J. P.

Loyd, William & Elizabeth Herris, 6 April 1782; Joseph Taylor, bm; James Jett, wit.

Loyd, William & Betsey Mangrom, 22 Feb 1797; Benjamin Thomson, bm; Richard Taylor, wit.

Loyd, William & Peggey Scott, 8 Dec 1791; Joshua Loyd, bm; Step. Sneed, wit.

Loyd, William & Mary Williams, 30 Sept 1829; Littleton Forkner, bm; David Laws, wit.

Loyd, William & Elizabeth Irby, 26 May 1832; Guilford Ball, bm; David Laws, wit.

Loyd, William R. & Virginia L. Roges, m 15 Sept 1867 by W. D. Allen, J. P.

Loyd, Willie & Dolley Roberson, 14 Jan 1809; Wilson Abbot, bm; Step. Sneed, wit.

Loyd, Willis & Emiline Cox, 22 Oct 1834; Wily Mangham, bm; Benja. Kittrell, wit.

Loyd, Wilson & Susan Ann Hicks, 31 Dec 1846; Robt. Elliott, bm; J. M. Wiggins, wit.

Loyd, Zadock & Elisabeth Thomerson, 13 Jan 1798; Valentine Loyd, bm; Step. Sneed, wit.

Loyed, Joseph & Mariah Buckhanon, 17 Dec 1838; William Royster, bm; M. J. Royster, wit.

Lozer, Lewis H. & Elizabeth Curtis, m 19 July 1866 by Jas. R. Duty, J. P.

Lucas, H. G. & Susan Jones, 29 March 1851; Joseph J. W. Jones, bm.

Lucas, Valentine & Rachel Pettiford, 12 Aug 1780; William Tabourn, bm; John Searcy Junr., wit.

Lucas, William H. & Susan D. Williams, 27 Dec 1852; Wm. B. Wolff, bm; m 27 Dec 1852 by A. C. Harris, M. G.

GRANVILLE MARRIAGES 1753-1868

Lumpkin, Anthony & Sarah Hunt, 12 Nov 1798; M. Satterwhite, bm; Smith Satterwhite, Mitchel Satterwhite, wit.

Lumpkin, Edmund & Elisabeth Barnett, 25 Dec 1805; Joseph Barnett, bm; Step. Sneed, wit.

Lumpkin, Fleming & Catey Parker, 9 Jan 1812; Jonas Parker, bm; W. M. Sneed, wit.

Lumpkin, Fleming & Mary Mayfield, 13 May 1833; James Cheatham Jr., bm; David Laws, wit.

Lumpkin, George W. & Martha C. Hicks, 30 Jan 1840; Thos. D. Hayes, bm.

Lumpkin, James R. J. & Louisa E. Cottrell, 4 Aug 1859; John S. Ellis, bm; Jas. R. Duty, wit; m 7 Aug 1859 by A. Barker, J. P.

Lumpkin, John & Ann Mayfield, 26 Oct 1835; George Wilborn, bm; Benja. Kittrell, wit.

Lumpkin, John & Betsey Rice, 22 May 1839; Jno. Kinton, bm.

Lumpkin, Robert & Nancy Hunt, 16 Dec 1799; John Moss, bm; James Sneed, wit.

Lunsford, Alexander & Maria Cozort, 21 Feb 1829; John H. Bobbitt, bm; L. Gilliam, wit.

Lunsford, Crockett & Nancy J. Cozort, 10 Dec 1860; m 13 Dec 1860 by Jeff Horsier(?), J. P.

Lunsford, Joseph & Betsey Howard, 29 Dec 1816; Jesse Lunsford, bm.

Lunsford, Joseph & Edney Fowler, 26 Dec 1848; Jones Peed, bm.

Lunsford, Volen B. & Elizabeth Bowen, 21 Feb 1836; John Tillison, bm; Benja. Kittrell, wit.

Lunsford, William & Martha Ann Worel, 17 Aug 1853; Sil. Naton, bm; John E. Montague, wit.

Lunsford, William A. & Mildred Tilley, 6 Oct 1864; J. Parrish, bm.

Lyerly, J. L. & Rebecker Walker, 27 Jan 1867; C. W. Walker, bm; W. H. Thomas, J. P., wit; m 29 Jan 1867 by R. J. Devin.

Lynam, George W. & Miranda G. Bailey, 27 Dec 1854; John T. Due, bm; m 28 Dec 1854 by Jas. J. Moore, J. P.

Lymon, William & Malisa A. Wilson, 4 Feb 1845; Geo. J. Rowland, bm.

Lynam, William & Telitha J. Robards, 20 Dec 1841; Charles Lynum, bm.

Lynch, Dennis & Phebe G. Morris, 2 July 1852; Doctor D. Clay, bm.

Lynch, Jeremiah & Barbary Blalock, 29 Feb 1772; John Blalock, bm; Reuben Searcy, wit.

Lynch, Thomas M. & Cecilia Dorsey, 15 May 1855; D. A. Paschall Jr., bm; m 15 May 1855 at the residence of Dr. Dorsey by Robt. B. Sutton, Rector of St. Stephen's Church, Oxford, a presbyter of the Protestant Episcopal Church.

Lynch, William F. & Mary T. Garrott, 14 June 1838; B. F. Williamson, bm.

Lyne, Henry Junr. & Lucey Martin, 9 Dec 1795; John Hare, bm; Step. Sneed, wit.

Lynum, Charles & Alcinda Bridges, 30 Oct 1841; Elijah Pruitt, bm; G. C. Wiggins, wit.

Lynum, William & Lucy Ann Roberts, 19 Dec 1837; John W. Merritt, bm; Tho. L. King, wit.

Lyon, Anthony, of color, son of Lovelace Russell & Fannie Lyon, & Maria Marrow, parents unknown, 22 July 1867; m 25 July 1867 by F. N. Whaley, a Minister of the Gospel.

Lyon, Clement & Catharine Wood, 15 Dec 1806; Thos. Jinkins, bm; W. M. Sneed, wit.

Lyon, E. H. & Nannie E. Beasley, 8 May 1866; m 10 May 1866 by W. C. Gannon, M. G.

Lyon, Edward B. & Amanda A. Floy, 14 March 1845; John G. Royster(?), bm; J. M. Wiggins, wit.

Lyon, Elkanah & Celia Fleming, 31 July 1813; William Flemming, bm; W. M. Sneed, wit.

Lyon, James E., son of Z. J. & Nancy B. Lyon, & Mittie E. Lyon, daughter of William H. & Betsy Ann Lyon, 22 July 1868; m 30 July 1868 by B. B. Hester, M. G.

Lyon, James W. & Celia White, 13 Oct 1842; John F. Lyon, bm; Wm. H. Whitfield, wit.

Lyon, James W. & Mary O. Waller, 17 Nov 1849; W. E. Bullock, bm.

Lyon, Jackson & Jennie Washington, m 10 Aug 1866 by W. C. Bullock, J. P.

Lyon, John M. & Elizabeth Wood, 11 April 1814; Clement Lyon, bm; W. M. Sneed, wit.

Lyon, Lewis & Fannie Dalby, freed people, 30 Sept 1865; m 10 Oct 1865 by R. B. Hester.

Lyon, Norflet & Mary Waller, 26 Aug 1857; B. L. Hester, bm; m 30 Aug 1857 by T. B. Lyon, J. P.

Lyon, Obediah & Phanny Stovall, 18 Sept 1802; John Stovall, bm; Step. Sneed, wit.

Lyon, Pomp & Sally Hayes, m 9 Oct 1866 by D. Tilly, J. P.(freed people); Henry Harris, bm; Francis J. Tilley, wit.

Lyon, Ralph & Ann Henderson, freed people, 10 Feb 1866; Saml. A. Williams, bm; A. Landis, wit; m 11 Feb 1866 by T. J. Horner.

Lyon, Richard A. & Ziby Ann Waller, 2 Nov 1850; W. Bullock, bm.

GRANVILLE MARRIAGES 1753-1868

Lyon, Thomas B. & Mary J. Christian, 9 Aug 1842; Edward B. Green, bm; Jas. M. Wiggins, wit.

Lyon, Thos. B. & Penelope Dalby, 26 March 1849; E. E. Freeman, bm; J. M. Wiggins, wit.

Lyon, William & Patsey Turner, 10 Dec 1816; John M. Lyon, bm; Step. K. Sneed, wit.

Lyon, William H. & Elizabeth Ann Hester, 29 Jan 1839; James T. Gill, bm; Jas. M. Wiggins, wit.

Lyon, William M. & Sarah Ann Crews, 3 Nov 1857; Robert L. Suit, bm; m 10 Nov 1857 by J. W. Floyd, Minister.

Lyon, William W. & Eliza Moore, 13 Aug 1853; James S. Finch, bm; A. Landis, wit.

Lyon, Woodson & Jemima Cozort, 17 Dec 1833; Thos. Strum, bm; Benja. Kittrell, wit.

Lyon, Z. E., son of John & Betsey Lyon, & Mary Jane Mitchell, daughter of William & Susan Mitchell, 14 Nov 1868; m 20 Nov 1868 by B. R. Hester.

Lyon, Zacheriah & Nancy Lanier, 6 Feb 1809; Clement Lyon, bm; Jun. Sneed, wit.

Mc--see also Ma, Me

McAlester, Garland & Salley Banks, 1 June 1784; William Reeves, bm; John Minor, wit.

McCadden, Addison & Ann Trimmon, 9 Nov 1865; D. A. Paschall, bm; G. W. Landis, wit; m 9 Nov 1865 by Thomas U. Faucette.

McCann, Jno. J. & Mrs. Ann D. Smith, m 16 Jan 1867 by W. Overby, J. P.

McCann, Owen & Sally Loftist, 29 Aug 1834; Anderson Holloway, bm.

McClenahan, William & Frances Blacknall, 14 Aug 1832; Jas. A. Russell, bm; David Laws, wit.

McCormick, Jeremiah & Damsel V. McC----, 24 June 1850; Wesley W. Young, bm.

McCraw, Armstead & Susan Davis, 29 Sept 1866; m 14 Oct 1866 by W. H. P. Jenkins, J. P.

McCraw, Frank M. & Bettie Wiggins, 27 Oct 1855; Wm. Brasius, bm; m 29 Oct 1855 by Wm. Holmes.

McCutchan, John S. & Elizabeth T. Salmon, 18 Sept 1837; Jesse Rankin, bm; Jas. M. Wiggins, wit.

McDaniel, George & Sarah Earl, 8 Sept 1779; Thomas McDaniel, bm; _____ Henderson, wit.

McDaniel, James & Nancey Rogers, 24 May 1790; Mark. White, bm; H. Potter, wit.

GRANVILLE MARRIAGES 1753-1868

McDaniel, Joseph of Cumberland County, & Sarah Fuller, daughter of Henry Fuller, of Granville County, 5 March 1761; Henry Jones, bm; J. D. Bowie, wit.

McDaniel, Joseph & Mary Parham, 25 July 1792; Mark White, bm; W. Norwood, wit.

McDaniel, William & Georgiana Clyburn, 8 Aug 1865; L. J. Kimbal, bm; m 9 Aug 1865 by Eld. J. M. Minnis.

McFarlin, Henry & Temperance Robards, 24 May 1817; Moses Jones Junr., bm; Daniel Winsted, Step. K. Sneed, wit.

McFarlin, Henry & Mary Parrish, 12 Sept 1826; Turner Johnson, bm; Wm. H. Owen, wit.

McFarlin, John & Sally Bearden, 5 Dec 1825; Willie Harris, bm; Wm. H. Owen, wit.

McFarlin, Moses & Ann Umsted, 18 July 1832; William Umsted, bm; A. Sneed, wit.

McFarlin, Robert H. & Virginia C. Allen, 15 July 1856; A. Landis, bm.

McFarling, Rasmus & Celia S. Parrish, 13 Nov 1832; Archibald Allen, bm; David Laws, wit.

McGee, Shem & Elizabeth Hawkins, 5 Feb 1805; Archibald Byram, bm; James Sneed, wit.

McGehe, Crafford & Elisabeth Priddy, 6 May 1806; Claborn Cook, bm; Step. Sneed, wit.

MeGehe, Josiah & Fanny Harris, 29 Sept 1827; Edward Kimball, bm; David Laws, wit.

McGehe, Nathan & Elizabeth Glasgow, 15 Jan 1787; Richard Glasgow(?), bm; Robert Searcy, wit.

McGehe, Nathan & Martha Brogden, 14 Oct 1842; Shem McGehe, bm; Wm. H. Whitfield, wit.

McGehee--see also Maggee

McGehee, Banks & Clary Priddy, 28 Oct 1806; Josiah McGehe, bm; W. M. Sneed, wit.

McGehee, Banks & Elizabeth Fuller, 13 Aug 1832; Thos. Leavister, bm; David Laws, wit.

McGehee, Claborn & Polley Woodley, 27 Sept 1814; Shem McGeehee, bm; W. M. Sneed, wit.

McGehee, Gilliam & Polly Megehee, 20 Dec 1812; Edmund Gilliam, bm; Thos. J. Hicks, wit.

McGehee, Henry & Emmilla Cogens, 7 May 1825; George Cogens, bm; Wm. Hayes Owen, wit.

McGehee, Henry & Julia Ann Day, 19 Feb 1844; George Anderson, bm; Wm. H. Whitfield, wit.

McGehee, Henry & Hixy Ross, 6 Aug 1844; J. E. Whitfield, bm; J. M. Wiggins, wit.

GRANVILLE MARRIAGES 1753-1868

McGehee, James & Winnie Champion, freed people, 6 Sept 1865; A. Landis, wit.

McGehee, John & Sally Boyce Harris, 14 Jan 1851; D. H. Whitfield, bm; A. Landis, wit.

McGehee, John T. & Susan E. Cannady, 4 Aug 1847; Jno. White, bm.

McGehee, Josiah, son of Banks McGehee & Elizabeth McGehee, & Minerva A. Brinkley, daughter of Hiriam & Annice Brinkley, 14 April 1868; m 16 April 1868 by Robt. L. Heflin, J. P.

McGehee, Josiah C. & Emiline Catlett, 21 Oct 1865; Z. T. McGehee, bm; m 25 Oct 1865 by A. B. Lyon, J. P.

McGehee, Lemuel & Susanna White, 10 Sept 1822; John M. Vincent, bm; Jas. M. Wiggins, wit.

McGehee, Lucius & Eliza Williams, 9 Oct 1850; George Catlett, bm.

McGehee, Shem & Eliza Jane Haswell, 7 Oct 1843; Henry McGehee, bm; J. M. Wiggins, wit.

McGehee, Shemuel & Patsy Cook, 2 Oct 1847; Benj. C. Cooke, bm.

McGehee, Silas E. & Mary E. Bradford, 3 May 1859; Shem McGehee, bm; A. Landis, wit.

McGehee, Washington & Leucy Fuller, 25 Dec 1834; Zacheriah Fuller, bm; Benja. Kittrell, wit.

McGehee, Wm., request for license with Saml. Clay, bm; 10 July 1805.

McGehee, William & Elizabeth L. Clay, 10 Aug 1805; Samuel Clay, bm; Jas. Sneed, wit.

McGehee, Zachariah & Martha Usry, 27 July 1858; W. D. Fuller, bm; A. Landis, wit; m 29 July 1858 by Geo. J. Rowland, J.P.

McGhee, Young & Elizabeth Biggs, 30 Aug 1828; W. F. McClanahan, bm; David Laws, wit.

McGhee, Young & Lucy Allen, 29 June 1839; Jos. B. Penn, bm.

McGloklen, Dawson & Jenney Fuller, 28 June 1816; David Thrift, bm; Step. K. Sneed, wit.

McIllroy, John & Rebecca Jones, 24 June 1762; Thos. Cook, bm; Jn. Bowie, wit.

McIntosh, George S. & Euphemia A. Hamilton, 30 April 1829; Robt. B. Gilliam, bm.

McIntosh, John W. & Phebe Overbey, 26 July 1859; Saml. A. Williams, bm; m 26 July 1859 by E. F. Beachum, a Minister of the Gospel.

McIver, Archibald D. & Augusta C. Chandler, 6 Nov 1860; Saml. A. Williams, bm; m 6 Nov 1860 by E. Hines.

McLemore, John & Sarah Carnes, 30 Dec 1780; James Claxton, bm; William Meryman, wit.

GRANVILLE MARRIAGES 1753-1868

McLin (Macklin), James & Elizabeth Bullock, 29 Nov 1792; John Brodie, bm; Step. Sneed, wit.

Macklin, Joseph & Susan Martin, 11 Sept 1834; R. N. Herndon, bm; Benja. Kittrell, wit.

Maclin, Nathaniel & Elisabeth Springer(?), 22 June 1799; William Bullock, bm; Step. Sneed, wit.

McMurry, Samuel & Margaret McMurry, 1 Dec 1764; James McMurry, bm; Charles Bruce, James Davenport, wit.

McNamee, Peter F. & Mary Miers, m 3 Oct 1866 by Joseph W. Murphy, Rector of Holy Innocents, Henderson, N. C.

McPherson, Joseph & Lucinda Pippins, 30 Oct 1843; Redman Forsyth, bm; Wm. H. Whitfield, wit.

Maben, Robert & Susan W. Davis, 27 April 1835; Jas. M. Wiggins, bm; Benja. Kittrell, wit.

Macay, Spruce & Fanney Henderson, 27 May 1785; B. Ridley, bm; _____ Stokes, wit.

Mackenzie, Charles & Ruthy Shadrach, 6 March 1851; Samuel P. Wilson, bm; A. Landis, wit.

Macon, Gideon H. & Martha Blacknall, 6 Aug 1834; Jas. A. Howze, bm.

Macon, John & Elisabeth Bowdon, 3 Jan 1786; Stephen Grisham, bm; Bennet Searcy, wit.

Macon, Miles & Frances Miller, 20 May 1816; Thomas B. Littlejohn, bm; W. M. Sneed, wit.

Macon, Nathaniel & Hannah Plummer, 29 Sept 1783; Ro. Burton, bm; Reuben Searcy, wit.

Macon, Nathaniel T. & Tabitha M. Kittrell, 21 Aug 1837; Theodor Hicks, G. C. Wiggins, bm; Jas. M. Wiggins, wit.

Maddox, Wm. O. & Mary A. Mitchell, 24 March 1830; Will. A. Ferrell, bm; David Laws, wit.

Madison, James & Phebe Forsythe, 25 Oct 1837; Erasmus McFarling, bm; J. M. Wiggins, wit.

Madison, Peyton & Elizabeth Bailey, 20 Feb 1785; Stephen Beley, bm; Richd. Harris Junr., wit.

Maggee, Benjamin & Mary Priddy, 23 Nov 1775; Wm. Nailing, bm.

Mahone, James H. & Martha A. Rowland, m 17 May 1866 by T. Page Ricaud.

Majors, John H. & Sarah Tuck, 9 Jan 1824; Robert Elliott, bm; Jno. P. Smith, wit.

Mallard, Thornton & Elizabeth Wright, 5 Jan 1789; Wm. Tatom, bm; A. Henderson, wit.

Mallory, Anderson & Roxanna Gregory, 9 March 1867; m 10 March 1867 by John W. York.

GRANVILLE MARRIAGES 1753-1868

Mallory, Charles & Elizabeth Horton, 24 Dec 1836; D. C. Herndon, bm; J. M. Wiggins, wit.

Mallory, James R. & Lucy P. Horner, 3 March 1866; m by Robt. L. Heflin, J. P., 6 March 1866.

Mallory, Rufus & Martha Howard, freed people, 23 Sept 1865; A. Landis, wit.

Mallory, William & Lucy Horne, 30 Jan 1815; Henry Ransom, bm; John Owen Junr., wit.

Mallory, William C. & Mildred A. Hunt, 20 July 1839; Isaac P. Hester, bm.

Mallory, William J. & Ann J. Clay, 26 May 1830; Oliver Higgs, bm; David Laws, wit.

Mallory, William J. & Mary H. Jackson, 21 Dec 1863; A. Landis, bm.

Malone, David & Aggy Anderson, 16 July 1787; Mitchel Burford, bm; B. Searcy, wit.

Malone, John & Anne Blackwell, 24 July 1786; George Malone, bm; Bennet Searcy, wit.

Malory, Charles & Rebeccah Norwood, 19 Nov 1797; Drury Kimbal Junr., bm; Step. Sneed, wit.

Mangram, Paton & Miss Lucey Emory, 30 Dec 1832; William Pack, bm; Jno. White, J. P., wit.

Mangram, Simson & Nancy Bradford, 6 Oct 1814; John Nevill, bm; Nat. Alexander, wit.

Mangrum, Augustin & Charity Joplin, 23 Aug 1814; Samuel Bailey, bm; W. M. Sneed, wit.

Mangrum, Josiah & Susannah Cooper, 10 Feb 1809; Fowler Hobgood, bm; W. M. Sneed, wit.

Mangrum, Pleasant & Anne Loyd, 15 Aug 1805; Isham Harris, bm; Steo. Sneed, wit.

Mangrum, William & Sarah Wilkerson, 7 Nov 1809; John Eastwood, bm; Step. Sneed, wit.

Mangrum, Willis & Myram Hayes, 28 Dec 1788; Benjamin Hayes, bm; A. Henderson, wit.

Mangum, Allen & Winefred Thomas, 10 Feb 1835; L. Gilliam, bm; Benja. Kittrell, wit.

Mangum, Archibald & Martha Parham, 12 Feb 1847; Zachariah Hines, bm; Jas. M. Wiggins, wit.

Mangum, Cadmus & Nancy Hampton, 19 Oct 1866; N. T. Green, bm.

Mangum, Dewitt & Mary Thomas Jenkins, 12 Nov 1858; Gaston Roberts, bm; m 18 Nov 1858 by J. W. Floyd, Minister.

Mangum, Fielding & Nancy Arnold, 4 Aug 1846; John Walker, bm.

GRANVILLE MARRIAGES 1753-1868

Mangum, George, of color, son of Tony Bailey & Charrity Mangum, & Betsy Bobitt, daughter of Billy Gilliam & Sarah Gilliam, m 2 Nov 1867 by W. D. Allen, J. P.

Mangum, Green A. & Jemima Veazey, _____; John C. Veazey, bm; Jas. M. Wiggins, wit.

Mangum, Haywood & Harriet Cannady, 4 Feb 1866; Sandy Mills, bm; m 4 Feb 1866 by W. D. Allen, J. P.

Mangum, Henry & Patsey Lewis, 14 Aug 1801; Abner Partee, bm; Step. Sneed, wit.

Mangum, Henry & Barbary Ellington, 28 Dec 1829; Thomas Rice, bm; David Laws, wit.

Mangum, James & Nancey Goss, 24 Sept 1807; Benjamin McFarland, bm; W. M. Sneed, wit.

Mangum, James & Debba Carey, 25 Jan 1852; Jesse Headspeth, bm; A. Landis, wit.

Mangum, James & Aley Washington, 10 Jan 1866; F. J. Tilley, bm; m 11 Jan 1866 by J. J. Lansdell, Minister of the Gospel.

Mangum, James M. & Mary Clark, 25 Dec 1839; Kennan Parham, bm; J. M. Wiggins, wit.

Mangum, Jesse & Polley Parish, 7 Jan 1819; Willie Robards, bm; W. M. Sneed, wit.

Mangum, John & Martha Loyd, 5 Jan 1824; Absalom Mangum, bm; Wm. H. Owen, wit.

Mangum, John & Rachel Cozort, 3 Nov 1829; Willis L. Gooch, bm; David Laws, wit.

Mangum, John & Mary Tippett, 21 Feb 1831; John H. Tippett, bm; David Laws, wit.

Mangum, John G. & Judith W. Higgs, 28 Feb 1860; William H. Kittrell, bm; m 28 Feb 1860 by L. K. Willie, M. G.

Mangum, Josiah & Louisa Kirkland, 18 Jan 1827; Joseph Bowlen, bm; Wm. H. Owen, wit.

Mangum, Moody & Betsey Bass, 28 May 1856; m 28 May 1856 by J. W. Floyd.

Mangum, Orastus P., son of Wily P. & Frances Mangum, & Martha Long, daughter of John & Patsy Long, m 16 Feb 1868 by W. D. Allen, J. P.

Mangum, Rives & Martha Wilkerson, 28 Nov 1818; Willis Bolling, bm; R. N. Herndon, wit.

Mangum, Silas & Martha Ann Curtis, 14 Jan 1854; D. L. Bullock, bm; m 15 Jan 1854 by Jno. Nance, J. P.

Mangum, Simpson & Edna Emory, 9 Jan 1860; Thades Canady, bm; m 17 Jan 1860 by W. D. Allen, J. P.

Mangum, Solomon & Elvey Meadows, 10 April 1839; Jno. Jones, bm; J. M. Wiggins, wit.

GRANVILLE MARRIAGES 1753-1868

Mangum, Theophilus P. & Eliza J. Emory, 31 Dec 1859; J. S. Morgan, bm; m 1 Jan 1860 by W. D. Allen, J. P.

Mangum, Wallas A. & Eliza P. Bullock, 22 Dec 1829; Albert Sneed, bm; Step. K. Sneed, wit.

Mangum, Washington & Anna Hobgood, 15 Jan 1832; Littleton Adcock, bm; David Laws, wit.

Mangum, Wiley & Lethey Loyd, 10 Nov (no year, probably 1826); Bevil Ellington, bm; Wm. H. Owen, wit.

Mangum, William & Rheney Duke, 7 June 1811; Riley Meadows, bm; W. M. Sneed, wit.

Mangum, William & Sarah Cannon, 19 Jan 1837; Zechariah OBriant, bm; J. M. Wiggins, wit.

Mangum, William & Martha G.(?) Adcock, 18 Dec 1847; Jn. Jones, bm; Jas. M. Wiggins, wit.

Mangum, William J. & Emma A. Weathers, m 18 Jan 1866 by B. B. Hester.

Mangum, William P. & Mary D. Higgs, 26 Aug 1854; J. S. Mangum, bm; m 26 Aug 1854 by Lewis R. Parham, J. P.

Mangum, Willie P. & Mary Ann Jones, 28 Sept 1865; G. W. Brinkley, bm; m 4 Oct 1865 by D. B. Johnson, J. P.

Mangum, Willis & Jane Hobgood, 30 July 1832; Joseph D. Hobgood, bm; Step. K. Sneed, wit.

Manier, Daniel Jackson & Anne Bullock Vandyke, 14 April 1796; James Vaughan, Sterling Yancey, bm; Wm. Robards, wit.

Manier, John B. & Mary J. Evans, 8 Feb 1825; Jesse J. Kelly, bm; Wm. Hayes Owen, wit.

Manier, John William & Patty Ogilvie, 19 Dec 1785; Sherwood Harris, bm; Wm. Jacob, wit.

Mann, Alexander & Dolly Franklin, 7 May 1799; John Pulliam, bm; Ro. Harris, wit.

Mann, Arnold & Rebecca Wright, 16 Nov 1779; Nathan Harris, bm; Asa Searcy, wit.

Mann, James & Polley Heflen, 4 April 1809; John Merrit Vincent, bm; W. M. Sneed, wit.

Mann, James A. & Abigail Mann, 7 Dec 1838; Willis Royrs, bm; J. M. Wiggins, wit.

Mann, Peter & Sarah Freeman, 5 March 1796; Elijah Bradford, bm; Step. Sneed, wit.

Mann, Thomas & Deliley Floyd, 17 June 1812; James White, bm; W. M. Sneed, wit.

Mann, William B. & Nancey Valentine, 26 Dec 1817; Pleasant Floyd, bm; W. M. Sneed, wit.

Mann, William B. & Elizabeth Ragsdale, 20 July 1851; Benj. C. Cooke, bm; m 21 July 1851 by E. Hines.

GRANVILLE MARRIAGES 1753-1868

Manson, Otis T. & Mary A. S. Bunnell, 16 Dec 1843; Jno. Hargrove, bm; W. T. Haynie, wit.

Marable, Mason, of color, son of Osborn & Mary Marable, & Charles Anna Herndon, daughter of Charles & Eliza Herndon, 7 Dec 1867; m 11 Dec 1867 by Lewis K. Willie, M. G.

Marable, Saml. & Polly Latham, freed people, 25 Sept 1865; A. Landis, wit; m 4 Nov 1865 by Wm. B. Hicks, J. P.

Marable, William & Mary Allen (freed people), 19 Aug 1865; Saml. A. Williams, bm; A. Landis, wit.

Marler, James & Mary Ann Jinkins, 15 Oct 1828; Jerry Estes(?), bm; David Laws, wit.

Marlow, Samuel & Nelly Ann Due, 4 April 1844; Jas. C. Cozart, bm.

Marrow, Alexander & Sarah Lewis (freed people), 11 Aug 1865; Madison Young, bm; m 13 Aug 1865 by H. H. Prout.

Marrow, Daniel & Fanney H. Smith, 31 Aug 1808; Wm. Blackwell, bm; Step. Sneed, wit.

Marrow, Daniel J. & Caladonai L. Ezzell, 19 Dec 1854; Jas. R. Duty, bm; m 21 Dec 1854 by E. Hines, Minr. of the Gospel.

Marrow, Eli & Bella Marrow, 11 Aug 1865 (freed people); Madison Young, bm; A. Landis, wit; m 12 Aug 1865 by H. H. Prout.

Marrow, Henry & Nelly Marrow, freed people, 11 Aug 1865; Madison Young, bm; m 12 Aug 1865 by H. H. Prout.

Marrow, Isaac & Rachel Marrow, 11 Aug 1865; freed people, Madison Young, bm; m 13 Aug 1865 by H. H. Prout.

Marrow, Sherwood & Lavina Stovall, freed people,; m 20 April 1867 by A. C. Harris, M. G."There were very old people".

Marrow, William, of color, son of Caesar & Amy Murrow, & Frances Smith, daughter of Sally Ann Smith, m 7 Sept 1867 by A. C. Harris, M. G.

Marrow, William D. & Mary Ann Marrow, 22 Oct 1858; Isham J. Cheatham, bm; J. M. Bullock, J. P.; m 27 Oct 1858 by A. C. Harris, M. G.

Marshall, John & Milky Arnold, 30 April 1813; Allen Howard, bm; Thos. J. Hicks, wit.

Marshall, John F. & Henrietta Duncan, 2 Nov 1818; Wm. B. Collins, bm; Sam. Sneed, wit.

Marsho, Anderson & Lucy Cole, 5 March 1820; David Due, bm; A. Sneed, wit.

Martin, James & Mary Morrow, 21 Aug 1866.

Martin, Stephen Taylor & Isabella Brown Venable, 23 Dec 1863; T. R. Carrington, bm; m 23 Dec 1863 by Edward Hines.

Martin, William K. & Lucy T. Jones, 26 May 1845; Sidney Winston, bm.

GRANVILLE MARRIAGES 1753-1868

Mask, Dudley & Anney Bare, 2 Jan 1781; James Bare, bm; Asa Searcy, wit.

Mason, Armstead G. & Angelina Due, 4 Aug 1832; Israel L. Dillard, bm; Step. K. Sneed, wit.

Mason, David & Rebecca Davis, 14 Nov 1788; Henry Potter, bm; A. Henderson, C. C., wit.

Mason, Frederick & John Shadwick (sic), 14 April 1809; John Paschal, bm; W. M. Sneed, wit.

Mason, James T. & Rebecca Williams, 24 Dec 1857; James M. Wood, bm; A. Landis, wit.

Mason, Jesse & Mary Ann Harris, 16 Dec 1800; Collin Pettiford, bm; Step. Sneed, wit.

Mason, John & Prissilla Wells, 26 July 1792; Elisha Wells, bm; W. Norwood, wit.

Mason, William & Phereby Shadwick, 27 Nov 1809; James Moore, bm; W. M. Sneed, wit.

Massey, John & Lydda Landland, 7 June 1779; Arthur Fuller, bm; Sherwood Harris, wit.

Massey, Simeon & Elizabeth Edwards, 12 Feb 1810; Pumphrey Edwards, bm; A. H. Sneed, wit.

Mathes, Kemp & Margaret Wilson, 17 Dec 1840; Green Culbreath, bm; W. T. Hargrove, wit.

Mathews, Erasmus & Mary A. Hester, 20 Dec 1839; John Culbreath, bm; J. M. Wiggins, wit; consent from Robert Hester, 20 Dec 1839; wit. by M. D. Royster, John Culbreath.

Mathews, James & Mary Ellis, 23 July 1822; Cephas Hudson, bm; Jas. M. Wiggins, wit.

Mathews, James & Jane Allen, 29 May 1847; Francis M. Wilkinson, bm; L. B. Stone, J. P., wit.

Mathews, James & Julia Ann E. Evans, 13 Dec 1853; A. Landis, bm.

Mathews, James & Sallie Guy, 17 Nov 1855; Leonidas F. Hicks, bm; m 19 Nov 1855 by Jno. R. Hicks, J. P.

Mathews, John & --ry West, 2 Aug 1800; Gideon Crews, bm.

Mathews, Thomas & Martha Cavenus, 21 Nov 1829; John T. Hunt, bm; David Laws, wit.

Mathis, Thomas & Ann Mathis, 5 March 1861; A. Landis, bm.

Mathus, William H. & Eddy Overbey, 5 Jan 1861; A. G. P. Pool, bm; m 5 Jan 1861 by L. B. Stone, J. P.

Matthews, Benjamin & Nancy Wilkins, 3 May 1789; Darvin Harris, bm.

Matthews, Henry & Martha Currin, 4 March 1864; Wm. Faucett, bm; A. Landis, wit; m 9 March 1864 by A. C. Harris, M. G.

GRANVILLE MARRIAGES 1753-1868

Matthews, Jesse & Elizabeth Twisdel, 26 Jan 1790; Thomas Collins, bm; A. Henderson, wit.

Matthews, William & Anne Hicks, 12 July 1787; Micajah Debruler, bm; Reuben Searcy, wit.

May, Babel & Temperance Fuller, 18 Sept 1819; James Estes, bm; W. M. Sneed, wit.

May, Green & Willis Cole (sic), 16 Feb 1809; Willis Cole, bm; W. M. Sneed, wit.

May, Robert & Ambrillas Walker, 12 Jan 1852; Jonan Jinkins, bm.

May, Thomas & Elizabeth Cole, 21 March 1821; Stephen Cooke, bm; Step. K. Sneed, wit.

May, Thomas & Elizabeth Parrish, 3 Feb 1829; Willis Hutchinson, bm; David Laws, wit.

May, W. C. & Louisa Kearney, 26 Nov 1866; T. H. May, bm; m 27 Nov 1866 by W. H. P. Jenkins, J. P.

May, William & Elizabeth Inscore, 14 Dec 1836; Hampton Fuller, bm; J. M. Wiggins, wit.

May, William & Direna Huddleston, 23 Jan 1866; Joseph Reddy, bm; m 13 Jan 1866 by R. B. Hester.

May, William G. & Mary Heflin, 20 Dec 1848; George T. Leavister, bm; J. M. Wiggins, wit.

Mayes, Frederick & Martha Hinton, 3 Oct 1792; James Akin, bm; W. Norwood, wit.

Mayes, Grandison, of color, son of Samuel & Linsey Mayes, & Ella Wilkerson, daughter of Elijah Wilkerson & Elizer Thorp, m 26 Dec 1867 by W. H. Puryear, J. P.

Mayes, Wm. W. & Martha A. S. Allen, 3 Jan 1848; Robt. L. Hunt, bm.

Mayfield, Daniel & Pheriba Ball, 8 Aug 1822; Richd. Holmes, bm; Jas. M. Wiggins, wit.

Mayfield, Daniel & Sarah Duke, 3 Feb 1858; Jas. J. Moore, bm; m 4 Feb 1858 by S. H. Cannady, J. P.

Mayfield, David, of color, son of Washington & Mary Mayfield, & Charlotte Williams, parents unknown, m 20 Aug 1867 by E. B. Lyon, J. P.

Mayfield, John & Massey Crews, 17 Dec 1798; Voluntine Mayfield, bm; Ro. Harris, wit.

Mayfield, John & Elizabeth Earl, 10 Feb 1806; Philip Kinemon, bm; A. H. Sneed, wit.

Mayfield, John & Fanny Bradford, 25 Aug 1807; William Heflin, bm; W. M. Sneed, wit.

Mayfield, Valentine & Anney Hunt, 8 April 1816; Thos. Barr, bm; Wm. Thomasson, wit.

GRANVILLE MARRIAGES 1753-1868

Mayho, Cuffee & Glathy Ann Hawkins, 29 Dec 1828; William Mayho, bm; David Laws, wit.

Mayho, Cuffee & Julia Ann Hawley, 11 Sept 1851; John Kates, bm; m 11 Sept 1851 by W. S. McClanahan, J. P.

Mayho, Elbridge & Sally Harris, 11 Jan 1840; John Howell, bm; J. M. Wiggins, wit.

Mayho, William H., colored, son of Sallie Ann Mayho, & Josephine Day, daughter of Robert & Rebecca Ann Day, m 4 Oct 1868 by G. W. Ferrill, M. G.

Mayhoe, Cuffee & Martha Boon, 22 Dec 1849; James Brandum, bm; A. Landis, wit.

Mayhoe, William & Joicey Chavis, 12 June 1834; William Chavers, bm; Benja. Kittrell, wit.

Mayhue, Hillman & Martha Dunson, 29 April 1852; Harrison Edward, bm; Eugene Grissom, wit; m by W. L. McClanahan, J. P.

Maynard, Bose, of color, son of Squire Fuller & Mary Maynard, & Anna Fuller, daughter of George & Henrietta Fuller, 25 Dec 1867; m 26 Dec 1867 by L. M. VanHook, J. P.

Maynard, James P. & Nancy G. Harris, 11 April 1855; H. A. Davis, bm; m 11 April 1855 by L. R. Parham, J. P.

Maynard, Robert C. & Sallie P. Hester, 15 Nov 1862; W. S. Chaffin, bm; m 18 Nov 1862 by W. S. Chaffin; (return titles groom The Revd. Robert C. Maynard of N. C. Camp).

Mayo, Henry & Jane Cole, 1 Jan 1838; Cuffee Mayo, bm; S. G. Shearmon, wit.

Mayo, Lorenso & Isabella Mitchell, 4 April 1866; m 5 April 1866 by George J. Rowland, J. P.

Mays, Autry D. & Martha T. Chavis, 14 Dec 1841; James H. Davis, bm; W. E. Wiggins, wit.

Mays, John & Martha Morgan, 20 Dec 1849; A. D. May, bm; A. Landis, wit.

Meacham, Sam B. & Martha Curron, 27 May 1834; Samuel Hunt, bm; Benja. Kittrell, wit.

Meaders, James & Polly Hobgood, 23 Dec 1818; Sherman Goss, bm; Zacha. Herndon, wit.

Meadows, Anderson C. & Margaret Kimball, __ Sept 1837; Washington Mangum, bm; J. M. Wiggins, wit.

Meadows, Anderson C. & Emily OBriant, 28 Dec 1840; G. G. Lawson, bm; Jas. M. Wiggins, wit.

Meadows, Brodie & Sally Ann Fraizer, 19 Jan 1846; F. B. Currin, bm; Jas. M. Wiggins, wit.

Meadows, Brodie & Rowena Minor, 6 Sept 1857; Stephen Satterwhite, bm; m 10 Sept 1857 by J. W. Floyd, Pastor.

Meadows, Daniel & Sarah Perdue, 7 May 1782; Blackmun Pardue, bm; John Mitchel, wit.

GRANVILLE MARRIAGES 1753-1868

Meadows, Daniel & Sally Tindall, 8 Nov 1805; James Cozart, bm; Jas. Sneed, wit.

Meadows, Deberry, son of Jesse & Saluda Meadows, & Nannie G. Thomasson, daughter of Benjamin & Polly Thomasson, m 23 Dec 1867 by T. J. Horner, Minister of the Gospel.

Meadows, Eldridge & Amanda Howard, 27 Aug 1866; m 28 Aug 1866 by B. D. Howard, J. P.

Meadows, Elijah & Sally Kimball, 7 Dec 1834; Littleton Adcock, bm; Benja. Kittrell, wit.

Meadows, Ephraim & Sylvia Jones, 3 Dec 1813; Thomas Goodrum, bm; W. M. Sneed, wit.

Meadows, Ephraim & Martha Arnold, 27 March 1815; William M. Sneed, bm; Step. Sneed, wit.

Meadows, Francis M. & Mary Jane Hobgood, 14 March 1855; J. J. Meadows, bm; m 15 March 1855 by R. J. Devin.

Meadows, Hawkins & Elizabeth Jenkins, 30 Oct 1854; Willis Meadows, bm; A. Landis, wit; m 2 Nov 1854 by Jeff Horner, J. P.

Meadows, Isaac & Molley Merryman, 20 Aug 1785; Blackmon Purdue, bm; Reuben Searcy, wit.

Meadows, James & Elizabeth Wheeler, 22 June 1853; Thomas Meadows, bm; A. Landis, wit; m 22 June 1853 by Cam. W. Allen, J. P.

Meadows, Jesse & Jemimah Adcock, 6 Nov 1817; John Meadows, bm; Step. Sneed, wit.

Meadows, Jesse & Orpha Tippitt, 7 Nov 1822; Lemuel Hobgood, bm; Jas. M. Wiggins, wit.

Meadows, Jesse Jr. & Saluda Kimball, 4 April 1843; William T. Tippett, bm; J. M. Wiggins, wit.

Meadows, John & Elizabeth Goss, 2 Aug 1808; James Mangum, bm; A. Wilkins, wit.

Meadows, John & Polly Bolling, 10 Oct 1817; James Cozart, bm; R. N. Herndon, wit.

Meadows, John J. & Nancy Gooch, 6 March 1860; J. W. Currin, bm; m 8 March 1860 by M. Caldwin.

Meadows, John S. & Elizabeth D. Hobgood, 29 May 1866; m 1 June 1866 by T. J. Horner.

Meadows, Pinkney & Rowan Blalock, 5 Jan 1847; John Meadows, bm; Jas. M. Wiggins, wit.

Meadows, Squire & Mary Philpott, 13 Dec 1836; Dave Meadows, bm; J. M. Wiggins, wit.

Meadows, William & Sarah Mangum, 10 Jan 1803; William Mangum, bm; Green Merritt, wit.

Meadows, William & Martha Allen, 16 Dec 1865; Rufus Avery, bm; A. Landis, wit; m 16 Dec 1865 by Robt. L. Heflin, J. P.

GRANVILLE MARRIAGES 1753-1868

Meadows, William & Elisabeth Meadows, 8 Nov 1809; Riley Meadows, bm; W. M. Sneed, wit.

Meadows, William & Rebecca Wheeler, 21 June 1830; Henry Wheeler, bm; David Laws, wit.

Meadows, William L. & Elizabeth C. Haskins, 21 Feb 1860; A. H. Cooke, bm; m 22 Feb 1860 by G. W. Ferrill, Minister of the Gospel.

Meadows, William L., son of William & Rebecca Meadows, & Ludie W. Walker, 29 June 1868; m 19 July 1868 by J. J. Lansdell, Minister of the Gospel.

Meadows, Willie & Elizabeth Robards, 5 Oct 1809; John Wilburn, bm; W. M. Sneed, wit.

Meadows, Willis & Fannie Waller, 30 Nov 1852; Thos. Meadows, bm: m 1 Dec 1852 by Cam. W. Allen, J. P.

Mealer, William L. & Frances Wilbon, 29 Nov 1853; Jones Moore(?), bm; J. E. Montague, wit.

Megehee, Asben & Rebecca Thammel, 31 Jan 1798; Miel Megehee, bm; Robt. Taylor, wit.

Megehee, Benjamin & Mourning Wormath, 2 Nov 1827; James Leavister, bm; David Laws, wit.

Megehee, Jesse & Elisabeth Wood, 8 Nov 179_; Meal Megehee, bm; Step. Sneed, wit.

Megehee, Mial & Susannah Inscore, 19 March 1803; Jonathan Inscore, bm; Green Merritt, wit.

Melone, John & Mary Flin, 24 June 1814; James Stone, bm; H. Young, wit.

Melton, James & Elizabeth Pettypool, 17 April 1821; James Sandford, bm; Jno. P. Smith, wit.

Melton, Pomphrett & Salley Adcock, 6 Feb 1813; David Adcock, bm; W. M. Sneed, wit.

Mennis, William & Julia Green, freed people, 5 Sept 1865; James E. Turner, bm.

Merit, William & Martha Cooke, 20 July 1767; William Davis, bm; John Oliver, Jesse Benton, wit.

Meritt, Henry & Mary Powel, 5 Feb 1819; Edmund Wooton, bm; Richd. Sneed, wit.

Merrit, Ephraim & Elisabeth McKlejohn, 29 March 1798; Reuben Ragland, bm; Step. Sneed, wit.

Meritt, Morris & Sally Powel, 23 Dec 1835; James Powell, bm; Benja. Kittrell, wit.

Meritt, Stephen & Winnefred Rose, 1 July 1771; Joseph Langston, Solomon Langston, bm; Jesse Benton, wit.

Merrett, James, son of William & Susan Merrett, & Priscella House, daughter of Macon & Rena House, 23 Nov 1868; m 2 Dec 1868 by W. A. Barnett, Minister.

GRANVILLE MARRIAGES 1753-1868

Merritt, Benjamin & Celia Bush, 19 Sept 1805; William Leeman, bm; Henry H. Newell, wit.

Merritt, Joel & Frances Merrett, 18 Dec 1837; John Merritt, bm; Jas. M. Wiggins, wit.

Merritt, Wm. & Martha Cocke, 20 July 1767; William Davis, John Compton, wit; (statement only that Martha Cocke is 20 years old).

Merritt, Dr. William, son of Daniel & Mary Merritt, & Mary C. Hamlet, daughter of William J. & Lucy Hamlet, 24 June 1868; m 25 June 1868 by E. Montague.

Merryman, Malachiah & Hannah Coleman, 17 Aug 1786; William Merryman, bm; Bennet Searcy, wit.

Merryman, Nicholas & Lethi Bonner, 18 July 1789; Malackiah Merryman, bm; A. Henderson, C. C., wit.

Mertin, Jacob, of color, son of Virey Marten, & Jemima Harp, daughter of Osborn & Lizzie Harp, 27 May 1868; m about 30 May 1868 by A. C. Harris, M. G.

Miller, Garnett & Frances Amelia, 28 March 1865; Lewis Jones, bm; A. Landis, wit; m 2 April 1865 by L. B. Stone, J. P.

Miller, H. M. & Isabella U. Hinton, 1 March 1826; Archibald E. Henderson, bm.

Miller, Henry M. of Raleigh, & Miss Lizzie D. Collins, of Granville County, 22 June 1861; Robt. B. Gilliam, bm; m 26 June 1861 by Al. Smedes.

Miller, Thomas & Mary Jane Robards, 26 Dec 1832; H. A. Miller, bm; Step. K. Sneed, wit.

Miller, Wm. A., son of Alford B. & Loisa Miller, & Mildred F. Jones, daughter of Thomas & Elizabeth Jones, 6 Feb 1868; m 6 Feb 1868 by L. B. Stone, J. P.

Mills, Bolling & Emily Harris, 28 Feb 1842; Wm. Bass, bm; J. M. Wiggins, wit.

Mills, Jack & Betsy Boon, 26 May 1855; W. B. Reid, bm.

Mills, Jack & Betsy Brown(?), m in Henderson, 26 May 1855 by A. C. Harris, M. G.

Mills, John H. & Elizabeth N. Williams, 28 Feb 1856; Eugene Grissom, bm.

Mills, William & Catharine Satterwhite, m 14 March 1867 by L. R. Parham, J. P.

Milton, John & Margaret Wilkerson, 25 Dec 1810; David Harris, bm; Saml. S. Downey, wit.

Milton, Stephen & Elizabeth Peryear, 25 Oct 1799; Thomas Puryear, bm; Step. Sneed, wit.

Mimas, Stokely & Jane Boyd, 20 June 1848; Han--- Loyd, bm; Jas. M. Wiggins, wit.

GRANVILLE MARRIAGES 1753-1868

Mimms, Theodrick F. & Cordelia L. Womack, 9 Oct 1858; John H. Terry, bm; m 9 Oct 1858 by L. B. Stone, J. P.

Minor, John Junr. & Lucey Mallory, 6 Nov 1807; Edmond Parham, bm; W. M. Sneed, wit.

Minor, John Sr. & Massey Hobgood, 9 Sept 1835; Wm. Jones, bm; Benja. Kittrell, wit.

Minor, Lazarus & Polley Jones, 4 Sept 1810; William Hester, bm; W. M. Sneed, wit.

Minor, Mark & Nancy Bullock, 23 Dec 1805; Richard Cook, bm; W. M. Sneed, wit.

Minor, Millis H. & Louisa Thomasson, 11 Jan 1849; Joseph Minor, bm.

Minor, Randal & Martha Hunt, 18 March 1809; Smith Satterwhite, bm; W. M. Sneed, wit.

Minor, Robert & Amy Minor, freed people, 16 Sept 1865; Jas. B. Crews, bm; m 16 Sept 1865 by T. W. Lynch, J. P.

Minor, William H. & Emily S. Rust, 5 March 1834; Allen Nance, bm; Benja. Kittrell, wit.

Minshew, Benjamin & Celia M. Sauls, 21 March 1855; A. H. Alley, bm; m 21 March 1855 by Wm. Holmes.

Mintus, Webb, of color, son of Nelson & Nancy Webb, & Roxanna Smith, daughter of Bella Smith, m 14 Sept 1867 by B. D. Howard, J. P.

Minzey, Dudley & Nancy Norwood, 27 Aug 1799; Stephen Clay, bm; Ro. Harris, wit.

Minzey, Dudley & Lidey Norman, 3 Aug 1824; Thomas Terry, bm; Wm. H. Owen, wit.

Mires, Jacob & Elizabeth Holsten, 15 Feb 1800; Joel Kittle, bm; Philip Bullock, wit.

Mirris, James & Mary G. Johnson, 24 July 1841; George T. Leavister, bm; J. M. Wiggins, wit.

Mise, Benjamin & Elisabeth Brinkley, 3 Nov 1795; Barnet Pulliam Esqr., bm.

Mitchel, Abraham & Messenier Davis, 22 Dec 1769; Michael Satterwhite, bm; Thos. Henderson, wit.

Mitchel, Charles & Mary Mitchel, 19 July 1781; Chas. Harris(?), bm; Asa Searcy, wit.

Mitchel, Charles & Jane Threft Critcher, 16 Dec 1785; Solo. Walker, bm; Martha Walker, Phereby Walker, wit.

Mitchel, Daniel & Mary Gregg, 26 Nov 1763; Wm. Gregg, bm; Jn. Bowie, wit.

Mitchel, Edward & Sophia Jane Taborn, 26 March 1836; Eben _____, bm; Tho. H. Willie, wit.

GRANVILLE MARRIAGES 1753-1868

Mitchel, Elijah & Salley Critcher, 3 March 1779; Thomas Critcher, bm; Charles Mitchel, wit.

Mitchel, Isham & Sarah Hudpeth, 13 April 1802; Benjamin Mitchel, bm; Philip Bullock, wit.

Mitchel, John & Phillis Williams, 22 Dec 1777; Reuben Searcy, bm; Asa Searcy, wit.

Mitchel, Major & Molley Wiggins, 26 Dec 1778; Dennis Driskil, bm.

Mitchel, Nelson & Nancey Harriss, 1 June 1825; Samuel Nance, bm; L. Gilliam, wit.

Mitchel, Robert B. & Martha Burton, 28 Nov 1800; Hutchings G. Burton, bm; James Sneed, wit.

Mitchel, Thomas & Nancy Mitchell, 16 May 1798; Thomas Potter, bm; J. Norman, wit.

Mitchel, William & Catey Rose, 8 Oct 1792; William Lanier, bm; Step. Sneed, wit.

Mitchel, William P. & Lucy F. Henderson, 5 Oct 1847; Benja. Wilson, bm; Jas. M. Wiggins, wit.

Mitchel, Zacheriah & Jain Anderson, 25 Aug 1795; Abel Anderson, bm; Step. Sneed, wit.

Mitchel, Zachriah & Eliza Bass, 23 Dec 1834; Iverson Mitchel, bm; Benja. Kittrell, wit.

Mitchell, A. C. & Sallie C. Hicks, 3 Jan 1866; Robert Hicks, bm.

Mitchell, Abraham & Missenier Davis (no date, consent from Solomon Davis, father of Messenier, only), Michl. Satterwhite, wit.

Mitchell, Alexander & Nancy S. Freeman, 20 Nov 1835; Robert Freeman, bm; Benja. Kittrell, wit.

Mitchell, Archibald & Rainy Ann Mitchell, 26 Oct 1825; Wm. S. Mitchell, bm; Jas. M. Wiggins, wit.

Mitchell, Barker A. & Betsey A. Hester, 15 Oct 1833; Guy Smith, bm; Benja. Kittrell, wit.

Mitchell, Benjamin & Winny Anderson, 19 Dec 1803; George Anderson, bm; A. H. Sneed, wit.

Mitchell, Charles & Nancey Waggstaff, 15 Sept 1809; John Mitchell, bm; W. M. Sneed, wit.

Mitchell, David & Polly Hackinyear, 1 Jan 1804; John Tyner, bm; Js. Sneed, wit.

Mitchell, David & Elizabeth Smith, 20 Feb 1809; Maurice Smith, bm; W. M. Sneed, wit.

Mitchell, Edmond & Mariah Bass, 5 Jan 1795; Thomas Bass, bm; L. Henderson, wit.

Mitchell, Evan & Charsly Harriss, 5 Nov 1798; Thomas Harris, bm; Step. Snee, wit.

GRANVILLE MARRIAGES 1753-1868

Mitchell, Freeman A. & Ann Cook, 2 Nov 1819; Caleb Brasfield, bm; Wm. E. Sturgis, wit.

Mitchell, Henry & Eliza Hagin, 3 Feb 1851, (colored); Rd. Sneed, bm; Jas. R. Duty, wit; m 3 Feb 1851 by A. C. Harris, M. G.

Mitchell, Henry & Eliza Richerson, 6 Sept 1852; Wesley Mitchell, bm; A. Landis, wit.

Mitchell, Iverson & Ann Jones, 10 July 1832; Littleton Taburn, bm; David Laws, wit.

Mitchell, Iverson & Peggy Boling, 6 Dec 1838; Richd. Mitchell, bm.

Mitchell, Iverson & Rebecca Boon, 7 June 1847; Abm. Plenty, bm; J. M. Wiggins, wit.

Mitchell, James & Elizabeth Bobbitt, 30 Nov 1847; George C. Compton, bm.

Mitchell, James & Ann Dickerson, 28 Dec 1850; Eppy Grissom, bm; A. Landis, wit.

Mitchell, John & Sarah Johnson, 8 Nov 1798; Evan Mitchell, bm; Step. Sneed, wit.

Mitchell, John & Jenney Minge Buxton, 2 Feb 1799; Benjamin Bullock, bm; Step. Sneed, wit.

Mitchell, John & Nancy Hawley, 29 Jan 1816; George Anderson, bm; Rhodes Herndon, wit.

Mitchell, John & Mary Tyler, 23 April 1833; Allen Atkins, bm; David Laws, wit.

Mitchell, John & Susan Parker, 13 April 1857; Samuel Carter, bm.

Mitchell, John & Polly Fleming, 20 Dec 1866; m 25 Dec 1866 by _____.

Mitchell, John, of color, son of Mark & Pattie Bullock, & Rhoda Ann Green, daughter of Ann Green, 18 Jan 1868; m 29 Jan 1868 by T. B. Lyon.

Mitchell, John, son of S. W. & Frances P. Mitchell, & Nancy Mangum, daughter of William & Martha Mangum, 3 Nov 1868; m 4 Nov 1868 by G. W. Ferrill, Minister.

Mitchell, John E. & Sophia W. Clay, 4 Nov 1845; Leroy Smith, bm; Jas. M. Wiggins, wit.

Mitchell, John G. & Elizabeth L. Allen, 25 Sept 1843; E. E. Freeman, bm; Wm. H. Whitfield, wit.

Mitchell, John W. & Emily H. Breedlove, 6 Nov 1856; Thomas E. Usry, bm; m 12 Dec 1856 by R. B. Hester, J. P.

Mitchell, Lemuel & Holly D. White, 4 Jan 1819; Lewis Heflin, bm; Z. Herndon Jr., wit.

Mitchell, Littleton & Winney Jones, 12 July 1823; Littleton Taborn, bm; Jas. M. Wiggins, wit.

GRANVILLE MARRIAGES 1753-1868

Mitchell, Mathew F. & Nancy Freeman, 21 Oct 1819; Gideon Freeman Jr., bm; S. K. Sneed, wit.

Mitchell, Michael & Lucy Bass, 25 April 1805; Sherwood Bryant, bm; Jas. Sneed, wit.

Mitchell, Philip C. & Charity Mangum, 8 Aug 1866; m 30 Oct 1866 by A. L. Davis, J. P.; (freed people).

Mitchell, Robert & Hannah Russell, 24 July 1817; Thos. Mitchel, bm; Step. K. Sneed, wit.

Mitchell, Robert & Sally Ann Day, 15 Dec 1852; John Chavis, bm; m 15 Dec 1852 by A. Hester, J. P.

Mitchell, Robert Davis, of color, son of Mary Davis & Elizabeth Parrish, parents unknown, m 3 May 1868 by W. N. Harris, J. P.

Mitchell, Rush J. & Virginia Dorsey, 8 Sept 1852; W. R. Wiggins, bm.

Mitchell, Solomon & Mary Macvedr(?), 4 Dec 1797; Levon Jackwall, bm; Step. Sneed, wit.

Mitchell, Solomon W. & Frances P. Kimball, 23 Nov 1843; Jno. Jnoes, bm; Wm. H. Whitfield, wit.

Mitchell, Thomas & Liley Hawley, 6 July 1811; Benjamin Evans, bm; W. M. Sneed, wit.

Mitchell, Thomas & Polly Reed, 14 Nov 1832; Littleton Mitchell, bm; Step. K. Sneed, wit.

Mitchell, Thomas A. & Martha Buckanan, 6 July 1816; Mastin Freeman, bm; W. M. Sneed, wit.

Mitchell, Wesley & Betsey Piles, 12 July 1842; Jas. B. Peace, bm; Wm. H. Whitfield, wit.

Mitchell, William & Bytha Headspeth, 11 Aug 1796; Darling Bass, bm; L. Hare, wit.

Mitchell, Wm. & Rachel Harden, 7 Dec 1800; Mathew Allin, bm.

Mitchell, William & Lucinda Richardson, 31 May 1830; Chesly Jones Mitchell, bm; Step. K. Sneed, wit.

Mitchell, William & Sarah Ross, 19 Oct 1831; Jonathan Lankford, bm; David Laws, wit.

Mitchell, William & Tassa Wells, 22 Aug 1833; L. Gilliam, bm; Benja. Kittrell, wit.

Mitchell, William & Sally Parrish, 4 Feb 1846; Ransom Baily, bm.

Mitchell, William & Mary Mason, 11 Dec 1860; m by Wm. Holmes.

Mitchell, Wm. L. & Sarah J. Lyon, 13 Jan 1859; Wm. E. Bullock, bm; m 26 Jan 1859 by R. B. Hester.

Mitchell, William S. & Candiss Mitchell, 15 Nov 1831; John Greeman, bm; David Laws, wit.

Mitchell, Willie & Rachel Morgan, 16 Dec 1844; John E. Tharington, bm; Wm. H. Whitfield, wit.

GRANVILLE MARRIAGES 1753-1868

Mitchell, Willie D. & Louisa J. Crews, 16 Dec 1856; T. W. McClanahan, bm; m 23 Dec 1856 by J. W. Floyd, Minister.

Mitchell, Willis P. & Susan Bullock, 9 Dec 1829; N. N. Bragg, bm; Step. K. Sneed, wit.

Mize, Alexander & Sarah E. OBrien, 9 Feb 1839; James P. OBrien, bm.

Mize, Edmund & Martha Jones, 17 Dec 1820; Howel Mize, bm; Step. K. Sneed, wit.

Mize, Henry & Lucey Justice, 16 Sept 1785; John Tuder, bm; Bennet Searcy, wit.

Mize, Howel & Elizabeth Jones, 3 Aug 1821; Lemuel Hobgood, bm; S. K. Sneed, wit.

Mize, James P. & Virginia Critcher, 3 Nov 1866; A. J. Critcher, bm; A. Landis, wit. m __ Nov 1866 by T. J. Horner, G. M.

Mize, Jonathan & Rachel Hopkins, 19 April 1808; Allin Mize, bm; W. M. Sneed, John H. Farrar, Alfred Wilkins, wit.

Mize, Lewis & Catey Lumpkin, 6 Nov 1798; Jesse Meadows, bm; Step. Sneed, wit.

Mize, Obediah & Sarah Frazier, 5 Jan 1802; Benjamin Mize, bm; P. Bullock, wit.

Mize, Solomon & Mary Ann Arnold, 11 Nov 1853; George P. Roberts. bm.

Mize, William & Elizabeth Meadows, 11 Dec 1829; John Wilkerson, bm; Step. K. Sneed, wit.

Mize, William & Rebecca OBrient, 23 Sept 1858; Alexander Mize, bm.

Mobley, Ransom & Precilla Bailey, 31 Jan 1820; William Bailey, bm; Step. K. Sneed, wit.

Moer, William & Mary Reed, 5 Sept 1811; John M. Peace, bm.

Monday, Stephen & Mary Puryear, 18 July 1830; Allin Yancy, bm.

Monroe, Johnson & Sarah Hanks, 28 Dec 1803; John Collins, bm; Robert Hester, wit.

Monroe, Johnson & Jane Roberts, 10 Feb 1830; John Clardy, bm; A. Sneed, wit.

Montague, Adolphus W., son of Samuel & Mary Montague, & Emily Usry, daughter of William & Jane Usry, m 30 Jan 1868 by George J. Rowland, J. P.

Montague, Alfred & Sarah Andrews, 8 May 1855; Geo. J. Rowland, bm; m 10 May 1855 by H. Hester, J. P.

Montague, Henry J. & Elizabeth N. Reeks, 6 Sept 1844; L. S. Philpott, bm; J. M. Wiggins, wit.

Montague, James P. & Jana E. Burnett, 6 March 1855; A. M. Cly, bm.

GRANVILLE MARRIAGES 1753-1868

Montague, John & Elizabeth Thomason, 21 Feb 1811; James Thomason, bm; W. M. Sneed, wit.

Montague, John E. & Barshaby Pittard, 8 Nov 1838; Latny Montague, bm.

Montague, Lewis & Hicsy Buchannan, 21 March 1820; James J. Ferrar, bm; Jas. M. Wiggins, wit.

Montague, Samuel & Mary Amis, 25 April 1818; Wm. Thompson, bm; A. Tomlinson, wit.

Montague, William & Polly Owen, 14 Jan 1795; William Owen, bm; L. H. Woodson, wit.

Montague, William & Mary Kimball, 23 April 1814; John Kimball, bm; W. M. Sneed, wit.

Montague, William & Barber Cook, 19 Dec 1818; Young Montague, bm.

Montague, Young & Sarah Pittard, 8 Feb 1784; Samuel Pittard, bm; Bennet Searcy, wit.

Montague, Young & Sally Cooke, 6 Nov 1820; Jas. Nuttall, bm; Step. K. Sneed, wit.

Montague, Young McC. & Mary E. Shanks, 28 Jan 1848; R. G. Dean, bm; Jas. M. Wiggins, wit.

Montgomery, Archibald & Eliza Lewis, 10 Dec 1822; Robert K. Clack, bm; Jas. M. Wiggins, wit.

Moody, Arthur & Mary Royster, 20 Nov 1829; John S. Overbey, bm; David Laws, wit.

Moody, Benjamin & Elizabeth Lumpkin, 19 Dec 1809; Fleming Lumpkin, bm; Richd. Sneed, wit.

Moody, Esau G. & Polly Burnett, 3 Oct 1854; Thos. W. McClanahan, bm; m 4 Oct 1854 by L. B. Stone, J. P.; Polly Burnett certifies that she is over 21 years of age.

Moon, William & D. Macon, 13 Oct 1833; Jos. B. Peace, bm.

Moore, Albert G. & Lilly Daniel, 17 Sept 1829; Henderson Moore, bm; Jno. P. Smith, wit.

Moore, Alvis L. & Correna H. Wilkerson, 6 April 1867; H. W. Jones, bm; F. J. Tilley, J. P., wit; m 11 April 1867 by Francis J. Tilley, J. P.

Moore, Arthur & Mary Cates, 3 Nov 1784; Bennet Searcy, wit.

Moore, Benjamin & Salley Washington, 18 March 1780; Jeremiah Bullock, bm; Jno. Hanon(?), wit.

Moore, Benjamin & Mary Harrison, 9 Dec 1798; William Harp, bm; Step. Sneed, wit.

Moore, Charles & Beckey Tudor, 14 April 1777; Jos. Peace, Jr., bm; Reuben Searcy, wit.

Moore, Charles & Sibba Harp, 1 Nov 1785; Samson Harp, bm; Bennet Searcy, wit.

GRANVILLE MARRIAGES 1753-1868

Moore, Charles & Elizabeth Carrel, 29 Jan 1812; John Harris, bm; W. M. Sneed, wit.

Moore, Demsey & Susanna Walker, 20 Aug 1778; Pleasant Henderson, bm; Reuben Searcy, wit.

Moore, Edward & Anne Chandler, 1 Sept 1779; Solomon Walker, bm; James Jett, wit.

Moore, Elijah & Mary Morgan, 16 Dec 1793; John Moore, bm; Step. Sneed, wit.

Moore, Franklin & Margaret E. Edwards, 12 May 1859; J. H. Horner, bm; m 19 May 1859 by B. M. Williams, Minister of the Gospel of Christ of the M. E. Church, South.

Moore, George & Sarah Wright, 14 Sept 1793; James Wright, bm; Step. Sneed, wit.

Moore, George & Sarah Freeman, 14 Jan 1829; Aaron Haskins, bm; David Laws, wit.

Moore, George H. & Mary E. Sadler, 31 March 1858; Archer C. Sadler, bm; m 31 March 1858 by James R. Duty, J. P.

Moore, George L. & Mary Phillip, 5 Jan 1783; Ralph Williams, bm; Sparks Bullock, wit.

Moore, George Thomas & Harriet Matterson, 25 March 1828; Thomas Roberts, bm; David Laws, wit.

Moore, Harper C. & Nancy Chandler, 20 Jan 1867; John W. Bowen, bm; m 20 Jan 1867 by L. B. Stone, J. P.

Moore, Henry & Caroline York, freed people, m 4 March 1866 by John W. York; M. C. Herndon, bm.

Moore, Henry F. & Martha J. Lyon, 2 July 1853; W. M. Lyon, bm; m 5 July 1853 by W. H. Lyon, J. P.

Moore, Henry M. & Jane E. Elam, m 25 Oct 1864(?) by Thos. Hester.

Moore, Henry W. & Jane E. Elam, 24 Feb 1864; James H. White, bm.

Moore, Hester & Ann E. Whitfield, 3 Nov 1834; Thomas Belborn, bm; S. Harris, wit.

Moore, James & Betty Yancey, 7 Jan 1765; Charles Bruce, bm.

Moore, James & Priscilla Williams, 1 Jan 1852; ___ Heflin, Robert Garner, bm.

Moore, Jefferson & Martha J. Haskins, 2 March 1852; P. P. Bullock, bm; A. Landis, wit; m 15 March 1852 by R. B. Hester, J. P.

Moore, Jeremiah & Mary Partee, 22 April 1797; Yerbey Partee, bm; Drury Kimbal Jr., wit.

Moore, John & Fanney Bradford, 30 Sept 1782; B. Bookerford, bm; Reuben Searcy, wit.

Moore, John & Sharolet(?) Garrott, 12 May 1796; Matthew Garrot, bm; Richard Taylor, wit.

GRANVILLE MARRIAGES 1753-1868

Moore, Jno. & Sarah Pruit, 10 May 1800; John Fradford Puet, bm; G. Brasfield, wit.

Moore, John & Holley Jones, 3 Nov 1821; Aaron Haskins, bm; Jas. M. Wiggins, wit.

Moore, John & Martha Harrison, 3 Jan 1825; Willis Johnson, bm; Step. K. Sneed, wit.

Moore, John W. & Maria A. Moore, 17 Jan 1842; John Talley, bm; J. M. Wiggins, wit; consent from George W. Moore, 15 Jan ____; John Talley attests to the consent of George W. Moore, father of Maria, and attests that she is above 15 years of age.

Moore, Joseph R. & Louvecy Averett, 8 Sept 1853; James S. Finch, bm; A. Landis, wit.

Moore, Josiah & Mary A. F. Hite, 22 Dec 1859; James R. Fortines. bm; m 22 Dec 1859 by L. B. Stone.

Moore, Lane & Nancey Adcock, 3 Nov 1790; Jeremiah Bullock, bm; H. Potter, wit.

Moore, Laune & Jensey Jenkings, 11 Dec 1806; Woodson Daniel, bm; W. M. Sneed, wit.

Moore, Lemuel & Lucrecia Rudd, 1 Aug 1814; Jeremiah Bailey, bm; Step. Sneed, wit.

Moore, Lucius & Dicey Rodgers, 25 Nov 1837; James T. Johnson, bm; J. M. Wiggins, wit.

Moore, Lucius & Quincy Marlow, 25 Aug 1845; James J. Thomas, bm.

Moore, Major & Lucretia Noland, 22 March 1780; James Blackwell, bm.

Moore, Nathaniel & Pitsey Steward, 2 Aug 1845; Jas. M. Wiggins, bm.

Moore, Pleasant & Elisabeth Stroud, 7 July 1804; Joel Moore, bm; Step. Sneed, wit.

Moore, Portius & Frances Webb, 28 March 1806; Benjamin Bullock, bm; Jun. Sneed, wit.

Moore, Potius & Lucy W. Pulliam, 4 July 1814; W. M. Sneed, bm.

Moore, Seawell H. & Martha Parrish, 2 Nov 1831; Moses Roberts, bm; Step. K. Sneed, wit.

Moore, Thomas & Lenney Bonner, 13 Aug 1802; Laine Moore, bm; Step. Sneed, wit.

Moore, Thomas & Julia Ann Royster, 5 Feb 1822; Tabern Royster, bm; Jas. M. Wiggins, wit.

Moore, Thomas E. & Indiana Hunt, 21 Dec 1853; Eugene Grissom, bm; m 22 Dec 1853 by A. C. Harris, M. G.

Moore, Thomas J. & Lucretia Dickens, 12 Nov 1807; William Robards, bm; L. Henderson, wit.

Moore, Thomas R. & Sarah Jane Coley, 10 March 1840; Isaac Haskins, bm; J. M. Wiggins, wit.

GRANVILLE MARRIAGES 1753-1868

Moore, William & Susanna Nichols, 12 Sept 1763; James Moore, bm.

Moore, William & Elisabeth Clark, 21 Nov 1784; Isham Johnson, bm; Bennet Searcy, wit.

Moore, William & Amey Martin, 30 Dec 1795; Saml. Worthington, Phill. Bullock, bm; Step. Sneed, wit.

Moore, William & Druciller Macon, 1 Nov 1834; W. B. Ellington, bm; Geo. Kittrell, wit.

Moore, William & Milley Barley, 13 May 1837; Green T. Partin, bm.

Moore, William & Nancy Overby, 17 June 1844; Leroy Wilkins, bm; Wm. H. Whitfield, wit.

Moran, Gabriel & Anna Roberds, _____ 1798; Samuel Themwell, bm; H. Williams, wit.

Moreland, Gabriel & Salley Harding, 15 Dec 1796; William Miner, bm; Richard Taylor, wit.

Morgan, Archelus & Mary Kirk, 15 Sept 1836; L. Gilliam, bm; J. M. Wiggins, wit.

Morgan, Archillus & Nancy Lad, 13 Nov 1808; Franklin Satterwhite, bm; Jas. Sneed, wit.

Morgan, Irvin & Agness Bullock, 25 Aug 1843; J. B. Allen, bm; Wm. H. Whitfield, wit.

Morgan, James D. & Elizabeth Puckett, 22 March 1844; Robt. H. Read, bm.

Morgan, John G. & Susan Ann Hudson, 14 Dec 1842; John Hudson, bm; J. M. Wiggins, wit.

Morgan, Orman & Charlsa(?) Jordan, 18 Jan 1774; Thos. Reeks, bm; Reuben Searcy, wit.

Morgan, Robert B. & Mary F. Cutts, 15 Dec 1865; Jos. B. Crews, bm; m 20 Dec 1865 by E. Hines.

Morgan, Robert E. & Susan Overbey, 17 Oct 1856; R. B. Hunt, bm; m 18 Oct 1856 by Jno. W. Stovall, J. P.

Morgan, William & Mary Ragsdale, 24 Aug 1811; Zadock Loyd, bm; Step. Sneed, wit.

Morgan, William D. & Mary Dyer, 4 Dec 1858; Robert E. Morgan, bm; A. Landis, wit.

Morgan, Winfield & Piety Weathers, 5 Dec 1807; Edward Weathers, bm; W. M. Sneed, wit.

Morris, Addicus & Elizabeth Hunt, 16 Jan 1844; Robert D. Jones, bm; J. M. Wiggins, wit.

Morris, Asa & Oney Mayfield, 29 Nov 1825; Henderson Morriss, bm; Wm. Hayes Owen, wit.

Morris, Henry & Nancy Cavndar, 2 Feb 1808; Tyre Morris, bm; W. M. Sneed, wit.

GRANVILLE MARRIAGES 1753-1868

Morris, Henry & Nancy Hobgood, 15 Sept 1855; John Kimball, bm.

Morris, J. H. & Mary F. Adcock, 24 April 1858; A. S. Newton, bm; m 26 April 1858 by S. Beasley, J. P.

Morris, John & Fanny Johnston, 5 Nov 1799; Anderson Freeman, bm; L. Henderson, wit.

Morris, Redding B. & Mary Longmire, 1 Jan 1826; Morris Byrum, bm.

Morris, Samuel & Phanney Eastwood, 17 Feb 1790; William Williams, bm; Step. Sneed, wit.

Morris, Stephen & Rodah Parham, 8 Feb 1792; Kannon Parham, bm; W. Norwood, wit.

Morris, Stephen H. & Sarah E. Critchen, 15 Oct 1840; Thomas Hester, bm; Jas. M. Wiggins, wit.

Morris, Thomas & Sary Johnson, 7 May 1794; James Johnson, bm; H. Seawell, wit.

Morris, Tyre & Elisabeth Hester, 12 Dec 1800; Garland Hester, bm; P. Bullock, wit.

Morris, Wesley & Susan Kinton, 1 April 1865; Z. Daniel, bm; A. Landis, wit.

Morris, William & Rebeccah Freeman, 17 Jan 1798; Gideon Mitchell, bm; Step. Sneed, wit.

Morris, William & Sally Busby, 26 Dec 1801; Robert Hargrove, bm; H. Sneed, wit.

Morris, William & Oney Crews, 4 Feb 1812; Stephen Bridges, bm; A. H. Sneed, wit.

Morris, William & Mary Brinkley, 10 July 1819; William Clark, bm; Step. K. Sneed, wit.

Morriss, Joseph & Elizabeth Harris, 28 Aug 1829; Henry P. Huddleston, bm; David Laws, wit.

Morriss, Littleton & Phoebe Murphy, 23 Oct 1832; Simon Hayes, bm; Step. K. Sneed, wit.

Morrow, Aaron & Susan Daniel, 19 Aug 1866.

Morrow, Anderson & Lucy Morrow, 1 Aug 1866.

Morrow, Auston & Ann Morrow, 31 July 1866.

Morrow, Drury S. & Susan P. Glover, 16 Nov 1829; James Anderson, bm; Albert Sneed, wit.

Morrow, Drury S. & Sallie Ann Clark, 4 Feb 1861; T. L. Hargrove, bm; m 13 Feb 1861 by E. Hines.

Morrow, Ebenezer & Pallatiah Clement, 2 Oct 1815; John T. Clement, bm; John C. Smith, wit.

Morrow, Edmund & Filis Feald, 6 Aug 1866.

Morrow, Henry & Caroline Lewis, 11 Aug 1866.

GRANVILLE MARRIAGES 1753-1868

Morrow, James & Louisa Tarreys, 31 July 1866.

Morrow, Stephen & Mary Ann Chandler, 3 May 1832; Wm. H. Hibb, bm; Step. K. Sneed, wit.

Morse, Franklin & Sarah Vaughan, 15 April 1812; Bennett Morse, bm; Step. Sneed, wit.

Morse, Samuel & Elizabeth Smith, 16 Dec 1794; Howel Morp, bm; Step. Sneed, wit.

Morton, Andrew J. & Mira Frances Fuller, 26 Jan 1867; John Rogers, bm; A. Landis, wit. m 27 Jan 1867 by W. H. P. Jenkins, J. P.

Morton, Billy, colored, son of York & Rhody Morton, & Margarate Taylor, daughter of Bella Hicks, 14 Nov 1868; m 21 Nov 1868 by A. C. Harris, M. G.

Morton, David F., son of John & Elizabeth W. Morton, & Martha E. Daniel, daughter of James B. & Jane E. Daniel, 13 Aug 1867; m 28 Aug 1867 by Edward Hines.

Morton, James & Frances Peace, 7 Oct 1836; Robert A. P. Jones, bm; J. M. Wiggins, wit.

Morton, John S. & Emmer L. Nowel, 31 May 1857; Saml. H. Davis, bm.

Morton, Joseph & Miss Ann E. Daniel, 26 April 1845; M. H. Daniel, bm.

Morton, Joseph & Christiana Hicks, 1 Feb 1867; Jonathan Jenkins, bm; m 3 Feb 1867 by W. H. P. Jenkins.

Morton, Lacy & Lucy Strong, 25 Aug 1866.

Morton, Nathaniel D., son of Joseph & Ann Morton, & Margaret S. Cole, daughter of Dr. B. L. Cole & Margaret Cole, m 22 Dec 1868 by E. Hines.

Morton, Robert, of color, son of Peter & Sarah Morton, & Martha Roberts, daughter of Syrus & Isabellah Robards, 30 July 1867; m 1 Aug 1867 by Jas. R. Duty, J. P.

Morton, Samuel S. & Martha E. Venable, m 11 Nov 1851 by E. Hines.

Morton, Samuel V. & Martha E. Venable, 2 Nov 1857; Geo. H. Venable, bm.

Mosely, Benjamin & Rhoda Woodlock, 25 May 1840; Jas. B. Peace, bm.

Mosely, Saml. & Susanna Bledsoe, 12 Aug 1786; John Mosely, bm; Thos. Ligon, wit.

Moses, Thomas C. & Sarah A. Moore, 18 Jan 1850; N. G. Whitfield, bm.

Mosley, William & Polley Ware, 8 Nov 1814; Thomas Knott, bm.

Moss, B. L. & Mary L. Bullock, 5 Sept 1854; Thos. W. McClanahan, bm; m 3 Oct 1854 by R. B. Hester, J. P.

Moss, Benjamin & Elizabeth C. Turner, 22 Dec 1824; Franklin Moss, bm; A. Sneed, wit.

GRANVILLE MARRIAGES 1753-1868

Moss, Benjamin F. & Lucy Freman, 11 Dec 1864; Isaac Birch, bm.

Moss, Charles & Cyntha Perkinson, 24 Dec 1852; Robert T. Stanton, bm; m 6 Jan 1853 by D. P. Paschall, J. P.

Moss, James & Lucy Collins, 3 Oct 1826; James Kendrick, bm; Wm. H. Owen, wit.

Moss, James C. & Fanny Adcock, 11 Jan 1851; A. Landis, bm.

Moss, James Madison & Charity Weathers, 12 Dec 1821; Benjamin Moss, bm; S. K. Sneed, wit.

Moss, John & Polly Kittrell, 27 April 1785; Saml. Goodwin, bm; B. Searcy, wit.

Moss, John & Mary Mitchell, 8 Sept 1830; Areil Mitchel, bm; S. K. Sneed, wit.

Moss, John & Frances C. Bullock, 3 Dec 1850; H. Bullock, bm.

Moss, Joseph Y. & Rowan Lawrence, 5 Jan 1866; W. J. Mitchell, bm; m 8 March 1866 by B. R. Hester.

Moss, Newton, colored, son of Iezor Eaton & Millie Moss, & Mary Dunston, parents unknown, m 26 Dec 1868 by T. S. Cook, M. G.

Moss, Reuben J. & Frances A. White, 4 Oct 1837; Benja. C. Cook, bm.

Moss, Richard & Frances Mitchell, 19 Nov 1833; John Moss, bm; Benja. Kittrell, wit.

Moss, Richard & Catharine Rowland, 15 Nov 1858; J. H. Gooch, bm; m 18 Nov 1858 by H. H. Rowland, J. P.

Moss, Richard A. & Hixy Jane Kittle, 16 Dec 1840; Elijah Fuller, bm; Jas. M. Wiggins, wit.

Moss, Richard A.& Mary Francis Montague, 19 Aug 1859; John Y. Smith, bm; A. Landis, wit; m 2 Sept 1859 by Geo. J. Rowland, J. P.

Moss, Robert E. & Sallie Ann Meadows, 18 Nov 1859; D. C. Reames, bm; m 6 Dec 1859 by B. B. Hester.

Moss, S. H., son of R. A. & Hicksey Moss, & Mary J. Overton, daughter of A. & Jane Overton, m 27 Oct 1867 by W. P. White, J. P.

Moss, Turner & Salley Reaves, 15 Nov 1797; Thos. Reaves, bm; Step. Sneed, wit.

Moss, Wm. & Martha Woodliff, 15 Dec 1853; Gilcrease Bailey, bm; m 22 Dec 1853 by D. P. Paschall, J. P.

Moton, Joseph & Elizabeth Ball, 25 Dec 1832; Thomas Leavick(?), bm; David Laws, wit.

Mulchi, George W. & Jane West, 6 Feb 1860; W. R. Tilletson, bm; A. Landis, wit; m 8 Feb 1860 by Thos. Hester.

Mulchi, William, son of Robert & Susan Mulchi, & Miss Bettie Loyd, daughter of James & Jane Loyd, 8 Dec 1868; m 10 Dec 1868 by R. J. Devin, M. G.

GRANVILLE MARRIAGES 1753-1868

Mullins, Robert W. & Mary C. Muller, 10 May 1845; William J. Carter, bm; W. T. Hayne, wit.

Munn, Alexander & Sally Gresham, 30 Dec 1823; Thomas P. Gresham, bm; S. K. Sneed, wit.

Munn, Alexander & Rebecca Gresham, 28 Oct 1855; John Gresham, bm; Jas. R. Duty, wit.

Munn, Wheeler & Agnes Smiley, m 25 April 1867 by Jos. E. Pattillo, J. P.

Munn, Wm. H. & Martha J. Newman, 19 July 1863; Jas. L. Norwood, bm; Jas. R. Duty, wit; m 19 July 1863 by Jas. R. Duty, J. P.

Munroe, John & Nancy F. Hudson, 7 Jan 1865; William Tillotson, bm; m 7 Jan 1865 by L. B. Stone, J. P.

Murphey, Alexander & Jenney Smith, 28 March 1797; Maurice Smith, bm; Jas. Smith, wit.

Murphey, John G. & Tabitha Bryant, 18 April 1807; John M. Peace, bm; W. M. Sneed, wit.

Murphey, William & Mary Inge, 17 May 1804; Wm. Blackwell, bm; Step. Sneed, wit.

Murphy, Daniel & Holly Traylor, 4 Jan 1831; D. J. Cardwell, bm; Step. K. Sneed, wit.

Murray, Hampton & Margaret Pinson, 17 Nov 1836; James Williamson, bm; Robert Clack, wit.

Murray, James & Elizabeth M. Duty, 10 April 1830; William B. Ellington, bm; David Laws, wit.

Murray, John T. & Elizabeth Sherman, 2 Nov 1858; William N. Fuller, bm; m 4 Nov 1858 by J. W. Floyd, Minister of the Gospel.

Murray, Richard A. & Ann Culbreath, 11 Aug 1847; Miles Cox, bm.

Murray, Thomas H. & Susan May, 2 Oct 1847; James O. Cooper, bm; J. M. Wiggins, wit.

Murrer, Oliver & Anna Shearman, 16 Nov 1812; John R. Hobgood, bm; Stephen D. Sneed, wit.

Murry, Edward & Mary Tillotson, 11 Aug 1852; G. W. R. Averot, bm; m 11 Aug 1852 by Jno. W. Stovall, J. P.

Murry, John H. & Harriet Elliott, 24 Dec 1851; John Elliott, bm; L. B. Stone, J. P., wit; m 24 Dec 1851 by L. B. Stone, J. P.

Murry, Willie M. & Nancy Daniel, 26 Dec 1854; Richard H. Murry, bm; John D. Wilkerson, wit; m 28 Dec 1854.

Murry, William & Masoury O. Phillips, 15 Aug 1864; Milton Keen, bm; m 15 Aug 1864 by L. B. Stone, J. P.

Mutter, Thomas & Elizabeth Moore, ___ July 1767; Wm. Moore, bm; Robert Goodloe, wit.

Mutter, Thomas & Ann Bull-- (no date, during admn. of Sam Johnston); A. Henderson, wit.

GRANVILLE MARRIAGES 1753-1868

Nailing, Nelson & Polley Rust, 27 Jan 1796; A. Champion, bm; Step. Sneed, wit.

Nailing, Willis A. & Mary Jane Evans, 24 Feb 1824; William P. Jinkins, bm; S. K. Sneed, wit.

Nall, Martin & Mary Blackwell, (no date, during admn. of Samuel Johnston); John Pope Jr., bm.

Nance, Agreppy & Sarah Hithel, 29 Nov 1815; Hezekiah Plummer, bm; Jno. Cobbs, wit.

Nance, Agrippa & Sally Inscore, 13 March 1834; Thomas Inscore, bm; Benja. Kittrell, wit.

Nance, Albert A. & Bethia Fowler, 28 Aug 1841; John Mitchell, bm; J. M. Wiggins, wit.

Nance, Allen & Ann Suit, 22 Dec 1849; A. B. Bullock, bm; A. Landis, wit.

Nance, Clement & Martha Ann Fowler, 19 Feb 1820; John Wilson, bm; Jas. M. Wiggins, wit.

Nance, David & Eliza Tanner, 8 Sept 1840; Jas. M. Wiggins, wit.

Nance, Frederick Woodson & Rachel Leathers, 26 June 1809; James Allison Jr., bm; W. M. Sneed, wit.

Nance, Frederick Wootsen & Aggy Bichett, 19 Apr 1793; Jas. Paschal, bm; W. Norwood, wit.

Nance, Herwood & Martha Cardwell, 9 May 1798; Philip Bullock, bm; Step. Sneed, wit.

Nance, Isham & Eady Fowler, 1 Dec 1841; James C. Cozart, bm; J. M. Wiggins, wit.

Nance, John & Phebey Fowler, 4 Sept 1795; James Gilcreast, bm.

Nance, Preston M. & Linly Goss, 1 Sept 1855; Harriston Wheeler, bm; m 2 Sept 1855 by Wm. H. Jones.

Nance, Samuel & Fanny Wilson, 16 Jan 1812; F. W. Nance, bm; W. M. Sneed, wit.

Nancy, James H. & Elizabeth Nunn, 25 Dec 1828; Geo. C. Smith, bm.

Nanny, Joseph B. & Mary B. Dunkly, 20 Dec 1854; William R. Tucker, bm; Jas. R. Duty, wit.

Neal, David & Beggy Puryear, 1 April 1811; Wm. Graves, bm; Oba. Farrar, wit.

Neal, Ralph & Jeany Jordon, 9 May 1780; William Thornton, bm; Asa Searcy, wit.

Neal, William R., son of John F. & Martha Neal, & Mary J. Barnett, daughter of James P. & Mary Barnett, 27 Feb 1868; m 27 Feb 1868 by J. A. Stradley, M. G.

Neale, Reuben & Sarah Jordan, 27 Dec 1779; Reuben Morn, bm; Asa Searcy, wit.

GRANVILLE MARRIAGES 1753-1868

Neele, Fielden & Rebeckah Reece, 4 Nov 1799; Richard Kemp, bm; Geo. Brasfield, wit.

Nelloms, Presley & Judith Edwards, 25 Aug 1820; John Vass, bm; Step. K. Sneed, wit.

Nelson, Howell Y. & Ann Winfrey, 3 July 1850; James T. Ramsay, bm.

Nelson, Hugh & Mary Ann Hunt, 19 Oct 1811; Thos. Hunt, bm; A. H. Sneed, wit.

Nelson, John & Bettie Lyle Royster, 8 Sept 1856; R. W. Lassiter, bm; m 17 Sept 1856 by N. Z. Graves.

Nelson, Major A. & Sarah Winfree, 4 Dec 1849; Henry R. Nelson, bm.

Nelson, Matthew & Rowan Hester, 5 July 1851; R. D. Jones, bm; m 8 July 1851 by R. J. Devin.

Nethery, George D. & Luisa Griffin, 21 Aug 1860; Richard E. Yancey, bm; m 21 Aug 1860 by L. B. Stone, J. P.

Nevell, John & Milley Fuller, 5 Jan 1817; John Estes, bm; James Ridley, wit.

Nevil, James R. & Sally C. Mangum, 8 Sept 1840; Peyton G. Mangum, bm; Jas. M. Wiggins, wit.

Newbey, James & Polley Demont, 26 Feb 1806; Thomas Dement, bm; W. M. Sneed, wit.

Newbill, John H. & Mary A. Bigger, 15 Sept 1827; Bozzal Burroughs, bm; S. Sneed, wit.

Newman, Thomas & Hester Smiley, 8 Dec 1818; Wm. W. Reaves, bm; James Wiggins, wit.

Newman, Thomas J. & Edney J. Wilson, 6 Sept 1859; Moses T. Riggan, bm; James R. Duty, J. P., wit; m 6 Sept 1859 by James R. Duty, J. P.

Newton, Alexander S. & Mary S. Elom, 4 Dec 1855; James R. Newton, bm; m 13 Dec 1855 by Jno. W. Stovall, J. P.

Newton, Alexander S. & Sarah A. Eaks, 18 Sept 1860; D. A. Hunt, bm; m 23 Sept 1860 by Thos. Hester.

Newton, George & _____, 24 Jan 1834; William Newton, bm; Benja. Kittrell, wit.

Newton, Haly & Milly Monroe, 21 Dec 1839; A. H. Hunt(?), bm; Wm. T. Hayne, wit.

Newton, Henry & Lucy Good, 19 June 1850; Henry W. Beasly, bm.

Newton, Henry A. & Martha Overton, 23 July 1856; J. H. Merritt, bm; m 24 July 1856 by A. C. Harris, M. G.

Newton, Isaac & Mary E. Currin, 23 Nov 1858; James Newton, bm.

Newton, James B. & Ann F. Blackwell, 10 Nov 1853; John Newton, bm; m 17 Nov 1853.

GRANVILLE MARRIAGES 1753-1868

Newton, James P. & Nancy S. Berkley, 3 Jan 1846; John Barkley, bm; J. M. Wiggins, wit.

Newton, John & Amey Newton, 20 Dec 1795; Robert Hargrove, bm; Step. Sneed, wit.

Newton, Jno. & Frances Clardy, 8 Nov 1841; A. H. Hanks, bm; Wm. H. Whitfield, wit.

Newton, John & Parthenia P. Currin, 25 Jan 1847; James Newton, bm; Jas. M. Wiggins, wit.

Newton, John & Luranian Belcher, 20 Dec 1860; Joseph Noble, bm; m 20 Dec 1860 by L. B. Stone, J. P.

Newton, Patrick J. & Nancy M. Daniel, 15 July 1858; Isaac Newton, bm; m 15 July 1858 by L. B. Stone, J. P.

Newton, Washington W. & Sally Loyd, 11 Jan 1865; Lewis H. Loyd, bm; m 11 Jan 1865 by L. B. Stone, J. P.

Newton, William & Letha Fitts, 27 Nov 1849; R. H. Jones, bm; L. B. Stone, J. P., wit.

Nichols, John & Linney Cash, 5 June 1809; Peter Cash, bm; W. M. Sneed, wit.

Nichols, Mathias & Elizabeth Daniel, 16 Jan 1814; Wm. Davidson, bm; W. M. Sneed, wit.

Nichols, Thomas & Sally Kinnamon, 1 March 1817; James R. Johnson, bm; Richd. Sneed, wit.

Nichols, W. R. & H. L. Philpott, 25 Oct 1866; W. N. Gooch, bm; C. E. Landis, wit; m 26 Oct 1866 by G. W. Ferrill, Minister of the Gospel.

Nicholson, Atkin & Elisabeth Knott, 7 Nov 1797; Wm. Fuller, bm; Step. Sneed, wit.

Nicholson, George Junr. & Jane Pope, 18 May 1775; John Pope, bm; Osborn Pope, wit.

Nicholson, Lewis & Polley Wortham, 18 July 1806; Wm. Blackwell, bm; Step. Sneed, wit.

Nicholson, Robert & Lucy Harris(?), 19 Nov 1808; Adam Nostedler (?), bm; A. H. Sneed, wit.

Nilson, William G. & Susan M. Stone, 16 Oct 1858; B. R. Williamson, bm; L. B. Stone, wit; m 17 Oct 1858 by R. J. Devin.

Nithery, Henry H. & Lucy F. Ligon, 26 March 1862; Wm. L. White, bm; m 26 March 1862 by L. B. Stone, J. P.

Noblen, Richard & Franky Daniel, 7 Oct 1843; Wilson Loyd, bm; Wm. H. Whitfield, wit.

Noblin, Joseph & Nancy S. Belcher, 7 Feb 1861; James Belcher, bm; m 7 Feb 1861 by L. B. Stone, J. P.

Noblin, Richard & Martha Daniel, 14 Oct 1854; Alexander G. Land. bm; m 20 Oct 1854 by Lewis Amis, J. P.

Noblin, Robert & Martha Adams, 24 Dec 1834; Leroy P. Wilkins, bm.

GRANVILLE MARRIAGES 1753-1868

Noblin, Spencer & Nancy West, 21 Jan 1826; James Loyd, bm; Robert K. Clack, wit.

Noblin, William & Kathern Murry, m 16 Jan 1867 by E. L. Parrish, J. P.; James Murry, bm.

Noel, James & Mary Downey, 2 Jan 1816; James Nuttall, bm; Wm. Lamasson, wit.

Noland, Bud & Elizebeth Mills, 20 Jan 1788; Charles Noland, bm; John Searcy, wit.

Noland, David & Mary Fuller, 26 Oct 1810; Daniel Fuller, bm; W. M. Sneed, wit.

Noland, Henry & Isbell Milner, 5 March 1782; Edwd. Noland, bm; Reuben Searcy, wit.

Noland, James & Patience Hook, 26 Oct 1784; Israel Judge, bm; Ephraim Hampton, wit.

Norman, Collier, colored, son of Anderson Wiggins & July Wiggins, & Caroline Hester, daughter of Billy & Tempy Hester, 14 Nov 1868; m by M. H. Vaughan, Rector of St. Stephen's Church, 14 Nov 1868.

Norman, Henry & Elizabeth Williams, 15 Dec 181_; Richd. Sneed, bm; John J. Strum, wit.

Norman, John & Prudence Maynard, 28 Dec 1801; Lewis Hening, bm; Jas. Bedford, wit.

Norman, John & Elizabeth Petiford, 17 March 1835; L. A. Paschall, bm; Benja. Kittrell, wit.

Norman, Mathew & Patsey Bryant, 2 Aug 1816; Dennis L. Kendrick, bm.

Norman, Richard & Mary Day, 9 Feb 1867; James Day, bm; m 10 Feb 1867 by W. H. Jordan.

Norman, Thomas W. & Salley Babler, 2 Nov 1814; William H. Gillian, bm; W. M. Sneed, wit.

Norman, Thomas & Sarah Lowe, 9 June 1773; William Potter, bm.

Norvell, Clinton & Polley Lane Jarratt, 2 Oct 1804; Wm. Norvell, bm; E. W. Parham, wit.

Norwell, Hugh of Mecklenburg County, Va. & Margaret Bugg, 7 Jan 1790; Young Norwell, bm; Henry Potter, wit.

Norwood, Benjamin & Mary Akin, 6 April 1782; Thomas Lena(?) Ford(?), bm; W. Hilton, wit.

Norwood, Benjamin & Elizabeth Kerron, 8 Jan 1858; James R. Duty, bm; m 14 Jan 1858 by Jno. W. Stovall, J. P.

Norwood, Benjamin & Mary Murray, 25 Dec 1860; W. M. Arrington, bm.

Norwood, Benja. Jr. & Catharin Norwood, 4 Feb 1845; G. W. Norwood, bm; J. M. Wiggins, wit.

GRANVILLE MARRIAGES 1753-1868

Norwood, David & Mary Satterwhite, 7 Oct 1843; John G. Barker, bm; Wm. H. Whitfield, wit.

Norwood, David & Martha Satterwhite, 9 Jan 1851; Stephen Currin, bm.

Norwood, David & Emily H. Davis, 5 Jan 1854; John T. C. Norwood, bm; Jno. W. Stovall, wit; m 5 Jan 1854 by Jno. W. Stovall, J. P.

Norwood, George & Mary Walters, 10 Dec 1799; Benjamin Norwood, bm; James Sneed, wit.

Norwood, George W. & Isabella Norwood, 4 Sept 1843; Wm. Barnett, bm; J. M. Wiggins, wit.

Norwood, Henderson, of color, son of Richard Royster & Fanny Sandford, & Metilda Smith, daughter of Squire & Mima Smith, m 5 Jan 1868 by Warren Overbey, J. P.

Norwood, James L. & Frances A. Norwood, 27 Jan 1841; Geo. W. Burroughs, bm; Jas. M. Wiggins, wit.

Norwood, James L. & Phebe Ann Norwood, 29 Nov 1855; James R. Duty, bm; m 29 Nov 1855 by Jas. R. Duty, J. P.

Norwood, James L. & Lucretia J. Crews, 24 June 1867; Jas. R. Duty, bm; m 27 June 1867 by Jas. R. Duty, J. P.

Norwood, James S. & Susan A. Norwood, 5 Jan 1841; Washington Burroughs, bm; J. M. Wiggins, wit.

Norwood, Jesse B. & Herriott Murry, 2 April 1861; Ruffin Puryear, bm; m 2 April 1861 by L. B. Stone, J. P.

Norwood, John & Mary Satterwhite, 28 Oct 1817; Andw. Rhea, bm; Richd. Sneed, wit.

Norwood, John & Penny Norwood, 16 Aug 1820; Charles Mallory, bm; W. M. Sneed, wit.

Norwood, John & Ann Eliza Curtis, 25 Dec 1858; Royal Anderson, bm; A. Landis, wit; m 25 Dec 1858 by W. R. Harris, J. P.

Norwood, John T. C. & Elizabeth S. Crews, 15 Jan 1856; John F. Harris, bm; m 16 Jan 1856 by Jno. R. Hicks, J. P. at the residence of Benjamin F. Crews.

Norwood, John T. C. & Frances A. E. Satterwhite, 20 Sept 1865; A. Landis, bm; m 3 Oct 1865 by E. F. Beachum, a regular G. M.

Norwood, Joseph & Sallie A. Watkins, 2 Sept 1857; Jno. R. Haskins, bm; A. Landis Jr., wit; m 3 Sept 1857 by J. M. Bullock, J. P.

Norwood, Joseph A. & Letuce Royster, 26 Dec 1815; Robert G. Norwood, bm; Step. Sneed, wit.

Norwood, Joseph G. & Elisabeth P. Glover, 21 Dec 1813; John Ricks, bm; Step. Sneed, wit.

Norwood, Joseph L. & Mary C. Tillotson, 20 Dec 1866; J. T. C. Norwood, bm; m 20 Dec 1866 by Jas. R. Duty, J. P.

GRANVILLE MARRIAGES 1753-1868

Norwood, Lewis B. & Jane D. Amis, 6 Jan 1846; Alexander Norwood, bm; S. Beasley Jr., wit.

Norwood, Nathaniel A. & Amelia Tillottson, m 24 Jan 1867 by E. L. Parrish, J. P.; John T. J. Norwood, bm.

Norwood, Nathaniel G. & Elizabeth Land, 6 Dec 1841; Stephen Satterwhite, bm; W. H. Whitfield, wit.

Norwood, Nathl. M. & Martha H. Burnett, 12 Feb 1834; Jas. R. Duty, bm.

Norwood, Nathaniel M. & E. Miller, 4 Feb 1841; W. Barnett, bm.

Norwood, Philip H. & Marinun Wilson, 2 May 1861; Jas. R. Duty, bm.

Norwood, Robert & Elisabeth Norwood, 14 Dec 1819; Henry Allen, bm.

Norwood, Robert & Ellen Cooper, 8 May 1866; m 20 May 1866 by John L. Carrole.

Norwood, Robert G. & Mary J. Breedlove, 23 Nov 1865; A. Landis, bm; m 26 Nov 1865 by John F. Harris, J. P.

Norwood, Solomon S. & Harnett S. Lemay, 4 Aug 1857; Eaton Haithcock, bm; m 9 Aug 1857 by Jas. R. Duty, J. P.

Norwood, Thomas & Mary Norwood, 11 Feb 1850; Jas. L. Norwood, bm; Jas. R. Duty, wit.

Norwood, Thomas J. & Mary A. Morgan, 27 March 1866; m 29 March 1866 by R. J. Devin.

Norwood, Thomas T. & Mary A. Morgan, 27 March 1866; Jas. R. Duty, bm.

Norwood, Weldon & Anne Harris, 22 Oct 1840; Henry Cousins, bm; Jas. M. Wiggins, wit.

Norwood, William & Rebecah Thomas, 9 Sept 1807; Joshua Mabry, bm; A. H. Sneed, wit.

Norwood, Wm. Senr. & Sally Thomas, 24 Oct 1805; Wm. Norwood Jr., bm; A. H. Sneed, wit.

Norwood, William B. & Dansel C. Dabnam, 1 Feb 1854; Jas. L. Reid, bm; m 2 Feb 1854 by A. C. Harris, M. G.

Norwood, William J. & Emily J. Veazey, 15 Jan 1856; Solomon Watterwhite, bm; m 20 Jan 1856 by A. M. Veazey, J. P.

Notgrass, James & Susanna Huffman, 10 June 1781; Joseph Landep, bm; Robert Harris, wit.

Notgrass, James & Sarah Turner, 5 Feb 1802; George Glimph, bm; P. Bullock, wit.

Nowell, David & Elisabeth Dauney, 18 Jan 1800; James Nowell, bm; Step. Sneed, wit.

Nowland, Jno. & Polley Taylor, (no date, during admn. of Gov. Samuel Johnston); Joseph Champion, bm; A. Henderson, wit.

GRANVILLE MARRIAGES 1753-1868

Nuckles, John, son of Wm. H. & Nancy Nuckles, & Charlotte Clarke, daughter of Adam Clarke, 6 Feb 1868; m 7 Feb 1868 by Wm. Holms, Minister of the Gospel.

Nuckles, Thomas & Elisabeth Bobbitt, 17 June 1854; James H. Nuckles, bm.

Nunn, Conrad B. & Emily E. Keen, 6 April 1866; m 6 April 1866 by L. B. Stone, J. P.

Nunn, Fautleroy & Elizabeth Overbey, 15 April 1833; Archd. Clark, bm; Jno. P. Smith, wit.

Nunn, Henry L. & Sorotha F. Elliott, 24 Nov 1859; Edwd. Overby, bm; L. B. Stone, J. P., wit; m 24 Nov 1859.

Nunn, James D. & Mary Jenkins, 6 Jan 1829; Augustin Davis, bm.

Nunn, Joshua & Mary Chandler, 15 Aug 1835; Jackson Chandler, bm; Wm. L. Owen, wit.

Nunn, Thomas & Polley Davis, 5 Dec 1797; Gulielnus Byars, bm; Step. Sneed, wit.

Nunn, Thomas & Sarah Head, 29 Jan 1814; Benj. Grisham, bm.

Nutall, John & Mary Alston, 29 Oct 1789; Reuben Butler, bm.

Nuttall, Charles & Fanny Blacknall, 25 Sept 1827; Thomas Blacknall, bm; S. K. Sneed, wit.

Nuttall, Edwin J. & Mrs. Sally E. Ware, 30 Oct 1851.

Nuttall, George & Sally M. Brodie, 8 Dec 1818; Nathl. Robards, bm.

Nuttall, George A. & Sarah Farrar, 28 Feb 1832; John B. Hutchinson, bm; David Laws, wit.

Nuttall, James & Emily Hawkins, 28 Feb 181_; Saml. Hillman, bm; Step. K. Sneed, wit.

Nuttall, John Junr. & Mary E. Smith, 14 March 1816; James Nuttall, bm.

Nuttall, John B. & Mary J. G. Patton, 12 Dec 1859; Lewis K. Willie, bm; m 14 Dec 1859 by L. K. Wille, M. G.

Oakeley, Barnett & Elizabeth Oakeley, 28 Feb 1855; John Oakely, bm; Benja. Kittrell, wit.

Oakeley, Simeon & Parthena Briggs, 23 Dec 1859.

Oakley, Alexander & Rachael F. Massy, 22 Dec 1863; m 4 Jan 1864 by Wm. S. Hobgood.

Oakley, Dolphus & Beady Ann Penny, 6 Aug 1861; Washington Mangum, bm.

Oakley, Dudley, of color, son of Robi. Tabon & Sylva Oakley, & Sabrina Thorp, parents unknown, m 31 Dec 1867 by B. D. Howard, J. P.

Oakley, Duncan & Caroline Roberts, 18 Sept 1857; Addison Oakly, bm; m 30 Sept 1857 by A. H. Cooke, J. P.

GRANVILLE MARRIAGES 1753-1868

Oakley, Durell & Harriett Cornelia Newton, 21 Dec 1859; James H. N. Russell, bm; A. Landis, wit.

Oakley, Haywood & Eliza Bullock, 5 July 1836; Rupert Parham, bm.

Oakley, Haywood & Elizabeth Traylor, 23 Oct 1866; Ridley Oakley, bm; A. Landis, wit; m 29 Oct 1866 by B. D. Howard, J. P.

Oakley, James & Rebeccah Goss, 6 Dec 1804; Thomas Banks, bm; Step. Sneed, wit.

Oakley, James T. & Mahala Fowler, 28 July 1838; Jas. M. Wiggins, wit.

Oakley, James W. & Mary Carnal, 6 Nov 1841; S. Terry, bm; Wm. H. Whitefield, wit.

Oakley, John & Ann Parker, 18 Dec 1815; Jesse Carnal, bm; W. M. Sneed, wit.

Oakley, John & Catharine Wood, 30 Jan 1816; Anthony B. Wood, bm; W. M. Sneed, wit.

Oakley, Richard & Winnefred Wheelor, 20 May 1788; William Oakely, bm; Reuben Searcy, wit.

Oakley, Simeon & Parthena Omerry, 23 Dec 1859; S. D. Ferrill, bm.

Oakley, Stephen & Sarrat Terry, 7 Feb 1804; Richard Wood, bm; A. H. Sneed, wit.

Oakley, Thomas & Joanna Wood, 25 Jan 1803; Jordan Bowles, bm; Green Merritt, wit.

Oakley, Tinsley & Susan Suit, 7 April 1851; M. Bullock, bm.

Oakley, William & Rebecca Oakley, 8 Feb 1814; Jesse C. Carnal, bm; W. M. Sneed, wit.

Oakley, William L. & Isabella Oakley, 7 March 1866; m 8 March 1866 by B. D. Howard, J. P.; C. Traylor, bm.

Oakley, William R., son of Hyram & Betsy Oakley, & Mrs. Emily F. Wood, daughter of Ransom & Sally Fowler, m 5 June 1867 by B. D. Howard, J. P.

Oakley, Yancey & Patsey Wood, 2 July 1814; Anthony Wood, bm; W. M. Sneed, wit.

Oakly, Jesse Jr. & Sarah N. Latta, 31 Dec 1855; Ezra Oakley, bm.

Oakly, Micajah & Sarah Perkinson, 3 Oct 1785; William Cole, bm; Bennet Searcy, wit.

OBrian, Gardner & Ann Eliza Hester, 4 Aug 1841; John W. Hunt, bm; J. M. Wiggins, wit.

OBriant, Dennis & Fanny Wilkerson, 30 July 1806; Georg. Landis, bm; W. M. Sneed, wit.

OBriant, Dennis & Frances Jones, 5 Sept 1854; Thomas Latta, bm.

OBriant, Edwin & Fanny W. Terry, 21 Dec 1837; C. Burton, bm; T. T. Wiggers, wit.

GRANVILLE MARRIAGES 1753-1868

OBriant, Gardner & Sophia Jane Hester, 2 Jan 1837; Harville Hester, bm; J. M. Wiggins, wit.

OBriant, James P. & Lucy Eastwood, 20 Aug 1844; A. C. Meadows, bm; Jas. M. Wiggins, wit.

OBriant, John & Sarah Slaughter, 25 Nov 1830; Sol. Philpott, bm; Step. K. Sneed, wit.

OBriant, Robert & Elizabeth Philpot, 22 Oct 1803; George Landis, bm; Green Merritt, wit.

OBriant, Robt. & Tabitha Chandler, 24 Nov 1824; Allen Yancy, bm; Jno. P. Smith, wit.

OBriant, William & Elisabeth Sanford, 23 Nov 1793; Reuben Ragland, bm; Step. Sneed, wit.

OBriant, William & Elisabeth Weaver, 18 Jan 1802; Jos. Wynne, bm; Step. Sneed, wit.

OBriant, Z. H., son of Z. & Elizabeth OBriant, & Sarah Hampton, daughter of J. H. & Sarah Hampton, 1 June 1868; m 2 June 1868 by F. J. Tilley, J. P.

OBriant, Zachariah & Elizabeth Mangum, 2 Nov 1830; Henry House, bm; David Laws, wit.

OBrien, Alexander P. & Emily C. Hobgood, 3 Nov 1866; James W. Badgett, bm; m 8 Nov 1866 by Samuel Hunt, J. P.

OBrien, James M. & Elizabeth S. West, 5 Feb 1861; A. Landis, bm; m 19 Feb 1861 by R. D. Puryear, J. P.

OBrien, Thomas & Parthena Oakley, 26 Aug 1833; T. B. Day, bm; S. Harris, wit.

OBrien, Zachariah & Rebecca Willowford, 16 Aug 1859; Emmett Gooch, bm; A. Landis, wit.

OBrient, Patrick & Faithey Hester, 19 March 1808; John Hester, Wiatt Currin, bm; W. M. Sneed, wit.

OBrient, Thomas & Elizabeth Gordon, 22 July 1835; Sol. Philpott, bm; Step. K. Sneed, wit.

OBryan, G. W. D. & Edney Daniel, 21 Nov 1842; William H. Reaves, bm; J. M. Wiggins, wit.

OBryant, James & Nancey Eastwood, 2 Nov 1837; Chas. Edwards, bm; J. M. Wiggins, wit.

OBryant, Philip & Lucy Bressie, 5 Dec 1801; Irby Bressie, bm; Phil. Bullock, wit.

O'Dear, William H. & Nancy Winston, 18 Oct 1848; Jo. B. Aleln, bm; Jas. M. Wiggins, wit.

Ogelvie, Harris & Elisabeth Amis(?), 26 Oct 1781; Wm. Lasseter, bm; Bennet Searcy, wit.

Ogilvie, John & Hannah Amis, 20 Nov 1792; Lewis Amis, bm; Step. Sneed, wit.

NOTE: For Ogilvie, Kimbrough through Overbey, John, see p. 370 (Additions)

GRANVILLE MARRIAGES 1753-1868

Overbey, John H. & Bettie Powell, 20 Oct 1863; A. Landis, bm; m 22 Oct 1863 by S. P. J. Harriss, M. G.

Overbey, Lafayett & Virginia Boyd, 30 Dec 1860; William Rice, bm; m 30 Dec 1860 by L. B. Stone, J. P.

Overbey, Obadiah & Nancy Winfree, 2 April 1867; m 4 April 1867 by L. B. Stone, J. P.

Overbey, Peter Junr. & Susanna Stovall, 1 July 1799; Philip Yancey Junr., bm; Sterling Yancey, wit.

Overbey, Warren & Sarah A. Norwood, m 11 July 1866 by R. J. Devin.

Overby, Bird & Caty Hight, 20 May 1813; William Overby, bm; H. Young, wit.

Overby, Henderson & Elizabeth Royster, 1 Nov 1826; Willis A. Royster, bm.

Overby, James W. & Lucy Hicks, 12 Sept 1842; J. C. Cooper, bm; Jas. M. Wiggins, wit.

Overby, James Y. & Mary A. Norwood, 1 Sept 1847; Will. B. Hughes, bm.

Overby, John & Ann Overby, 9 Dec 1830; Henry Overby, bm; Jno. P. Smith, wit.

Overby, John S. & Elizabeth Puryard, 21 Jan 1845; R. H. Kingsbury, bm; J. M. Wiggins, wit.

Overby, L. Cain & Elizabeth Loyed, 24 Oct 1861; m 24 Oct 1861 by Wm. M. Bennett, J. P.

Overby(?), Larkin W. & Emily F. Griffin, 26 Nov 1854; William R. Tucker, bm; Jas. R. Duty, wit; m _____ by Jas. R. Duty.

Overby, Larkin W. & Mary Loyd, 16 Sept 1858; William R. Tuck, bm; Jas. R. Duty, wit; m 16 Sept 1858 by Jas. R. Duty, J. P.

Overby, John & Mary Ann Chandler, 6 May 1829; Jas. M. Overby, bm; D. J. Young, wit.

Overby, John & Sarah Chandler, 29 March 1836; Edward Hite, bm; Robert K. Clack, wit.

Overby, Obediah & Harriet Booth, 31 Dec 1830; W. H. Farrar, bm.

Overby, Robert & Panthea Culbreath, 2 Oct 1843; Kemp Methis, bm; W. T. Hayne, wit.

Overby, Robert & Mary Culbreath, 27 Dec 1854; James R. Duty, bm; m 27 Dec 1854 by James R. Duty, J. P.

Overstreet, William & Henretta McCan, 17 June 1858; P. H. Yancey, bm; m 17 June 1858 by L. B. Stone, J. P.

Overton, Aurelious & Mahala S. Dement, 10 Oct 1866; A. Landis, bm; m 17 Oct 1866 by E. B. Lyon, J. P.

Overton, Benjamin & Harriet Powell, 4 Jan 1831; J. C. Smith, bm; David Laws, wit.

GRANVILLE MARRIAGES 1753-1868

Overton, Elisha & Letha Hunt, 4 Nov 1818; John Hunt, bm; Rhodes N. Herndon, wit.

Overton, Graton & Dilly Powell, 3 Feb 1829; Elisha Overton, bm; David Laws, wit.

Overton, Hartwell & Susan Dickerson, 22 Dec 1834; Samuel W. Dickerson, bm; Benja. Kittrell, wit.

Overton, James & Mary P. Jeeter, 9 Dec 1833; Robert Kinton, bm; Benja. Kittrell, wit.

Overton, James Arther & Jane R. Dickerson, 8 May 1833; Benjamin Merrett, bm; David Laws, wit.

Overton, John & Mary Craig (no date, during admn. of Gov. Alexander Martin); John Washington, bm; A. Henderson, wit.

Overton, John & Drucilla Kearney, 30 Oct 1866; m 31 Oct 1866 by Joseph K. Reddick; Redden Knight, bm.

Overton, Joseph & Hannah Hunt, 2 Oct 1824; Fielding Kittrell, bm; S. K. Sneed, wit.

Overton, Joshua & Elizabeth Turner, 15 Dec 1866; David A. Stone, bm; C. E. Landis, wit.

Overton, Osburn & Kizia Smith, 10 May 1794; Isaiah Smith, bm; L. Henderson, wit.

Overton, Robert P. & Mrs. Maria R. Cole, 19 April 1866; m 29 April 1866 by M. J. Hunt.

Overton, William & Lucy C. Longmire, 6 May 1854; George Hays, bm; m 11 May 1854 by D. P. Paschall, J. P.

Owen, Alexander & Elizabeth Bowen, 9 Dec 1858; James R. Blanks, bm; m 9 Dec 1858 by L. B. Stone, J. P.

Owen, Anderson & Frances Stephens, 4 June 1830; Jacob Owen, bm; Robert K. Clack, wit.

Owen, David & Rebecah L. Farrar, 5 Oct 1825; Alexander Farrar, Alexr. Smith, bm; G. W. Farrar, wit.

Owen, David A., son of David & Elizabeth Owen, & Caroline V. Hays, daughter of Avory & Phebe Morris, 11 Sept 1867; m 12 Sept 1867 by Wm. D. Hicks, J. P.

Owen, Evan & Oney Hester, 22 Dec 1828; Joseph Hart, bm; D. J. Young, wit.

Owen, Jacob & Elizabeth Crisp, 2 May 1862; Jas. Mathews, bm; A. Landis, wit; m 3 May 1862 by Saml. Hunt, J. P.

Owen, John & Sarah Walace, 5 Jan 1773; James Williams, bm; Reuben Searcy, wit.

Owen, John & Ellen Howard, 12 Jan 1803; Thomas Owen, bm; Green Merritt, wit.

Owen, John & Eliza Yancey, 13 March 1843; James Neal, bm; Wm. H. Whitfield, wit.

GRANVILLE MARRIAGES 1753-1868

Owen, John & Frances Overbey, 12 Jan 1853; Obadiah Christmas(?), bm; A. Landis, wit.

Owen, John Junr. & Rebeccah Ballard, 5 March 1804; William H. Lanier, bm; A. H. Sneed, wit.

Owen, John Junr. & Polly A. Goodwin, 16 Dec 1812; William Webb, bm; Thos. J. Hicks, wit.

Owen, John A. & Emily Wilson, 16 Jan 1860; E. W. Harris, bm; m 19 Jan 1860 by William M. Bennett, J. P.

Owen, John H. & Ann A. Parham, 3 Nov 1842; T. B. Barnett, bm; Joseph W. Barnett, wit.

Owen, John H. & Rowan Owen, freed people, 21 Oct 1865; A. Landis, bm; A. R. Burwell, wit.

Owen, Levi & Elizabeth Ashley, 6 Sept 1821; Willis Bowling, bm; Jas. M. Wiggins, wit.

Owen, Melchisedek & Margaret Downey, 3 Oct 1847; A. Owen, bm; L. B. Stone, wit.

Owen, Moses, of color, son of Wallace Blackley & Juda Owen, & Ann McKeever, daughter of Babby McKeever, 24 Aug 1867; m 12 Oct 1867 by M. H. Vaughan, Rector of St. Stephen's Church.

Owen, Thos. & Elisabeth Webb, 6 Jan 1794; Allen Howard, bm; Step. Sneed, wit.

Owen, William & Charlotte Montague, 12 Dec 1793; Richardson Owen, bm; Step. Sneed, wit.

Owen, William & Elizabeth J. Chandler, 1 March 1838; Ebey. Allen, bm; M. D. Royster, wit.

Owen, William & Sally Ann Wood, 11 March 1848; Jos. McGehee, bm; Jas. M. Wiggins, wit.

Owens, James & Martha Proctor, 23 Aug 1842; William Wilson, bm; Wm. H. Whitfield, wit.

Owens, Levi & Elvey Bolling, 27 Nov 1810; Thomas Owens, bm; W. M. Sneed, wit.

Owens, Thomas & Mehalcy Moadows, 27 Nov 1810; Levi Owens, bm; W. M. Sneed, wit.

Owens, Tidy, of color, son of Wallace & Judy Owens, & Jane Heggs, daughter of Meremon & Debby Heggs, 1 Nov 1868; m 7 Nov 1868 by Aron Pratcher.

Page, Isom, of color, son of Frank & Milia Rogers, & Jane Holloway, daughter of Green & Philis Holloway, 9 Sept 1867; m 9 Sept 1867 by J. D. C. Pool, J. P.

Paine, John & Susanna Satterwhite, 11 Jan 1769; John Satterwhite, David Mitchel, bm; Cha. Bruce, Jesse Sanders, wit.

Palmer, Elias & Nancy Hardwick, 15 Nov 1807; Levy Vasser, bm; Thos. Falconer, J. P., wit.

Palmer, William & Mary Brisse, 25 May 1776; James Yancey Jr., bm.

GRANVILLE MARRIAGES 1753-1868

Pannill, William & Martha Walker, 26 April 1794; Leonard Henderson, bm; Charles Mitchel, wit.

Parham, Aaron, of color, son of Jesse Willie & Hahhan Parham, & Maria Flag, daughter of Samuel & Fannie Flag, 29 Nov 1867; m 29 Nov 1867 by B. T. Winston, J. P.

Parham, Albert C. & Sarah C. Cheatham, 21 Feb 1856; Thos. R. Bobbitt, bm; m 24 Feb 1856 by L. K. Willie, M. G.

Parham, Alphus & Emeline Riggin, 8 Dec 1855; Dennis Lynch, bm.

Parham, Asa & Dilly H. Reavis, 22 March 1824; John Moore, bm; Wm. H. Owen, wit.

Parham, Asa C. & Sallie A. Paschall, 16 Feb 1864; Stephen Satterwhite, bm; m 24 Feb 1864 by E. F. Beachum, G. M.

Parham, Charles W. & Harriett Suit, 19 Nov 1851; Archd. Taylor, bm.

Parham, Cyrus & Frances Hester, 26 Dec 1866; m 26 Dec 1866 by R. B. Hester.

Parham, Edmond & Polly Bearden, 22 July 1807; W. M. Sneed, bm; Randal Minor, wit.

Parham, Ephraim & Nancy McGloclin, 17 June 1791; Willie Reeves, bm; Step. Sneed, wit.

Parham, Fredrick & Mary Rogers, 21 Aug 1801; Simeon Hayes, bm; Step. Sneed, wit.

Parham, George & Elizabeth Brinkley, 15 Dec 1815; Isham Cheatham, bm; Leslie Gilliam, wit.

Parham, George K. & Martha L. Pleasants, 22 Nov 1851; George A. Mangum, bm.

Parham, Isham Jr. & Polley Harrison, 1 Feb 1799; Frederick Parham, bm; Step. Sneed, wit.

Parham, James & Abbie Parham, 1 Feb 1867; James Hays, bm; C. E. Landis, wit.

Parham, James A. & Martha E. Davis, 19 Aug 1865; William A. Parham, bm; m 19 Oct 1865 by W. C. Gannon.

Parham, Jasper & Lucinda K. McCannde, 18 Dec 1867; m by G. W. Ferrill, Minister.

Parham, John & Mary Shamwell, 4 Sept 1792; Zacheriah Shamwell, bm; Step. Sneed, wit.

Parham, John & Elisabeth Reaves, 7 March 1793; Isham Parham, bm; Step. Sneed, wit.

Parham, Joseph B., son of Asa & Delia H. Parham, & Emma J. Hunt, daughter of George W. & Susan C. Hunt, 3 Oct 1868; m 4 Oct 1868 by L. K. Willie, M. G.

Parham, Kennon & Milley Parham, 28 July 1787; Lewis Parham, bm; B. Searcy, wit.

GRANVILLE MARRIAGES 1753-1868

Parham, Kennon Junr. & Tabitha Morris, 13 May 1825; Thompson
Parham, bm; Step. K. Sneed, wit.

Parham, Lewis & Rachel Amis, 5 Oct 1816; John W. Amis Junr., bm;
Rt. Herndon, wit.

Parham, Lewis & Agness Tuck, 10 Dec 1828; William Floyd, bm;
David Laws, wit.

Parham, Lewis & Elizabeth Barnett, 22 June 1859; D. A. Paschall,
bm; m 26 June 1859 by J. S. Purifoy, Minister of the Gospel.

Parham, Lewis R. & Mary Hicks, 1 April 1835; Lewis W. Parham,
bm.

Parham, Lewis W. & Julian J. Howard, 7 Nov 1838; Joseph Howard,
bm.

Parham, Mark & Hannah Harris (freed people), 5 Aug 1865; A.
Landis, bm; m 6 Aug 1865 by Robt. S. Heflin, J. P.

Parham, Nathan & Ellen Young, colored, m 26 Dec 1866 by Joseph
W. Murphy, Rector of Holy Innocents, Henderson.

Parham, Richard & Rhoda Thomson, 26 Dec 1788; Ephraim Parham,
bm; A. Henderson, wit.

Parham, Rowland & Maria Parrish, 4 April 1829; William B. Parrish, bm; Wm. H. Owen, wit.

Parham, Rupert & Eliza A. Sadler, 21 June 1831; Edward Burton(?),
bm; David Laws, wit.

Parham, Samuel & Elizabeth Talley, 18 Dec 1810; Lewis Parham,
bm; W. M. Sneed, wit.

Parham, Samuel A. & Mary A. W. Upchurch, 2 July 1859; J. J.
Clark, bm; m 7 July 1859 by _____, J. P.

Parham, Saml. R., son of Lewis W. & Julie Ann Parham, & Martha
J. Eaks, daughter of Woodson & Jane Gilliam Eaks, 23 Nov
1868; m 1 Dec 1868 by R. J. Devin, M. G.

Parham, Thomas & Winefred Jett, 1 June 1782; Gedion Johnson,
bm; Bennet Searcy, wit.

Parham, Thomas & Agness Hicks, 19 April 1785; E---- Parham, bm;
B. Searcy, wit.

Parham, Thomas W. & Patsey Bearden, 24 July 1809; John Hawkins,
bm; W. M. Sneed, wit.

Parham, Thompson & Winea J. T. House, 19 Dec 1815; Asa Parham,
bm; W. M. Sneed, wit.

Parham, Thompson & Miss Elizabeth G. Briggs, 2 Dec 1819; John
Moore, bm; Z. Herndon, J. P., wit.

Parham, Thornton & Sarah Rogers, 20 Dec 1794; Thorp Parham, bm;
Step. Sneed, wit.

Parham, Thornton & Elizabeth Gregory, 6 Sept 1815; Thomas Atkins,
bm; John C. Smith, wit.

GRANVILLE MARRIAGES 1753-1868

Parham, Warner G. & Mary W. Higgs, 10 Nov 1831; Sothoron H. Thomasson, bm; Step. K. Sneed, wit.

Parham, William & Elizabeth Powell, 20 Sept 1853; Charles W. Parham, bm; m 22 Sept 1853 by L. R. Parham, J. P.

Parham, Wm. A. & Mary J. Cheatham, 19 Aug 1865; James A. Parham, bm.

Parham, Williamson & Judith Amis, 12 Dec 1807; Samuel Parham, bm; W. M. Sneed, wit.

Parham, Willie J. & Elizabeth Clark, 13 May 1815; Saml. LeMay, William Gilliam, bm; W. M. Sneed, wit.

Parham, Willis & Rosanna Alston (freed people), 13 May 1867, m by G. W. Ferrill, Minister.

Parish, Claibourne & Judith Parish, 6 Feb 1779; David Parish, bm; Reuben Searcy, wit.

Parish, David & Ellender Shemwell, 13 Dec 1787; Isaac Shemwell, bm; Reuben Searcy, wit.

Parish, Ellison & Tempy Harriss, 28 Oct 1817; Jesse Whitlow, bm; R. N. Herndon, wit.

Parish, George & Jane Brown, 24 June 1837; Hillyard Parish, bm; Jas. M. Wiggins, wit.

Parish, James W. & Mary E. Blackley, 14 Oct 1857; Thos. F. Brummett, bm; A. Landis, wit; m 15 Oct 1857 by D. P. Paschall, J. P.

Parish, John & Polley Harris, 26 Dec 1798; Archer Johnson, bm; Step. Sneed, wit.

Parish, Langford & Lidia Parham, 29 Dec 1802; Saml. Parham, bm; P. Bullock, wit.

Parish, Presley & Aggness Malory, 4 Aug 1818; Nathl. Robards, bm; James Wiggins, wit.

Parish, Ransom & Celia Goss, 18 March 1809; James Cooper, bm; W. M. Sneed, wit.

Parish, Sherwood & Dilly Parish, 17 Nov 1799; Valentine Parish, bm; James Sneed, wit.

Parish, Volentine & Betsey Parish, 23 Dec 1789; Wm. Parish, bm; A. Henderson, C. C., wit.

Parish, Woody & Beersheba Lumpkin, 6 May 1819; Solomon Satterwhite, bm; W. M. Sneed, wit.

Park, Robert & Sarah E. Long, 28 Sept 1809; James Vaughan, bm; A. H. Sneed, wit.

Parke, William & Sinah Perry, 31 Jan 1787; Thomas Willey, bm; Jno. Cooke, wit.

Parker, Alfred & Melvina Evans, 20 Nov 1854; Henry Parker, bm; A. Landis, wit; m 30 Nov 1854 by W. D. Allen, J. P.

GRANVILLE MARRIAGES 1753-1868

Parker, Cader & Phebah Wright, 25 Dec 1801; Jordan Wright, bm; P. Bullock, wit.

Parker, Cader & Nancey Adcock, 27 May 1809; Wm. Adcock, bm; W. M. Sneed, wit.

Parker, Cader & Jincy Tippet, 14 June 1813; Thomas D. Ridley, bm; Thos. J. Hicks, wit.

Parker, David & Cloe Adcock, 4 Jan 1792; Linem Adcock, bm; W. Norwood, wit.

Parker, Davy, of color, son of Davy & Lotty Parker, & Betsy Masenburg, daughter of Washington & Peggy Masenburg, m 19 Jan 1868 by W. D. Allen, J. P.

Parker, Elijah & Mary Harris, 3 Feb 1789; Jonathan Badgett, bm; Henry Potter, wit.

Parker, George & Lucy Wilkinson, 10 Dec 1789; Bowling Adcock, bm; A. Henderson, wit.

Parker, George & Piety Harris, 7 Aug 1792; Thomson Harris, bm; W. Norwood, wit.

Parker, Giles & Betsy Pettiford, 8 March 1862; Henry Parker, bm; A. Landis, wit; m 8 March 1862 by E. B. Lyon, J. P.

Parker, James A. & Elvira S. Wilson, 8 Oct 1865; Jas. R. Duty, bm; m 11 Oct 1865 by J. F. Harris, J. P.

Parker, Jepthah & Elisabeth Talley, 20 Dec 1783; Peter Badget, bm; Dennis Reardon, wit.

Parker, John Bunyan & Mary Ann Brandum, 9 June 1863; Giles Parker, bm; A. Landis, wit; m 16 June 1863 by E. B. Lyon, J. P.

Parker, Packaline & Rhoda Anderson, 8 May 1866; m 9 May 1866 by W. P. White, J. P.

Parker, Richard H. & Mollie L. Burwell, 4 Oct 1865; J. Beverly Hunter, bm; m 5 Oct 1865 by M. H. Vaughan, Rector of St. Stephen's Church.

Parker, Saml. & Lucy Harris, 14 Dec 1784; Saml. Harris, bm; Bennet Searcy, wit.

Parker, William & Emma Pettiford, 28 Aug 1863; Henry Parker, bm; m 29 Aug 1863 by E. B. Lyon, J. P.

Parkes, John & Jane Mailling, 26 Dec 1789; Robert Pretty, bm; Step. Sneed, wit.

Parks, John & Mary Lyle, 13 June 1826; Archer Cauthon, bm; S. K. Sneed, wit.

Parmer, William T. & Sarah J. Dickerson, 5 Dec 1862; James N. Crenshaw, bm; m 5 Dec 1862 by Jno. W. Stovall, J. P.

Parnell, Wm. W. & Mary M. Traylor, 25 July 1865; A. S. West, bm; A. Landis, wit; m 26 July 1865 by Wm. R. Hicks, J. P.

Parrish, Absolem Duke & Judy W. Roffe, 30 Jan 1817; Woodson Roffe, bm; Step. K. Sneed, wit.

GRANVILLE MARRIAGES 1753-1868

Parrish, Artemus, of color, son of Dunk Taborn & Lerty Parrish, & Mary Harris, daughter of Sim & Sallie Harris, 23 July 1868; m 25 July 1868 by E. J. Montague, M. G.

Parrish, Barsher & Sucky Highfield, 11 Dec 1803; Reubin Parrish, bm; A. H. Sneed, wit.

Parrish, Chas. H. & Ann E. Knight, 5 May 1845; Edwin W. Kittrell, bm.

Parrish, Charles T. & Ruthy Smith, 6 Aug 1850; Johnathan Woodlieff, bm.

Parrish, David & Peggy Volentine, 22 March 1817; William Beck, bm; Step. K. Sneed, wit.

Parrish, David & Lively Muller, 4 Feb 1828; Richd. H. Umstead, bm; David Laws, wit.

Parrish, Edward & Miss Mildred Bryant, 4 June 1829; William Dutton, bm.

Parrish, Elba L. & Harriet Ellington, 1 Dec 1836; Reuben Parrish, bm; J. M. Wiggins, wit.

Parrish, Elijah & Jane Spaigg, 29 Nov 1800; James Bradley, bm; P. Bullock, wit.

Parrish, Elijah & Gilla Clopton, 30 Sept 1851; A. Landis, Clk.; m 7 Oct 1851 by Saml. S. Hicks, J. P.

Parrish, Elijah S. & Gilla Clopton, 30 Sept 1851; F. Harrington, bm; A. Landis, wit.

Parrish, Erasmus & Seley M. Wheeler, 4 Aug 1829; Alfred Jones, bm; David Laws, wit.

Parrish, George & Happy Parrish, 1 Feb 1827; Reuben Parrish, bm; Step. K. Sneed, wit.

Parrish, Hilliard J. & Ava Jane Inscore, 15 Dec 1846; H. C. Lashly, bm.

Parrish, J. W., son of J. M. & N. A. Parrish, & Ellanoro A. Marshall, daughter of Wm. P. & Susan Marshall, 21 Aug 1867; m 21 Aug 1867 by E. L. Parrish, J. P.

Parrish, John & Elisabeth Suit, 13 Jan 1797(?); George Harrison, bm; Step. Sneed, wit.

Parrish, John & Nancy Howel, 15 July 1820; Bartlett Andrews, bm; Step. K. Sneed, wit.

Parrish, John M. & Julia E. Finch, 27 Feb 1861; John M. Ellington, bm; m 27 Feb 1861 by Wm. _____.

Parrish, Nelson & Martha Clay, 2 May 1843; B. C. Cozort, bm; Wm. H. Whitfield, wit.

Parrish, Nelson, son of David & Polly Parrish, & Mary Moore, daughter of Hesler & Ann Moore, 17 Dec 1867; m 25 Dec 1867 by F. J. Tilley, J. P.

Parrish, Nelson G. & Laura W. Hailey, 23 Jan 1866; Francis J. Tilley, bm.

GRANVILLE MARRIAGES 1753-1868

Parrish, Octon & Messa Starks, 21 July 1792; Volentine Parrish, bm; W. Norwood, wit.

Parrish, Pleasant & Salley Driskel, 22 May 1804; Auston Parrish, bm; A. W. Parham, wit.

Parrish, Presly & Nancy Alen, 8 July 1806; William Dodson, bm; Richd. Sneed, wit.

Parrish, Presly & Elizabeth Vincent, 18 Nov 1834; Fleming Lumpkim, bm; Benja. Kittrell, wit.

Parrish, Ralph & Mary Ann Upchurch, 10 Sept 1838; G. C. Wiggins, bm; S. G. Shearmon, wit.

Parrish, Robert & Lucy Demont, 11 Dec 1850; D. A. Paschall, bm; Sam. W. Dickerson, wit.

Parrish, Rubin & Elizabeth Hyfell, 1 Nov 1801; Brasy Parrish, bm; A. Sneed, wit.

Parrish, Samuel & Margaret Bryant, 11 May 1821; Gideon Davis, bm; Jas. M. Wiggins, wit.

Parrish, Shadrack & Betsey Smith, 16 Sept 1807; John Sears, bm; W. M. Sneed, wit.

Parrish, Sihon & Celia Robards, 9 Dec 1808; George Robarts, bm; W. M. Sneed, wit.

Parrish, Sion & Sarah Adams, 22 Nov 1823; Francis H. Worsham, bm; Jas. M. Wiggins, wit.

Parrish, Sterling L. & Lucy Ann Wright, 8 Aug 1865; A. Landis, bm.

Parrish, Thomas & Nancey Lankford, 1 June 1787; Stephen Lankford, bm; John Searcy Junr., wit.

Parrish, William & Sabey Parrish, 12 Jan 1781; William Desha, bm; Asa Searcy, wit.

Parrish, William & Polly Jones, 2 Nov 1820; John Jarret, bm; S. K. Sneed, wit.

Parrish, William & Elizabeth Hicks, 28 April 1827; John Jenkins (of William), bm; Step. K. Sneed, wit.

Parrish, William B. & Elizer Cheatham, 19 Dec 1833; Ralph J. Parrish, bm; S. Harris, wit.

Parrish, William & Sally Roberts, 3 Aug 1833; Alfred Jones, bm; Benja. Kittrell, wit.

Parrish, William & Agnis Hopkins, 14 Jan 1835; T. Lewis, bm; Benja. Kittrell, wit.

Parrish, William & Charlotte Roberts, 5 Nov 1847; William Suit, bm; Jas. M. Wiggins, wit.

Parrish, William S. & Mary A. W. Veazey, 3 Nov 1846; Moses H. Roberts, bm.

Parrish, Williamson & Isabella Clement, 29 Oct 1827; James T. Terry, bm; David Laws, wit.

GRANVILLE MARRIAGES 1753-1868

Parrish, Willis & Mary Smith, 27 Aug 1809; Thomas White, bm; A. H. Sneed, wit.

Parrot, Henry F. & Mary Jane Brummet, 27 May 1843; David B. Allen, bm; J. M. Wiggins, wit.

Parrot, James & Eliza Miller, 21 June 1848; Jas. M. Wiggins, bm.

Parrot, Thomas & Susan Evans, 29 Aug 1821; Lemuel McGehee, bm; Jas. M. Wiggins, wit.

Parrott, James & Ailsey Cooke, 12 Dec 1829; Step. K. Sneed, bm.

Parrott, Jas. & Salley Cooke, 13 Aug 1822; Willis Nailing, bm; Jas. M. Wiggins, wit.

Parrott, James P. & Nancy Hester, 8 May 1867; m 12 May 1867 by E. F. Beachum, R. G. Minister.

Parrott, Levinous & Cynthia Ann Hays, 10 Apr 1865; L. D. McMahan, bm; A. Landis, wit; m 20 April 1865 by R. J. Mitchell, J. P.

Parrott, Mark E. & Meriah Caroline Brummitt, 29 Jan 1853; A. Landis, bm.

Parrott, Nathaniel & Mary Glover, 15 March 1784; Nathaniel Norwood, bm; Reuben Searcy, wit.

Parrott, William & Mary Fleeman, 29 Dec 1796; Robert Hargrove, bm; Step. Sneed, wit.

Parsh, Jonathan & Keziah Fuller, 17 Dec 1794; James Laurence, bm; Step. Sneed, wit.

Partee, Abner & Polley Shearman, 7 Nov 1797; Earbe Partee, bm; Step. Sneed, wit.

Partee, Benjamin & Elisabeth Grigg, 19 Dec 1775; Edmund Partee, bm; Abraham Potter, wit.

Partee, Henderson & Dinecy Shearman, 22 May 1818; John Shearman, bm; Step. K. Sneed, wit.

Partee, Lockhart & Marshy Dickens, 27 Jan 1813; Henry Chambless, bm; Thos. J. Hicks, wit.

Partin, Sam B. & Elizabeth R. Cobb, 21 Aug 1865; Thos. A. Park, bm; m 21 Aug 1865 by R. H. Kingsbury, J. P.

Paschal, James O'Kelly & Francis J. Clibourne, 23 Sept 1854; W. A. Chapman, bm; m 23 Sept 1854 by C. R. Eaton, J. P.

Paschal, Silas & Jina Taylor, 18 Sept 1787; John Holt, bm; John Searcy, wit.

Paschall, Anderson & Mary Harris, 25 Oct 1820; Richd. Sneed, bm; S. K. Sneed, wit.

Paschall, D. A. & Ann R. Hicks, 9 Sept 1836; Alfred Knight, bm; J. M. Wiggins, wit.

Paschall, Daniel & Sarah Wood, 15 Oct 1824; John Moore, bm; S. K. Sneed, wit.

GRANVILLE MARRIAGES 1753-1868

Paschall, Dennis & Sally W. Hilyard, 19 Jan 1824; Thos. W. Norman, bm; Wm. H. Owen, wit.

Paschall, Donaldson P. & Lettica Hicks, 16 Oct 1830; Isham Cheatham, bm; David Laws, wit.

Paschall, Edward & Viney Venable, freed people, 31 Aug 1866.

Paschall, Edwin & Harriet W. Hillyard, 25 Dec 1822; Leslie Gilliam, bm; Tho. M. Norman, wit.

Paschall, Edwin P. & Mary E. Kittrell, 12 June 1848; Henry C. Herndon, bm.

Paschall, Henderson, colored, son of Luke & Dilly Paschall & Emely Montague, daughter of Umphry Montague, 24 Nov 1868; m 25 Nov 1868 by G. W. Ferrill, Minister.

Paschall, Isaiah M. & Virginia C. Yancey, 1 Sept 1840; J. Abbot, bm; Jas. M. Wiggins, wit.

Paschall, James & Candess Welden, 15 June 1824; Matthew Blalock, bm; Step. K. Sneed, wit.

Paschall, James P. & Lucy T. Paschall, 14 March 1859; Geo. B. Reavis, bm; m 15 March 1859 by L. K. Willie, M. G.

Paschall, Jesse (Jyse) & Mary Freeman, 26 Aug 1819; William D. Paschall, bm; W. M. Sneed, wit.

Paschall, Jesse M. & Martha Garrett, 17 Jan 1856; John E. Mitchell, bm; A. Landis, wit; m 20 Feb 1856 by B. R. Hester.

Paschall, John & Elizabeth Ann Ross, 5 Dec 1837; Josephus Moss, bm; J. M. Wiggins, wit.

Paschall, John & Mary Shadrick, 28 Aug 1851; William F. Freeman, bm.

Paschall, Jno. Wm. H. & Mary A. Rideout, 30 June 1864; m 30 June 1864 by J. H. Wheeler, M. M. E. C. S., Ridgeway, N. C.

Paschall, Junius & Ellen J. Forrest, 24 Nov 1854; Henry C. Herndon, bm; m 6 Dec 1854 by Rev, John H. Pickard.

Paschall, L. A. & Fannie B. Landis, 31 Jan 1865; R. A. Hunt, bm; m 31 Jan 1865 by Maurice H. Vaughan, Rector of St. Stephen's Church.

Paschall, Lunsford A. & Cary Ann Taylor, 10 Aug 1829; Nathan Dabney, bm; Step. K. Sneed, wit.

Paschall, Masey & Maney Mangum, 26 Jan 1836; John Paschall, bm; Benja. Kittrell, wit.

Paschall, Richard & Martha Rochelle, 11 Dec 1829; Joseph Perkinson, bm; Step. K. Sneed, wit.

Paschall, Richard & Martha Heggs, 31 Dec 1833; James Paschal, bm; Benja. Kittrell, wit.

Paschall, Robert & Sophia Wagstaff, 7 April 1849; Jno. Y. Smith, bm; J. M. Wiggins, wit.

GRANVILLE MARRIAGES 1753-1868

Paschall, Robert & Barbary A. Smith, 29 July 1854; L. B. Kittle, bm; m 5 Sept 1854 by B. B. Hester, J. P.

Paschall, Silas & Winney Mayfield, 8 Aug 1800; James Burchet, bm; W. M. Sneed, wit.

Paschall, William H. & Judith W. Parham, 19 Jan 1837; S. W. Dunston, bm; J. M. Wiggins, wit.

Paschall, William H. & Tyson Qualls, 31 Dec 1846; Frances Allen, bm; Jas. M. Wiggins, wit.

Paschall, Wm. V. & Mary A. Spencer, 28 July 1847; R. W. Lassiter, bm; Jas. M. Wiggins, wit.

Paschall, Zebulon M. & Eliza C. Spencer, 25 Oct 1837; Jas. A. Russell, bm; Jas. M. Wiggins, wit.

Paskill, Silas & Eliza Blalock, 6 Nov 1792; James Paskill, bm; W. Norwood, wit.

Patient, Job & Rhodey Grisham, 30 Oct 1798; Leonard Cardwell, bm; W. M. Sneed, wit.

Patillo, Anderson & Cathrine Harper, 20 Oct 1792; Robt. Hyde, bm; Step. Sneed, wit.

Patillo, John F. & Ann Webb, 22 Sept 1808; Wm. Pattillo, bm; James B. Jones, Robt. Pattillo, wit.

Patterson, Andrew & Elisabeth White, 3 Feb 1813; Jonathan Higgs, bm.

Patterson, Charles G. & Lucy C. Fleming, 25 Dec 1869; m 25 Dec 1869 by John F. Harris, J. P.

Patterson, Hardy & Lucy Rice, 26 Aug 1837; Math. Weathers, bm; Jas. M. Wiggins, wit.

Patterson, James & Elisabeth Jones, 10 Feb 1786; William Laurence, bm; Bennet Searcy, wit.

Patterson, James B. & Eliza Stovall, 16 Aug 1824; Hardy Patterson, bm; A. Sneed, wit.

Patterson, James W. & Martha A. May, 12 Oct 1861; Eugene Grissom, bm.

Patterson, John H. & Susan Rowland, 16 April 1845; D. T. Barket, bm.

Patterson, Robert A. & Indianna Boyd, 21 July 1852; W. W. Young Jr., bm.

Patterson, Thomas & Martha Fleming, 15 Dec 1839; Kizah J. Stark, bm; J. M. Wiggins, wit.

Pattillo, George & Nancy Hart, freed people, m 26 Dec 1866 by James E. Pattillo, J. P.

Pattillo, Wm. J. & Dianna M. Harper, 21 Dec 1794; L. Henderson, bm; H. Seawell, wit.

Patton, James & Mary Nuttall, 6 May 1825; M. N. Henderson, bm; L. Gilliam, wit.

GRANVILLE MARRIAGES 1753-1868

Patton, James A. & Isabella Nuttall, 7 Dec 1858; A. Landis, bm; m 7 Dec 1858 by A. H. Cooke, J. P.

Patton, William C. & Isabella G. A. Nuttall, 27 Sept 1830; John Blacknall, bm; David Laws, wit.

Peace, Abner & Lucy Williams, 27 Dec 1809; William Peace, bm; Stephen Sneed Jun., wit.

Peace, Anderson & Judith McGehee, 26 Dec 1832; W. D. Allen, bm; S. K. Sneed, wit.

Peace, Harry, of color, son of Polbus & Martha Peace, & Maria Kittrell, daughter of John & Peggy Kittrell, 6 Feb 1868; m 8 Feb 1868 by J. H. Riddick.

Peace, Henry & Frances Spears(?), 13 Feb 1814; Parker F. Stone, bm; W. M. Sneed, wit.

Peace, James & Eliza Cooke, 18 Dec 1814; James Jenkins, bm; Step. K. Sneed, wit.

Peace, John & Betty Smith, 9 May 1795; John Finch, bm; H. Seawell, wit.

Peace, John & Eady Winston, 4 May 1830; Daniel Grisham, bm; David Laws, wit.

Peace, John C. & Emily Kittrell, 29 Oct 1842; John B. Moore, bm; J. M. Wiggins, wit.

Peace, John M. & Frances Maria Reed, 31 July 1810; W. M. Sneed, wit.

Peace, Joseph & Elizabeth Corthan, 7 Oct 1799; Samuel Peace, bm; W. M. Sneed, wit.

Peace, Joseph & Elizabeth Brummitt, 18 Dec 1830; Cleary(?) Dement, bm; David Laws, wit.

Peace, Meredith & Seley Cauthen, 19 Nov 1801; Samuel Peace, bm; Junius Sneed, wit.

Peace, Peter, colored, son of Benj. Blacknall & Cely Peace, & Jacksey Person, daughter of Tom Person & Winnie Johnson, 28 Doc 1868; m 29 Dec 1868 by Moses J. Hunt, M. G.

Peace, Pleasant & Peggy Reed, 21 Dec 1808; John G. Murphey, bm; W. M. Sneed, wit.

Peace, Samuel & Charity Parham, 4 Nov 1800; N. Wood, bm; Step. Sneed, wit.

Peace, Thomas & Elizabeth Vass, 31 Jan 1832; Henry McDaniel, bm.

Peace, William & Lenney Stalings, 20 Jan 1814; Noble Ladd, bm; H. Young, wit.

Peace, William & Charity Winston, 3 Feb 1834; John E. Peace, bm; Benja. Kittrell, wit.

Peace, Wm. H. & Lucy Walker, 23 Nov 1801; Jno. M. Peace, bm; Phil Bullock, wit.

GRANVILLE MARRIAGES 1753-1868

Peace, William J. & Sarah A. Cheatham, 28 Nov 1859; J. M. Hockaday, bm; m 12 Dec 1859 by J. W. Floyd, Minister.

Peace, William K. & Mary A. Nevill, 18 Nov 1857; James N. Peace, bm.

Peak, Gilford & Holand Perry, 25 Nov 1866; m by A. S. Davis, J.P.

Peak, Philip R. & Rowan Duke, _____; W. P. S. Slaughter, bm.

Pearce, Herod & Sarah Hester, 4 Nov 1817; Robert Hester, bm; S. K. Sneed, wit.

Pearce, Wesley & Frances Lowery, 28 Dec 1861; W. D. Bailey, bm.

Pearce, Wesley & Francis Lowry, 29 Dec 1865; m by Wm. D. Davis, J. P.

Pearce, Willis & Frances Johnson, 22 Feb 1854; Thomas W. Bragg, bm.

Peck, David & Leacey Garner, 6 Feb 1798; Elijah Green bm; Step. Sneed, wit.

Peck, Philip & Mary H. Duncan, 16 May 1835; Sterling H. Duncan, bm; Howel G. Pittard, wit.

Pedefoot, Pomphret & Ann Curtis, 11 Dec 1862; Thos. Kinton, bm; m 11 Dec 1862 by Thos. Hester, J. P.

Peed, David & Elizabeth Adcock, 8 Sept 1818; David Adcock, bm.

Peed, Jesse & Rebecca Hudgings, 10 May 1859; G. W. Peed, bm.

Peed, Shermon & Malinda Falkner, 9 Jan 1847; Henry Parrish, bm; J. M. Wiggins, wit.

Peed, Thomas & Elizabeth Shearman, 12 Dec 1812; Jeremiah Roberts, bm; Stephen D. Sneed, wit.

Peed, William H. & Virginia Waller, 10 Nov 1865; Francis J. Tilley, bm; m 16 Nov 1865 by Francis J. Tilley, J. P.

Peede, William & Elizabeth Mize, 21 June 1821; John Shearman, bm; Sam. F. Sneed, wit.

Peek, Robert & Nancy Ansley, 11 Feb 1790; Ellis West, bm; Henry Potter, wit.

Peek, William Burford & Elisabeth Griggs, 14 July 1796; Bryon Stonum, bm; Step. Sneed, wit.

Peel, John & Margaret Howell, 22 Nov 1865; Henry Berry, bm; m 23 Nov 1865 by B. T. Winston, J. P.

Peel, Joseph & Jane Pettiford, 18 May 1822; Willis Bass, bm; Jas. M. Wiggins, wit.

Peel, Josiah & Margaret Garrott, 31 Aug 1853; m 1 Sept 1853.

Pegram, George W. & Mary Watkins, 22 Dec 1856; James M. Vaughan, bm; m 24 Dec 1856 by Wm. Holmes.

Pegram, John J. & Ella Reavis, 31 July 1865; R. L. Harris, bm; m 1 Aug 1865 by H. H. Rowland, J. P.

GRANVILLE MARRIAGES 1753-1868

Pemberton, Smith, of color, son of Edmund & Hester Pemberton & Rebecca Gilliam, daughter of Mima Kittrell, 4 Aug 1867; m 15 Aug 1867 by M. H. Vaughan, Rector of St. Stephen's Church.

Penerton, Junius & Frances M. Minor, 28 Dec 1831; William J. Mallory, bm; Step. K. Sneed, wit.

Penney, Joseph & Huldy F. Jackson, 1 Dec 1841; F. Keith, Wesley Keith, bm; J. M. Wiggins, wit.

Penny, Ezekiel & Catharine Winston, 19 Jan 1835; John D. Peace, bm; Benja. Kittrell, wit.

Perdue, Macon L. & Lucy V. Harris, 16 Jan 1844; Thos. H. Cristmus, bm; Jas. M. Wiggins, wit.

Perdue, Macon L. & Elizabeth H. Stone, 5 Nov 1853; Jas. L. Reid, bm; m 9 Nov 1853 by A. C. Harris, M. G.

Perdue, Robert & Ann Faulkner, 9 Dec 1857; James H. Ball, bm; m 9 Dec 1857 by A. C. Harris, M. G.

Perdue, Roland & Martha Weaver, 15 Nov 1817; Samuel Edwards, bm; A. Sneed, wit.

Pergason, Seth & Mary Hicks, 22 Nov 1843; Gilford Ellington, bm; Wm. H. Whitfield, wit.

Perkerson, Joseph & Unity Paschall, 11 Jan 1823; Wills B. Traylor, bm; L. Gilliam, wit.

Perkins, J. H., son of William Perkins & Mrs. Mary A. Parker, & India F. Turner, daughter of the late H. H. Turner & Mrs. Mary A. Turner, m 22 Jan 1868 by Joseph H. Riddick.

Perkinson, Henry & Sarah Jane Collins, 5 Sept 1862; D. A. H. Hays, bm.

Perkinson, John & Emily Dement, 1 Oct 1846; Robert Paschal, bm; Jas. A. Wiggins, wit.

Perkinson, Ransom & Pricilla Powell, 13 Jan 1834; John Prewit, bm; Benja. Kittrell, wit.

Perkinson, Seth & Mary Wilson, 19 Dec 1814; John Reeks, bm; Spencer OBrien, wit.

Perkinson, Ransom & Martha Moss, 19 July 1851; Charles Moss, bm; B. C. Cooke, wit.

Perkinson, Ransom & L. Martha Moss, m 29 July 1851 by D. J. Paschall, J. P.

Perkinson, Robert & Louisa Wagstaff, 23 June 1858; G. A. Dement, bm; m 6 July 1858 by B. B. Hester.

Perkinson, Travis & Elizabeth Parham, 7 May 1817; Ransom Walker, bm; A. Sneed, wit.

Perry, Alston, of color, son of Henry Jones & Harriet Perry, & Mary Sutton, daughter of Harry Powel & Julia Sutton, m 25 Sept 1867 by W. H. P. Jenkins, J. P.

Perry, Booth & Mary Fuller, 1 Feb 1763; Joseph Johnson, bm; Jno. Bowie, wit.

GRANVILLE MARRIAGES 1753-1868

Perry, Calvin & Mahalia Fuller, 25 June 1833; Hilliard Welch, bm; David Laws, wit.

Perry, Charles & Elisabeth Burton, 5 March 1851; Isaac M. Davis, bm.

Perry, Elijah, son of Thomas & Maria Perry, & Mary Emma Jones, daughter of Jubal R. & Cynthia A. Jones, m 3 Nov 1867 by Eugene Grissom, J. P.

Perry, Jasiel H. & Sally W. Godden, 5 March 1835; Jas. Blackley, bm.

Perry, Jesse & Sally Tarver, 21 Dec 1806; John Snipes, bm; W. M. Sneed, wit.

Perry, John & Nancy Brogdon, 11 Feb 1831; Michael Beck, bm; David Laws, wit.

Perry, John R. & Sarah E. Coley, 6 Dec 1860; m 13 Dec 1860 by Jas. W. Dalby, J. P.

Perry, John W. & Sarah F. Mitchell, 16 Sept 1865; Samuel H. Perry, bm; m 21 Sept 1865 by B. B. Hester.

Perry, Jordan & Elizabeth Barr, 30 Dec 1818; David J. Young, bm; Step. K. Sneed, wit.

Perry, Joshua & Martha Crudup, 3 May 1842; J. H. Davis, bm; Wm. H. Whitfield, wit.

Perry, Minton L. & Martha Williams, 13 Dec 1852; Clinton H. Perry, bm.

Perry, Peter & Nancey Perry, 28 Feb 1783; John Amos, bm; Bartlet Searcy, wit.

Perry, Peter & Sarah Harris, 8 Nov 1837; Thos. Harris, bm.

Perry, Samuel H. & Sarah E. Perry, 15 March 1866; R. H. Hobgood, bm; m 22 March 1866 by R. H. Hobgood, J. P.

Perry, Solomon & Catharine Beck, 28 Sept 1838; John Byrd, bm.

Perry, Stephen & Anney Clement, 4 Feb 1783; Samuel Clement, bm; Sherwood Harris, wit.

Perry, Thomas & Linna Brogdon, 2 Jan 1836; Robt. Harris, bm; Benja. Kittrell, wit.

Perry, Thomas & Mariah Beck, 18 Dec 1841; J. B. Barnett, bm; J. M. Wiggins, wit.

Perry, Willie L. G. & Martha B. Brogden, 1 Sept 1859; Jos. C. Davis, bm; m 5 Sept 1859 by R. B. Hester.

Perry, Zachariah & Rebecca Mitchell, 16 April 1866; m 16 April 1866 by Thos. B. Lyon.

Person, Archibald & Dicey Culbrath, 28 Dec 1829; Peyton West, bm; S. K. Sneed, wit.

Person, Benjamin F. & Margarett J. Stegall, 24 Dec 1857; Job Osborn, bm; A. Landis, wit; m 24 Dec 1857 by Thos. U. Faucette, Minister of the Gospel.

GRANVILLE MARRIAGES 1753-1868

Person, Gilbert, of color, son of Richard Person & Lindy Manning, & Martha Thomas, daughter of Haywood & Serry Thomas, m 4 Oct 1867 by W. H. P. Jenkins, J. P.

Person, Thomas & Joana Thomas, 24 June 1765; Philip Taylor, bm; Sam. Clay, Thomas Sanders, wit.

Person, William Jr. & Martha Eaton, 27 Sept 1759; Thos. Lowe, bm; Jno. Bowie, wit.

Petegrew, Hans & Elisabeth Edy, 19 May 1781; Nathanel Clark, bm; Asa Searcy, wit.

Peters, Luther C. & Sallie J. Speed, 7 March 1854; A. Landis, bm; m 17 May 1852 by E. Hines, Minister of the Gospel.

Peterson, Roberson & Lucy Ann Parker, 11 March 1865; Henry Parker, bm; m ____ March 1865 by E. B. Lyon, J. P. (license has groom as Isham Peterson).

Petteford, Austin & Oliver Evans, 31 Dec 1814; James Dorom, bm; Step. Sneed, wit.

Petteford, Moses & Sally Hawley, 24 March 1816; Franklin Satterwhite, bm; Richd. Sneed, wit.

Petteford, William H. & Avarilla Guy, 7 April 1842; Thomas Petteford, bm; Wm. H. Whitfield, wit.

Pettegrew, James & Elisabeth Jarrett, 14 Sept 1796; Peyton Maderson, bm; M. Bullock, wit.

Pettey, Joseph & Lucy Brinkley, 7 Nov 1797; Joseph Hart, bm; Step. Sneed, wit.

Pettiford, Allsey & Eliza Jefferson, 16 Jan 1833; Wm. Conyers, bm; David Laws, wit.

Pettiford, Anderson & Anny Anderson, 4 Dec 1817; Horace Anderson, bm; Leslie Gilliam, wit.

Pettiford, Colins, of color, son of William & Susan Pettiford, & Eliza Pain, parents unknown, 17 Sept 1868; m 17 Sept 1868 by M. H. Vaughan, Rector of St. Stephen's Church.

Pettiford, Collin & Polly Chavis, 16 June 1802; Leonard Cardwell, bm; Junius Sneed, wit.

Pettiford, Drury & Tycey Bass, 12 Nov 1781; Right Bass, bm; Bennet Searcy, wit.

Pettiford, Edmund & Rebecca Johnson, 19 March 1832; George Anderson, bm; David Laws, wit.

Pettiford, Evans & Martha Brandum, 30 Sept 1840; Abram Plenty, bm; J. M. Wiggins, wit.

Pettiford, George & Taby Johnson, 1 May 1837; Edmond Pettiford, bm; G. C. Wiggins, wit.

Pettiford, Lewis & Elisabeth Sweat, 2 Jan 1788; Elias Petteford, bm; Asa Searcy, wit.

Pettiford, Lewis & Disey Bass, 23 Dec 1809; Elijah Valentine, bm; W. M. Sneed, wit.

Pettiford, Lewis & Matilda Paschall, 4 July 1846; Richd. Mayhoe, bm; J. M. Wiggins, wit.

Pettiford, Meredith & Ann Tylor, 6 Aug 1818; Littleton Mitchel, bm; R. N. Herndon, wit.

Pettiford, Minniard & Beady Pettiford, 1 April 1865; Henry Parker, bm; A. Landis, wit; m 2 April 1865 by E. B. Lyon, J. P.

Pettiford, Reuben & Parky Jones, 27 Oct 1812; Robert Jones, bm; W. M. Sneed, wit.

Pettiford, Reuben & Rebecca Ann Chavis, 1 Sept 1836; Littleton Mitchell, bm; J. M. Wiggins, wit.

Pettiford, Solomon & Henrietta Evans, 5 Feb 1865; Jas. R. Duty, bm; m 6 Feb 1865 by Jas. R. Duty, J. P.

Pettiford, Stephen & Mary Cozens, 16 March 1824; Robert Roach, bm; Wm. H. Owen, wit.

Pettiford, Tharington Y. & Elizabeth Hookram(?), 13 Sept 1852; Arthur Tabern, bm; A. Landis, wit.

Pettiford, Thomas & Patsey Tyner, 1 Sept 1807; Jonathan Tyner, bm; Jun. Sneed, wit.

Pettiford, Thomas & Polly Parker, 17 Jan 1829; Joseph Peal, bm; David Laws, wit.

Pettiford, Thomas & Faithy Anderson, 4 June 1839; Major Evans, bm; J. M. Wiggins, wit.

Pettiford, William & Rosa Durham, 30 Dec 1822; John Durham, bm; W. Sneed, wit.

Pettiford, William & Susan Brandom, 3 Jan 1846; Sterling Chavis, bm; Jas. M. Wiggins, wit.

Pettifort, Collins & Hopsey Kersey, 17 Dec 1837; Joseph Beal, bm; M. D. Royster, wit.

Pettigrue, John & Lear Owins, 21 Feb 1800; Reuben Baxter, bm; Philip Bullock, wit.

Pettipool, Logustin & Patsey Satterwhite, 28 July 1794; Smith Satterwhite, bm; H. Seawell, wit.

Pettit, John & Betsy Kennon, 4 Dec 1787; Robert Lewis, bm; Elizabeth Lany, wit.

Pettus, George & Mary L. Daniel, 9 July 1866; James Warren, bm; L. B. Stone, wit; m 9 July 1866 by L. B. Stone, J. P.

Petty, Rasha & Mary Hart, 29 Sept 1795; Gideon Williams, bm; Step. Sneed, wit.

Pettygrew, Charles & Elizabeth Cash, 6 Dec 1810; Henry Going, bm; Fanny M. Sneed, wit.

Pettypool--see also Pool

Pettypool, Caldwell & Patsey Pettypool, 21 Jan 1808; Seth P. Pool, bm; Thos. Falconer, wit.

GRANVILLE MARRIAGES 1753-1868

Pettypool, Logustine & Letty Wilkerson, 18 July 1805; Thomas Knott, bm; Jas. Sneed, wit.

Pettypool, Philip & Anna Winfrey, 7 April 1808; Collins Winfree, bm; Thos. Falconer, wit.

Pettypool, William & Frances Owen, 6 Feb 1797; Stephen Satterwhite, bm; M. Satterwhite, Mitchel Satterwhite, wit.

Pewit, John & Elizabeth Bradford, 28 Aug 1769; John Bradford, bm; Jesse Benton, wit; consent from Thos. Bradford, father of Elizabeth, 21 Aug 1769.

Peyear, Samuel & Sarah Newton, 5 Dec 1844; James Newton, bm; T. B. Barnett, wit.

Peyton, Puryear & Frances Amis, 5 Nov 1822; Stephen Melton, bm; Jas. M. Wiggins, wit.

Peyton, Thomas & Rachal Rogers, 8 Oct 178_; William Rogers, bm; Asa Searcy, wit.

Philips, Bennet & Ezebell Moore, 10 Feb 1786; James Haskins, bm; Bennet Searcy, wit.

Philips, Howel & Susan A. Wilson, 5 Feb 1866; L. Wilson, bm; A. Landis, wit.

Philips, James & Martha Culbreath, 17 April 1843; Allen Tilletson, bm; W. S. Hargrove, wit.

Philips, William & Mary Culbreth, 24 Jan 1834; Francis Wilson, bm; S. Harris, wit.

Phillips, Albert H. & Jane E. Hutcherson, 6 Jan 1831; Geo. Floyd, bm; Step. K. Sneed, wit.

Phillips, Benjamin & Mary Woodliff, 23 July 1839; Joel Merritt, bm; J. M. Wiggins, wit.

Phillips, David & Susannah Mangum(?), 5 Nov 1793; Jonathan Harris, bm; W. Norwood, D. C., wit.

Phillips, Francis B. & Mahaley Bledsoe, 18 Sept 1813; Jechonias Bledsoe, bm; W. M. Sneed, wit.

Phillips, Nelson & Susan Lemay, 29 Oct 1828; Saml. L. Holt, bm; Step. K. Sneed, wit.

Phillips, Thos. H. & Susannah Hanks, 10 Dec 1794; Wm. Pattillo, Leonard Henderson, bm; H. Seawell, wit.

Phillips, William & Nancy Phillips, 22 Dec 1822; James M. Coley, bm; (uncertain as to which is groom and which is bm); James M. Wiggins, wit.

Phillips, Zachariah & Sally Phillips, 31 Dec 1834; Warren Hester, bm; Benja. Kittrell, wit.

Philpott, Edward, of color, son of Amy Philpott & Fannie Russell, daughter of Joe & Patsy Russell, m 1 Aug 1867 by W. T. Winston, J. P.

Philpott, Grandison & Elizabeth Clements, 25 Jan 1825; Solomon Philpott, bm; Step. K. Sneed, wit.

GRANVILLE MARRIAGES 1753-1868

Philpott, John & Mary Thomas, 11 March 1805; William Penn, bm; Jas. Sneed, wit.

Philpott, Lindon S. & Nancy S. Clement, 15 May 1846; J. H. Gooch, bm.

Philpott, Thomas & Mimah Cozart, 9 Aug 1799; John Philpott, bm; Step. Sneed, wit.

Philpott, William A. & Mary Puryear, 1 May 1839; Lindon S. Philpott, bm.

Philpott, William A. & Ann T. Puryear, 15 Oct 1853; Joseph H. Gooch, bm; m 17 Oct 1853 by G. W. Ferrill.

Physioc, Jas. E. & Miss Mary F. Bennett, 12 Jan 1859; Louis J. Peoples, bm; W. M. Sneed, J. P.; m 12 Jan 1859 by W. M. Sneed, J. P.

Pierce, James T. & Elizabeth Jane Bragg, 20 Dec 1860; W. D. Laws, bm.

Pigott, Jennings & Ann Eliza Moseley, 26 Nov 1857; Thomas N. Griffin, bm; A. Landis, wit; m 3 Dec 1857 by E. Hines.

Piles, Reuben & Elesh Rogester, 13 Nov 1770; Thomas Critcher, bm; Michael Wilson, wit.

Pinson, Zachariah & Sally Phillips, 31 Dec 1834; Warren Hester, bm; Benja. Kittrell, wit.

Piper, Nathan H. & Lucy A. Cozort, 21 May 1866; m by T. J. Horner, 22 May 1866.

Piper, Wesley Y. & Cornelia P. Hutcherson, 22 Sept 1858; Wm. L. Bledsoe, bm; m 22 Sept 1858 by Gaston Farrar, G. M.

Pitchford, Daniel & Rebecca Davis, 31 Dec 1786; Augustin Davis, bm; Robert Searcy, wit.

Pitchford, Wesley B. & Nancy Norwood, 5 March 1827; Thomas Barnett, bm.

Pitchford, William J. & Sally Philpott, 17 Nov 1863; L. A. Paschall, bm; m 17 Nov 1863 by L. K. Willie, M. G.

Pittard, Elijah & Barshaba Hays, 16 Dec 1805; Williamson Wynne, bm; A. H. Sneed, wit.

Pittard, George & Elizabeth R. Shanks, 2 Nov 1846; Young MaC. Montague, bm; Jas. M. Wiggins, wit.

Pittard, Grandison & Elizabeth Wagstaff, 14 Oct 1835; L. Gilliam, bm.

Pittard, James M. & Sarah F. Montague, 14 Dec 1853; Wm. T. Hodges, bm; m 14 Dec 1853 by R. J. Devin, V. D. M.

Pittard, James M. & Francis A. Montague, 13 Dec 1859; A. Landis, bm; m 13 Dec 1859 by E. F. Beachum, a regular Minister of the Gospel.

Pittard, John W. & Martha Montague, 14 Dec 1841; John Brummet Jr., bm.

GRANVILLE MARRIAGES 1753-1868

Pittard, John Jr. & Dolley Graves, 24 Dec 1804; Nathaniel Graves, bm.

Pittard, Thomas J. & Ann W. Royster, 6 Sept 1843; A. M. Cloy, bm; Wm. H. Whitfield, wit.

Pittard, William & Maria Weaver, 11 Jan 1832; W. B. Ellington, bm; David Laws, wit.

Pittiard, Abner & Fanny Hightour, 25 Dec 1811; Samuel Pittiard, bm; Stephen K. Sneed, wit.

Pitts, Pitmon & Polly C. Andrews, 7 Sept 1811; John Smith, bm.

Pleasant, John L. & Cornelia Lawrence, 13 Sept 1862; m 14 Sept 1862 by R. B. Hester.

Pleasants, James & Martha Mayes, 7 Oct 1844; John J. Bobbitt, bm; Jas. M. Wiggins, wit.

Pleasants, Thomas T. & Susan Jane Parham, 11 Oct 1852; Archd. H. Upchurch, bm; A. Landis, wit; m 18 Oct 1852 by D. J. Paschall, J. P.

Pleasants, William & Malinda S. Powell, 1 Aug 1865; L. K. Willie, bm.

Pleasants, William B. & Angelina Hicks, 29 Dec 1846; C. H. Wiley, bm.

Pledger, Murrel & Elizabeth Thomas, 23 Dec 1791; Jonathan McKissack, bm; W. Norwood, wit.

Pledger, Thomas & Nancy Leaverton, 15 March 1785; James Leaverton, bm; Bennet Searcy, wit.

Plenty, Abraham & Fanny Fuller, 11 April 1829; George Anderson, bm; Step. K. Sneed, wit.

Plenty, Abraham & Ruthy Valentine, 16 May 1836; J. Orsborn, bm; J. M. Wiggins, wit.

Plummer, Ezekiah & Susannah Speers, 13 Dec 1801; Joseph Rogers, bm; A. H. Sneed, wit.

Plummer, Kemp & Susannah Martain, 30 Sept 1794; Benjamin Moss, bm; B. Davis, wit.

Plummer, Thomas & Pencey Booker, 14 Dec 1800; John Wilson, bm.

Poindexter, Francis & Jane Lanier, 26 May 1786; Henry Pattillo, bm; William Pattillo, wit.

Pollard, Major, of Wake County, & Charity Jones, 4 April 1778; Woodson Daniel, bm; Reuben Searcy, wit.

Pollard, Major & Susannah Davis, 2 Dec 1818; John Holloway, bm; Step. K. Sneed, wit.

Pollard, William & Phereby Jones, 10 Dec 1784; James Smith, bm; David Mason, wit.

Pollard, Willie & Anny Davis, 6 Aug 1816; John Enry, bm; Rhodes Herndon, wit.

GRANVILLE MARRIAGES 1753-1868

Pool--see also Pettypool

Pool, Burgess & Sarah Clardy, 20 Nov 1811; Thos. Murrey, bm; Step. Sneed, wit.

Pool, Leonidas & Melcene Dent, 28 July 1858; C. H. Perry, bm; m 1 Aug 1858 by James S. Purefoy, Baptist Minister.

Pool, Spencer P. & Martha P. Pool, 9 Sept 1858; R. P. Wilbourn, bm; A. Landis, wit; m 9 Sept 1858 by L. B. Stone, J. P.

Pool, Thomas & Nancy Duncan, 6 Jan 1815; John Ricks, bm; Step. Sneed, wit.

Pool, Thomas W. & Sarah D. Hicks, 18 Oct 1845; John F. Sandford, bm; Jas. M. Wiggins, wit.

Pool, William & Elizabeth Stovall, spinster, aged 20 years, 15 Dec 1760; Bartlet Yancey, bm.

Pope, John & Martha Carey, 6 Jan 1857; A. Landis, bm.

Potter, Archibald & Lemender Harris, 5 June 1795; Thomas Potter, bm; Step. Sneed, wit.

Potter, Henry & Patsey Moore, 11 Jan 1794; William Norwood, bm; Leon. Henderson, wit.

Potter, Jordan & Harriett Lewis, 27 Oct 1865; m 27 Oct 1865 by Thomas A. Faucette, M. G.

Potter, Robert & Isabella A. Taylor, 9 April 1828; Step. K. Sneed, bm.

Potter, Thomas & Susannah Walker, 23 June 1798; Thomas Taylor, bm; Step. Sneed, wit.

Potter, William & Elizabeth Barr, 9 Nov 1773; Abraham Potter, bm; William Rardon, wit.

Potters, Thomas & Salley Mitchell, 1 Aug 1812; Henry Lyne, bm; Step. Sneed, wit.

Powel, Enoch & Amey Merritt, 17 Dec 1835; Benjamin Overton, bm; Tho. L. King, wit.

Powell, Charles P. & Lucy Jordan, 7 May 1866; m 8 May 1866 by W. M. Wingate, M. G.

Powell, Edmund & Elisabeth York, 15 July 1799; Thomas York, Jr., bm; Step. Sneed, wit.

Powell, Erastus, son of Henry & Elizabeth Powell, & Elizabeth C. Falkner, daughter of Noel J. & Eliza Falkner, 1 Oct 1868; m 1 Oct 1868 by J. H. Gilbreath, M. G.

Powell, George & Quincy Strickling, 29 Dec 1836; Honor Powell, bm; Tho. L. King, wit.

Powell, James & Harriet Thomasson, 18 Aug 1829; Wm. S. McClanahanm, bm; David Laws, wit.

Powell, John & Elvey Parham, 23 Dec 1831; J. W. Smith, bm; Step. K. Sneed, wit.

GRANVILLE MARRIAGES 1753-1868

Powell, John & Elizabeth Davis, 5 Dec 1847; James C. Davis, bm.

Powell, John B. & Malinda S. Dickerson, 14 Dec 1857; N. B. Montague, bm; m 14 Dec 1857 by L. K. Willie, M. G.

Powell, Robert & Esther Tompson(?), 10 Feb 1779; William Colclough, bm; Samuel Searcy, wit.

Powers, James & Julian Parham, 31 Jan 1835; James Redford, bm; Benja. Kittrell, wit.

Poytress, George Y. & Permelia S. Redman, 13 May 1861; John T. Rodman, bm; m 16 May 1861 by Peterson Thorp, J. P.

Preddy, Benjamin & Bedy Preddy, 27 Jan 1813; Willis Cole, bm; Thos. J. Hicks, wit.

Preddy, William & Sarah Matlock, 6 Sept 1781; William Skelton, bm; Reuben Searcy, wit.

Prens (Irens?), John & Martha Harris, 12 Jan 1854; m by W. D. Allen, J. P.

Pretty, Alexander & Lavenia Henley, 3 April 1860; William Bradford, bm; m 4 April 1860 by W. D. Allen.

Pretty, William & Phanney Pretty, 5 March 1790; Harler Pretty, bm; Step. Sneed, wit.

Prew, George & Mary Mitchell, 9 Jan 1860; Wm. B. Mann, bm; m 21 Jan 1860 by T. A. Stewart, J. P.

Prewett, Robert & Harriett Norwood, 28 Dec 1849; Green B. Elliott, bm; A. Landis, wit.

Prewit, Alexander & Martha Vaughan, 9 Jan 1854; W. H. Cutts, bm.

Prewit, David & Elizabeth Williams, 7 May 1822; Wm. Estes, bm; Jas. M. Wiggins, wit.

Prewit, Jacob & Mary Seaborn, 12 March 1784; John Searcy Jur., bm; Bennet Searcy, wit.

Prewit, Joseph & Susanna Gill, 2 Aug 1790; Isaac Gill, bm; H. Potter, wit.

Prewit, Parker & Elizabeth Collins, 21 May 1811; Jesse Barnott, bm; Oba. Farrar, wit.

Prewit, Richard & Jane Vaughan, 10 April 1857; W. H. Cutts, bm.

Priddy, George & Eliza May, 8 Jan 1849; B. Walker, bm; J. M. Wiggins, wit.

Priddy, Harley & Prissilla Rust, 12 Jan 1809; John Priddy, bm; W. M. Sneed, wit.

Priddy, John & Polly Biggs, 8 Jan 1810; Harley Priddy, bm; W. M. Sneed, wit.

Priddy, Joseph & Polly Clopton, 19 Aug 1828; A. P. Hall, bm; David Laws, wit.

Priddy, Joseph & Jane Holmes, 21 Dec 1865; Alex Priddy, bm; m 24 Dec 1865 by E. B. Lyon, J. P.

Priddy, Robert & Elisabeth Champion, 25 March 1783; Wm. Nailing, bm; Reuben Searcy, wit.

Priddy, Thomas & Elizabeth Whitfield, 8 Dec 1806; Ninum Ball, bm; W. M. Sneed, wit.

Priddy, William & Mildred Stroud, 28 Nov 1855; W. A. Philpott, bm; A. Landis, wit.

Pridy, Herlow & Rebekah Smith, 16 Nov 1802; Martin Pridy, bm; Edmund F. Taylor, wit.

Priglger, William & Suffia Waller, 20 Dec 1780; Wm. Bonner, bm; Bennet Searcy, wit.

Primrose, Thomas & Priscilla Wade, 2 Jan 1810; John Haskins, bm; W. M. Sneed, wit.

Primrose, William & Elizabeth Culverhouse, 28 May 1821; Jas. Primrose, bm; Jas. M. Wiggins, wit.

Pritchet, William & Sally Ann Thacker, 31 Dec 1845; Joel Coral, bm; Jas. R. Duty, wit.

Privett, Mathew & Nancey Oneal, 23 Feb 1805; John Gober, bm; Jun. Sneed, wit.

Proctor, Charles M. & Tabitha Simmons, 18 May 1821; Benjamin Davis, bm; Jas. M. Wiggins, wit.

Proctor, Frank J. & Frances Owen, m 22 June 1865 by E. Hines.

Proctor, Joseph & Dicy Owen, 10 Feb 1799; Gideon Williams, bm; James Sneed, wit.

Proctor, Joseph & Nancy Smith, 15 Nov 1825; Charles Barnett, bm; S. K. Sneed, wit.

Prophet, Garret & Rebeca Arnold, 6 Nov 1833; Evan Ratin, bm; Benja. Kittrell, wit.

Prosise, Thomas & Frances Vaughan, 26(?) June 1757; Jacob Somerin, Daniel Pegram, bm.

Prosise, Thomas & Frances Vaughn, 27 June 1757; Priscilla Macon, Daniel Pegram, wit; (request for license only).

Pruett, Thos. & Salley Estis, 1 Oct 1801; Wm. Estis, bm; Danl. Bridges, wit.

Pruit, Alexander & Martha Vaughan, m 10 Jan 1855 by E. Hines, Minister of the Gospel.

Pruit, Dokes & Milley Hanks, 27 Sept 1799; Robert Shanks, bm; Step. Sneed, wit.

Pruit, Robert & Jane Vaughn, m 11 April 1857 by E. Hines, Mins. of the Gospel.

Pruitt, David & Kizzy Blalock, 27 March 1826; William Allen, bm; Wm. H. Owen, wit.

Pryor, Haden & Elizabeth Wade, 9 Sept 1769; Micajah Bullock, bm.

GRANVILLE MARRIAGES 1753-1868

Pryor, Pleasant & Elizabeth Palmer, 25 March 1795; John Moss, bm; Step. Sneed, wit.

Puckett, Stephen R., son of Shep. A. & Susan Puckett, & Mary Jane Norwood, daughter of _____ & Harriett Norwood, 10 Dec 1867; m 21 Dec 1867 by Wm. H. Puryear, J. P.

Puckram, Elias & Chaney Scott, 24 June 1824; Moses Jones Junr., bm; Wm. H. Owen, wit.

Pugh, Alexander & Mahala Blacknall (or Blackwell), 18 Aug 1866; m by W. C. Gannon, M. G.

Puit, Ancil & Nancy Joyner, 10 Oct 1823; Matthew Joyner, bm; Wm. H. Owen, wit.

Pulley, Daniel, son of John & Ann Pulley, & Lina Fitts, daughter of Henry & Fanny(?) Fitts, 4 Dec 1867; m 10 Dec 1867 by J. D. C. Pool, J. P.

Pulley, Lindsay & Susan Petteford, 6 Feb 1861; C. H. Horton, bm; m 24 Feb 1861 by H. B. Bridgers.

Pulliam, Barnett Jr. & Peggy Norman, 12 Sept 1801; William Kittrell, bm; Phil. Bullock, wit.

Pulliam, John B. & Temperance Norman, 7 May 1800; Thomas Potter, bm; Step. Sneed, wit.

Pulliam, Theophilus M. & Elizabeth Ann Butler, 10 Nov 1827; William S. McClenahan, bm; Step. K. Sneed, wit.

Purcell, John H. & Jane H. Chism, 25 May 1853; James Wilmoth, bm; L. B. Stone, J. P., wit; m 25 May 1853 by L. B. Stone, J. P.

Purdue, Blackman & Rachel Meadows, 10 March 1780; John Shearman, bm; Thomas Hicks, wit.

Purdue, George & Salley Roland, 8 May 1785; Richard Stringfellow, bm; Bennet Searcy, wit.

Puryear, Alexander & Mrs. Mary Shotwel, 5 Dec 1852; William P. Newton, bm; L. B. Stone, J. P.

Puryear, Alexander S. & Mary P. Butler, 16 Dec 1835; J. C. Trewolla, bm; Benja. Kittrell, wit.

Puryear, Anderson & Jemima Adcock, 25 Oct 1844; Peterson Thorp, bm; J. M. Wiggins, wit.

Puryear, Applin & Frances Wilkerson, 27 Jan 1830; Harmon Puryear, bm.

Puryear, Ellis & Lucy Beasley, 23 Feb 1867; (freed people), m 26 March 1867 by B. T. Winston, J. P.

Puryear, Henry E. & Mary An Reeks, 7 July 1826; Danl. Easley, bm; D. J. Young, wit.

Puryear, Isaiah & Sarah A.F. Shotwell, 24 July 1862; Thomas T. Ware, bm; m 24 July 1862 by L. B. Stone, J. P.

Puryear, James & Caroline Hunt, 5 Feb 1840; Jas. M. Heggie, bm; Jas. M. Wiggins, wit.

GRANVILLE MARRIAGES 1753-1868

Puryear, James D. & Susan A. Tuck, 6 Nov 1861; R. Amis, bm.

Puryear, John & Sally Lasiter, 7 Sept 1818; Charles Yancey, bm; Rhodes N. Herndon, wit.

Puryear, Joseph R., son of Peyton & Francis Puryear, & Maggie Hill, daughter of W. W. & Mary Hill, 3 Nov 1868; m 12 Nov 1868 by Richard D. Jones, J. P.

Puryear, Lovelace & Ellen Steward, 2 March 1867; Isasah Cash, bm; m 3 March 1867 by R. H. Hobgood, J. P.

Puryear, Richard & Mary Green, 23 Aug 1860; Isaiah Puryear, bm; m 23 Aug 1860 by L. B. Stone, J. P.

Puryear, S. L., son of Peyton Puryear & Francis Puryear, & Elmira C. Amis, daughter of John & Catherine Amis; m 6 Dec 1868 by J. A. Stradley, M. G.

Puryear, William & Frances H. Blackwell, 29 Dec 1831; Jesse Daniel, bm; Step. K. Sneed, wit.

Puryear, William G. & Irana Wright, 6 Jan 1867; Ed Dixon, bm; L. Parrish, wit; m 6 Jan 1867 by E. L. Parrish, J. P.

Puryear, Wm. H. & Mary J. M. McCannde, 3 Nov 1856; H. S. Puryear, bm; m 21 Nov 1855 by G. W. Ferrill, Minister of the Gospel.

Qualls, Allen & Prudence Adcock, 25 Oct 1839; J. M. Wiggins, wit.

Qualls, Chesly & Eliza Hudkey, 19 June 1832; Jordan Moss, bm; David Laws, wit.

Qualls, Henry & Elizabeth Allen, freed people, 13 Aug 1866; m by W. P. White, J. P. on 14 Aug 1866.

Qualls, James & Judith Ross, 23 Dec 1831; B. A. Mitchell, bm; Step. K. Sneed, wit.

Qualls, James & Frances Qualls, 3 Feb 1852; Jas. R. Brummitt, bm.

Qualls, John & Matilda Fowler, 8 Sept 1840; David Nance, bm; James M. Wiggins, wit.

Qualls, John & Elizabeth Bullock, 7 Nov 1815; John Mitchell, bm; W. M. Sneed, wit; (groom signed by mark, John Nytchell).

Qualls, Richard & Emily Frances Fuller, 6 April 1858; Rufus Bobbitt, bm; m 8 April 1858 by S. H. Cannady, J. P.

Qualls, William & Nancey Freeman, 14 Dec 1807; Gideon Freeman, bm; W. M. Sneed, wit.

Qualls, William & Frances Fowler, 23 Dec 1839; Benjamin Bowles, bm; J. M. Wiggins, wit.

Qualls, William E., of color, son of William & Mary Qualls, & Any Ann Bobbitt, of color, Daughter of Asinda Bobbitt, 27 Dec 1867; m 28 Dec 1867 by Jas. B. Floyd.

Quinchett, Wilbourn & Franky Trevain, 17 Feb 1841; Branch Hughes, bm; D. L. Reavis, wit.

GRANVILLE MARRIAGES 1753-1868

Quinishe, John & Susan Parker, 26 Dec 1836; Allen Cousens, bm; M. D. Royster, wit.

Rabion, Alfred & Nancy Champion, 23 May 1861; Merrett Champion, bm; A. Landis, wit.

Radford, Joseph & Martha Mitchell, 9 March 1843; James O. Cogwill, bm; Jas. M. Wiggins, wit.

Ragan, Samuel & Nancy Slaughter, 18 Nov 1847; John Ragin, bm; Jas. M. Wiggins, wit.

Ragland, Evan & Agey Williams, 6 March 1802; Saml. Craft, bm; Jun. Sneed, wit.

Ragland, George & Anney Merritt, 3 Oct 1783; A. Barker, bm; Robert Searcy, wit.

Ragland, James Madison & Martha Wilkerson, 22 Feb 181_; Richd. Sneed, bm; S. K. Sneed, wit.

Ragland, John & Mary Harris, 12 Feb 1826; James T. Johnson, bm; Benja. Kittrell, wit.

Ragland, John P. & Ann P. Beasley, 15 Oct 1849; Leonard H. Norwood, bm.

Ragland, Littleton & Anny Jones, 23 Feb 1828; Willis Snipes, bm; D. J. Young, wit.

Ragland, Obrien & Catharien Lasiter, 14 Nov 1816; Philip Inge, bm; Richd. Sneed, wit.

Ragland, Reuben & Mary Obriant, 7 Sept 1790; Ro. Harris, bm; Step. Sneed, wit.

Ragland, William & Elizabeth Bates, 12 May 1809; Abner Boothe, bm; A. H. Sneed, wit.

Ragland, William & Mary Kinton, 20 Dec 1843; J. C. Cooper, bm; Wm. H. Whitfield, wit.

Ragsdale, Edward & Jincey Oliver, 3 Aug 1791; Wm. Fowler, bm; Step. Sneed, wit.

Ragsdale, John & Mary Peace, 21 April 1800; Dudley Minzey, bm; Step. Sneed, wit.

Ragsdale, John H. & Susan M. Lemay, 16 Feb 1828; Thomas L. Lemay, bm; David Laws, wit.

Ragsdale, Jones W. & Millicent Young, 10 April 1804(?); Robert Potter, bm; E. W. Parham, wit.

Ragsdale, Smith Y. & Amanda H. Royster, 3 May 1853; Thos. Hester, bm; m 18 May 1853 by J. E. Montague.

Rainey, Allen & Martha Kittrell, 19 Jan 1811; Michael Hunt, bm; W. M. Sneed, wit.

Rainey, Horace D. & Eliza Summerhill, 17 Oct 1822; Horace Summerhill, bm; S. K. Sneed, wit.

Rainey, Lemuel & Ann T. Hunt, 7 Nov 1816; Thomas Hunt, bm; R. N. Herndon, wit.

GRANVILLE MARRIAGES 1753-1868

Ramey, Randal & Genny Hunt, 4 Dec 1802; John A. Hutchings, bm; A. H. Sneed, wit.

Ramsay, Warren & Frances Twisdale, 22 Dec 1858; m 23 Dec 1858 by Jno. W. Stovall.

Ramsay, William & Margaret Slucer, 17 July 1858; Thos. Cox, bm; A. Landis, wit; m 22 Aug 1858 by Thos. Hester, J. P.

Ramsey, Baldy & Avarilla Lumpkin, 23 Sept 1828; Woodson J. Ramsey, bm.

Ramsey, David & Artimilia Lumpkin, 21 Dec 1830; John H. Caviner Jr., bm; David Laws, wit.

Ramsey, James W. & Mary A. E. Sanford, 8 Oct 1851; R. T. Beasley, bm; L. B. Stone, J. P., wit.

Ramsey, John & Mary Hester, 25 Jan 1832; Young Culbreath, bm; A. Sneed, wit.

Randall, Silas & Jane Cook, freed people, 17 Aug 1865; ____ H. Williams, bm; A. Landis, wit; m by Maurice H. Vaughan, Rector of St. Stephen's Church, 20 Aug 1865.

Raney, Charles W. & Sallie C. Kittrell, 21 July 1866; m 26 July 1866 by Jos. Jas. Ridley, D. D.

Raney, Lewis, of color, son of Henry & Annie Raney, & Lizzie Scott, daughter of Alonzo & Rowan Scott, 8 April 1868; m 11 ____ 1868 by Edward Hines, M. G.

Ranschau, Carl Frederick (Charles Fredrick Rhinshaw) & Mary Hill, 29 Sept 1795; John Hill, bm; Step. Sneed, wit.

Ransom, James & Priscilla Macon, 9 Feb 1763; Will Johnson, bm; Danl. Weldon, wit.

Ravens, John Junr. & Frances Amis, 7 Nov 1797.

Rawles, Hillyard O. & Ann Eliza Butler, 5 Jan 1863 (sic); m 6 Jan 1864 by William C. Butler.

Rawlins, Samuel D. & Mary A. E. Hunt, 7 May 1817; Thomas Hunt, bm; A. Sneed, wit.

Ray, Benton & Ellen Paschall, 11 July 1850; Jas. S. Leathers, bm.

Ray, Henry C. & Harriett Arnold, 15 Dec 1856; William H. Pulley, bm; m 17 Dec 1856 by W. A. Atkinson.

Ray, John & Elisibeth Mize, 2 Sept 1783; Bennet Searcy, bm; Joseph More, wit.

Ray, Willie P. & Eliza Arnold, 15 Jan 1857; Alexander Perry, bm; m 18 Feb 1857 by T. B. Lyon, J. P.

Reace, Beverly M. & Prudence Chandler, 25 May 1863; James B. Blanks, bm; m 25 May 1863 by L. B. Stone, J. P.

Read, Aron & Jemima Claxton, 27 Feb 1783; James Clanton, bm; Sherwood Harris, wit.

GRANVILLE MARRIAGES 1753-1868

Read, Elijah & Annelize Mason, 10 Nov 1859; William Green, bm; m 10 Nov 1859 by D. E. Ginney, J. P.

Read, John & Sallie G. Sneed, 22 July 1845; Dabney Farrar, bm.

Read, Joseph & Ursula Williams, 19 Dec 1761; Benjamin Goodman, bm; Thos. Lowe, Thos. Conti, wit.

Read, Moses & Isabellah Mayfield, 18 June 1867; Ovil Henderson, bm; Jas. R. Duty, wit.

Read, Thomas A. & Martha H. Norwood, 4 May 1861; Wm. S. Holloway, bm; m 9 May 1861 by W. H. Jordan.

Reade, Robert & Elizabeth Davis, 9 July 1794; J. Vaughan, bm; H. Seawell, wit.

Reames, David C. & Louisa Moss, 8 Sept 1857; B. F. Bullock, bm; m 9 Sept 1857 by B. B. Hester.

Reams, Alexander & Roxy Ann Yancey, 26 July 1853; J. H. W. Hester, bm; m 4 Aug 1853 by R. J. Devin, V. D. M.

Reams, Cornelius & Lucinda A. Parham, 31 May 1858; m 3 June 1858 by R. J. Devin, M. G.

Reams, George W. & Martha C. Parham, 13 Dec 1862; C. R. Cauthon, bm; m 18 Dec 1862 by E. F. Beachum.

Reams, Green A. & Isabella J. Turner, 18 Oct 1857; J. R. Bucanon, bm; m 22 Oct 1851 by Wm. M. Blackwell, J. P.

Reams, Isaiah M. & Lucinda A. Howard, 18 Dec 1854; Z. M. Paschall, bm; m 21 Dec 1854 by H. Hester, J. P.

Reams, John & _____ Mayfield, 15 ____ 1824; Thomas G. Morris, bm; Wm. H. Owen, wit.

Reams, Wesly H. & Rachel Brinkley, 20 April 1829; Archibald Crafts, bm; David Laws, wit.

Reanes, Wm. H. & Elizabeth Horner, 11 Dec 1847; James W. Freeman, bm; Jas. M. Wiggins, wit.

Reaves, John B. M. & Clony Brinkley, 6 March 1819; R. S. P. Jones, bm; M. Jones Jr., wit.

Reaves, Robert & Rebecca Vaughan, 21 Feb 1824; Reeves Turner, bm; A. Sneed, wit.

Reaves, Thomas & Lucy D. Amis, 20 Oct 1837; James J. Bryant, bm.

Reavis, George B. & Sarah Jane Taylor, of Oxford, 11 Aug 1852; T. T. Best, bm; m 11 Aug 1852 by A. C. Harris, M. G.

Reavis, George J. & Damsel R. McCraw, 30 Sept 1850; J. B. Kingsbury, bm.

Reavis, George J. & Martha H. Debnam, 12 Nov 1857; W. H. Rowland, bm.

Reavis, Lewis & Mary R. Coghill, 5 Aug 1833; Peter Reavis, bm; David Laws, wit.

GRANVILLE MARRIAGES 1753-1868

Reavis, Rufus, of color, son of Thos. Durm & Elisn Reavis, & Sarah Rodgers(?), daughter of Stephen & Angelin Young, 20 Dec 1868; m 20 Dec 1868 by Aaron Pratcher, Minister of the Gospel.

Reavis, Stephen, of color, son of Warren & Martha Reavis, & Emily Durham, daughter of Thomas Smith & Catherine Durham, m 29 Dec 1867 by Aaron Prather, M. Gospel.

Reavis, Thomas & Elisabeth Marshall, 23 April 1796; Howel Morse, bm; Step. Sneed, wit.

Reavis, Whitfield & Elizabeth Wiggins, 25 Oct 1807; William Jones, bm; Jun. Sneed, wit.

Reavis, William A. & Lizzie Cheatham, 13 Dec 1866; Isham C. Bobbitt, bm; m 19 Dec 1866 by L. K. Willie, M. G.

Reavis, Woodson & Alice Taylor, m 27 Dec 1865 by Thos. U. Faucette.

Red, William & Rebecca Bowen, 7 Nov 1843; William Bowen, bm; Wm. H. Whitfield, wit.

Reed, Elijah & Lucretia Bailey, 1 Dec 1806; Robert Bailey, bm; A. H. Sneed, wit.

Reed, John D. & Nancy Rodgers, 22 Sept 1834; Tryon Yancey, bm; S. Harris, wit.

Reeks, John & Salley Kimball, 13 Oct 1795; Philip Bishop, bm; J. Hara, wit.

Reeks, Thomas & Agness W. Norman, 20 Jan 1808; Robert Hamilton, bm; W. M. Sneed, wit.

Rees, Richard H. Sr. & Martha G. Keeton, 23 Dec 1858; Thomas B. Wood, bm; L. B. Stone, J. P., wit.

Reeves, Allen & Nancy Whiten, 10 Aug 1780; Blake Mauldin, bm; John Searcey Jr., wit.

Reeves, Frederick & Elisabeth Thompson, 27 Dec 1780; Bartlet Wright, bm; William Hester, wit.

Reeves, Willy & Rebeka Thomson, 24 Nov 1788; Abner Reeves, bm; A. Henderson, wit.

Regan, Moses T. & Maria E. Smiley, 2 March 1863; O. S. Christmas, bm.

Reid, William B. & Martha A. Crandell, 15 Feb 1855; Jno. E. Clark, bm; m 15 Feb 1855 by A. C. Harris, M. G.

Register, Anthony J. & Eliza D. Tinsley, 2 Jan 1839; G. Stanton, bm.

Reires, Henderson & Hanah Chapell, 24 Oct 1864; Bolden Wilson, bm.

Renbey, James & Nancy Brinkley, 29 March 1794; William Brinkley, bm; Step. Sneed, wit.

Rencher, John Grant & Anne Lewis, 11 Sept 1781; Elijah Veazey, bm; Richd. Searcy, wit.

GRANVILLE MARRIAGES 1753-1868

Reney, John & Polly McGehee, 29 Oct 1827; William Levister, bm; David Laws, wit.

Renn, Green C. & Nancy Faulkner, 28 May 1855; W. H. Rowland, bm; m 28 May 1855 by A. C. Harris, M. G.

Renn, Herman H. & Nancy G. Strum, 16 April 1848; Wm. T. Rice, bm; Jas. R. Duty, wit.

Renn, James H. & Jackey Faulkner, 19 Oct 1854; John W. Merrit, bm; m 19 Oct 1854 by A. C. Harris.

Renn, Thomas M. & Elizabeth Hope, 27 Dec 1849; H. H. Rowland, bm; Jas. R. Duty, wit.

Renwick, William & Frances Huddleston, 21 Sept 1822; W. M. Sneed, bm.

Retter, James & Martha Willburn, m 27 Oct 1861 by Wm. M. Bennett, J. P.

Reynolds, Thomas & Mary Griffen, 10 Nov 1846; Wm. K. Cargo, bm; Jas. M. Wiggins, wit.

Reynolds, William & Rebecca Jenkins(?), 16 Dec 1821; Lyman Latham, bm; Jas. M. Wiggins, wit.

Rhen, Joseph & Elisabeth Jackson, 28 Dec 1799; John Riley, bm; Step. Sneed, wit.

Rhodes, John W. & Mary D. Glover, 1 Nov 1866; m by Jas. R. Duty, J. P.

Rhodes, Willie & Elizabeth Curtis, 9 Aug 1854; G. F. Bullock, bm; A. Landis, wit.

Rice, Basdil & Martha Pruett, 13 April 1801; Wm. Taylor, bm; W. M. Robards, wit.

Rice, David & Elisabeth Satterwhite, 21 Dec 1812; Michael Hunt, bm; Step. Sneed, wit.

Rice, Fleming & Martha Arrington, 26 March 1838; Matthew Cottrell, bm.

Rice, John & Elisabeth Fleming, 13 March 1785; Rhodam Cole, bm; Bennet Searcy, wit.

Rice, Lemuel & Sally Ball, 16 Jan 1806; David Rice, bm; W. M. Sneed, wit.

Rice, Lewellin & Jemima Hester, 19 Dec 1806; Joel Boothe, bm; W. M. Sneed, wit.

Rice, William & Francis Right, 24 March 1830; Lemuel Hobgood, bm; David Laws, wit.

Rice, William & Nancey Charinge, 24 Sept 1831; Thomas Chillion, bm; Willis Royster, J. P., wit.

Rice, William T. & Martha J. Jenkins, 22 Nov 1855; James R. Duty, bm.

Rice, Zadock & Amy Satterwhite, 6 Nov 1817; William Sears, bm; A. Sneed, wit.

GRANVILLE MARRIAGES 1753-1868

Richards, Green & Elizabeth Hayes, 9 May 1812; Nathaniel Thomason, bm; W. M. Sneed, wit.

Richards, James & Mary Ann Haswell, 17 Dec 1838; Wm. Salmon, bm.

Richards, John H. & Mary A. Royster, 9 Oct 1844; Jas. Young, bm; J. M. Wiggins, wit.

Richardson, Allen & Fanny Merrett, 6 Aug 1838; William Kersey(?), bm; S. G. Shearmon, wit.

Richardson, Allen & Eliner Mitchell, 27 Dec 1847; Thos. T. Pleasants, bm.

Richardson, Applewhite & Martha Stone, 7 April 1849; Benj. C. Cooke, bm; J. M. Wiggins, wit.

Richardson, Benjamin & Nancy Richardson, 7 Feb 1816; Meredith Pettiford, bm; Step. K. Sneed, wit.

Richardson, George & Joanna Heardin, 2 Oct 1865; m 28 Oct 1865 by Wm. C. Bullock, J. P.

Richardson, John & Sarah Bass, 22 March 1802; Absalem Bass, bm; P. Bullock, wit.

Richardson, John A. & Mary F. Lipford, 1 July 1850; William Cleator, bm; Jas. R. Duty, wit.

Richardson, Martin B. & Elizabeth Harris, 22 Dec 1819; Thos. Marrow, bm; Jas. M. Wiggins, wit.

Richardson, Nathaniel & Mary Ann Hawley, 20 Nov 1845; Sterling Chavis, bm; J. M. Wiggins, wit.

Richardson, Saml. & Lucy Ann Chavis, 28 Jan 1842; Sam. Richardson, bm; J. M. Wiggins, wit.

Richerson, Allen & Maryann Coley, 9 Aug 1842; Alkerson Anderson, bm; Wm. H. Whitfield, wit.

Richerson, Benjamin & Mary Bass, 13 Feb 1783; Phil. Patteford, bm; Elisebeth Sarcy, wit.

Richerson, Benjamin & Frances Tyler, 27 Feb 1867; Benjamin Williams, bm; m 2 July 1867 by Wm. R. Hicks, J. P.

Richerson, Beverly & Isabella Vaughan, 27 Dec 1850; A. Landis, bm; Samuel Hunt, wit.

Richerson, Beverly & Edney Ann Mayho, 21 March 1857; A. Landis, bm; m 22 March 1857 by L. R. Parham, J. P.

Richerson, George & Isabella Harris, 31 Dec 1853; Thos. Jones, bm; A. Landis, wit; m 3 Jan 1854 by D. P. Paschall, J. P.

Richerson, George & Mary Evans, 2 Aug 1858; Jorden Harris, bm.

Richerson, Henry & Martha Lynes, 11 June 1861; Robert Anderson, bm; A. Landis, wit.

Richerson, Samuel & Emily Kersey, 19 Oct 1833; Waddy Jones, bm; S. Harris, wit.

Richerson, Samuel & Emily Kersey, 17 Oct 1833; S. Harris, bm.

Richerson, William T. & Ellen Brandum (colored people), 31 May 1866; m 7 June 1866 by Joseph W. Murphey, Rector of the Church of the Holy Innocents, Henderson.

Ricketts, Jas. H. & June Harris, 2 April 1831; Thos. Beck, bm; David Laws, wit.

Ricks, Charles W. & Mary Ann Hunt, 14 March 1833; John Hunt Jr., bm; David Laws, wit.

Ricks, John W. & Sarah G. Hunt, 15 Feb 1837; John P. Butler, bm.

Rideout, James & Catharina Hall, 4 May 1843; J. W. Hargrove, bm.

Ridley, Archibald & Henrietta Maria R. Lewis, 1 March 1812; William M. Sneed, bm; Thos. D. Ridley, wit.

Ridley, Arin & Chlora Sumner, freed people, 14 Aug 1865; A. Landis, bm.

Ridley, Bromfield & Frances Keeling, 18 Feb 1770; John Keeling, Samuel Henderson Jr., bm; Jesse Benton, wit.

Ridley, Dolphin & Mary Ridley, 27 Dec 1865; Geo. W. Landis, wit; m 13 May 1866 by R. J. Devin.

Ridley, James & Elizabeth Lewis, 14 Oct 1801; Hutchins G. Burton, bm; A. Sneed, wit.

Ridley, Joseph J. & Eliza Kingsbury, 17 Oct 1836; Jas. C. Cooper, Andw. H. Christian, bm; J. M. Wiggins, wit.

Ridley, Robert, son of Frank Farrow & Tisha Ridley, & Merrear Hicks, daughter of Elisha Hunt & Kittie Hicks (colored), 30 Sept 1868; m 1 Oct 1866 by J. A. Stradley, M. G.

Ridley, Thomas D. & Mary B. Blunt, 9 Aug 1830; William M. Sneed, bm.

Ridley, William & Elisabeth Lewis, 7 Feb 1780.

Ridley, William M. & Caroline G. Pickett, 11 March 1838; H. L. Robards, bm.

Ridout, George L. & Sarah Joye, 13 Dec 1853; D. T. Ridout, bm; C. R. Eaton, wit; m 13 Dec 1853 by C. R. Eaton, J. P.

Rigan, Moses T. & Maria E. Smiley, 10 March 1863; m by E. Hines.

Riggan, Jacob J. & Catherine Rideout, 18 Dec 1855; James R. Duty, bm.

Riggan, Jas. M. & Francis Currin, 1 April 1866; C. M. B. Hunt, bm; Jas. R. Duty, wit; m 1 April 1866 by Jas. R. Duty, J. P.

Riggins, James M. & Rebecca Blackwell, 27 Feb 1842; William F. Toom, bm; W. S. Haynie, wit.

Riggan, John H. & Martha A. Rideout, 13 Sept 1863; Jas. R. Duty, bm; m 15 Sept 1863 by J. H. Wheeler, Ridgeway, N. C.

Riggins, Geo. W. & Miss Ella A. Parish, 16 April 1860; m 17 April 1860 by Wm. Holmes.

GRANVILLE MARRIAGES 1753-1868

Riggs, George & Sarah Brinkley, 20 May 1864; D. C. Cozert, bm; m 22 May 1864 by Robt. L. Heflin, J. P.

Riley, Eliza & Ann Abbott, 3 Aug 1852; James Riley, bm; A. Landis, wit.

Rivers, Green & Frances M. Hardaway, 9 Dec 181_; James Atkins, bm; Richd. Sneed, wit.

Rives, James & Elizabeth Hood, 1 Sept 1825; Stephen R. Turner, bm; A. Sneed, wit.

Rives, Thomas & Mary B. Collens, 19 Oct 1813; John Turner, bm; Richd. Sneed, wit.

Roanoke, John, colored, son of Jack Lynes & Eda Lynes, & Nancy Bell, parents unknown, m 24 Dec 1868 by J. A. Bullock, J. P.

Robards, Alexander, of color, son of Cammell Eaton & Lucy Norman, & Susan Oliver, daughter of Orsborne & Lucinda Marable, 11 Dec 1867; m 11 Dec 1867 by M. H. Vaughan, Rector of St. Stephen's Church.

Robards, Anderson & Susan Davis, 3 Dec 1818; Gideon Davis, bm; R. N. Herndon, wit.

Robards, David & Mary Robards, 28 Oct 1838; John G. Merritt, bm; S. G. Shearmon, wit.

Robards, George & Nancey Mize, 15 Nov 1810; Ralph Jones, bm; W. M. Sneed, wit.

Robards, James & Rebecca Jones, 5 Nov 1812; George Robards, bm; W. M. Sneed, wit.

Robards, James B. & Mary Jane Fowler, 19 Dec 1861; A. Robards, bm; A. Landis, wit.

Robards, Jeremiah & Rebeca Jones, 15 Oct 1820; John Jarret, bm; S. K. Sneed, Clk., wit.

Robards, Jesse & Martha Turner, 24 Sept 1802; James Nutgrass, bm; Philip Bullock, wit.

Robards, John & Elisabeth Jones, 2 Sept 1782; Fowler Jones, bm.

Robards, Nathan & Jemima Meadows, 27 April 1814; George Robarts, bm; W. M. Sneed, wit.

Robards, Nathaniel & Mary Ridley, 2 Dec 1805; Jas. Sneed, bm.

Robards, Presley & Nancy B. Jenkins, 12 July 1842; Ralphe Jones, bm; Wm. H. Whitfield, wit.

Robards, Shadrack & Rebecca Veazey, 10 Dec 1808; Ezekiel Veazey, bm; W. M. Sneed, wit.

Robards, Thomas & Tilly Willeford, 28 Dec 1802; George Bullock, bm; P. Bullock, wit.

Robards, Thomas G. & Rebecca Brame, 1 Dec 1843; John M. Ellington, bm; Jas. M. Wiggins, wit.

Robards, William & Ann K. Satterwhite, 8 Dec 1802; Hutchins G. Burton, bm; Richd. Henderson, wit.

GRANVILLE MARRIAGES 1753-1868

Robards, William H. & Lucy A. J. Lynam, 17 Dec 1855; John B.
Debramp(?), bm; m 19 Dec 1855 by A. C. Harris, M. G.

Robards, William L. & Mary Jane Hargrove, 20 Jan 1866; James Y.
Landis, bm; m 24 Jan 1866 by W. C. Gannon, M. G.

Robards, William N. & Polly Ann Solomon, 2 Nov 1852; Robert
Brame, bm; A. Landis, wit; m ___ 1852 by A. C. Harris, M. G.

Robards, Wyatt & Adeline Hayes, 1 Nov 1865; A. Landis, wit; m
26 Nov 1865 by T. U. Faucette.

Robbins, Jessee B. & Mary A. Jenkins, 23 Nov 1858; James T. Hunt,
bm.

Roberds, Isaac & Ann Thomasson, 4 Oct 1785; Richard Thomasson,
bm; Bennet Searcy, wit.

Roberson, Bannister & Sophia Wilkerson, 18 Aug 1851; Thos. J.
Hicks, bm; A. Landis, wit.

Roberson, Charles & Sarah W. Roberson, 19 Feb 1820; Willie Loyd,
bm; Step. Sneed, wit.

Roberson, Christopher & Winnefred Gillam, 2 July 1771; Isham
Parham, bm; Jesse Benton, wit.

Roberson, Ellis & Martha Jane Roberds, 23 Dec 1861; m 23 Dec
1861 by William B. Mann, J. P.

Roberson, Erasmus & Rosey Munro, 31 Dec 1833; William M. Walker,
bm; Benjs. Kittrell, wit.

Roberson, George & Susannah Johnson, 13 Dec 1809; Israel Hargrove, bm; A. H. Sneed, wit.

Roberson, George & Marinda Clark, 8 Nov 1859; B. Burroughs, bm;
m 10 Nov 1859 by E. L. Parrish, J. P.

Roberson, Higdon & Elisabeth King, 21 Jan 1799; Green Merritt,
bm; Step. Sneed, wit.

Roberson, James L., son of ___ & N. C. Roberson, & Martha Finch,
daughter of William Finch, 6 June 1868; m 9 June 1868 by
William Holmes.

Roberson, John & Susan Mangum, 22 May 1826; Dorris Canaday, bm;
Step. K. Sneed, wit.

Roberson, John & Barbary Parham, 8 Sept 1860; Wm. A. Upchurch,
bm; A. Landis, wit; m 9 Sept 1860 by A. H. Cooke.

Roberson, John T. & Gertrude E. White, m 2 May 1861 by Jas. R.
Duty, J. P.

Roberson, Leonard H. & Amelia Wilkerson, 18 June 1846; Thomas
A. Lewis, bm; W. A. Chapman, wit.

Roberson, Major & Mary Ladd, 10 Dec 1855.

Roberson, Nathaniel & Martha Yancy, 22 Dec 1819; Wm. Hargrove,
bm; Jas. M. Wiggins, wit.

Roberson, Norphlet Y. & Rhoda J. Falkner, 24 Aug 1863; W. H.
Upchurch, bm; m 25 Aug 1863 by T. A. Stewart, J. P.

GRANVILLE MARRIAGES 1753-1868

Roberson, Paul & Eliza Parrish, 27 May 1833; Riley Suit, bm.

Roberson, Samuel & Mary Jane Robards, 5 March 1861; m 20 March 1861 by G. G. Walker; (certificate has name of groom as Lemuel Roberson).

Roberson, Willeford & Milley Falkner, 25 Oct 1820; Robert Roberson, bm; Step. K. Sneed, wit.

Roberson, William & Narcissa Garrett, 3 Dec 1849; A. Landis, bm.

Roberts, A. D., son of M. P. & Rebecca Roberts, & Elizabeth Jones, daughter of Littleton & Edna Jones, 23 Dec 1868; m 24 Dec 1868 by G. W. Ferrill, Minister.

Roberts, Aaron & Nancey Green, 26 Feb 1813; John Stephenson, bm; W. M. Sneed, wit.

Roberts, Anderson & Susannah Davis, 28 Nov 1818; Lewis Roberts, bm; Step. K. Sneed, wit.

Roberts, Abner & Winnah F. Bonner, 4 May 1790; William Roberts, bm; A. Henderson, wit.

Roberts, Charles & Frances Langston, 12 Jan 1782; John Horton, bm; William Skelton, wit.

Roberts, George P. & Ailey Jones, 7 Nov 1851; William Horn, bm; m 19 May 1851 by Saml. S. Hicks, J. P.

Roberts, Ira & Sarah Hester, 4 Dec 1829; William Hester, bm; David Laws, wit.

Roberts, Jacob & Dolly Freeman, 19 March 1825; Elisha Roberts, bm; Wm. Hayes Owen, wit.

Roberts, James & Sarah Ellis, 1 Jan 1787; Moses Jones, bm; James Jett, wit.

Roberts, James & Miss Elizabeth Newton, 21 April 1859; W. H. D. Stanton, bm; D. E. Young, wit; m 21 April 1859 by D. E. Young, J. P.

Roberts, Jesse V. & Lavanie P. Cozort, 4 Dec 1855; H. W. Lanes, bm; m 19 Dec 1855 by R. J. Devin.

Roberts, John & Judy Clement, 13 Sept 1828; Jacob Roberts, bm; David Laws, wit.

Roberts, Joseph & Parthenia Gooch, 12 Feb 1824; Henry Tilley, bm; Step. K. Sneed, wit.

Roberts, Lewis & Fanny Goss, 8 July 1814; Bruce Boyd, bm; W. M. Sneed, wit.

Roberts, Mark & Selva Roberts, 27 Oct 1835; Zachariah Philpott, bm; Benja. Kittrell, wit.

Roberts, McKensie P. & Rebecca Jones, 21 Oct 1843; Alfred Brinkley, bm; Wm. H. Whitfield, wit.

Roberts, Moses & Elizabeth Robards, 11 Sept 1833; Seawell H. Moore, bm; Benja. Kittrell, wit.

GRANVILLE MARRIAGES 1753-1868

Roberts, Philip & Lucy Parrish, 7 May 1793; John Spears, bm; W. Norwood, wit.

Roberts, Phillip & Emaline Day, 14 July 1866; Richard Peed, bm; F. J. Tilley, wit.

Roberts, Philip & Emiline Bowers (colored), 14 July 1866; m 21 July 1866 by J. J. Lansdill, Minister of the Gospel.

Roberts, Robert S. & Martha J. Crute, 17 May 1852; John W. Thomas, bm; m 17 May 1852 by L. B. Stone, J. P.

Roberts, Thomas & Martha Bledsoe, 12 July 1828; Moses Wheeler, bm; David Laws, wit.

Roberts, Thomas & Lively Roberts, 31 Oct 1837; W. S. McClanahan, bm.

Roberts, William & Lucy Umsted, 29 Dec 1781; Joseph Walker, bm; Bennet Searcy, wit.

Roberts, William & Martha Morris, 20 Jan 1794; Champion Allin, bm; W. Norwood, wit.

Roberts, Wm. & Barbara Brinkly, 16 Sept 1823; Bumpass Brinkley, bm; Jas. M. Wiggins, wit.

Roberts, William McB. & Mary E. Hicks, 28 Sept 1866; m 1 Oct 1866 by T. H. Pegram, Minister of the Gospel.

Roberts, Willie & Rowan Washington, 11 July 1848; Woodson Washington, bm; Jas. M. Wiggins, wit.

Roberts, Willis B. & Catharine H. Coley, 10 Jan 1832; Allen Smith, bm; David Laws, wit.

Robertson, Benjamin P. & Sallie C. Skinner, 14 Dec 1864; A. Landis, bm; m 15 Dec 1864 by Jos. Jas. Ridley, D. D.

Robertson, Haley & Miss Christian Fuller, m 26 Feb 1853 by A. C. Harris; Hohn H. Grissom, bm.

Robertson, Haley & Indiana Fuller, 18 Dec 1854; George W. Brame, bm; m 21 Dec 1854 by A. C. Harris, M. G.

Robertson, Hillman B. & Jane Robertson, 11 June 1852; Robert House(?), bm.

Robertson, John & Mary Robertson, 25 Nov 1853; Geo. W. Brame, bm; m 30 Nov 1853 by D. E. Young, J. P.

Robertson, John T. & Gertrude E. White, 2 May 1861; William T. Fowlkes, bm.

Robertson, Leonard & Sarah Johnson, 1 Sept 1804; Gilliam Hargrove, bm; Step. Sneed, wit.

Robertson, Lewis & Elizabeth Short, 2 March 1857; A. Landis, bm; David W. Knott, wit.

Robertson, Peter & Mary Falconer, 25 Dec 1837; Gilbert Denes, bm; Jas. M. Wiggins, wit.

Robertson, Silas F. & Eliza Ann Coly, 19 Dec 1837; Robt. R. Sweaney, bm; Jas. M. Wiggins, wit.

GRANVILLE MARRIAGES 1753-1868

Robertson, Thomas & Elisabeth Gomer, 29 May 1784; Thomas Roberson, bm; Bennet Searcy, wit.

Robertson, Thomas & Miss Betsy Clarke, 14 Nov 1861; m 14 Nov 1861 by E. L. Parish, J. P.

Robertson, Thomas B. & Mary Ann Arnold, 20 May 1848; William E. Akin, bm; Jas. M. Wiggins, wit.

Robertson, Dr. W. H. & Miss Corinna Hunter, 12 March 1862; J. C. Howard, bm; m 12 March 1862 by R. J. Devin.

Robertson, William & Elisabeth Collins, 20 June 1778; Absolem Davis Jr., bm; Pomt. Davis, wit.

Robertson, William & Matilda C. Chappel, 6 Aug 1839; Major H. Chappel, Richard Chappel, bm.

Robertson, William W. & Clary Falconer, 22 Jan 1816; Stephen Dodson, bm.

Robertson, Zach. & Indiana Robertson, 8 Oct 1856; G. W. Clopton, bm.

Robinson, James & Ann Henderson Jones, 2 Dec 1817; David L. Evans, bm.

Robinson, Mark & Martha Clardy, 21 July 1790; William Duncan, bm; H. Potter, wit.

Robison, William & Nancy Akin, 22 Nov 1790; Wm. Sears, bm; H. Potter, wit.

Rochell, James & Siloah Jordan, 16 Feb 1775; George Jordan, bm; Wm. Reardon, wit.

Rochelle, Willie & Nancy Fuller, 2 Oct 1823; Anson Ball, bm; S. K. Sneed, wit.

Rockett, Richard & Mary Abernathy, 27 June 1763; William Sims, bm; Jn. Bowie, wit; consent from Robt. Abernathy, father of Mary, 27 June 1763.

Rodgers, Essix & Lucy Cook (colored), 27 Dec 1866; m 27 Dec 1866 by Lewis H. Kinte(?), J. P.

Rodgers, Henry, colored, son of Matilda Rodgers, & Mary Rodgers, parents not known, 13 Oct 1868; m 15 Oct 1868 by R. B. Hester, M. G.

Roe, Charles & Elizabeth Taborn, 11 Dec 1797; Solomon Harriss, bm; H. Williams, wit.

Roe, Jiles & Agness Harris, 16 July 1822; Ransom Roe, bm; Jas. M. Wiggins, wit.

Roe, John & Tamer Bass, 2 Dec 1801; George Petiford, bm; J. Hutchings, wit.

Roe, Ransom & Nancey Harris, 23 Dec 1817; William Harris, bm; W. M. Sneed, wit.

Roe, Willis & Matilda Harp, 31 Dec 1845; Wm. Harp, bm; Jas. M. Wiggins, wit.

GRANVILLE MARRIAGES 1753-1868

Roffe, Woodson & Patience Williams, 16 Jan 1823; Jonathan Knight, bm; Jas. M. Wiggins, wit.

Rogers, Benjamin B., son of John & Mary Rogers, & Luvenia T. Jones, daughter of Jubilee & Sintha Jones, 17 Oct 1867; m 17 Oct 1867 by James J. Moore, J. P.

Rogers, Clinton & Elizabeth R. A. Hockaday, 7 Oct 1865.

Rogers, George, of color, son of Horace & Lucretia Rogers, & Sarah Garrett, daughter of Henson & Maria Garrett, 13 April 1868; m 16 April 1868 by George J. Rowland, J. P.

Rogers, George W. & Ann Bullock, 5 Nov 1855; William Cook, bm.

Rogers, Harvey, of color, parents unknown, & Caroline Holloway, daughter of Green & Philis Holloway, 3 Sept 1867; m 9 Sept 1867 by J. D. C. Pool, J. P.

Rogers, James & Nelly Raily, 14 July 1794; William Stanton, bm.

Rogers, Jefferson & Mary Jeter, 25 Oct 1829; William Allen, bm; Step. K. Sneed, wit.

Rogers, Job & Sarah Rust, 28 Nov 1791; Saml. Rust, bm; W. Norwood, wit.

Rogers, John & Ellender Preddy, 22 Dec 1802; Mack Robards, bm; P. Bullock, wit.

Rogers, John & Mary Ann Cozort, 22 Dec 1834; Simeon Cozort, bm.

Rogers, Jonathan T. & Frances Jeter, 15 Dec 1827; Anthony Clement, bm; David Laws, wit.

Rogers, Joseph & Dera Kittrell, 14 Oct 1797; John Kittrell, bm; Step. Sneed, wit.

Rogers, Josiah C. & Julia Ann Mitchell, 29 Sept 1853; A. Landis, bm; m 27 Oct 1853 by B. B. Hester, J. P.

Rogers, Madison, of color, son of Dilliard Rogers & Martha Higgs, & Delia Burwell, daughter of Josiah & Hannah Burwell, 13 Feb 1868; m 15 Feb 1868 by Jos. H. Reddick.

Rogers, Peleg & Elizabeth Baily, 15 ___ 1794; Geo. Brasfield, bm; H. Seawell, wit.

Rogers, Peter & Ellen Grissom, 28 Aug 1866; m 29 Aug 1866 by Jas. B. Floyd, J. P.

Rogers, Randal & Ann Lyon, freed people, 11 Sept 1865; m 12 Sept 1865 by L. A. Paschall, J. P.

Rogers, Samuel & Sarah Harris, 28 Dec 1829; Woodson Knight, bm; David Laws, wit.

Rogers, Stephen & Permellah Wood, 12 Aug 1782; Jas. Bristow, bm; John Duncan Jr., wit.

Rogers, Thomas & Drucilla Brassfield, 16 Dec 1822; Anthony Clement, bm; S. K. Sneed, wit.

Rogers, Thomas & Amanda Fuller, 23 Aug 1864; m 24 Aug 1864 by J. G. McGehee, J. P.; Thomas Fowler, bm.

GRANVILLE MARRIAGES 1753-1868

Rogers, Thomas J. & Nancy H. Mangum, 10 Dec 1856; H. Rogers, bm; m 14 Dec 1856 by B. B. Hester, J. P.

Rogers, Willie & Frances A. Bullock, 12 April 1857; Benj. C. Cooke, bm.

Rogers, Willis & Loretta Z. Kittrell, 4 May 1847; William Radcliff, bm.

Rogers, Willis & Meriah J. Kittrell, 14 Sept 1852; Wm. J. Hunt, bm.

Ron, William & Elisabeth Merrit, 18 March 1772; Ellis Drury, James Langston, bm; Reuben Searcy, wit.

Rose, Henry & Elisabeth Johnson, 12 Dec 1798; Leonard Cardwell, bm; Step. Sneed, wit.

Rose, Howel & Mary Willis, 19 Feb 1795; John C. Russell, bm; Step. Sneed, wit.

Rose, Thomas & Barbary Crenshaw, 10 Feb 1787; Henry Fowler, bm; Robt. Searcy, wit.

Ross, Charles & Nancy Izzard, 7 May 1838; John E. Peace, bm.

Ross, Elias & Lucey Smith, 24 Nov 1808; William Blackley, bm; W. M. Sneed, wit.

Ross, Hinton & Maria Garner, 3 Aug 1866; m 3 Aug 1866 by L. A. Paschall, J. P.

Ross, James & Nancy Paschall, 31 Jan 1849; C. H. Dement, bm; J. M. Wiggins, wit.

Ross, James P. & Jane Eaks, 15 Jan 1855; J. H. Crorom(?), bm; A. Landis, wit.

Ross, John & Tabitha Parish, 22 June 1808; John Amis, bm; J. J. Tanar, wit.

Ross, John & Elizabeth A. Ferguson, 22 Sept 1842; Docter W. Byrum, bm; Wm. H. Whitfield, wit.

Ross, Patrick & Elizabeth Dickerson, 21 Sept 1831; Anthony W. Cole, bm; David Laws, wit.

Ross, William Edwin, son of Charles & Nancy Ross, & Lucy J. Jackson, daughter of Ransom & Caroline Jackson, m 29 Dec 1867 by W. D. Allen, J. P.

Rottenbury, William & Sarah Jane Jeffreys, 3 Dec 1856; James Philpot, bm; m 4 Dec 1856 by Allen Cozart, J. P.

Rowland, Benjamin Wood & Annie S. Gooche, 11 Nov 1867; m 13 Nov 1867 by S. P. J. Harris.

Rowland, Daniel & Lucy Lemay, 26 Dec 1865; John Smith, bm; m 27 Dec 1865 by J. F. Harris, J. P.

Rowland, George J. & Eliza Horner, 9 Aug 1853; Jeff Horner, bm; m 20 Aug 1853 by R. B. Hester, J. P.

Rowland, Henry & Sally Barnes, 2 June 1801; John Ellington, bm; A. Sneed, wit.

GRANVILLE MARRIAGES 1753-1868

Rowland, Horace H. & Martha Cheatham, 22 Feb 1840; John Barns(?), bm; J. M. Wiggins, wit.

Rowland, Isham & Elizabeth Wilson, 17 Dec 1792; Geo. Perdue, bm; Step. Sneed, wit.

Rowland, Jas. & Edney H. Wiggins, 15 Oct 1833; Robert Rowland, bm; Benja. Kittrell, wit.

Rowland, James H. & Milley Rowland, 13 July 1840; S. R. Watson, bm; Jas. M. Wiggins, wit.

Rowland, Jesse & Betty Merrian, 22 Jan 1781; William Quarles, bm; Asa Searcy, wit.

Rowland, Pleasant & Polly Wilson, 16 Dec 1799; Henry Rowland, bm.

Rowland, Presley & Kiza Harris(?), 22 Dec 1811; William Purdue, bm; Stephen K. Sneed, wit.

Rowland, Presley & Mary Paschall, 13 Sept 1851; Jas. R. Duty, bm.

Rowland, Presley & Mary Paschall, 13 Sept 1851; m 14 Oct 1851 by E. E. Freeman.

Rowland, Samuel H. & Betsey Satterwhite, 21 Dec 1830; William B. Ellington, bm; David Laws, wit.

Rowland, Stephen & Phebe Rowland, 2 Jan 1866; John Smith, bm.

Rowland, Thomas & Mary Harrison, 4 Oct 1798; George Perdue, bm; Step. Sneed, wit.

Royall, Joseph & Nancey Hayes, 23 July 1808; Levi Higgs, bm; A. H. Sneed, wit.

Roycroft, Kinchen & Arena Cash, 1 Dec 1851; A. Landis, Clk.; m 7 Dec 1851 by J. E. Hester(?).

Roycroft, Ruffin & Elisabeth Cash, 31 Aug 1850; Kinchen T. Roycroft, bm.

Roycroft, Ruffin T. & Eliza Cash, 17 Jan 1856; Willis Gorden, bm; A. Landis, wit; m 19 June 1856 by E. Hester.

Royster, Alec. & Melissa Hughes (freed people), 14 April 1866; m by Joseph W. Murphy, Rector of the Ch. of Holy Innocents, Henderson.

Royster, Ben & Alcy Long, freed people, m 1 April 1866 by J. A. Stradley, M. G.

Royster, David & Mary Daniel, 11 Jan 1775; Thomas Henderson, bm; Reuben Searcy, wit.

Royster, David, colored, son of Horace & Emily Royster, & Parthena Burton, daughter of Randel Beird & Mary Burton, m 25 Dec 1868 by Richard D. Jones, J. P.

Royster, Dennis & Fanny Amis (freed people), 26 Dec 1865.

GRANVILLE MARRIAGES 1753-1868

Royster, Edmund, of color, son of (slave not known) & Emily Satterwhite, daughter of (slave not known), 7 Aug 1868; m 9 Aug 1868 by R. J. Devin, M. G.

Royster, Edward & Frances Ragland, 21 Jan 1824; D. E. Young, bm; D. J. Young, wit.

Royster, Fabian A. & Eliza P. Lasier, 26 Nov 1825; Marquis Royster, bm; Wm. H. Owen, wit.

Royster, Francis & Elizabeth Shepard, 6 May 1789; James Bedford, bm; A. Henderson, C. C., wit.

Royster, Franklin & Frances Duncan, 24 Aug 1866; m 25 Aug 1866 by Wm. H. Puryear, J. P.

Royster, George & Mary Hendrick, 24 July 1815; Corbin Jackson, bm; H. Young, wit.

Royster, Harmon & Mildred R. Harrison, 17 Feb 1821; Alexander Smith, bm.

Royster, Henry & Eliza Lassiter, m 3 Feb 1867 by Wm. H. Puryear, J. P.

Royster, Henry, of color, son of Henry Hunt & Caroline Royster, & Lea Allen, of color, daughter of Chesteen Allen & Fannie Allen, 30 Dec 1867; m by James E. Patillo, J. P.

Royster, Horace T. & Insianna W. Jones, 4 Sept 1829; William F. Henderson, bm; A. Sneed, wit.

Royster, Horace T. & Mary E. Royster, m 21 Nov 1866 by Joseph W. Murphy, Rector of Ch. of Holy Innocents, Henderson, N. C.

Royster, James, of color, son of Raleigh & Martha Royster, & Emily Read, daughter of Ransom & Christian Read, 2 May 1868; m 3 May 1868 by J. J. Speed, J. P.

Royster, James, colored, son of Ras Chandler & Edity Royster, & Bella Young, daughter of George Young & Mary Hart, 30 Dec 1868; m 30 Dec 1868 by James Puryear, J. P.

Royster, James A. & Virginia E. Shanks, 29 March 1866; m by A. C. Harris, M. G.

Royster, Jethro & R. Mason, 3 Feb 1800; Leonard Cardwell, bm; W. M. Sneed, wit.

Royster, Jethro & Martha Stanback, 1 Sept 1804; Thomas Mitchell, bm; Step. Sneed, wit.

Royster, John & Pheby Stovall, 6 Aug 1792; Thomas Apling, bm; W. Norwood, wit.

Royster, John, of color, son of Henry Royster & Martha Overbey, & Luisa Nelson, daughter of Jacob & Ann Nelson, 13 March 1868; m 13 March 1868 by B. T. Winston, J. P.

Royster, John F. & Maria Beasley, 24 Jan 1851; Stephen L. Puryear, bm; L. B. Stone, J. P., wit.

Royster, John H. & Esta A. Stovall, 22 Dec 1859; Hartwell F. Ezell, bm; m 5 Jan 1860 by A. C. Harris, M. G.

GRANVILLE MARRIAGES 1753-1868

Royster, M. D. & Frances Webb, 12 Oct 1843.

Royster, Moses & Rhoda Bullock (freed people), 8 Dec 1865; m 28 Dec 1865 by A. C. Harris.

Royster, Moses, of color, son of Juda Royster & Elizabeth Boom, of color, daughter of Martha Boom, 1 Dec 1867; m 1 Dec 1867 by B. T. Winston, J. P.

Royster, Pleasant, of color, son of Maria Royster, & Malissa Beasley, of color, daughter of Stephen Puryear & Pollie Beasley, 12 Aug 1867; m 18 Aug 1867 by R. J. Devin.

Royster, Raff, colored, son of Solomon Wilkerson & Judy Wilkerson, & Jane Roberts, daughter of Moses & Muel Roberts, 23 Dec 1868; m 24 Dec 1868 by W. A. Belvin, J. P.

Royster, Robert D. & Elizabeth Hayes, 10 Dec 1853; Thomas Royster(?), bm; m 21 Dec 1853 by D. S. Wilkerson, J. P.

Royster, Robert L., son of F. A. & E. P. Royster, & Virginai C. Paschall, daughter of Wm. V. & Mary A. Paschall, 30 Sept 1867; m 2 Oct 1867 by M. H. Vaughan, Rector of St. Stephen's Church.

Royster, Rufus & Elisabeth Green, 9 March 1867.

Royster, Rufus & Elisabeth Evans, freed people, m March 1867 by B. T. Winston, J. P.

Royster, Spotswood B. & Mary C. Puryear, 14 March 1839; W. A. Philpott, bm.

Royster, Stephen J. & Jane E. Robards, 2 Dec 1841; Edwd. H. Carter, bm; J. M. Wiggins, wit.

Royster, William & Sarah Puryear, 28 June 1779; William Puryear, bm; John Gwin, wit.

Royster, William & Mary Ann Downey(?), 12 Dec 1834; Joshua Nunn, bm.

Royster, William & Ann Hart, 7 Dec 1840; James D. Shotwell, bm; T. B. Barnett, wit.

Royster, William & Mary S. Norwood, 5 April 1859; m 13 April 1859 by T. J. Horner, M. G.; Henry Carver, bm.

Royster, William E. & Mary Ann OBrien, 2 Dec 1856; D. S. Wilkerson, bm; m 11 Dec 1856 by D. S. Wilkerson, J. P.

Rucks, Josiah & Elizabeth Taylor, 14 Aug 1788; Edm. Taylor, John Marshall, bm; Dennis Reardin, wit.

Rudd, Barnett & Anna Loyd, 11 Nov 1860; Charles Ross, bm; m 11 Nov 1860 by W. D. Allen, J. P.

Rudd, Barney(?) & Peggy Bragg, 20 Dec 1836; Jas. Blackley, bm; J. M. Wiggins, wit.

Rudd, James T. & Eliza Haskins, 27 July 1850; James S. Finch, bm.

Rudd, John D. & Elizabeth Floyd, ____ 18__; A. Landis, bm.

GRANVILLE MARRIAGES 1753-1868

Rudd, John D. & Mary Volentine, 17 Dec 1824; Wm. Volentine, bm; Wm. H. Owen, wit.

Russel, William D. & Semender Potter, 4 March 1819; Randel Minor, bm.

Russell, Burnel & Martha Ann Jeter, 14 Jan 1837; William P. Gunn, bm; Robert K. Clack, wit.

Russell, Isaac, of color, son of Grandison & Rose Russell, & Mary Ann Flag, daughter of Samuel & Fannie Flag, 28 Nov 1867; m 29 Nov 1867 by B. T. Winston, J. P.

Russell, Jas. A. & Lucy Ann Heflin, 13 Jan 1841; Robt. B. Gilliam, bm.

Russell, James H. N. & Amanda Clark, 4 May 1860; John G. Russell, bm; m 10 May 1860 by W. E. Oakley.

Russell, John C. & Hannah Walker, 25 April 1802; William Butler, bm; James Butler, wit.

Russell, Jno. C. & Emma L. Harris, 30 Jan 1867; A. Landis, bm; m 31 Jan 1867 by J. L. Carroll, Minister.

Russell, Joseph & Meriah McGill, 28 Dec 1838; G. Stanton, bm; Tho. A. King, wit.

Russell, Joseph & Patsy Royster, freed people, m 5 April 1866 by R. J. Devin.

Russell, Sherwood & Mary Jones, 2 April 1835; J. E. Allen, bm; Benja. Kittrell, wit.

Russell, Timothy & Elizabeth West, 27 Aug 1809; Richard Briggs, bm; W. M. Sneed, wit.

Russell, William Henry & Elmira F. Ramsay, 1 Dec 1862; A. Landis Jr., bm; m 1 Dec 1862 by A. W. Jones, J. P.

Russell, Willis & Elizabeth Craft, 5 May 1832; D. P. Laman, bm; David Laws, wit.

Russil, George & Rebeckah Richards, 11 Sept 1769; George Waggoner, Henry Waggoner, Joseph Langston, bm; Jesse Benton, wit.

Russill, William & Anney Russill, 6 April 1801; James Brinkley, bm; P. Bullock, wit.

Rust, Benjamin S. & Mary Ann McGehee, 18 Feb 1839; George T. Leavister, bm; J. M. Wiggins, wit.

Rust, George & Justina Banks, 9 April 1781; Ralph Banks, bm; Asa Searcy, wit; consent from Thos. Banks, 9 April 1781, wit. by R. Banks.

Rust, James & Betsey Gooch, 20 June 1819; Nelson Cole, bm; Step. K. Sneed, wit.

Rust, Jeremiah & Sarah Mills, 11 Nov 1802; James Mills, bm; Green Merritt, wit.

Rust, Jeremiah & Sarah Miles, 6 Feb 1805; Claborn Cook, bm.

GRANVILLE MARRIAGES 1753-1868

Rust, John & Nancy Cooke, 31 March 1823; Nelson Cole, bm; Jas. M. Wiggins, wit.

Rust, Lemuel & Nancey Cooke, 12 Sept 1796; Roling Cook, bm; Step. Sneed, wit.

Rust, Matthew & Priscilla Mills, 2 July 1791; William Mills, bm; Step. Sneed, wit.

Rust, Samuel & Lucey Frances, 25 Aug 1787; John Rust, bm; B. Searcy, wit.

Rust, Samuel & Sarah C. Wilson, 28 Oct 1826; Claiborn Stone, bm; Wm. H. Owen, wit.

Rust, Vincent & Anna Bradford, 31 July 1797; Jeremiah Rust, bm; H. Williams, wit.

Rust, William & Nancy McGee, 3 Jan 1811; Benjamin Priddy, bm; W. M. Sneed, wit.

Ryecroft, Thomas & Glafrey H. Walker, 24 Oct 1866; Wiley L. Emery, bm.

Sack, John & Jane Semple, 15 May 1782; Thomas Williams, bm; Bennet Searcy, wit.

Sadler, Robert & Elizabeth J. West, 15 Jan 1866; W. R. Tilletson, bm; A. Landis, wit.

St. Lawrence, Henery & Thamer Duke, 30 April 1804; Valentine White, bm; Step. Sneed, wit.

Salmon, William & Nancy Smith, 24 June 1820; Anderson Smith, bm; Jas. M. Wiggins, wit.

Sammonds, William & Mrs. Sally McCan, 25 May 1853; Robert Puryear, bm; L. B. Stone, J. P., wit; m 25 May 1853 by L. B. Stone, J. P.

Samon, James G. & Abiail Haywood, 20 Nov 1815; Wm. H. Gilliam, bm; Step. K. Sneed, wit.

Sample, Alexander & Peggey Waller, 7 Nov 1797; Jesse Bonner, bm; Step. Sneed, wit.

Sample, William & Nancy Fraizer, 10 Dec 1803; Henry Walker, bm; A. H. Sneed, wit.

Samuel, Andrew & Mary Norwood, 24 Oct 1828; Smith Cooly, bm.

Samuel, Andrew & Letta Twisdale, 29 Dec 1852; Wm. Williamson, bm; A. Landis, wit; m 30 Dec 1852 by Jno. W. Stovall, J. P.

Samuel, James & Angelina Mayho, 13 May 1859; John T. Jenkins, bm; A. Landis, wit.

Samuel, Zachariah & Mary Clay, 24 March 1819; William Thomasson, bm; Step. K. Sneed, wit.

Sanderford, Jerimiah & Sophronia Ann Smith, 23 Nov 1864; J. L. Smith, bm; A. Landis, wit; m 26 Nov 1864 by Geo. J. Randall (?), J. P.

GRANVILLE MARRIAGES 1753-1868

Sanderford, Munroe & Malissa Blackley, 6 Feb 1866; m 7 Feb 1866 by R. B. Hester(?).

Sanders, Edward & Jane Yancey, 22 Dec 1774; Jesse Sanders, bm; Robert Harris, wit; consent from James Yancey, 11 Dec 1774.

Sanders, James & Hannah Mitchel (no date, during admn. of Gov. Sam. Johnston); F. Dixon, bm.

Sanders, Jesse & Annis Yancey, 19 Oct 1765; James Yancey, bm.

Sanders, Wiley & Selah Puett, 20 July 1804; Henry Puett, bm; Danl. Bridges, wit.

Sandford, Green & Jane Weathers, 2 Jan 1843; M. Z. Whitfield, bm; J. M. Wiggins, wit.

Sandford, John B. & Faithy West, 18 June 1840; David Wilkerson, bm; Jas. M. Wiggins, wit.

Sanford, Giles & Cynthia Tanner, 16 July 1831; Jas. B. Peace, bm; Step. K. Sneed, wit.

Sandford, Robert & Milly Knott, 6 Jan 1829; Henry Sanford, bm; David Laws, wit.

Sandford, Stephen & Lucy Frazier, 16 Aug 1850; Pomphret Blackwell, bm; B. C. Cooke, wit.

Sandifer, Charles, son of Green & Jane Sandifer, & Ellen Harris, daughter of Thomas & Prudence Harris, 3 Nov 1868; m 15 Dec 1868 by Willie Rogers, J. P.

Sandifer, Joel & Jane Allen, 17 June 1841; Absalom Harris, bm; J. M. Wiggins, wit.

Sandlen, Crawford W. & Mary G. May, 16 Dec 1847.

Sandlin, Henry K. & Mary E. Jeffreys, 8 July 1854; S. H. Benney, bm; m 9 July 1854 by Jas. J. Moore, J. P.

Sandling, Caswell & Rebecca Jeffries, 19 May 1851; W. R. Levister, bm.

Sanford, Henry & Nancey Fraizer, 17 Dec 1828; Abner Currin, bm; David Laws, wit.

Sanford, James & Miss Hannah Amis, 22 April 1822; David J. Young, bm.

Sanford, Joel & Lucy Allen, 2 Sept 1854; Rives Adcock, bm; A. Landis, wit.

Sanford, William T. & Permelia T. Bullock, 8 Feb 1861; Augustus Blackley, bm; m 9 Feb 1861.

Satterwhite, Adam, of color, son of Robt. & Liza Satterwhite, & Frances Downey, of color, daughter of Woodson & Anna Downey, 31 March 1868; m 5 April 1868 by R. J. Devin.

Satterwhite, Alexander & Amy P. Hart, 14 Feb 1852; John T. C. Norwood, bm; m 26 Feb 1852 by C. Barker, J. P.

Satterwhite, Booker, colored, & Kermiller Ann Kittrell, 4 May 1867; m 4 May 1867 by Lewis H. Kittle, J. P.

GRANVILLE MARRIAGES 1753-1868

Satterwhite, Charles & Narcissa Veazey, 31 Aug 1853; John H. Norwood, bm; m 31 Aug 1853 by A. M. Veazey.

Satterwhite, David & Sophia Hunt, 18 May 1814; Step. Sneed, Clk., wit; Howel Satterwhite, bm.

Satterwhite, Edwin & Susan Ann Satterwhite, 3 Nov 1840; William Perkinson, bm; Jas. M. Wiggins, wit.

Satterwhite, Elijah & Elizabeth D. Marrow, 7 July 1854; H. J. Robards, bm; m 8 July 1854 by J. P. Moore.

Satterwhite, Howel & Nancy Rowland, 25 Jan 1809; Solomon Hunt, bm; Step. Sneed, wit.

Satterwhite, James & Frankey Childs, 26 May 1778; John Childs, bm; Sherwood Harris, wit.

Satterwhite, James & Susan A. Satterwhite, 23 June 1853; S. Satterwhite, bm; James R. Duty, wit.

Satterwhite, James Jr. & Susannah Wilson, 24 Dec 1805; Solomon Hunt, bm; Step. Sneed, wit.

Satterwhite, James A. & Susan A. Scott(?), m 24 June 1853 by Jas. R. Duty, J. P.

Satterwhite, James E. & Mary E. Patterson, 5 April 1866; m by Jas. R. Duty, J. P.

Satterwhite, James F. & Lucretia Norwood, 26 March 1861; J. G. Barker, bm;

Satterwhite, James J. & Susan Wilson, 3 Dec 1842; D. T. Barker, bm; J. M. Wiggins, wit.

Satterwhite, James M. & Martha Vass, 16 Dec 1831; Robert H. Vass, bm; David Laws, wit.

Satterwhite, James M. & Sally M. Downey, 15 Oct 1847; Stephen Satterwhite, bm.

Satterwhite, John & Sally White, 14 Dec 1835; John G. Barker, bm; Benja. Kittrell, wit.

Satterwhite, Joseph M. & Manerva G. White, m 13 Feb 1867 by R. J. Devin; Jas. R. Duty, bm.

Satterwhite, Joseph P. & Louisa G. White, 15 Sept 1839; Stephen Satterwhite, bm; J. M. Wiggins, wit.

Satterwhite, Michael & Amey Wilkerson, 12 May 1812; James Satterwhite, bm; A. H. Sneed, wit.

Satterwhite, Mitchel & Lucy Knott, 3 Jan 1799; Thomas Daniel, bm; M. Satterwhite, Thomas Poyner, wit.

Satterwhite, Nathan & Lucey Mabry, 31 Dec 1816; Anderson Sears, bm.

Satterwhite, Nathan & Ellen Stovall, 4 March 1851; Thomas B. Hester, bm; m 6 March 1851 by C. Barker, J. P.

Satterwhite, Simon & Polly Satterwhite, freed people, 11 Aug 1865; Madison Young, bm; m 12 Aug 1865 by H. H. Prout.

GRANVILLE MARRIAGES 1753-1868

Satterwhite, Soloman & Amanda J. Walker, 20 Dec 1856; James R. Duty, bm; m 21 Dec 1856 by Robt. B. Sutton, Rector of St. Stephen's Church, Oxford.

Satterwhite, Solomon & Anne Smith Butler, 24 Dec 1805; Solomon Hunt, bm; Step. Sneed, wit.

Satterwhite, Solomon & Mary Jane Land, 6 Dec 1841; Stephen Satterwhite, bm; Wm. H. Whitfield, wit.

Satterwhite, Stephen & Nancy Knott, 6 Aug 1795; Jesse Davis, bm; Step. Sneed, wit.

Satterwhite, Thomas & Ann Keeling, 15 Oct 1772; Reuben Searcy, bm.

Satterwhite, Thomas & Ann Martin, 29 Nov 1790; A. Henderson, bm.

Satterwhite, Thomas & Martha White, 17 Dec 1831; Ambrose Barker, bm; David Laws, wit.

Satterwhite, William & Mary Ann E. Strum, 8 Jan 1846; Nathan Satterwhite, bm; Jas. M. Wiggins, wit.

Satterwhite, Wm. L. & Martha E. Kelley, 2 Nov 1847; John M. Banner, bm.

Saunders, Robert & Susan Hoard, 17 March 1803; John Hargrove, bm; Step. Sneed, wit.

Scales, Alfred M. & Kate B. Henderson, 2 March 1863; W. M. Sneed, bm; m 2 March 1863 by H. H. Prout.

Scales, Junius & Effie H. Henderson, 12 Dec 1859; A. M. Scales, bm.

Schoht, William, son of Frederick & Prissilia Schoht, & Luanzy Bragg, daughter of Malsy Bragg, m 3 Jan 1868 by W. D. Allen, J. P.

Scot, Daniel & Margaret Anne Elliot, 18 April 1781; Richard Hargrove, bm; Bennet Searcy, wit.

Scot, Pryor & Sarah Pool, 18 Dec 1833; Thomas R. Dewbey, bm.

Scot, W. R., son of Nathan & Susan Scot, & Martha R. Link, daughter of Barton & Wilmus Link, m 22 Dec 1867 by L. B. Stone, J. P.

Scott, Archibald H. & Ann C. McIntyre, 28 Dec 1816; Thos. A. Holden, bm.

Scott, Henderson & Adeline Parham, 2 Feb 1867; Richard Parham, bm; m 2 Feb 1867 by L. R. Parham, J. P.

Scott, Henry, of color, son of Louis Henderson & Lucy Scott, & Martha Ann Russell, daughter of Grandison & Rose Russell, m 13 July 1867 by Maurice H. Vaughan, Rector of St. Stephen's.

Scott, John & Sally E. Taburn, 15 June 1849; Warrington Pitteford, bm; Jas. M. Wiggins, wit.

Scott, John & Martha Lankister, 10 Jan 1860; A. L. Davis, bm; m 13 Jan 1860 by Wm. D. Davis, J. P.

GRANVILLE MARRIAGES 1753-1868

Seagrove, John Jr. & Sarah Priddy, 26 April 1779; John Pitty-
Cobb, bm; Reuben Searcy, wit.

Seagrove, John Jur. & Phebe Cooke, 11 June 1781; Williamson
Rogers, bm; Asa Searcy, wit.

Seamon, William & Elizabeth Blackwell, 22 Dec 1825; Jesse Bull,
bm; D. J. Young, wit.

Searcy, Charles & Mary Morse, 19 Aug 1787; Thos. Ligon, bm;
John Searcy Junr., wit.

Searcy, Reuben & Susannah Henderson, _____ 1760; consent from
Saml. & Elisabeth Henderson, parents of Susannah, stating
that she is under the age of 21 years, 27 March 1760; Richd.
Henderson, Ann Henderson, wit.

Searcy, Richard & Anne Lindsey, 15 June 1787; Thomas Parham, bm;
R. Searcy, wit.

Searcy, Samuel & Salley Wilkerson, 21 Oct 1783; J. Howard, bm;
William Rooker, wit.

Sears, Anderson & Alley White, 3 Feb 1807; Richard Gresham, bm;
W. M. Sneed, wit.

Sears, Bevel & Ann Cottrell, 8 Aug 1837; Hanson Breedlove, bm.

Sears, John & Temperence Sears, 30 May 1803; Wm. Sears, bm;
Green Merritt, wit.

Sears, John & Harriet Crews, 28 Dec 1839; Wm. Sears, bm; J. M.
Wiggins, wit.

Sears, John & Sally Sears, 5 May 1840; S. H. Parish, bm.

Sears, John Jr. & Frances Hester, 22 Dec 1797; John Barnett, bm;
Step. Sneed, wit.

Sears, John Junr. & Mary Parrish, 27 Jan 1808; Richard Grisham,
bm; W. M. Sneed, wit.

Sears, Mordecai & Maggie E. Tunstall, 28 Nov 1859; Jerome Tunstall, bm; m 13 Dec 1859 by L. K. Willie, M. G.

Sears, Thomas & Nancey Ellis, 5 Sept 1817; Anderson Sears, bm;
Step. K. Sneed, wit.

Sears, Thomas & Elizabeth R. White, 31 July 1833; James Cheatham Jr., bm; David Laws, wit.

Sears, Vinson & Lunday Kimball, 24 Dec 1817; Anderson Sears, bm;
Rhodes N. Herndon, wit.

Sears, Washington & Dolly Ellis, 14 Dec 1825; Isaac Cheatham,
bm; Wm. Hayes Owen, wit.

Sears, Wiett & Franky Wilkerson, 28 Oct 1817; Zadock Rice, bm;
Richd. Sneed, wit.

Sears, William & Judith Robison, 22 Nov 1790; Wm. Robison, bm;
H. Potter, wit.

Seawell, Gideon & Dianna Smith, 4 April 1809; W. M. Sneed, bm.

GRANVILLE MARRIAGES 1753-1868

Seawell, James & Lucy Anne Lewis, 7 Dec 1805; Thos. Lewis, bm; Jas. Sneed, wit.

Self, Joseph & Nancy J. Sanford, 22 Jan 1853; Bowlin W. Wilson, bm; A. Landis, wit; m 27 Jan 1853 by B. B. Hester, J. P.

Self, Witter & Pattey Gilliam, 28 June 1794; William Gilliam, bm; Step. Sneed, wit.

Sexton, Caswell C. & Mary R. York, 30 Aug 1847; John Norwood, bm.

Shadrick, Allen & Nancy Hayes, 11 Feb 1857; A. Landis, wit; m 22 Feb 1857 by Geo. J. Rowland, J. P.

Shadrick, Daniel & Rosa Huddleston, 11 Sept 1856; James Hayes, bm; A. Landis, wit.

Shadwick, Henry & Salley Bowers, 7 Feb 1820; Wm. Adcock, bm; Jas. M. Wiggins, wit.

Shadwick, Paskel & Lucy Fowler, 21 Feb 1817; William Adcock, bm; Leslie Gilliam, wit.

Shammell, Zachariah & Mary Suit, 23 July 1794; Jorge Handock(?), bm; H. Seawell, wit.

Shank, James & Susan A. Royster, m 1 April 1861 by Wm. M. Bennett, J. P.

Shanks, Robert & Betsey Royster, 15 March 1800; James Christopher, bm; W. M. Sneed, wit.

Shanks, William & Lucy Gooch, 17 Dec 1832; Allen **Gordon**, bm; Step. K. Sneed, wit.

Shanks, William & Ann Moody, 27 Nov 1840; Robert H. Sharpe, bm; Wm. T. Hargrove, wit.

Shanks, William, son of William Hicks & Mary Shanks, & Lucy Currin, daughter of Robert Currin, m 27 Feb 1868 by E. F. Beachum, R. G. Minister.

Sharp, Isaac & Rachael Gooch, 11 Oct 1816; Thos. P. Downey, bm; Richd. Sneed, wit.

Shaver, George & Nancy May, 28 Dec 1841; John W. Paschal, bm; J. M. Wiggins, wit.

Shaver, James & Mary Perkerson, 9 June 1813; Charles Moore, bm; Tho. J. Hicks, wit.

Shaw, Gabriel, of Wake County, & Marah Mobley, 17 April 1778; John Shaw, bm; Henry Pattillo, wit.

Shearin, John & Betsey Lock, 4 Nov 1833; W. M. A. Gill, bm; Benja. Kittrell, wit.

Shearman, Charles & Susannah Justus(?), 15 July 1797; Abner Partee, bm; Step. Sneed, wit.

Shearman, Squire & Dancey Partee, 26 April 1805; David Landers, bm; Jas. Sneed, wit.

Shearman, Thomas J. & Rebecca E. Boswell, 16 March 1855; Samuel D. Murray, bm.

GRANVILLE MARRIAGES 1753-1868

Shearmon, John & Hannah Jones, 6 May 1815; George Knott, bm; W. M. Sneed, wit.

Shearrin, John M. & Mary Perry, 7 Oct 1831; Step. K. Sneed, bm.

Shearrin, William & Lucey Nance, 20 Jan 1809; James Wheeler, bm; W. M. Sneed, wit.

Shelton, Absolem & Polley Belcher, 25 May 1803; Jesse Johnson, bm; Step. Sneed, wit.

Shelton, William T. & Elen A. Almon, 27 Nov 1850; James Cole, bm; L. B. Stone, J. P., wit.

Shemwell, James & Barbery Suit, 7 Aug 1797; Sham Parham, bm.

Shemwell, Samuel & Jenney Dickerson, 14 July 1798; Thornton Harden, bm; Wm. Robards, wit.

Shenin, John W. & Riney Cash, 16 March 1864; W. A. Philpott, bm; m 14 April 1864 by R. B. Hester, M. G.

Shenin, William & Mary Adams, 11 April 1855; A. Landis, bm; Thos. W. McClanahan, wit; m 15 April 1855 by E. Hester.

Shepard, Samuel & Lucy Huskey, 14 Nov 1781; (bondsman and wit. torn off).

Shepard, William & Angelina Oliver, 24 June 1836; J. C. Trevelle, bm.

Sheppard, William Jr. & Mary A. Haywood, 1 May 1816; Saml. Hillman, bm; Stephen K. Sneed, wit.

Sherin, Aaron & Lucy Akin, 1 Oct 1819; Joseph Wiggins, bm; S. K. Sneed, wit.

Shermon, Alfred & Frances Williams, 13 Sept 1848; James B. Jackson, bm; J. M. Wiggins, wit.

Shermon, Petre & Felice Waller, freed people, m 25 Jan 1867 by Dennis Tilley; Kerson Parrish, bm; D. Tilley, wit.

Sherrin, Aaron & Elizabeth Chapel, 7 Jan 1809; Samuel Chapel Senr., bm; W. M. Sneed, wit.

Sherrin, Buckner L. & Sarah K. Freeman, 7 Jan 1851; James R. Suit, bm.

Sherrin, Drury & Eliza Sherrin, 7 Dec 1844; G. W. Greer, bm; J. M. Wiggins, wit.

Sherrin, James R. & Narcissa Dilliard, 1 Dec 1857; J. A. Battle, bm; m 3 Dec 1857 by W. T. Walters, Minister of the Gospel.

Sherrin, John & Riney Robertson, 19 Dec 1849; Moses Gannen, bm.

Sherrin, Major A. & Mary Beck, 23 Oct 1847; J. H. Gooch, bm.

Sherrin, Moses A. & Jemima Harris, 11 June 1846; J. M. Wiggins, wit.

Shore, William & Fanny Anderson Taylor, 9 June 1819; James H. Cobbs, bm; Step. K. Sneed, wit.

GRANVILLE MARRIAGES 1753-1868

Short, Edward & Hulda Falconer, 13 Feb 1840; Jas. R. Duty, bm; Jas. M. Wiggins, wit.

Short, J. F. & Susan Newton, 6 Dec 1866; D. R. Boyd, bm; C. E. Landis, wit; m 9 Dec 1866 by Jas. R. Duty, J. P.

Short, James N. & Nancy Harris, 19 Jan 1846; Samuel D. Edwards, bm; Jas. M. Wiggins, wit.

Short, Jas. S. & Virginia F. Clark, 15 Nov 1866; Thos. S. Bull, bm; C. E. Landis, wit.

Short, James T. & Virginia F. Clark, 15 Nov 1866; m 17 Nov 1866 by E. F. Beachum, R. G. Minister.

Short, John R. & Emily Royster, freed people, 30 Dec 1865; m 31 Dec 1865 by L. K. Willie, M. G.

Short, Thomas W. & Sarah A. Stone, 23 Aug 1842; A. B. Grissom, bm; Wm. H. Whitfield, wit.

Short, Vines & Susan A. Hays, 3 Jan 1824; Samuel Edwards, bm; Wm. H. Owen, wit.

Short, William & Happy Hayes, 15 Jan 1807; Wyatt Short, bm; Jun. Sneed, wit.

Short, William H. & Permelia Loyd, 15 Oct 1855; Champion Faulkner, bm; m 16 Oct 1855 by A. C. Harris, M. G.

Short, Wyatt & Martha Smith, 30 March 1808; Dudley Weaver, bm; Step. Sneed, wit.

Shotwell, James H. & Rebecca G. Hart, 2 Feb 1841; Robert H. Vass, bm.

Shotwell, Thomas S. & Mary Jane Smith, 24 April 1844; Burwell Taylor, bm; Wm. H. Whitfield, wit.

Sikes, Henry & Frances H. York, 6 Feb 181_; Henry B. Lawrence, bm; Step. K. Sneed, wit.

Sikes, William M. & Mary T. Haswell, 15 Nov 1842; Adnah Roberson, bm; Wm. H. Whitfield, wit.

Simmons, Thomas & Agness Brogdon, 5 Feb 1794; Elijah Ball, bm; Leonard Henderson, wit.

Sims, Gilford & Jacksey White, 19 Nov 1833; Thomas Hicks, bm.

Sims, Harvel & Elizabeth Beavish(?), 23 July 1804; Allin Sims, bm; Danl. Bridges, wit.

Sims, James B. & Virginia L. Ridley, 28 July 1846; R. H. Kingsbury, bm.

Sims, Joseph & Peggy German, 17 Jan 1867; m 17 Jan 1867 by Joseph H. Riddick.

Sims, Martin & Anna Howard, 20 Jan 1782; James Searcy, bm; Bishop Hicks, wit.

Sims, Swepson & Jane Paine, 19 Dec 1799; James Ridley, bm; James Sneed, wit.

GRANVILLE MARRIAGES 1753-1868

Sims, William & Lundy Gilliam, 8 Nov 1800; Thom. Robards, Ro. Burton Jr., bm; A. Sneed, wit.

Sims, Zacheriah & Sarah Mitchel, 7 Sept 1801; Franklin Satterwhite, bm; Jun. Sneed, wit.

Sisemore, Daniel & Elisabeth Sisemore, 30 Nov 1809; William Newton, bm; H. Young, wit.

Sizemore, James D. & Alavenia B. Mason, 2 Jan 1847; Jas. R. Cooke, bm.

Sizemore, John & Catharine Cooly, 6 Jan 1816; Bird Sizemore, bm; H. Young, wit.

Sizemore, Leroy & Susan W. Keeton, 18 Dec 1851; George W. Royster(?), bm; L. B. Stone, J. P., wit.

Sizemore, William J. & Jemima Solomon, 11 Oct 1852; W. H. Solomon, bm; L. B. Stone, J. P., wit; m 11 Oct 1852 by L. B. Stone, J. P.

Sizemore, William P. & Elizabeth J. Dean, 2 Oct 1861; B. F. ___, bm.

Skelton, William & Jane Fleming, 10 Feb 1782; Bennet Searcy, bm; Samuel Searcy, wit.

Skidmore, Ferry & Jinny Nelson, 27 March 1867, m by Maurice H. Vaughan, Rector of St. Stephen's.

Skinner, William C. & Caroline M. Hicks, 13 Nov 1838; H. L. Robards, bm.

Skinner, Wm. S., son of William C. & C. M. Skinner, & Cynthia Landis, daughter of Augustine & Francis Landis, 24 Nov 1868; m 25 Nov 1868 by John Tillett.

Skipwith, Sir Peyton, baronet, & Jane Miller, 25 Sept 1788; Ro. Burton, Esq., bm; A. Henderson, C. C., wit.

Slagle, John & Ann C. Owen, 11 Feb 1858; William D. Glasscock, bm; m by L. B. Stone, J. P.

Slaughter, Abraham & Anne Scott, 27 Sept 1800; Isaac Slaughter, bm; P. Bullock, wit.

Slaughter, Abraham & Charity S. Slaughter, 3 Aug 1841; Isaac Duncan, bm; J. M. Wiggins, wit.

Slaughter, Abraham S. & Mary Ann W. Asque, 1 Feb 1846; Solomon Slaughter, bm; Jas. M. Wiggins, wit.

Slaughter, David & Susan Duncan, 8 Sept 1825; Stephen Terry, bm; Wm. Hayes Owen, wit.

Slaughter, Isaac & Lottey Scrugg, 23 Dec 1799; John Slaughter, bm; W. M. Sneed, wit.

Slaughter, Isaac Junr. & Tabitha Lemmons, 14 Jan 1821; Sterling H. Duncan, bm; Step. K. Sneed, wit.

Slaughter, Jacob & Laner Slotter (Slaughter), 7 Jan 1782(?); Robert Adcock, bm; B. Searcy, wit.

GRANVILLE MARRIAGES 1753-1868

Slaughter, Jacob & Susannah Nutgrass, 4 Aug 1801; Frederick Beck, bm; P. Bullock, wit.

Slaughter, Jacob G. & Elizabeth P. Howard, 15 Jan 1838; Jacob L. Slaughter, bm; Jas. M. Wiggins, wit.

Slaughter, Jacob L. & Alice G. Slaughter, 2 Aug 1836; Anderson L. Dunkin, bm; G. C. Wiggins, wit.

Slaughter, Martin & Martha Duncan, 28 Feb 1826; John Duncan, bm; Wm. H. Owen, wit.

Slaughter, Martin C. & Minerva Ann Jones, 19 Dec 1843; Abraham Slaughter, bm; J. M. Wiggins, wit.

Slaughter, Solomon G. & Sarah P. Duncan, 5 Nov 1844; A. R. B. Slaughter, bm.

Slaughter, T. S. & Mary Cutts, 25 Dec 1844; Jas. Cutts, bm; J. M. Wiggins, wit.

Slaughter, Thomas & Charlotte Evans, 15 Sept 1824; Masten Slaughter, bm; L. Gilliam, wit.

Slaughter, William P. S. & Caty Ascue, 12 Feb 1862; William N. Slaughter, bm; A. Landis, wit; m 13 Feb 1862 by Peterson Thorp, J. P.

Sledge, O. A. & M. J. Goodwin, 8 May 1863; m 8 May 1863 by Wm. Holmes.

Sledge, Willie & Lucey Smith, 25 June 1816; Willie Smith, bm; John M. Williams, wit.

Slicer(?), George W. & Tabitha Phillips, 29 Jan 1835; Howel Phillips, bm; Benja. Kittrell, wit.

Smallman, John & Mary Franklin, 5 Feb 1843; O. F. Manson, bm; W. T. Haynes, wit.

Smiley, William & Talitha Guy, 17 Dec 1845; D. S. Barker, bm; J. M. Wiggins, wit.

Smiley, William & Mary Guye, 15 May 1850; D. J. Kinchen, bm; Jas. R. Duty, wit.

Smith, Adam, son of Lun & Celia Smith, colored, & Rachiel Marrow, parents unknown, 23 Dec 1868; m 25 or 26 Dec 1868 by A. C. Harris, M. G.

Smith, Addam & Elisabeth Cook, 7 May 1782; John Gwin, bm; Reuben Searcy, wit.

Smith, Alexander & Anne Bearley, 5 Sept 1811; Maurice Smith, bm; Mary W. Smith, wit.

Smith, Alexander & Elizabeth Mitchell, 18 June 1835; Josephus Moss, bm; Benja. Kittrell, wit.

Smith, Alexander C. & Permelia A. Grissom, 19 March 1866; m 19 March 1866 by W. D. Allen, J. P.

Smith, Anderson & Salley Hunt, 15 Oct 1782; Wm. Hunt, bm; Elizabeth Searcy, wit.

GRANVILLE MARRIAGES 1753-1868

Smith, Anderson & Silvia Johnson, 17 Dec 1800; Archibald Duglass, bm; _____ Sneed, wit.

Smith, Anderson & Betsey Moore, 25 June 1803; Wiley Smith, bm; Step. Sneed, wit.

Smith, Anderson & Barbary Haswell, 7 Aug 1821; Willie Grisham, bm; Jas. M. Wiggins, wit.

Smith, Anderson & Martha Williams, 2 April 1855; George W. Anderson, bm; A. Landis, wit; m 10 April 1855 by Jeff Horner, J. P.

Smith, B. W. & Harriett Dean, 17 Jan 1866; T. H. Smith, bm; m 4 Feb 1866 by G. W. Ferrill, Minister.

Smith, Benjamin & Sarah Lankford, 16 March 1784; Elijah Parrish, bm; Bennet Searcy, wit.

Smith, Benjamin & Patsey Jenkins, 13 July 1813; Joseph M. Smith, bm; W. M. Sneed, wit.

Smith, Benjamin W. & Anne Potter, 26 April 1826; Lyman Latham, bm; Wm. H. Owen, wit.

Smith, Cager, of color, son of Stephen & Rosella Smith, & Amy Harris, daughter of James & Betsy Harris, 18 Dec 1867; m 22 Dec 1867 by W. H. Puryear, J. P.

Smith, Charles & Rodah Vass, 2 May 1793; David Smith, bm; W. Norwood, wit.

Smith, David W. & Mary Wilkerson, 19 June 1821; Robert L. Blackwell, bm; Jno. P. Smith, wit.

Smith, Edmond & Elisabeth Daniel, 25 Jan 1779; Joseph Daniel, bm; John Searcy Jr., wit.

Smith, Francis & Charlotte Brodie(?), 25 June 1811; James Vaughan, bm; Step. Sneed, wit.

Smith, George C. & Martha C. Gooch, 26 April 1826; Richd. Allen, bm; S. K. Sneed, wit.

Smith, George W. & Jane Boen, 3 Oct 1833; Peter G. Vaughan, bm; Willie Royster, J. P., wit.

Smith, Guy & Prudence H. Kittle, 22 June 1831; Leroy E. Smith, bm; Step. K. Sneed, wit.

Smith, Harry & Louisa Daniel, 7 Jan 1867; m 12 Jan 1867 by B. D. Howard, J. P.

Smith, Henry & Polly Clifford, 23 Aug 1778; Richd. Henderson, bm; Oswald Towns, wit.

Smith, Henry & Elizabeth C. Smith, 26 Dec 1825; Samuel Smith, bm; A. Sneed, wit.

Smith, Henry & Agness Mitchel, 5 Nov 1835; Guy Smith, bm; Benja. Kittrell, wit.

Smith, Henry P. & Evria Ann B. Land, 18 Aug 1847; D. S. Barker, bm; Jas. M. Wiggins, wit.

GRANVILLE MARRIAGES 1753-1868

Smith, James & Nancey Strem, 22 Dec 1800; Wm. Taylor, bm; Step. Sneed, wit.

Smith, James & Harriot W. Pulliam, 11 July 1822; Will. F. Smith, bm; Jas. M. Wiggins, wit.

Smith, James & Isabella Buchannan, 5 Nov 1824; D. E. Young, bm; David J. Young, wit.

Smith, James & Relly Ann Hart, 6 Feb 1844; Wm. H. Gilliam, bm; Wm. H. Whitfield, wit.

Smith, James (son of John) & Sally Kittle, 20 April 1820; Edward Atkinson, bm; Step. K. Sneed, wit.

Smith, James & Britania Wagstaff, 7 March 1854; Jas. Heflin, bm; m 9 April 1854 by B. B. Hester, J. P.

Smith, James & Elennor Vass, m 18 Nov 1866 by Wm. H. Puryear, J. P.; Louis Smith, bm; C. E. Landis, wit.

Smith, Dr. James A., son of Maurice & Amy W. Smith, & Alice G. Daniel, daughter of Nathaniel & Ann Daniel, 2 Dec 1867; m 2 Dec 1867 by Edward Hines, M. G.

Smith, Jas. W. & Polly Downey, ___ Dec 1791; Lewis Lanier, bm; William J. Pattillo, wit.

Smith, James W. & Mary Webb, 16 March 1839; James Cooper, bm.

Smith, John & Elisabeth Blackley, 1 May 1778; James Blackley, bm; Jam. Jett, wit.

Smith, John & Martha Peace, 15 Sept 1783; Justice Parrish, bm; Wm. Hunt, wit.

Smith, John & Judah Prew, 20 Dec 1813; Samuel Brummit, bm; J. P. Sneed, wit.

Smith, John & Mary Cox, 9 March 1816; Thos. Daniel(?), bm; Rich. Sneed, wit.

Smith, John & Sarah Bradford, 22 Feb 1826; Elias Huskey, bm; Sm. H. Owen, wit.

Smith, John H. & Obedience Rogers, 4 Oct 1854; H. A. Davis, bm; m 5 Oct 1854 by W. D. Allen, J. P.

Smith, John P. & Eliza Coulton, 18 Dec 1816; Henry C. Walton, bm; Rhodes N. Herndon, wit.

Smith, John P. & Mary E. Smith, 15 Dec 1846; Jas. Elles, bm; Jas. M. Wiggins, wit.

Smith, John Prior & Frances Harper, 26 Sept 1788; Robt. Hyde, bm; A. Henderson, wit.

Smith, John W. & Ruth Powell, 2 Aug 1830; G. Stanton, bm; Step. K. Sneed, wit.

Smith, John W., son of Wm. H. & Mahala Smith, & Caroline F. Crews, daughter of James A. & Martha Crews, 28 Dec 1867; m 29 Dec 1867 by T. J. Horner, G. M.

Smith, John Y. & Mary Ann Kittle, 14 Dec 1853; m 18 Dec 1853 by
G. C. Compton.

Smith, John Y. & Mary Ann Giliam, 14 Dec 1853.

Smith, Joseph & Sarah Knott, 15 Feb 1791; Lewis Lemay, bm; H.
Potter, wit.

Smith, Joseph & Sarah Fuller, 16 April 1791; Saml. Fuller, bm;
A. Potter, wit.

Smith, Joseph L. & Martha A. Jeffreys, 14 May 1867; L. B. Wagstaff, bm; m 15 May 1867 by W. D. Allen, J. P.

Smith, Joseph W. of Petersburg, Va. & Miss Mollie Hicks, of
Granville Co., N. C., 14 Jan 1864; Thomas S. Gilliam, bm; m
14 Jan 1864 by Thomas U. Faucette.

Smith, Kannon & Polley Finch, 5 Feb 1799; Wm. Peace, bm; Step.
Sneed, wit.

Smith, Larkin & Stella Parker, 4 March 1865; Henry Parker, bm;
m 5 March 1865 by E. B. Lyon, J. P.

Smith, Lemuel & Nancey Smith, 24 Dec 1823; Peyton Puryear, bm;
Jno. P. Smith, wit.

Smith, Leonard & Polly Collins, 13 Oct 1789; John Collins, bm.

Smith, Leroy & Martha Mitchell, 7 Sept 1833; W. B. Witehill, bm;
Benja. Kittrell, wit.

Smith, Lewis T. & Nancy G. Howel, 11 Jan 1855; Chas. W. Clay Jr.,
bm; m 17 Jan 1855 by James S. Purifoy, M. G.

Smith, Maurice & Frances Goodwin, 27 June 1814; W. M. Sneed, wit.

Smith, Maurice & Amey Webb, 10 April 1829; Anne Smith, bm.

Smith, Mead A. & Eliza Avery, 9 June 1841; Person Williams, bm.

Smith, Meade A. & Elizabeth A. Williams, 2 Nov 1830; Aug. Landis,
bm; David Laws, wit.

Smith, Owen & Mary M. Campbell, 9 June 1863; Saml. A. Williams,
bm; m 9 June 1862 by Wm Hodges, Rector of Emmanuel Ch., Warrenton, N. C.

Smith, Patrick H. & Martha A. Compton, 2 Sept 1845; C. Osborn,
bm; J. M. Wiggins, wit.

Smith, Peter P. & Peggy Smith, 17 Jan 1807; Charles Smith, bm;
W. M. Sneed, wit.

Smith, Ransom & Elizabeth Morse, 26 Aug 1783; Edmond Smith,
bm; _____ Harris, wit.

Smith, Ransom & Mary Hicks, 29 Nov 1820; Nathaniel Robards, bm;
Step. K. Sneed, wit.

Smith, Redman R. & Rebecca Farrah, 11 Jan 1837; John Hargrove,
bm; W. T. Hargrove, wit.

Smith, Richard & Fanny Stone, m 7 Aug 1867 by L. B. Stone, J. P.

GRANVILLE MARRIAGES 1753-1868

Smith, Richd. J. & Mary A. G. Smith, 3 April 1835; Wm. A. Maddox, bm; Benja. Kittrell, wit.

Smith, Robert & Salley Moss, 9 May 1789; Joseph Totten, bm; A. Hederson, wit.

Smith, Robert O. & Fannie R. Cottrell, 19 Nov 1866; W. H. Daniel, bm; C. E. Landis, wit; m 21 Nov 1866 by L. K. Willie, M. G.

Smith, Sammuel & Nancy Dodson, 14 Feb 1781; Charles Dodson, bm; William Skelton, wit.

Smith, Samuel & _____ ; John Owen, A. Satterwhite, bm; 11 April 1805; Richd. Sneed, wit; "It is conjectured that Saml. Smith is married or was intended to Sally Williams."

Smith, Samuel S. & Elizabeth Satterwhite, 17 Oct 1825; D. E. Young, bm.

Smith, Samuel W. & Hester Ann Hargrove, 22 July 1830; Maurice Smith, bm.

Smith, Samuel W. & Isabella H. Green, 27 Nov 1841; John Sherman, bm.

Smith, Sehon & Elizabeth Owen, 22 May 1793; William Owen, bm; W. Norwood, wit.

Smith, Sterling & Catharine Parish, 1 Jan 1817; David Thrift, bm; Step. K. Sneed, wit.

Smith, Thomas & Mary Scott, 6 Jan 1787; Ben. Hancock, bm; Thos. Ligon, wit.

Smith, Thomas & Salley Oakly, 18 March 1809; Augustine Anderson, bm; W. M. Sneed, wit.

Smith, Thomas & Arey Heflin, 3 Jan 1824; Jonathan Osborn, bm; Wm. H. Owen, wit.

Smith, Thomas & Emerly Royster, 8 Aug 1866.

Smith, Thomas J., son of William H. & Mahaly G. Smith, & Sallie M. Cozart, daughter of James C. & Jane Cozart, 17 Dec 1867; m 17 Dec 1867 by T. J. Horner, G. M.

Smith, William & Gilley Fuller, 1 Sept 1780; Ezekiel Fuller, bm; Peyton Wood, wit.

Smith, William & Litha Eaton, 8 Aug 1797; Alexander Smith, bm; Jas. W. Smith, wit.

Smith, William & Susanah Brack, 31 July 1809; Thos. H. Phillips, bm; John G. Gunn, William Brack, wit.

Smith, William & Frances Smith, m 26 Aug 1866 by B. T. Winston, J. P.

Smith, William A. & Elizabeth N. A. Chandler, 24 June 1857; Johnathan H. Tippett, bm; m 25 June 1857 by J. M. Satterwhite.

Smith, William C. & Rebecca Dickerson, 11 Oct 1858; A. C. Smith, bm; m 12 Oct 1858 by Geo. J. Rowland, J. P.

GRANVILLE MARRIAGES 1753-1868

Smith, William F. & Mary K. B. Clark, 29 Oct 1822; James Noel, bm; Jas. M. Wiggins, wit.

Smith, William H. & Eliza J. Wheeler, 19 June 1861; m 20 June 1861 by R. J. Devin.

Smith, Willis & Lucy S. Hayes, 22 April 1846; John M. Floyd, bm; Jas. M. Wiggins, wit.

Smith, Wilson & Winney Roberson, 22 Nov 1800; Green Merritt, bm; W. M. Sneed, wit.

Smity, Wyat & _____; 14 Feb 1807; Daniel Estes, bm; Wm. Pannell, Howell L. Jeffries, wit.

Smithea, Spencer & Francis Fuller, 1 Oct 1835; T. S. Walthall, bm; S. G. Shearmon, wit.

Smither, John M. & Mary L. Bagby, 20 Dec 1858; Saml. A. Williams, bm; m 21 Dec 1858 by L. K. Willis, M. G.

Smithson, Francis L. & Sarah S. Brame, 5 Oct 1847; Robert G. Cheatham, bm; J. M. Wiggins, wit.

Smithwick, Madison, of color, son of Robt. & Louisa Smithwick, & Rowan Peace, daughter of Edmund Peace & Nancy Parham, 23 Aug 1868; m 25 Aug 1868 by R. E. Young, J. P.

Smyth, Joseph L. & Mary P. Compton, 31 Dec 1863; W. H. Moss, bm; m 31 Dec 1863 by B. B. Hester.

Sneed, Albert & Maria J. Bullock, 24 Nov 1825; Mark M. Henderson, bm; W. Sneed, wit.

Sneed, John R. & Elizabeth Veazey, 19 Feb 1825; Francis Timberlake, bm; Wm. Hayes Owen, wit.

Sneed, Joseph P. & Edney Satterwhite, 23 July 1818; David Satterwhite, bm; Step. K. Sneed, wit.

Sneed, Madison, of color, son of Moses & Isabella Sneed, & Crecy Williams, daughter of Alfred & Julia Williams, 15 Dec 1868; m 17 Dec 1868 by Andrew Williams, J. P.

Sneed, Peter B. & Elizabeth F. Tilletson, 23 July 1865; m 24 July 1865 by E. F. Beachum, M. G.

Sneed, Philip & Jemiah Ann Mitchel, 9 March 1788; Barnet Jeter, bm; Reuben Searcy, wit.

Sneed, Richard & Lucy F. Henderson, 22 Dec 1814; Samuel Hillman, bm; H. Satterwhite, E. Sneed, wit.

Sneed, Stephen & Mary Williams, 27 Dec 1779; Bishop Hicks, bm; James Jett, wit.

Sneed, Stephen K. & Ann M. Lyne, 18 June 1817; Leslie Gilliam, bm.

Sneed, William B. G. & F. A. Henderson, 17 April 1848; Jno. Read, bm; Rd. Sneed, wit.

Sneed, William M. & Sarah A. Bullock, m 14 March 1866 by H. H. Peart.

GRANVILLE MARRIAGES 1753-1868

Sneed, William Morgen & Francis Ridley, 21 Dec 1802; John Mitchel, bm; Jos. Wynne, wit.

Sneed, William R. & Lucy R. Mosley, 30 June 1852; W. S. Tolley, bm.

Snelling, Barnet & Lucey Farrar, 3 May 1790; Wm. H. Searcy, bm; H. Potter, wit.

Snelling, Hugh & Ann Snelling, 30 Aug 1779; Bartlet Tylor, bm.

Snipe, Matthew & Mary Crews, 6 Feb 1788; John Thomason, bm; A. Henderson, C. C., wit.

Snipes, James & Sarah Liles, 1 Jan 1807; Lewellen Rice, bm; Jun. Sneed, wit.

Snipes, Thomas & Mary Hunt, 28 Dec 1793; John Harris, bm; Step. Sneed, wit.

Snipes, Thomas, son of James & Nancy Snipes, & Lucy Ann Oakley, daughter of Barnett & Betsey Oakley, daughter of Barnett & Betsey Oakley, 27 Dec 1867; m by W. E. Oakley, Minister of The Gospel at Barnet Oakley's.

Soloman, Armstead & Edney Winfree, 19 April 1821; Gabriel Jones Junr., bm; Jno. P. Smith, wit.

Solomon, Benjamin & Nancey Hide, 20 May 1819; John P. Smith, bm.

Solomon, Jordan & Mary Ann Biggs, 23 Jan 1860; Jos. Hunt, bm; m 2 Feb 1860 by Wm. B. Mann, J. P.

Solomon, William & Penny Bird, 11 Jan 1804; James W. Green, bm; Wm. Walker, wit.

Solomon, William & Matilday Weaver, 10 Jan 1835; Thomas Edwards, bm; Benja. Kittrell, wit.

Somervell, Jas. & Agnes B. Taylor, 26 Sept 1836; Robt. B. Gilliam, bm; J. M. Wiggins, wit.

Somervell, John & Mary Goodloe, 10 Aug 1779; Len. Henley Bullock, bm; Reuben Searcy, wit.

Somerville, John Jr. & Francis A. Taylor, 8 Dec 1804; William Taylor, bm; Step. Sneed, wit.

Southerland, Solon & Mary Jourdan, 17 Dec 1834; Sabat Southerland, bm.

Spear, Wiles & Lucy King, 12 Jan 1801; Thomas Ricks, Junr., bm.

Spears, John & Catharine Kittral, (no date, during admn. of Gov. Samuel Johnston); James McDaniel, bm; A. Henderson, C. C., wit.

Spears, Philip Hunt & Penney Kittrell, 1 March 1785; Parish Lanford, bm; Reuben Searcy, wit.

Spears, Saml. & Nancy Eeart, 21 Dec 1818; Micklejohn Kittrell, bm; Rhodes N. Herndon, wit.

Spears, William Jr. & Martha Woodlif, 24 Jan 1781; Leonard Higgs, bm; Zacharias Higgs, wit.

GRANVILLE MARRIAGES 1753-1868

Speed, David S. & Louisa Wyche, 7 Nov 1843; S. A. Paschall, bm; Wm. H. Whitfield, wit.

Speed, Edward & Francis E. Young, 1 April 1830; Fredk. Lewis, bm.

Speed, Edward & Mary A. Young, 8 Nov 1853; L. A. Paschall, bm.

Speed, James & Mary Jane Royster, 10 Aug 1866.

Speed, James H. & Emily Lewis, 8 Dec 1827; Maurice Smith, bm.

Speed, Jordon, of color, son of Thos. Jones & Lucy Jones, & Nancy Yancey, daughter of Joe Young & Vilet Lewis, m 19 Dec 1867 by E. L. Parrish, J. P.

Speed, Joseph & Mary Goodloe Harper, 22 Dec 1796; Wm. Shepard Jr., bm.

Speed, Peter & Mary Blackwell, free persons, m 1 April 1866 by W. H. Puryear, J. P.

Speed, Thomas & Ann T. Young, 17 Sept 1837; L. A. Paschall, bm; Jas. M. Wiggins, wit.

Speller, Thomas K. & Mary Ridley, 22 May 1828; Jos. H. Bryan, bm; David R. Laws, wit.

Spencer, Alexander F. & Sarah T. Paschall, 7 Dec 1846; H. C. Herndon, bm; Jas. M. Wiggins, wit.

Spencer, Shadrick & Amelia Downey, 24 Dec 1866; H. J. Hester, bm; m 26 Dec 1866 by Wm. H. Puryear, Esq.

Spivey, William & Eliza Cooke, 26 May 1792; Saml. Fuller, bm; W. Norwood, wit.

Spragins, Melchizedec & Frances Lanier, 10 March 1784; Robt. Williams, bm; Jo. Williams, wit.

Springer, John & Catherine Bullock, 24 Dec 1779; Howell Lewis, Sen., bm; R. Searcy, wit.

Stainback, Forister & Winefred Morse(?), 2 Oct 1800; John Wilson, bm; Step. Sneed, wit.

Stamper, Daniel & Fanny Robards, 7 June 1819; William Thomasson, bm; Step. K. Sneed, wit.

Stamper, John & Jane Chandler, 21 July 1792; William Stamper, bm; W. Norwood, wit.

Stanback, William & Martha Ann Brame, 3 May 1845; William J. Edwards, bm; Jas. M. Wiggins, wit.

Stanback, William & Elizabeth F. Cox, 2 Feb 1858; John Fleming, bm; m 10 Feb 1858 by S. G. Wilson, J. P.

Stanback, William P. & Octavia R. Chandler, 26 Oct 1853; James D. Pemberton, bm; m 26 Oct 1853 by R. J. Devin, V. D. M.

Standly, James & Lucy Pratt, 15 Dec 1766; Barthw. Stovall, bm; Ch. Bruce, wit.

Stanley, Dickerson & Isabellah Torean, 14 March 1838; L. A. Blankenship, bm.

GRANVILLE MARRIAGES 1753-1868

Stanley, Ezekiel & Dinecy Vaughan, 22 June 1853; Paul Walker, bm; m 25 June 1853 by A. M. Veazey.

Stanley, Thos. & Elizabeth Cuts, 28 Dec 1826; John Amis, bm; David J. Young, wit.

Stanley, William & Pene Cash, 16 Oct 1852; Ezekiel Stanley, bm; A. Landis, wit; m 16 Oct 1852 by A. M. Veazey.

Stanton, George G. & Hollis E. Sims, 28 Sept 1865; W. H. Smith, bm.

Stanton, Green & Mary Thomasson, 25 Oct 1823; James Dickerson, bm; Wm. H. Owen, wit.

Stanton, Green & Betsey Moore, 6 Aug 1847; D. A. Paschall, bm.

Stanton, Lewis & Elisabeth Smith, 3 Sept 1798; Thomas Smith, bm; James Sneed, wit.

Stark, James & Sarah T. Strum, 1 Aug 1810; Henry N. Rowland, bm.

Stanton, Robert T. & Mary Ann Hayes, 8 Feb 1856; George Stanton, bm; A. Landis, wit.

Stanton, Robert T. & Martha Ann Hayes, 8 Feb 1856; m by D. J. Paschall, J. P., 12 Feb 1856.

Stark, Benjamin & Sally Hays, 7 Oct 1802; Harrison Fussell, bm; A. H. Sneed, wit.

Stark, James R. & Amelia W. Turner, 6 Feb 1849; Jno. G. Ellis, bm.

Stark, James T., son of Kyzer J. & Julia Stark, & Larcena Wheeler, daughter of Moses & Elvira Wheeler, 1 Dec 1868; m 3 Dec 1868 by G. W. Ferrill, Minister.

Stark, John & Sarah Neal, 30 Oct 1792; Edmond Smith, bm; W. Norwood, wit.

Stark, Kyras & Julia A. Wilson, 19 ___ 1840; B. Montgomery, bm; Jas. Nuttall, wit.

Stark, Kyzer J. & Dionysthea T. Wilson, 25 Nov 1854; John G. Barker, bm; m 7 Dec 1854 by S. G. Wilson, J. P.

Stark, Robt. W. & Martha A. Daniel, 20 Oct 1848; D. R. Fern, bm; W. R. Wiggins, wit.

Stark, Samuel & Dollie Cox, 24 Feb 1858; John Fleming, bm; m 25 Feb 1858 by S. G. Wilson.

Starke, Christopher R. & Rebecca Parham, 14 Oct 1852; B. M. Fulford, bm; m 14 Oct 1852 by L. K. Willie, M. G.

Starke, James & Sally Moss, 3 Feb 1818; William H. Gilliam, bm; A. Sneed, wit.

Starke, Rufus H. & Louisa Satterwhite, 1 Oct 1856; Tolivar Satterwhite, bm.

Starke, William & Massey Parish, 11 March 1788; Timothy Eaks, bm; Reuben Searcy, wit.

GRANVILLE MARRIAGES 1753-1868

Starret, Emsley & Ann M. Bragg, 10 April 1835; William Bragg, bm; S. G. Shearmon, wit.

Steed, Edward M. & Lucy Ann McGraw, 25 April 1842; Wm. W. White, bm; J. M. Wiggins, wit.

Steel, Thomas & Lydia Graves, 18 Nov 1789; William Graves, bm; Henry Potter, wit.

Steele, Robert Johnson & Pattey Graves, 16 Oct 1795; Nathaniel Graves, bm; Step. Sneed, wit.

Steen, James & Sarah Bullock, 2 Nov 1813; Aaron Farabough, bm; T. J. Hicks, wit.

Stegall, George & Louisa Vincent, 31 Oct 1857; Leonard Stegall, bm; A. Landis, wit; m 5 Nov 1857 by James R. Duty, J. P.

Stegall, Leonard & Mary Chapman, 17 Jan 1839; C. M. Hargrove, bm.

Stegall, William L. & Rutha F. Scot, 10 July 1862; Gordan T. Powell, bm; m 10 July 1862 by L. B. Stone, J. P.

Stem, Asa & Nancy Cardwell, 30 Dec 1813; Aaron Farabough, bm; Jno. Cobbs, wit.

Stem, George C. & Lucinda Hunt, 2 May 1857; Henry A. Gooch, bm; m 3 May 1857 by Geo. J. Rowland, J. P.

Stem, Jacob & Polley Herkins, 25 Feb 1785; William Green, bm; Bennet Searcy, wit.

Stem, Jacob & Mary Primrose, 10 Jan 1808; George Bullock, bm; John H. Farras, wit.

Stem, John & _____, 20 Jan 1816; Asa Stem, bm; W. M. Sneed, wit.

Stem, Robert J. & Lydia A. Jenkins, 13 July 1846; Jas. B. Webster, bm; J. M. Wiggins, wit.

Stephens, Green & Susannah Williams, 11 Dec 1816; Thos. L. Williams, bm; Richd. Sneed, wit.

Stephenson, Arthur & Jane Green, 21 Nov 1816; Jno. Stephenson, bm; R. N. Herndon, wit.

Stephenson, Arthur & Nancy Bullock, 24 Oct 1846; Tarlton Johnson, bm; Jas. M. Wiggins, wit.

Stephenson, Green & Isabella Frances Allen, 23 Feb 1847; Paul H. Wheeler(?), bm; Jas. M. Wiggins, wit.

Stephenson, Jno. & Barbara Green, 21 Nov 1816; Isaiah Holder, bm; R. N. Hernson, wit.

Stephenson, Joseph & Susan Madison, 25 Jan 1823; Jesse Wheeler, bm; Jas. M. Wiggins, wit.

Stephenson, Wm. & Polley Green, 5 March 1816; Edward Jones, bm; W. M. Sneed, wit.

Sterk, James & Edna Rowland, 11 Aug 1826; James M. Ragland, bm; Wm. H. Owen, wit.

GRANVILLE MARRIAGES 1753-1868

Stern, Richard H. & Sally R. Garrott, 15 July 1839; Thos. S. Jenkins, bm; Jas. M. Wiggins, wit.

Stern, William T. & Mary J. Jones, 6 Nov 1843; Aron Haskins, bm; Wm. H. Whitfield, wit.

Stevall, Moses & Eliza Rice, freed people, 13 July 1867; m 13 July 1867 by A. C. Harris, M. G.

Stevalo, Sifax, of color, son of Matilda Stevalo & Silva Saterwhite, daughter of Balaam Hurt & Becky Satterwhite, m 23 Nov 1867 by A. C. Harris, M. G.

Stevens, Joshua & Phanney Kitchen, 13 Jan 1801; John Castor, bm; Step. Sneed, wit.

Stewart, Manson & Delila Chavis, 31 July 1858; Baldy Keargen, bm; A. Landis, wit; m 1 Aug 1858 by L. K. Willie, M. G.

Stewart, Manson & Elizabeth Curtis, 7 Aug 1860; Presley Day, bm.

Stewart, Pettes & Armin Kearsey, 21 Oct 1840; Martin Anderson, bm.

Stinback, John & Pattey Davis, 7 July 1769; Robert Reid, William Wilson, bm; Saml. Benton, C. C., Jas. Litterel, wit.

Stokes, Benjamin & Mary Royster, freed people, m 1 Sept 1866 by W. Overbey, J. P.

Stokes, Grey, colored, son of Alfred & Hester Stokes, & Annie Williams, daughter of Peter Williams & Penny Williams, 22 Oct 1868; m 24 Oct 1868 by J. H. Reddick.

Stone, Claborn & Mary F. Russ, 7 April 1817; Lemuel Megehe, bm. R. N. Herndon, wit.

Stone, Daniel & Mary Ann Fletcher Hicks, 14 Jan 1822; Isaac Cheatham, bm; Step. K. Sneed, wit.

Stone, David N. & Sally M. Hunt, 10 Jan 1840; H. H. Hight, bm; J. M. Wiggins, wit.

Stone, Francis M. & Sarah H. Dent, 21 May 1861; James A. Winston, bm; m 4 Jan 1861 by James J. Purefoy, Bapt. M.

Stone, James A. & Matilda Stacy, 1 March 1847; Thos. W. Short, bm.

Stone, James P. & Sarah Thompson, 26 Feb 1828; Wm. S. McClanahan, bm.

Stone, John & Sarah Walker, _____ 1780; William Walker, bm; Bennet Searcy, wit.

Stone, John B. & Elisabeth H. Lenoir, 25 March 1812; William G. Boers, bm; Step. Sneed, wit.

Stone, Littleberry & Elizabeth Stovall, 16 July 1832; William Stovall, bm; Rowlen Stone, wit.

Stone, Littleberry & Mary G. Medley, 28 Oct 1846; Willis A. Royster, bm; D. S. Wilkerson, wit.

Stone, Marvel G. & Martha Stovall, 7 April 1832, Eli Stone, bm.

GRANVILLE MARRIAGES 1753-1868

Stone, Parker F. & Kindness Hicks, 9 Jan 1813; Thos. J. Hicks, bm; Isaiah Holden, wit.

Stone, Robert R. & June A. Hester, 23 Oct 1851; Francis Hester, bm.

Stone, Robert T. & Lucinda H. Hunt, 17 Dec 1850; E. H. Overton, bm.

Stone, Ruffin J. & Harriott N. Elum, 2 June 1865; Jordan Stone, bm.

Stone, Samuel & Priscilla Hight, 23 Jan 1816; Richardson Gill, bm; W. M. Sneed, wit.

Stone, Thomas A. & Rosa A. Kittrell, 24 April 1866; m 24 April 1866 by W. C. Gannon, M. G.

Stone, William Nichols & Salley Thomason, 19 Dec 1808; William Thomasson, bm; W. M. Sneed, wit.

Stovall, Elijah & Elina Jones, freed people, 1 Jan 1867; m 12 Jan 1867 by Wm. H. Puryear, Esq.

Stovall, Henderson & Martha Ann Smith, 17 Oct 1840; L. B. Stone, bm; Jas. M. Wiggins, wit.

Stovall, John & Susannah Boswell, 19 March 1803; William Griffin, bm; Step. Sneed, wit.

Stovall, John W. & Lucy B. Barnett, 7 Jan 1835; George L. Duty, bm; Thos. F. Mallone, wit.

Stovall, John W. & Lucy Daniel, 18 Dec 1838; John Hargrove, bm.

Stovall, Richd. & Jane Mayfield, freed people, m 21 July 1866 by Lewis H. Kittle, J. P.

Stovall, Thomas & Emily Overby, 17 Oct 1838; W. W. Vass, bm; _____ Hargrove, wit.

Stovall, Wilkins & Leonora Ellen Tanner, 4 Sept 1865; John R. Currin, bm; m 27 Dec 1865 by A. C. Harris, M. G.

Stovall, William & Margaret Stovall, 18 Jan 1803; John Stovall, bm; Step. Sneed, wit.

Stovall, Wilkins & Hester Marrow, 16 March 1810; Drury Marrow, bm; Step. Sneed, wit.

Stovall, William & Sarah Scot, 22 Feb 1768; Bartholomew Stovall, bm; Saml. Benton, wit.

Straeter, Adam & Mary Strater, 3 Dec 1799; James Leathers, bm; W. M. Sneed, wit.

Strange, Albert & Mary Ellexon, 4 April 1861; B. F. Young, bm; m 4 April 1861 by L. B. Stone, J. P.

Strange, Samuel & Elizabeth Knott, 27 Sept 1842; Jas. R. R---, bm; Wm. H. Whitfield, wit.

Strayhorn, Calvin G. & Lucie B. Cannady, 30 Oct 1860; W. E. Cannady, bm; m 1 Nov 1860 by R. B. Jones, M. G.

GRANVILLE MARRIAGES 1753-1868

Strickland, Clayton & Mary Ann Harp, 21 Oct 1846; Jordan D. Moss, bm; J. M. Wiggins, wit.

Strong, Esicks & Chovar Morton, 31 July 1866.

Strong, James & Nicy Strong, 8 Aug 1866.

Strong, Joel & Elisabeth Young, 18 Nov 1814; John Reeks, bm; Step. Sneed, wit.

Strong, Joel & Lizzie Johnson, 10 Dec 1853; m 10 Dec 1853 by Jas. M. Heggie, J. P.

Strong, Meshack & Joysa Strong, 17 Aug 1866.

Strother, James L. & Malissa Bobbitt, 1 Jan 1848; Henry H. Cook, bm.

Strother, Christopher & Peggy Lemay, 30 Sept 1819; William G. Bowers, bm; Tho. Y. Cook, wit.

Strother, Henry & Mary A. Macon, 16 Dec 1857; m 17 Dec 1857 by Wm. Arendell.

Strother, W. Henry & Mary A. Macon, 16 Dec 1857; Hugh S. Hayes, bm.

Stroud, George & Rachel Inscore, 23 Aug 1799; Wm. Inscore, bm; Step. Sneed, wit.

Stroud, George C. & Francis Ross, 6 Oct 1858; J. H. Gooch, bm; m 6 Oct 1858 by George J. Rowland, J. P.

Stroud, John & Harriet L. Tippett, 13 Dec 1826; Peter Vincent, bm; Wm. H. Owen, wit.

Stroud, Ransom & Martha Thomasson, 26 Nov 1851; m 26 Nov 1851 by W. S. McClanahan, J. P.

Stroud, Richardson & Rutha Bradford, 5 Sept 1854; Junius Hays, bm; m 15 Sept 1854.

Stroud, Richerson F. & Nancy Grey Blackley, 22 July 1834; Woodson D. Blackley, bm; L. A. Paschall, wit.

Stroud, Thomas & Sarah Moss, widow, 24 March 1763; Wm. Stroud, bm; Jno. Bowie, wit.

Stroud, William B. & Rebecca Ann Baldwin, 4 March 1856; E. B. Lyon, bm.

Stroud, William C. & Ann Gilliam, 1 Jan 1850; John Stroud, bm; Benj. C. Cooke, wit.

Strum, Almon & Mary Duke, 14 Sept 1859; J. R. Fuller, bm; m 21 Sept 1859 by W. B. Mann, J. P.

Strum, Bartholomew & Martha Johnston, 6 April 1784; Jas. Smith, bm; Bennet Searcy, wit.

Strum, Hezekiah & Susannah Gooch, 7 Oct 1799; Bartholomew Strum, bm; W. M. Sneed, wit.

Strum, William & Ann Hester, 19 Sept 1844; James Griffin, bm; Jas. M. Wiggins, wit.

GRANVILLE MARRIAGES 1753-1868

Taburn, Harrison & Isabella Jones, 4 Sept 1845; Chesly Bass, bm; Jas. M. Wiggins, wit.

Taburn, John & Minerva Corn, 27 Dec 1845; Drury Sherrin, bm; Jas. M. Wiggins, wit.

Tait, James G. & Elizabeth Kittrell, 10 Jan 1822; Wm. S. McClanahan, bm; S. K. Sneed, wit.

Taliafero, Henry & Emily Harperding(?), 16 Sept 1843; J. A. Geoghegan, bm; T. B. Barnett, wit.

Talley, Greef G. & Francis Lawteffe, 11 April 1832; Pyer Scot, bm; Willie Royster, J. P., wit.

Talley, John & Jincy Eacks, 16 Feb 1788; Josh. Parker, bm; John Sidney Jr., wit.

Talley, John W. & Martha Overbey, 7 Dec 1866; L. W. Rice, bm; m 7 Dec 1866 by L. B. Stone, J. P.

Talley, Peyton R. & Nancy Butler, 3 Oct 1850; John E. Montague, bm; L. B. Stone, J. P., wit.

Tally, Howard & Sarah Perry, 9 Feb 1827; Matthew Chandler, bm; H. C. Walton, wit.

Tally, James & Lucy Walker, 26 Feb 1818; Henry H. Allin, bm; Richd. Sneed, wit.

Tally, James H. & Eliza T. Eaks, 7 May 1858; A. Landis, bm; m 11 May 1858 by Thos. Hester, J. P.

Tally, Richard & Margarett Rear, 29 Dec 1815; Obryant Ragland, bm; Richd. Sneed, wit.

Tally, Stephen B. & Parmelia Fortener, 1 Sept 1817; Allin Petty Pool, bm.

Tanner, David & Sally Cash, 5 Feb 1824; Willie Pollard, bm; Wm. H. Owen, wit.

Tanner, Leach(?) & Sarah Fowler, 5 Aug 1818; John Nance, bm; G. Herndon, wit.

Tanner, Moses & Patience Paschall, 21 Aug 1828; John Haley, bm; David Laws, wit.

Tanner, Moses & Elisabeth Haley, 28 Dec 1850; William Hailey, bm; A. Landis, wit.

Tanner, William & Synthia Adcock, 11 July 1825; William Adcock, bm; L. Gilliam, wit.

Tanner, Wm. & Rebeccah Qualls, 2 Dec 1819; Richd. Hutcheson, bm; R. N. Herndon, wit.

Tapp, George & Massaniah Howard, 28 Nov 1796; Sterling Yancey, bm; John OBryant, wit.

Tapp, Lewis & Jenny Yancey, 2 Jan 1797; Chas. Yancey, bm; Wm. Robards, wit.

Tarry, George & Mary E. Hamilton, 27 April 1832; Albert Sneed, bm.

GRANVILLE MARRIAGES 1753-1868

Tarwal, George T. & Helen Nelson, 22 Sept 1833; S. Harris, bm; Wm. A. Maddon, wit.

Tate, James G. & Birchett Solomon, 7 Jan 1832; John Fuller, bm; Step. K. Sneed, wit.

Tatom, Barnet & Mary Thompson, 20 Aug 1778; Solomon Walker, bm; P. Henderson, wit.

Tatom, John & Peggey Phillops, 13 Jan 1781; Fowler Jones, bm; Asa Searcy, wit.

Tatom, John & Mary Write, 20 Oct 1783; James Cash, bm; Henry Potter, wit.

Tatom, John Jr. & Martha Hicks, 1 Aug 1782; William Hicks, bm; Bennet Searcy, wit.

Tatum, Henry & Patty Bass, 12 Nov 1838; Littleton Mitchell, bm; J. M. Wiggins, wit.

Tatom, Stephen & Salley Owen, 27 Dec 1799; George Browning, bm; H. Dalley, William Byars, wit.

Tatom, William & Margret Wright, 29 Dec 1781; Fowler Jones, bm; Bennet Searcy, wit.

Tayloe, Edmund, the younger, & Polley Robards, 10 Sept 1798; Joseph White, bm; B. Bullock, wit.

Tayloe, Mills & Jenny Hicks, 18 Feb 18--(probably 1808); Alexander Hamilton, bm; A. H. Sneed, wit.

Taylor, Anderson & Jane Young, 20 Dec 1790; John Young Jr., bm; Saml. Griffin, wit.

Taylor, Arthur & Annie Coghill, m 23 March 1867 by H. G. Hill, Minister.

Taylor, Benjamin & Anna Taylor, m 27 Dec 1865 by Thos. U. Faucette.

Taylor, Burwell & Sarah Jane A. Paschall, 23 Sept 1844; James A. Collins, bm; Jas. M. Wiggins, wit.

Taylor, Charles & Esther Ann Tanner, 3 Feb 1866; Philip Bullock, bm; Jas. R. Duty, wit; m 3 Feb 1866 by H. H. Prout.

Taylor, Charles, son of John & Pinkey Taylor, & Harriet Hamme, daughter of Joe & Pollie Hammie (colored), 24 Dec 1868; m 29 Dec 1868 by Jefferson Burrell, M. G.

Taylor, Cato, of color, son of David & Nancy Taylor, & Panthea Fields, daughter of Howard & Caroline Fields, of color, 7 Aug 1868; m 12 Aug 1868 by Wyatt A. Belvin, J. P.

Taylor, Dennis & Isabella Freeman, 2 Nov 1838; Thomas Green, bm; S. G. Shearmon, wit.

Taylor, Edmund & Betsey Lewis, 24 April 1790; Henry Potter, bm; Anderson Taylor, wit.

Taylor, Francis & Elizabeth Burwell, m 21 Nov 1866 by Jas. R. Duty, J. P.

GRANVILLE MARRIAGES 1753-1868

Taylor, George & Jerusha Buchanan, 16 Dec 1793; Silas Paschall, bm; Step. Sneed, wit.

Taylor, George W. & Sarah Ann Loving, 24 Sept 1834; George F. Munford, George T. Hayten, bm; Robert K. Clack, wit.

Taylor, Henry, of color, son of Jack & Ava Taylor, & Maria Turner, daughter of Lewis & Christian Turner, m 26 Dec 1867 by Wm. R. Hicks, J. P.

Taylor, Horace & Leathy Taylor, freed people, m 7 April 1866 by M. H. Vaughan, Rector of St. Stephen's.

Taylor, James & Sary Eaton, 19 Nov 1786; Bennet _____, bm; Thomas Lyon, wit.

Taylor, James & Betsy Roberds, 15 Oct 1797; Edmund Taylor, bm; H. Williams, wit.

Taylor, James & Caroline Cooper, 15 Sept 1866; m by Lunsford A. Paschall, 15 Sept 1866.

Taylor, James H. & Mary G. Eaton, 9 Aug 1827; Moses Neal, bm; A. Sneed, wit.

Taylor, James H. & Victoria A. Moore, 21 May 1861; S. V. Daniel, bm; m 22 May 1861 by John B. Colhoun, Rector of St. Stephen's Church, Oxford.

Taylor, John & Susannah Bullock, 16 March 1784; Edmund Taylor, bm; Bennet Searcy, wit; consent from Lend. H. Bullock, father of Susannah, 15 March 1783.

Taylor, John & Mary Smith, 28 June 1800; James Jones, bm; Step. Sneed, wit.

Taylor, John & Mary Knott, 21 May 1801; Smith Satterwhite, bm; M. Satterwhite, Stephen Satterwhite, wit.

Taylor, John & Lucy A. Boyd, 27 Sept 1815; James Lewis Jr., bm; Richard Sneed, wit.

Taylor, John C. & Mary R. Ridley, 31 Aug 1842; R. H. Kingsbury, bm; J. M. Wiggins, wit.

Taylor, John W. & Jane O. Marable, 17 Oct 1866; m 17 Oct 1866 by M. H. Vaughan, Rector of St. Stephen's Church; Benjamin Burwell, bm; C. E. Landis, wit.

Taylor, Joseph & Maranda Forsyth, 22 Aug 1834; Wm. Mangum, bm; S. A. Paschall, wit.

Taylor, Joseph, of color, son of not known & Dolly Taylor, & Mary Allen, daughter of not known and Marsha Mallory, m 15 June 1868 by Rev. Wyatt Walker.

Taylor, Lawson G. & Augusta J. Rawlings, 4 June 1833; Benjamin Hines, bm; David Laws, wit.

Taylor, Mat, colored, son of Horace & Nancy Taylor, & Francis Downey, daughter of Isiah & Nicy Downey, m 23 Nov 1868 by L. K. Willie.

Taylor, Nathan & Isabella Tarry, 12 May 1867; m 13 May 1867 by Ira T. Wyche, Minister of the Gospel.

GRANVILLE MARRIAGES 1753-1868

Taylor, Richard & Lucy Byne, 7 Feb 1775; Joseph Taylor, bm; William Reardon, wit.

Taylor, Richard & Martha B. Norman, 2 May 1838; H. L. Robards, bm.

Taylor, Robert & Sarah Pelham, 11 July 1809; Warner Taylor, bm; Jun. Sneed, wit.

Taylor, Robt. & Mildred Kennon, 24 April 1816; Jno. Cobbs, bm; W. M. Sneed, wit.

Taylor, Stephen & Francis Currin, 6 June 1845; Risdon Jones, bm; J. M. Wiggins, wit.

Taylor, Thos. J. & Rosalia Speed, 2 Oct 1843; T. H. Gregory, bm; Wm. H. Whitfield, wit.

Taylor, Warner & Polly Johnson, 9 Sept 1829; Tho. L. King, bm; Step. K. Sneed, wit.

Taylor, William & Elisabeth H. Smith, 8 Dec 1804; John Somerville Jr., bm; Step. Sneed, wit.

Taylor, William & Francis Wilson, 9 March 1836; M. N. Hope, bm; Benja. Kittrell, wit.

Taylor, William C. & Clarasa Eaker, 11 Dec 1816; John OBriant, bm.

Taylor, William L. & Sally M. Gregory, 11 Jan 1845; T. J. Gregory, bm; Jas. M. Wiggins, wit.

Taylor, William V. & Fanny M. Henderson, 21 June 1814; William M. Sneed, bm.

Taylor, Woodley, of color, son of Scipio & Betsy Taylor, & Lizzie Currin, daughter of Mary Currin now Hart, 27 Dec 1867; m 27 Dec 1867 by A. C. Harris, M. G.

Teasley, Willey & Parthenia Bass, 7 May 1856; John Buller, bm; Eugene Grissom, wit; m 12 May 1856 by Jas. J. Moore, J. P.

Terrell, Jephtha & Nancey Allen, 9 Sept 1807; Robert Jeter, bm; Jun. Sneed, wit.

Terrell, Jephthah & Nancy Hockaday, 24 Dec 1821; Anthony Clement, bm; S. K. Sneed, wit.

Terrell, John & Susana Douglass, 17 April 1760; Sugar Jones, John Terrell, bm; Danl. Weldon, wit.

Terrell, John & Susana Douglass, 17 April 1760; Sugar Jones, bm; Will. Johnson, wit.

Terrell, Thomas J. & Mary B. Johnson, 22 Dec 1857; Wm. K. Brasius bm; m 3 Jan 1858 by Wm. T. Brooks.

Terry, Benjamin & Easter Dorset, 9 April 1834; James Beck, bm.

Terry, Benjamin & Frances Tippett, 7 March 1853; B. F. Jenkins, bm; m 9 March 1853 by H. W. Jones, J. P.

Terry, Benjamin J. & Virginia Thomasson, m 28 April 1867 by A. C. Harris, M. G.

GRANVILLE MARRIAGES 1753-1868

Terry, James & Sarah Thorp, 5 April 1780; Terry Thorp, bm; Bennet Searcy, wit.

Terry, James & Mary Gooch, 3 Jan 1792; John Gooch, bm; W. Norwood, wit.

Terry, James & Prudence Gooch, 18 Aug 1816; John Gooch, bm; Wm. Thomasson, wit.

Terry, James T. & Susanna Slaughter, 14 Dec 1830; James Oakley, bm; David Laws, wit.

Terry, John & Sarah Terry, 26 Sept 1798; James Terry, bm; Step. Sneed, wit.

Terry, Joseph & Edie Hopgood, 8 Feb 1797; Wm. Dickins, bm; Step. Sneed, wit.

Terry, Josiah & Polly Lanier, 12 Feb 1825; Nathaniel Speer, bm; Wm. Hayes Owen, wit.

Terry, Kertis & Judith Gooch, 12 July 1803; James Terry, bm; Green Merritt, wit.

Terry, Stephen & Elisabeth Barnet, 7 March 1785; James Byars, bm; John Stamped(?), wit.

Terry, Stephen & Marlitia(?) Dean, 13 Oct 1842; Wm. Dean, bm; Wm. H. Whitfield, wit.

Terry, Thomas & Elizabeth Smith, 21 Dec 1810; Thos. Shapard, bm; Jun. Sneed, wit.

Terry, Thomas Chamr. & Nancy Pools, 10 Jan 1788; Benj. Harris, bm; Asa Searcy, wit.

Terry, Wm. & Nancy Gooch, 11 Feb 1793; Daniel Gooch, bm; W. Norwood, wit.

Terry, William & Parthenia Dean, 1 April 1829; John Shearman, bm; Step. K. Sneed, wit.

Tharington, John E. & Martha Johnson, 24 Oct 1846; Samuel H. Jeffreys, bm; Jas. M. Wiggins, wit.

Tharington, Ruffin T., son of Thos. & Harriet Tharrington, & Eliza H. Clay, daughter of Allen Clay & E. Oakley, m 6 Feb 1869 by B. Walker, J. P.

Tharington, Willie & Mary Sykes, 21 Oct 1865; Edward T. Gooch, bm; m 29 Oct 1865 by Eugene Grissom, J. P.

Tharp, Benjamin & Jane Taylor, 6 Jan 1800; Robt. Taylor, bm; Rd. Sneed, wit.

Thomas, Alfred, of color, son of Granville Jordan & Eliza Thomas, & Elizabeth Bullock, daughter of Alexander Mason & Deliley Bullock; m 9 April 1868 by Jas. R. Duty, J. P.

Thomas, Anthony & Allis Smith, 25 Dec 1866; Anthony Walker, bm; W. S. H. Thomas, J. P.; m 26 Dec 1866 by Wm. H. Puryear, Esq.

Thomas, Drewry & Sarah Wilson, 8 Dec 1847; L. S. Philpott, bm; Jas. M. Wiggins, wit.

GRANVILLE MARRIAGES 1753-1868

Thomas, Ferny, of color, son of Haywood & Seny Thomas, & Betsy Perry, daughter of Henry Perry & Harriet Williams, m 4 Oct 1867 by W. H. P. Jenkins, J. P.

Thomas, Howel & Elizabeth Murry, 7 Jan 1854; Charles Kearson, bm; A. Landis, wit; m 10 Jan 1854 by Jno. W. Stovall, J. P.

Thomas, James & Elizabeth Keeton, 18 March 1862; Richard Reece, bm; m 18 March 1862 by L. B. Stone, J. P.

Thomas, James & Mary Winston, m 3 Aug 1866 by L. K. Willie, M. G.

Thomas, John & Anne Holt, 8 Oct 1784; James Holt, bm; Bennet Searcy, wit.

Thomas, John & Susannah Duty, 16 Oct 1798; Sam. F. Williams, bm; Step. Sneed, wit.

Thomas, John & Elizabeth Pinson, 26 Sept 1853; William Davis, bm; Jno. W. Stovall, wit; m 26 Sept 1853 by Jno. W. Stovall, J. P.

Thomas, John, colored, son of Madison Lewis & Eliza Lewis, & Elizabeth Thomas, daughter of Richard & Ann Thomas, 22 Dec 1868; m 25 Dec 1868 by James Puryear, J. P.

Thomas, Joseph L. & Louisa A. Sanford, 20 Dec 1856; J. W. Thomas, bm; m 24 Dec 1856 by James King.

Thomas, Maurice S., son of W. H. Thomas & Caroline Thomas, & Fannie A. Pittard, daughter of Thomas J. & Ann Pittard, 23 Oct 1868; m 29 Oct 1868 by R. J. Devin, M. G.

Thomas, Peter & Jane Smith, 2 Nov 1867; James Thomas, bm; W. S. H. Thomas, J. P., wit; m 3 Nov 1867 (colored), by W. H. Puryear, J. P.

Thomas, Philip H. & Elizabeth A. Taylor, 22 April 1823; Warner M. Lewis, bm; Step. K. Sneed, wit.

Thomas, Philip H. & Mary E. Taylor, 16 Aug 1853; Jas. R. Duty, bm; m 24 Aug 1853 by Thos. F. Davis, Rector of Episc. Church in Wmsboro.

Thomas, Robert W. & Virginia M. Beasley, 12 Jan 1866; R. S. Barnett, bm; m 24 Jan 1866 by R. J. Devin.

Thomas. Walker & Eler OBrien, 6 _____ 1843; A. H. Hanks, bm.

Thomas, Washington H. & Caroline Royster, 24 May 1830; Wm. L. Owen, bm.

Thomas, Wesley G. & Mary Ann Perkinson, 18 Dec 1855; R. T. Overton, bm; m 20 Dec 1855 by D. J. Paschall, J. P.

Thomas, William & Frances Pettaford, 24 April 1858; O. L. Burch, bm; J. C. Hester, wit.

Thomas, William & Audney Coley, 5 June 1866; m 10 June 1866 by R. H. Hobgood.

Thomas, William B. & Susan Lewis, 28 Nov 1828; Wm. L. Owen, bm.

Thomas, William J. & Mary T. Jordan, 26 Dec 1821; Robert Jones, bm; L. Gilliam, wit.

GRANVILLE MARRIAGES 1753-1868

Thomason, Garland & Lucy W. Smith, 22 May 1829; Alexander Montague, bm; David Laws, wit.

Thomason, George & _____, ____ 178_; Richard Hudspeth, bm.

Thomason, John & Betsey Ann Freeman, 10 Nov 1804; Thomas Ricks, bm.

Thomason, Nathaniel & Elisabeth Cottrell, 7 Nov 1796; James Thomason, bm; Step. Sneed, wit.

Thomason, Richard P. & Mary Higgs, 22 Dec 1801; Louthern Higgs, bm; P. Bullock, wit.

Thomason, Thomas & Susanna Price Clay, 6 Dec 1810; Doctor Daniel, bm; Fanny M. Sneed, wit.

Thomason, William & Betsey Walker, (no date, during admn. of Gov. Nathaniel Alexander); Gleming Thomasson, bm; W. M. Sneed, wit.

Thomason, William J. & Virginia V. Ellis, 31 Oct 1860; James R. Duty, bm.

Thomasson, Benjamin & Dolly Flemming, 5 Nov 1839; William W. Parkinson, bm; G. C. Wiggins, wit.

Thomasson, Chas. R., son of Benj. Thomasson & Polly Thomasson, & Nancy L. Brinkley, daughter of Hiriam & Annice Brinkley, 17 July 1868; m 19 July 1868 by Robt. L. Heflin, J. P.

Thomasson, James G. & Adeline F. Byram, 10 Jan 1867; W. P. Mitchell, bm.

Thomasson, James M. & Frances Cottrell, 17 Dec 1854; Jas. R. Duty, bm; m 20 Dec 1854 by James R. Duty, J. P.

Thomasson, Jones & Lucy Proctor, 25 Dec 1815; Bannester Royster, bm; Step. K. Sneed, wit.

Thomasson, Nelson & Martha Johnson, 10 Dec 1808; John Thomasson, bm; W. M. Sneed, wit.

Thomasson, Samuel & Polly Ann Terry, 9 Feb 1861; J. P. Kinten, bm; m 10 Feb 1861 by H. W. Jones, J. P.

Thomasson, Thomas M. & Catharine Gorden, 28 July 1853; Alexander A. Hunt, bm; m 29 July 1853 by D. J. Paschall, J. P.

Thomasson, Upton & Mary Williams, 5 Jan 1820; Leonard Cardwell, bm; Jas. M. Wiggins, wit.

Thomasson, William & Mary Reeves, 23 Nov 1782; _____ Johnson, bm; Bennet Searcy, wit.

Thomasson, William & Candis Terry, m 2 Oct 1867 by G. W. Ferrill.

Thomasson, William Jr. & Tureacy McC. Allen, 27 Nov 1837; William J. Mallory, bm.

Thompson, Andrew & Lucy Ann Cox, 20 April 1855; H. H. Rowland, bm; m 22 April 1855 by A. C. Harris, M. G.

Thompson, Henderson & Martha Tucker, 8 Feb 1825; Richard W. Booker, bm; A. Sneed, wit.

GRANVILLE MARRIAGES 1753-1868

Thompson, James & Phoebe Williams, 14 Sept 1808; Joseph Shearing, bm; W. M. Sneed, wit.

Thompson, Nicholas & Sally A. Thompson, 11 Feb 1836; John McGlenchey(?), bm; Benja. Kittrell, wit.

Thompson, Randolph & Mary White, 13 July 1827; Jno. Bucknall, bm.

Thompson, S. H. & Minty W. Higgs, 6 March 1835; James Kittrell, bm; Benja. Kittrell, wit.

Thompson, Walter A. & Sally Reavis, _____ 185_; A. H. Alley, bm.

Thompson, William & Isabella Cobb, 5 Aug 1816; Jno. Cobb, bm; Rhodes N. Herndon, wit.

Thompson, William & Milley Cash, 31 Dec 1831; Peter Cash, bm; Step. K. Sneed, wit.

Thompson, William & Mary Cash, 25 March 1842; George Emry, bm.

Thompson, William J. & Virginia V. Ellis, 31 Oct 1860; m by Jas. R. Duty, J. P.

Thompson, Wynn & Martha Style, 24 Dec 1809; Samuel Hogg, bm; A. H. Sneed, wit.

Thomson, John & Christan Redwine, 23 Oct 1782; Michael Redwine, bm; Asa Searcy, wit.

Thorn, Charles & Delilah Tilliam, 22 July 1794; Wm. C. Beckham, bm; L. Henderson, wit.

Thornton, James & Elisabeth Jones, 22 March 1762; Jno. Hawkins, bm; Thos. Lowe, Thos. Conti, wit.

Thornton, Richard & Sarah T. Puryear, 13 Jan 1836; Robt. W. Lassiter, bm.

Thornton, Solomon & Rebeccah Simmons, 1 Oct 1794; Thomas Harp, bm; Step. Sneed, wit.

Thornton, William & Fanney Mitchel, 18 Jan 1781; Ralph Neal, bm; Reuben Searcy, wit.

Thorp, Anderson & Lucinda Thorp, m 27 Dec 1866 by M. H. Vaughan, Rector of St. Stephen's Church.

Thorp, Benjamin, of color, son of Young & Burchett, a slave, & Lucy Webb, daughter of Nelson & Nancy Webb, m 30 June 1867 by Samuel Hunt, J. P.

Thorp, Benjamin P. Jr. & Ann Eliza Norman, 8 Feb 1837; Richd. P. Taylor, bm; G. C. Wiggins, wit.

Thorp, Ephraim & Lizzie West, free persons, m 30 Dec 1865 by W. H. Puryear, J. P.

Thorp, Federick, colored, son of Dick & Riah Lewis, & Sallie Ann Pete Thorp, daughter of Happy Pete & George Pete Thorp, 10 Oct 1868; m 12 Oct 1868 by James Puryear, J. P.

Thorp, George, of color, son of Elijah Smith & Abbie Thorp, & Lizzie Morton, daughter of Alonzo Fields & Rowan Morton, 13 July 1867; m by Samuel Hunt, J. P., 14 July 1867.

GRANVILLE MARRIAGES 1753-1868

Thorp, Gideon & Rosena Jones, m 20 April 1867 by W. H. Thomas, J. P.

Thorp, Harry & Julia Jenkins, 27 Dec 1866; David Stumper, bm.

Thorp, James, of color, son of Juba Slaughter & Kizzie Thorp, & Dorcas Cash, daughter of Stephen Young & Bella Philpott, of color, m 7 Dec 1867 by W. H. Puryear, J. P.

Thorp, John & Patsy Howard, 27 June 1792; William Gooch, bm; W. Norwood, wit.

Thorp, Jordan & Peggy Smith, 25 Feb 1867; David Slaughter, bm; (freed people); m 3 May 1867 by B. D. Howard, J. P.

Thorp, Lewis & Mildred C. Lewis, 14 Oct 1842; Arch. Taylor, bm; Wm. H. Whitfield, wit.

Thorp, Lewis, of color, son of Silla Oakley, & Rebecca Wilkerson, daughter of George & Patsy Wilkerson, m 4 July 1867 by J. L. Carroll, Minister.

Thorp, Lucius & Eliza Longmire, 18 Jan 1866; Daniel J. Gooch, bm; m 21 Jan 1866 by H. W. Jones, J. P.

Thorp, Martin, of color, son of Richd. Young & Mariah Lewis, & Tempy Davis, daughter of Jerry Davis, m 19 Sept 1868 by William S. Hester.

Thorp, Micajah & Amelia Satterwhite, 25 Jan 1866; freed people; m 25 Jan 1866 by J. M. Satterwhite, J. P.

Thorp, Stephen, of color, son of Parthenia Thorp, & Hannah Chavis, daughter of Anderson Chavis & Critty Waller, 1 Aug 1868; m 1 Aug 1868 by J. L. Carroll, Minister.

Thorp, William & Arrabella Young, 3 Aug 1847; John Blacknall Jr., bm; Jas. M. Wiggins, wit.

Thorp, William & Lucy Gregory, 4 March 1862; A. Landis, bm; m 26 March 1862 by L. K. Willie, M. G.

Thorp, Willie & Henrietta Smith, freed people, m 10 March 1866 by T. T. Grandy, J. P.

Throgmorton, Wilson & Caroline Glover, 17 Nov 1866; C. E. Landis, bm; m 2 Dec 1866 by J. J. Speed, J. P.

Tiggle, John & Sarah Bradford, 29 Nov 1784; Bennet Searcy, bm; Elisabeth Searcy, wit.

Tiler, Pink & Lucy Bass, 25 Sept 1797; Able Anderson, bm; Jno. Hall, wit.

Tillett, John & Elizabeth J. Wyche, 4 Oct 1841; Robert H. Wyche, bm.

Tillett, Rev. John & Louisa Y. Speed, 3 Feb 1863; Jno. S. Burnett, bm; m 4 Feb 1863 by J. H. Wheeler.

Tilley, Dennis & Sallie Jenkins, 11 Jan 1854; Wilie Ashley, bm; m 11 Jan 1854 by Jeff Horner, J. P.

Tilley, F. J. & Sallie A. Coley, 28 Aug 1865; A. H. Gooch, bm; m 29 Aug 1865 by R. B. Hester.

GRANVILLE MARRIAGES 1753-1868

Tilley, Francis J. & Ann O. Waller, 31 Dec 1858; Willie Meadows, bm; m 4 Jan 1859 by Jeff Horner, J. P.

Tilley, George & Mary Jones, 7 Aug 1843; Henry Tilley, bm; Wm. H. Whitfield, wit.

Tilley, Henderson & Sallie Barnett, 18 Dec 1857; Anson Critcher, bm; A. Landis, wit; m 22 Dec 1857 by W. J. Devin.

Tilley, James & Temp. Roberts, 23 Feb 1829; Henry Tilley, bm; Step. K. Sneed, wit.

Tilley, James D. & Mildred E. Waller, 6 April 1866; m by Dennis Tilley, J. P.

Tilley, John & Martha Jones, 13 Sept 1850; Dudley B. Johnson, bm.

Tilley, Richard & Atelia Jones, freed people, 7 March 1866; F. J. Tilley, bm; m 4 March 1866 by Dennis Tilley, J. P.

Tilley, Willie R. & Virginia K. Priddy, 7 Jan 1862; Dennis Tilley, bm; m 22 Jan 1862 by R. G. Tinnin.

Tillotson, Allen & Mary Hunt, 11 Sept 1828; Anderson Owin, bm; Robert K. Clack, wit.

Tillotson, Henry & Elizabeth Morgan, 21 Dec 1841; John H. Richards, bm; J. M. Wiggins, wit.

Tillotson, Martin & Martha Cutts, 3 Dec 1844; William H. Cutts, bm; Wm. H. Whitfield, wit.

Tillotson, Martin & Elizabeth Butler, 24 Oct 1855; J. H. Strum(?), bm.

Tillotson, Robert & Mrs. Susanna Daniel (no date, request for license from Susanna Danel, wit by Samuel Tillotson).

Tillotson, Robert & Susannah Dannel, 15 Dec 1843; Samuel Dannel, bm; J. M. Wiggins, wit.

Tillotson, Woody & Amanda Yancey, 20 Jan 1846; Hezekiah Yancy, bm; Jas. M. Wiggins, wit.

Tillottson, Allen & Mrs. Margaret Murry, 23 July 1851; James M. Overbey, bm; L. B. Stone, J. P., wit; m 23 July 1851 by Littlebury Stone, J. P.

Tillottson, William R., son of William & Julia Tillottson, & Martha Clark, daughter of William & Nancy Clark, 5 Nov 1867; m 6 Nov 1867 by E. L. Parrish, J. P.

Tilly, Haskins & Susan Walker, 8 March 1860; Moody Fowler, bm.

Tindal, John & Elisabeth Nunnery, 3 March 1795; John Johnson, bm; Step. Sneed, wit.

Tingen, Garret & Joanna Duncan, 8 Jan 1815; Elijah Carnal, bm; W. M. Sneed, wit.

Tingen, Sterling H. & Ellenor D. Duncan, 2 Feb 1857; Jacob L. Slaughter, bm; m 19 Feb 1857 by Peterson Thorp, J. P.

Tingen, William W. & Jackey E. Landis, 1 Dec 1847; S. H. Duncan, bm; Jas. M. Wiggins, wit.

GRANVILLE MARRIAGES 1753-1868

Tingen, Zachariah H. & Ailey Ann Duncan, 30 Nov 1857; Robt. Wade, bm; A. Landis, wit; m 21 Jan 1858 by Peterson Thorp, J. P.

Tingin, Garrett R. & Emily P. OBriant, 14 Jan 1856; Howell Duncan, bm.

Tippet, John Junr. & Lucy Bearden, 22 Sept 1820; Cader Parker, bm; Step. K. Sneed, wit.

Tippet, Jonathan & Mary Wade, 13 Oct 1798; Michael Wood, bm; W. M. Sneed, wit.

Tippett, David & Lucy Mangum, 1 Nov 1859; Benjamin Terry, bm.

Tippett, Eli & Elizabeth Hobgood, 12 Dec 1831; Lemuel Hobgood, bm; David Laws, wit.

Tippett, James & Nancey Morris, 3 _____ 1819; Archibald Cauthon, bm; Richd. Sneed, wit.

Tippett, John H. & Mary Jones, 10 June 1837; John B. Moore, bm.

Tippett, Jonathan & Louisa Cawthorn, 17 Dec 1859; John C. Peace, bm; A. Landis, wit; m 18 Dec 1859 by H. R. Bridgers.

Tippett, Jonathan & Ariella M. Overton, 23 Nov 1865; Samuel T. Dickerson, bm.

Tippett, Simeon & Elizabeth A. Peace, 23 Sept 1865; T. E. Bobbitt, bm; m 24 Sept 1865 by Jas. S. Purifoy, Minister of the Gospel.

Tippett, Thomas & Jane Morriss, 3 Jan 1829; Sol. Philpott, bm; D. J. Young, wit.

Tippett, William & Arena Adcock, 28 Dec 1831; Lemuel Hobgood, bm; David Lewis, wit.

Tippit, John H. & Roberta Chambless, 5 May 1835; Lemuel Hobgood, bm; Benja. Kittrell, wit.

Tippit, Luke & Mary Vincent, 27 Dec 1792; Joseph Wesley, bm; W. Norwood, wit.

Todd, Henry W. & Anne W. Hull, 1 Sept 1804; Thomas Taylor, bm; Step. Sneed, wit.

Tolar, William & Susan Cousin, 10 Nov 1838; Alexr. Howell, bm.

Toomi(?), Jackson & Sarah J. Elam, 25 Aug 1838; Wm. R. Jeffries, bm; M. D. Royster, wit.

Toone, William F. & Sarah A. Stovall, 5 July 1842; Elijah Satterwhite, bm; Wm. T. Hargrove, wit.

Tooni, William J. & Ann Eliza Floyd, 5 Feb 1861; Thomas G. Kittrell, bm; m 6 Feb 1861 by L. K. Willie.

Toryan, John & Nancy Ann Wornal, 6 Dec 1859; Gordan T. Powell, bm; L. B. Stone, wit; m 6 Dec 1859 by L. B. Stone, J. P.

Totten, Joseph & Elisabeth Griggs Scott, 20 Sept 1796; John OBryant, bm; Step. Sneed, wit.

GRANVILLE MARRIAGES 1753-1868

Townes, Edmond & Elizabeth T. Hunt, 29 Oct 1832; Memican Hunt, bm.

Townes, Isaac, of color, son of John Small & Nancy Small, & Henrietta Bullock, daughter of Henry & Matilda Bullock, m 14 July 1867 by Jas. R. Duty, J. P.

Townes, Wesley & Julia Speed, m 24 Nov 1866 by Was. H. Thomas, J. P.; Peter Speed, bm; C. E. Landis, wit.

Townley, Henry & Agness Rich, 19 Sept 1776; Shadrach Rich, bm; Jesse Newley, wit.

Tranum, Lazarus & Judith Owen, 25 April 1800; Gideon Williams, bm; Step. Sneed, wit.

Traylor, John & Delilah Huddleston, 28 April 1795; James Tuill, bm; Step. Sneed, wit.

Traylor, Thompson & Anne Anderson, 24 Sept 1820; Robert Kinton, bm; Samuel Hillman, wit.

Traylor, William & Fanny Jeffreys, 9 June 1816; Eaks Huddleston, bm; W. M. Sneed, wit.

Trevan, Mongomery & Edney Wever, 18 March 1867; Thomas Pedaford, bm; m 19 March 1867 by John W. York.

Trewollee, Henry P. & Eliza G. Poytress, 12 May 1833; Peyton Hayes, bm; Jno. P. Smith, wit.

Trim, Robert B. & Ann J. Harris, 10 Nov 1860; B. D. Howard, bm; m 17 Nov 1860 by F. M. Jordan.

Trisdal, George W., son of Wm. & Nancy Trisdal, & Ginna Strum, daughter of Jas. A. Strum & Ritter Hester, m 22 March 1867 by E. L. Parrish, J. P.

Troler, James & Betsy Norwood, m 25 Jan 1862 by Wm. M. Bennett, J. P.

Troler, William Anderson, son of Eliza Toler, of color, & Martha Boone, of color, daughter of Fannie Curtis, 1 May 1868; m 1 May 1868 by B. T. Winston, J. P.

Truman, Hanson & Hannah Norman, 16 June 1815; Leonard Henderson, bm; Richd. Sneed, wit.

Trustee, John & Levicy Partee, 23 Jan 1782; Edmd. Partee, bm.

Tuck, John & Martha Hester, 29 Nov 1802; James Hester, bm; Jun. Sneed, wit.

Tuck, John & Mary Fletcher, 9 Nov 1814; Wm. Lassiter, bm; _____ Sneed, wit.

Tuck, John & Abby W. Tuck, freed people, m 15 July 1867 by W. Overbey, J. P.

Tuck, John, son of Paul & Mary C. Tuck, & Elizabeth Murry, daughter of Richard & Nancy Murry, 26 Dec 1867; m 26 Dec 1867 by L. B. Stone, J. P.

Tuck, John W. & Lucy P. Sandford, 20 May 1841; Gabriel Jones, bm; Jas. M. Wiggins, wit.

GRANVILLE MARRIAGES 1753-1868

Tuck, P. R. T. & Matilda Tuck, 17 Jan 1864; R. B. Tuck, bm; m 19 Jan 1864 by L. B. Stone, J. P.

Tuck, Paul L. & Nancy R. Nelson, 6 Nov 1865; E. A. Tuck, bm; m 6 Nov 1865 by Alfred Apple, M. G.

Tuck, Powell, son of Nathan F. & Drana A. Tuck, & Martha Wilkerson, daughter of Spencer & Tabitha Wilkerson, m 3 Jan 1868 by L. B. Stone, J. P.

Tuck, Tom & Mary Eliza Sanford, m 24 Dec 1866 by L. B. Stone, J. P.; John Tuck, bm.

Tuck, William M. & Jane O. Wilkerson, 12 Nov 1859; Powell Tuck, bm; L. B. Stone, J. P., wit; m 12 Nov 1859 by L. B. Stone, J. P.

Tucker, Berry T. & Mary Adams, 25 Nov 1852, m by Jas R. Duty(?), J. P. (return only).

Tucker, Berry T. & Rebecca Seats, 28 May 1866; m 30 May 1866 by James E. Pattillo, J. P.

Tucker, Charles D. & Martha Newton, 9 May 1818; Littlebery Tucker, bm; A. Sneed, wit.

Tucker, Daniel & Sarah Shearmon, 19 April 1800; William Pannill, Benjamin Hilliard, bm.

Tucker, George & Sally Reeks, 6 Feb 1836; L. Huddleston, bm; Benja. Kittrell, wit.

Tucker, George W. & Harritt P. Neal, 18 Nov 1828; John Puryear, bm; D. J. Young, wit.

Tucker, Green & Elisabeth Hurt, 8 Aug 1849; Green Elliott, bm; A. Landis, wit.

Tucker, Henry & Ann B. Yates, 28 July 1835; Wm. H. Poindexter, bm; Robert K. Clack, wit.

Tucker, Henry & Adabyron Taylor, 2 July 1857; William R. Tucker, bm; m 2 July 1857 by James R. Duty, J. P.

Tucker, John B. & Sarah E. Wood, 12 Oct 1865; John W. York, Jr., bm.

Tucker, John L. & Patsey Kimball, 12 Jan 1843; Stephen Satterwhite, bm; J. M. Wiggins, wit.

Tucker, Littleberry & Mary Lumpkin, 15 July 1828; Harriss Williams, bm; David Laws, wit.

Tucker, Richard G. & Mary Vincent, 1 Nov 1864; A. J. Peoples, bm; m 1 Nov 1864 by W. M. Sneed, Jr.

Tucker, Robert & Nancey Peak, 10 Jan 1791; Wm. Peek, bm; H. Potter, wit.

Tucker, Robert C. & Martha C. Curtis, 9 Nov 1824; Henderson Thompson, bm; A. Sneed, wit.

Tucker, Thomas & Merina Howel, 13 March 1828; Samuel Hunt, bm; David Laws, wit.

GRANVILLE MARRIAGES 1753-1868

Tucker, William & Hawkins Chappell, 10 Dec 1858; Ephm. Emory, bm;
A. Landis, wit; m 12 Dec 1858 by Thos. B. Lyon, J. P.

Tucker, William R. & Mary F. Griffin, 9 Sept 1852; m by Jas. R.
Duty, J. P.

Tuder, John Jr. & Martha Searcy, 22 July 1779; Richd. Searcy,
bm; Reubin Searcy, wit.

Tudor, James & Joannah Martin, 20 June 1781; John More, bm; Asa
Searcy, wit.

Tudor, Valentine & Bettey Hicks, 17 March 1784; Henry Tudor, bm;
Bennet Searcy, wit.

Tunstall, Patrick A. & Celestia A. Vaughan, 22 March 1859; R. A.
Tunstall, bm; m 24 March 1859 by W. H. Hight.

Tunstall, Robert A. & Louisa F. Hayes, 10 June 1863; C. J.
Bobbitt, bm; m 10 June 1863 by J. W. Floyd, Minister.

Tuppence, James & Jincey Tabourn, 5 Aug 1826; Step. K. Sneed, bm.

Turnbull, Hay 7 Martha Field, 18 April 1763; James Forsyth, bm;
Jno. Bowie, wit.

Turner, Charles R. & Talitha Turner, 17 Dec 1807; James M. Burton, Jr., bm; Jun. Sneed, wit.

Turner, Drury R. & Elizabeth F. Moss, 26 April 1828; L. Paschall,
bm; S. K. Sneed, wit.

Turner, Drury T. & Sarah Brame, 6 June 1847; Wm. W. Perkinson,
bm; Benj. C. Cooke, wit.

Turner, Henry & Margaret M. Hunt, 6 Aug 1832; Thomas Hunt, bm;
Step. K. Sneed, wit.

Turner, James A. & Sallie H. Kittrell, 26 May 1857; L. A. Paschall, bm; m 27 May 1857 by W. K. Willie, M. G.

Turner, James A. & Rebecca Cheatham, 19 Oct 1860; G. W. Allen,
bm; m 23 Oct 1860 by L. K. Willie.

Turner, James E. & Margarette E. Whitfield, 17 Nov 1852; D. C.
Bullock, bm; A. Landis, wit.

Turner, John & Polly Williams, 6 Nov 1798; William Bonner, bm;
W. M. Sneed, wit.

Turner, John & Polly Haily, 9 Sept 1826; Willie Pollard, bm;
Wm. H. Owen, wit.

Turner, John & Minerva Hawkins, 12 Aug 1865; Peter Fains, bm;
Jas. R. Duty, wit.

Turner, John J. & Martha Floyd, 25 Dec 1833; Wm. Floyd Jr., bm.

Turner, Reeves & Lumaga Vaughan, 25 March 1817; John Wiggins,
bm; Samuel Sneed, wit.

Turner, Richard H. & Elizabeth M. Satterwhite, 13 Dec 1853;
Henry Davis, bm; m 15 Dec 1853 by S. G. Wilson, J. P.

Turner, Samuel D. & Geneva F. Lyman, m 22 Aug 1867 by W. D. Allen,
J. P.

GRANVILLE MARRIAGES 1753-1868

Turner, Sion & Polley Hart, 27 Jan 1789; Samuel Pittard, bm; A. Henderson, C. C., wit.

Turner, Simon T. & Rosabella B. Wainwright, 18 Feb 1858; B. J. Jinkins, bm; m 21 Feb 1858 by T. J. Horner, M. G.

Turner, Dr. Vines, son of A. A. & Mary A. Turner, & Miss Zena H. Lassiter, daughter of James H. & A. Lassiter, 22 Sept 1868; m 24 Sept 1868 by A. McDowell.

Turner, William & Frances Dodson, 30 Dec 1791; William Dodson, bm; W. Norwood, wit.

Turner, William R. & Lucretia H. Stark, 5 Jan 1859; C. R. Cawthom, bm; m 12 Jan 1859 by L. K. Willie, M. G.

Twisdale, James & Elisabeth Hunter Mason, 15 Oct 1798; David Mason, bm.

Twisdale, John & Lettey Williams, 17 Aug 1809; Thomas Mitchell, bm; Lewis Yancey, wit.

Twisdall, Green & Mary Brame, 12 Oct 1844; William P. Edwards, bm; Wm. H. Whitfield, wit.

Tyler, Anderson & Laney Hawley, 13 July 1814; Lemuel Tyler, bm; J. C. Smith, wit.

Tyler, James & Nancy Evans, 2 March 1843; Thomas Anderson, bm; Wm. H. Whitfield, wit.

Tyler, Lemuel & Winny Anderson, 7 Dec 1811; Benjamin Evans, bm; Stephen K. Sneed, wit.

Tyler, William & Patsey Day, 4 April 1821; George Anderson, bm; W. M. Sneed, wit.

Tyler, William L. & Martha Ann Due, 14 May 1857; Edward Mayo, bm; A. Landis, wit.

Tyner, James & Betsey Bass, 5 Jan 1805; James H. Butler, bm; J. Sneed, wit.

Tyner, John & Betty Bass, 5 Jan 1796; Uriah Tyner, bm; William Robards, wit.

Tyner, Jonathan & Pheby Bass, 9 July 1804; Arthur Tyner, bm; Step. Sneed, wit.

Tynes, William,& Luviney Davis, 4 April 1778; Absolem Davis Jr., bm; Reuben Searcy, wit.

Umstead, Abraham & Beedy Parish, 22 Feb 1822; Jeremiah Bullock, bm; Step. K. Sneed, wit.

Umstead, John H. & Luisa G. Waller, 26 March 1867; R. C. Tilley, bm; D. Tilley, wit; m 28 March 1867 by A. W. Mangum.

Umstead, Richard & Levina Wheeler, 23 March 1825; John Nance Jr., bm; Wm. Hayes Owen, wit.

Umstead, Squire & Martha Waller, 17 Jan 1835; Alfred Jones, bm; Benja. Kittrell, wit.

Umstead, William & Frankey Waller, 10 Jan 1825; Robt. F. P. Jones, bm.

GRANVILLE MARRIAGES 1753-1868

Umsted, John & Betsey Diskill Chettam, 21 Jan 1796; Daniel Green, bm; Philip Bullock, wit.

Umsted, Richard & Rebeca Baxter, 25 May 1794; Elijah Veazey, bm; H. Seawell, wit.

Upchurch, A. H. & Mary E. Dement, 12 Nov 1859; William Deckerson, bm; m 13 Nov 1859 by S. J. Horner, M. G.

Upchurch, Henry & Mary Parrish, 14 Dec 1840; Rowland Parham, bm; J. M. Wiggins, wit.

Upchurch, John & Anne Harris, 21 June 1790; Wm. Currin, bm; Henry Potter, wit.

Upchurch, John G. & Rebecca Barnett, 24 Oct 1866; m 24 Oct 1866 by L. M. VanHook, J. P.

Upchurch, William & Anita Jenkins, 2 March 1803; Valentine White, bm; Green Merritt, wit.

Uphris, James M., of Person County, & Elizabeth Daniel, of Granville Co., 11 July 1857; m 30 Aug 1857 by James King.

Usery, Joel & Susan Lemay, 29 Jan 1828; Mitchell Daniel, bm; David Laws, wit.

Usery, John & Elisabeth Priddy, 2 Sept 1851; B. J. Blackly, bm.

Usry, Freeman & Ellen Montague, 23 Jan 1866; Geo. J. Rowland, bm; m 23 Jan 1866.

Usry, Richard, son of William & Jane Usry, & Martha Burnett, daughter of Addison R. & Mildred Burnett, 3 July 1868; m 5 July 1868 by George J. Rowland, J. P.

Usry, Thomas R. & Mary A. Harris, 5 Nov 1852; Eugene Grissom, bm.

Usry, Washington, son of William & Jane Usry, & Mary Hunt, daughter of James & Lucinda Hunt, 29 Aug 1868; m 3 Sept 1868 by T. J. Horner, G. M.

Usry, William T. & Ann Hawkins Qualls, 11 Nov 1856; Allen Adcock, bm; A. Landis, wit; m 12 Nov 1856 by W. D. Allen, J. P.

Ussery, Freeman & Ann Peace, 29 Sept 1819; Richd. B. Taylor, bm; S. K. Sneed, wit.

Ussery, John & Tempey Wilson, 13 May 1820; Joseph White, bm; Jas. M. Wiggins, wit.

Ussery, William & Jane Fowler, 30 April 1834; C. W. Walker, bm; Benja. Kittrell, wit.

Uzzell, William B. & Amanda C. Catlett, 11 Nov 1864; Jas. J. Moore, bm; m 1 Dec 1864 by T. Page Ricaud, Minister of the Gospel, Franklinton, N. C.

Valentine, Austin & Nancy Mitchell, 21 May 1823; Amos Coe, bm; Jas. M. Wiggins, wit.

Valentine, Chesley Jones & Jane Hayne, 13 Sept 1800; John Valentine, bm; Step. Sneed, wit.

GRANVILLE MARRIAGES 1753-1868

Valentine, Elijah & Polley Bass, 28 June 1806; Benjamin Mitchell, bm; W. M. Sneed, wit.

Valentine, James Alexander & Elizabeth Pettiford, 10 March 1840; Cuffe Mayo, bm; J. M. Wiggins, wit.

Valentine, John A. J. & Elisabeth Hayne, 13 Sept 1800; Chesley James Valentine, bm; Step. Sneed, wit.

Valentine, John W. & Polly A. Rice, 9 Sept 1835; W. B. Ellington, bm; Benja. Kittrell, wit.

Valentine, Pleasant & Lucinda Parrish, 30 Sept 1845; Abel Valentine, bm; Jas. M. Wiggins, wit.

Valentine, Pomfrett & Margaret Howell, 25 April 1845; Abel Valentine, bm; Jas. M. Wiggins, wit.

Valentine, Robert & Mary Howell, 15 July 1848; Pleasant Valentine, bm.

Valentine, Robert & Mary Ann Steward, 7 Sept 1857; Robert Anderson, bm; A. Landis, wit; m 9 Sept 1857 by John Mallory.

Vann, A. R. & Elisabeth F. Canaday, 29 March 1850; W. M. Cannady, bm.

Vann, Lewis & Amanda Fuller, 10 Aug 1866; m 24 Aug 1866 by G. N. Hicks, J. P.

Vass, George, son of Benaham & Ooney Vass, & Larcissa Curtis, daughter of Peter & Isabella Curtis, m 3 Jan 1869 by John H. Webb, J. P.

Vass, John & Peggy Edwards, 10 Feb 1816; John Hart, bm; W. M. Sneed, wit.

Vass, Reuben & Elizabeth Pool, 1 March 1813; John Hart, bm; W. M. Sneed, wit.

Vass, Robert & Ann Satterwhite, 29 Oct 1831; Wm. S. McClanahan, bm; Step. K. Sneed, wit.

Vass, Thomas Junr. & Phoebe A. Howard, 18 Dec 1830; W. S. McClanahan, bm; David Laws, wit.

Vaughan, Amis & Polley Obrian, 19 Nov 1811; Dennis Obriant, bm; W. M. Sneed, wit.

Vaughan, Arthur & Susan Bridges (freed people), 21 Sept 1866; m 22 Sept 1866 by Wyatt Walker, M. Gospel.

Vaughan, Brewer (alias Brewer King) & Sarah Ashley, 4 April 1811; Thomas King, bm; _____ Sneed, wit.

Vaughan, Edward & Julia Glasscock, 26 Dec 1848; William Glasscock, bm; L. B. Stone, J. P., wit.

Vaughan, Evy & Mary Ann Griffin, 11 March 1843; Thos. _____, bm; Wm. H. Whitfield, wit.

Vaughan, Henry & Fanny Mayo, 24 Jan 1831; Step. K. Sneed, bm; David Laws, wit.

GRANVILLE MARRIAGES 1753-1868

Vaughan, Henry & Susan Richardson, 10 Jan 1833; William Mayo, bm; Step. K. Sneed, wit.

Vaughan, James M. & Elizabeth Leneve(?), 7 Feb 1855; William Clyborne, bm; m 8 Feb 1855 by Thos. Hester.

Vaughan, John & Rebecca Ann Wall, 10 March 1819; John Wiggins, bm; Richd. Sneed, wit.

Vaughan, John W. & Martha J. Reavis, 24 May 1854; Geo. B. Reavis, bm.

Vaughan, John W., son of Orsborn & Polly Vaughan, & Mary L. Reavis, daughter of Lewis & Mary Reavis, m 25 July 1867 by Ira T. Wyche, Minister of the Gospel.

Vaughan, Martin & Mary A. Noblin, 13 April 1853; Henry Tillottson, bm; L. B. Stone, J. P., wit; m 13 April 1853 by L. B. Stone, J. P.

Vaughan, Revd. Maurice H. & Miss Sarah A. Hamme, 7 Feb 1866; Geo. W. Landis, bm; m 8 Feb 1866 by Joseph W. Murphy, Rector of Holy Innocents Ch., Henderson.

Vaughan, Munroe & Elizabeth Hampton, 31 Dec 1855; Ezra Oakley, bm; m 27 Dec 1855 by Allen Cozart, J. P.

Vaughan, Peter & Frances Parrish, 15 May 1823; Pocaman Wilkins, bm; Jas. M. Wiggins, wit.

Vaughan, Reuben A. & Susan A. Whitt, 12 Aug 1867; A. Landis, bm; m by W. Overbey, J. P.

Vaughan, Seborn & Fanny Noblen, 9 Feb 1853; John S. Overbey, bm; Thos. Hester, J. P., wit; m 2 May 1853 by Thos. Hester.

Vaughan, Stephen & Eliza Chandler, 26 June 1847; F. T. deGraffenriedt, bm; L. B. Stone, J. P., wit; statement from Edwin Chandler, father of Eliza, of Mecklenburg County, Va., 24 June 1847 that she is 19 years of age and has his consent; R. H. Nance, T. G. De Graffenriedt, Richard H. Walker, wit.

Vaughan, Vince(?) & Elizabeth T. Reavis, 8 Nov 1834; William Bowdon, bm; Benja. Kittrell, wit.

Vaughan, William & Sally Griffin, 20 Oct 1835; James H. Griffin, bm; Robert D. Clack, wit.

Vaughan, William & Margaret Newton, 23 Dec 1848; Hamon Newton, bm; L. B. Stone, J. P., wit.

Vaughan, Winmond & Dilly Reavis (freed people), m 8 March 1866 by Joseph W. Murphy, Rector of Holy Innocents, Henderson.

Vaughan, Arther, colored, parents unknown, & Mary Parker, daughter of Henry & Haly Parker, 12 Oct 1868; m __ Oct 1868 by Jeffires Burwell, M. G.

Vaughn, John & Caroline Collier, 8 Feb 1838; James Curtis, bm; M. D. Royster, wit.

Vaughn, John G., son of James & Polly Vaughn, & Henrietta A. Catlett, daughter of George & Caroline Catlett, m 4 June 1868 by J. W. Wellons, Minister of the Gospel.

GRANVILLE MARRIAGES 1753-1868

Veasley, Stephen Junr. & Elizabeth H. Puryear, 25 April 1838; T. S. Beasley, bm; J. T. Beasley, wit.

Veazey, Abner & Elizabeth Jones, 4 Nov 1845; Geo. Haskins, bm; J. M. Wiggins, wit.

Veazey, Alfred M. & Margaret F. Umstead, 13 Nov 1844; Benj. C. Cook, bm.

Veazey, Andrew J. & Frances Clements, 9 Feb 1843; L. S. Philpott, bm; Wm. H. Whitfield, wit.

Veazey, Elijah H. & Luetta Ellis, 11 July 1867; F. J. Tilley, bm; m 14 July 1867 by Elder D. R. Moore.

Veazey, Ezekiel & Frankey Hester, 27 Feb 1809; Thomas Cooke, bm; W. M. Sneed, wit.

Veazey, Fielding & Nancy Howard, 20 May 1843; J. H. Gooch, bm; J. M. Wiggins, wit.

Veazey, Fielding L. & Polley Bowden, 12 Dec 1818; L. Gilliam, bm; W. M. Sneed, wit.

Veazey, Isham E. & Leticia Huddleston, 28 Oct 1857; Fielding Veazey, bm; L. A. Paschall, wit.

Veazey, James L. & Elizabeth Waller, 20 June 1837; E. Hester, bm; J. M. Wiggins, wit.

Veazey, John, of color, son of John Puckrom & Tiny Veazey, & Jane Holoway, daughter of Charles & Rebecca Holoway, 13 Nov 1867; m 17 Nov 1867 by John J. Lansdell, Minister of the Gospel.

Veazey, Marcellus W. B., son of Alfred M. & Margaret F. Veazey, & Louisa L. Peed, daughter of John & Susan Peed, 21 Nov 1867; m 28 Nov 1867 by John J. Lansdell.

Veazey, Mark & Polly Williams, 22 April 1803; Leavin Carey, bm; Green Merritt, wit.

Veazey, William & Nancey Hester, 13 June 1807; Thomas Gooch, bm; W. M. Sneed, wit.

Venable, T. Brown & Delia Kingsbury, 11 Jan 1854; T. L. Hargrove, bm; m 12 Jan 1852 by E. Hines, Minister of the Gospel.

Vincent, Henry & Elizabeth Adcock, 30 Sept 1805; William Leathers, bm.

Vincent, Henry H. & Susannah Mann, 27 Aug 1808; William Vincent, bm; W. M. Sneed, wit.

Vincent, John M. & Polley White, 20 March 1811; Wm. Butler, bm; W. M. Sneed, wit.

Vincent, Peter & Nancey Roffe, 7 March 1815; Henry H. Vincent, bm; W. M. Sneed, wit.

Vincent, William & Fanny Heflin, 3 Dec 1799; John Mitchell, bm; W. M. Sneed, wit.

Vincent, Willis & Rachel Vincent, 19 Oct 1781; John Suttan, bm; William Searcy, wit.

GRANVILLE MARRIAGES 1753-1868

Vinson, Richard & Sarah Beves, 9 Sept 1797; Evan Freeman, bm; Step. Sneed, wit.

Volentine, Archer & Ruthy Anderson, 14 July 1820; Thomas Anderson, bm; Step. K. Sneed, wit.

Volentine, John & Parthenia Anderson, 15 March 1847; William _____, bm; N. H. Wiggins, wit.

Volentine, Meshack & Nancy Pendergrass, 22 Oct 1823; Eligh Volentine, bm; Jas. M. Wiggins, wit.

Volentine, Rigdon & Dilly York, 8 March 1791; William Garrot, bm; A. Potter, wit.

Volentine, William R. & Mary P. Stone, 2 Feb 1826; Thomas Powel, bm; Step. K. Sneed, wit.

Vowel, Obediah & Rachel Frazier, 6 Sept 1786; John Findal, bm; Robert Searcy, wit.

Vowel, Thornar & Nancy Simmons, 7 July 1815; Mathew Vowel, bm; J. S. Young, wit.

Waddle, Thomas F. & Amelia S. Cook, 6 Nov 1851; Young A. Minnes, bm.

Wade, Benja. & Amey Jordan, 11 May 1762; Philip Taylor, bm; D. Weldon, wit.

Wade, Joseph & Elisabeth Allin, 30 Sept 1766; Benjamin Wade, bm; Cha. Bruce, wit.

Wade, Josiah & Isabella Smith, 17 Nov 1831; William P. Logan, bm; Jno. P. Smith, wit.

Wade, Memucan & Nancey Stem, 19 Oct 1796; Benjamin Moore, bm; M. Bullock, wit.

Wade, Richard & Elizabeth Edwards, 22 Nov 1790; Wm. Edwards, bm; H. Potter, wit.

Wade, Robert & Rebecka Downey, 8 Aug 1785; Robert Downey, bm; Bennet Searcy, wit.

Wadford, Alexander & Lucresia More, _____ 1854; A. Landis, bm; Jas. J. Moore, wit; m 16 July 1854 by W. D. Allen, J. P.

Wadford, William & Candis Sherrin, 31 Dec 1856; Lemuel Moore, bm; m 31 Dec 1856 by W. D. Allen.

Wagoner, John H., son of John & _____, & Lucy Ellis, daughter of _____ & Tilda Ellis, 2 Oct 1867; m 2 Oct 1867 by Francis J. Tilley, J. P.

Wagstaff, Joseph G. & Eugenia C. Paschall, 15 Dec 1849; Thadeus O. McClanahan, bm; A. Landis, wit.

Wagstaff, Joseph G. & Mary N. Blacknall, 15 Sept 1853; Will. Hicks, bm.

Wagstaff, Lee R., son of John S. & Frances Wagstaff, & Nancy Freeman, daughter of William F. & Rebecca Freeman, 31 Dec 1867; m 10 Jan 1868 by D. H. D. Bullock, J. P.

GRANVILLE MARRIAGES 1753-1868

Wainwright, Kennon H. & Narcissa A. Cooke, 18 Dec 1847; Isaac P. Hester, bm.

Waldo, S. P., son of Jos. & Catherine Waldo, & Alice M. Owen, daughter of E. W. & Margaret Owen, 30 Dec 1868; m 31 Dec 1868 by John Tillett.

Walker, Anderson H. & Sison W. White, 26 Nov 1830; Elias Jinkins, bm; Step. K. Sneed, wit.

Walker, Burnis & Martha Ann Wiggins, 6 Nov 1851; S. H. Petegrew, bm.

Walker, C. W. & Martha J. Champion, 20 April 1842; Jas. B. Peace, bm; Wm. H. Whitfield, wit.

Walker, Charles & Glafrey H. Tucker, 17 Oct 1864; Silas A. Cross, bm;

Walker, Daniel & Nancy Baily, 27 June 1798; Wm. Walker, bm; Jno. Thorman(?), wit.

Walker, Daniel & Rena Carey, 8 Nov 1851; Willie Mangum, bm.

Walker, David & Martha Gooch, 17 Jan 1792; Nicholas Green, bm; W. Norwood, wit.

Walker, Dudley & Susan Laws, 3 Oct 1857; Wilie Ashley, bm.

Walker, Ellis & Dicey Maderson, 25 Feb 1834; Joseph Walker, bm.

Walker, Ellis Jr. & Mary Walker, 5 May 1843; John Emry, bm; Wm. H. Whitfield, wit.

Walker, Elliss & Elizabeth Pettigrew, 31 March 1809; Ezekiel Jackson, bm; W. M. Sneed, wit.

Walker, George & Dicky Laws, 25 Jan 1805; James Walker, bm; Junius Sneed, wit.

Walker, Henry & Mary Sample, 28 Dec 1795; John Beck(?), bm; Step. Sneed, wit.

Walker, Henry, of color, son of Coley & Emily Walker, & Martha Hayes, daughter of Alvan & Milly Hayes, 14 March 1868; m 18 March 1868 by F. J. Tilley, J. P.

Walker, James & Polley Suit, 6 Dec 1804; Eless Walker, bm; E. W. Parham, wit.

Walker, James & Polly Baxter, 22 Feb 1810; Solomon Nipper, bm; Jas. Sneed, wit.

Walker, Jarrott & Lucy Walker, 5 March 1844; L. Latham, bm; J. M. Wiggins, wit.

Walker, Jeremiah & Hannah Daniel, 11 Feb 1775; Woodson Daniel, bm; Reuben Searcy, wit.

Walker, John & Salley Fuller, 5 July 1804; Samuel Kittrell, bm; Edmund W. Parham, wit.

Walker, John & Betsey Bryant, 10 Dec 1804; Washington Fuller, bm; E. W. Parham, wit.

GRANVILLE MARRIAGES 1753-1868

Walker, John & Nancey Garner, 2 April 1810; Bryan Cash, bm; W. M. Sneed, wit.

Walker, John & Lucy McFarlin, 12 March 1823; Jarrot Walker, bm; Jas. M. Wiggins, wit.

Walker, John B. & Elizabeth Laws, 24 Nov 1853; John Garner, bm; A. Landis, wit; m 11 Dec 1853 by Jno. Nance, J. P.

Walker, John P. & Ann Walker, 5 Aug 1853; Saml. P. Forsyth, bm; m 5 Aug 1853 by Jno. Nance, J. P.

Walker, Joseph & Susannah Laws, 18 June 1814; George Walker, bm; Richd. Sneed, wit.

Walker, Joseph & Margaret Laws, 18 March 1857; Nathan Walker, bm.

Walker, Julius & Mary Homes, 6 Nov 1788; Henry Fuller, bm; A. Henderson, wit.

Walker, Nathaniel & Susan Forsythe, 23 May 1860; W. A. Laws, bm.

Walker, Paul J. & Saluda Waller, 3 March 1856; W. Green, bm; m 10 March 1856 by A. M. Veazey, J. P.

Walker, Solomon & Martha Mitchel, 9 Aug 1779; F. Satterwhite, bm; Wm. Ridley, wit.

Walker, Thomas & Mrs. Mary Ann Parham, 5 Dec 1865; John G. Upchurch, bm; A. Landis, wit; m 5 Dec 1865 by ____ Hicks, J. P.

Walker, William & Feraby Fuller, 8 Oct 1781; Samuel Hunt, bm; Bennet Searcy, wit.

Walker, William & Sally Jarrot, 4 Feb 1799; James Forsith, bm; Ro. Harris, wit.

Walker, William & Rutha Baxter, 31 July 1824; Jarret Walker, bm; Step. K. Sneed, wit.

Walker, William & Reany Walker, 3 Dec 1836; Jarrat Walker, bm; J. M. Wiggins, wit.

Walker, Wm. M. & Eliza W. Gorden, 11 Sept 1839; James S. Lewis, bm; Wm. T. Haynie, wit.

Walker, William M. & Elizabeth Newton, 21 Aug 1849; James R. Duty, bm.

Walker, Willis & Elizabeth Pettigrue, 4 May 1843; Calvin Gordon, bm; Wm. H. Whitfield, wit.

Walker, Willis & Martha Laws, 27 Dec 1851; Nathaniel Walker, bm.

Wall, Burgess & Catey Omerry, 10 May 1805; Owen Omerry, bm; Jun. Sneed, wit.

Wall, Charles H. & Dicey Overbey, 21 Jan 1833; Granderson Glascock, bm; Jno. P. Smith, wit.

Wall, Miles S. & Martha Wilkerson, 24 July 1865; H. Cadden, bm; m 30 July 1865 by W. H. Puryear, J. P.

Wall, Stephen R. & Elizabeth H. Vaughan, 16 Dec 1852; Charles P. Boyd, bm; L. B. Stone, wit; m 16 Dec 1852 by L.B. Stone, J. P.

GRANVILLE MARRIAGES 1753-1868

Wall, William C. & Rebecca C. Green, 2 Oct 1815; Jesse Craddock, bm; H. Young, wit.

Wallace, William & Mary Moss, 19 April 1769; John Walker, James Hunt, bm; Jesse Benton, wit.

Waller, Allen & Clarry Cozort, 19 Nov 1829; Rowland Goss, bm; David Laws, wit.

Waller, Allen & Nancy S. Philpott, 8 Oct 1851; Benj. C. Cooke, bm; m 8 Oct 1851 by Cam. W. Allen, J. P.

Waller, Calvin & Mary Veazey, 13 May 1839; M. A. Smith, bm; Jas. M. Wiggins, wit.

Waller, Carter & Margaret Cuzort, 25 Aug 1829; John Waller, bm; David Laws, wit.

Waller, David & Rebecka Adams, 6 Dec 1790; David Brundige, bm; A. Henderson, C. C., wit.

Waller, Franklin M. & Rutha J. Peed, 2 Aug 1859; John Peed, bm.

Waller, Henry & Frances Bullock, 17 Nov 1864; Franklin Chavis, bm; T. G. Tilley, wit.

Waller, Henry & Frances Bullock, freed people, m 18 Nov 1866 by Francis J. Tilley, J. P.

Waller, James & Elizabeth Jones, 11 Dec 1833; Wm. R. Searcy(?), bm; J. Harris, wit.

Waller, Job, of color, son of Job & Patience Waller, & Tuesa Bullock, of color, daughter of Fuster & Mima Bullock, 6 May 1868; m 7 May 1868 by F. J. Tilley, J. P.

Waller, John & Isabella Umstead, 27 Dec 1851; Philip Forsythe, bm; A. Landis, wit; m 4 Jan.

Waller, John A. & Saluda W. Peed, m 16 May 1867 by F. J. Tilley, J. P.; M. W. B. Veazey, bm.

Waller, Joseph & Brigett Lockwell, 14 Nov 1796; William Arnold, bm; Micajah Bullock, wit.

Waller, Nathaniel & Oty Chambles, 11 Feb 1804; James Leathers, bm; E. R. Parham, wit.

Waller, Nathaniel A. & Sarah Walker, 31 Dec 1852; L. W. Umstead, bm; m 14 Jan 1853 by A. M. Veazey.

Waller, William & Rena Walker, 21 Aug 1830; Wm. R. Jones, bm; Step. K. Sneed, wit.

Waller, William M. & Eliza R. Mutter, 20 Sept 1815; Thomas B. Littlejohn, bm; Step. K. Sneed, wit.

Waller, Zephaniah & Nancey Forsyth, 18 Dec 1804; Thomas Gooch, bm; Step. Sneed, wit.

Wallers, John & Patsey Meadows, 5 Feb 1806; Randal Minor, bm; W. M. Sneed, wit.

Walters, Banister & Margret A. Qualls, freed people, 13 Aug 1866; m 14 Jan 1867 by W. P. White, J. P.

GRANVILLE MARRIAGES 1753-1868

Walters, Edward P., son of John & Lucy Walters, & Mary Newton, daughter of William & Mary Newton, 16 Nov 1868; m 24 Nov 1868 by E. J. Montague, G. R.

Walters, John & Mary Lumpkin, 10 Oct 1843; Hilliard Welch, bm; Wm. H. Whitfield, wit.

Walters, R. D. & Mary C. Cannady, 10 Dec 1857; S. H. Cannady, bm; m 16 Dec 1857 by W. M. Wingate, M. G.

Walthall, Francis A. & Sarah F. Wilson, 17 Dec 1837; B. F. Williamson, bm; Wm. M. Daniel, wit.

Walton, John T. & Susan C. Eaton, 6 Feb 1838; H. L. Robards, bm.

Walton, Scot & Fanny Eaton, 15 Dec 1866; m 26 Dec 1866 by Joseph W. Murphy, Rector of Holy Innocents, Henderson.

Walton, Timothy & Mary Tayloe, 26 Aug 1817; Richard Taylor, bm; Richd. Sneed, wit.

Wamsley, Thomas & Patsey Floyd, 29 Aug 1804; Thomas Floyd, bm; E. W. Parham, wit.

Ward, Joseph & Charity Low, 6 Jan 1808; Jehu Sherrin, bm; W. M. Sneed, wit.

Ward, Willis & Martha Woodliff, 2 Feb 1841; P. G. Mangum, bm; J. M. Wiggins, wit.

Warde, Gorge & Nancy D. Winston, 19 April 1839; James Winston, bm; J. M. Wiggins, wit.

Ware, Henry F. & Sally Hicks, 7 July 1830; Step. K. Sneed, bm; David Laws, wit.

Ware, Richard & Mary A. Hopkins, 29 July 1830; David Perkins, bm.

Ware, Thomas T. & Rebecca Puryear, 30 Nov 1848; Samuel Puryear, bm; L. B. Stone, J. P., wit.

Warler, Squire & Ferriby Forsythe, 2 Dec 1832; Jno. Jarratt, bm; Albert Sneed, wit.

Warmath, William W. & Mary E. Brogden, 30 Nov 1842; Zacheriah Fuller, bm; Wm. H. Whitfield, wit.

Warmouth, Nathaniel & Jinney McGehee, 24 Nov 1807; Crafford Megehee, bm; W. M. Sneed, wit.

Washington, Alexander & Mary Goss, 15 Dec 1846; Wm. Goss, bm; Jas. M. Wiggins, wit.

Washington, George & Sally Jones, 16 Jan 1849; Young Jones, bm; J. M. Wiggins, wit.

Washington, Millington & Nancy Hill, 14 Feb 1856; G. R. Livingston, bm; m 24 Feb 1856 by Jno. Nance, J. P.

Washington, Robert & Agnis Terrell, 4 Sept 1761; Jas. Washington, bm.

Washington, Robert & Elizabeth Sneed, 19 Dec 1842; Alexander Washington, bm; J. M. Wiggins, wit.

GRANVILLE MARRIAGES 1753-1868

Washington, Samuel P. & Lucy Nance, 12 May 1862; D. G. Hobgood, bm.

Washington, William & Elizabeth Jones, 1 Aug 1807; Daniel Dean, bm; W. M. Sneed, wit.

Washington, Wm. G. & Sarah Basey, 5 Jan 1848; W. W. Fuller, bm; Jas. M. Wiggins, wit.

Washington, Woodson & Sally Blalock, 2 Sept 1817; Samuel Philpott, bm; Step. Sneed, wit.

Watkins, Alexander, of color, son of Fannie Watkins, & Luvenia Watkins, parents unknown, m 9 Feb 1868 by R. J. Devin.

Watkins, Ben & Rebecer Sneed, 29 July 1866.

Watkins, Benjamin & Elizabeth Woodliff, 4 April 1846; Jos. B. Ellington, bm; Jas. M. Wiggins, wit.

Watkins, Benjamin & Celestia Woodliff, 4 Aug 1864; Wm Torenton, bm.

Watkins, Charles & Mary E. Watkins, 12 Dec 1851; Macon G. Newman, bm.

Watkins, Charles E. & Mary E. Watkins, 12 Dec 1851.

Watkins, Dempsey & Catharine Stewart, 28 Sept 1838; David Clark, bm; J. M. Wiggins, wit.

Watkins, Edmund & Minerva Ann Stone, 17 Nov 1849; Benjamin W. Hicks, bm.

Watkins, George W. & Mary E. Elliott, 14 Dec 1861; Robt. Elliott, bm; m 15 Dec 1861 by S. T. Winston, J. P.

Watkins, Henry P. & Charlott T. Lawrence, 23 March 1841; Demcy Watkins, bm; D. S. _____, wit.

Watkins, Henry T. & Ann Eliza Bullock, m 16 April 1851 by E. Hines; W. B. Hunt, bm.

Watkins, James & Rebecca Chrismas, 21 Sept 1853; W. Thomas Terrell, bm; A. Landis, wit; m 17 Nov 1853 by J. E. Montague.

Watkins, John & Susannah Daniel, 26 Oct 1798; Stepn. Satterwhite, bm; M. Satterwhite, Woodson Daniel, wit.

Watkins, John & Jane M. Clardy, 20 Feb 1837; Thomas Johnson, bm; W. S. Haynne, wit.

Watkins, Joshua & Emily Due, 31 Dec 1828; Uriah Dickens(?), bm; David Laws, wit.

Watkins, Josiah & Mildred W. B. Watkins, 1 June 1831; J. M. Rowlett, bm.

Watkins, N. V. & Nannie V. Daniel, m 16 Dec 1857 by E. Hines.

Watkins, Nathaniel W. & Nannie V. Daniel, 23 Nov 1857; C. R. Daniel, bm.

Watkins, Sandy T. & Lucy P. Johnson, 1 Sept 1862; m 9 Sept 1862 by Ira T. Wyche, Minister.

GRANVILLE MARRIAGES 1753-1868

Watkins, Smith & Harriett Kingsbury, freed people, 7 Oct 1865; A. Landis, bm.

Watkins, Thomas & Ann Jane Hester, 31 July 1847; Elijah R. Frazer, bm; Jas. M. Wiggins, wit.

Watkins, Thos., colored, son of James & Barbara Watkins, & Matilda Lewis, daughter of Paul Brackley & Winnie Brackley, 7 Nov 1868; m 15 Nov 1868 by A. C. Harris, M. G.

Watson, James, of color, son of Guilford Thrush & Leitha Thrush, & Lucinda Bridges, of color, daughter of Marcus & C--- Briges, 25 Dec 1867; m 26 Dec 1867 by Wyatt Walker, M. Gospel.

Watson, James R. & Sarah Blanks, 15 Nov 1832; Samuel Blanks, bm; Jno. P. Smith, wit.

Watson, Jesse & Catharen Carnal, 31 Oct 1813; Elijah Carnal, bm; _____ Hicks, wit.

Watson, Lota G. & Martha M. P. Hillyard, 31 Oct 1820; James Nuttall, bm; Step. K. Sneed, wit.

Watson, William & Martha Lanier, 1 Dec 1770; Joseph Williams Jr., bm; Sam. Benton, wit.

Weatherford, John & Emily B. Riggans, 25 Dec 1828; Riley Suit, bm.

Weatherford, Patrick A. & Virginia S. Gillespie, 15 Feb 1845; Burwell Barnes(?), bm.

Weathers, Charles H. & Mary Ann Williams, 10 Nov 1845; Rufus C. Freeman, bm; J. M. Wiggins, wit.

Weathers, Edward & Mary Fletcher, 17 Nov 1845; Benj. C. Cook, bm; J. M. Wiggins, wit.

Weathers, George & Malissa Chappell, 7 Nov 1854; Eugene Gressom, bm; A. Landis, wit.

Weathers, James & Nancy Williams, 21 Dec 1841; James B. Peace, bm; J. M. Wiggins, wit.

Weathers, John P. & Sally Nuttall, 6 Feb 1855; Elijah Winston, bm; m 8 Feb 1855 by B. B. Hester, J. P.

Weathers, Nathaniel H. & Francis M. Jackson, 12 Dec 1833; Lorenzo D. Jackson, bm; Benja. Kittrell, wit.

Weathers, Orsborn & Mary Bullock, 20 April 1841; Arill Mitchell, bm; J. M. Wiggins, wit.

Weathers, William & Prescilla Parker, 8 Feb 1803; Stephen Bridges, bm.

Weathers, William P., son of James & Nancy Weathers, & Loury A. Dent, daughter of Thomas & Eliza Dent, m 20 Dec 1867 by Moses J. Hunt, M. G.

Weaver, Absolom & Sarah Arnold, 8 Nov 1809; Riley Meadors, bm; W. M. Sneed, wit.

Weaver, Adam & Sarah Tippet, 3 May 1788; Sherwood Harris, bm; Reuben Searcy, wit.

GRANVILLE MARRIAGES 1753-1868

Weaver, Dudley & Elenor Cox, 20 Dec 1806; Jones Ellington, bm; Junius Sneed, wit.

Weaver, Dudley & Nancy Cox, 6 Feb 1844; Horace H. Rowland, bm; Wm. H. Whitfield, wit.

Weaver, George W. & Elizabeth Jenkins, 18 Nov 1855; Jas. R. Duty, bm.

Weaver, Isaac & Mary Hill, 17 Oct 1795; James Forsythe, bm; Step. Sneed, wit.

Weaver, Isaac & Fanny Cole, 5 May 1818; Levi Owens, bm; W. Sneed, wit.

Weaver, Isaac & Elizabeth J. Kinton, 26 Feb 1853; John G. Watson, bm; m 30 March 1853.

Weaver, James & Mary Johnson, 3 July 1829; George Anderson, bm; David Laws, wit.

Weaver, James & Emily Pettiford, 31 Jan 1842; Gavin Bookram, bm; J. M. Wiggins, wit.

Weaver, James & Mary Jane Pettiford, 2 Nov 1850; Manson Stewart, bm; A. Landis, wit.

Weaver, John & Amey Weaver, 12 Aug 1793; Richard Stringfellow, bm; W. Norwood, wit.

Weaver, John & Nancy Glenn, 2 May 1820; Absolem Weaver, bm; Jas. M. Wiggins, wit.

Weaver, John & Jane Knight, 8 March 1853; Nathan Breedlove, bm.

Weaver, John W. & Amy Pinson, 14 Feb 1821; Franklin Moss, bm; A. Sneed, wit.

Weaver, Joseph & Susan Mangum, 18 May 1858; H. Latta, bm; A. Landis, wit.

Weaver, Litte & Emily Petteford, 8 Nov 1859; John W. Bragg, bm.

Weaver, Mouns & Betsy Clardy, 23 Oct 1820; Wm. Marshall, bm; Jas. M. Wiggins, wit.

Weaver, Paul & Nancy Bookram, 23 Sept 1857; John Laws, bm; A. Landis, wit.

Weaver, Robert & Patsey Perdue, 8 Dec 1801; William Barner, bm; W. M. Robards, wit.

Weaver, Spencer A. B., son of William G. & Susan Weaver, & Elizabeth Harris, parents unknown (both dead), 16 Nov 1867; m 17 Nov 1867 by E. B. Lyon, J. P.

Weaver, Spencer O. & Martha M. Griffin, 15 July 1852; _____, bm.

Weaver, William & Lucy Rowland, 24 March 1781; Richard Stringfellow, bm; Asa Searcy, wit.

Weaver, William & Rebeca Wilson, 11 Sept 1797; John Wilson, bm; Wm. Robards, wit.

GRANVILLE MARRIAGES 1753-1868

Weaver, William G. & Susan M. Pinson, 8 March 1827; James Brame, bm; Wm. H. Owen, wit.

Weaver, William H. & Nelly A. Daniel, 27 Dec 1853; Jas. R. Duty, bm; m 27 Dec 1853 by James R. Duty, J. P.

Webb, Alexander, son of Nelson & Nancy Webb, & Lizzie Cooper, daughter of Philip & Mary Cooper, colored, m 19 Dec 1868 by R. J. Devin.

Webb, Benjamin & Nansey Eatling, 8 Feb 1794; James Brewer, bm; Step. Sneed, wit.

Webb, James & Ann H. Smith, 8 Feb 1803; Thomas Owen, bm; Step. Sneed, wit.

Webb, Jas. T. & Mary L. Daws, 22 April 1850; Wesley J. Newton, bm.

Webb, John Jr. & Margaret Howard, 17 April 1802; Baxter Davis Jr., bm; P. Bullock, wit.

Webb, John H. & Judith F. Amis, 28 June 1855; M. T. Smith, bm.

Webb, John H. & Lucy T. Daniel, 6 Dec 1864; J. C. Cooper, bm; m 7 Dec 1864 by Edwards Hines.

Webb, John P. & Amy B. Pattillo, 21 May 1845; S. W. Smith, bm; J. M. Wiggins, wit.

Webb, Lewis & Ann N. Nutall, 7 Jan 1818; Saml. D. Daniel, bm.

Webb, Squire & Betsy Daniel, 27 Dec 1865; Isaac Clay, bm; A. Landis, wit.

Webb, Thomas & Mary Jones Thomas, 6 May 1800; John Norman, bm; Step. Sneed, wit.

Webb, Thomas & Martha Dickins, 3 Dec 1805; Brodie Howard, bm; W. M. Sneed, wit.

Webb, Thomas Jr. & Martha P. Smith, 11 Oct 1824; James Beasley, wit; David J. Young, wit.

Webb, William & Frances Young, 15 July 1771; Samuel Smith (Grassey Creek), bm; Jesse Benton, bm.

Webb, William & Elizabeth Pulliam, 11 Sept 1813; Thomas J. Hicks, bm; Wm. Mallory Jnr., wit.

Webb, William, colored, son of Edmund & Polly Webb & Martha Daniel, daughter of David & Harriett Daniel, m 5 Dec 1868 by James Puryear, J. P.

Webb, William H. & Elizabeth W. Patillo, 29 March 1834; Wm. L. Owen, bm; Benja. Kittrell, wit.

Webb, William P. & Martha Ann Webb, 24 Nov 1852; Benjamin P. Thorp Jr., bm; m 1 Dec 1852 by G. W. Ferrill.

Webster, James B. & Eliza Wheeler, 2 Jan 1844; Aron Haskins, bm; Wm. H. Whitfield, wit.

Weddell, Alexander W. & Pencie M. Wright, 24 Jan 1866; B. A. Capehart, bm.

GRANVILLE MARRIAGES 1753-1868

Welbourn, Washington & Martha Mealor, 24 Nov 1831; Matthew Chandler, bm; Jno. P. Smith, wit.

Welch, Hilliard & Tempey Fuller, 31 Aug 1832; David Jenkins, bm; S. K. Sneed, wit.

Welch, John & Mary Pope, 20 May 1786; Shem Cook, bm; William Cooper, wit.

Welch, Robert & Betsy Mafield, 28 Dec 1801; Herbert Gilliam, bm; P. Bullock, wit.

Welden, William & Nancey Welch, 11 Jan 1830; John Reeves, bm; David Laws, wit.

Weldon, Dangerfield & Polly Shaver, 4 Sept 1827; William Amis, bm; S. K. Sneed, wit.

Weldon, Daniel & Miss Bett Eaton, 17 Jan 1753; Blake Baker, bm; Saml. Swann Jr., wit.

Weldon, Martin & Rachel Mitchell, 21 Dec 1836; Jackson Prissom, bm; J. M. Wiggins, wit.

Wells, Samuel & Elizabeth Oakley, 22 Feb 1794; Stephen Oakley, bm; W. Norwood, wit.

West, Abraham & Nancy Pinson, 17 Nov 1803; Peter West, bm; A. H. Sneed, wit.

West, Alexander & Elizabeth Jane West, 20 Feb 1864; Hardemon West, bm; A. Landis, wit; m 21 Feb 1864 by Thos. Hester.

West, Alfred & Susannah Currin, 19 Dec 1837; Richard Noblen, bm; M. D. Royster, wit.

West, Benjamin H. & Margaret B. West, 2 Oct 1862; m by D. S. Wilkerson, J. P.

West, Charles F. & Frances Usry, m 20 June 1866 by Geo. J. Rowland, J. P.

West, Daniel & Judith Fraizer, 7 Feb 1803; William West, bm; Green Merritt, wit.

West, George S. & Margaret Jones, 23 Jan 1860; Wm. R. Beasley, bm; m __ Feb 1860 by Jeff Horner, J. P.

West, Hardemon & Adeline Daniel, 15 Jan 1856; Thos. Loyd, bm; A. Landis, wit; m 18 Jan 1856 by Thos. Hester, J. P.

West, Hardiman & Susan West, 12 Sept 1839; William Stevens(?), bm; T. B. Barnett, wit.

West, James & Henrietta Lock, 15 Jan 1828; Abner Currin, bm; Step. K. Sneed, wit.

West, James & Nancy Currin, 19 Dec 1836; Hardiman West, bm; Robert K. Clack, wit.

West, James R. & Elizabeth King, 29 Sept 1866; m 2 Oct 1866 by A. C. Harris, M. G.

West, James W. & Mary E. Newton, 26 Aug 1867; B. H. West, bm; W. S. H. Thomas, J.P., wit; m 1 Sept by W. H. Puryear, J. P.

GRANVILLE MARRIAGES 1753-1868

West, John & Ann J. Wilkerson, 16 Dec 1822; Mastin Fraizer, bm; S. K. Sneed, wit.

West, John & Mary West, 23 Dec 1840; James West, bm; T. B. Barnett, wit.

West, John & Susan West, 4 Aug 1848; William Bladen, bm; J. M. Wiggins, wit.

West, John & Elizabeth J. Philips, 21 June 1860; Jas. R. West, bm; m 27 June 1860 by Thomas Hester.

West, John L. & Nancy Loyd, 17 June 1858; Cephus Hudson, bm; m 23 June 1858 by Thos. Hester, J. P.

West, Joseph & Lucinda West, 29 May 1841; David Wilkerson, bm; T. B. Barnett, wit.

West, Peyton & Norma(?) Somerhill, 16 Nov 1833; Jesse Daniel, bm; S. Harris, wit.

West, Stephen & Sally Ann West, 19 Nov 1860; Joseph West, bm; m 19 Nov 1860 by A. C. Harris, M. G.

West, Thomas & Mildred Currin, 18 Dec 1838; James Elliott, bm; J. M. Wiggins, wit.

West, William & Michael Fraizer, 29 Dec 1802; Shadrach Fraizer, bm; P. Bullock, wit.

West, William & Mary Lock, 11 Aug 1831; David Wilkerson, bm; David Laws, wit.

West, Willis & Sarah Ann Adcock, 4 April 1846; Alex. West, bm; Jas. M. Wiggins, wit.

Westmoreland, Shaderick & Sally Coon, 18 Aug 1789; Gilliam Norwood, bm.

Wheeler, America & Rachel Primrose, 7 Aug 1820; William Primrose, bm; Jas. M. Wiggins, wit.

Wheeler, Benjamin & Winnefred Turner, 14 Dec 1781.

Wheeler, Benjamin & Elizabeth Robertson, 7 March 1828; Francis Robertson, bm; David Laws, wit.

Wheeler, Dudley & Emeline Peed, 20 Feb 1860; James H. Cozart, bm; m 22 Feb 1860 by Jeff Horner, J. P.

Wheeler, Ezekiel & Lucy Green, 5 May 1818; Redford Gooch, bm; Rhodes N. Herndon, wit.

Wheeler, Harrison & Sarah Nance, 2 Feb 1856; W. P. Roberts, bm.

Wheeler, Harrison & Mary J. Farebow, 19 Oct 1865; Saml. P. Washington, bm; m 22 Oct 1865 by Robt. L. Heflin, J. P.

Wheeler, Henry & Celiah Wheeler, 7 Aug 1817; Richard Arnold, bm; Step. K. Sneed, wit.

Wheeler, J. Y. & Frances Meadows, 21 March 1864; m __ March 1864 by T. J. Horner.

GRANVILLE MARRIAGES 1753-1868

Wheeler, James & Elizabeth Nance, 7 May 1811; Jacob Hoofman, bm; W. M. Sneed, wit.

Wheeler, Jefferson & Martha Roberts, 16 Sept 1857; Thos. Adcock, bm.

Wheeler, Jesse & Sarah Oslin, 3 Aug 1813; Moses Jones, bm; W. M. Sneed, wit.

Wheeler, John & Rachel Ferrell, 13 Sept 1783; Elijah Veazy, bm; Bennet Searcy, wit.

Wheeler, Martain & Selah Jones, 13 Aug 1796; Aaron Jones, John Turner, bm; Micajah Bullock, wit.

Wheeler, Moses & Elizabeth Jinkins, 22 July 1820; Lazarus Minor, bm; Rhodes N. Herndon, wit.

Wheeler, Moses & Elsey Landers, 21 March 1831; Elijah Avery, bm; Step. K. Sneed, wit.

Wheeler, Willie & Polly Wheeler, 11 Sept 1816; Ezekiel Wheeler, bm.

Wheeles, John W. & Eliza Haley, 21 March 1851; A. Landis, Clk., wit.

Whit, Jessee & Nancy Knorden, 1 July 1793; James Knowling, bm; W. Norwood, wit.

Whitaker, William M. & Celestia H. P. Moore, 10 Dec 1855; Benja. F. Hancock, bm; m 23 Dec 1856 by B. B. Hester, J. P.

White, Asbury & Prudence Buchanan, 7 Jan 1832; W. D. Allen, bm; Step. K. Sneed, wit.

White, Blumer & Phereba Morris, 25 May 1784; Dennis Reardon(?), bm; Bennet Searcy, wit.

White, Coleman & Polley Cole, 26 Sept 1812; Joshua White, bm; W. M. Sneed, wit.

White, Colemon & Celah Bradford, 13 March 1786; John Champion, bm; Bennet Searcy, wit.

White, David & Geney Trusty, 11 Dec 1781; John Trusty, bm; Bennet Searcy, wit.

White, Eaton J. & Catharine Spears, 4 Jan 1826; Hinton G. Hester, bm; Step. K. Sneed, wit.

White, Edward & Cary Heflin, 10 Jan 1804; Robert Foster, bm; Danl. Bridges, wit.

White, Henry & Anne Priddy, 6 Sept 1781; William Skelton, bm; Reuben Searcy, wit.

White, James & Martha Mann, 17 Feb 1812; Mark White, bm; W. M. Sneed, wit.

White, James & Ann Robards, 7 Feb 1840; _____ Haskins, bm; Wm. T. Hargrove, wit.

White, John & Betsey Harris, 10 March 1798; Richard Taylor, bm; Robt. Taylor, wit.

GRANVILLE MARRIAGES 1753-1868

White, John & Hicksey Cole, 30 Nov 1825; Thos. J. Carter, bm; Wm. H. Owen, wit.

White, John & Mildred Champion, 14 May 1861; Alexander Wadford, bm.

White, Joseph & Nancey Mason, 24 Oct 1799; Joshua White, bm; Step. Sneed, wit.

White, Joseph & Charity A. Clay, 6 July 1867; Robert White, bm; m 9 July 1867 by Jas. B. Floyd.

White, Joshua & Rachael Allen, 7 Jan 1805; George White, bm; Jn. Sneed, wit.

White, Kinelm & Elizabeth Higgs, 8 Feb 1825; Henry H. Brinkley, bm; Wm. H. Owen, wit.

White, Larkin & Zorbey(?) Parker, 15 Jan 1814; Zacheriah Glascock, bm; H. Young, wit.

White, Mark & Sarah McDonald, 22 Dec 1784; Jas. McDaniel, bm; Elisabeth Searcy, wit.

White, Mark Junr. & Martha Brinkley, 2 Nov 1813; Richard Wood, bm; W. M. Sneed, wit.

White, Philip & Jemima White, 17 Sept 1783; William Priddy, bm; Bennet Searcy, wit.

White, Philip & _____, 7 Feb 1797; Coleman White, bm; John Brodie, wit.

White, Philo W. & Nancy M. Mitchell, 7 Sept 1858; John W. Meherell(?), bm; m 6 Oct 1858 by B. B. Hester.

White, Robert & Jane Bobbitt, 28 Oct 1865; Siah Moss, bm; A. Landis, wit; m 5 Nov 1865 by R. H. Hill, J. P.

White, Serril & Susanah Lankford, 20 Nov 1785; Jesse Lankford, bm; John Searcy, wit.

White, Thomas & Elizabeth Higgs, 3 Oct 1809; Levi Higgs, bm; W. M. Sneed, wit.

White, Thomas P. & Rebecca Kittrell, 2 Sept 1840; Lewis H. Kittle, bm; Jas. M. Wiggins, wit.

White, Valentine & Polley Huckebey, 27 Oct 1802; William Taylor, bm; Jun. Sneed, wit.

White, William & Jane Coleman, 22 Dec 1838; John Newton, bm.

White, William G. C. & Maranda R. Hester, __ Sept 1836; Elias J. Jenkins, bm; J. M. Wiggins, wit.

White, William H. & Tabitha Ann Kittrell, 30 Nov 1847; James A. Bledso, bm; J. M. Wiggins, wit.

White, William H. & Mary Jane Floyd, 23 Oct 1866; George R. Davis, bm.

White, William T. & Mary V. C. Yancey, 8 Jan 1850; B. B. Barnes(?), bm.

GRANVILLE MARRIAGES 1753-1868

White, William W. & Mariah L. Stanton, 3 Nov 1841; H. G. Robards, bm; Jas. M. Wiggins, wit.

Whitlock, Jeremiah & Patsey Crenshaw, 4 March 1797; Robert Malone, bm; Step. Sneed, wit.

Whitloe, Cocker & Ann Hicks Whitloe, 7 May 1787; Wm. Hunt, bm; B. Searcy, wit.

Whitloe, Lot & Susannah Farrar, 31 Jan 1789; Lewis Page, bm; A. Henderson, C. C., wit.

Whitloe, Pleasant & Tabitha Tuder, 11 Jan 1786; Henry Tudor, bm; J. Searcy, wit.

Whitlow, Champion & Nancy Husten, 23 March 1837; Henry Barnes, bm.

Whitlow, Champion & Sarah Malone, 3 Jan 1850; Henry H. Newton, bm; L. B. Stone, J. P.

Whitmore, Mathew J. & Sarah Hunt, 24 Oct 1831; A. Landis, bm; S. K. Sneed, wit.

Whitlow, Thomas R. & Nancy Briant, 26 Sept 1835; Thos. P. Bryan, bm; Wm. L. Owen, wit.

Whitworth, Thomas C. & Ann C. Pope, 16 Oct 1816; Leonard Cardwell, bm; Richard Sneed, wit.

Wicker, Thomas & Salley Talley, 27 Dec 1780; William Austen(?), bm; Bart. Wright, wit.

Wicker, Thomas & Massey Chuer, 11 Oct 1786; Matthew Simpson, bm; Bennet Searcy, wit.

Wicker, William & Martha Talley, 2 March 1784; John _____, bm; Bennet Searcy, wit.

Wier, William T. & Ann L. Barnes, 15 Oct 1857; James Grady, bm; Jas. R. Duty, wit; m 22 Oct 1857 by James R. Duty, J. P.

Wiggers, Elijah & Polly Roycraft, 23 Sept 1817; Edward Chappell, bm; R. H. Herndon, wit.

Wiggers, Hinton W. & Delila M. Watkins, 15 Nov 1858; Henry A. Edwards, bm; m 18 Nov 1858 by Wm. N. Bragg, Minister.

Wiggins, David W. & Agnes A. Basket, 20 Dec 1858; Wm. K. Brosius, bm; m 23 Dec 1858 by Lewis K. Kissle(?), J. P.

Wiggins, Eli & Bettie Tabern, 28 Jan 1859; Wm. Headspeth, bm; A. Landis, wit.

Wiggins, Frederic & Sarah Smith, 8 Feb 1775; Turner Jordan, bm; Wm. Reardon, wit.

Wiggins, Frederick & Nancy Jordan, 15 Dec 1783; Ransom Smith, bm; W. F. Searcy, wit.

Wiggins, Fredr. & Nancy Preddy, 1 Jan 1827; Fredk. Wiggins Senr., bm; A. Sneed, wit.

Wiggins, Hendley & Dolley Stark, 10 Nov 1818; Thomas Daniel, bm.

GRANVILLE MARRIAGES 1753-1868

Wiggins, James H. & Mary E. Debram, 21 Dec 1840; G. Harris, bm; J. M. Wiggins, wit.

Wiggins, James M. & Susan P. Russell, 13 Dec 1826; Lemuel Potter, bm; S. K. Sneed, wit.

Wiggins, Jaquelin & Lucy W. Daniel, 4 Dec 1816; Thomas Daniel, bm.

Wiggins, John & Susannah Hester, 5 Nov 1811; William H. Gilliam, bm; Richd. Sneed, wit.

Wiggins, John J. & Martha Ann Strum, 5 Feb 1846; Beverly Sears, bm; Jas. M. Wiggins, wit.

Wiggins, Loton A. & Martha A. Wiggins, 17 Jan 1848; D. A. Paschall, bm; J. M. Wiggins, wit.

Wiggins, Thomas & Frances Grisham, 5 Nov 1796; Step. Sneed, wit; Wm. Robards, wit.

Wiggins, Thomas & Sealy Mitchell, 27 Dec 1802; Samuel Denton, bm; Jun. Sneed, wit.

Wiggins, Thomas T. & Lucy Ann Lewis, 23 Jan 1839; D. R. Goodloe, bm.

Wilborn, George W. & Elizabeth Lumpkin, 3 Dec 1832; Joseph Loyd, bm; Jno. P. Smith, wit.

Wilbourn, John & Mary Hampton, 8 April 1783; Lewis Webb, bm; Bennet Searcy, wit.

Wilburn, Thomas W. & Susan Ramsay, 27 Jan 1855; James Hanns(?), bm; m 27 Jan 1855 by S. Beasley Jr., J. P.

Wilburn, Zacariah & Jemima White, 30 Jan 1781; Sherwood Harris, wit.

Wiles, Overton & Peggy Franklin, 7 Nov 1806; Thomas Yancey, bm; Jun. Sneed, wit.

Wiles, William & Rhodey Harding, 12 Nov 1816; Absalom D. Parish, bm; W. M. Sneed, wit.

Wilkerson, Alexander & Mary Ann Royster, 30 Oct 1839; Burgess Adcock, bm; Jas. M. Wiggins, wit.

Wilkerson, Albert, son of Harris & Martha Wilkerson, & Indianna Eakes, daughter of Zachariah Eakes & Jane Eakes, 22 April 1868; m 5 May 1868 by R. J. Devin.

Wilkerson, Allen & Lethy Preers, 28 Nov 1817; Semore Puryear, bm; Rhodes N. Herndon, wit.

Wilkerson, Allen & Rebecca Evans, 8 Feb 1833; Howel Briggs, bm; Step. K. Sneed, wit.

Wilkerson, Allen & Rebecca Ann Hampton, 20 Oct 1848; Oxford Moise, bm.

Wilkerson, Ansel & Elizabeth Madison, 23 March 1816; Zephaniah Waller, bm; Step. K. Sneed, wit.

GRANVILLE MARRIAGES 1753-1868

Wilkerson, Benj. C. & J. A. T. Boswell, 7 Aug 1860; Benj. B. Hicks, bm; m 12 Aug 1860 by E. F. Beachum.

Wilkerson, Burwell & Patsey Parrish, 7 Aug 1807; Stephen Satterwhite, bm; Jun. Sneed, wit.

Wilkerson, David & Jane West, 15 Dec 1829; Charles Duncan, bm; S. K. Sneed, wit.

Wilkerson, David, son of Franklin & Nancy Wilkerson, & Emily Glasscock, daughter of Thomas & Betsy Glasscock, 29 Dec 1867; m 29 Dec 1867 by L. B. Stone, J. P.

Wilkerson, David S. & Martha R. Neal, 23 Oct 1830; Darman Puryear, bm; Jno. P. Smith, wit.

Wilkerson, Dudley & Elizabeth Jones, 14 Dec 1809; Howell Satterwhite, bm; A. H. Sneed, wit.

Wilkerson, Elijah & Henrietta Akin, 9 Nov 1815; Robert Norwood, bm; Richard Sneed, wit.

Wilkerson, Elijah & Permelia Huchins, 7 Jan 1830; Jno. Ricks, bm; A. Sneed, wit.

Wilkerson, Erastus W. & Ann H. Overbey, 15 Oct 1850; Jno. D. Wilkerson, bm; L. B. Stone, J. P., wit.

Wilkerson, Francis & Ursle Saterwhite, 16 April 1783; Benjamin Hawkins, bm; Reuben Searcy, wit.

Wilkerson, Francis & Lucy Hester, 14 March 1807; Zacheriah Hester, bm; Junius Sneed, wit.

Wilkerson, Francis & Martha Tuck, 26 Nov 1851; Major A. Nelson, bm; m 26 Nov 1851 by A. Apple.

Wilkerson, George & Henrietta Harris, 16 Jan 1799; David Wilkerson, bm; M. Satterwhite, Wm. Gill, wit.

Wilkerson, George & Emily Eaks, 18 Dec 1827; Henry Sandford, bm; David Laws, wit.

Wilkerson, George & Lucy C. Brame, 19 Nov 1836; Jas. Mathews, bm; Jas. M. Wiggins, wit.

Wilkerson, Howell T. & Isabella Fraizer, 10 Jan 1839; John Brodio, bm.

Wilkerson, James & Sarah Sanford, 19 Jan 1802; John Eastwood, bm; Nancy Bullock, wit.

Wilkerson, John & Elizabeth Smith, 20 Dec 1837; John H. Royster, bm; S. G. Shearmon, wit.

Wilkerson, John D. & Judith M. Beasley, 11 Nov 1853; T. L. Hargrove, bm; m 23 Nov 1853 by L. K. Willie, M. G.

Wilkerson, John H., son of James H. & Susan Wilkerson, & Emaly D. Wilkerson, daughter of George W. & Elizabeth J. Wilkerson, m 26 Dec 1867 by L. B. Stone, J. P.

Wilkerson, John H., son of Spencer G. & Tabby B. Wilkerson, & Bettie Noblin, daughter of Richard & Patsey Noblin, 8 Dec 1868; m 10 Dec 1868 by Richard D. Jones, J. P.

GRANVILLE MARRIAGES 1753-1868

Wilkerson, John Q. & Louisa Sandford, 14 Feb 1822; Semore Puryear, bm; Jno. P. Smith, wit.

Wilkerson, Joseph A. & Margaret A. Gold, 19 Feb 1851; William Goll, bm; L. B. Stone, J. P., wit.

Wilkerson, Joseph P. & Martha Pool, 8 Nov 1804; Logustine Pool, bm; Jas. Sneed, wit.

Wilkerson, Lewis & Tempy Ball, 17 Aug 1865; Stephen Taylor, bm.

Wilkerson, Merrideth & Nancy Yancey, 30 Dec 1866; Calvin Yancey, bm; m 30 Dec 1866 by E. L. Parrish, J. P.

Wilkerson, Nicholas & Amey Darden, 16 Nov 1809; David Perkins, bm; H. Young, wit.

Wilkerson, Peter, son of Royal & Margaret Wilkerson, & Viney Eaks, daughter of Bevily & Ibbie Eaks, 16 Jan 1868; m 19 Jan 1868 by W. H. Puryear, J. P.

Wilkerson, Randal & Susannah Daniel, 31 May 1814; Logustus P. Pool, bm; W. M. Sneed, wit.

Wilkerson, Richard & Maria A. Lockett, 15 May 1831; E. A. Holloway, bm.

Wilkerson, Richard & Martha Adcock, 11 Dec 1858; Rufus R. Slaughter, bm.

Wilkerson, Robert & Emaly Mealer, 26 Feb 1852; Nathan F. Tuck, bm; L. B. Stone, J. P., wit; m 26 Feb 1852 by L. B. Stone, J. P.

Wilkerson, Robert D. & Martha A. Permelia Eaks, 23 July 1866; m 19 Aug 1866 by John L. Carroll, Minister.

Wilkerson, Smith & Sally Smith, 25 March 1822; Step. K. Sneed, bm.

Wilkerson, Stephen & Emily Talley, 19 Jan 1853; William L. Talley, bm; m 20 Jan 1853 by J. E. Montague, M. G.

Wilkerson, Thomas B. & Rosa E. Chandler, 8 May 1866; m 22 May 1866 by E. Hines.

Wilkerson, Washington & Lucy Ann Shanks, 10 Oct 1856; Young Montague, bm.

Wilkerson, William & Nancy C. Royster, 24 Nov 1860; William P. Hobgood, bm; m 28 Nov 1860 by R. D. Puryear, J. P.

Wilkerson, William & Perlona Yancey, 17 Dec 1860; m 20 Dec 1860 by E. F. Beachum; Benj. W. Yancey, bm.

Wilkerson, William & Jane Moore, 2 Oct 1865; W. R. Beasley, bm; m 5 Oct 1865 by E. Hines.

Wilkerson, Wm. E., son of Charles & Ann Wilkerson, & Elizabeth Glasscock, daughter of Anderson & Lucy Glasscock, 29 Dec 1867; m 29 Dec 1867 by L. B. Stone, J. P.

Wilkins, Clement & Mary W. Gunn(?), 8 Sept 1848; Richd. D. Taylor, bm.

GRANVILLE MARRIAGES 1753-1868

Wilkins, Elijah & Thomas Perry (sic), 11 Aug 1859; Joshua Inscore, bm; A. Landis, wit.

Wilkins, Hinton & Lucy C. Sherrin, 15 Jan 1861; Darlin A. Chappell, bm.

Wilkins, James & Frances Minor, 23 May 1824; John Wood, bm; Wm. H. Owen, wit.

Wilkins, John & Elizabeth Chambless, 24 Jan 1811; Robert Chambliss, bm; W. M. Sneed, wit.

Wilkins, John & Elizer Helen Grissom, 15 Feb 1832; R. B. Laurence, bm; Step. K. Sneed, wit; application dated 14 Feb 1832 from Wake County, N. C., signed by E. H. Grissom.

Wilkins, John W. & Betty A. Harriss, 31 Aug 1867; William H. Harriss, bm; m 4 Sept 1867 by D. Tilley, J. P.

Wilkins, Leroy B. & Mary Ann Adams, 11 Nov 1834; F. M. Elliott, bm.

Wilkins, Leroy S. & Caroline V. Wilkins, 23 Sept 1860; Alfred T. Bowen, bm; m 23 Sept 1860 by L. B. Stone, J. P.

Wilkins, Richard & Mary Parham, 28 Feb 1790; Seamore Duncan, bm; Henry Potter, wit.

Wilkins, William & Susanna Hicks, 20 July 1784; Darvin Herris, bm; Bennet Searcy, wit.

Wilkins, Wm. R. & Mary F. Wilkerson, 30 May 1867; Spencer Noblin, bm; E. L. Parrish, wit.

Wilkinson, A. D. & Naknie O. Brame, 7 May 1856; Geo. W. Gunns, bm; m 8 May 1856 by R. J. Devin.

Wilkinson, Jordon & Nancey Anderson, 6 Nov 1810; Howell Briggs, bm; Step. Sneed, wit.

Wilkinson, Richard & Nancy P. Avarett, 22 Dec 1848; Wyatt Avarett, bm; L. B. Stone, J. P., wit.

Wilks, Daniel J. & Charlotty Champion, 17 Jan 1866; Henry Hailey, bm; m 17 Jan 1866 by R. B. Hester.

Wilks, Washington & Kittey Christopher, 11 Feb 1819; Stephen Bryant, bm; Sam. Sneed, wit.

Willeford, Lunsford, of color, son of Peter Curtis & Susan Willeford, & Harriet Curtis, daughter of Squire Allen & Nancy Curtis, 21 Dec 1867; m 22 Dec 1867 by B. D. Howard, J. P.

Williams, Alfred & Sally Ann Hancock, 19 Feb 1847; Daniel Clayton, bm; L. B. Stone, J. P., wit.

Williams, Alfred & Happy Caughon, 23 Sept 1851; Rd. Sneed, bm; m 23 Sept 1851 by E. E. Freeman.

Williams, Allen & Betsey Duty, 14 July 1807; Willie Williams, bm; Jun. Sneed, wit.

Williams, Archabald D. & Lucy Ann Lewis, 21 April 1843; H. H. Kingsbury, bm; Wm. H. Whitfield, wit.

GRANVILLE MARRIAGES 1753-1868

Williams, Benjamin & Milley Carpendar, 21 April 1807; David Beck, bm; W. M. Sneed, wit.

Williams, Benjamin & Henrietta Croft, 23 Dec 1828; Wm. Croft, bm; David Laws, wit.

Williams, Benjamin & Sarah P. Smith, 30 May 1832; John McFarling, bm; David Laws, wit.

Williams, Berry & Leathy Anderson, 17 June 1857; P. Valentine, bm; A. Landis, wit; m 17 June 1857 by D. A. Paschall, J. P.

Williams, Calup & Martha Brown, 10 Oct 1804; Thomas Williams, bm; J. Sneed, wit.

Williams, Charles & Hannah Chewell (?), 28 Feb 1797; Daniel Morrow, bm; Step. Sneed, wit.

Williams, Charles & Beady Chavis, 20 Nov 1845; Henry Gates, bm; Jas. M. Wiggins, wit.

Williams, Charles & Rosa Harte, 7 April 1867; D. D. Allen, bm; m 7 April 1867 by E. B. Lyon, J. P.

Williams, Crudup, son of Johnathan & Mary Williams, & Nancy Mason, daughter of Samuel & Pevey Mason, 10 Nov 1867; m by J. W. Wellons.

Williams, Daniel & Ann Henderson, 31 July 1765; Saml. Henderson, Joseph Williams, bm; Charles Bruce, wit.

Williams, David A. & Mary Jane Currin, 18 Oct 1861; Robert Williams, bm; A. Landis, wit; m 19 Oct 1861 by Jesse Satterwhite, J. P.

Williams, Edward & Elizabeth Craft, 2 March 1845; M. A. Smith, bm; J. M. Wiggins, wit.

Williams, Erasmus & Caroline Dement, freed people, 22 Aug 1865; Geo. W. Barnes, bm; A. Landis, wit.

Williams, Erastus B. & Angeline Pearce, 15 April 1862; Wm. D. Davis, bm; m 16 April 1862 by Wm. D. Davis, J. P.

Williams, General W. & Priscilla Sandiferd, 3 Jan 1848; Allen Qualls, bm; Jas. M. Wiggins, wit.

Williams, George & Elizabeth Henley, 16 July 1844; Henry Williams, bm; Jas. Wiggins, wit; m _____ 1844 by J. K. Cole, M. G.

Williams, Henry & Prisy Glover, 5 Sept 1782; George Hopkins, bm; Bennet Searcy, wit.

Williams, Henry & Arina A. Priddy, 23 Nov 1838; John H. Hester, bm; J. M. Wiggins, wit.

Williams, Howell & Phanney Pittard, 26 Dec 1801; William Summerhill, bm; Step. Sneed, wit.

Williams(?), Israel & Vilet Sneed, 19 Aug 1866.

Williams, James & Elizabeth Wheeler, 10 Jan 1807; John Turner, bm; W. M. Sneed, wit.

GRANVILLE MARRIAGES 1753-1868

Williams, James & Sarah Ellison, 8 Oct 1808; Abner Peace, bm; Edwin T. Satterwhite, wit.

Williams, James & Amanda OBrient, 8 Nov 1859; P. Williams, bm; m on the third Sunday of Nov. 1859 by D. S. Wilkerson, J. P.

Williams, Jesse & Maria T. Worrell, 25 Oct 1826; David P. Damon, bm; Wm. H. Owen, wit.

Williams, John & Agnes Keeling, 12 Nov 1759; John Bullock, bm; Jno. Bowie, wit.

Williams, John & Mary Burton, 25 Feb 1783; Allen Burton, bm; Bennet Searcy, wit.

Williams, John & Sarah Estridge, 13 June 1786; Benjamin Johnston, bm; Reuben Searcy, C. C., wit.

Williams, John & Mary Somerhill, 30 Aug 1799; Thomas Williams, bm; Step. Sneed, wit.

Williams, John & Milley Hester, 3 March 1800; Samuel Craft, bm.

Williams, John & Mima Goss, 8 Feb 1825; Lemuel Hobgood, bm; Wm. Hayes Owen, wit.

Williams, John & Alice Allen, 13 June 1845; John Williams, bm; Benj. C. Cook, wit.

Williams, John & Miss Mariam Hester Grandy, of Oxford, m 17 Dec 1868 by John H. Phillips, Baptist Minister.

Williams, John D. & Winniford Hayes, 30 Oct 1821; Clement Wilkins, bm; Jas. M. Wiggins, wit.

Williams, John H. & Martha J. OBrien, 15 Dec 1855; A. Sherman, bm; A. Landis, wit; m 19 Dec 1855 by G. W. Ferrill, wit.

Williams, John S. & Mary Y. Mallory, 9 May 1844; Chas. E. Russ, bm; Wm. H. Whitfield, wit.

Williams, Joseph & Sarah Lanier, 3 June 1766; Robert Lanier, bm; Cha. Bruce, wit.

Williams, Joseph Jr. & Rebecca Lanier, 11 Sept 1772; John Henderson, bm; Reuben Searcy, wit.

Williams, Joseph Jr. & Rebekah Lanier, 11 Sept 1772 (consent from Thomas Lanier, father of Rebekah only).

Williams, Joseph Junr. & Susannah Martin Taylor, 8 July 1806; Jas. Sneed, bm; Step. Sneed, wit.

Williams, Joshua, of color, son of John Blackwell, a slave, & Lucy Williams, a slave, both of the parents has been dead for 40 years or more, & Petta Raney, m 12 Jan 1868 by E. B. Lyon, J. P.

Williams, Joshua & Sally Cannady, freed people, m 19 April 1866 by W. P. White, J. P.

Williams, Nathaniel Junr. & Elisabeth Neal, 29 Dec 1801; Leonard Williams, bm; Step. Sneed, wit.

Williams, Nelson & Frances Peace, m 4 Aug 1866 by E. B. Lyon, J.P.

GRANVILLE MARRIAGES 1753-1868

Williams, Nimrod & Amey Bobbet, daughter of Lewis Bobbet, 9 March 1762; Robert Williams, bm; consent from Lewis Bobbett, 8 March 1762.

Williams, Person & Mary Ann Knott, 15 April 1841; Mead A. Smith, bm; J. M. Wiggins, wit.

Williams, Presley & Ann Ellixon, 9 March 1855; A. Sheman, bm; A. Landis, wit; m 29 March 1855 by Peterson Thorp, J. P.

Williams, Ralph & Ann Walker, 27 Aug 1778; Solomon Walker, bm; Reuben Searcy, wit.

Williams, Robt. & _____, (no date, probably colonial period); Thos. Lowe, bm.

Williams, Robert & Anne Edwards, 29 Oct 1762; (request for license from Elizabeth Edwards & Anne Edwards only).

Williams, Robert & Sarah Williams, 13 Sept 1774; request for license wit. by Catey Allin & Thos. Lanier.

Williams, Robert & Sarah Williams, 10 Oct 1774; Duncan Campbell, bm; William Mackenzie, wit.

Williams, Robert & Susannah Keneday, 6 Aug 1788; J. Williams, John Larmer, bm; A. Henderson, wit.

Williams, Robert & Nancy Kimball, 23 Dec 1850; Brodie Meadows, bm; B. C. Cooke, wit.

Williams, Robert & Mary Howel, 9 Oct 1804; Archibald Gordon, bm; E. W. Parham, wit.

Williams, Robert & Elizabeth F. Daniel, 11 March 1867; m 11 March 1867 by W. H. Thomas, J. P.

Williams, Robert A. & Fannie Taylor Jinkins, 1 May 1856; William G. Williams, bm; m 1 May 1856 by Jas. R. Duty, J. P.

Williams, Rueben & Ursula Satterwhite, 20 Dec 1836; John G. Barker, bm; J. M. Wiggins, wit.

Williams, Samuel & Nancy H. Reavis, 14 March 1838; Saml. Kirkland, bm; Jas. M. Wiggins, wit.

Williams, Samuel & Frances P. Bridges, 18 Oct 1853; George Catlett, bm; A. Landis, wit; m 25 Oct 1853 by R. C. Maynard.

Williams, Saml. Farrar & Hannah Sneed, 16 Jan 1782; Bennet Searcy, bm; Reuben Searcy, wit.

Williams, Simon & Dilley Ann Evans, 3 Dec 1845; Geo. Haskins, bm; J. M. Wiggins, wit.

Williams, Simon & Eliza Inscore, 14 July 1852; Wm. D. Williams, bm.

Williams, Thomas & Elizabeth Semple, 5 Dec 1781; Samuel Walker, bm; Bennet Searcy, wit.

Williams, Thomas & Mary Conyers, 7 Sept 1819; Isaac Winston, bm; Step. K. Sneed, wit.

Williams, Thomas C. & Mary W. Smith, 7 Oct 1831; Wm. T. Hargrove, bm.

GRANVILLE MARRIAGES 1753-1868

Williams, Varnold & Elizebeth Thomas, 22 Nov 1796; Richard Taylor, bm; S. Higgs, wit.

Williams, William & Peggey Patterson, (no date, during admn. of Gov. Richd. D. Spait); John Mangrum, bm; Step. Sneed, wit.

Williams, William & Sarah Pean, 29 March 1798; William Williams Jr., bm; H. Williams, wit.

Williams, William & Sarah Elliot Western, 5 Feb 1799; Allen Howard, bm; Micajah Bullock, wit.

Williams, William & Betsey Allison, 3 Nov 1800; Wilson Jenkins, bm; _ P. Bullock, wit.

Williams, William & Patsey Mosly, 1 June 1802; Fowler Hobgood, bm; Nancy Bullock, wit.

Williams, Wm. & Susannah Barns, 11 Aug 1804; John Ellington, bm; J. Sneed, wit.

Williams, William & Polley Ramey, 15 Dec 1806; W. M. Sneed, bm.

Williams, Wm. & Elizabeth Crews, 24 Feb 1816; Adnah Robinson, bm; W. M. Sneed, wit.

Williams, William & Frances Williams, 18 Feb 1817; Archibald E. Brown, bm; A. Sneed, wit.

Williams, Wm. & Obedience Childers, 17 Feb 1818; Eldrige Dunovan, bm; Rhodes N. Herndon, wit.

Williams, William & Nancy Fletcher, 2 June 1832; Jery Estes, bm; David Laws, wit.

Williams, William & Susan Short, 27 Feb 1839; Willis Loyd, bm.

Williamson, William & Polly Ann Twisdale, of Mecklenburg County, Va., 23 Dec 1846; John Noblin, bm; Jas. M. Wiggins, wit.

Williams, William & Candis Bridges, 29 May 1854; N. G. Whitfield, bm; A. Landis, wit; m 31 May 1854 by James S. Purifoy, Minister of the Gospel.

Williams, William Jr. & Miss Nancy Fletcher, 2 June 1832; William C. York, wit.

Williams, William G. & Sarah Hadspeth, 7 April 1866; m 8 April 1866 by T. M. Lynch, J. P.

Williams, William Rose & _____, 2 Feb 1790; Solomon Williams, bm; Henry Potter, wit.

Williams, William T. & Catharine S. Holms, 17 Sept 1866; m 20 Sept 1866 by J. W. Wellons.

Williams, Willie & Jinsey Bishop, 20 Jan 1808; John Ricks, bm; W. M. Sneed, wit.

Williamson, Dr. A. N. & Virginia L. Griffin, 26 Oct 1859; Thomas N. Griffin, bm; m 20 Dec 1859 by E. Hines.

Williamson, Henry & Adeline Tillotson, 6 Nov 1860; Wm. M. Bennet, bm; m 22 Nov 1860 by Wm. M. Bennett, J. P.

GRANVILLE MARRIAGES 1753-1868

Williamson, Hugh L. & Harriott Ann Cox, m 15 March 1866 by L. B. Stone.

Williamson, J. C., son of Jas. R. & Melinda Williamson, & Roxanna Phillips, daughter of Jas. & Martha Phillips, 21 Nov 1868; m 22 Nov 1868 by E. L. Parrish, J. P.

Williamson, James & Malinda S. Murray, 23 Dec 1836; Joseph Yancy, bm; Robert K. Clack, wit.

Williamson, Lewis P. & Mary E. Littlejohn, 31 Dec 1823; Thomas M. Littlejohn, bm; Step. K. Sneed, wit.

Williamson, William & Mary Smith, 19 Feb 1799; Morris Smith, bm; Step. Sneed, wit.

Williamson, William & Winny Samuel, 16 Dec 1860; Thomas Matthews, bm; m 20 Dec 1860 by Wm. A. Bennett, J. P.

Willie, Thomas H. & Nancey W. Kennon, 11 Dec 1813; Thos. B. Littlejohn, bm; Js. Sneed, wit.

Williford, Augustus & Laura Jane Curtis, 25 Dec 1865; m 26 Dec 1865 by W. A. Currin, J. P.

Williford, Lewis D. & Parthena Meadows, 28 March 1842; Thos. Blalock, wit.

Williford, Squire & Jane Owen, 11 Jan 1845; William Dean, bm; J. M. Wiggins, wit.

Willingham, Isaac & Pattsey Brasfield, 6 Feb 1787; Willis Roberts, bm; _____ B. Searcy, wit.

Wilmond, Pleasent & Sally Thomas, 3 June 1839; William Thomas, bm; S. Beasley Jr., wit.

Wilmuth, Miles & Elizabeth Hughs, 21 Dec 1835; Henry Childres, bm; Robert K. Clack, wit.

Wilson, Benjamin & Lethe Wilson, (of Robert), 25 Feb 1824; Step. K. Sneed, bm; Wm. H. Owen, wit.

Wilson, Benjamin & Harriett Newman, 18 Dec 1854; Kyzer J. Stark, bm; m 22 Dec 1854 by S. G. Wilson, J. P.

Wilson, Bowling & Susan Tanner, 29 Sept 1851; Charles E. Jeffreys, bm; m 29 Sept 1851 by John N. Gill, J. P.

Wilson, Edmund & Temperance Ussery, 12 Oct 1832; Samuel P. Wilson, bm; David Laws, wit.

Wilson, Francis & Martha Phillips, 15 Jan 1835; John Wilson, bm; Benja. Kittrell, wit.

Wilson, Frank Jr. & Elvira S. Dunn, m 2 May 1853 by A. Harris, M. G.

Wilson, Grandison & Mary Bouldin, 19 Dec 1829; Henry Bouldin, bm; Robert K. Clack, wit.

Wilson, Henry & Marey Wicker, 16 Dec 1785; James Bishop, bm; George Harris, wit.

GRANVILLE MARRIAGES 1753-1868

Wilson, James & Elizabeth Mathis, 28 Feb 1861; Henry H. Nethery, bm; m 28 Feb 1861 by L. B. Stone.

Wilson, James A. & Harriet Gordon, 5 Nov 1846; Manson Breedlove, bm.

Wilson, John & Mary Weaver, 15 Feb 1797; Henry Wilson, bm; Wm. Robards, wit.

Wilson, John & Charity Ragland, 23 Dec 1807; Thos. Mitchel, bm; Jun. Sneed, wit.

Wilson, John & Lizza Adcock, 26 April 1820; John White, bm; Step. K. Sneed, wit.

Wilson, John R. & Parthena A. Sears, 4 Jan 1864; W. H. Hart, bm; m 6 Jan 1864 by John F. Harris, J. P.

Wilson, John W. & Lucy C. Sherrin, 5 Dec 1861; A. Landis, bm.

Wilson, Joseph & Eliza Parham, 17 Jan 1861; James A. Parham, bm; m 23 Jan 1861 by E. F. Beachum.

Wilson, Joseph P. & Frances E. Grisham, 31 Oct 1839; Granville Grisham, bm.

Wilson, Joseph G., son of S. P. & Martha Wilson, & Lucy F. Daniel, daughter of Willis & Elisabeth Daniel, m 9 Dec 1868 by L. K. Willie, M. G.

Wilson, Lee, son of Frank & Martha A. Wilson, & Hester Ann Overby, daughter of Obediah & Hariet Overby, 16 Dec 1868; m 22 Dec 1868 by James A. Bullock, J. P.

Wilson, Lewis & Mary Weaver, 7 May 1812; Howel Satterwhite, bm; Stephen K. Sneed, wit.

Wilson, Lewis & Elisabeth Pollen, 20 Jan 1815; Robert Wilson, bm.

Wilson, Lewis & Jane S. Parrish, 21 Sept 1851; A. Landis, bm; Wesley W. Young, wit.

Wilson, Lewis & Jane S. Parish, 21 Sept 1851; A. Landis, wit; m 21 Sept 1851 by D. J. Paschall, J. P.

Wilson, Marion M. & Amey F. Knott, 18 July 1863; A. Landis, bm; m 19 July 1863 by J. F. Harris, J. P.

Wilson, Mathew & Elizabeth Peace, 8 Dec 1802; Joshua White, bm; P. Bullock, wit.

Wilson, Robert & Rebeccah Hester, 10 Oct 1798; Henry Rowland, bm; Step. Sneed, wit.

Wilson, Robert Jr. & Elizabeth Gresham, 7 Nov 1811; Labon Gresham, bm; Saml. Hogg, wit.

Wilson, Robert A., son of Solomon & Priccilla Wilson, & Cornelia A. Barker, daughter of David T. & Martha Barker, m 24 Dec 1868 by W. C. Kennett, Minister.

Wilson, Robert S. & Martha R. Robertson, 5 March 1867; m 6 March 1867 by J. E. Pattillo, J. P.

GRANVILLE MARRIAGES 1753-1868

Wilson, Samuel P. & Martha Baker, 12 Dec 1836; John C. Lemay, bm; J. M. Wiggins, Clk., wit.

Wilson, Solomon G. & Priscilla Stark, 19 Dec 1840; C. Barker, bm; J. M. Wiggins, wit.

Wilson, Solomon G. & Mary Jane Philpott, 21 Feb 1853; J. R. Fuller, bm; Jno. G. Watson, wit; m 21 Feb 1853 by J. R. Devin.

Wilson, Tapley & Jane Wood, 8 April 1819; William P. Rose, bm; Jno. Wms. Burton, wit.

Wilson, Thomas & Milly Obrien, 6 Nov 1820; Robert Wilson, bm; Richd. Sneed, wit.

Wilson, William & Mary Sims, 16 April 1774; Lennard Sims, bm; Reuben Searcy, wit.

Wilson, William & Lucy A. Davis, 28 Dec 1814; James Guy, bm.

Wilson, William & Amey Boyd, 20 May 1816; Robert Wilson, bm; H. Young, wit.

Wilson, William & Elizabeth Morrow, 23 Feb 1830; John Ramsey, bm; A. Sneed, wit.

Wilson, William & Elizabeth Franklin, 4 Feb 1845; John H. Owen, bm.

Wilson, William & Eliza Toon, 29 Dec 1849; John Clarke, bm; Jas. R. Duty, wit.

Wilson, William & Martha Hester, 28 Aug 1851; Obadiah Christmas, bm; B. C. Cooke, wit.

Wilson, William & Harriett Sherrin, 29 Nov 1852; John Wilson, bm; A. Landis, wit; m 9 Dec 1852 by E. Hester, Minister of the Gospel.

Wilson, William & Elizabeth Strum, 15 Nov 1861; Robert R. Rowland, bm; Jas. R. Duty, wit.

Wilson, Wm. D. & Virginia Ann Toone, 21 Dec 1857; Granville ____, bm; m 21 Dec 1857 by John W. Kelly, J. P.

Wimbish, John & Bettie Thomas, 9 Nov 1857; R. N. Herndon, bm; m at Pool's Rock by Robt. B. Sutton, Rector of St. Stephen's Church, Oxford, 25 Nov 1857.

Wimbish, Samuel P. & Elizabeth T. Townes, m 18 July 1868 by H. H. Prout, Rector of St. John's Church, Williamsboro.

Wimbush, Jessie, son of Peter & Caroline Wimbush, & Lina Fields, son of Howard & Rosa Fields, 14 Dec 1868; m 16 Dec 1868 by Andrew Williams, J. P.

Winckler, Matthew T. & Christiana E. Turner, 21 Nov 1857; H. A. Davis, bm; m __ Nov 1857.

Winfree, James & Nancy Blanks, 24 Feb 1830; D. J. Young, bm.

Winkfield, Henderson & Sarah Durham, 16 Sept 1858; Jos. J. Wagstaff, bm; W. M. Sneed, wit; m 17 Sept 1858 by W. R. Hunt, J. P.

GRANVILLE MARRIAGES 1753-1868

Winn, John P. & Harriet C. Winn, 18 Dec 1849; Wesley W. Young, bm.

Winney, James & Mary Morgan, m 17 Sept 1865 by Jas. J. Moore, J. P.

Winningham, Sherwood & Susanna Huskey, 12 Jan 1782; Nathan Harris, bm; Bennet Searcy, wit.

Winslow, Edward Lee & Sally Little, 7 May 1835; Thos. Landford, bm.

Winstead, Alexander & Martha C. Puryear, 15 Oct 1831; Stephen Munday, bm; Jno. P. Smith, wit.

Winston, Anthony & Elisabeth Garrett, 5 Feb 1782; Joseph McGehe, bm; ___ Henderson, wit.

Winston, B. T. & Susan A. Downey, 25 Jan 1851; Robert A. Hicks, bm.

Winston, Benjamin & Elizabeth Hendly, 4 Oct 1825; Samuel Bailey, bm; Step. K. Sneed, wit.

Winston, Bridges T. & Mary E. Overbey, 5 May 1863; A. Landis, bm; m 17 May 1863 by Ro. H. Marsh, Minister of the Gospel.

Winston, David & Candace Jeter, 28 Oct 1824; Richard Allen, bm; Wm. H. Owen, wit.

Winston, David C. & Martha A. Bragg, 6 Feb 1860; William Card, bm; m 8 Feb 1860 by W. D. Allen, J. P.

Winston, George & Hixey White, 7 Oct 1819; Clement Wilkins, bm; Step. K. Sneed, wit.

Winston, Jacob & Harriett Hester, freed people, 29 March 1866; m 31 March 1866 by Wm. E. Bullock, J. P.

Winston, John & Adeline Usry, freed people, m 14 Oct 1866 by William E. Bullock, J. P.; A. Landis, bm; Jos. J. Egerton, wit.

Winston, John B. & Mary Elizabeth Cannady, 17 Oct 1860; E. Winston, bm; m 21 Oct 1860 by R. B. Jones, M. G.

Winston, Moses & Polly Weathers, 25 Oct 1805; Edward Weathers, bm; Jas. Sneed, wit.

Winston, Obediah & Parmelia Bullock, 7 May 1832; John McFarling, bm; Step. K. Sneed, wit.

Winston, Rufus & Mary E. Mitchell, 11 March 1848; Joseph Peace, bm; Jas. M. Wiggins, wit.

Winston, Wiley & Elizabeth Blackwell, 9 Jan 1794; Athansius Thomas, bm; W. Norwood, D. C., wit.

Widsom, Jessee & Elizabeth Griffin, 1 July 1819; Charles Yancey, bm; Jechonias Yancey, wit.

Witherspon, Lewis M., son of Hyram & Nannie Witherspon, & Jennie E. Royster, daughter of William & Ann Royster, 4 Aug 1868; m 4 Aug 1868 by J. H. Stradley, M. G.

GRANVILLE MARRIAGES 1753-1868

Womack, Abraham & Martha Mitchel, spinster, 31 Mah 1763; John Mitchel, bm; Jno. Bowie, wit.

Womack, Charles L. & Ann Stegall, 7 Dec 1859; Bedford L. Stigall, bm; L. B. Stone, wit; m 7 Dec 1859 by L. B. Stone, J. P.

Womack, Jesse & Elisabeth Johnson, 15 Nov 1796; Isaac Johnson, bm; Step. Sneed, wit.

Wommoth, Richard & Nancy Sandling, 15 Jan 1851; Samuel H. Jeffrys, bm; A. Landis, wit.

Wood, Alexander & Sarah Landis, 3 Nov 1846; William W. Dun, bm; Jas. M. Wiggins, wit.

Wood, Alexander F. & Emily F. Fowler, 11 Aug 1865; Roberson R. Hobgood, bm; m by Hartwell Arnold.

Wood, Alexander S. & Loueasa Ann Moss, 7 Nov 1844; William C. Wood, bm.

Wood, Anthony & Fanny Hege(?), 11 Dec 1822; Yancy Oakley, bm; Jas. M. Wiggins, wit.

Wood, Carter & Sarah Heveler, 19 Dec 1801; Benjamin Clardy, bm; Step. Sneed, wit.

Wood, George & Nancey Terry, 18 July 1814; William Terry, bm; W. M. Sneed, wit.

Wood, John & Sarah, daughter of William Hendrick, 1 Oct 1763; Anne Spivey, bm; Jno. Bowie, wit.

Wood, John & Anne Minor, 11 July 1815; William Bartlet, bm; Step. Sneed, wit.

Wood, Lewis & Bella Graves, colored, 8 Oct 1867; m 10 Oct 1867 by Aron Protcher(?).

Wood, Richard & Elizabeth Lyon, 4 Aug 1830; McVay Chandler, bm; David Laws, wit.

Wood, Richard S. & Samantha A. Fuller, 10 April 1863; Jacob Satterwhite, bm; m 26 April 1863 by L. K. Willie, M. G.

Wood, Samuel Chester & Susannah Clemens, 19 Dec 1794; John Thorp Jr., bm; L. Henderson, wit.

Wood, William C. & Jane C. Redman, 26 Nov 1861; J. Terry, bm; m 28 Nov 1861 by Peterson Thorp, J. P.

Wood, William R. & Bettie Smith, 29 Feb 1860; W. R. Brasius, bm.

Woodley, William B. & Polly Richards, 10 Jan 1860; Wm. D. Davis, bm.

Woodlief, Corneleous Junr. & Martha Woodlief, 15 Nov 1837; James Powel, bm; Tho. L. King, wit.

Woodlief, John & Molley Cooper, 9 May 1786; John Cooper, bm; Reuben Searcy, C. C., wit.

Woodlief, Patrick & Hester Ann Edwards, 23 Sept 1852; Charles T. Parrish, bm.

GRANVILLE MARRIAGES 1753-1868

Woodliff, B. H. & Mary A. Stanton, 17 Oct 1865; J. B. Woodliff, bm; m 18 Oct 1865 by E. H. Overton, J. P.

Woodliff, Benjamin T., son of John & Ann Woodliff, & Lucy C. Pergurson, daughter of Ransom & Martha Pergurson, m 17 Oct 1867 by Joseph H. Riddick.

Woodliff, Charles & Sally Merrett, 13 Oct 1840; Ira E. Arnold, bm; Jas. M. Wiggins, wit.

Woodliff, John & Ann Powell, 20 Nov 1832; J. J. Hunt, bm; David Laws, wit.

Woodliff, John & Mary Woodliff, 17 Oct 1840; James R. Cook, bm; Jas. M. Wiggins, wit.

Woodliff, John B. & Mary W. Hight, 24 Feb 1866; John Headspeth, bm; A. Landis, wit.

Woodliff, Joseph & Mary Hunt, 15 Oct 1851; Jas. M. Wiggins, bm; m 20 Oct 1851 by D. P. Paschall, J. P.

Woodliff, Joseph & Emily Garrett, 5 Feb 1856; Woodson D. Blacklay(?), bm; m 7 Feb 1856 by J. W. Floyd, Minister.

Woodliff, Joseph J. & Mary R. Wrenn, 4 Oct 1858; W. Z. Renn, bm.

Woodliff, Littleberry & Rebecah Cook, 3 May 1814; Claborn Stone, bm; Step. Sneed, wit.

Woodliff, Nathaniel A. & Roberta A. Edwards, 16 Sept 1864; Jno. M. Ellington, bm.

Woodliff, Thomas & Letha Parrish, 17 Dec 1844; Hilliard Powell, bm; Jas. M. Wiggins, wit.

Woodliff, Thomas & Sarah Ann Wynn, 18 Dec 1849.

Woodliff, William & Mary Crowder, 2 Nov 1834; William Brown, bm; W. M. Spears, wit.

Woodliff, William A., son of Cornelius & Martha Woodliff, & Mary E. Overton, daughter of James & Jane H. Overton, m 30 Oct 1867 by J. H. Riddick, M. G.

Woodliff, William H. & Abigail Overton, 7 April 1862; Wm. J. Hight, bm.

Woods, Wilas & Cindarilla Holmes, 2 May 1856; Samuel Longmire, bm; A. Landis, wit; m 2 May 1856 by J. W. Floyd, Minister.

Woods, William & Nancy Roberts, 1 Oct 1859; P. A. T. Farabow, bm.

Woodward, Robert & Salley Bass, 3 Oct 1822; Leonard Worthan, bm; Jas. M. Wiggins, wit.

Woody, Joseph & Martha Norman, 23 July 1839; Robert Michel, bm.

Woody, Reubin J. & Matilda B. Overbey, 11 Jan 1866; m 14 Jan 1866 by E. Hines; Charles E. Landis, bm.

Wooton, John & Poley Johnston, 26 July 1796; Joseph Johnson, bm; Richard Taylor, wit.

GRANVILLE MARRIAGES 1753-1868

Wooton, John & Mary Fuller, 3 May 1827; Wm. S. Kibble, bm; Step. K. Sneed, wit.

Wooton, William & Nancy Adcock, 16 Jan 1824; James Wooton, bm; S. K. Sneed, wit.

Worph, George & Martha Brack, 9 June 1785; William Parish, bm; Reuben Searcy, wit.

Worrel, John & Elizabeth Chadwick, 14 Jan 1788; Charnock Cox, bm; A. Henderson, wit.

Worrell, Thomas & Rebecca Smith, 24 Nov 1825; Thomas Chapman, bm; Jas. Sneed, wit.

Worsham, Francis & Nancy Parish, 17 Nov 1812; William Robards, bm; Thos. J. Hicks, wit.

Worsham, Joshua & Ann Hopkins, 15 Jan 1794; George Hopkins, bm; W. Norwood, wit.

Wortham, Alexander W. & Lucy W. Reavis, 12 Jan 1858; m 14 Jan 1858 by A. C. Harris.

Wortham, Edwd. W. & Harriet J. McGraw, 5 Sept 1848; R. J. Wortham, bm.

Wortham, Edward W. & Sarah A. E. Harris, 30 July 1858; A. Landis, bm; m 2 Aug 1858 by H. H. Rowland, J. P.

Wortham, George & Virginia L. Ridley, 3 Aug 1846; J. M. Wiggins, wit.

Wortham, James & Sarah Lewis, 20 Sept 1789; William Marshall, bm; Henry Potter, wit.

Wortham, James & Martha J. Green, 2 Oct 1848; A. H. Cooke, bm; J. M. Wiggins, wit.

Wortham, James L. & _____ Washington, 15 Aug 1820; Wm. Blackwell, bm; A. Sneed, wit.

Wortham, John D. & Naknie Blackwell, 14 April 1866; m 19 April 1866 by T. Page Ricaud, Minister of the Gospel.

Wortham, Robert H. & Lucy A. Webb, 15 Dec 1847; Jas. T. Gill, bm.

Wortham, William D. & Fanny A. Blackwell, 6 April 1825; Richard Allen, bm; Step. K. Sneed, wit.

Wren, William Z. & Mary McGhee, 10 Dec 1853; Wm. E. Jones, bm; m 21 Dec 1853 by A. C. Harris, M. G.

Wright (Right), Anderson & Jane Clopton, 23 March 1843; Jas. Blackly, bm; Wm. H. Whitfield, wit.

Wright, Daniel A. & Lucy Ann Turner, 9 April 1859; John L. Wright, bm; m 13 April 1859 by E. F. Beachum, M. G.

Wright, George & Morning Hunt, 17 Feb 1825; Randol Minor, bm; L. Gilliam, wit.

Wright, Geo. W. & Fannie R. Collins, 7 Nov 1865; A. Landis, bm; m 6 Dec 1865 by E. F. Beachum, a regular M. G.

GRANVILLE MARRIAGES 1753-1868

Wright, Gideon & Nancy Kittrell, 17 Nov 1805; George W. Harris, bm; Jas. Sneed, wit.

Wright, James & Tabithey Smith, 7 Dec 1793; George Moore, bm.

Wright, John, of color, son of Woodson & Frances Wright, & Mary Williford, daughter of Peter Curtis & Susan Williford, m 8 Dec 1867 by John H. Webb, J. P.

Wright, John L., son of John H. & Sophia C. Wright, & Mildrid N. Fuller, daughter of J. R. & Mary H. Fuller, 20 Jan 1868; m 22 Jan 1868 by E. F. Beachum, a regular G. Min.

Wright, John T. & Adeline Waller, 12 June 1848; L. S. Philpott, bm.

Wright, Jordan & Polley Nellums, 27 Dec 1804; Cader Parker, bm; E. W. Parham, wit.

Wright, Joshua K. & Martha E. Kittrell, 20 Aug 1828; Benja. Kittrell, bm.

Wright, Lawson & Ann Eliza Hunt, 26 Dec 1865; A. Landis, wit; m 28 Dec 1865 by W. G. Gannon, M. G.

Wright, Priesly & Nancey OBrien, 5 Feb 1828; Wm. Jones, bm; David Laws, wit.

Wright, Richard & Elisabeth Phillips, 1 Nov 1800; John Moore, bm; Philip Bullock, wit.

Wright, Robt. & Louisa Speed, m 23 June 1866 by Wyatt Walker, M. G.

Wright, Thomas & Anne Haynes, 18 June 1809; David Landers, bm; Jun. Sneed, wit.

Wright, Thomas & Mary Brantly, 20 Jan 1825; Willie Jones, bm; W. Hayes Owen, wit.

Wright, Thomas D. & Elizabeth G. Harris, 30 Nov 1838; Benj. F. Harris, G. C. Wiggins, bm.

Wright, W. B. & Eliza G. Gilliam, 14 April 1831; Jas. T. Gilliam, bm; Step. K. Sneed, wit.

Wright, William & Mary Harter, 9 Jan 1797; William Hester, bm; Step. Sneed, wit.

Wright, William O. & Mary E. Crews(?), 1 April 1835; Benj. F. Harris, bm; Benj. Kittrell, wit.

Wright, Woodson & Frances Curtis, 18 Jan 1847; Chas. Curtis, bm; Jas. M. Wiggins, wit.

Wyche, P. W. & Rebecca J. Southall, 18 July 1854; W. H. Rowland, bm; m 19 July 1854 by J. Tillett.

Wyche, Parry, of color, son of George & Anna Wyche, & Parthenia Minor, parents unknown; 23 Jan 1868; m 26 Jan 1868 by S. P. J. Harris.

Wyche, William E. & Sally T. Reavis, 10 June 1833; G. E. Allen, bm; Step. K. Sneed, wit.

GRANVILLE MARRIAGES 1753-1868

Wynn, Charles Jr. & Repsey Spivy, 19 May 1818; Landey L. A. Thurman, bm; Zach. Herndon Jr., wit.

Wynne, Thomas & Judith Blackwell, 28 Jan 1823; John P. LeMay, bm; S. K. Sneed, wit.

Yancey, Albert & _____, 26 Dec 1866; William Yancey, bm; E. L. Parrish, wit.

Yancey, Boyd, of color, son of Sam & Sena Yancey, & Amanda Williamson, daughter of Lonia Williamson, m 12 Feb 1868 by B. T Winston, J. P.

Yancey, Henry & Elizabeth Royster, 15 Jan 1805; Obediah Farrar, bm; Jas. Sneed, wit.

Yancey, Henry, of color, son of Selina Harris, & Rebecca Green, of color, daughter of Rose Green, 23 Dec 1868; m 6 Jan 1869 by E. Hines, M. G.

Yancey, James & Mary Bracey, 15 Aug 1765; William Moore, bm.

Yancey, Lyon & Sarah Stovall, 15 Nov 1798; Sterling Yancey, bm; Betsey Yancey, wit.

Yancey, Meredith & Elizabeth C. Allen, 23 Oct 1829; Jordan D. Moss(?), bm; Step. K. Sneed, wit.

Yancey, Philip & Polly Diah Hester, 25 Aug 1818; Absolem Yancey, bm.

Yancey, Robert & Susan Griffin, 12 May 1832; Jas. Wiles, bm; Jno. P. Smith, wit.

Yancey, Thomas & Margaret Mulky, 20 Nov 1856; Henry Tillottson, bm; m 20 Nov 1856 by L. B. Stone, J. P.

Yancey, Thornton & _____, _____ (no date, colonial period); document not completed; Wm. Allin, bm.

Yancey, Tryon & Sarah Brooks Blacknall, 10 Sept 1834; Jas. Russell, bm.

Yancey, Warren, of color, son of Lucy Harris, & Hannah Jones, daughter of Roger & Martha Jones, m 10 Aug 1867 by W. H. Thomas, J. P.

Yancey, William & Abigail Hicks, 13 Nov 1767; James Yancey Junr. bm; Jesse Benton, wit.

Yancey, William, of color, son of William Cutts & Martha Cutts, & Martha An Winbush, daughter of Gabe & Lucy Winbush, m 26 Dec 1867 by E. L. Parrish, J. P.

Yancy, Albert & Elizabeth Jones, freed, 26 Dec 1866; m 26 Dec 1866 by E. L. Parrish, J. P.

Yancy, C. F., son of John H. & Lucy Yancy, & A. M. Royster, daughter of Charles M. & Mariller Royster, 27 Nov 1867; m 27 Nov 1867 by L. B. Stone, J. P.

Yancy, John & Indianer Yancy, freed people, 8 June 1867; Wm. Yancey, bm; E. L. Parrish, wit; m 8 June 1867 by E. L. Parrish, J. P.

GRANVILLE MARRIAGES 1753-1868

Yancy, William & Avarilla Lawson, 26 July 1826; Danl. Easley, bm.

Yarbrough, Dud & Winey Edmunds, 5 Oct 1865; m 25 Dec 1865 by Wm. Hicks, J. P.

Yarbrough, Green & Candis Lawrence, 19 Jan 1867; Jonathan Jenkins, bm; m 20 Jan 1867 by W. H. P. Jenkins, J. P.

Yarbrough, Dewit C. & Caroline M. Jones, 22 July 1856; John B. Day, bm; m 24 July 1856 by T. J. Horner, M. G.

Yarbrough, William & Anne Clement, 6 June 1808; John Clement, bm; James J. Tarrar, wit.

Yates, C. G. & Martha E. Doab, 21 Oct 1850; Thos. T. Best, bm.

Yeargan, son of James Yeargan & Susan Yeargan, & Betsy Bailey, daughter of Gilcrease Bailey & Fanny Bailey, 8 Feb 1868; m by W. D. Allen, J. P.

Yeargin, David & Caroline F. Knight, 11 Dec 1847; William T. Garshan(?), bm; J. M. Wiggins, wit.

Yeargin, Thos. & Nelly Parham, 19 Dec 1821; Dorris Yeargin, bm; S. K. Sneed, wit.

York, Edward T., son of William & Margerite York, & Louisiana Grissom, daughter of James D. & Patsey Grissom, 15 Dec 1868; m 6 Feb 1869 by B. Walker, J. P.

York, Philemon & Lucy Powel, 1 July 1786; John York, bm; B. Searcy, wit.

York, Thomas & Mary Finch, 24 July 1793; William Garrett, bm; W. Norwood, D. C. C., wit.

York, Thomas Jr. & Maria Loyd, 3 Dec 1828; William Peek, bm; David Laws, wit.

York, William C. & Peggy Fletcher, 1 March 1825; John Wesley Finch, bm; S. K. Sneed, wit.

Young, Allen L. & Lucy C. White, 28 Sept 1843; Henry G. Green, bm; Wm. T. Hargrove, wit.

Young, Commodore & Nancy Turner, m 21 Dec 1866 by Joseph W. Murphy, Rector of the Church of the Holy Innocents, Henderson.

Young, David J. & Julian Hutchison, 12 Dec 1821; William Terry, bm.

Young, Demetrus E. & Mary A. W. D. Jones, 30 Dec 1835; L. Gilliam, bm; Benja. Kittrell, wit.

Young, Henry & Ann L. Taylor, 25 June 1808; James Young, bm; Step. Sneed, wit.

Young, Henry & Nancey Pettigrew, 14 Aug 1811; Elless Walker, bm; W. M. Sneed, wit.

Young, Capt. Isaac J. & Miss Elizabeth M. Southall, m 23 March 1864 by Jos. W. Murphy, Rector of Ch. of Holy Innts. Henderson.

GRANVILLE MARRIAGES 1753-1868

Young, John & Francis Young, 20 Sept 1786; John Young, bm; Bennet Searcy, wit.

Young, John, of color, son of John George & Jane Ezel, & Isabella Jordan, daughter of Harrison & Sarah Jordan, 19 Dec 1867; m 19 Dec 1867 by Jas. R. Duty, J. P.

Young, John H. & Lucy F. Jinkins, 20 Nov 1845; L. A. Paschall, bm; J. M. Wiggins, wit.

Young, John H. & Sally John Eaton, 25 Sept 1854; T. L. Hargrove, bm; m 26 Sept 1854 by Thomas U. Faucette, Oxford, N. C.

Young, John W. & ____ A. M. Kittrell, 18 July 1836; Wm. W. Young, bm; J. M. Wiggins, wit.

Young, Jonathan & Dochia Clay, 15 April 1830; Wm. Jones, bm; Step. K. Sneed, wit.

Young, Joseph, a freed man, & Gooding Ford, 3 April 1866; L. B. Stone, J. P., wit.

Young, Joseph & Goodding Ford, 3 April 1866; m 3 April 1866 by L. B. Stone, J. P.

Young, Madison & Patsy Satterwhite, freed people, 11 Aug 1865; Henry Marrow, bm.

Young, Peter W. & Jane E. Cooper, 19 April 1852; P. T. Beasley, bm; m 21 April 1852 by G. W. Farrill.

Young, Richd. A. & Mary Ellen Jeggetts, 15 Aug 1848; Jno. Johnson, bm.

Young, Robert E. & Pattie W. Harris, 9 June 1864; m 9 June 1864 by J. L. Michaux, Minister of the Gospel.

Young, Samuel & Sarah Whitfield, 4 May 1791; Wm. Smith, bm; W. Norwood, wit.

Young, Sol., son of James Herndon & Susan Young, & Anne Bradford, daughter of Cresey Bradford, m 26 Dec 1868 by R. T. Overton, J. P.

Young, Street & Judy Cooper, freed people, 8 Oct 1865; Peter Hunt, bm; A. Landis, wit; m 8 Oct 1865 by Maurice H. Vaughan, Rector of St. Stephen's Church.

Young, Sydney, colored, son of Ab & Louisa Young, & Aliza Marrow, daughter of Peter & Sarah Marrow, 25 Dec 1868; m 28 Dec 1868 by Edward Hines.

Young, Thomas & Agnes Herndon, 10 Feb 1866; A. Landis, wit; m 12 Feb 1866 by L. K. Willie, M. G.

Young, Thomas & Caroline P. Parham, freed people, m 28 July 1866 by J. F. Harris, J. P.

Young, Thomas W. & Ann Allen, 11 Nov 1844; Abner Veazey, bm; J. M. Wiggins, wit.

Young, Wesley W. & Ann Eliza Young, 26 June 1858; Samuel D. Young, bm.

GRANVILLE MARRIAGES 1753-1868

Young, William W. & Lucy F. Kittrell, 21 March 1834; Frances Winston, bm.

Young, Willie & Eliza Dew, 12 Oct 1835; John Young, bm; Benja. Kittrell, wit.

Younger, George & Elizabeth Sears, 24 Sept 1824; Jesse Rice, bm; A. Sneed, wit.

Yourk, John & Salley Coopper, 12 June 1786; Benjamin Coopper, bm; John Searcy, wit.

ADDITIONS

Ogilvie, Kimbrough & Nansey Harris, 25 Sept 1782; Robert Harris, bm; Asa Searcy, wit.

Oliver, Berrien & Mary B. Royster, 13 Nov 1821; Willis A. Royster, bm.

Oliver, Dyonisius & Polley Oliver, 26 Jan 1790; Joseph Smith, bm; A. Henderson, wit.

Oliver, Francis H. & Mary Owen, 2 April 1817; Robert Blackwell, bm; R. N. Herndon, wit.

Oman(?), Jesse & Martha Ann Briggs, 7 March 1846; Thos. Jones, bm; J. M. Wiggins, wit.

Omarry, Richard & Mary Ann Washington, 8 Oct 1839; Jn. Jones, bm; J. M. Wiggins, wit.

Omary, Jesse & Rebeca Fosset, 12 June 1810; Richard Omary, bm.

Omary, Silas, son of John & Tinna Omary, & Luetta Jenkins, daughter of William & Martha Jenkins, 11 May 1868; m 12 May 1868 by F. J. Tilley, J. P.

Omerry, Owen & Elizabeth Wall, 10 May 1805; Burgess Wall, bm; Jun. Sneed, wit.

Omerry, Thomas, son of not known, & Parthenia Omerry, & Eliza Adcock, daughter of not know & Jackey Adcock, m 1 May 1868 by B. C. Howard, J. P.

Omshundro, William & Mary Clareton, 22 Dec 1794; George Bullock, bm; Step. Sneed, wit.

Oneal, William & Fanny J. Inscore, 11 Sept 1861; m 18 Sept 1861 by Wm. D. Davis, J. P.

ONeil, Hardy & Candy J. Davis, 22 Sept 1852; Wm. A. Davis, bm.

Orell, Joseph N. & Elizabeth G. Edwards, 24 Oct 1866; W. J. Stewart, bm.

Orrell, William L. & Frankey Robertson, 8 June 1838; Rufus A. Bullen, bm.

Orsborn, D. S. & Martha R. Daws, 24 Dec 1851; S. S. Parrott, bm; m 24 Dec 1851 by Thomas U. Faucett.

Orsborn, Job & Caroline A. H. Davis, 15 Sept 1847; A. Landis, bm.

Orsborne, Jonathan & Mrs. Elizabeth C. Allen, 3 Nov 1863; A. Landis, bm; m 5 Nov 1863 by Thos. U. Faucette.

Overbey, David Jr. & Ellen H. Hicks, 19 Jan 1853; D. A. Paschall, bm; m 19 Jan 1853 by R. J. Devin.

Overby, Ditrion & Elizabeth A. Overbey, 8 July 1863; J. W. Ladd, bm; m 8 July 1863 by L. B. Stone, J. P.

Overbey, Edward & Mary Griffin, 9 Dec 1858; m 9 Dec 1858 by L. B. Stone, J. P.

Overbey, John H. & Nancy T. Griffin, 25 Nov 1846; William Henry Summerhill(?), bm; L. B. Stone, wit.

INDEX

(?), Amanda 85
(?), B. F. 301
(?), Bennet 319
(?), David 75
(?), Dosha 51
(?), Eben 227
(?), Fielding A. 58
(?), Granville 360
(?), Hutchins 179
(?), James 16
(?), John 349
(?), Leza 77
(?), Liddy 151
(?), Marcus 342
(?), Martha 112
(?), Penolepee 130
(?), Thomas 153
(?), Thos. 333
(?), Will 110
(?), William 119, 153, 336
(?), Wm. A. 49
Abbot, J. 259
  Wilson 210
Abbott, Ann 282
  Mary 186
Abernathy, Mary 286
  Robt. 286
Adams, Benjamin 114, 131
  Edmond 1
  Elizabeth 17, 118
  Isaac 3
  Lucy 1
  Martha 146, 242
  Mary 1, 299, 329
  Mary Ann 353
  Rebecka 339
  Robert C. 64
  Sarah 257
  William 1
Adcock, Adeline 86
  Allen 332
  Arena 327
  Barnett 147
  Bowling 255
  Burgess 350
  Charity 121
  Cloe 255
  David 225, 262
  Delphy Ann 4
  Eliza 47, 370
  Elizabeth 2, 51, 262, 335
  Fanny 238
  Frances 38
  Jackey 370
  James 3
  Jas. W. 51
  Jemima 273
  Jemimah 224
  Jincey 194
  Josey 136
  Linem 255

Adcock (cont.)
  Littleton 219, 224
  Lizza 359
  Martha 153, 352
  Martha Ann 182
  Martha G.(?) 219
  Mary 166
  Mary F. 81, 236
  Mary Hillman 120
  Nancey 234, 255
  Nancy 14, 193, 364
  Nancy M. 119
  Parthena A. (Mrs.) 167
  Piety 145, 204
  Prudence 274
  Rhoda L. 14
  Rives 294
  Roan 90
  Robert 301
  Ruth 44
  Salley 225
  Sally 190, 197
  Sarah Ann 346
  Synthia 317
  Thos. 347
  William 2, 298, 317
  Wm. 2, 255, 298
  Wm. H. 142
Adkins, Allen 86
Afscue, Susanna 180
Aiken, Margaret 105
Aikin, Adeline H. 23
  Ann Eliza 62
  Rebecca F. 32
Akin, Ann 3
  Elizabeth 194
  Henrietta 351
  James 222
  James, Sr. 3
  Joseph 134
  Joseph, Jr. 194
  Lucy 299
  Mary 243
  Mary H. 155
  Nancy 286
  W. E. 23
  William 3, 174
  William E. 23, 286
Akins, Frankey 111
Aleln, Jo. B. 248
Alen, Nancy 257
Alexander, Nathaniel (Gov.) 323
  Patsy 4
  Richard H. 183, 192
Allen, A. A. 170
  Adeline 54
  Alice 355
  Ann 6, 368
  Archibald 214
  Barbara 57
  Charles 139, 179
  Charlotte 87

Allen (cont.)
  Chas. 7
  Chesteen 290
  Cornelia 56
  Cynthia 145
  D. D. 354
  David B. 56, 258
  Desdimonia 132
  Ebey. 251
  Eliza J. 148
  Elizabeth 141, 274
  Elizabeth C. 179, 366
  Elizabeth C. (Mrs.) 370
  Elizabeth H. 144
  Elizabeth L. 229
  Emeline H. 6, 63
  Emily 104
  Fannie 290
  Fanny 97, 179
  Frances 7, 179, 260
  G. E. 365
  G. W. 330
  Garland 5, 34, 42, 88, 182
  Henry 245
  Hy. 6
  Isabella Frances 311
  J. B. 235
  J. E. 292
  James 117
  Jane 221, 294
  Jas. E. 121
  John 43
  L. F. 6
  Lea 290
  Louisa 177
  Lucy 215, 294
  Lydia Ann 145
  Malinda 123
  Martha 17, 156, 224
  Martha A. S. 222
  Mary 220, 319
  Mary Ann 144
  Mary C. 157
  Mary E. 203
  Matthew 70
  Nancey 320
  Nilly 6
  P. W. 182
  Permelia W. 185
  Phebe 5
  Pissillar 4
  Polly Ann 56
  Qualls 354
  Queen 123
  Rachael 348
  Rebecca 50
  Richard 135, 361, 364
  Richd. 209, 303
  Ruth Ann 63
  Samuel, Jr. 192
  Sarah 40, 142, 191
  Sarah E. 148
  Solomon 5

Allen (cont.)
  Squire 353
  Susan L. 143
  Susannah 4
  Tureacy McC. 323
  Virginia C. 214
  W. D. 42, 44, 67, 85,
    104, 167, 179, 203,
    261, 347
  William 6, 272, 287
  Willie 141
  Winney 183
  Wm. D. 63
  Zelpha 4
Alley, A. H. 36, 174,
  227, 324
Allgood, Martha M. 117
Allin, Champion 285
  Elisabeth 336
  Henry H. 317
  John 80
  Mathew 230
  Mildred 25
  Sarah 178
  Wm. 366
Allison, Betsey 357
  James, Jr. 240
  Jennet 188
  John 7
  Polley 188
Almon, Elen A. 299
Alston, Anne 177
  Charity 189, 315
  Frances 193
  Geo. 93
  James 66, 165
  Martha 177
  Mary 246
  Rosanna 254
  Sarah 156
  Solo., Jr. 189
  Solomon 7, 177
  Woodson 167
Amelia, Frances 226
Amis, Catherine 274
  Elizabeth 8, 42, 130
  Elmira C. 274
  Fanny 289
  Frances 267, 276
  Francis 198
  Hannah 149, 248, 294
  Harriot 42
  J. S. 8
  Jane D. 245
  John 8, 171, 274,
    288, 310
  John W., Jr. 253
  Jonathan 164
  Joseph 130
  Judith 254
  Judith F. 344
  Lewis 248
  Lucy D. 277
  Marlta 8
  Martha H. 61
  Mary 232
  Nancy 43, 130
  Nancy R. 188
  Nanny R. 189
  R. 274
  Rachel 253
  Rosa A. 8
  Salley 42
  Sam 121
  Sarah 60
  Stephen 58
  Susan 121
  Warren 76

Amis (cont.)
  William 345
Amos, John 264
An-(?), Albert 114
Anderson, Abel 8, 9, 89,
    105, 106, 228, 316
  Able 325
  Abraham 59
  Adeline 8
  Aggy 217
  Alkerson 280
  Anne 328
  Arabella 79
  Augustine 306
  Betsey Ann 172
  Bolling 20
  Delila 316
  Dennis 11, 20
  Elizabeth 106
  Emily 10
  Faithy 266
  Frankey 106
  Geo. 9, 151
  Geo. W. 10
  George 9, 10, 21, 30,
    36, 86, 105, 125,
    138, 149, 151, 179,
    189, 214, 228, 229,
    265, 269, 331, 343
  George W. 303
  Hannah 105
  Henry 20
  Jacob 9, 21
  Jain 228
  James 60, 184, 236
  Jerry 8, 79
  Jerry R. 10
  John 18
  King D. 9
  Kisiah 151
  Kissey 10
  Leathy 354
  Lewis 11, 106
  Lidda 106
  Lottie 86
  Lucey 89
  Lues 9
  Martin 11, 60, 133,
    312
  Mary 131
  Mary Ann 10, 11
  Mary D. 150
  Mary Jane 151
  Nancey 353
  Nancy 20
  Nelson 10
  Parthenia 336
  Permilia J. 191
  Peter 20
  Polly 200
  Rebecca 61, 125
  Rhoda 255
  Rhody 20
  Ritter 11
  Robert 280, 333
  Royal 172, 244
  Ruthy 336
  Sallie 8
  Sarah 59
  Susan 36
  Susan Ann 10
  Susan J. 162
  Thomas 9, 20, 21, 331
    336
  William 9, 86, 316
Anderson(?), William A.
    11
Anderson, Winney 20

Anderson (cont.)
  Winny 228, 331
Andrews, Bartlett 256
  Mary 142
  Polly C. 269
  Sarah 122, 231
Angel, William J. 135
Ansley, Nancy 262
Anthony, N. A. S. 166
Apling, Thomas 290
Apperson, Malinda L. 165
Apple, Juda 11
Appling, Thomas 27
Arnold, Betsy 38
  Eliza 276
  Hannah 131
  Harriett 169, 276
  Ira C. 144
  Ira E. 11, 128, 143,
    144, 146, 156, 169,
    363
  James 189
  Jane 85
  Joseph 67
  Malinda 169
  Martha 224
  Martha Ann 111
  Mary Ann 231, 286
  Milky 220
  Nancy 217
  Nancy Hawkins 104
  Polly 189
  Rebeca 272
  Richard 346
  Sally 39
  Sarah 342
  William 339
Arrington, Ann 193
  Emily 97
  Lucy 52
  Martha 279
  Martha A. 97
  Mary Eliza 110
  W. M. 243
  Willis 97
  Wm. 105
Ascew, Abigal 16
Ascue, Caty 302
Ash, Saml. (Gov.) 130
Ashley, C. 12
  Elizabeth 251
  J. M. 48
  Sarah 195, 333
  Wilie 325, 337
Ashman, Leavis 92
Ashworth, William 12
Asque, Mary Ann W. 301
Atkerson, Elizabeth 19
Atkins, Allen 229
  Elizabeth 11
  James 282
  Lucy A. E. 169
  Nancey 198
  Thomas 253
Atkinson, Edward 304
  Roger P. 187
  Sallie J. 196
Attwood, Elisabeth 125
  Martha 125
  Martha G. 125
Atwood, Mary 144
Aubrey, Dulcena 110
Austen(?), William 349
Averett, Louvecy 234
  Sallie 173
Averot, G. W. R. 239
Avery, Elijah 347
  Eliza 305

Avery (cont.)
  Martha 155
  Rufus 224
Avorett, Delia Ann 208
Avrett, Henry M. 13
B-(?), Heinrich 201
Babb(?), James 113
Babler, Salley 243
Babtist, William 13
Bacon, Millissia A. 73
  Mont. S. 194
Badger, George 151
Badget, Andrew 13
  Benton 13
  Peter 255
Badgett, Drucilla 19, 161
  James 14
  James W. 248
  Jesse 161
  Jonathan 255
  Rebecca 78
  Samuel 78
  Samuel P. 14
  Sarah 14
  Thomas 14
  Thomas E. 14
Bagby, Mary L. 307
Bagly, Milly 21
Bailey, Alsey 15
  Anderson 93
  Betsy 367
  Candis 84, 90
  Clara 178
  Clarey 203
  Clay 90
  Darda 204
  Davis D. 84
  Delila 167
  Elizabeth 14, 203, 209, 216
  Emeline 209
  F. J. 121
  Fanny 367
  Frances 14
  Gilcrease 90, 238, 367
  Glafney 15
  Israel 15, 90
  Israel, Jr. 85
  Jackobina 84
  Jackobina L. 84
  James 12
  Jeremiah 234
Bailey(?), John 15
Bailey, John 15, 148
  Lucretia 66, 278
  Mahala 90
  Martha 14, 15
  Mary 171
  Middy 15
  Miranda G. 211
  Nancey 15, 23
  Peleg 15, 116, 119
  Phanney 127
  Precilla 231
  Prescilla 14
  Ransom 14, 140
  Robert 278
  Samuel 14, 119, 217, 361
  Stephen 111
  Tison Ann 93
  Tony 218
  W. D. 262
  William 231
  William Y. 93
Baily, Elizabeth 287
  Nancy 337

Baily (cont.)
  Ransom 230
Baits, Susannah 172
Baker, Blake 345
  Martha 360
  Phoebe Ann 118
  Vandelia V. 103
Baldwin, M. 196
  Rebecca Ann 314
Balely, Penelope 150
Ball, Anson 185, 286
  Betsy A. 163
  Chesley 16
  Dansel 89
  Dennis H. 16
  Elijah 55, 300
  Elizabeth 238
  Erasmus 17
  Frances 107
  Guilford 210
  Isham 107
  James 1, 99
  James H. 263
  Jas. 16
  Jordan 46
  Martha 16
  Nancy 63
  Ninum 272
  Pheriba 222
  Rhoda 68
  Sally 90, 279
  Tempy 352
  William 210
  Winney 140
  Wm. 210
Ballard, Elisabeth 123
  Rebeccah 251
Balton, Lethy 173
Baly, John 192
Baned(?), T. B. 5
Banks, Justina 292
  Ralph 292
  Salley 213
  Salley Chandler 27
  Susannah 50
  Thomas 27, 247
  Thos. 27
Banner, John M. 296
Baptist, Ellen 53
Bare, Anney 221
  James 221
Barker, A. 275
  Ambrose 124, 205, 296
  C. 360
  Cornelia A. 359
  D. S. 302, 303
  D. T. 194, 295
  David T. 359
  Eugenia F. 65
  J. G. 295
  John G. 244, 295, 310
  Julia 150
  Leathy 123
  Martha 359
  Sarah P. 78
  Temperance W. 102
Barket, D. T. 250
Barkley, John 242
Barley, Milley 235
  Nancy 51
Barner, William 343
Barnes, Ann L. 349
Barnes(?), B. B. 348
Barnes(?), Burwell 342
Barnes, Elizabeth 101
  Frances 202
  Geo. W. 354
  Henry 349

Barnes (cont.)
  Hilman 62
  John 100
  Mildred 18
  Pamelia 203
  Sally 288
  Susan 68
  William 18
  Winney 17
  Wm. 47
Barnet, Elisabeth 321
  Nancy 18
Barnett, Charles 21, 272
  Elijah 183
  Elisabeth 211
  Elizabeth 106, 253
  Franklin 208
  J. A. 22
  J. B. 264
  James 18
  James P. 240
  Jesse 18, 19, 271
  John 18, 297
  Joseph 18, 211
  Joseph W. 8
  Julia 205
  Lucy B. 313
  Luetta 202
  Lucy C. 75
  Martha F. 100
  Mary 125, 240
  Mary A. 56
  Mary J. 143, 240
  Milfred 182
  Patsey 115
  R. G. 75
  R. S. 322
  Rebecca 332
  Rebeccah 7
  Sallie 326
  Sarah 18
  T. B. 19, 251
  Tabitha 75
  Thomas 268
  Thos. 18
  Thos. B. 19
  W. 245
  Wm. 19, 244
  Wm. 244
Barns, Amey 12
  Anneney 100
Barns(?), John 289
Barns(?), Nelson 37
Barns, Susannah 357
Barr, Elizabeth 264, 270
  Jas. 197
  Mary 108
  Mildred 108
  Thos. 222
Barrett, Eliza G. 97
Barritt, Wm. F. 185
Bartlet, William 362
Barton, Benjamin 198
  Eliza 9
  Nancy 116
  William 116
Basey, Sarah 341
Baskerville, Alice 176
  Charles 19
  Faithy 19
Basket, Agnes A. 349
  Joseph 200
Baskett, Hixie B. 146
Basnick, Clarasa 20
Bass, Absalem 280
  Absalom 20
  Barnett 11
  Ben., Jr. 59

Bass (cont.)
  Benjamin 20
  Betsey 218, 331
  Betty 331
  Chesly 317
  Darling 60, 230
  Disey 265
  Eliza 228
  Elizabeth Ann 150
  Elizah 203
  Ellen 120
  Hardey 21
  Henrietta 316
  Honor 190
  Jesse 21, 60, 316
  John 9
  Lucy 230, 325
  Mariah 79, 228
  Martha 20, 21
  Mary 280
  Moses 106
  Mourning 10
  Nancy 9, 86
  Parthenia 320
  Patsy 20
  Patty 317
  Pheby 331
  Polley 8, 9, 104, 333
  Pricey 10
  Prissey 86
  Reubin 20
  Right 265
  Rubin 19
  Salley 106, 363
  Sarah 21, 280
  Susan 150
  Tamer 286
  Thomas 228
  Tycey 265
  William 20
  Willis 20, 262
  Wm. 226
Baswell, Betsey 21
  Jordan 21
Bates, Elizabeth 275
  Frankey 158
Battle, J. A. 299
Baxter, Elizabeth 42
  Polly 337
  Rebeca 332
  Reuben 266
  Rutha 338
Bayley, Tildathe 84
  William 84
Baynes, Mary 187
Beachum, E. F. 109
Beal, Edwin 21
  Joseph 266
  Mary 108
Bearden, Benjamin 102
  Elisabeth 147
  John 147
  Letty 198
  Lucy 327
  Patsey 253
  Polly 252
  Sally 214
Beardin, Sarah 118
  William 22
Beardon, Patsey 116
Bearley, Anne 302
Beasley, Amy F. 130
  Ann P. 275
  Fleming 22
  Flemming 77
  Isabella 145
  James T. 15, 102
  Judith M. 351

Beasley (cont.)
  L., Jr. 2, 175
  L. H. 62
  Lucy 273
  Malissa 291
  Maria 290
  Mildred T. 201
  Nannie E. 212
  P. T. 368
  Pollie 291
  R. T. 276
  Stephen 22
  Stephen H. 81
  T. S. 335
  Virginia M. 322
  W. R. 51, 74, 176, 352
  Wm. R. 345
Beasly, Anna Y. 149
  Elizabeth 201
  Henry W. 241
  James M. 95
  S. H. 174
  Sally P. 15
Beaver, Margaret 47
Beavish(?), Elizabeth 300
Beck, Catharine 264
  David 104, 179, 354
  Elizabeth 3
  Francis 103
  Frederick 23, 55, 302
  J. M. 156
  James 55, 320
Beck(?), John 337
Beck, John 55, 67, 103, 121, 191, 193
  Mariah 264
  Mary 299
  Michael 264
  Robert H. 3
  Sarah 40
  Thos. 281
  William 50, 256
Beckham, Wm. C. 324
Beckwith, Jesse 12
Bedford, Elisabeth 69
  Frances 70
  J. 161
  James 163, 194, 290
Bedwile, Sarah 198
Beech, Elizabeth 23
Beeks, Martha 18
Beird, Randel 289
Belborn, Thomas 233
Belcher, James 242
  Luranian 242
  Nancy S. 242
  Polley 299
Beley, Stephen 216
Bell, Elisabeth 143
  Hester C. 109
  Isaac 26, 129
  John 66
  Joshua 125
  Nancy 282
  Robt. 128
  Sarah 39
  Susanna 27
  Benjamin, Burwell 319
  Evans 331
Bennet, Susannah 195
  Wm. M. 357
Bennett, Alice 51
  Christian U. 198
  Lewis 126
  Mary F. 268
  Mary J. 126

Bennett (cont.)
  Wm. M. 279
Benney, S. H. 294
Benont, Delila 186
Benton, Bettey 41
  F. N. W. 167
  Sml. 201
Berkley, Amanda M. 205
  Nancy S. 242
Berkly, B. 192
  Mary 192
  Roxa M. 122
Berry, Henry 262
  Mary Jane 10
Best, Henry 55, 198
  T. T. 277
  Thos. T. 367
Betterson, Archd. 51
Bettes, Wm. 194
Betts, Winny 58
Bevell, Sarah 61
Beverly, Thos. 111
Beves, Sarah 336
Beville, Bennet W. 183
Bichett, Aggy 240
Bigger, Mary A. 241
Biggs, Elizabeth 215
  Fanney 146
  Mary Ann 308
  Polly 271
Birch, Isaac 238
Bird, Maron(?) 60
  Penny 308
Bishop, James 358
  Jinsey 357
  Philip 278
Black, Charles 179
Blacklay(?), Woodson D. 363
Blackley, Ann 69
  Augustus 294
  B. J. 38
  Charles 130, 179
  Chas. 42
  Elisabeth 304
  Elizabeth 135
  Hallyard 69
  Halyard 68, 157
  Howel 141, 144
  James 67, 304
  Jane 153
  Jas. 264, 291
  Leathy 26
  Lucy 88
  Lucy C. 144
  Malissa 294
  Maria 153
  Martha 145
  Mary 42
  Mary E. 254
  Mary H. 141
  Miranda S. 162
  Nancy Grey 314
  Thompson 135
  Thomson 26
  Wallace 251
  William 179, 288
  Woodson D. 314
Blackly, B. J. 332
  C. R. 144
  Harriott 144
  Jas. 4, 66, 364
Blacknall, Anna 196
  Benj. 261
  Elizabeth 69, 77, 191
  Emily 15
  Fanny 246
  Frances 213

Blacknall (cont.)
　George 26
　John 25, 261
　John, Jr. 325
　Lucy 161
　Mahala 273
　Martha 216
　Mary 69
　Mary N. 336
　Nancy 184
　R. P. 173
　Sarah Brooks 366
　T. H. 133
　Thomas 246
　Wm. 191
Blacknell, Sarah 77
Blackwel, Frances 155
Blackwell, Ann 58, 154
　Ann F. 241
　Anne 217
　Caroline 81
　Elizabeth 115, 144, 297, 361
　Fanny A. 364
　Frances A. 78
　Frances H. 274
　Isabella 49
　James 164, 234
　James A. 81
　Joanna 92
　John 355
　Judith 366
　Mahala 273
　Mary 100, 240, 309
　Mary Ann 116
　Meriah 30
　Naknie 364
　Nancy 67
　Nutty 74
　Phoebe 77
　Polley 132
　Pomphret 29
　Rebecca 78, 281
　Robert 117, 370
　Robert L. 303
　Rose 66
　Sally 77
　Sary 65
　Stephen 77
　Temprance 69
　Thos. G. 51
　Wm. 220, 239, 242, 364
　Wm. M. 49
Bladen, William 346
Blair, Mary 20
Blalock, Barbary 211
　David 155
　Eliza 260
　Jincy 178
　Jn. P. 166
　John 211
　Kizzy 272
　Luetta 31, 187
　Mary T. 86
　Matthew 259
　Nancey 56
　Nancy 166
　Rebecca 166
　Rowan 224
　Sally 341
　William 178
Blankenship, L. A. 70, 138, 309
Blanks, Elizabeth 157
　Elvira H. 122
　J. R. 165
　James B. 28, 276

Blanks (cont.)
　James H. 28
　James R. 250
　Nancy 360
　Samuel 342
　Sarah 342
Bledso, James A. 348
Bledsoe, Amanda 54
　Catharine 114
　Jechonias 54, 267
　Jinsey 6
　Macon 123
　Mahaley 267
　Martha 285
　Susanna 237
　Terrell B. 6
　Wm. L. 268
Blount, Sarah L. 81
Blunt, Mary B. 281
Bobbet, Amey 356
　Averellah 164
　Charity 186
　Lewis 356
　William 186
　Wm. 28
Bobbett, Lewis 356
Bobbitt, Ann H. 99
　Any Ann 274
　Asinda 274
　Barbara 83
　Britain 110
　C. J. 330
　Catharine E. 162
　D. E. 29, 34
　David 44
　Elisabeth 246
　Elizabeth 229
　Harriet 68
　Isham C. 278
　J. H. 204
　Jane 348
　Jno. J. 190
　John H. 211
　John J. 42, 190, 269
　Malissa 314
　Margaret B. 42
　Martha E. 42
　Patsey 29
　Rowan E. 47, 48
　Rufus 29, 181, 274
　T. E. 327
　Thos. R. 252
　Wm. O. 29
Bobitt, Betsy 218
Boen, Jane 303
Boers, William G. 312
Boling, Peggy 229
Bolling, Elvey 251
　James 29
　Polly 224
　Willis 218
Bonner, Betsey 136
　Charity 53
　Jesse 293
　Lenney 234
　Lethi 226
　Moses 53
　Moses H. 40, 137
　Nevison 136
　Thomas 316
　William 330
　Winnah F. 284
　Wm. 272
Booker, Emma C. 202
　Joseph 196
　Mary 92
　Pencey 269
　Richard W. 323

Bookerford, B. 233
Bookram, Dilley 316
　Emiline 155
　Gavin 343
　John 152
　Mary 60
　Nancy 343
Boom, Elizabeth 291
　Martha 291
Boon, Betsy 226
　Emeline J. 151
　Martha 223
　Rebecca 229
　Ruthy Ann 10
Boone, Martha 328
Booswell, Elizabeth 28, 197
Booth, Ann Eliza 189
　Eliza 115
　Harriet 249
　Thomas 30
Boothe, Abner 275
　George 97
　Joel 78
　Lemuel 279
　Mary Ann 169
　William 133
Borough, Mary 176
Boswell, J. A. T. 351
　John H. 144
　Mary 42, 155, 189
　Raney 81
　Rebecca E. 298
　Susannah 313
Bouldin, Henry 358
　Mary 358
Bouls, Oney 53
Boummitt, John 88
Bowden, Jackey 171
　Parthenia 31
　Polley 335
　Wm. 31
Bowdon, Elias 113
　Elisabeth 216
　Francis 113
　William 31, 334
Bowen, Alfred T. 353
　Angelina 200
　Elizabeth 124, 211, 250
　Elizabeth C. 195
　Elizabeth J. 165
　John 41
　John W. 233
　Martha Ann 41
　Minerva 31
　Rebecca 278
　William 278
　William G. 5
　William T. 32
　Wm. 124
Bowers, Camella F. 77
　Emiline 285
　Martha 28
　Midda 43
　Priscilla 25
　Salley 298
　William 28, 154
　William G. 198, 314
　Wm. G. 32
Bowie, John 119
Bowlen, Joseph 218
Bowles, Ann 12
　Benjamin 274
　Harriett 182
　Jane 105
　John, Jr. 32
　Jordan 247

375

Bowling, Presley 32
  Willis 251
Bowls, Elizabeth 148
  Samuel 123
Boyd, Amey 360
  Anderson 81
  Bruce 33, 116, 149, 284
  Charles P. 338
  D. R. 300
  George 81
  Indianna 260
  J. A. 33
  Jane 226
  Lucy A. 319
  Margaret A. 116
  Mary A. 136
  Panthea B. 4
  Robert 33
  Robt. 33
  Sarah 116
  Virginia 249
Bracey, Mary 366
Brach, Nancy 33
  Sarah 138
  William 33
Brack, Martha 364
  Mary 83
Brackley, Paul 342
  Winnie 342
Bracy, Jane 122
Bradford, Anna 293
  Anne 368
  Ava 56
  Barbara 149
  Benjamin 3, 121
  Booker 34
  Celah 347
  Cresey 368
  Elijah 141, 219
  Elizabeth 267
  Fanney 233
  Fanny 222
  Hicksey 159
  James 34
  Jemima 38
  Jolin 267
  Joseph 119
  Judith 6
  Lucy 27
  Mary E. 215
  Melvina 208
  Nancy 163, 217
  Polley 38
  Polly 110
  Rutha 314
  Ruthy 5
  Sarah 120, 152, 304, 325
  Thos. 267
  William 174, 271
Bradiway, Grassie 56
Bradley, Isaac 52, 170
  James 256
  Samuel 114
Bragg, Ann M. 311
  Beady 164
  Benjamin 35
  C. A. 133
  Elizabeth Jane 268
  Fanny 14
  Indianah H. 120
  John H. 34
  John W. 343
  Luanzy 296
  Malsy 296
  Martha 157
  Martha A. 3, 361

Bragg (cont.)
  Mary 11
  Mary A. 179
  Mary E. 182
  N. N. 231
  Nancy E. 56
  Peggy 291
  Robert 76
  Sicily 55
  Thomas W. 262
  W. W. 34
  William 311
Brame, Elizabeth A. (Mrs.) 18
  Ellen H. 156
  Emily J. 195
  Geo. W. 285
  George W. 25, 285
  James 36, 344
  James W. 35
  John 72
  John J. 146
  Julia Ann 135
  Lucy C. 351
  Martha Ann 309
  Mary 143, 331
  Mary T. 35
  Naknie O. 353
  Nelson 62, 96
  Rebecca 282
  Robert 283
  Sarah 330
  Sarah S. 307
  Susan 194
  Thomas 36
Brandam, Jane 36
Brandom, Jane 71
  Susan 266
Brandon, Betsey 36
  Betsy 172
  Burwell 118
  Hilliard 36
  Mary 207
  Panthea 172
Brandum, Bivens 96
  Ellen 281
  James 223
  Jas. 96
  Martha 265
  Mary Ann 255
  Nettie 147
Branson, Leonard 83
Brantly, Mary 365
Brasel, Wright 36
Brasfield, Caleb 229
  Elizabeth 5
  Frances 24
  Geo. 287
  George 98
  Mary 65
  Nancy 65
  Pattsey 358
  Rebekah 51
  Sally 199
Brasford, George 33
Brasius, W. R. 362
  Wm. 213
  Wm. K. 320
Brasley, Rebeca 22
Brassfield, Ann 183
  Drucilla 287
Bratcher, Caroline 110
Bray, Martha J. 62
Breadlove, William 100
Breedlove, Emily H. 229
  Hanson 297
  Manson 70, 73, 359
  Manson H. 37

Breedlove (cont.)
  Martha P. 37
  Mary J. 245
  Nathan 343
  Wm. 164
Brem, Jos. C. 25
Bressie(?), Frances 186
  Irby 248
  Lucy 248
Brewer, James 344
  John 22
  Mary 22
Briant, Nancy 349
Bridges, Alcinda 212
  Allen 5, 104, 120
  Amanda 168
  Candis 357
  Drury 56
  Frances 56
  Frances P. 356
  Harriot 135
  James 38
  Joseph 6
  Lucinda 342
  Mary 150
  Polly 38
  Stephen 38, 149, 150, 156, 236, 342
  Suckey 48
  Susan 333
Briges, C-(?) 342
Briggs, Elisabeth 81
  Elizabeth 189
  Elizabeth G. 253
  Henry 68, 95
  Howel 350
  Howell 96, 149, 353
  Lethe 95
  Lucy 68
  Massy 174
  Parthena 246
  Richard 292
Brightwell, F. A. 165
  Olivia(?) A. 41
  Runnold 93
  Salley 93
Briky, James 160
Brinkley, Agness 182
  Alfred 284
  Annice 215, 323
  Biddy 201
  Elisabeth 227
  Elizabeth 252
  G. W. 219
  Henry A. 39
  Henry H. 348
  Hiriam 215, 323
  James 39, 149, 187, 292
  John H. 38
  Lucy 265
  Malinda 46
  Martha 348
  Martha Ann 370
  Mary 144, 236
  Minerva A. 215
  Nancy 278
  Nancy L. 323
  Pheriba 124
  Rachel 277
  Raney 133
  Rebecca 160, 185
  Sarah 282
  William 278
Brinkly, Barbara 285
  Bumpass 285
  Richard 2
  Robert 172

Brisse, Martha Dianne 187
Mary 251
Bristow, Jas. 287
John 95
Brock, Burwell 39
Brodie, Ann T. 198
Brodie(?), Charlotte 303
John 3, 68, 121, 216, 351
L. J. 132
Melviney 19
Sally M. 246
Thomas 190
Brodiway(?), Grassie 56
Brogden, James 40
Martha 214
Martha B. 264
Mary E. 340
Polly 40
Susan Ann 179
Brogdon, Agness 300
David 4, 40, 108
Elizabeth 108
George 180
Isaac 40
James 53
Linna 264
Nancy 264
Palley 54
Parker 136
Robert H. 58
Brome, Elizabeth 122
Mary 101
Brooks, William C. 52
Broom, Melus 73
Brosius, W. K. 66, 99, 207
Wm. K. 95, 349
Browder, Nancy 101
Brown, Archibald E. 357
Brown(?), Betsy 226
Jane 254
Martha 354
Nancy 86
Rachael 141
Richard H. 178
William 186, 363
Browning, George 317
Bruce, Charles 233
Nancey 122
Brume, Arabelah 93
Brummet, Ellender 117
James 26
John 88, 186
John, Jr. 268
Leroy 117
Mary Jane 258
Brummett, James R. 135
John 90, 139
John, Jr. 110
Lucy W. 134
Margaret E. C. 34
Martha 42
Patsey 129
Pryey 186
Salley 90
Thos. F. 254
Wesley 42
Brummit, John 88
Nancy 11
Polley 186
Samuel 186, 304
Wesley 88
Brummitt, Elizabeth 261
Jas. R. 274

Brummitt (cont.)
Meriah Caroline 258
T. J. 135
Brundige, David 339
Bruno, Samuel 96
Bryan, Jos. H. 309
Joseph H. 12
Mary E. 179
Thos. P. 349
Bryant, Betsey 337
Isaac 43
James H. 43, 63
James J. 42, 277
Lucy 8
Margaret 257
Mary Ann 196
Mildred 256
Nancy 120
Patsey 243
Polley 66
Polly 151
Rachiel 43
Rosey 198
Rowland 115, 153, 177
Rowland, Jr. 143
Sherwood 230
Stephen 353
Tabbie 197
Tabitha 239
William 197
Buchanan, Agness 178
David 43
Frances 209
Georg. W. 43
Isabella 304
Jerusha 319
John 43
Prudence 347
Rosa B. 67
Sarah 147
Virginia A. 51
Buchannan, Hicsy 232
Buckanan, Martha 230
Buckhana, David R. 100
Buckhanon, Elizabeth 152
Mariah 210
Bucknall, Jno. 324
Buckner, John 56
Sherrin 315
Bugg, Margaret 243
N. C. 145
Watkins M. 43
Bull, Jesse 297
Thos. S. 300
Bull-(?), Ann 239
Bullen, Rufus A. 370
Buller, John 320
Bullock, A. B. 240
Agnes 127
Agness 235
Angeline 75
Ann 287
Ann Eliza 341
Anny 46
B. F. 80, 277
Benj. F. 143
Benjamin 12, 229, 234
Benjamin F. 111
Betsey 156
Buck 75, 182
Carlina 154
Catherine 146, 309
Charles 56, 111
D. C. 330
D. L. 6, 218
Deliley 321
Edward 45
Elisabeth 178

Bullock (cont.)
Eliza 247
Eliza P. 219
Elizabeth 13, 170, 216, 274, 321
Ellender 24
Frances 19, 33, 111, 339
Frances A. 288
Frances C. 238
Francis C. 203
Fuster 339
G. F. 168, 169, 279
George 68, 126, 201, 282, 311, 370
H. 238
H. A. 114
Harisson 206
Harrison 138
Henrietta 328
Henry 328
J. M. 175
James, Jr. 28
James T. 114
Jeremiah 126, 174, 187, 232, 234, 331
Jesse 146
Jno. 46, 131, 192, 206
John 355
John D. 154
John F. 209
Joshua 127, 316
Judy 146
Len. Henley 308
Lend. H. 319
Leonard H. 182
Leonard Henley 45
Louisa 28
Lucy 53, 206
Lucy O. 132
M. 247
Malinda 126
Maria J. 307
Mark 229
Mary 96, 146, 168, 342
Mary L. 237
Matilda 328
Micajah 177, 272
Mima 339
Mordcai 13
Nancy 182, 227, 311
Nancy Jane 169
P. P. 233
Parmelia 361
Pattie 229
Permelia T. 294
Philip 29, 30, 240, 318
Phill. 235
R. 83
R. H. D. 46
Rhoda 96, 291
Richard 35
Rowan 67
Sally 160
Saml. 16
Samuel 44, 46
Sarah 13, 46, 159, 204, 311
Sarah A. 307
Sophia 154
Susan 108, 204, 231
Susan A. 126
Susannah 86, 319
Thomas 184
Tuesa 339
W. 212

Bullock (cont.)
  W. A. 165
  W. E. 155, 212
  Will. H. 44
  William 45, 156, 216
  Wm. E. 230
  Wm. M. 45
Bumpass, Alfred 315
  Robert D., Jr. 46
  Robt. L., Jr. 94
Bunnell, Mary A. S. 220
Bunton, Irby G. 89
Burch, O. L. 322
Burchet, Davy 47
  James 260
Burchett, (?) 324
  Agness 25
  Green 47
  Mildred 3
  Prissy 47
Burford, Mitchel 217
  Wm., Jr. 65, 109
Burge, Mary J. 170
  Rebecca A. H. 75
  William 51
Burkley, Elizabeth 174
Burnet(?), Lewis D. 33
Burnett, Elisabeth 173
  Emma R. 208
  Frances 186
  Jana E. 231
  Jno. S. 325
  Martha 332
  Martha A. 208
  Martha H. 245
  Mildred 332
  Patsey 157
  Polly 232
Burns, B. 123
  Mary H. 45
  Tom 120
Burroughs, B. 283
  Bozzal 241
  Geo. W. 244
  Stephen 19
  Washington 244
Burrows, Robena 159
Burtch, Robert 12
Burton, Allen 355
  C. 247
  Edmer 145
  Edmund 48
Burton(?), Edward 253
Burton, Edwd. 118, 171
  Elisabeth 264
  Fanny Henderson 90
  Hutchings G. 228
  Hutchins 92
  Hutchins G. 281, 282
  James M. 208
  James M., Jr. 330
  Jesse J. 108
  Martha 228
  Martha A. 36
  Mary 48, 289, 355
  Parthena 289
  Ro. 216, 301
  Ro., Jr. 301
  Robert 42, 178
  Sarah 22, 48
Burwell, A. R. 33
  Agnes 139
  Alice 157
  Betsey Ann 139
  Christian B. 98
  Delia 287
  Elizabeth 318
  Fanny 148

Burwell (cont.)
  H. H. 139
  Hannah 287
  Josiah 287
  L. D. 187
  Leathy 100
  Martha 121, 177
  Mary 49, 175
  Matilda B. 49
  Mollie L. 255
  Richard 60
  Sally T. 98
  T. G. 13
Busbee, Anne 49
  Perrin 49
Busbey, Elizabeth 202
  James 202
Busby, Sally 236
Bush, Celia 226
Butler, Ann Eliza 276
  Anne 45
  Anne Smith 296
  Betsey 131
  Betty 92
  E. G. 70
  Elisabeth 143
  Elizabeth 91, 326
  Elizabeth Ann 273
  James H. 331
  John P. 281
  Lucinda 175
  Martha 11
  Mary P. 273
  Nancy 92, 317
  Polley 85
  Reuben 246
  Saml. P. 196
  Samuel 152
  Solomon 92
  William 42, 49, 136, 292
  Wm. 22, 69, 137, 335
Buxton, Jenney Minge 229
By-(?), John W. 104
Byard, George 168
Byars, Ann 115
  Barbara 23
  Gulielnus 246
  Henry 167
  James 321
  Jane 63, 134
  Martha 50
  Nicholas 55
  Salley 83
Byers, Elizabeth 50
Byne, Lucy 320
Bynum, J. W. 170
  Martha 2
Byram, Adeline F. 323
  Archibald 214
Byrd, Alex 7
  Ann E. 7
  Helen 7
  James 59
  Jim 50
  John 121, 264
  Marullus 50
  Victoria C. 64
Byrum, Archibald 50
  Cynthia 50
  Henry K. 134
  Jacob 50
  John 50, 143
  Kinchen 50
  Maurice 38
  Morris 236
  W. (Doctor) 288
Cabiniss, Courtland 10

Cadden, H. 338
  Hugh A. M. 2
Callaham, Edward D. 90
Calleham, Emily A. 82
Callifer, Emily 315
Calvert, Mary 54
Campbell(?), David D. 195
  Mary M. 305
  Sarah 63
  Serah 50
Can-(?), S. B. 53
Canaday, Dorris 283
  Elisabeth F. 333
  Wm. 51
Canady, Thades 218
  Wyatt 172
Caniel, Elizabeth D. 117
Cannaday, Misanday D. 5
  Nancy E. 163
  W. M. 333
Cannady, Amanda M. 37
  Ann E. 34
  Dorris 12, 54
  Gracy 146
  Harriet 218
  John F. 95
  Lucie B. 313
  Mary C. 340
  Mary Elizabeth 361
  S. H. 340
  S. M. 15
  Sally 355
  Susan E. 215
  W. E. 313
  Wyatt 1
Cannon, Linda 51
  Ned 51
  Sarah 219
Cape, John Williamson 155
Capehart, B. A. 344
Card, Leonard 207
  Susan 40
  William 361
Carden, Celia 120
  Dicey 12
  James 12
Cardin, James 120
  Robert 52
Cardwell, D. J. 239
  Dorey N. 184
  Leonard 7, 12, 16, 47, 110, 194, 195, 260, 265, 288, 290, 323, 349
  Leonard H. 205
  Lethe 315
  Martha 240
  Nancy 311
  Polley 34
  Susan 47
  William N. 144
Carey, Debba 218
  Leavin 335
  Martha 270
  Rena 337
Cargill, Mary J. 173
  Victoria E. 93
Cargo, Wm. K. 279
Carnal, Catharen 342
  Elijah 94, 326, 342
  Jesse 247
  Jesse C. 247
  Louisa E. A. 94
  Mary 247
Carnal(?), Moses 52, 105
Carnal, Nancy Ann 46

Carnel, Elizabeth 87
  William 52, 87
Carnell, Sally F. 95
Carnes, Sarah 215
Carol(?), Sally 120
Carpendar, Milley 354
Carr, William 164, 205
Carrel, Elizabeth 233
  John 52, 93, 177
  Patsey 34
Carrington, John J. 53
  N. M. 38
  T. R. 220
Carson, Lucy 129
Carter, Edwd. H. 291
  Elisabeth 41
  Jesse 53
  Margaret N. 13
  Mary 30, 118
  Molly 118
  Nancy A. 207
  Samuel 229
  Thos. J. 348
  William J. 239
  Wm. H. 102
Cartis, Martha 30
Carver, Henry 291
Cash, Angeline 67
  Arena 289
  Barshaba 67
  Benjamin 140
  Brian 103
  Briant, 76
  Bryan 338
  Comfort 56
  Crissey 40
  Dorcas 325
  Edney 37
  Elisabeth 289
  Eliza 289
  Elizabeth 266
  Emily J. 32
  Frances 129
  Frances C. 67
  Isasah 274
  James 54, 317
  John 54
  Joseph 53
  Josias 134
  Linney 242
  Lucretia 40
  Mary 40, 324
  Milley 324
  Oaly 102
  Pene 310
  Peter 53, 54, 55,
    242, 324
  Polly 53
  Prudence 55
  Ransom 162
  Riney 299
  Sally 317
  Susannah 134
  Valentine 55
  William 40
Caskey, Mary 183
Cassady, William M. 72
Castor, John 312
Caswell, Richd. 155
Cates, Mary 232
Catlett, Amanda C. 332
  Caroline 334
  Emiline 215
  George 16, 215, 334,
    356
  Henrietta A. 334
  Laborn 16, 34
  Martha 106, 143

Catlett (cont.)
  Rachel 143
  Sally 34
  Samuel 55
  Sarah Ann 76
  Wm. 55
Caudle, Dolly 56
  Jas. 56
  Susannah 43
Caughon, Happy 353
Cauthen, J. H. 34
  James H. 148
  Seley 261
Cauthon, Archer 255
  Archibald 327
  C. R. 277
  John C. 145
Cavenah, Bryan 119
Cavendar, Bryant 38
Cavender, Bryant 37
  Needham 141
  Polley 37
Cavendish, Lucy 80
Caveness, John 76
Cavennah, Elizabeth 119
Cavenus, Martha 221
Caviner, John H. 276
Caviness, Phebe 24
Cavndar, Nancy 235
Cawhon, James H. 146
Cawthom, C. R. 331
Cawthon, John C. 208
Cawthor, Lottey 88
Cawthorn, A. L. 56
  Ann 197
  Archibald 114
  Elizabeth 56
  Louisa 327
  Phebe 42
Chadwick, Elizabeth 364
  Polley 2
Chaffin, W. S. 223
Chain, Nancy 181
Chambers, Betsy 175
  Lucy R. 138
  Viney 175
Chambles, Oty 339
Chambless, Betsey 45
  Elizabeth 353
  Henry 258
  Robert 57
  Roberta 327
  Susannah 126
Chambliss, Henry 45
  Lucy 203
  Polly 204
  Robert 353
  Salley 316
Champain, Merrit 93
Champen, John 57
Champion, A. 240
  A. M. 57, 108
  Amanda E. 108
  Anne 178
  Aramanta B. 192
  Bennett 144
  Charlotty 353
  Elisabeth 272
  Elizabeth 155
  Frances 27
  Jerry 143
  John 7, 142, 347
  Joseph 245
  Lucy 56
  Martha J. 337
  Mary 142
  Merit 110
  Merrett 275

Champion (cont.)
  Mildred 348
  Miranda 148
  Nancy 275
  Rebecca 4
  Richard 4, 57
  Susan 4
  Winnie 215
  Wm. 4
Chandler, Almira 117
  Andrew J. 133
  Ann E. 117
  Anne 233
  Augusta C. 215
  Edwin 334
  Eliza. 334
  Elizabeth 251
  Elizabeth N. A. 306
  Emily Catharine 78
  J. H. 51
  Jackson 246
  Jane 309
  L. V. 108
  Lucy A. J. 196
  Martha 191
  Mary 100, 246
  Mary Ann 237, 249
  Mathew, Jr. 103
  Matthew 82, 317, 345
  McVay 83, 362
  Nancy 233
  Octavia R. 309
  Phebe 123
  Prudence 276
  Ras 290
  Rosa E. 352
  Rowan 116
  Salome H. 158
  Sarah 249
  Sarah Ann 139
  Stephen 82
  Tabitha 248
  Valleria 128
  Wm. C. 57, 139
Chane, Polly T. 192
Chapel, Elizabeth 299
  Samuel, Sr. 299
Chapell, Hanah 278
Chapman, George 140
  Mary 311
  Thomas 364
  W. A. 258
Chappel, Edward 50, 83
  Major H. 286
  Matilda C. 286
  Richard 286
Chappell, A. J. 103
  A. R. 45
  Anna 58
  Bennett 145
  Betsy Ann 55
  Darlin A. 353
  Darling A. 104
  Edward 349
  Hawkins 330
  Henriettae 55
  Jack 55
  Jane A. 40
  Malissa 342
  Richard 58
  Saml., Jr. 200
  Samuel 202
Charinge, Nancey 279
Chavas, Lucy 59
Chavers, Jas. 59
  John 8
  Nancy 20
  Olive 21

Chavers (cont.)
  William 223
Chaves, Peter 9, 59
Chavis, Anderson 325
  Angeline 59
  Ann Rebecca 48
  Beady 354
  Charles 59
  Delila 312
  Emily 42
  Evans 36
  Frances 21
  Franklin 339
  Hannah 325
  Harriet 191
  James 187
  Jno. 316
  John 230, 316
  John H. 86
  Joicey 223
  Joins 59
  Julia Ann 110
  Lottey 316
  Lucy 84
  Lucy Ann 280
  Martha 10
  Martha T. 223
  Mary 36
  Moses 86
  Nelly Ann 187
  Polly 30, 265
  Rebecca 79
  Rebecca Ann 266
  Ritter 59
  Sallie 86
  Sally 106
  Sterling 106, 148, 266, 280
  Susannah 59
  William 60, 86, 191
  Willie 71, 84
Chavus, Tabitha 20
Cheatham, (?) 170
  C. A. 127
  Cynthia A. 61
  Cynthia R. 127
  Elizer 257
  Isaac(?) 100
  Isaac 61, 69, 127, 185, 297, 312
  Isham 98, 145, 252, 259
  Isham J. 220
  James 158, 189
  James, Jr. 75, 120, 211, 297
  Jane 18
  Lizzie 278
  Lucy A. 29
  Malissa 19
  Martha 289
  Mary 163
  Mary J. 254
  Nancy 74
  Parthenia J. 18
  Rebecca 330
  Robert G. 307
  Sarah A. 262
  Sarah C. 252
  Thomas 142
  Thos. G. 84
Chebers, Margarett 145
Cheek, Robt. 25
Chesley, Martha T. 85
Chettam, Betsey Diskill 332
Chevers, Mary 125
Cheves, Caswell 145

Cheves (cont.)
  Eliza 145
Chewell, Hannah 354
Childers, Obedience 357
Childres, Henry 358
Childs, Frankey 295
  John 295
  Nathan 186
Chiles, John 45
  Lusey 186
Chillion, Thomas 279
Chism, Jane H. 273
Chisum, Ann 206
Chotman, Thomas 88
Chrismas, Rebecca 341
Christian, Mary J. 213
Christie, Danl. Harvey 61
Christmas(?), Obadiah 251
Christmas, Obadiah 360
  Rose 132
Christopher, Betsey 195
  James 61, 298
  Kittey 353
Chuer, Massey 349
Chumbly, James 61
Clack, Robert K. 232
Claiborne, Sarah 196
Claiton, William 41
Clanton, James 276
Clardey, Polley 68
Clardy, Benjamin 362
  Betsy 343
  Elisabeth 154
  Frances 242
  Jane M. 341
  John 231
  Martha 286
  Milley 185
  Sarah 270
  Susey 95
Clareton, Mary 370
Clark, Allen 180
  Amanda 292
  Ann Meriah 37
  Archd. 246
  Aroma 152
  Benjamin 129
  Betsey 16
  Cordelia Ann 210
  Cornelia Ann 154
  David 107, 341
  E. 62
  Eaton 62
  Elisabeth 235
  Eliza 56
  Elizabeth 254
  Emila 120
  Emily (Mrs.) 200
  J. J. 253
  Jas. 62
  Joanah 83
  Jno. E. 278
  John 16, 62
  Joseph 63, 315
  Luetta 95
  Marinda 283
  Martha 326
  Mary 178, 218
  Mary Ann 23
  Mary H. 120
  Mary J. 47
  Mary K. B. 307
  Mary L. 144
  Nancy 62, 63
  Nanvy 210
  Nathanel 265

Clark (cont.)
  Rebecca 67
  Reuben 90, 135
  Salina 165
  Sallie Ann 236
  Sam. 120
  Susan Ann 22
  Timothy 199
  Virginia F. 300
  W. D. 97
  William 63, 236, 326
  Wm. 121
Clarke, Adam 246
  Allen 56
  Betsy 286
  Charlotte 246
  Ellen 37
  John 8, 360
  Mary 167
  Polly 134
  Rhoda 210
  Sarah C. 62
  Susan A. 118
  William 18, 107
Clary, Elizabeth 104
Claxton, James 137, 197, 215
  Jemima 276
Clay, Allen 80, 203, 321
  Ann J. 217
  Archibald W. 80
  C. W., Jr. 172
  Catharine 152, 154
  Charity A. 348
  Chas. W., Jr. 305
  D. (Doctor) 211
  Dochia 368
  Docia Ann 208
  Dosha 5
  Dosia 117
  Eliza H. 321
  Elizabeth L. 215
  Fanny J. 135
  Isaac 344
  Isabella 145
  James 31
  Martha 108, 256
  Mary 293
  Mary Eliza 203
  Melana H. 190
  Sam. 265
  Saml. 184
  Samuel 215
  Sarah 15
  Sarah G. 69
  Sophia 64
  Sophia W. 229
  Stephen 227
  Susanna Price 323
Clayton, Daniel 353
  Danl. 64
  Liza 64
  Nancy 72
  William 64
  Wm. T. 196
Cleator, William 280
Clemens, Susannah 362
Clement, Anna 46
  Anne 367
  Anney 264
  Anthony 287, 320
  Isabella 257
  John 46, 367
  John T. 236
  Judy 284
  Maria 64
  Martha 46
  Nancy 65

Clement (cont.)
  Nancy S. 268
  Pallatiah 236
  Samuel 187, 264
  Sarah 187
  Simon 65
  William 36
  Zephaniah 65
Clements, A. 5
  Elisabeth 68
  Elizabeth 267
  Frances 335
  Peyton 121
Clemment, Isabella 117
Clerk, Jane 134
  Nathaniel 65
Cliborn, Martha 135
  Susan A. 195
Clibourne, Francis J. 258
Clifford, Polly 303
Clopton, Devereaux 85
  G. W. 286
  Gilla 256
  Jane 364
  Polly 271
  Rosa C. 192
  Roza 43
Closwell, Alexr. 49
Cloy, A. M. 269
Cloyer, J. C. 182
Cly, A. M. 231
Clyborne, William 334
Clyburn, Georgiana 214
Cobb, Elizabeth R. 258
  Isabella 324
  Jno. 324
  Susan 45
  William J. 87
Cobbs, Eliza 206
  James H. 206, 299
  Jno. 70, 320
Cocke, Elizabeth 141
  James 133
  Martha 226
Coe, Amos 332
Cogens, Emmilla 214
  George 214
Coghill, Ann Elizabeth 175
  Annie 318
  Damsel V. 87
  Lucy 25
  Lucy W. 174
  Mary F. 174
  Mary R. 277
  P. F. 175
  Sabrina H. 135
  Thomas 94, 143
  Thos. 41
  W. E. 25
Cogwell, Martha 28
Cogwill, James O. 275
Cokely, Nancy 35
Colclough, Alexander 156
  William 271
Cole, (?) (Doctor) 178
  Anne 109
  Anthony W. 26, 50, 84, 288
  B. L. (Dr.) 237
  Celey 38
  Dilley 103
  Elizabeth 222
  Fanny 69, 343
  Haley 127, 128
  Haskey 68
  Hicksey 348

Cole (cont.)
  James 299
  Jane 223
  Jincy 105
  Lucy 220
  Margaret 237
  Margaret S. 237
  Maria R. (Mrs.) 250
  Marina Ann 143
  Martha 119, 127
  Mary 192
  Nelson 292, 293
  Polley 347
  Rhodam 279
  Tabitha 12
  Thomas 69, 204
  William 247
  Willis 222, 271
Coleman, Hannah 226
  Jane 348
Coley, Audney 322
  Catharine H. 285
  Edmund 67
  Frances 45, 54
  Hasseltine 54
  Henrietta A. 137
  James 67
  James M. 267
  John 55
  Mary 3
  Maryann 280
  Richard H. 67
  Sallie A. 325
  Sarah 54
  Sarah E. 264
  Sarah Jane 234
  William 67, 167
Collar, William 61
Collens, Mary B. 282
  Thomas 138
  William 61, 154
Collier, Anne 121
  Caroline 334
  Cole 68
  Elizabeth H. 141
  Maranda A. 44
  Tempey 16
  Thomas 67
Collifer, Ellinoir 315
Collins, Edward 121
  Elisabeth 61, 286
  Elizabeth 271
  Fannie R. 364
  Isham 68
  James A. 318
  John 151, 231, 305
  Lizzie D. 226
  Lois 121
  Lucy 238
  Permelia 68
  Polly 305
  Robert 96
  Sarah 125
  Sarah Jane 263
  Thomas 68, 222
  William 41, 61, 95
  Wm. B. 220
Collinsworth, Lueilla 173
Coly, Eliza Ann 285
Comer, Elisabeth 84
  James 64
Compton, Elisabeth M. 29
  George C. 229
  Martha A. 305
  Mary P. 307
Connell, G. C. 68

Connell (cont.)
  Usley 68
Conyers, Horace 265
  Mary 356
Cook, Amanda C. 55
  Amelia S. 336
  Ann 45, 229
  B. 107
  Barber 232
  Benj. C. 72, 106, 147, 179, 335, 342
  Benja. C. 238
  C. 184
  Claborn 93, 214, 292
  Clairborne 31
  David T. 68
  Elisabeth 302
  Elizabeth 57
  James R. 363
  Henry H. 314
  Jane 276
  Lucy 286
  Mariah 183
  Mary 68
  Patsy 215
  Rebecah 363
  Richard 227
  Roling 293
  Shem 345
  Shemuel 40
  Stephen 115, 119, 181
  Tho. 49
  Thos. 215
  William 68, 76, 287
  Wm. 76
Cooke, A. H. 24, 29, 198, 225, 364
  Ailsey 258
  B. C. 175
  Benj. C. 22, 25, 29, 49, 103, 109, 118, 148, 161, 183, 195, 196, 202, 215, 219, 280, 288, 339
  Caroline 55
  Claborn 20
  Claiborn 181
  Cynthia M. 139
  Elisabeth 155
  Eliza 261, 309
  Eliza Frances 308
  Elizabeth 26
  James 99, 123
  Jane 16
  Jas. R. 301
  Jno. D. 155
  Louisa B. 41
  Martha 67, 225
  Nancey 293
  Nancy 198, 293
  Narcissa A. 337
  Phebe 297
  Precilla 201
  Salley 81, 258
  Sally 232
  Stephen 193, 222
  Thomas 69, 335
  Thos. Y. 9
  Wm. 81
Cooley, Lucy 67
Cooly, Catharine 301
  Smith 293
Coon, Sally 346
Coop, Ben. 90
Cooper, Cannon 5, 70
  Caroline 319
  Caty 190
  Clarias 126

Cooper (cont.)
　Dorthey 108
　Ellen 245
　Elvice 149
　Frances G. 99
　Harriett 190
　J. C. 4, 59, 163,
　　182, 249, 275, 344
　James 162, 176, 254,
　　304
　James O. 239
　Jane E. 368
　Jas. C. 131, 208, 281
　Jeannette T. 101
　John 362
　Judy 368
　Kannon 149
　Leviney 206
　Lizzie 344
　Mary 143, 343
　Mary A. 159
　Mary Ann 188
　Molley 362
　Moses 190
　Philip 344
　Polly Ann 126
　Ransom 51
　Sinia 126
　Susannah 217
　Wesley 126
　Willis 153
Coopper, Benjamin 369
　Salley 369
Copeland, Mana 106
　N. P. 182
　Wm. 185
Coral, Joel 272
Corn, Eliza 148
　Minerva 317
Corthan, Elizabeth 261
Cottrel, Eliza 68
Cottrell, Ann 297
　Elisabeth 323
　Fannie R. 306
　Frances 323
　James 115
　Louisa E. 211
　Matthew 279
　Solomon 162
Couch, Juda 22
Coulton, Eliza 304
Cousens, Allen 275
Cousin, Frances 84
　Martha Ann 71
　Susan 327
Cousins, Betsey 149
　Burton 172
　Happy 86
　Henry 10
　Henry 245
　Margaret 36
　Martin 71
　Nancy 71
Covington, Eliza 150
Coward, Nancy 96
Cox, Aletha 181
　Betsey 101
　Charnock 364
　Dolley 33
　Dollie 310
　Elenor 343
　Elizabeth F. 309
　Emiline 210
　Faithy 183
　Harriott 358
　Lucy Ann 323
　Mary 304
　Mary Ann 194

Cox (cont.)
　Mary Jane 57
　Miles 71, 239
　Nancy 343
　Polley 71
　Thos. 276
Cozart, Allin 184
　D. C. 64
　Hubbard 72
　James 29, 224
　James C. 240, 306
　James H. 346
　Jane 306
　Jas. C. 32, 220
　Jiney 148
　Mimah 268
　Sallie M. 306
Cozens, Mary 266
　Wiley 72
Cozert, D. C. 282
Cozins, Nancey 59
Cozort, B. C. 256
　Catharine 91
　Clarry 339
　D. C. 72
　Ellendar 88
　Fanny 53
　Hannah 127
　Jemima 213
　John 127
　Lavanie P. 284
　Lucy A. 268
　Maria 211
　Mary A. 52
　Mary Ann 287
　Nancy 65
　Nancy J. 211
　Rachel 218
　Rebecca 83
　Sarah 64
　Simeon 287
　Winney 171
Crabtree, James 100
　Lucy 186
　R. 25
Craddock, Jane 10
　Jesse 339
Craft, Elizabeth 292,
　354
　John, Jr. 75
　Lethe 183
　Saml. 275
　Samuel 355
　Sarah 133
Crafts, Archibald 277
Cragett, Diner 132
　George 132
Craig, Mary 250
Crandell, Martha A. 278
Crawley, Hannah 64
　Robert 64
Creath, Samuel, Jr. 157
Creedle, Thomas 49
Creekmore, Martha L.
　182
Crenshaw, Barbary 288
　Daniel 182
　James N. 255
　Martha 49
　Patsey 349
　Polly 58
　R. 129
　Rehab. 129
　Thomas 49, 149
Creth, Jane 163
　Mary A. R. 120
Crews, Abram 74
　Alex 182

Crews (cont.)
　Anderson 74
　Ann H. 121
　Benjamin F. 18
　Caroline F. 304
　Caroline S. 45
　Colbe 42
　Crity 205
　Elizabeth 78, 357
　Elizabeth S. 244
　Emily 11, 74, 123
　Frances 74
　Gideon 73, 82, 221
　Hannah 75, 99
　Harriet 297
　Isabella J. 161
　J. B. 78
　James A. 304
　Jane 205
　Jas. B. 227
　Jemima 78
　Jos. B. 235
　Joseph 78
　Littleberry 198
　Louisa J. 231
　Lucretia J. 244
　Lucy 75
　Lucy Ann 70
　Martha 304
　Malissa F. 161
　Martha M. 176
　Martha P. 37
　Mary 42, 308
　Mary Ann 158
Crews(?), Mary E. 365
Crews, Massey 222
　Meredith 168
　Milley 158
　Oney 236
　Rebecca A. 60
　Salley 192
　Sallie P. 159
　Sarah Ann 213
　Solomon B. 75
　Susan C. 175
　William H. 65
　Wm. B. 74, 122
Crisp, Elizabeth 250
Cristmas, O. S. 278
Cristmus, Thos. H. 263
Critchen, Sarah E. 236
Critcher, A. J. 231
　Anson 13, 75, 326
　Frances J. 64
　Jane Threft 227
　Martha Jane 82
　Mary E. 135
　Rebecca G. 18
　Salley 228
　Thomas 21, 228, 268
　Thos. 75
　Virginia 231
　Wm. 75
Croft, Henrietta 354
　Wm. 354
Crorom(?), J. H. 288
Cross, Amos G. 76
　Cherry 75
　Eliza 76
　Jack 75
　Silas A. 337
Crouder, Kessiah 202
Crowder, Caroline 180
　Elisabeth 137
　Isaac 183
　John 89
　Lucy 16
　Mary 363

Crowder (cont.)
  Uel 138, 139
Cruce, Joseph 74
Crudup, Edward A. 27
  Lucy 197
  Martha 264
  Temperance 31
Crump, Emeline 76
  John C. (Gen.) 76
Crutchen, Matilda A. E. 52
Crutcher, Rebecah 154
Crute, Martha J. 285
Crymes, Mary S. 41
Cudden, William 34
Culbrath, Dicey 264
Culbreath, Ann 239
  Green 221
  John 194, 221
  Martha 267
  Mary 249, 267
  Panthea 249
  Rowan 152
  Young 276
Culverhouse, Elisabeth 130
  Elizabeth 272
  Jane 150, 157
Culverhouse(?), Joseph 157
Culverhouse, Lidia 80
  Thomas 121, 195
  Thomas Wilmon 54
Cunningame, Sally 91
Cunningham, Ransom 149
Curne, Mary 199
Curren, Chesly 38
  Sally 77
Currin, Abner 115, 294, 345
  Cornelia 14
  David 58, 77
  E. L. 77
  Elizabeth 115, 191
  Ellen Maria 14
  Ezekiel B. 113
  F. B. 223
  Fleming B. 14
  Frances 157
  Frances A. 204
  Francis 281, 320
  Hamilton 166
  Hampleton 78
  Hugh 200
  Indiana 188
  Isabella F. 122
  J. B. 77
  J. H. 78, 116
  J. M. 175
  J. W. 224
  John R. 313
  John W. 116
  Larkin 173
  Lizzie 320
  Lotan G. W. 77
  Lucy 298
  Lucy A. 102
  Lucy M. 132
  Martha 221
  Martha Ann 82
  Martha G. 27
  Mary 78, 149, 320
  Mary Ann 157
  Mary E. 241
  Mary Jane 199, 354
  Mildred 200, 346
  Mildred F. 200
  Nancy 173, 345

Currin (cont.)
  Parthenia P. 242
  Rebecca Frances 149
  Robert 298
  Sallie P. 77
  Sarah 58, 74, 204
  Selona 132
  Stephen 77, 204, 244
  Susannah 345
  W. A. 78, 166
  Wiatt 248
  William 199
  William A. 78, 80
  Wm. 142, 332
Curring, F. B. 117
  J. W. 148
Currins, Mary Jane 196
  Stephen 177
Curron, Martha 223
Curry, Susan 14
Curtice, Eliza Ann 78
Curtis, Alexr. 79
  Ann 167, 262
  Ann Eliza 179, 244
Curtis(?), Benjamin 61
  Chas. 365
  Delia 184
  Elisabeth 173
  Eliza Jane 79
  Elizabeth 210, 279, 312
  Fannie 328
  Frances 365
  Francis 86
  Harriet 353
  Isabella 333
  James 334
  Jas. 80
  Jemima 87
  Larcissa 333
  Laura Jane 358
  Lewis 10, 32
  Lucinda 87
  Martha 136
  Martha Ann 218
  Martha C. 329
  Mary Ann 84
  Minerva A. 10
  Moses 79
  Nancy 79, 353
  Peter 333, 353, 365
  Silas 79
  Terrell 79, 151
  Thos. 60
Cuts, Elizabeth 310
Cutts, Jas. 302
  Martha 326, 366
  Mary 302
  Mary F. 235
  W. H. 271
  William 366
  William H. 326
Cuty, Nanny 195
Cuzort, Margaret 339
Cuzzort, Nancy 181
Cworn(?), Abner 78
Dabnam, Dansel C. 245
Dabney, Nathan 259
  Nathaniel 203
Dailey, Nancey 144
Dalbey, Permelia 45
  William 111
Dalby, Annie E. 123
  Arrena 67
  E. 44
  Fannie 212
  Penelope 213
Dallyr, E. 59

Daly, George L. 163
Dameron, Judith 1
Damon, David P. 355
Dance, Mayze 23
Daniel, (?) (Doctor) 323
  Adeline 345
  Ailcy 50
  Alice G. 304
  Ann 304
  Ann E. 237
  Ann Eliza 97
  Armstead 82
  Barbary L. 153
  Benj. 111
  Betsy 344
  Beverley 199
  C. R. 341
  Celia 44
  Charlotte 199
  Cloe 31
  Daphney 82
  David 344
  Edney 248
  Elenor 194
  Elijah 56
  Elisabeth 65, 85, 303, 332, 359
  Eliza 82
  Eliza Jane 80
  Elizabeth 169, 174, 242
  Elizabeth F. 356
  Ellen 82
  Francis C. 46
  Franky 242
  Geo. 14
  Geo. W. 32
  Hannah 337
  Harriet 33
  Harriett 344
  Hester 96
  James 131
  James B. 237
  Jane 147
  Jane E. 237
  Jerry 50
  Jesse 274, 346
  Jno. 146
  John 7, 80
  Joseph 81, 82, 303
  Josiah, Jr. 200
  Judah 161
  Lilly 232
  Louisa 303
  Lucy 313
  Lucy F. 359
  Lucy T. 344
  Lucy W. 350
  M. H. 237
  Martha 80, 242, 344
  Martha A. 310
  Martha E. 237
  Martha I. 8
  Martha T. 95
  Mary 96, 194, 289
  Mary L. 266
  Mauris S. 82
  Minerva 31
  Mitchell 332
  Nancy 130, 239
  Nancy M. 242
  Nannie V. 341
  Nathaniel 304
  Nelly A. 344
  Patsey 41
  Penny 50
  Polley 71, 72
  S. V. 319
  Salley 193

Daniel (cont.)
  Saml. 62
  Saml. D. 344
  Sarah 138, 146
  Sarah V. 33
  Seley 159
  Stark 56
  Susan 82, 236
  Susanna (Mrs.) 326
  Susannah 341, 352
  Tamer 82
  Teressey E. 154
  Thomas 41, 117, 160, 205, 295, 349, 350
  Thos.(?) 304
  Thos. B. 191
  W. H. 306
  Whitfield 31
  William 181
  Willis 37, 73, 359
  Woodson 7, 234, 269, 337
  Z. 81, 236
Daniels, Samuel D. 85
Dannel, Samuel 326
  Susannah 326
Darden, Amey 352
Darman, Puryear 351
Dauney, Elisabeth 245
Davenport, Joseph 73
Davidson, Wm. 242
Davies, Susannah Frazer 3
Davis, A. 4
  A. E. 85
  A. L. 296
  A. S. 85, 262
  Absolem, Jr. 286, 331
  Agathey 19
  Alexander L. 85
  Alfred 137
  Ann 183
  Ann Eliza 135
  Anny 269
  Archibald 141
  Augustin 246, 268
  Baxter 60
  Baxter, Jr. 344
  Benj. 157
  Benjamin 272
  Betsey 29
  Candy J. 370
  Caroline A. H. 370
  Chesley 83
  Cyrus 50
  Cyrus, Jr. 50
  Dolphin 84
  Eaton 14
  Elisabeth 155
  Elisabeth A. 87
  Elizabeth 146, 166, 271, 277
  Elizabeth H. 139
  Emily H. 244
  Fanny 134
  Frances 84
  George R. 348
  Gideon 257, 282
  H. A. 223, 304, 360
  Harriett 66
  Henry 330
  Isaac M. 264
  J. 83, 90
  J. H. 264
  James C. 271
  James H. 83, 223
  James M. 64

Davis (cont.)
  Jas. 84
  Jas. J. 196
  Jerry 325
  Jesse 296
  Jno.(?) 198
  Davis(?), John 31
  Davis, John 86
  John W. 184
  Jonathan 65
  Joseph P. 85
  Julia 182
  Lavina 30
  Louisa W. 80
  Lucinda 85, 133
  Lucy 20
  Lucy A. 28, 360
  Luviney 331
  Lynda 84
  Martha E. 252
  Martha G. 61
  Mary 230
  Mary A. 19, 85
  Mary E. 58
  Mary Eliza 109
  Mary G. 33
  Mary J. 61
  Messenier 227, 228
  Missenier 228
  Nancy 60
  Niah 23
  Pattey 312
  Phoebe 125
  Polly 28, 246
  Rebecca 221, 268
  Sallie 53
  Sally 133
  Saml. H. 237
  Sarah 105
  Solomon 228
  Susan 213, 282
  Susan W. 216
  Susannah 269, 284
  Tempy 325
  William 8, 225, 322
  Wm. A. 370
  Wm. D. 354, 362
  Zereviah 3
Daws(?), Anne 108
  Elisabeth 112
  Martha R. 370
  Mary L. 344
  Matilda 86
Dawson, Jessie A. 49
Day, Ann 13
  Beady 11
  Betsey 87
  Bowling 1
  Dicey 151
  Elizabeth 11, 55, 71
  Emaline 285
  Ferrabay 316
  Francis 316
  Henry 145
  James 79, 243
  Jesse 86
  John 11
  John B. 367
  John L. 140
  Josephine 223
  Julia Ann 214
  Lucy 86
  Luiza 59
  Maney 10
  Mary 60, 243
  Patsey 331
  Phereby 20
  Polly Ann 80

Day (cont.)
  Presley 80, 312
  Rebecca Ann 223
  Reuben 20, 86
  Robert 223
  Salley 11
  Sally 71
  Sally Ann 230
  Saml. 86
  Susan 151
  T. B. 248
  Wm. 80
Dean, Daniel 341
  Elizabeth 52
  Elizabeth J. 301
  Frances 116
  Geo. W. 41
  Harriett 303
  Margaret 52
  Marlitia(?) 321
  Parthenia 321
  R. C. 91
  R. G. 232
  Sally Jane 128
  Sarah 87
  William 358
  Wm. 87, 321
  Wm. W. 128
Deas, William 87
Debman, Lucy 83
Debnam, Damsel R. 35
  Dolly 198
  Fanny W. 203
  John B. 35
  Martha H. 277
  Matilda 35
  Virginia V. 84
Debram, Mary E. 350
Debramp(?) John B. 283
Debruler, Micajah 222
Deckerson, William 332
Dedman, Henry H. 133
deGraffenriedt, F. T. 334
Delap, Daniel 210
Dement, A. L. 42
  Asbury 64
  C. H. 288
  Caroline 354
  Cleary(?) 261
  Eliza 208
  Emily 263
  G. A. 208, 263
  Henderson 87
  Hilman 50
  Jane 90
  M. 26
  Mahala S. 247
  Martha 115
  Mary Ann 315
  Mary E. 332
  Thomas 241
  W. 198
  W. W. 134
  Wilson W. 88, 151
Demont, Cassy 42
  Lucy 257
  Polley 241
  Thomas 26, 42
Denes, Gilbert 285
Denman, Ellen R. (Mrs.) 3
Denny, Fanny 55
Denson, Edna Bailey 91
Dent, Eliza 168, 342
  Francis 168
  Loury A. 342
  Melcene 270
  Mary B. 7
  Sarah H. 312

Dent (cont.)
　Thomas 342
Denton, Benjamin 72, 90
　Benjn. 73
　John 23, 88
　Mary 23
　Reuben 136
　Rosey 112
　Samuel 350
Derieus, Francis 174
Derieux, Sophia 174
Desha, William 257
Devin, R. J. 6
　Robert J. 132
Dew, Eliza 369
　John T. 6
　Otamour 186
Dewbey, Thomas R. 296
Dickens, Lucretia 234
　Marshy 258
　Martha 344
　Parthenia 91
Dickens(?), Uriah 341
Dicker, Henry 164
　Susannah 164
Dickerson, Ann 229
　Duke 89
　Elisabeth 121, 186
　Elizabeth 133, 152, 288
　Eppy 93
　James 310
　Jane R. 250
　Jenney 299
　Jno. 152
　John 152, 153
　John, Jr. 121
　Leonidas 315
　Lotty 69
　Lucy Ann 2
　Malinda 271
　Martha 144, 315
　Mary 69
　Nancey 36, 65, 163
　Polly 89
　Ransom 36
　Rebecca 93, 306
　Sally 19
　Sally A. 147
　Samuel T. 327
　Samuel W. 250
　Sarah 93, 140
　Sarah J. 255
　Susan 250
　Susannah 93
　Thos. 89
Dickerson(?), William 210
Dickerson, William 17, 89, 118, 186, 210
　Wm. 89
Dickins, Salley 61
　William 91
　Wm. 61, 321
Dickinson, Zachr. 110
Dickson, Keziah 170
Dillard, Cornelia 85
　Hilsmon 14
　Israel L. 221
Dilliard, Israel F. 209
　Narcissa 299
Dinkins, Winney 188
Dixon, Ed 274
　F. 294
　Joanah 94
　Samuel A. 52
　Sarah J. 204
Doab, Martha E. 367

Dock, David A. 73
Docry, Robert 91
Dodson, Betsey 140
　Brister 91
　Charles 140, 306
　Frances 331
　Lucy 91
　Mary 73
　Nancy 306
　Polley 111
　Stephen 286
　Susan 91
　William 91, 257, 331
Dolby, Knight 68
　Macajah B. 91
Dorcy, George 103
Dordeg(?), Z. M. P. 149
Dorom, James 265
Dorset, Easter 320
Dorsey, Cecilia 212
　Virginia 230
Douglass, Susana 320
Dowdy(?), John 201
Downes, Elizabeth 8
Downey, Amelia 309
　Ann A. 84
　Anna 70, 294
　Currell 126
　Frances 294
　Francis 319
　Harriett 200
　Isabella 177
　Isiah 319
　Jane 140
　Jane S. 162
　Jas. T. 32
　John 62, 126
　Letha 132
　Margaret 251
　Mary 92, 243
Downey(?), Mary Ann 291
Downey, Mary Ann 102
　Nicy 91
　Polly 304
　Rebecka 336
　Robert 336
　Sally M. 295
　Samuel S. 59
　Susan A. 6, 361
　Thomas 92
　Thos. P. 298
　Woodson 294
Downing, Saml. S. 22
Downy, John 61
　Nancy 199
Draper, Lucinda 126
Drew, Mary 30
Drew(?), Squire 143
Drewry, Amey 41
Driskel, Dennis 195
　Frankey 39
　Salley 257
Driskil, Dennis 228
Driver, Bird 52
Drumright, Mary A. E. 145
Drury, Ellis 288
Drury(?), Peter 115
Due, Angelina 221
　David 220
　Dicey 20
　Emily 341
　Fanny 79
　John T. 211
　Martha Ann 331

Due (cont.)
　Mary 28
　Nelly Ann 220
Dueberry, Ann 46
Duff, Fleming 57
　Hugh 93
Duffy, Patrick 169
Dufoy, Allce 109
Duggar, Mourning 167
Duglass, Archibald 303
Duke, Ann 94
　Britty Ann 52
　Dicey 28
　Eliza M. 113
　Lucy T. 172
　Martha R. 37
　Mary 30, 314
　Mary Jane 164
　Rheney 219
　Rowan 262
　Sallie M. 198
　Sarah 222
　Tabithey 179
　Thamer 293
　Thomas 94
　Thomas V. 135
　Thos. V. 187
Dun, William W. 362
Duncan, (?) 128
　Ailey Ann 327
　Alfred 96
　Anderson 94
　Charles 12, 351
　Charles K. 94
　David 95
　Delia Ann 194
　Elizabeth 95
　Ellenor D. 326
　Frances 91, 290
　Henrietta 220
　Howel 94
　Howell 94, 327
　Isaac 94, 301
　James H. 94
　Joanna 105, 326
　Joannah 94
　John 12, 38, 46, 152, 153, 302
　John B. 95
　Martha 302
　Mary H. 262
　Nancy 91, 194, 270
　Rebecca 94
　Rebecca J. 94
　S. D. 94
　S. H. 326
　Sarah 96
　Sarah P. 302
　Seamore 58, 353
　Sterling H. 262, 301
　Susan 301
　William 286
Dunigan, Charles 175
Dunkin, Alfred 90
　Anderson 94
　Anderson L. 302
　Mary A. E. 90
Dunkly, Mary B. 240
Dunlop, Isabella L. 95
　James 95
Dunn, Elvira S. 358
Dunn(?), J. N. 95
Dunn, John 49, 92
　Martha F. 36
　R. W. 171
　Sarah 41, 95
　William 95
Dunovan, Eldridge 357

Dunson, Martha 223
Dunstan, G. (Admiral) 136
  Henrietta 136
Dunston, Charles 96
  Eleany 190
  Martha Ann 96
  Mary 96, 238
  S. W. 260
Durham, Catherine 35, 278
  Emily 278
  Frances 96
  John 266
  Nanney 96
  Peggy 32
  Rosa 266
  Sarah 360
Durm, Thos. 278
Dutton, Betsey 15
  William 256
  Zachariah 96
Duty, Adeline 66
  Betsey 153
  Eliza 97
  Elizabeth M. 239
  George L. 97, 313
  Harriet A. 187
  Indiana 196
  Jabez 19
  James R. 9, 46, 47, 58, 79, 93, 96, 101, 102, 103, 160, 162, 195, 199, 243, 244, 245, 249, 279, 281, 296, 323, 338
  Jas. R. 8, 12, 36, 79, 101, 108, 122, 142, 143, 162, 185, 196, 220, 245, 255, 266, 281, 289, 295, 300, 322, 323, 343, 344
  Lucy Ann 175
  Martha 118
  Mary A. 84
  Matilda B. 71
  Parthenia F. 103
  Sallie 152
  Saml. 163
  Sarah 128, 148
  Susan 92
  Susannah 322
  Warren 113
Dyer, Linney 54
  Mary 235
  Molley 157
  Patience 31
Eacks, Jincy 317
Eaker, Clarasa 320
Eakes, Edmund 199
  Indiana 350
  Jane 350
  William S. 33
  Zachariah 350
Eaks, Agga 173
  Bevily 352
  Carolina 209
  Eliza 62
  Eliza T. 317
  Emily 351
  Frances 174
  Ibbie 352
  Jane 97, 288
  Jane Gilliam 253
  Martha 199
  Martha A. Permelia 352
  Martha J. 253
  Mary 194

Eaks (cont.)
  Robt. S. 97
  Sarah 199
  Sarah A. 241
  Timothy 310
  Viney 352
  Woodson 97, 253
  Zachariah 97
Earl, Elisabeth 74
  Elizabeth 222
  John 24
  Martha B. 198
  Mary 119
  Polley 190
  Sally 74
  Sarah 213
Earle, John 161
Easley, Danl. 273, 367
Easter, Mary 136
Eastes, Nancy 65
Eastland, Dorcas 92
Eastridge, Lucretia 15
  Lydda 153
  Nancey 184
Eastwood, Charity 131
  Dicey 187
  John 122, 189, 190, 217, 351
  Lucy 248
  Nancey 248
  Phanney 236
  Rebeccah 122
Eatling, Nansey 344
Eaton, Adam 24
  Bett 345
  Cammell 282
  Christiana B. 180
  Elisabeth 92
  Fanny 340
  Iezor 238
  Jas. W. 19, 21
  Litha 306
  Martha 265
  Mary 19, 36
  Mary (Mrs.) 209
  Mary G. 319
  Panthea 36
  Polly 24
  Robert V. 67
  Sallie T. 181
  Sally John 368
  Sarah A. 67
  Sary 319
  Susan C. 340
  Willm. 209
  Wm. A. 180
Edmonds, Jas. W. H. 122
Edmunds, Winey 367
Edward, Harrison 223
Edwards, Anne 356
  Beverly 81
  Catherine 91
  Charles 73
  Chas. 248
  Clora 123
  Devreaux 99
  Dilly 113
  Elisabeth 184
  Elizabeth 221, 315, 336
  Elizabeth G. 370
  Frances 32
  Francis 110
  George R. 99
  Henry A. 349
  Hester Ann 362
  J. 176
  James 199

Edwards (cont.)
Edwards(?), Jno. W. 7
  Judith 241
  L. C. 15, 184
  L. R. 1
  Laura 1
  Leander R. 57
  Lucy 2
  Margaret E. 233
  Martha 107
  Mary 27
  Mary J. 88, 121
  Peggy 333
  Pumphrey 221
  Roberta A. 363
  Samuel 29, 66, 99, 263, 300
  Samuel D. 110, 300, 315
  Samuel F. 153
  Sarah Ann 140
  Sefroney E. J. 99
  Thomas 308
  Thomas S. 99
  William 170
  William J. 309
  William P. 331
  Wm. 336
Edy, Elisabeth 265
Eeart, Nancy 308
Elam, Harriet 77
  James D. 147
  Jane E. 233
  Martha A. 77
  Richard 77
  Sarah J. 327
Elexon, Mary 73
Elexson, Jno. A. 100
  John D. 100
  Synthia 2
Elixson, Alexander 64, 147
  Caroline 43
  James B. 31
Ell-(?), Arch 110
Elles, Jas. 304
Ellexon, Mary 313
Ellington, Albert 16
  Amey Ann 162
  Amy Ann 162
  Barbary 218
  Berelle 210
  Bevelle 62, 133
  Bevil 37, 219
  David 101
  Fannie 101
  Gilford 263
  Harriet 256
  Jas. M. 100
  Jno. M. 173, 363
  John 36, 100, 101, 161, 288, 357
  John M. 109, 164, 256, 282
  Jones 101, 343
  Jos. B. 341
  Louisa 101
  Lucy 162, 163
  Martha 154
  Mary 101
  Meradith 35
  Meredith 35, 43
  Thos. S. 25
  W. B. 235, 269, 333
  William B. 177, 239, 289
  Wright 73
Elliot, Green B. 43
  Margaret Ann 296

Elliott, Bartlet 95
  Charles 201
  Chas. 196
  Eliza 133
  Elizabeth 17
  Elizabeth J. 102
  Elizabeth N. 200
  F. M. 353
  Fannie E. 200
  Green 102, 329
  Green B. 271
  Harriet 239
  James 158, 346
  John 200, 239, 315
  L. F. 102
  Laura 102
  Louiza Jane 101
  Lucy Ann 158
  Marshall 101
  Martha 102, 158
  Mary E. 341
  Mary Jane 78
  Robert 179, 200, 216
  Robt. 92, 210, 341
  Ruben 102
  Sarah 124
  Sorotha F. 246
  Susan A. 158
  William 15
  Wm. 102
Ellis, Dolly 297
  Elizabeth 82
  J. S. 63
  James 101
  Jno. G. 310
  John S. 211
  Lucy 336
  Luetta 335
  Mary 221
  Nancey 297
  Sabriner 2
  Sarah 284
  Susan 18
  Tilda 336
  Virginia V. 323, 324
Ellison, Sarah 355
Elliss, Fanny 73
Ellixon, Ann 356
Ellixson, Ann Hunt 51
  Isabella 43
  Peggey 195
Elom, Mary S. 241
Elum, Harriott N. 313
Emery, Ephraim E. 58
  Henry 103
  John 91, 103
  Lewis 103
  Pattey 91
  Polley 91
  Susan 58
  W. L. 103
  Wiley L. 103, 293
  Willis 142
Emory, Edna 218
  Eliza J. 219
  Elitha T. 58
  Ephm. 330
  Lucey 217
  Susan 40
Emrey, George 144
Emry, George 324
  John 337
  John 269
Eperson, Susanna 51
Eppes, Sarah C. 133
Epps, Elizabeth Lewis 159
Estes, Caroline H. 85

Estes (cont.)
  Daniel 307
  Dicy 179
  Drury 4
  Israel 157
  J. W. 14
  James 222
Estes(?), Jerry 220
Estes, Jerry 169
  Jery 357
  John 241
  John B. 150
  Lucy 111
  Nathl. 105
  Patsy 104
  Rebecca 179
  Romulus 104
  W. T. 60
  William 178
  Wm. 14, 271
Estis, Charlott 140
  Salley 272
  Wm. 272
Estridge, Ann 209
  Elizabeth 85
  Sarah 355
Evans, Abram 95
  Babby 87
  Benjamin 230
  Betsey 142
  Burwell 106
  Charles 60, 96
  Charlotte 302
  Coleman 87
  David L. 286
  Dilley Ann 356
  Dolly 144
  Elisabeth 291
  Elizabeth 59, 79
  Elizabeth J. 197
  Fanny 5
  Frances 89
  Francis 29
  Griffin 106
  Harriett 172
  Helen 17
  Henrietta 266
  Hilliard 106
  Howel 12
  Isaac 105
  James 60
  Julia Ann E. 221
  Keziah 145
  Lewis 79, 145
  Lucy 198
  Mahala 145
  Major 266
  Malinda 5
  Margaret 187
  Martha 60, 135, 207
  Mary 280
  Mary J. 219
  Mary Jane 106, 240
  Mason 21
  Melvina 254
  Morris 188
  Nancy 87, 160, 331
  Oliver 265
  Patsey 30
  Peter 41, 135
  Rebecca 350
  Richard 105
  Sally Ann 36
  Sarah 9
  Susan 258
  Thomas 106, 136
  Thos. 30
  W. B. 137

Evans (cont.)
  William 106, 162
Evins, Susannah 8
Ezel, Jane 368
Ezell, Hartwell F. 290
Ezzell, Caladonai L. 220
F-(?), William 131
Fain, Alfred 51
  Caroline 51
  Delphia 194
  Isabella 138
  Jane 49
  Maria 194
  Sallie 51
Fains, Peter 330
Falconer, (?) (Doctor) 17
  Clary 286
  Hulda 300
  Mary 285
Falkner, Areline E. 57
  Bartholomew 63
  Eliza 270
  Elizabeth 62
  Elizabeth C. 270
  Hardy 172
  Huldy 153
  Jas. 195
  Jno. 135
  Littleton 108
  Lucy Ann 53
  Malinda 262
  Margaret (Mrs.) 18
  Milley 284
  Milly Jane 17
  Noel J. 270
  Rhoda J. 283
  Wm. A. J. 107
Fannett, Nancy 109
Farabough, Aaron 34, 108, 311
  William 150
Farabow, P. A. T. 46, 132, 363
  Susan 108
  William 108
Farbanks, Jerusha E. 199
Farebow, Mary J. 346
Farmer, Catharine 194
  Lodowick 108
Farmer(?), Mary 76
Farmer, Rebeccah 63
  Thomas 63
Farrall, Abel 162
Farrar, Alexander 250
  Anne 111
  Dabney 277
  Frances 156
  G. C. 99
  George 178
  James J. 25, 66
  Jane 167
  Judith 154
  Lucey 308
  Lucy 141, 198
  Martha A. B. G. 141
  Mary 76
  Obediah 366
  Peter 154
  Rebeccah L. 250
  Sarah 246
  Susannah 349
  Tabitha H. 56
  W. H. 249
  William 108, 115
Farror, Lucy 185
Farrow, Frank 281
Faucett, Wm. 221
Faucette, Thomas U. 196

Faucette (cont.)
 Thos. U. 278
Faukner, Nelly 108
Faulkner, Ann 263
 Asa 109
 Champion 300
 Jackey 279
 Nancy 279
 Roxana 23
 Sallie 108
 Sally W. 62, 63
 Thos. 21
 Wm. 108
Fazrier, Jeremiah, Jr. 38
Feald, Filis 236
Ferabow, Uphemia E. 44
Ferebough, Mary 84
Ferguson, Elizabeth A. 288
 Richard 40
Fern, D. R. 310
Ferrar, James J. 232
Ferrell, J. W. 67
 Rachel 347
 S. H. 103
 Will. A. 216
Ferrill, Eliza 109
 Fanny 77
 S. D. 155, 247
 William 109
Field, Martha 330
 Mary 131
Fields, Alonzo 324
 Caroline 318
 Howard 318, 360
 Lina 360
 Panthea 318
 Rosa 360
Figg, Priscilla 124
Filcher, Ann 22
Fillpott, Margaret J. 58
Finch, Barbary 28
 Elbert 106
 Elijah 110
 Eliza 110
 Elizabeth 182
 James 154
 James S. 150, 213, 234, 291
 Jane 90
 Jas. S. 44
 John 110, 261
 John Wesley 367
 Julia E. 256
 Martha 156, 283
 Mary 367
 Mary W. 25
 Nancey 182
 Nancy 16
 Patsey 181
 Patsy 110
 Polley 305
 Rosa 174
 Salley 170
 Sucey 164
 William 110, 176, 283
Findal, John 336
Finley, Thomas 315
Fitts, Fanny(?) 273
 Henry 273
 Letha 242
 Lina 273
 Olivia D. 92
 R. W. 52
Flag, Fannie 252, 292
 Mary Ann 292
 Maria 252

Flag (cont.)
 Samuel 252, 292
Fleeman, Mary 258
Flemin, Mary 111
 William 111
Fleming, Alex 159
 Alice 15
 Andrew 75
 Ann M. 3
 Babby 84
 Celia 212
 Daniel 15
 Delila J. 109
 Elisabeth 279
 Elizabeth 109
 Frances 111
 Hannah 67
 Henrietta E. 44
 J. W. 111
 James 195
 Jane 301
 John 47, 159, 309, 310
 Lishia 111
 Louisa J. 74
 Lucy C. 260
 Mariah F. 80
 Martha 129, 260
 Mary 63
 Polly 229
 Rowan 109
 Sally 50
 Sarah 159
 Sarah F. 101
 Sarah Jane Caster 202
 Susan A. F. 159
 William 125
Flemming, Dolly 323
 John 80
 William 46, 67, 212
Fletcher, Elizabeth 83
 G. W. 36
 Mary 328, 342
 Nancy 357
 Peggy 367
 Sally 2
Flin, Mary 225
 James M. 1
 Margaret 1
 Phoebe Ann 1
Floid, Elizabeth 58
Floy, Amanda A. 212
Floyd, Amey 125
 Ann Eliza 327
 Ann Maria 88
 Catharine 198
 Charles 120
 Delila 164
 Deliley 219
 Elisabeth 98
 Elizabeth 291
 Frankey 208
 Geo. 267
 George 98, 124, 207
 Henderson 171
 Henry 52
 Hickman 113
 John M. 307
 Leah E. 84
 Martha 330
 Martha Ann 68
 Mary 68, 110
 Mary Jane 348
 Nancy 161
 Patsey 340
 Pleasant 219
 Polley 134
 Presly 120

Floyd (cont.)
 Sarah 153, 207
 Susan G. 88
 Susannah 52
 Thomas 113, 340
 William 68, 253
 Wm. 112
 Wm., Jr. 330
Foard, Fanny 2
Foeest, James 98
Fogg, Sarah 26
Ford, David 82
 Goodding 368
 Gooding 368
 James 37
 Martha 86
 Mary F. 43
 Mildred C. 24
 Sarah 37
 Susan 203
Ford(?), Thomas Lena(?) 243
Forker, James 48
 Jas. 184
 Lucy 113
Forkner, Littleton 210
Forlines, Frances 133
Forrest, Anna T. 152
 Ellen J. 259
 William P. 87
Forsith, James 338
Forsyth, James 164, 330
 Maranda 319
 Nancey 339
 Redman 216
 Saml. P. 338
Forsythe, Ferriby 340
 Helen F. 83
 James 343
 John 12, 129
 Nancy 169
 Phebe 216
 Philip 48, 339
 Samuel 131, 151, 191
 Sarah K. 1
 Susan 338
 Thomas 165
 W. P. 200
 William 114, 129
Fortener, Parmelia 317
Fortines, James R. 234
Fortner, Elizabeth 16
Fosset, Rebeca 370
Foster, Lily 114
 Robert 347
Fouler, Mary Ann 4
Fowler, Benjamin 147
 Bethia 240
 Betsey 139
 Betsy 113
 Catharine 90
 Daniel 40, 42, 83, 84
 Danl. 139
 Eady 240
 Edney 211
 Elizabeth 115
 Emily F. 362
 Frances 274
 Henry 288
 Jacky 156
 James 115
 Jane 332
 John 23
 Larceny M. 2
 Lucy 298
 Mahala 83, 247
 Martha 160
 Martha Ann 240

Fowler (cont.)
 Mary Ann 4
 Matilda 274
 Moody 326
 Phebey 240
 Ransom 247
 Sally 247
 Sarah 317
 Thomas 169, 287
 William 70, 95, 185
 Wm. 275
Fowlkes, William T. 285
Fr-(?), Robert 177
Frainer, Shadrick 73
Fraizer, Anne 33
 Ephraim 27, 38, 116, 197
 Faithy 160
 Frances 101
 Franklin 199
 Howel 116
 Isabella 27
 James 100
 Jane 116
 Jeremiah 22
 Judith 345
 Levina 27
 Lucey 77
 Mary Jane 97
 Masten 116
 Nancey 22
 Nancy 42
 Polley 114, 128
 Polly 199
 Robert 117
 Salley 1
 Sally Ann 223
 William 116
Frances, Lucey 293
Franklin, Dolly 219
 Elizabeth 360
 Mary 302
 Peggy 350
Frashier, Sarah 129
Frazar, W. 116
Frazer, Arthur 32, 92
 Elijah R. 342
 Howel 117
 Jeremiah 37
 Ransom 115
 Susannah 37
 Thomas S. 97
Frazier, Barnett 195
 Charity Caroline 95
 Charles F. 116
 Delia Ann 171
 E. R. 117
 Elijah R. 209
 Elisabeth 161
 Ephm 195
 Ephraim 117
 Elizabeth 33
 Harriet 166
 Isabella 351
 James M. 117
 Jane 7
 Lucy 294
 Margaret 158
 Margaret A. 116
 Mary 160
 Mary Ann 78
 Mastin 346
 Michael 346
 Nancey 294
 Nancy 293
 Rachel 336
 Rebecca 166
 Robert H. 160

Frazier (cont.)
 Rowan 129
 Sarah 231
 Shadrach 346
 Thomas B. 27
 William B. 116
Freear, Margaret H. 19
Freeman, Anderson 236
 Betsey 69
 Betsey Ann 323
 Betsy 42
 Calvin 42
 Claborn A. 117
 Dolly 284
 E. E. 213, 229
 Edmund A. 162
 Eliza 59
 Elizabeth 114
 Emily 64
 Evan 155, 336
 Evan E. 117
 Eveline D. 52
 Francis C. 117
 Gideon 274
 Gideon, Jr. 118, 230
 Haley 118
 Hatchwell 118
 Isabella 318
 James A. 117, 118
 James W. 277
 Jane 50
 Jenny 56
 John E. 26, 120, 174
 Lucretia Weldon 117
 Lucy 118
 Lucy Frances 42
 Martha 46
 Mary 44, 259
 Mary E. 125
 Masten 118
 Mastin 230
 Nancey 274
 Nancy 230, 336
 Nancy S. 228
 Nathaniel 47
 Olive(r) 16
 Pheba 16
 Rebecca 336
 Rebeccah 236
 Robert 118, 228
 Rufus C. 120, 342
 Sally G. 142
 Sarah 219, 233
 Sarah K. 299
 Susan 131
 William F. 259, 336
Freezar, A. D. 87
Freman, Lucy 238
Fulford, B. M. 310
Fuller, A. E. 113
 Allsey 6
 Amanda 287, 333
 Anna 223
 Arthur 137, 221
 Benjamin 121
 Betsey 119
 Catherine 140
 Chamsy 124
 Charlotte 57
 Christian 285
 Daniel 119, 243
 Delilah 177
 Elijah 1, 238
 Elisabeth 52
 Elizabeth 137, 215
 Emily 6
 Emily Frances 274
 Ezekiel 306

Fuller (cont.)
 F. T. 152
 Fanny 9, 269
 Feraby 338
 Festus M. 164
 Frances 7, 95
 Francis 307
 George 223
 Gilley 306
 Hampton 222
 Henrey 34
 Henrietta 223
 Henry 112, 119, 153, 214, 338
 Henry A. 120
 Hicksey 26
 Indiana 285
 Isom 118
 J. R. 62, 121, 314, 360, 365
 James 112, 124
 Jane 47
 Jenney 215
 John 145, 163, 317
 Johnathan 4
 Joseph 119, 155
 Judith 66
 Keziah 258
 Leucy 215
 Louisa J. 89
 Louisa P. 89
 Lucy 104, 115
 Mahala 68
 Mahalia 264
 Martha 25
 Mary 15, 16, 132, 243, 263, 364
 Mary Ann 193
 Mary H. 365
 Mary M. 135
 Massay 39
 Mildrid N. 365
 Milley 241
 Mira Frances 237
 Nancy 286
 Polly 16
 Robert 62
 Robt. 63
 Salley 337
 Samantha A. 362
 Saml. 186, 305, 309
 Samuel 113, 120
 Sarah 168, 214, 305
 Selah 118
 Squire 223
 Stephen 52
 Susan 51
 Temperance 222
 Tempey 345
 W. D. 119, 215
 W. W. 341
 Washington 337
 William N. 66, 239
 Wm. 242
 Zacheriah 215, 340
 Zuluka K. 66
Furgerson, Clary 180
 Frances 118
Fussell, Harrison 310
Fynch, Nancy 16
Gains, Elizabeth 103
Gales, Ned 121
Gallohoon, Temperance 135
Gannen, Moses 299
Gannon, Wm. C. 48
Garett, Rowan 13
Garland, Ned 121
Garner, Aily E. 23

Garner (Cont.)
  Ann E. 121
  Beckey 61
  Conrad 191
  Creassey 53
  Eliza 109
  Fanny 4
  Joanna 191
  John 104, 169, 338
  Leacey 262
  Leanna(?) 191
  Louisa 58
  Margarett J. 167
  Maria 288
  Mary 54
  Nancey 338
  Nancy R. 51
  Phanney 104
  Rebeccah 54
  Robert 40, 51, 233
  Robt. 30
Garrat, Isabella 177
Garratt, Lucy 52
Garrett, Edwd. W. 91
  Elisabeth 361
  Emily 363
  George 142
  Henson 287
  Maria 287
  Martha 259
  Martha Jane 47
  Mary 6
  Narcissa 284
  Rowan 13
  Sarah 287
  Seth J. 67
  Stephen 119
  William 367
Garrot, Matthew 233
  William 336
Garrott, Mary T. 212
  Margaret 262
  Sally R. 312
  Sharolet(?) 233
  Stephen 197
  Wm. 90
Garshan(?), William T. 367
Gatch, Benj. W. 121
  Martha R. 121
Gates, Caty 121
  Henry 354
  Henry W. 93
Gaven(?), Moses 179
Gentry, (?) 183
Geoghegan, J. A. 317
George, Helen 176
  Polly 88
German, Peggy 300
Gibbs, A. N. 178
Giffers, T. 54
Gilcreast, James 240
Giles, John 140
  Mary U. P. William 157
Giliam, Mary Ann 305
Gill, Drusilla 206
  Frances 51
  Isaac 271
  James T. 54, 169, 213
  Jas. T. 364
  John N. 3
  Levi 4
  Lutitia 123
  Martha 1
  Nancy M. 86
  Pleasant 123
  Ransom 122

Gill (cont.)
  Richardson 313
  Sally T. 185
  Sarah T. 46
  Susanna 271
  W. M. A. 298
  William A. 161
Gillam, Amey 148
  Charles 73, 91
  Frances 91
  Francis 91
  Harris 123
  John 91
  Joshua 123
  Priscilla 144
  Robert 123
  Winnefred 283
Gillespie, R. O. 207
  Virginia S. 342
Gilliam, Ann 123, 314
  Billy 218
  Dolley 196
  Dolly 102
  Edmund 214
  Eliza G. 365
  Elizabeth 146
  Elizabeth L. 196
  Herbert 345
  Jas. T. 365
  John 102, 142
  L. 1, 76, 77, 126, 144, 159, 186, 217, 230, 235, 268, 335, 367
  Leslie 85, 259, 307
  Lesly 30, 84, 194
  Lucinda 75
  Luncy 301
  Martha 193
  Mary 142
  Mary A. 15
  Myrick 69
  Nancy 181
  Pattey 298
  Rebecca 263
  Robt. B. 99, 215, 226, 292, 308
  Sarah 218
  Thomas S. 305
  William 254, 298
  William H. 82, 310, 350
  Wm. H. 293, 304
Gillian, William H. 243
  Wm. H. 11
Gillis, Daniel T. 90
  Mary 81
  Mary Jane 81
  W. A. 146
Gilmour, John 19
Gilpin, Henry 109
Glamp, Francis 73
Glascock, Zacheriah 348
Glasgow, Elizabeth 214
  Francis 96
  Harriett 96
  James 186
  John 112, 197
  Nancy 98
  Rebecah 178
Glasgow(?), Richard 214
Glasscock, Anderson 352
  Ann 32
  Betsy 351
  E. B. 124
  Elizabeth 124, 352
  Emily 351
  Granderson 338

Glasscock (cont.)
  Jane 95
  Julia 333
  Lucy 352
  Martha A. 102
  Sally 101
  Sandford 124
  Sarah 124
  Sylvania 123
  Thomas 124, 351
  William 333
  William D. 301
  Zachariah 82
  Zacheriah, Jr. 95
  len, Isabella 99
Glenn, Fanny 29
  John S. 13
  Nancy 343
  Pleasant 29
Glimph, George 245
Glover, Caroline 325
  Daniel 125
  Elisabeth P. 244
  Elizabeth P. 144
  Jos. 125
  Mary 258
  Mary A. 61
  Mary D. 279
  Mary J. 47
  Parthena 74
  Phebe M. 133
  Prisy 354
  Susan P. 236
  Wallace 61
Gober, John 125, 272
  Mary 125
  Nancey 125
  William 125
Godden, Sally W. 264
Going, Henry 266
Gold, Elizabeth J. 128
  Margaret A. 352
  Mary A. 24
Goll, William 352
Gomah, Sarrah 125
Gomer, Elisabeth 286
  Mary 109
  William 109
Gooch, A. H. 325
  Betsey 292
  C. 202
  D. T. 127
  Daniel 127, 321
  Daniel J. 325
  Daniel T. 61
  David 65
  Dudley S. 127
  Edward T. 321
  Elisabeth 126
  Elizabeth 127, 191
  Emmett 103, 248
  Emmit 126
  Esther 31
  Frances 126
  Henry A. 311
  J. H. 26, 46, 142, 155, 209, 238, 268, 299, 314, 335
  James 53, 166
  Jane 65
  Jane D. 28
  John 321
  John T. 204
  Jos. H. 177, 204
  Joseph H. 268
  Judith 321
  Lucy 31, 298
  Malinda 129

Gooch (cont.)
　Martha 142, 337
　Martha C. 303
　Mary 92, 191, 321
　Nancy 61, 127, 224, 321
　Nancy P. 51
　Parthenia 284
　Patsy 126
　Polly 127, 147
Goodwin, Polly A. 251
　Prudence 35, 321
　Pumphrett 129
　Rachael 1, 298
　Rachel 171
　Redford, 191, 346
　Rosa 4
　Rowland 126
　Sallie H. 61
　Sarah 127, 129
　Susannah 201, 314
　Thomas 335, 339
　Viney 205
　W. N. 242
　W. T. 3
　William 126, 325
　Willis 142
　Willis L. 218
　Wm. 31
Gooche, Annie S. 288
Good, Lucy 241
Goode(?), Barrott 200
Goodloe, D. R. 350
　Elizabeth 191
　Mary 308
　Robert 45
　Susannah 45
Goodman, Benjamin 277
Goodrum, Jincey 116
　Polly 115
　Thomas 224
Goodson, Barbara 25
Goodwin, Frances 305
　M. J. 302
　Saml. 238
Gordan, Allen 116
Gorden, A. 94
　Alfred 91
　Catharine 323
　Eliza W. 338
　Judith 171
　Mildred 77
　Samuel 32
　Rebecca 171
　William 78, 128
　Willis 289
　Willis L. 21
　Wm. H. 77
Gordon, Allen 298
　Archabald 128
　Archd. 102
　Archibald 356
　Calvin 338
　Elizabeth 248
　Harriet 359
Gordun, Howell 11
　Jane 79
Goss, Babby 39
　Celia 254
　Elisabeth 166
　Elizabeth 224
　Fanny 284
　Jemima 194
　Linly 240
　Lively 129
　Martha 170
　Mary 72, 340
　Mary Thomas 114

Goss (cont.)
　Mary W. 315
　Mima 355
　Nancey 218
　Nancy F. 44
　Rebecca 129
　Rebeccah 247
　Robert 129
　Rowland 339
　Sarah 73, 167
　Sarah Ann 53
　Sherman 223
Goss(?), Thomas 127
Goss, Thomas 129, 167
　William 127
　Wm. 340
　Wm. D. 62
Gould, Geo. L. 133
Grady, James 349
Graham, Joanna 132
　June 148
　Saml. L. 128
Grandy, Edla L. 73
　Louisa 115
　Mariam Hester 355
　Sarah 129
Granger, Lucy 139
　Jane 117
Grave, Catharine 171
Graves, Anne 81
　Bella 362
　Betsey Newberry 108
　David 108
　Dolley 269
　Elisabeth 117
　Lydia 311
　Mary 158
　Mary L. 199
　Nathaniel 269 311
　Pattey 311
　Rebecka 149
　Robert 190
　Sarah 190
　William 73, 311
　Wm. 240
Gravett, Elizabeth 209
　Margaret F. 209
　Wm. 209
Greeman, John 230
Green, Allen 168
　Ann 229
　Anna 130
　Anne 130
　Barbara 311
　Betsey 114
　Catharine 131
　Daniel 332
　Edward B. 213
　Elijah 262
　Elisabeth 131, 291
　Eliza C. 108
　Elizabeth 105
　Frank 130
　Green Berry 195
　Henry 188
　Henry G. 367
　Isabella 5
　Isabella H. 306
　Jacob 131
　James W. 308
　Jane 311
　Jno. B. 54, 159
　Job 130
　John 31, 134
　Julia 225
　Lilia 131
　Lucy 142, 346
　Malinda 44

Green (cont.)
　Martha J. 364
　Mary 185, 274
　Mary Ann 22
　Mary J. 44
　N. T. 217
　Nancey 284
　Nancy 45
　Nicholas 130, 131, 337
　Osborn 131
　Polley 61, 311
　Rachel 207
　Rebecca 129, 366
　Rebecca C. 339
　Rebecha 188
　Rhoda Ann 229
　Robert 30
　Rose 61, 366
　Sarah 12
　Spence 22
　Susan 108, 131
　Susan M. 108
　Thomas 108, 113, 131, 318
　Thornberry 1
　W. 338
　William 66, 277, 311
　Willis 61
　Wm. 96
Greenhill, Samuel 28
Greenway, John E. 78
Greer, G. W. 299
　Nancy 188
Gregg, Mary 227
　Wm. 227
Gregory, Adeline 65
　Eliza Ann 129
　Elizabeth 253
　Frances 18
　Johnson 65
　Lucy 325
　Nancy 49
　Roxanna 216
　Sally M. 320
　Sarah 80
　T. H. 320
　T. J. 320
Grenaway, Betsey 202
　Denis 78
　Dicey 173
　John E. 132
　Susey 173
Gresham, A. A. 78
　Anney 143
　Archabal A. 159
　Daniel 133
　Elizabeth 359
　Elizabeth A. 50
　George 129
　John 133, 143, 164
　Labon 359
　Mary 133
　Richard 297
　Salby 239
　Thomas P. 239
　Wheeler 133
Griffen, Mary 279, 370
Griffin, Elizabeth 361
　Emily F. 249
　Frankey 39
　James 314
　James H. 334
　John R. 25
　Lucey 31
　Luisa 241
　Margaret 107
　Martha M. 343
　Mary Ann 333

391

Griffin (cont.)
  Mary F. 330
  Nancy T. 370
  Petronella C. 69
  Sally 334
  Spencer C. 76
  Susan 366
  Tabby 56
  Thomas N. 268, 357
  Virginia L. 357
  William 313
Grigg, Elisabeth 258, 262
Griggis, Nanncy 56
Griggs, Elizabeth 131
  Jemimah 30
  Nancy 33
  Robert 54
Grinneway, Elizabeth 79
Grisham, Agnes 143
  Anderson 133
  Benj. 246
  Catharine 148
  Daniel 261
  Danl. 152
  Elizabeth 92
  Elizabeth J. 134
  Frances 350
  Frances E. 359
  Frankey 135
  Granville 359
  Hilliard J. 134
  James 134
  Mary M. 134
  Neill S. 106
  Randal A. 62
  Randolph Hilliard 134
  Rhodey 260
  Richard 297
  Sally 133
  Sarah 163
  Stephen 216
  Susanna 195
  Thomas P. 135
  Wheler 134
  William T. 88
  Willie 69, 141, 303
Grissam, Agley(?) 89
  Willie 89
Grissom, A. B. 300
  Electra 67
  Elizabeth J. 42
  Elizer Helen 353
  Ellen 287
  Eppy 229
  Eugene 29, 64, 83, 106, 112, 152, 161, 167, 226, 234, 260, 332
  Hohn H. 285
  Jacobina L. 14
  James D. 367
  John W. 35
  Kevia Ann 43
  Lewis T. 135
  Louisiana 367
  Mary E. 50
  Mary F. 16
  Patsey 367
  Permelia A. 302
  Sally 85
  Susan 135
  Thomas 134, 135
  Timinina 316
  Virginia C. 119
  Willie 203
Grissum, Richd. 144
Guarner, Elizabeth A. 58

Guest, Sarah 39
Gum, John 159
Gunn, Addison W. 33
Gunn(?), Mary W. 352
Gunn, William P. 292
Gunns, Geo. W. 353
Gupton, C. 140
  Stephen 96
Guy, (?) 144
  Avarilla 265
  Delila 59
  Delilah 145
  Enicey 43
  James 360
  Lucy P. 49
  Mins 59, 136
  Nicey 77
  Polly 136
  Sallie 221
  Sally 83
  Talitha 302
  Thomas T. 136
Guye, Mary 302
Gwin, John 203, 302
  John 302
  Mary 146
H-(?), John 112
Hack, Nancey 129
Hackinyear, Polly 228
Hadspeth, Sarah 357
Hagin, Eliza 229
Hagues, Patsey 20
Hailey, Elizabeth 198
  Henry 6, 189, 353
  John 137
  Laura W. 256
  Prudence 189
  William 317
Hailley(?), Henderson 170
Hailly, Richard 198
Hailstock, Susan 79
Haily, Polly 330
Hair, Sally 170
Haithcock, Eaton 245
  Sarah 315
Haladay, Lucy 1
Haley, Anne 40
  Catharine 137
  Elisabeth 317
  Eliza 347
  Elizabeth 204
  John 23, 49, 317
  Mariah 139
  Nancy 54
  Peggie 102
  Polley 54
  Sally 49
  Susan 53
  Wm. H. 53
Hall, A. P. 271
  Catharine 281
  Fruitrel 134
  Futrall 76
  Henry 137
  Jehu 27
  Joseph 137
  Joseph Cash 137
  Rebecca 137
  Susannah 121
Ham, Lucy 140
Hambett, Addie 41
  Alexander 318
  Anthoney, Sr. 138
  Deana 208
  Euphemia A. 215
  Isabella A. 19
  James 138

Hamilton (cont.)
  Jas. 133
  John 45
  Joseph 173
  Mary E. 317
  Robert 278
  Sarah 138
  Souless 99
  Temperance 138
Hamlet, Elizabeth P. 168
  Lucy 226
  Mary C. 226
  William J. 226
Hamlett, Lucy A. 159
Hamme, Harriet 318
  Sarah A. 334
Hammie, Joe 318
  Pollie 318
Hammond, Frederick 96
Hampton, Elizabeth 334
  Ephraim 17
  J. H. 248
  Kizziah 100
  Mary 64, 350
  Nancy 217
  Noland 182
  Rebecca Ann 350
  Sarah 248
  Wilburn L. 138
Hamson, Elizabeth G. 164
Hancock, B. F. 92
  Ben. 306
  Benja. F. 347
  Benone 139
  Elisabeth 169
Hancock(?), J. W. 41
Hancock, Sally Ann 353
Handock(?), Jorge 298
Hanes, Nancy 89
  Wm. 176
Hanks, A. H. 242, 322
  Elijah 139
  John D. 139
  Mary 155
  Milley 272
  Sarah 231
  Susannah 267
  William 139
Hanns(?), James 350
Hanon, W. D. 36
Hanton, John 172
Harbauk, Rebecca 161
Hard, Edward D. 72
Hardaway, Frances M. 282
Harden, Phereba 41
  Priscilla 88
  Rachel 230
  Thornton 299
Harding, Lydda 76
  Molley 76
  Nancy 60
  Rhodey 40, 350
  Salley 235
Hardwick, Nancy 251
Hardy, Ben. 41
  Mary 165
Hare, Agnes B. 177
  John 156, 212
  Martha 160
  William B. 129
Harget, John J. 66
Hargraves, Frances 139
  Million 139
  Polley 34
  Richard 139
Hargrove, Amey 140
  Amy 140

Hargrove (cont.)
  Burwell 140
  C. M. 201, 311
  E. M. 100
  G. 140
  Gilliam 285
  Hester Ann 306
  Israel 140, 155, 283
  J. W. 281
  James 106
  Jno. 220
  John 111, 134, 139,
    296, 305, 313
  John S. 49
  Kizziah 140
  Lucy 49
  Mary Jane 283
  Nancey 42
  Nancy J. 139
  Polley 139
  Rebecca 140
  Richard 296
  Robert 3, 51, 236,
    242 258
  Susan C. 49
  T. L. 25, 139, 191,
    199, 236, 335, 351,
    368
  William R. 85
  William T. 49
  Wm. 91, 283
  Wm. T. 356
Hargroves, Ellendar 111
  Richard 24
Haris, Robert 35
Harkney, Nancy 95
Harp, Jemima 226
  John 16, 140, 150
  Lizzie 226
  Mary Ann 314
  Matilda 286
  Molley 16
  Mourning 150
  Osborn 226
  Polley 184
  Samson 140, 184, 232
  Sibba 232
  Tabitha 137
  Thomas 324
  William 140, 148,
    232
  Wm. 286
Harper, Cathrine 260
  Dianna M. 260
  Elisabeth 178
  Frances 304
  Jesse 178
  Joseph 41
  Lottey 165
  Mary Goodloe 309
Harperding(?), Emily
  317
Harral(?), William 17
Harrington, F. 256
  S. H. 66
Harris, (?) 77
  A. C. 29, 154, 197
  Abram 143
  Absalom 147, 294
  Agness 286
  Alex 26, 144
  Allen 142
  Amanda M. 146, 148
  Amy 303
  Ann 146, 172, 191
  Ann Eliza 60
  Ann J. 328
  Anne 245, 332

Harris (cont.)
Harris(?), Arnold 34
Harris, Arrene 80
  Augustine 37
  Barbary 141
  Bed 144
  Benj. 321
  Benj. F. 365
  Benjamin 188
  Betsey 347
  Betsy 303
  Bettie 130
  Beverly 1, 117, 118
  Bitsey 66
  C. 285
  Charity 137
Harris(?), Chas. 227
Harris, Claborn 39
  Cornelia A. 200
  Daniel 196
  Darvin 221
  David 226
  Deritha 170
  E. W. 106, 251
  Edward 191
  Eliza 189, 193
  Eliza G. 43
  Elizabeth 161, 201,
    236, 280, 343
  Elizabeth G. 365
  Ellen 294
  Emily 226
  Emily Ann 106
  Emily S. 26
  Emma L. 292
  Fanny 96, 143, 214
  Fanny H. 97
  Fielden 13
  Frances 104, 180
  G. 350
  G. T. 145
  George 119
  George W. 365
  Gideon 147
  Hannah 131, 253
  Hardy 93
  Harriet 170
  Harriett F. 147
  Harriot 158
  Henrietta 351
  Henry 130, 146, 212
  Isabella 280
  Isah 146
  Isaiah 11
  Isham 217
  Ivey 148
  J. 77, 169, 189
  James 11, 148, 303
  James C. 202
  Jane 172
  Jemima 123, 299
  Jno. L. 53
  John 5, 13, 69, 89,
    105, 233, 308
  John F. 244
  Jonathan 16, 267
  Jorden 280
  Joseph 141
  Josiah 11
  Julia 35
  Julia Ann 43, 66
  June 281
Harris(?), Kiza 289
Harris, Lemender 142,
  270
  Letha 3, 26
  Lethe 60
  Lucinda 167

Harris (cont.)
  Lucy 130, 189, 242,
    255, 366
  Lucy A. G. 148
  Lucy V. 263
  Martha 1, 106, 271
  Marthey 16
  Mary 1, 14, 21, 255,
    256, 258, 275
  Mary A. 332
  Mary Ann 221
  Mary E. 90
  Mary E. J. 83
  Mary G. 148
  Matilda 130
  Milchisa 208
  Mima 146
  Minerva 145
  Mourning 142
  Nancey 119, 157, 286
  Nancy 20, 22, 60, 96,
    205, 300, 315
  Nancy G. 223
  Nansey 370
  Nathan 91, 219, 361
  Norwood 151
  O. 142
  Osborn 141
  Oxford 189
  Pattie W. 368
  Penny 131
  Phebe 144
  Piety 57, 255
  Polley 136, 254
  Polly 115, 163
  Prudence 294
  R. L. 262
  Ransom 179
  Rebecca 41
  Richard 146
  Richd. W. 147
  Riney 147
  Ro. 275
  Robert 53, 370
  Robert, Sr. 68
  Robt. 1, 264
  S. 26, 104, 146, 166,
    280, 318
  Salley 151, 206
  Sallie 256
  Sally 1, 19, 164, 168,
    181, 223
  Sally Boyce 215
  Sally W. 41, 126
  Saml. 56, 188, 255
  Samuel 4, 168
  Sanders 145
  Sarah 151, 264, 287
  Sarah A. E. 364
  Selina 366
  Selina T. 163
  Seney 72
  Sherwood 17, 72, 201,
    219, 342
  Sim 256
  Spears, 198
  Stephen 5, 140
  Sterling 145
  Susan 141
  Temperance 37
  Thomas 131, 142, 228,
    294
  Thomson 174, 255
  Thos. 146, 147, 264
  Tiery 146
  Tildy 146
  Tyre 145
  Tyre, Jr. 22

Harris (cont.)
  W. H. 7
  William 90, 286
  William H. 106
  Willie 214
Harrison, Betsey 14
  Eliner 88
  Elizabeth 139
  Elleanor 175
  G. W. 56
  George 256
  H-(?) 198
  Isham 82, 144
  Jane 92
  Lotty 140
  Lucy A. D. 197
  Margaret 13
  Martha 163, 234
  Mary 232, 289
  Mildred R. 290
  Orpha 198
  Polley 252
  Rebecca 164
Harriss, Asa P. 26
  Betty A. 353
  Charsly 228
  Henry 149
  Martha A. 149
  Nancey 228
  Solomon 286
  Tempy 254
  William H. 353
Harrisson, Elisabeth 82
  Martha 70
Hart, Amy P. 294
  Ann 291
  Elisabeth 73, 130
  Eliza 20
  James, Jr. 77, 150, 160
  Jane 209, 210
  John 333
  Joseph 48, 209, 250, 265
  Lidia 33
  Lizza 150
  M. S. 149, 199, 206
  Martha A. 168, 185
  Mary 19, 266, 290, 320
  Mary A. 18
  Mary K. 185
  Nancy 160, 260
  Osborn 150
  Pleasant 176
  Polley 331
  Priscilla 123
  Rebecca Ann E. 106
  Rebecca G. 300
  Rebekah 199
  Relly Ann 304
  Robert D. 185
  Salley 116, 209
  Sally 33
  Sarah 149
  Selina 32
  W. H. 359
Harte, Joseph 19
  Rosa 354
Harter, Mary 365
Hartgrove, Nancey 68
Haskins, (?) 347
  Aaron 45, 233, 234
  Allen 150, 187
  Aron 312, 344
  Creed 192
  Eliza 291
  Elizabeth 100, 183

Haskins (cont.)
  Elizabeth C. 225
  Geo. 335, 356
  George 150, 183
  Henry 180
  Isaac 234
  James 267
  Jno. R. 244
  John 34, 272
  Lettie 114
  Martha J. 233
  Mollie 114
  Nancy 180
  Rachel 131
  Susan 44
  Thomas 76
Haswell, Barbary 303
  Edward 151
  Eliza Jane 215
  Frances 6
  Hawkins 66
  Helen 164
  Jane 151
  Jno. R. 150
  Julia A. 178
  Martha A. 151
  Mary 66
  Mary Ann 280
  Mary T. 300
  Nancy 151
  Nathan 151
  Penny 93
  Reddin 93
Hathcock, Kintchin 40
Haven(?), Latha 81
Haweley, Henderson 79
Hawkins, Ann 188
  Benjamin 83, 351
  Betsey 147
  Edward 13
  Elizabeth 214
  Emily 246
  Fanny 45
  Glathy Ann 223
  James 45
  Jno. 131, 324
  Jno. Henry 189
  John 1, 45, 69, 142, 147, 186, 192, 253
  Lucy Ann 67
  Mary 45
  Minerva 330
  Pheby 132
  Sallie 151
  Sarah 116, 126
  William 151
Hawley, Betsey 193
  Elizabeth 86
  Julia Ann 223
  Laney 331
  Liley 230
  Mary Ann 280
  Nancy 229
  Pearson 59
  Sally 265
  Samuel 151
Hayes, Adeline 283
  Alvan 337
  Benjamin 217
  Catharine 196
  Elizabeth 95, 100, 280, 291
  Emily 166
  Fama 67
  Fern 105
  Frances 43
  Frances A. 197
  Happy 300

Hayes (cont.)
  Hardy 98
  Henry 152
  Hugh S. 314
  Isabella R. 120
  James 95, 152, 298
  Jesse 108, 141
  John 112
  John W. 118
  Joshua 209
  Len. 137
  Lethe 26
  Louisa F. 330
  Lucy S. 307
  Margaret 133
  Martha 198, 337
  Martha Ann 310
  Mary Ann 310
  Mildred 166
  Milly 337
  Minta 208
  Myram 217
  Nancey 289
  Nancy 298
  Peyton 328
  Piety 152
  S. G. 47
  Sally 212
  Samuel L. 89
  Sarah C. 89
  Selea 112
  Simeon 252
  Simon 236
  Tabitha 109
  Thos. D. 211
  Thos. S. 10, 139, 200
  Winney P. H. 110
  Winniford 355
  Wm. S. 109
Haylander, Catharine 63
Hayley, Nancy 124
Hayne, Elisabeth 333
  Jane 332
Haynes, Anne 365
  Elizabeth 110
  John 140
Hays, Amy 145
  Barshaba 268
  Benj. 41
  Betsy 154
  Caroline V. 250
  Cynthia Ann 258
  D. A. H. 263
  Delilah 108
  Eliza 138
  Ezeliel 152
  George 250
  James 252
  Jessey 154
  John W. 92
  Junius 314
  Levizah 26
  Lucey 88
  Marenah 154
  Mariah 118
  Mary 179
  Mary A. C. 140
  Molley 41
  Octavia 118
  Patsey 154
  Peter 154
  Sally 310
  Sarah 46
  Susan A. 300
  Susannah 178
  T. P. 118
  Tempey 108
Hayten, George T. 319

Haywood, Abigail 293
  Mary A. 299
Hazwell, Pully 5
Hazzard, Jane 200
Head, Sarah 246
Headspeth, Amelia F. 106
  Bytha 230
  Jesse 30, 104, 218
  John 363
  Moses 30, 316
  Wm. 349
Heap, Sarah 110
Heardin, Joanna 280
Heavlin, R. A. 24
Hedgepeth, Sarah 172
Hedgespeth, Indianna 47
  James 47
  Patsy 47
Hedgpeth, Sallie 9
Hedspeth, Elizabeth 110
  Mary Ann 88
  Polley 116
Heffernon, William 155
Hefflen, John 189
  James 120
Hefil(?), Hesekiah 112
Heflen, Cary 103
  Polley 219
Heflin, (?) 233
  Arey 306
  Cary 347
  Charles 155
  Chs. 15
  Ellenor 189
  Fanny 335
  Harriet 155
  James 16, 111, 159, 185
  Jas. 51, 304
  John 155
  Lewis 155, 185, 229
  Lucy Ann 292
  Martha 111
  Martha A. C. 111
  Mary 222
  Miranda 315
  Nancy 119
  Nancy W. 76
  Phebe 56
  R. L. 127
  Susanna 155
  William 66, 222
  Wm. D. 155
Hege(?), Fanny 362
Heggie, Jas. M. 97, 273
  Jas. W. 115, 125
  Jos. M. 175
  Mary 64, 176
  Parthenia H. 125
Heggs, A. H. 148
  Debby 251
  Jane 251
  Levi 198
  Martha 259
  Meremon 251
Hellier, Margaret 173
Hencook, Mary 100
Henderson, A. 296
  A. E. 48
  Ann 212, 354
  Archibald E. 226, 315
  Betsey 26
  Effie H. 296
  Elisabeth 297
  Elizabeth 23
  F. A. 307
  Fanney 216

Henderson (cont.)
  Fanny M. 320
  John 355
  Kate B. 296
  L. 188, 260
  Leonard 7, 96, 252, 267, 328
  Louis 296
  Lucy F. 228, 307
  M. N. 260
  Mark M. 15, 63, 307
  Ovil 277
  Peter 74
  Phebe 74
  Pleasant 233
  Priscilla 74
  Richard 31
  Richd. 303
  Sallie S. 46
  Saml. 156, 297, 354
  Samuel, Jr. 281
  Susannah 297
  Thomas 289
  William F. 290
Hendisy, Patsey 113
Hendley, Arena 168
  Henry 55, 204
  Jean 204
  Mary 119
  Mary A. 119
  Nansey 207
  Patsey 205
  Sarah 38
  Susan 15
Hendly, Elizabeth 361
  Henry 35, 119
Hendrick, Mary 290
  Rufus 53
  Sarah 362
  William 362
Hening, Fanney 41
  Lewis 243
Henley, Burwell 145
  Elizabeth 354
Henley, Lavenia 271
  Thos. 3
Henlig, William 65
Henning, Eliza F. 64
  Jane 113
Henry, Virginia 22
Henson, Elisabeth 138
  John 136
Herkins, Polley 311
Herndon, Agnes 201, 368
  Charles 220
  Charles Anna 220
  Cynthia R. 89
  D. C. 40, 217
  D. O. 69
  Eliza 220
  Elizabeth 175
  H. C. 121, 177, 309
  Henry C. 108, 259
  James 368
  Jno. R. 47, 121, 165
  M. C. 233
  Matilda 126
  R. 144
  R. N. 23, 98, 216, 360
  Rhodes N. 8, 31, 67, 183
  Rholles N. 42
  Sallie S. 98
  Zachr. 92
Herris, Darvin 353
  Elizabeth 210
Hesketh, Elias 47

Hester, Affey 94
  Agness 47
  Ann 314
  Ann Eliza 247
  Ann Jane 342
  Appha 176
  Aramanta P. 131
  B. L. 212
  Benjamin 112, 158
  Benjamin B. 203
  Betsey A. 228
  Bettie J. 149
  Billy 243
  Caroline 175, 243
  Chapman 173
  Chisem 175
  Daniel 28, 68
  Delia 162
  E. 335
  Elijah 1
  Elijah J. 158
  Elisabeth 21, 30, 62, 236
  Elizabeth 78, 135, 158, 195, 200
  Elizabeth Ann 213
  Elizabeth J. 117
  F. B. 49, 69, 148
  F. J. 97
  Faithey 248
  Fanney 73
  Frances 117, 252, 297
  Frances B. 31
  Frances L. 111
  Francis 158, 160, 313
  Frankey 335
  Garland 153, 236
  Graves 130
  Green 160
  H. G. 197
  H. J. 160, 309
  Hamilton 77
  Harriett 99, 361
  Harville 248
  Hinton G. 347
  Indiana 162
  Isaac 102
  Isaac P. 217, 337
  J. C. 50, 168
  J. G. 111
  J. H. W. 277
  J. P. 16, 46, 72, 161, 199
  James 57, 78, 157, 200, 328
  Jamima 127
  Jane 81, 199
  Jemima 279
  John 17, 77, 248
  John C. 90, 166
  John G. 117
  John H. 354
  Joseph 161, 206
  Judah 160
  Katharine A. 117
  Laura 160
  Lawrence 160
  Lethe 33
  Lethe Ann 77
  Lizy 160
  Lucy 133, 351
  Maranda R. 348
  Martha 38, 102, 178, 360
  Mary 62, 102, 158, 159, 276
  Mary A. 160, 221
  Mary Ann 166

Hester (cont.)
  Mary C. 200
  Mary E. 3, 32
  Mary T. 35
  Martha 328
  Milley 153, 355
  Nancey 335
  Nancy 78, 126, 129, 149, 258
  Oney 250
  Pathenia R. 158
  Patsey 155
  Pattie 111
  Polley 130
  Polly 128, 153, 157
  Polly Diah 366
  R. B. 117
  Rebecca 63
  Rebeccah 359
  Retis(?) 175
  Ritter 328
  Robert 33, 47, 150, 157, 158, 160, 199, 262
  Rowan 241
  Sallie 176
  Sallie P. 223
  Sarah 33, 177, 181, 262, 284
  Sarah A. 166
  Sarah Jane 209
  Sophia Jane 165, 248
  Stellarah 63
  Stephen 128, 158
  Susan 87
  Susan A. 161
  Susannah 350
  T. K. 4
  Tempy 243
  Tho. T. 73
  Thomas 32, 149, 158, 150, 236
  Thomas B. 295
  Thos. 275
  Thos. T. 145
  Warren 267, 268
Hester(?), William 41
Hester, William 97, 129, 153, 157, 158, 159, 227, 284, 365
  William F. 102
  Zacheriah 351
Heveler, Sarah 362
Hewit, Polly 137
Hibb, Wm. H. 237
Hickman, Wiatt 161
Hicks, Abigail 366
  Abner 97
  Absalom 133
  Agness 253
  Amanda J. 121
  Amelia 67
  Angelina 269
  Ann Eliza 175
  Ann R. 258
  Ann W. 101
  Anne 222
  Bella 67
  Benj. B. 351
  Benjamin W. 341
  Bettey 330
  Bettie 26, 202
  Bishop 307
  Caroline 50
  Caroline M. 301
  Cary Ann 113
  Cassanda 104
  Catharine 70

Hicks (cont.)
  Cherry 113
  Christiana 237
  E. H. 39
  Elizabeth 172, 257
  Elizabeth T. 182
  Ella 190
  Ellen H. 370
  G. N. 34, 135
  Harris 25
  Jas. F. 6
  Jenny 318
  Jno. 144
  John 190
  John B. 71
  John W. 203
  Jos. T. 15
  Kindness 313
  Kittie 281
  Kitty 175
  Leonidas F. 221
  Lettica 259
  Lucretia R. 201
  Lucy 249
  Margaret 68
  Maria 145
  Maria G. 6
  Martha 107, 317
  Martha C. 211
  Martha J. 85
  Mary 87, 162, 253, 263, 305
  Mary Ann Fletcher 312
  Mary E. 285
  Merrear 281
  Millie 305
  Molly 78
  Nash 10, 153
  Nelson N. 163
  Pattie Ann 157
  Priscilla 95
  Rebecca W. 119
  Richard 70
  Robert 24, 228
  Robert A. 361
  Salley 123
  Sallie C. 228
  Sallie R. 128
  Sally 340
  Samuel S. 162
  Sarah Ann 209
  Sarah D. 270
  Steaven 137, 162
  Susan Ann 210
  Susan T. 121
  Susanna 353
  T. W. 54, 197
  Thomas 162, 184, 300
  Thomas C. 121
  Thomas J. 344
  Thos. J. 283, 313
  Thos. W. 110
  Will. 336
  William 161, 298, 317
  Willis 70
  Wm. 180
  Wm. D. 101
  Wm. R. 110
Hide, Dianna 155
  Nancey 308
Hiefield, Precilla 164
Hifield, Priscilla 164
Higgs, A. 61
  A. H. 71
  Allen 63
  Elisabeth 186
  Elizabeth 348

Higgs (cont.)
  George 19
  Jacksy L. 29
  John 186
  Jonathan 260
  Judith W. 218
  Leonard 308
  Levi 163, 164, 289, 348
  Louthern 323
  Martha 287
  Mary 186, 323
  Mary D. 219
  Mary W. 254
  Melvina 39
  Minty W. 324
  Nancey 147
  Oliver 217
  Rebecca 83
  Sarah 39
  Sothoron 178
  Zachariah 112
High, Alsey 180
Highfield, Anne 26
  Margaret 158
  Nelley 165
  Sucky 146, 256
Highfill, Hezekiah 112, 113
Hight, Caty 249
  Charnell 110
  H. H. 312
  Lively 28
  Lucy M. 93
  Mary W. 363
  Polly 67
  Priscilla 313
  Richard 164
  Sarah E. 74
  Thos. D. 164
  Wm. J. 363
  Wm. M. 161
Hightour, Fanny 269
Hill, Betsey 64
  Charles A. 122
  Eliza 8
  Green 69
  J. J. 165
  John 165, 276
  Maggie 274
  Mary 274, 276, 343
  Nancy 69, 340
  Pattey 134
  W. W. 274
Hilliard, Benjamin 329
  D. B. 8
  Jeremy 165
Hillman, Saml. 246, 299
  Samuel 307
Hillyard, Benja. 206
  Harriet W. 259
  Martha M. P. 342
Hilyard, Sally W. 259
Hines, Benjamin 319
  Melethan 9
  Nancey 20
  Polley 21
  Thomas 205
  Thos. 165
  Zachariah 217
Hinneberry, P. 197
Hinton, Elizabeth A. 206
  Isabella U. 226
  Martha 222
  Spence 78
  William 140
Hite, Bedford 11
  Edward 249

Hite (cont.)
  Louisa 128
  Mary A. F. 234
  Ryley H. 188
Hithel, Sarah 240
Hix, Sarah 24
Hoard, Broady 175
  Susan 296
Hobgood, Alfred 107
  Ann E. 78
  Anna 219
  Caroline V. 175
  D. G. 341
  Elizabeth 327
  Elizabeth D. 224
  Emily C. 248
  Fowler 217, 357
  George W. 166
  Henry 78
  Hezekiah 88, 166
  J. D. 28
  James 172
  James L. 51
  James S. 100, 149
  Jane 219
  Jemima 188
  John R. 239
  Joseph 72, 189
  Joseph D. 219
  Jos. D. 202
  Jos. F. 175
  Joseph D. 31
  Lemuel 166, 224, 231,
    327, 355
  Logan 167
  Louisa 3
  Lucy Ann 77
  Lucy H. 78
  Mary Jane 116, 224
  Massey 227
  Nancy 236
  Perthena 166
  Polly 223
  R. H. 264
  Rebecca 199
  Robt. H. 78, 117
  Rowland 166
  Sally 78
  Sarah 14, 88
  Shelton 100, 194
  Thomas 165
  Virginia 157
  William 143
  William P. 352
Hobkins, Polly 147
Hobson, John 12
Hockaday, Elizabeth R.
  A. 287
  J. M. 262
  Nancy 320
Hockady, Judith 110
Hockerday, Sally 182
Hodge, Fannie 167
  Milly 191
  W. H. 177
  Wm. H. 167
Hodges, Winfred K. 112
  Wm. T. 268
Hogg, Samuel 81, 324
Holcomb, Priscilla 92
Holden, Betsy A. 26
  Lewis 167
  Silvia 167
  Thos. A. 296
Holder, Isaiah 311
Holeby, Mary 47, 149
Holeman, H. F. 165
Holloway, Anderson 213

Holloway (cont.)
  Caroline 287
  E. A. 352
  George W. 41
  Green 251, 287
  Jane 251
  John 269
  Philis 251, 287
  Sarah E. 202
  Wm. B. 181
  Wm. S. 277
Holmes, Bettie 57
  Cindarilla 363
  Jane 271
  Mary 181
  Milley 180
  Nancy 168
  Richd. 222
  Sarah E. 36
  William 68, 168
Holms, Catharine S. 357
Holoway, Charles 335
  Jane 335
  Rebecca 335
Holsten, Elizabeth 227
Holt, Anne 322
  Elisabeth 25
  James 168, 322
  John 205, 258
  Lucy An 205
  Saml. L. 267
Homer, Mary 48
Homes, Elizabeth 181
  Mary 338
  Virginia H. 13
Hood, Elizabeth 282
Hoofman, Betsey 40
  Christian 23
  Cressey 55
  Jacob 347
  Phillipina 55
  Susannah 40
Hook, Patience 243
Hooker, Elizabeth 177
  Fanny 123
  John 17
  Keronhappuck 17
  Massey 118
  Nancy 120
  Rutha 117
  Ruthy 17
  Sarah 117
Hookram(?), Elizabeth
  266
Hoover(?), Christopher
  50
Hope, Elizabeth 279
  M. N. 320
Hopgood, Edie 321
Hopkins, Agnis 257
  Ann 364
  Cannon 169
  Charity 83
  George 354, 364
  Jane 205
  Mary A. 340
  Rachel 231
Horn, William 284
Horne, Lucy 217
Horner, Bettie 39
  Billy 169
  Eliza 288
  Elizabeth 277
  Evelina 162
  Indiana 75
  J. H. 233
  Jeff 288
  Lucy P. 217

Horner (cont.)
  Rily 75
  Samuel 169
  T. J. 268
  Thos. J. 112
Hornsby, Engelina Mary
  203
Horton, Betsey 103
  C. H. 273
  Elizabeth 217
  John 284
Hosbrey(?), John W. 13
Hostein, Catherine 170
Hotsteen, Katharine 197
Houler, John B. 86
Hour, Sary 9
House, Dudley P. T. 315
  Eliza 9
  Elizabeth 166
  Henry 166, 248
  James 78
  Macon 225
  Margaret 196
House(?), Martha 135
House, Martha 55
  Mary 171
  Priscella 225
  Rena 225
House(?), Robert 285
House, Thomas 126
  Thos. 170
  Winea J. T. 253
Houze, Isaac 128
  Mary 10
Howard, Allen 171, 220,
    251, 357
  Amanda 224
  Ann Eliza 205
  Anna 300
  Armelia 7
  B. D. 88, 328
  Barnard 171
  Betsey 211
  Betty 13
  Brodie 72, 184, 344
  Caroline 83
  Elisabeth 12, 206
  Ellen 250
  Elizabeth 302
  Fannie 143
  Frances 72
  Groves 206
  Isabella 157
  J. 297
  J. C. 87, 286
  James 171
  James A. 171
  Joh. C. R. 127
  John T. 171
  Joseph 253
  Julian J. 253
  Leah 3
  Lucey 175
  Lucinda A. 277
  Lucy 21
  Margaret 344
  Mark 198
  Martha 217
  Mary 72
  Massaniah 317
  Nancy 184, 335
  Patsy 325
  Phebe 171
  Phoebe 333
  Pidy 171
  Polley 183
  Priscilla 50
  Rebecca 13

Howard (cont.)
  Sarah 176
  Susanna 170
  Thomas 170
Howe, Joseph 30
  L. H. 107
Howel, Alexander 71
  James 129
  John 128
  Mary 356
  Merina 329
  Nancy 256
  Nancy G. 305
Howell, Alex 172
  Alexr. 107, 327
  Benja. 134
  Betsy Ann 172
  Elijah 79
  Eliza 112
  Elizabeth 128
  Fortune 39
  Isabella 60
  Indiana 193
  John 223
  Kesiah 138
  Linda 9
  Margaret 262, 333
  Martha 71, 157
  Mary 333
  Mary Ann 149
  Polly Ann 79
  Wm. 172
Howen, Tho. W. 180
Howze, Abbey 93
  Jas. A. 216
Hoyle(?), Frances N. 107
Huccabey, Susanna 21
Huchins, Permelia 351
Huckabay, William 135
Huckebey, Polley 348
Huckeby, Sally 57
Huddleston, Delilah 328
  Direna 222
  Eaks 328
  Ezekiel 173
  Frances 279
  Henry P. 236
  Jesse 173
  Jessee 157
  John 23
  L. 329
  Leticia 335
  Rosa 298
Huddleton, Elizabeth 38
  Ezekiel 56
Hudgings, Elizabeth F. 32
  Rebecca 262
Hudkey, Eliza 274
Hudleston, Lambert 149
Hudpeth, Sarah 228
Hudson, Agnes P. 176
  C. 85
  Caleb A. 128
  Cephas 110, 221
  Cephus 108, 346
  Creed 199
  Eleanor 136
  Elizabeth 178
  Frances 149
  John 235
  Mary 199
  Nancy F. 239
  Paschall 94
  Susan Ann 235
Hudspeath, Sary 185
Hudspeth, Lucy 115
  Richard 323

Hudspeth (cont.)
  Richd. 56
Huey, L. 45
Huffman, Susanna 245
Huggins, John C. 179
Hughes, Branch 274
  Elizabeth 76
  Louise 174
  Melissa 289
  Samuel M. 174
  Will. B. 249
  Will. R. 154
Hughs, Ann Eliza 103
  Elizabeth 358
  Lucinda 169
Hull, Anne W. 327
Humphries, Adonirim 174
Humphris, B. E. 2
Humsted, Richd. 203
Hunger, James P. 103
Hunt(?), A. H. 241
Hunt, Adelia 194
  Alexander A. 323
  Amanda F. 23
  Amy J. 122
  Anderson 103, 176
  Ann 94, 99, 176, 202
  Ann Eliza 365
  Ann T. 275
  Anna 60
  Anne 7
  Anney 222
  Betsey 107
  C. M. B. 281
  Caroline 273
  D. A. 241
  David 157, 180
  David A. 121, 203
  E. M. 66
  Edmund 130, 176
  Edward 73, 210
  Edward, Jr. 27
  Elisha 281
  Eliza 59, 70
  Elizabeth 208, 235
  Elizabeth P. 150
  Elizabeth T. 328
  Emma J. 252
  Frances 38, 158, 177
  Frankey 176
  Franky 202
  G. W. 17, 131
  Genny 276
  George 175, 186
  George W. 22, 77, 176, 252
Hunt(?), Hamilton 171
Hunt, Hannah 73, 250
  Harriet 59
  Henry 290
  Indiana 114, 234
  Isabella 102, 116
  J. J. 363
  J. T. 168
  James 107, 108, 171, 176, 208, 332, 339
  James P. 124
  James T. 72, 283
  Jane 170
  Jas. P. 120
  Jas. T. 156
  Jas. Y. 98
  Jemima 137
  Jno. W. 142
  John 28, 250
  John, Jr. 281
  John T. 45, 221
  John W. 174, 247

Hunt (cont.)
  Jos. 308
  Jos. P. 42
  Joseph 70
  Joseph P. 37
  Judah 180
  June 35
  Letha 250
  Liddey 160
  Lucinda 311, 332
  Lucinda H. 313
  Lucy E. (Mrs.) 171
  Lucy P. 136
  M. 48
  Margaret M. 330
  Maria 70
  Martha 37, 227
  Martha E. 66
  Mary 8, 11, 12, 68, 116, 308, 326, 332, 363
  Mary A. 166
  Mary A. E. 276
  Mary Ann 156, 241, 281
  Mary E. 60
  Memican 328
  Michael 175, 177, 195, 202, 275, 279
  Mildred A. 217
  Millie 208
  Morning 364
  Mourning 163
  Nancey 195
  Nancy 129, 211
  Nath. 34
  Nelley 179
  Peter 44, 368
  Polley 49
  Polly A. 29
  R. A. 259
  R. B. 235
  R. H. 180
  R. L. 175
  R. S. 56
  Rebecah 172
  Rebecca 102
  Richard B. 7
  Richard H. 125, 193
  Robt. L. 222
  Robt. S. 118
  Salley 302
  Sallie F. 74
  Sally 312, 315
  Saml. 208
  Samuel 173, 175, 179, 223, 329, 338
  Samuel, Jr. 102, 157
  Samuel A. 116
  Sarah 110, 211
  Sarah G. 281, 349
  Solomon 91, 295, 296
  Sophia 295
  Sophia J. 165
  Sophronia 78
  Stephen 175
  Susan C. 37, 252
  Susannah B. 7
  Thomas 74, 128, 141, 175, 275, 276, 330
  Thos. 129, 241
  W. B. 341
  W. T. 133
  Weldon E. 14
  William 102, 197
  William H. 153
  William J. 164
  Wm. 302, 349

Hunt (cont.)
  Wm. J. 288
Hunter, Corinna 286
  Elisabeth 123
  Elizabeth 122
  Henrietta 114
  J. Beverly 255
  John W. 177
  William 85, 161
  Wm. 189, 204
Hurt, Balaam 312
  Elisabeth 329
  Susanna 17
Huskath, M. D. 150
Husketh, Isaac 34
  Isham 177
  John 178
Huskey, A. 57
  Archibald 4, 7
  Elias 28, 304
  Elizabeth 197
  Emeline 183
  Lacy Ann 66
  Lucy 299
  Rebeckah 52
  Sarah 52
  Susanna 361
  William 57
  Wm. J. 5
Husky, Archd. 6
  William 178
Husten, Nancy 349
Hutcherson, Cornelia P. 268
  Jane E. 267
  L. 72
  Thos. 143
  Virginia 173
Hutcheson, Richd. 317
Hutchings, H. 59
  John 162
  John A. 276
Hutchinson, John B. 246
  Mary 50
  Thomas 153
  Willis 43, 222
Hutchison, Julian 367
  Pamelia P. 66
Hutson, John 207
  Morning 128
  Susan M. 121
Hyde, Robt. 146, 260, 304
Hyfell, Elizabeth 257
Ihappell, Sarah M. 114
Inge, Mary 239
  Philip 275
  Richard 49
Ingram, Sarah J. 29
Inschere, Milley 90
Inschore, Jonathan 90
Inscoe, Reuben, Jr. 26
Inscore, Ava Jane 256
  Benjamin 179
  Eliza 356
  Elizabeth 200, 222
  Fanny J. 370
  Jonathan 93, 225
  Joshua 353
  Lotty 139
  Lucy 179
  Milley 26
  Rachel 314
  Sally 240
  Stephen 137
  Susannah 225
  Thomas 240
  William 179

Inscore (cont.)
  Wm. 314
Irby, Elizabeth 73, 210
  James 209
  Mary 73
  William 73
Isaiah, Smith 250
Isbell, Mary 186
Ivens, Frances 29, 208
Ivy(?), Frederick 42
Izzard, Alice 57
  Frances 4
  Nancy 288
  Rebecca 168
Jackson, Aramitta 9
  Arter 179
  Caroline 288
  Chesley L. 167
  Corbin 290
  Elisabeth 162, 172, 279
  Ezekiel 337
  Frances 38
  Francis 180
  Francis M. 342
  Gilley Ann 193
  Helon 40
  Huldy F. 263
  Isaac 114
  James B. 299
  Jerusha 55
  Lacy 76
  Lorenzo D. 342
  Low 131
  Lowe 180
  Lucy 180
  Lucy J. 288
  Mary 151
  Mary H. 217
  Mary R. 150
  Nancey 150
  Petsey 179
  Priscillah 5
  Ransom 288
  S. J. 2, 162
  Susan 179
  Thos. 16
Jackwall, Levon 230
James, George W. 57
  Thos. A. 193
Jarratt, Jno. 340
  Polley Lane 243
Jarret, John 257, 282
Jarrett, Elisabeth 265
Jarrot, Sally 338
Jarrott, Nancey 15
Jeeter, Mary P. 250
Jeetor, Mary 83
Jeffers, John 123
  Nancy 152
Jefferson, Eliza 265
  Polly 123
Jeffreys, Charles 135
  Charles E. 358
  Eliza 181
  Green 181
  Louisa 174
  Martha A. 305
  Mary E. 294
  Mary M. 170
  Samuel H. 173, 321
  Stephen 181
  Susan Artelia 135
  Tison 135
  William 328
  Willis B. 69
Jeffries, Luther R. 43
  Rebecca 294

Jeffries (cont.)
  Wm. R. 327
Jeffrys, Samuel H. 362
Jeggetts, Mary Ellen 368
Jenkings, Jensey 234
Jenkins, Adkin 50
  Angie C. A. 29
  Anita 332
  Ann S. 101
  Anna 64
  B. F. 320
  Charey 6
  Charity 65
  David 345
  E. A. T. 152
  Easter 65
  Edney 39
  Elias J. 348
  Elizabeth 26, 81, 170, 224, 343
  Frances 46
  Hannah 182
  James 261
  James L. 151
  Jesse 181, 182, 183
  John 257
  John T. 44, 82, 182, 293
  Jonan. 76
  Jonathan 51, 182, 237, 367
  Julia 325
  Luetta 370
  Lydia A. 311
  Martha 192, 370
  Martha J. 279
  Mary 246
  Mary A. 283
  Mary Thomas 217
  Nancy 84
  Nancy B. 282
  Patsey 303
  R. A. 85
  Rachael 65
Jenkins(?), Rebecca 279
Jenkins, Sallie 325
  Sally 84
  Thos., Sr. 182
  Thos. S. 312
  W. H. P. 6
  William 5, 257, 370
  Wilson 182, 357
  Wm. 65, 182
Jeter, Allen 5
  Barnet 307
  Candace 361
  Catharine 36
  Elizabeth 5
  Frances 287
  Martha Ann 202
  Mary 287
  Mary Ann Elizabeth 198
  Robert 320
  Saml. 83
Jett, Stephen 137
  Winefred 253
Jinkins(?), A. T. 121
  Ann 31
  B. J. 331
  Elias 81, 337
  Elias S. 66
  Elizabeth 347
  Fannie Taylor 356
  James 110
  John 39, 45
  Jonan 222
  Joseph T. 99
  Lucy F. 368

Jinkins (cont.)
  Mary A. 149
  Mary Ann 220
  Thos. 212
  W. D. 50
  William 39, 137
  William P. 240
Jnoes, Jno. 230
John, Obedyah 27
Johnson, (?) 323
  Anderson 315
  Archer 254
  Benjamin 68
  Canon 190
  Catharine J. 207
  Caty 172
  Celestia R. 197
  D. B. 102, 169
  Daniel 185
  Dudley B. 326
  Elisabeth 68, 135, 288, 362
  Elizabeth 43, 136, 181
  Elizabeth H. 163
  Ephraim D. 202
  Frances 260
  Gedion 253
  Henry 184
  Isaac 157, 362
  Isham 235
  J. 49
  James 236
  James R. 242
  James T. 234, 275
  Jas. 174
  Jesse 299
  Jno. 368
  Jno. C. 185
  John 59, 74, 104, 171, 194, 326
  John N. 186
  Jos. 177
  Joseph 263, 363
  Kissy 3
  Laura A. 155
  Lizzie 314
  Lucey 93
  Lucinda A. 192
  Lucy P. 341
  Macon 39
  Manuel 138
  Martha 321, 323
  Martha E. 203
  Mary 163, 343
  Mary B. 320
  Mary G. 227
  Milley 39
  Nancy 100
  Noel 171
  Parmenus 41
  Pascal 5, 118
  Polly 320
  Rebecca 265
  Salley 157, 179
  Sallie A. 122
  Sally 164
  Sarah 2, 229, 285
  Sary 236
  Sealey 107
  Shaw 164
  Silvia 303
  Stephen 159
  Susannah 209, 283
  Tabitha 140
  Taby 265
  Tallon 150

Johnson (cont.)
  Tarlton 44, 45, 127, 176, 311
  Thomas 341
  Turner 214
  Will 276
  William 315
  Willis 163, 234
  Winnie 261
Johnston, Abigail 5
  Ann 186
  Benjamin 186, 355
  Elizabeth 3, 61
  Fanny 236
  Frances 111
  H. E. 19
Johns(t)on, James 63
Johnston, Jane 150
  Jesse 14
  Joshua 85, 184
  Judia 117
  Larkin 142
  Lucey 201
  Martha 99, 314
  Mildred 184
  Milly 85
  Noel 99
  Patsey 159
  Patsy 154
  Poley 363
  Sam 239
  Samuel 240
  Samuel (Gov.) 169, 245, 308
  Susanah 163
  Susanna 207
  W. A. 101
  William 203
  William Moore 152
Jones, (?) (Major) 5
  A. N. 108
  Aaron 190, 347
  Abigale 69
  Abner 61, 110, 130, 188, 189, 192
  Adeline 171
  Ailey 284
  Ailsey 127, 191
  Alex 191
  Alexr. S. 109
  Alfred 256, 257, 331
  Alice C. 22
  Allen 191, 192
  Amelia R. 64
  Amenuel Scott 105
  Amey 175
  Ann 207, 229
  Ann Henderson 286
  Anna 188
  Anny 275
  Aron 181
  Atelia 326
  Benson F. 13
  Betsey 173
  Bettie 146, 190
  Brerton 192
  Caroline 59, 169
  Caroline M. 367
  Catron 207
  Celia 131
  Cuffee 65
  Cynthia A. 264
  David 173
  E. A. (Prof.) 149
  Edd 187
  Edna 284
  Edney 189

Jones (cont.)
  Edward 12, 72, 165, 189, 311
  Edward A. 28
  Elina 313
  Elisabeth 189, 260, 282, 324
  Eliza 129, 170
  Elizabeth 21, 105, 226, 231, 284, 335, 339, 341, 351, 366
  Elizabeth A. 11
  Fanny 144
  Fowler 282, 316, 317, 318
  Frances 1, 137, 247
  Francis 30, 189
  Gabriel 132, 328
  Gabriel, Jr. 308
  Green 86
  H. W. 232
  Hannah 299, 366
  Harriet 59, 88
  Henry 131, 155, 214, 263
  Henry R. 153
  Henry W. 98
  Holley 234
  Insianna W. 290
  Isaac 190
  Isaac N. 81
  Isabella 11, 317
  J. G. 4
  J. R. 187
  James 22, 319
  Jane 21, 115
  Jane J. 71
  Jenny 64, 190
  Jim 64
  Jn. 219, 370
  Jn. G. 86
  Jno. 2, 32, 218
  John 30, 43, 140, 190
  John S. 79
  Jonathan 69
  Jos. J. W. 188
  Joseph J. W. 210
  Jubal R. 264
  Jubilee 105, 287
  L. W. 68
  Leanna 112
  Leonnera 203
  Lewis 226
  Littleton 284
  Littleton Z. 189
  Lucy 114, 309
  Lucy H. 149
  Lucy T. 220
  Luvenia T. 287
  M. H. 190
  Madison 10
  Malina 64
  Margaret 345
  Margaret An 9
  Marget T. 203
  Martha 57, 82, 231, 326, 366
  Martha A. 57, 158
  Martha C. 34
  Martha E. 36
  Mary 113, 146, 149, 292, 326, 327
  Mary A. 66
  Mary A. W. D. 367
  Mary Ann 189, 219
  Mary E. 72
  Mary Emma 264
  Mary F. 114, 126

Jones (cont.)
　Mary J. 312
　Mary P. 23
　Mary R. 128
　Mat. 21
　Matella 192
　Melly 104
　Mildred F. 226
　Minerva Ann 302
　Moses 80, 187, 284, 347
　Moses, Jr. 191, 204, 214, 273
　Nancey 117
　Nancey Norwood 30
　Nancy 111, 131, 141, 164, 182, 189
　Parky 266
　Patsy 132
　Peggy 83
　Phereby 105, 269
　Polley 136, 227
　Polly 136, 257, 315
　R. D. 241
　R. H. 242
　R. S. P. 277
　Ralph 187, 207, 282
　Ralphe 282
　Rebeca 282
　Rebecca 187, 189, 215, 282, 284
　Rebecca A. 123
　Reuben 34, 207
　Risdon 320
　Robert 322
　Robert A. 189
　Robert A. P. 237
　Robert D. 235
　Robert F. P. 103, 127
　Robt. F. P. 331
　Roger 366
　Rosena 325
　Rufus P. 187
　Sally 340
　Sarah 95, 156, 172
　Sarah E. E. 123
　Selah 347
　Sintha 287
　Sterling 191
　Sugar 320
　Susan 77, 126, 210
　Susanah P. 162
　Sylvia 224
　Thomas 226
　Thos. 10, 280, 309, 370
　Thos. S. 118
　Tiley 169
　Tingnal 57
　Tom 188
　Viney 191
　Waddy 280
　William 131, 187, 189, 192, 203, 278
　William, Jr. 127
　Willie 365
　Winnefred 133
　Winney 229
　Wm. 126, 146, 202, 207, 227, 365, 368
　Wm. E. 365
　Wm. H. 39, 185
　Wm. R. 339
　Young 44, 46, 340
Joplin, Charity 217, 269
　Frances 50
Jordan, Alice 138

Jordan (cont.)
　Amey 336
　Archabald, Jr. 153
　Arthur 196
　Burchet 315
　Charlsa(?) 235
　Elisabeth 7, 81
　Elizabeth 153
　George 286
　Granville 321
　Harrison 138, 368
　Isabella 368
　Lucy 270
　Margarett H. 17
　Mary 84, 190
　Mary T. 322
　Nancy 349
Jordan(?), Nimrod 145
　Sarah 138, 162, 240, 368
　Siloah 286
　Tabitha 109
　Thomas 31, 170
　Thos. 144
　Turner 349
　Willie T. 141
Jorden, Julius 87
Jordon, Jeany 240
Jourdan, Mary 308
Joye, Sarah 281
Joyner, Matthew 273
　Nancy 273
Judge, Israel 243
Jurphy(?), Mary Ann 25
Justice, Frances 113
　Lucey 231
Justus(?), Susannah 298
Karrel, Nancy 34
Kates, John 30, 71, 172, 223
Keargen, Baldy 312
Kearney, Drucilla 250
　Ellen J. 38
　Henry 193
　John 193
　Judy 167
　Louisa 222
　Martha 181
　Nancy 193
　Patience 167
　Susan 185
Kearsey, Anne 11
　Armin 312
　Mary 174
　Sally 10
　William 193
Kearson, Charles 322
Kearzey, Archibald 185
　Baldy 60
　Frances 60
　Sophiah 11
Keath, Geloann 193
　Wesley 193
Keaton, Thomas 209
Keeling, Agnes 355
　Ann 296
　Elizabeth 156
　Frances 281
　John 281
Keen, Emily E. 246
　Milton 239
　Nancy 31
Keeth, Bernulah 7
Keeton, Elizabeth 322
　Martha G. 278
　Nancy E. 184
　Susan W. 301
Keith, Elizabeth 104

Keith (cont.)
　F. 263
　George 7
　Lemuel 104, 124
　Saml. 193
　Samuel 18
　Wesley 179, 263
Kelley, Martha E. 296
　Thos. 68
Kelly, George J. 18
　Jesse J. 219
　John 23
Kemp, Burrel 89
　Murphey 194
　Richard 241
Kendrick, Dennis L. 243
　James 238
Keneday, Jemima 29
　Susannah 356
Kennedy, John 130
Kennett, W. C. 122
Kennon, Betsy 266
　Maria P. 39
　Mildred 320
　Nancey W. 358
Kenton, Robert 173
Ker(?), William 150
Kernall, Jane 38
Kerney, Eve 34
　Margret 6
　Mary 34
Kerron, Elizabeth 243
Kersey, Emily 280
　Hopsey 266
　Nancy 183
　Sarah 59
Kersey(?), William 280
Kess, James P. 89
Keter, Elizabeth 56
　Jane 56
　Joseph 56
Keyton, Charlotte 31
Kibble, Wm. S. 364
Kilzer, James B. 188
Kimbal, Cathorine 204
　Drury, Jr. 217
　L. J. 214
　L. L. 160
　Pleasant 97, 100
Kimball, Drury 134
　Edward 195, 214
　Frances P. 230
　John 232, 236
　Lethy 161
　Lucretia 2
　Lunday 297
　Margaret 223
　Mary 232
　Mary A. 195
　Nancy 356
　Patsey 329
　Salley 278
　Sally 224
　Saluda 224
　Susan 41
Kimbell, Bartholomew 163
Kimbral, Nancy 111
Kimbrall, Frances 97
Kinchen, D. J. 302
　Henry M. 27
Kindrach, Amey P. 149
Kindrick, Mary 185
Kinemon, Philip 222
King, Brewer 196, 333
　Elisabeth 157, 283, 345
　George 148
　James A. 190

King (cont.)
　John 204
　Lang 113
　Lucy 308
　Susan Ann 195
　Tho. L. 154, 320
　Thomas 93, 140, 195,
　　333
　William 191
Kingsbury, Amanda 107
　Delia 335
　Eliza 281
　H. H. 353
　Harriett 342
　J. B. 277
　R. H. 4, 26, 39, 131,
　　202, 249, 300, 319
Kinnamon, Sally 242
Kinten, J. P. 323
Kinton, Elizabeth J. 343
　Jno. 211
　John 38, 194
　Mary 275
　Robert 37, 97, 250,
　　328
　Susan 236
　Thos. 262
Kirk, Mary 235
Kirkland, Louisa 218
　Sally 32
　Saml. 356
　Selina H. 182
Kirton, Robert 172
Kitchen, Phanney 312
Kitley, Christopher 27
Kittle, Bettie 121
　Hixy Jane 238
　Joel 227
　L. B. 260
　Lewis 348
　Lewis H. 197
　Mary 147
　Mary Ann 305
　Molley 155
　Nancy 47
　Prudence H. 303
　Sally 304
Kittral, Catharine 308
　Wiley 119
Kittrall, Ann A. 190
Kittrel, Ruth 197
Kittrell, (?) A. M. 368
　(?) R. 178
　Ann N. 163
　Benja. 365
　Caroline 164
　Dera 287
　Eaton H. 44, 101, 156
　Edwin W. 134, 135,
　　256
　Elizabeth 317
　Emily 261
　F. 26
　Fielding 250
　James 324
　John 198, 261, 287
　Jonathan 163, 198
　Julia E. 125
　Kermiller Ann 294
　Leah 167
　Loretta Z. 288
　Louisiana 25
　Lucy F. 369
　Maria 261
　Martha 42, 275
　Martha A. O. 30
　Martha Ann 175
　Martha E. 365

Kittrell (cont.)
　Mary 27
　Mary E. 259
　Meriah J. 288
　Micklejohn 308
　Mima 263
　Nancey 34
　Nancy 190, 365
　Nanney 177
　Owen 15
　Peggy 261
　Penney 308
　Polly 238
　Priscilla 101
　Rebecca 348
　Robert W. 198
　Rosa A. 313
　Salley 39
　Sallie C. 276
　Sallie H. 330
　Samuel 337
　Sarah 163
　Tabitha 141
　Tabitha Ann 348
　Tabitha M. 216
　Thomas G. 327
　William 154, 198, 273
　William H. 218
　Winnefred 167
　Wm. F. 50
　Wm. H. 37
Knight, Alfred 164, 258
　Ann E. 256
　Benja. 69
　Caroline F. 367
　Elisabeth 8
　Jane 343
　John 204, 208
　Jonathan 208, 287
　Judah 65
　Judith 8
　Martha 126
　Mary 124
　Mary T. 108
　Milley 165
　Polley 8
　Redden 250
　Rosey 34
　Susan 148
　William 198
　Woodrow 94
　Woodson 8, 172, 287
Knoll, Charity 77
Knorden, Nancy 347
Knott, Amey F. 359
　Annah(?) 77
　Bartlet 33
　Bartlett 196, 197
　David 199
　David W. 85, 200
　Elisabeth 242
　Elizabeth 199, 313
　Fannie A. 56
　Frances 199
　Frances P. 92
　George 199, 299
　George W. 199
　J. D. 165
　James 199
　James C. 136
　Jane 78
　Jane Ann 117
　John 92, 199
　Julia H. 85
　Lucinda 80
　Lucy 295
　Lundy 85, 200
　Martha 132

Knott (cont.)
　Mary 84, 319
　Mary Ann 356
　Mary C. 200
　Mildred 199
　Milly 199, 294
　Mollie 160
　Nancy 296
　Part-(?) 160
　Patsey 177
　Polly 92
　Rebeccah 73
　Rhoda Ann 58
　Robert 200
　Sallie J. 150
　Sarah 305
　Thomas 237, 267
Knowland, Mary 17
Knowling, James 347
Kraider, Catherine 168
Kyle, Robert 105
Lad, Nancy 235
　Rebecca 136
Ladd, Elizabeth 103
　J. W. 370
　Martha G. 200
　Mary 283
　Noble 261
　William 13
Lafield, Smullen 103
Laman, D. P. 292
Lamay, Polly 162
Lamon, Abigail S. 30
Land, Alexander G. 101,
　　242
　Braxton 177
　Evria Ann B. 303
　Elizabeth 245
　James 201
　James M. 1, 315
　John B. 102
　Louisa 82
　Mary Jane 296
　Mildred 81
　Susan 177
　Susan R. 102
Landep, Joseph 245
Landers, Abraham 125,
　　188, 201
　David 298, 365
　Elsey 347
　George 65
　John 201, 202
　Joseph 23
　Mary 68
　William 201
Landess, John 3
Landford, Thomas J. 115
　Thos. 361
Landis, A. 2, 4, 7, 8,
　　20, 23, 24, 25, 28,
　　35, 37, 40, 41, 46,
　　48, 55, 57, 58, 60,
　　61, 62, 66, 69, 74,
　　75, 77, 78, 79, 80,
　　84, 85, 86, 92, 101,
　　104, 110, 115, 119,
　　133, 146, 150, 151,
　　152, 156, 159, 162,
　　169, 173, 175, 177,
　　192, 193, 203, 204,
　　208, 214, 217, 221,
　　238, 244, 245, 248,
　　249, 251, 253, 257,
　　258, 261, 265, 268,
　　270, 280, 281, 284,
　　285, 287, 291, 292,
　　299, 317, 325, 334

Landis, A. (cont.)
  336, 342, 349, 359, 361, 364, 370
  A., Jr. 152, 176, 292
  Abel 62
  Aug. 305
  Augustine 11, 45, 106, 301
  C. E. 14, 15, 51, 66, 149, 325
  Candis 87
  Charles E. 60, 363
  Cynthia 301
  Elizabeth 84
  Fannie B. 259
  Frances 83
  Francis 301
  Geo. W. 124, 170, 205, 334
  Georg. 247
  George 14, 23, 248
  George W. 18, 175
  Jackey E. 326
  James Y. 4, 149, 283
  Jas. J. 168
  Jas. Y. 73
  John 94
  Joseph 23
  Martha Ann 98
  Sarah 362
  Virginia C. 100
Landiss, William 138
Landland, Lydda 221
Landrum, Rhoda 128
Landus, George 201
Lanes, H. W. 284
Lanford, Parish 308
Langford, Johnathan 76
  Judah 194
  Polley 163
  Sarah 169
Langly, Thos. A. 102
Langston, Frances 284
  James 288
  Joseph 33, 225, 292
  Solomon 225
Langwood(?), M. M. 25
Lanier, Elizabeth 201
  Frances 309
  Jane 269
  Lewis 195, 304
  Lucey 55
  M. V. 128
  Martha 81, 342
  Nancy 213
  Polly 321
  Rebecca 355
  Rebekah 355
  Robert 355
  Sarah 355
  Thomas 355
  Thos. 178
  William 203, 228
  William H. 13, 35, 123, 251
  Wilmouth 1
  Wm. 96
Lankford, Isabella 15
  Jesse 348
  Jonathan 76, 230
  Nancey 257
  Parish 203
  Sarah 303
  Stephen 257
  Susanah 348
  Tabitha 179
Lankister, Martha 296
Larmer, John 356

Larrane, Sarah 201
Lashly, Anne 38
  H. C. 256
Lasier, Eliza P. 290
Lasiter, Catharien 275
  Elisabeth 316
  Sally 274
Lasseter, R. W. 116
  Wm. 248
Lassiter, A. 331
  Ann 27
  Eliza 290
  Fannie C. 66
  Harriet 27
  James H. 143, 331
  Jane 200
  Joanna R. 143
  Lovea 76
  Mattie S. 76
  R. W. 1, 74, 84, 207, 241, 260
  Riddick 76
  Robt. W. 324
  Wm. 328
  Zena H. 331
Latham, Eunice 93
  Francis 93
  L. 77, 337
  Lyman 93, 153, 161, 279, 303
  Polly 220
Latta, H. 39, 343
  Isaac 126
  Mary 126
  Sallie T. 4
  Sarah N. 247
  Thomas 192, 247
Laughter, John L. 202
  Sarah C. M. 77
Laurance, John 164
Laurence, Anne 52
  Charity 157
  James 258
  Lucy 135
  Mary 152
  Mary Gwin 109
  N. M. 203
  Peggy 187
  R. B. 139, 353
  William 109, 260
Laurence(?), William T. 84
Laurence, William T. 14, 15
  Wm. T. 52, 203
Lawrance, Betsey 25
Lawrence, Candis 367
  Charlott T. 341
  Cornelia 269
  Elizabeth 63
  Francis C. 203
  Henry B. 300
  J. P. 20
  Margaret 121
  Martha 112
  Mary A. 203
  Robt. 203
  Rowan 238
Laws, Caroline 114
  Dicky 337
  Elizabeth 338
  John 343
  Margaret 338
  Martha 338
  Susan 337
  Susannah 338
  W. A. 338
  W. D. 268

Laws (cont.)
  William A. 113
Lawson, Avarilla 367
  G. G. 223
  Gabe 204
  Margaret 24
  Martha G. 98
  Mary 184
  Polly 204
Lawteffe, Francis 317
Leach, John 136
Leathers, James 313, 339
  Jas. S. 276
  Martha 137
  Rachel 240
  William 335
Leavel, Nancy 126
Leaverton, James 269
  Nancy 269
Leavick(?), Thomas 238
Leavil, Elizabeth 14
Leavin, George T. 55
Leavister, G. T. 208
  George T. 222, 227, 292
  James 225
  Lavina 193
  Thomas 120
  Thos. 214
  W. R. 193
  William 181
  William R. 168
Ledbetter, James Wall 24
Leeman, William 226
Lemay, Caroline H. 137
  Ellen 79
  Harnett S. 245
  John C. 200, 204, 360
  LeMay, John P. 366
  Lemay, Kittey 73
  Lewis 305
  Lucy 288
  Lundy W. 182
  Miles S. 185
  Mildred 200
  Mildred H. 204
  Peggy 314
  Saml. 205
LeMay, Saml. 254
Lemay, Samuel 205
  Sarah C. 82
  Susan 267, 332
  Susan M. 275
  Temperance 74
  Thomas L. 275
Lemmons, Tabitha 301
Leneve(?), Elizabeth 334
Leneve, Louisa 47
Lenoir, Elisabeth H. 312
Leny, Elizabeth 18
Levester, Susey 205
  Temperance 70
Levett(?), Chs. L. 3
Levingston, Catharine 48
Levington, Wilson 38
Levister, Boson 143
  Elizabeth 93
  James 205
  Susan 35
  W. R. 294
  William 156, 279
Lewis, Anne 66, 278
  Betsey 318
  C. R. 177
  Caroline 236
  Catherine 45
  Charles 66
  Chas. 206

Lewis (cont.)
　Dick 324
　Dolly 205
　Elisabeth 140, 281
　Eliza 118, 232, 322
　Elizabeth 83
　Emily 70, 309
　Esther 20
　Fanny 53
　Frances 44, 165
　Fras. 205
　Fredk. 309
　Harriett 270
　Henrietta 8
　Henrietta Maria R. 281
　Howell 66
　Howell, Sr. 309
　Isabella 17
　James 61
　James, Jr. 6, 319
　James S. 338
　Jane 132, 165
　Jas. S. 107
　John 48
　Lucy Anne 298, 350, 353
　Luvenia 69
　Madison 322
　Mariah 325
　Marina (Mrs.) 176
　Martha 125
　Mary 48, 140, 194
　Matilda 342
　Mildred 66
　Mildred C. 95, 325
　Patsey 218
　Permelia 205
　Robert 113, 266
　Rosa A. 95
　Rose 24
　Saml. 205
　Sarah 61, 220, 364
　Sarah A. 44
　Sarah C. 208
　Sarah Ellen 175
　Susan 322
　Susan A. 107
　T. 257
　T. B. 33
　Thomas A. 283
　Thos. 298
　Warner M. 322
　Willis (Dr.) 95
Lightfoot, Anne C. 205
Ligon, Lucy F. 242
　Mary 53
　Thos. 297
Lile, Charlotte 114
　James H. 206
　Rebecca 45
　Salley 124
　Sandal 131
　William 206
Liles, Sarah 308
　Wm. 24
Lilly, Henry 188
Linch, Marget 80
Lindsey, Anne 297
　Caleb 112
　West 209
Linear, Susanna 195
Link, Barton 296
　Martha R. 296
　Wilmus 296
Linn(?), Eliz. 138
Linsey, Phebey 90
　Sarah 169

Linster, Rebecca 209
Linum, Louisa 25
　Sarah J. 161
Lipford, Mary F. 280
　Pattie E. 67
Lipscomb, William A. 207
Lisemore, Lenny 124
Little, Sally 361
　Susannah 89
Littlejohn, Anne W. 187
　Elizabeth 192
　Elizabeth W. 189
Littlejohn(?), Frances B. 109
Littlejohn, Margaret M. 13
　James F. 49
　Lillie L. 49
　Lucinda J. 187
　Mary E. 358
　Thomas B. 28, 216, 339
　Phoebe D. 49
　Thomas M. 358
　Thos. B. 358
Livingston, G. R. 340
Lock, Betsey 173, 298
　Henrietta 345
　Hezekiah 110
　John 39
　Martha 112
　Mary 346
　Rhoda 153
　Stephen 114
Lockett, Maria A. 352
Lockhart, Samuel 170
Lockwell, Bridgett 339
Loften, Harbert C. 191
Loftin, Emaly 53
Loftist, Sally 213
Logan, Peter, Sr. 207
　William P. 336
Loging, Mary 107
Long, Alcy 289
　Charles 125
　Chas. 104
　Elizabeth 208
　John 125, 218
　John C. 137
　Martha 218
　Patsy 218
　Richd. 207
　Robert A. 16
　Sarah E. 254
　Virginia A. 35
Longmire, Delia Ann 99
　Dilly 88
　Elijah 52
　Elisabeth 7, 24
　Eliza 64, 325
　Emily B. 131
　John 170
　Lucey C. 250
　Martha 75
　Mary 236
　Robert 22
　Salley 176
　Samuel 363
　Sophia 169
　William 7, 13, 208
　Wm. 146
Lord, Arthur 131
Lormier, W. B. 22
Lovett, Mary 53
Loving, Sarah Ann 319
Low, Charity 340
Lowe, Sarah 243

Lowe (cont.)
　Thos. 45, 265, 356
Lowery, Frances 262
　Henry 209
　Mary Ann 209
　Rebecca Ann (Mrs.) 124
Lowrey, Jas. G. 2
Lowry, Francis 262
　Z.M.P. 157
Loyd, Agnes 76
　Anna 291
　Anne 217
　Arryann 190
　Betsey 76
　Bettie 238
　Caroline 145
　Elisabeth 206
　George W. 191, 209
　Han-(?) 226
　Happy 70
　Henry 15
　Isaac 63
　Isabella 41
　James 41, 146, 209, 238, 243
　Jane 238
　Jarrett 206
　John 209
　Joseph 83, 350
　Joseph S. 85
　Joshua 210
　Juliann 183
　Lethey 219
　Lewis H. 242
　Louisa H. 83
　Lunsford 63
　Malissa 37
　Margaret 159
　Maria 367
　Martha 152, 218
　Mary 13, 249
　Molley 195
　Nancy 52, 93, 346
　Peggy 52
　Permelia 300
　Polley 91
　Sally 103, 242
　Terrel 114
　Thos. 345
　Valentine 210
　William 19, 103, 195
　Willie 91, 283
　Willis 194, 357
　Willison 167
　Wilson 242
　Wm. J. 55, 76
　Zadoc 27
　Zadock 235
Loyed, Elizebeth 249
　Jariot 123
Loyls, Nansey 180
Lumley, Candis H. 8
Lumpkin, Abigail 9
　Artimilia 276
　Avarilla 276
　Beersheba 254
　Catey 231
　Elizabeth 232, 350
　Fleming 86, 232, 257
　George 173
　George W. 75
　Mary 329, 340
Lunsford, Elender 148
　Jane 124
　Jesse 211
　Valen. V. 148
Luveesey(?), Sarah Y. 200
Lyle, Clary 24

Lyle (cont.)
  Mary 255
Lyman, Geneva F. 330
Lynam, George W. 93
  Lucy A. J. 283
Lynch, Denis 64
  Dennis 23, 252
Lyne, Ann M. 307
  Henry 270
  Nancey 79
  Nancy 79
  Susan P. 48
Lynes, Eda 282
  Jack 282
  Martha 280
Lynum, Charles 211
Lyon, Ann 287
  Betsey 213
  Betsy Ann 212
  Clement 212, 213
  Clement B. 111
  E. B. 16, 314
  Edward B. 208
  Elizabeth 362
  Emily F. M. 85
  Fannie 212
  Frances C. 117
  James Catharine 166
  Jane 85
  John 213
  John F. 137, 212
  John M. 213
  Liddy 84
  Martha J. 233
  Mittie E. 212
  Nancy B. 184, 212
  Nancy W. 111
  Rowan 137
  Sarah 168, 182
  Sarah A. 46
  Sarah J. 230
  W. M. 233
  W. W. 59
  William H. 212
  Z. J. 212
  Zachariah 84
Lyons, Thos. B. 23
Maben, Mary H. 4
  Robert 108
Mabery, Nancy 115
Mabry, Joshua 245
  Lucey 295
Macem(?), Wm. C. 158
Macklin, Nancy 81
Macon, D. 232
  Druciller 235
  Mary A. 314
  Priscilla 276
Macvedr(?), Mary 230
Madderson, James 99
Maddocks, Patsey 88
Maddox, Wm. A. 306
Maderson, Dicey 337
  Peyton 265
Madison, Elizabeth 204, 350
  Jane 183
  Margaret 48
  Mariah 48
  Mary 140
  Patsey 48
  Peyton 15
  Polley 12
  Sally 195
  Susan 311
Mafield, Betsy 345
Magby, David 115
Magee, Frances 174

Magehee, Susannah 76
Mahan, Minerva 145
Mailling, Jane 255
Major, Barnard 7
  Wm. T. 14
Majors, Amey 72
MaL-(?), James 174
Mallory, Ann Eliza 182
  Caroline 6
  Charles 244
  Lucey 227
  Marsha 319
  Mary G. 71
  Mary Y. 355
  Nancey 168
  Nancy R. 107
  Phebe 75
  Sally Ann 139
  Sarah A. 162
  William, Jr. 199
  William J. 263, 323
Malone, Elizabeth 95
  George 217
  Pattsy 13
  Robert 349
  Roxanna 66
  Sarah 349
Malory, Aggness 254
Man, Elisabeth 33
  Fanny 33
Mangham, Joseph 71
  Wily 210
Mangrom, Betsey 210
  Mary 70
Mangrum, Charlott 105
  Elisabeth 194
  John 359
  Mimy 130
  Samuel 144
  Sarah 19
  Wm. 72
Mangum, (?) 209
  Absalom 218
  Allen 142
  Amanda 105
  Arch. 154
  Arena 10
  Charity 230
  Charrity 218
  D. L. 208
  Elizabeth 78, 248
  Emily 63
  Fielding 52
  Frances 104, 218
  Francis 104
  George A. 252
  Green A. 94
  Helen 50
  J. S. 219
  James 113, 224
  Kate 141
  Lucy 107, 327
  Maney 259
  Martha 32, 184, 210, 229
  Mary 103
  Mary Jane 62
  Moody 60
  Nancy 94, 229
  Nancy H. 288
  P. G. 340
  Peggy 209
  Peyton G. 241
  Rachel 142
  Rebecca 118
  Sally A. 167
  Sally C. 241
  Sarah 110, 166, 224

Mangum (cont.)
  Sol. 118
  Susan 25, 142, 169, 283, 343
Mangum(?), Susannah 267
Mangum, Tabitha A. 107
  Washington 223, 246
  William 2, 32, 194, 224, 229
  Willie 204, 337
  Wily P. 218
  Wm. 316, 319
Manier, John B. 194
Mann, Abigail 219
  Ailsy 12
  Aremisa 161
  Dolley 182
  Julia 110
  Martha 110, 347
  Martha S. 103
  Nancey 120
  Narcissa J. B. 160
  Obedience 112
  Peter 44, 168
  Susannah 335
  William B. 99
  Wm. B. 271
Manning, Lindy 265
  Wm. O. 150
Manson, O. F. 302
Marable, Bob 126
  Caroline 70
  Edward T. 138
  Jane 25
  Jane O. 319
  Lucinda 282
  Mary 220
  Orsborne 282
  Osborn 220
Marlow, Quincy 234
Marron, D. J. 30
Marrow, Aliza 368
  Anderson 76
  Anna 104
  Bella 220
  Drury 313
  Elizabeth D. 295
  Henry 368
  Hester 313
  Lizzie 19
  Lucy 76
  Maria 212
  Mary 220
  Mary Ann 220
  Milly 180
  Nancey 206
  Nelly 220
  Permelia 17
  Peter 368
  Rachel 220
  Rachiel 302
  Rebecca 76
  Sarah 368
  Thos. 280
Marshal, Nancy 208
  Sarah 75
  Wm. 178
Marshall, Elisabeth 278
  Elizabeth 27
  Elizabeth C. 124
  Ellanoro A. 256
  Fanny R. 18
  John 291
  Mary 49
  Phebe 170
  Susan 256
  William 364
  Wm. 53, 343

Marshall (cont.)
  Wm. P. 256
Martain, Susannah 269
Marten, Virey 226
Martin, Alexander (Gov.)
    178, 250
  Amey 235
  Ann 296
  Joannah 330
  Lucey 212
  Mary F. 183
  Sarah 119
  Susan 216
Masenburg, Betsy 255
  Peggy 255
  Washington 255
Mason, Alavenia B. 301
  Alexander 321
  Ann Eliza 84
  Anna 106
  Annelize 277
  Benjamin 55
  Cargelia 87
  David 123, 331
  Elisabeth Hunter 331
  Frederick 2
  Harriet 179
  Joshua 105
  Mary 230
  Nancey 348
  Nancy 354
  Pevey 354
  R. 290
  Samuel 55, 354
Massy, Rachael F. 246
Mathews, Jas. 250, 351
  Mary 174
  Thomas 56
  Thos. 80
Mathis, Ann 221
  Elizabeth 359
Matilda, Avin 12
Matison, Polly 103
Matlock, Sarah 271
Matterson, Bedey 113
  Harriet 233
  Peyton 121
  Susannah 121
Matthews, Alexander 178
  Elizabeth 71
  Jos. 108
  Mary 108
  Thomas 358
Mauldin, Blake 143, 278
May, A. D. 223
  Ann 62
  Celestia 154
  Eliza 271
  Elizabeth J. 120
  Frances 181
  Francis 84
  John 168
  M. G. 131
  Martha A. 260
  Martha J. 140
  Mary G. 294
  Mary M. 183
  Nancy 298
  Susan 239
  Susan A. 28
  Susanna 89
  T. H. 222
  Thos. 89
  Unity 119
  William 119
Mayes, Frances E. 7
  Linsey 222
  Martha 269

Mayes (cont.)
  Mary Ann 190
  Mary S. 124
  Samuel 222
  Virginia C. 191
Mayfield, (?) 277
  Ann 211
  Isabellah 277
  Jane 313
  Mary 211, 222
  Nancy 185
  Oney 235
  Patsey 53
  Sallie 146
  Susan 16
  Voluntine 222
  Washington 222
  Winney 260
Mayho, Angelino 293
  Cuffee 93
  Delia 188
  Edney Ann 280
  Edridge 192
  Eldridge 21
  Elizabeth 13, 138
  Frances 160
  Isabella 30
  Joycy 191
  June 48
  Mary 10
  Norrell W. 110
  Parthena 106
  Sallie Ann 223
  Sally Ann 11
  William 223
Mayhoe, Elizabeth 71
  Richd. 112, 266
Maynard, James P. 112
  Jennie 156
  Mary 223
  Mary Ann 112
  Phillis 71
  Prudence 243
Maynor, Polley 158
Mayo, Cuffe 333
  Cuffee 147, 151, 223
  Edward 26, 331
  Elizabeth 147
  Fanny 333
  William 207, 334
Mayson, Sally 105
McAden, Jno. 68
McC-(?), Damsel V. 213
McCadden, Elizabeth A.
    111
  H. C. 130
  Hugh 91
  Sarah M. 69
McCan, Henretta 249
  Sally 293
McCannde, Lucinda K.
    252
  Mary J. M. 274
McCaraga(?), (?) 189
McCargo, Martha Jane
    132
McCarter, Dilsey 66
  Warren 66
McCartey, Caroline 124
McCartney, James 209
McClanahan, Catharine
    27
  Judith 101
  Louisa 26
  T. O. 191
  T. W. 10, 231
  Thadeus O. 336
  Thos. W. 175, 232, 237

McClanahan (cont.)
  W. F. 215
  W. J. 187
  W. S. 120, 126, 285,
    333
  Wm. 27
  Wm. S. 17, 312, 317,
    333
  Wm. T. 171
McClanahanm, Wm. S. 270
McClanhan, Daniel 123
McClarin, Elizabeth 113
McClenachan, Peggy 124
McClenahan, Spence 162
  W. S. 155
  William 113
  William S. 273
  Wm. S. 38
McClennahan, Spence 112
McClove, Peggey 103
McCraw, Damsel R. 277
  Mary R. 72
McDaniel, Henry 261
  James 154
  Jas. 348
  Jos. 167
  Joseph 119
  Thomas 213
McDonald, Flora 62
McDonald, Sarah 348
McFarland, Benjamin 218
  John 168
  Susan 168
McFarlin, Lucy 338
  Susan 204
  Thornton 316
McFarling, Celia 2
  Erasmus 216
  Henry 114
  John 50, 140, 168,
    190, 354, 361
  Rebecca 99
  Wm. 167
McGee, Mary 69
  Nancy 293
McGehe, Betsey 10
  Gilley 178
  Joseph 361
  Josiah 214
  Martha 119
  Shem 214
McGehee, Ann 121
  Banks 215
  Becky Jane 80
  Cary 144
  Delaney 140
  Elizabeth 193, 215
  Fanny 148
  Henry 215
  Jeremiah 15
  Jinney 340
  Jos. 2, 251
  Joseph 121
  Judith 261
  Lemuel 106, 182, 258
  Martha 168
  Mary Ann 292
  Meal 225
  Miel 225
  Nancey 68
  Polly 214, 279
  Sallie 193
  Sally Ann 16
  Shem 144, 193, 214,
    215
  Shemwell 115
  Solomon 69
  Susan 204

McGehee (cont.)
  Z. T. 215
McGhee, John W. 15
  Mary 364
  Sarah L. 86
McGill, Meriah 292
McGlenchey(?), John 324
McGlocin, Nancy 252
McGraw, Harriet 364
  Lucy Ann 311
McGwin, Martha 139
McIntyre, Ann C. 296
McKeever, Ann 251
  Babby 251
  Elvira 175
McKenzie, Jos. 202
McKlejohn, Elisabeth 225
McLan-(?), James 176
McLemore, John 130
  Mary 123
McMahon, L. D. 258
McMilian, Alexander 23
McMillian, Margaret 125
  Mathew 23
McMurry, James 216
  Margaret 216
Meachum, Saml. B. 193
Meador, Elizabeth 11
  Wm. M. 11
Meadors, Elijah 2
  F. M. 152
  Riley 342
Meadows, A. C. 248
  Brodie 356
  Elizabeth 2
  Dave 224
  Elisabeth 225
  Elizabeth 231
  Elvey 218
  Emah F. 34
  Frances 346
  Harriett 188
  J. J. 224
  J. S. 127
  James 166
  Jemima 282
  Jesse 224, 231
  John 224
  Margaret 94
  Mehaley 251
  Parthena 358
  Patsey 113, 339
  Rachel 273
  Rebecca 225
  Riley 219, 225
  Sallie Ann 238
  Saluda 224
  Sarah 52
  Susan 34
  Thomas 224
  Thos. 225
  William 225
  Willie 326
  Willis 224
Mealer, Emaly 352
  John F. 82
Mealor, Martha 345
  Mary 82
Mearemon, Ann 141
Medler, Gilley 5
Medley, Mary G. 312
Megehe, Josiah 70
  Lemuel 136
Megehee, Crafford 340
Meherell(?), John W. 348
Melton, Catharine 201

Melton (cont.)
  Henry 85, 116
  Jane 105
  Joanney 159
  Stephen 27, 138, 267
  William T. 13
Merimond, Pheby J. 74
Merit, James 208
Merrett, Benjamin 250
  Fanny 280
  Frances 226
  Sally 363
  Susan 225
  William 225
Merrian, Betty 289
Merrit, Elisabeth 288
  John W. 279
  Louisa 139
  Mary 33
Merritt, Abigail 164
  Amey 270
  Anney 275
  Daniel 226
  Green 47, 64, 119, 196, 283, 307
  J. H. 241
  Joel 267
  John 226
  John G. 282
  John W. 212
  Mary 226
  Mary A. C. 209
Merryman, Malackiah 226
  Molley 224
  P. R. 170, 192
  William 226
Methis, Kemp 249
Micheau, Sophie M. 207
Michel, Robert 363
Michell, Mary 98
Middleton, James 23
Miers, John 197
  Mary 216
Miles, Sarah 292
Miller, Alford B. 226
  E. 245
  Eliza 258
  Frances 216
  H. A. 226
  Jane 301
  Lizzie Ann 129
  Loisa 226
  Patsy 24
  Ruffin 24
  Sandy 129
  Sergina 24
Mills, Elizebeth 243
  James 292
  Priscilla 293
  Sandy 218
  Sarah 292
  William 141, 293
Milner, Isbell 243
Milton, Betsey 116
  Sarah 142
  Stephen 142
  Susan 180
Mimms, Thomas 98
Minnes, Young A. 336
Minnis, Leveny 6
  Young A. 16
Minor, Amy 227
  Anne 362
  Clary 186
  Elizabeth 22, 99
  Frances 353
  Frances M. 263
  Joseph 227

Minor (cont.)
  Lazarus 160, 347
  Martha 202
  Martha M. 27
  Mary 28
  Nancy 129
  Parthenia 365
  R. 186
  R. N. 137
  Randal 339
  Randel 292
  Randol 364
  Robt. W. 60
  Rowena 223
  Wm. H. 27
Minzey, Dudley 275
Mirchel, John 163
Mires, Sally 188
Mise, Benjamin 39
Mise(?), James O. 3
Mitchel, A. 162
  Agness 118, 303
  Anson 70
  Areil 238
  B. A. 159
  Benjamin 228
  David 251
  Elisabeth 18
  Fanney 324
  Hannah 294
  Iverson 228
  James 90
  Jane 192
  Jemiah Ann 307
  John 308, 362
  Kissey 13
  Littleton 266
  Lucy Ann 127
  Martha 338, 362
  Mary 47, 227
  Mary Ann 125
  Matthew 63
  Milley 181
  Nancey 35, 60
  Pamale T. 63
  Rebecka 43
  Sarah 301
  Thos. 230, 359
  William 155
Mitchell, Amy 161
  Ann 16
  Ann H. 46
  Archer 168
  Arill 342
  B. A. 274
  B. J. 68
  Benj. 8
  Benjamin 88, 333
  Candiss 230
  Chesly Jones 230
  Christian A. 52
  Daniel 117
  David 204
  Dolly 161
  Eliner 280
  Elisabeth 88
  Elizabeth 89, 106, 302
  Emeline 118
  Evan 137, 229
  Fanny 91
  Frances 80, 238
  Frances P. 229
  Frankey 9
  Gideon 111, 236
  Harriet 5, 124
  Henrietta 86
  Hunley 144
  Isabella 223

Mitchell (cont.)
  Iverson 10, 139
  Jane 124
  Jacksey E. 29
  James 45
  Jane 92
  John 61, 228, 240, 274, 335
  John E. 63, 259
  John W. 34
  Julia Ann 287
  L. 98
  Leander 316
  Littleton 230, 317
  Lucey 105
  Lucy Ann 127
  Margaret 131
  Martha 275, 305
  Martha Ann 96
  Mary 45, 135, 204, 238, 271
  Mary A. 216
  Mary E. 361
  Mary Jane 213
  Mary L. 96
  Minerva Ann 14
  Nancey 49
  Nancy 9, 118, 228, 332
  Nancy M. 348
  Narcissa 196
  Ned 131
  Peggy 134
  Polley 20
  R. J. 4, 18, 25, 75, 147, 186, 202, 204
  Rachel 345
  Rainy Ann 228
  Rebecca 264
  Richd. 229
  S. W. 72, 106, 229
  Salley 270
  Sarah F. 264
  Sealy 350
  Sophia 131
  Susan 213
  Tealey 45
  Thomas 290, 331
  W. J. 156, 238
  W. P. 323
  Wesley 229
  William 213
  William S. 21
  Willis B. 118
  Wm. 20, 86
  Wm. L. 159
  Wm. S. 228
  Zachariah 315, 316
Mize, Alexander 231
  Allin 231
  Benjamin 231
  Betsey 114
  Elizabeth 262, 276
  Howel 231
  Howel L. 173
  Nancey 282
  Obadiah 114
  Sarah 32
  Sarah O. 173
Mobley, Marah 298
Mobly, Ledy 192
Moise, Oxford 350
Moize, Emily J. 55
  Oxford 127
Monroe, Milly 241
Montague, (?) 208
  Alexander 323
  Alexander B. 43

Montague (cont.)
  Catharine Y. 63
  Charlotte 251
  Ellen 332
  Emely 259
  Frances 130
  Francis A. 268
  Francis L. 63, 66
  John E. 121, 142, 317
  Latny 232
  Martha 198, 268
  Martha Y. 162
  Mary 231
  Mary A. 4
  Mary Francis 238
  N. B. 271
  Saml. 174
  Samuel 43, 231
  Sarah F. 268
  Umphry 259
  William 130, 183
  Y. 85
  Young 132, 232, 352
  Young, Jr. 8
  Young MaC. 268
Montgomery, B. 310
Montigue, Mary 132
Moody, Ann 298
  Dolly 210
  Fanny 119
  Michal S. 206
  Sabelia B. 25
Moon(?), Charles 34
Moon, Patey 148
Moore, Alley G. 97
  Amie M. 64
  Ann 130, 256
  Arthur 190
  Benjamin 336
  Betsey 303, 310
  Celestia H. P. 347
  Charles 12, 34, 298
  Charly 57
  Chastool 89
  Chloe 94
  Christiana 29
  Dicey 89
  Elisabeth 12
  Eliza 213
  Elizabeth 188, 239
  Ezebell, 267
  George 114, 365
  George W. 234
  H. F. 44
  Harriet Jane 33
  Henderson 232
  Hesler 256
  Hester 185, 190
  James 221, 235
  Jane 352
  Jas. J. 222, 332
  Joel 234
  John 18, 60, 120, 147, 233, 252, 253, 258, 365
  John B. 261, 327
Moore(?), Jones 225
Moore, Joseph R. 188
  Lain 130
  Laine 234
  Lemuel 147, 336
  Luvisa 110
  Maria A. 234
  Martha 190
  Mary 57, 256
  Mary J. (Mrs.) 136
  Nancy 150
Moore(?), Patey 148

Moore (cont.)
  Patsey 270
  Philip 156
  Philip P. 41
  Rebecah 186
  Salley 141
  Sarah A. 237
  Seawell H. 284
  T. B. 34
  Tabitha 114
  Victoria A. 319
  Violett 315
  W. 111, 125
  W. H. H. 87
  William 366
  Wm. 159, 179, 239
More, Betsey 137
  John 330
  Lucresia 336
Morgain, Edy 137
Morgan, Amarilla 5
  Charlotte 156
  Elizabeth 326
  Elizabeth W. 167
  Frances 97
  J. S. 219
  Julia 5
  Lucy 43
  Martha 223, 285
  Mary 233, 361
  Mary A. 245
  Mary Jane 122
  Milley 7
  Nancy 35
  Penny 159
  Rachel 230
  Rebecca 180
  Robert E. 235
  Susan 97
Morn, Howel 139
  Reuben 240
Morp, Howel 237
Morris, Avory 250
  Blunt 171
  Caroline 154
  Elizabeth 153
  George J. 152
  John 95, 184
  John, Jr. 164
  Martha 51
  Martha A. 171
  Martha Ann 75
  Martha L. 167
  Mary 72
  Matilda 173
  Mathew J. 187
  Milley 50
  Mollie T. 22
  Movey 50
  Nancey 327
  Nancy 6, 98
  Patty 171
  Phebe 250
  Phebe G. 211
  Pheby 156
  Phereba 347
  Rebecca 130
  Richard A. 62
  Sally 179
  Sarah 32
  Susan 25, 171
  Tabitha 253
  Thomas G. 277
  Thos. G. 151
  Thos. S. 58
  Tyre 235
Morriss, Henderson 235
  Jane 327

Morriss (cont.)
  Pheby 38
  Wm. 65
Morrow, Ann 236
  Daniel 354
  Dianer 27
  Elizabeth 360
  Lucy 236
  Martha 98
  Mary 27
Morse, Bennett 237
  Elizabeth 305
  Howel 88, 278
  Mary 297
  Patsey 182
  Pattey 73
  Peggy 61
Morse(?), Reuben 146
Morse, Reuben 192
Morse(?), Sarah 61
  Winefred 309
Morton, Ann 237
  Betsy 155
  Bettie W. 15
  Chovar 314
  Elizabeth W. 237
  Henry 109
  John 237
  Joseph 155, 237
  Joseph H. 163
  Lizzie 324
  Martha A. 163
  Martha E. 138
  Narcissa C. 155
  Peter 237
  Rhody 237
  Rowan 324
  Sarah 237
  York 237
Moseley, Ann Eliza 268
  Josiah 30
Moseley(?), Thomas B. 132
Mosely, John 237
  Polley 100
Mosley, Lucy R. 308
Moses, Thos. C. 64
Mosly, Patsey 357
Moss, Amanda P. 2
  Ann 106
  Ann E. G. 160
  Benjamin 238, 269
  Catharine 61
  Charles 152, 263
  Elizabeth 31, 330
  Fanny 102
  Franklin 237, 343
  Franky 142
  Haly 12
  Hicksey 238
  Isabella 142
  Jane 185
  John 211, 238, 273
  Jordan 274
Moss(?), Jordan D. 366
Moss, Jordan D. 314
  Josephus 47, 259, 302
  Joshua 209
  Loueasa Ann 362
  Louisa 1, 277
  Louisa A. 112
  Lucy 15
  Malissa L. 118
  Martha 35, 263
  Mary 339
  Millie 238
  Nancy 40

Moss (cont.)
  Polly 208
  R. A. 238
  Reuben 146
  Ritter 142
  Salley 306, 310
  Sally 140
  Sally H. 2
  Sarah 314
  Sarah Ann D. 72
  Siah 348
  Susan 12
  Susan A. 118
  W. H. 307
  Wm. 164
Motlow, Stephen 113
Moton, Nancy F. 55
Mottaugh(?), Martha 57
Mulchi, Robert 238
  Susan 238
Mulky, Margaret 366
Mullen, Ann Eliza 201
Muller, Lively 256
  Mary C. 239
Munday, Stephen 361
Munford, George F. 319
Munn, Rebecca G. 120
Munro, Rosey 283
Murphey, Delila M. 111
  John G. 261
  Mary 188
  Wm. 103
Murphy, Phoebe 236
Murrah, Mary 32
Murray, Elizabeth 194
  John S. 94
  Malinda S. 358
  Mary 243
  Nancey E. 102
  Sally 152
  Samuel D. 298
Murrey, Thos. 270
Murrow, Amy 220
  Caesar 220
Murry, Elizabeth 322, 328
  Emaly J. 53
  Herriott 244
  James 243
  John H. 102
  Kathern 243
  Margaret (Mrs.) 326
  Martha 138
  Nancy 328
  Richard 328
  Richard H. 239
Mutter, Elisabeth 7, 207
  Eliza R. 339
  Margaret 28
  Thomas, Jr. 207
Myars, Sally 151
Myze, Frances 95
Nailing, John R. 198
  Nelson 169
  Willis 258
  Wm. 181, 216, 272
Nance, Albert D. 32
  Allen 227
  David 274
  Dolley 202
  Elizabeth 347
  Elizabeth Ann 168
  F. W. 240
  Fannie 189
  Frederick W. 204
  Jinny 185
  Jno. 59
  John 189, 202, 317

Nance (cont.)
  John, Jr. 331
  Lucey 299
  Lucy 341
  Lucy P. 206
  Margaret F. 113
  Rebecca 315
  Ruth 47
  Samuel 47, 228
  Sarah 190, 346
  Virginia 189
Nanny, Charles 104
  Minerva 104
Nants, Richd. 90
Nash, Jno. W. 33
  Martha P. 134
Naton, Sil. 211
Neal, Amanda 30
  Elisabeth 355
  Harritt P. 329
  James 98, 250
  John F. 168, 240
  Louisa B. 19
  M. 138
  Martha 240
  Martha R. 168, 351
  Minerva W. 116
  Moses 73, 98, 156, 319
  Ralph 324
  Sarah 310
Neale, Mary 145
Neel, Locky Ann 124
Neele, Fielden 194
Nellums, Polley 365
Nelms, Sally 100
Nelson, A. (Major) 95
  Ann 290
  Helen 318
  Henry R. 241
  Howel S. 51
  Jacob 290
  Jinny 301
  Luisa 290
  Major A. 351
  Nancy R. 329
Nethery, Henry H. 359
  Sarah E. 156
Nevel, Elisabeth 104
  John 104
Nevels, Angaline 23
  Mary 123
Nevill, John 217
  Mary A. 262
Newman, Caroline J. 58
  Harriett 358
  Macon G. 341
  Martha J. 239
Newton, A. S. 236
  Amey 242
  Ceb 124
  Elizabeth 284, 338
  Hamon 47, 334
  Hamon W. 189
  Harriett Cornelia 247
  Henry 71
  Henry H. 349
  Isaac 242
  James 241, 242, 267
  James H. 132
  James R. 241
  John 151, 166, 241, 348
  Lethy 190
  Margaret 334
  Martha 173, 329
  Mary 166, 340
  Mary E. 345

Newton (cont.)
  Maz 166
  Parthena 149
  Reuben H. 124
  Sally 159
  Sarah 267
  Susan 300
  Susan Ann 24
  Wesley J. 344
  William 241, 301, 340
  William P. 273
Nichols, Susanna 235
Night, Nancy 164
Nipper, Mary 51
  Solomon 337
Noble, Joseph 242
Noblen, Fanny 334
  Lucy 80
  Mary 209
  Richard 345
Noblin, Bettie 351
  Elizabeth 62
  Jno. 159
  John 357
  Jose 82
  Joseph 24
  Mary A. 334
  Patsey 351
  Richard 351
  Spencer 353
Noel, James 307
Noland, Charles 243
  Edwd. 243
  Lucretia 234
Norman, Agness W. 278
  Ann Eliza 324
  Bearsha 160
  Betsey 106
  Bettie K. 48
  Elisabeth 159
  Elizabeth 144, 191
  Hannah 328
  Henry 39, 60, 159, 160
  Laura N. 121
  Lidey 227
  Lucy 282
  Martha 363
  Martha B. 320
  Mary 161
  Peggy 273
  Prudence 99
  Temperance 273
  Thos. W. 259
  Wm. 159
Normion, Mary 197
Norris, Caroline Wake 73
Norton, Elizabeth 170
  Presley 170
Norvell, Wm. 243
  Young 243
Norwood, Alexander 245
  Ann 80
  Ann S. 150
  Arianna 53
  Benjamin 244
  Betsy 328
  Catharin 243
  Elisabeth 245
  Eliza 75
  Emily R. 46
  Faney 47
  Frances A. 244
  G. W. 243
  Gilliam 100, 346
  Harriett 271, 273
  Harriett S. (Mrs.) 200

Norwood (cont.)
  Isabella 169, 244
  J. T. C. 244
  Jas. L. 239, 245
  John 10, 84, 298
  John H. 295
  John T. C. 244, 294
  John T. J. 245
  Leonard H. 275
  Lucretia 295
  Martha H. 277
  Mary 92, 140, 245, 293
  Mary A. 19, 249
  Mary Jane 273
  Mary S. 291
  N. M. 150
  Nancey 208
  Nancy 47, 227, 268
  Nathaniel 258
  Penny 244
  Phebe Ann 244
  Phobe 3
  Raymond 182
  Rebeccah 217
  Robert 351
  Robert G. 244
  Sallie Ann 185
  Sally 60
  Sarah A. 249
  Susan A. 244
  Norwood, W. 133, 167
  Washington 165
  William 270
  Wm., Jr. 245
  Wm. S. 148
Nostedler(?), Adam 242
Notgrass, Critia 173
Nothern, Tamor 68
Nowel, Emmer L. 237
Nowell, James 245
Nuckles, James 246
  Nancy 246
  Wm. H. 246
Nunn, Elisabeth 174, 240
  Joshua 291
  Lucey 50
  Polley 3
  Thomas 136
Nunnery, Elisabeth 326
Nutall, Ann N. 344
Nutgrass, James 282
  Susannah 302
Nuttall, Ann 31
  Anna 120
  Geo. 34
  Geo. A. 31
  Isabella 261
  Isabella G. A. 261
  James 32, 68, 123, 163, 183, 200, 246, 342
  Jas. 31, 53, 232, 243
  M. 121
  Mary 260
  Mary E. 164
  Mary J. 26
  Sally 342
  Thomas 42
Oakeley, Elizabeth 246
Oakely, John 246
  William 247
Oakley, Barnett 308
  Betsey 308
  Betsy 247
  Brady Ann 39
  Celia 10
  Deborah 32

Oakley (cont.)
  Demarcus 10
  Dolphin 64
  E. 321
  Elizabeth 345
  Ezra 247, 334
  Ferebey 180
  Henry 190
  Hyram 247
  Isabella 247
  James 32, 321
  Lucy Ann 308
  Parthena 248
  Pheebey 115
  Polley 52
  Rebecca 55, 247
  Ridley 247
  Sarah 162
  Silla 325
  Stephen 73, 345
  Sylva 246
  Thomas C. 83
  William 52
  Yancy 362
Oakly, Addison 246
  Celia 52
  Emily C. L. 91
  George 55
  Salley 306
  Yancy 53
Oaks, B. D. 193
  Jane 181
Obrian, Polley 333
  Thos. A. 55
OBriant, Ailey G. 94
  Alice 117
Obriant, Dennis 333
OBriant, Elizabeth 103, 248
  Emily 223
  Emily P. 327
  Gardner 149, 157
  Henry 57
  James M. 58
  Jas. 126
  John 320
Obriant, Martha 26
  Mary 275
OBriant, Milley 117
  Nancey 201
  Nancy 39
  Patrick 158
  Z. 248
  Zachariah 167
  Zechariah 219
Obrien, Coateny J. 49
OBrien, Eler 322
  Elizabeth 170
  James P. 231
Obrien, John 43
OBrien, M. D. 26
  Martha J. 355
  Mary Ann 291
Obrien, Milly 360
OBrien, Nancey 365
  Parthena Ann 3
  Rebecca 14
  Sarah E. 231
  Zachariah 170
OBrient, Amanda 355
  Frances 201
  Rebecca 231
  Sally 96
OBryant, John 327
  Mary Jane 192
Ogilby, Sineth 208
Ogilvie, Patty 219
  Richard 7

Ogilvie (cont.)
  William 146
  Wm. 168
Oglesey, Nansey 7
Okley, Addison 51
Oliver, Angelina 299
  Jincey 275
  Polley 370
  Susan 282
Omary, John 370
  Parthenia 147
  Richard 370
  Tinna 370
Omerry, Catey 338
  Eliza 72
  Owen 338
  Parthena 247
  Parthenia 370
  Richard 54
Omry, George 58
Oneal, Nancey 272
Ooten, Jas. 48
  Martha 2
Orsborn, J. 269
Osborn, C. 305
  Job 264
  Jonathan 306
Oslin, Sarah 347
Overbey, Ann H. 351
  Chaves 188
  David 58
  Dicey 338
  Eddy 221
  Edwd. 246
  Elizabeth 246
  Elizabeth A. 370
  Fortune 58
  Frances 251
  James 67
  James M. 18, 326
  John S. 31, 232, 334
  Martha 290, 317
  Mary Ann 181
  Mary E. 361
  Matilda B. 363
  Mealy Ann 58
  Milley 82
  Nancy 156, 235
  Nathan 25
  Phebe 215
  Rebeca Susan 121
  Susan 235
  Susan J. 82
  Tabitha 76
Overby, Aney 11
  Ann 249
  Emily 313
  Hariet 359
  Henry 249
  Hester Ann 359
  Jas. M. 249
  July 92
  Lucy T. 159
  Marshal 128
  Obediah 359
  Reuben 92
  Susan Ann 5
  W. 108
  William 249
Overton, A. 238
  Abigail 363
  Ardelia Aregon 89
  Ariella M. 327
  Benjamin 270
  E. H. 120, 313
  Elisha 250
  Fanny 164
  Harriet 69

Overton (cont.)
  Hartwell 90
  James 363
  Jane 238
  Jane H. 363
  Martha 241
  Mary E. 363
  Mary J. 238
  Melvina 34
  R. T. 322
  Robert T. 164
Owen, A. 251
  Alice M. 337
  Ann C. 301
  Ann Eliza 87
  Ann H. (Mrs.) 193
  Bettie A. 165
  David 177, 250
  Dicy 272
  Elizabeth 11, 250, 306
  E. W. 337
  Frances 73, 267, 272
  Jacob 250
  Jane 358
  John 306
  John H. 122, 360
  Juda 251
  Judith 328
  Louisa 95
  Margaret 337
  Mary 370
  Mildred 97
  Moses 83
  Nancy 86
  Polly 232
  Rebecca 28
  Richardson 251
  Rowan 251
  Salley 317
  Thomas 11, 171, 206, 250, 344
  Thomas, Jr. 171
  William 232, 306
  Wm. L. 22, 322, 344
Owens, Daniel 158
  Judy 251
  Levi 251, 343
  Lucy 56
  Thomas 251
  Wallace 251
Owin, Anderson 326
Owins, Lear 266
P-(?), Elizabeth 122
Pack, William 217
Padgett, William 13
Page, Lewis 349
Pain(?), Elisabeth 155
Pain, Eliza 265
Paine, Jane 300
Paller, Sarah 36
Palmer, Dicey 123
  Lucy 80
  Pleasant 273
  William 80, 123, 187
Pannill, William 329
Pardue, Blackmun 223
  J. A. 96
  S. O. 122
Parham, Abbie 154, 252
  Adeline 296
  Albert C. 161
  Ann. A. 251
  Asa 8, 252, 253
  Asa C. 36, 89
  Asenath F. 61
  Barbary 283
  C. W. 315

Parham (cont.)
  Caroline P. 368
  Charity 261
  Charles W. 254
  Delia H. 252
  E-(?) 253
  Edmond 227
  Elisha B. 176
  Eliza 120
  Eliza. 359
  Elizabeth 152, 263
  Elvey 270
  Emily S. 180
  Ephraim 253
  Eveline 150
  Fanny 22
  Franky 172
  Frederick 154, 186, 252
  Geo. K. 107
  George 38
  George K. 99
  Hahhan 252
  Isham 252, 283
  James 86
  James A. 153, 254, 359
  Judith W. 260
  Julia Ann 134
  Julian 271
  Julie Ann 253
  Kannon 236
  Kennan 134, 218
  Lewis 112, 129, 252, 253
  Lewis, Jr. 42
  Lewis W. 253
  Lidia 254
  Louisa 86
  Lucey 154
  Lucinda A. 277
  Lucretia R. 35
  Lucy 150
  Martha 113, 217
  Martha C. 277
  Martha G. 74
  Mary 113, 214, 353
  Mary A. D. 171
  Mary Ann (Mrs.) 338
  Mary J. 74
  Mary Jane 121, 152
  Milley 120, 252
  Nancy 42, 307
  Nancy L. 29
  Nelly 367
  Patsey 18
  Rebecca 310
  Richard 296
  Rodah 236
  Rowland 332
  Rupert 24, 247
  Saml. 254
  Saml. J. 87
  Samuel 18, 254
  Sarah 112
  Sarah E. 172
  Sham 299
  Susan Jane 269
  Thomas 22, 172, 297
  Thompson 253
  Thorp 253
  William 150
  William A. 252
Paris, Mary 201
Parish, Absalom D. 350
  Ann E. 42
  Bannister 81
  Beedy 331
  Betsey 254

Parish (cont.)
  Betty Johnston 202
  Catharine 306
  Claibourn 21
  David 254
  Dilly 254
  Dize 196
  Elijah 202
  George 40
  Hillyard 254
  Hillyard J. 134
  Jane S. 359
  Judith 96, 254
  Keziah 112
  Malinda 171
  Mary 39
  Mary R. 41
  Massey 310
  Nancey 88
  Nancy 364
  Omey 96
  Phanney 21
  Pleasant 134
  Polley 218
  Ralph 39
  S. H. 297
  Susanna 97
  Tabitha 288
  Valentine 254
  W. A. 72, 205
  William 72, 88, 97, 364
  Willis 202
  Wm. 254
Park, Thos. A. 258
Parker, Ann 247
  Anne 205
  Cader 114, 327, 365
  Catey 211
  Charlotte 157
  David 2
  Davy 255
  Elisabeth 159
  Elizabeth 72
  Giles 255
  Haly 334
  Heddy 316
  Henry 36, 254, 255, 265, 266, 305, 334
  John Y. 106
  Jonas 211
  Jonathan 177
  Josh. 317
  Lotty 255
  Lucy Ann 265
  Margaret 10
  Mary 334
  Mary A. (Mrs.) 263
  Nancey 190
  Polly 266
  Prescilla 342
  Sarah 177, 189
  Stella 305
  Susan 229, 275
  Zorbey(?) 348
Parkinson, William W. 323
Parkman, Henry 156
  Mary 156
Parnell, Wm. 192
Parrett, Jane 198
Parrish, A. D. 139
  Absolam 40
  Absolam D. 1, 170
  Ailcy 72
  Ann 145
  Auston 257
  Brasy 257

Parrish (cont.)
  Charles T. 362
  Charrity 161
  Celia S. 214
  David 256
  Eady 187
  Elijah 303
  Eliza 284
  Elizabeth 222, 230
  Ella A. 281
  Elmira 184
  Elijah 201
  Frances 169, 334
  Frances L. 101
  George 2
  Happy 256
  Henry 262
  J. 211
  J. M. 256
  Jane 39
  Jane S. 359
  John 112, 157
  John M. 101
  Justice 304
  Kerson 299
  Lerty 256
  Letha 363
  Lewis 3
  Lucey 38
  Lucinda 333
  Lucy 25, 285
  Maria 253
  Martha 234
  Mary 214, 297, 332
  Mary A. 75
  Mary M. 100
  N. A. 256
  Patsey 351
  Polly 256
  Ralph J. 257
  Reuben 256
  Reubin 256
  Sabey 257
  Sally 230
  Sherwed 161
  Volentine 257
  William 161
  William B. 253
  William S. 115
Parrot, Elizabeth 136
  Mary Jane 133
Parrott(?), S. S. 24
  James 39
  S. S. 69, 198, 370
Partee, Abner 14, 204, 218, 298
  Arhey 2
  Dancey 298
  Earbe 258
  Edmd. 258
  Edmund 258
  Levicy 328
  Leviney 14
  Locker 38
  Mary 233
  Nancy 204
  Yerbey 233
Partin, Green T. 235
Paschal, James 43, 259
  Jas. 240
  Jas. O. K. 58
  John 221
  John W. 298
  Robert 263
Paschall, Benja. J. 139
  D. A. 12, 44, 74, 88, 111, 123, 135, 143, 213, 253, 257, 310,

Paschall, D. A. (cont.) 350, 370
  D. A., Jr. 212
  D. J. 94
  D. P. 172
  D. T. 60
  Dilly 259
  E. P. 197
  Elizabeth M. 108
  Ellen 276
  Eugenia C. 336
  Harriett 17
  James 179
  James P. 51
  Jas. P. 157
  John 259
  L. 330
  L. A. 59, 126, 243, 268, 309, 330, 368
  L. A., Jr. 201
  Lucy 34, 94, 197
  Lucy T. 259
  Luke 259
  Martha A. 109
  Mary 289
  Mary A. 291
  Matilda 266
  Milly B. 94
  Nancy 288
  Patience 317
  S. A. 309
  Sallie A. 252
  Sarah Jane A. 318
  Sarah T. 309
  Sarah W. 24
  Silas 319
  Unity 263
  Virginai C. 291
  W. 152
  William D. 259
  Wm. 4
  Wm. V. 291
  Z. M. 277
Paschell, William 4
Paskill, James 260
Patience, Rhody 90
Patillo, Mary 91
Paton, Mary 153
Patsey, Talley 87
Patteford, Phil. 280
Patterson, Christian 188
  Hardy 68, 260
  James 98
  Mary E. 295
  Nathan 178
  Peggey 357
Patillo, Elizabeth W. 344
Pattillo, Amy B. 344
  Anderson 61
  Henry 44, 269
  John F. 195
  Mary 133
  Milley 195
  Wm. 165, 260, 267
  Mary J. G. 246
Paulk, John 128
Peace, Abner 111, 355
  Ann 332
  Cely 261
  Charlotte 198
  Edmund 307
  Elisabeth 168
  Elizabeth 359
  Elizabeth A. 327
  Frances 182, 237, 355
  Henry 36
  J. A. 15
  James 118

Peace (cont.)
  James B. 105, 342
  James N. 262
  Jaqulin 99
  Jas. B. 106, 230, 237, 294, 337
  Jas. J. 177
  Jno. M. 261
  John 19
  John C. 144, 327
  John D. 263
  John E. 119, 261, 288
  John M. 154, 205, 231, 239
  Jos. B. 11, 51, 232
  Jos., Jr. 232
  Joseph 361
  Judith 145
  Lucey 184
  Lucy 205
  Maredeth 184
  Martha 261, 304
  Mary 275
  Patsey 104
  Pleasant 134
  Polbus 261
  Polley 197
  Rosa 183
  Rowan 307
  Samuel 261
  Sarah W. 77
  Viney 194
  William 261
  Wm. 305
Peak, Nancey 329
Peake, Lucy 36
  Mary 32
Peal, Joseph 266
Pean, Jos. B. 37
  Sarah 357
Pear(?), Thomas F. 78
Pearce, Angeline 354
  Tison 6
Pearson, Gibs W. 194
Pease, Thos. F. 82
Peck, Lucy 316
Pedaford, Thomas 328
Pedeford, Manery 145
Peebles, Robert B. 91
Peed, Anna 30
  Dudley 169
  Emeline 346
  G. W. 262
  John 335, 339
  Jones 211
  Louisa L. 335
  Polly 71
  Rebecca Ann 114
  Richard 285
  Rutha J. 339
  Saluda 339
  Susan 335
Peek, William 367
  Wm. 329
Peel, Sally 96
Pegram, Daniel 272
Pelham, Sarah 320
Pemberton, Edmund 263
  Hester 263
  James D. 309
Pendergras, Macen 154
Pendergrass, India 153
  Jesse 135
  Nancy 336
Penick, Danl. A. 81
Penn, Frances 176
  Jos. B. 215
  William 268

Penny, Beady Ann 246
  Riley 53
Peoples, A. J. 329
  L. J. 41
  Louis J. 268
  Martha A. 136
  Mary J. 207
Perdue, Geo. 289
  George 136, 289
  Harris 25
  Patsey 343
  Phileman 107
  Sarah 223
  Teresa 192
Pergurson, Lucy C. 363
  Martha 363
  Ransom 363
Perkerson, Chancy 130
  Mary 298
  Mary Ann 101
Perkins, David 340, 352
  Ezekiel B. 133
  William 263
Perkinson, Cyntha 238
  Joseph 259
  Mary 4, 134
  Mary Ann 322
  Pamelia 100
  Sarah 247
  William 295
  Wm. W. 330
Perry, Alexander 276
  Betsy 322
  C. H. 270
  Cealy 5
  Clinton H. 264
  Elizabeth 104
  Frances 103
  Harriet 131, 263
  Harriot 28
  Henry 322
  Holand 262
  Louisa 200
  Margaret Isabella 109
  Maria 109, 264
  Mary 299
  Mary E. 58
  Mary Eliza 85
  Nancey 264
  Nancy 18
  Peter 189
  Rebecca 147
  Reney 58
  Sally 12
  Samuel H. 264
  Sarah 317
  Sarah E. 264
  Sinah 254
  Telitha T. 103
  Thomas 58, 109, 264, 353
  Thos. 40
  Wiley L. G. 37
  Willie L. 58
Person, Benjamin 24, 69
  Benjamin E. 71
  Jacksey 261
  Mary 207
  Richard 265
  Sarah B. 151
  Thomas 165, 194
  Tom 261
Peryear, Elizabeth 226
Petegrew, S. H. 337
Petiford, Elizabeth 243
  George 286
Pettaford, Frances 322

Petteford, Anderson 11
  Ann 110
  Austin 96
  Elias 265
  Emily 343
  Evan 71
  Louiza 36
  Mary 96
  Rubin 21
  Stephen 86
  Susan 273
  Tarry 8
  Thomas 265
  Tony 79
  William 9
Pettegrue, Mary 54
Petterford, Averilla 21
  Betsey 21
  William 21
Petteway, John 177
Pettiferd, Evans 71
Pettiford, Beady 152, 266
  Betsey 20, 255
  Betsy Ann 93
  Collins 36, 221
  Drury 21
  Edmond 265
  Elizabeth 11, 191, 316, 333
  Emily 343
  Emma 255
  Fanny 96
  George 20
  Gilly Ann 36
  Hicksy 80
  Jane 262
  Julia A. 21
  Julia Ann 151
  Margaret 79
  Mary 172, 197
  Mary Jane 343
  Meredith 280
  Milley 19
  Nancy 10, 138
  Peggy 172
  Rachel 210
  Rebecca Ann 59
  Sallie Ann 30
  Sarah O. 9
  Solomon 139
  Susan 265
  Terry 143
  Thomas 174
  William 96, 265
Pettigrew, Elizabeth 337
  Nancey 367
Pettigrue, Elizabeth 338
Pettigure, Delila 54
Petty, Eliza 116
Pettypool, Elizabeth 225
  Patsey 266
Pewet, Joseph 34
Pewett, Lyddy 203
Peyton, Elisabeth 95
Philips, Anne 76
  Elizabeth 71
  Elizabeth J. 346
  John 76
  Thomas 101
  William 183
Phillip, Mary 233
Phillips, Elisabeth 146, 365
  Elizabeth 202
  Howel 302
  Jas. 358

Phillips (cont.)
  Martha 358
  Mary 23, 44
  Masoury O. 239
  Nancy 67, 267
  Nancy 267
  Robert A. 205
  Roxanna 358
  Sally 267, 268
  Tabitha 302
  Thomas 138
  Thomas H. 83
  Thos. H. 35, 306
  William 44, 67, 267
  Willis R. 109
Phillops, Peggey 317
Philpot, Elizabeth 248
  James 288
  Molly 34
  Nancey 62
  Rebecah 28
  Sarah 146
Philpott, Amy 267
  Bella 325
  Emily W. 187
  H. L. 242
  James 54
  Jemima 54
  Jno. 72
  John 268
  L. L. 35
  L. S. 47, 182, 231, 321, 335, 365
  Lindon S. 268
  Louisa M. 127
  Mary 43, 224
  Mary Jane 360
  Mildred A. F. 47
  Nancy S. 339
  Phyllis 81
  Sally 268
  Saml. 28
  Samuel 341
  Sol. 58, 248, 327
  Solomon 267
  Thos. 28, 43
  W. A. 69, 176, 272, 291, 299
  William 113
  Zachariah 284
Phips, Frances 54
Pickett, Caroline G. 281
  Mary M. 202
Pickrel, Mary 186
Pierce, John 168
Piles, Betsy 230
Pinson, Aaron 89, 343
  Elizabeth 322
  Julia 36
  Margaret 239
  Nancy 345
  Susan B. 344
Piper, Elvira A. 171
Pippins, Lucinda 216
Pitchford, Harriet 88
  Hezekiah 173
  Nancy (Mrs.) 31
  W. J. 173
Pittand, G. W. 205
Pittar, Samuel 162
Pittard, Ann 322
  Barshaby 232
  Fannie A. 322
  Harrel G. 106
  Howel G. 160
  Howell G. 8
  James 130

Pittard (cont.)
  James M. 166
  Mary Ann 80
  Mary M. 118
  Nancy A. 43
  Phanney 354
  Rebecca S. 63
  Samuel 149, 331
  Sarah 232
  Thomas 40, 63
  Thomas J. 62, 322
Pitteford, Warrington 296
Pittiard, Samuel 269
Pitty-Cobb, John 297
Pleasants, Martha L. 252
  Mary G. 12
  Thos. T. 280
  W. D. 89
Plenty, Abm. 229
  Abram 29, 172, 265
Plumer, Hezekiah 151
Plummer, Hannah 216
  Henry L. 179, 207
  Hezekiah 135, 145, 240
Poe, John C. 75
Poindexter, Wm. H. 329
Poll, J. T. 147
Pollard, Cynthia 58
  Major 84
  Willey 2
  Willie 58, 317, 330
Pollen, Elisabeth 359
Pomfrett, Staley 22
Pookrum, Sally 155
Pool, A. G. P. 221
  Allin Petty 317
  Cary Ann 22
  Ceney 168
  Elbert S. P. 189
  Elizabeth 333
  Logustin P.201
  Logustine 352
  Logustus P. 352
  Martha 352
  Martha P. 270
  Rachal 187
  Roda P. 82
  S. P. 40
  Salley P. 13
  Sarah 296
  Sept. P. 174, 266
  Stella Francis 40
  Susanner 89
  Thomas 46, 86
  Thos. 17
  Thos. W. 135, 154
  William 132
Poole, Elizabeth P. 177
  Frances B. 177
  John E. 177
Pools, Nancy 321
Pope, Ann C. 349
  Jane 242
  John 242
  John, Jr. 240
  Mary 345
  Temperance 27
Potter, Abraham 270
  Anne 303
  Betsey 165
  Elisabeth 196
  Elizabeth 41
  Henry 191, 221, 318
  John 163
  Lemuel 350
  Lewis 33, 165

Potter (cont.)
  Mary 115
  Robert 115, 116, 121, 141, 185, 275
  Sarah 116
  Semender 292
  Thomas 92, 147, 170, 186, 228, 270, 273
  William 243
Pound, Jane 151
Powel, Edmon 169
  Harry 263
  James 362
  Lucy 367
  Mary 225
  Mary A. 99
  Mildred 119
  Peggie 164
  Sally 225
  Thomas 336
Powell, Ann 363
  Bettie 249
  Dilly 250
  Elizabeth 107, 254, 270
  Gordan T. 311, 327
  Harriet 249
  Henry 270
  Hilliard 363
  Honor 270
  James 225
  John 62, 83, 152
  Judith 15
  Malinda S. 269
  Mary Ann 164
  Pricilla 263
  Ruth 304
Poytress, Eliza G. 328
Pratcher, Mary 48
Prather, Wm. H. 72
Pratt, Lucy 309
Preddy, Bedy 271
  Ellender 287
  Lucy 5
  Nancy 349
Preers, Lethy 350
Pretty, Harler 271
  Hod 43
  Phanney 271
  Robert 255
Previt, Mary 34
Prew, Judah 304
Prewett, Benja. 25
  Elisabeth 203
Prewit, Ancell 105
  John 263
  Nancy 25
Prewitt, Rebecca Ann 105
Priddy, Alex 271
  Anne 347
  Arina A. 354
  Benjamin 293
  Clary 214
  Elisabeth 214, 332
  Eliza 193
  Fanney 115
  George 193
  Harley 271
  John 271
  Joseph 57
  Mary 216
  Mary Frances 193
  Molsey 34
  Sarah 297
  Tempey 16
  Virginia K. 326
  William 348
  Wm. 25

Pridy, Joseph 16
  Martin 272
Primrose, Franky 76
  Jas. 272
  Mary 311
  Rachel 346
  William 346
Prissom, Jackson 345
Prittey(?), William 70
Proctor, Caroline 60
  Lucy 323
  Martha 109, 251
Pruett, Martha 279
Pruit, Chas. 206
  Elizabeth R. 35
  John Bradford 38
  Sarah 234
Pruitt, Elijah 212
  Jno. 124
  Lucy 181
Pryor, Francis 45
Pucket, Martha Jane 82
  Sarah J. 2
Puckett, Elizabeth 235
  Shep. A. 273
  Susan 273
Puckrom, John 335
Puet, John Fradford 234
  Thomas 144
Puett, Henry 294
  Selah 294
Pugh, Maria A. 207
Puliam, Martha 200
Pulley, Ann 273
  John 273
  Nancy E. 173
  William H. 276
Pulliam, Barnet 159, 227
  Elizabeth 344
  Harriot W. 304
  John 219
  Lucy W. 234
  Mary J. 49
  Nancy W. 89
Pullin, George 208
Purdue, Blackmon 224
  Nancy 99
  William 289
Purkins, Drury 141
Puryard, Elizabeth 249
Puryear, Alexander 31, 102
  Ann T. 268
  Beggy 240
  Cornelia F. 189
  Dolly 13
  Eliza 174
  Elizabeth 8
  Elizabeth A. 176
  Elizabeth H. 335
  Elizabeth Jane 25
  Elizabeth W. 49
  Francis 274
  Frem 11
  H. E. 43
  H. S. 274
  Harmon 273
  Irena P. 206
  Isaiah 274
  Jno. P. 13
  John 329
  Lydia 138
  Martha 132
  Martha C. 361
  Martha P. 33
  Mary 231, 268

Puryear (cont.)
  Mary A. 76
  Mary C. 291
  Mary S. 207
  Mima 81
  Permelia C. 90
  Peter 33
  Peyton 274, 305
  Rebecca 340
  Robert 293
  Ruffin 244
  Samuel 340
  Sarah 33, 291
  Sarah An 58
  Sarah T. 324
  Semore 350, 352
  Stephen 291
  Stephen L. 290
  Thomas 226
  William 73, 206, 291
Puryer, Rebeccah 206
Qualls, Adkin 6, 182
  Alcey 186
  Ann Hawkins 332
  Frances 274
  Margret A. 339
  Mary 274
  Mary Ann 114
  Nancy 6, 182
  R. C. 120
  Rebecca W. 89
  Rebeccah 317
  Rowan 90
  Tyson 260
  William 274, 289
Quarles, Candis 152
  Polly 168
Quols, Chesly 178
R-(?), Jas. R. 313
Rabon, Nancy 110
Radcliffe, William 288
Raggland, Frances 30
Ragin, John 275
Ragland, Amey 124
  Bettie 78
  Charity 359
  Elizabeth 64
  Emily 172
  Evan 125
  Evan, Jr. 17
  Frances 290
  Littleton 36
  Mary Ann 17
  Nancey 73, 192
  Obryant 317
  Reuben 225, 248
  Reubin 73
Ragsdale, Elizabeth 219
  Frances Y. 160
  Henry 87
  Jno. H. 163
  John H. 82
  Mary 235
  Rhoda T. 83
Raily, Nelly 287
Rainey, Anne E. 165
  C. W. 165
  Enid 170
Ramey, Elisabeth 24
  Nancy 83
  Polley 357
Ramsay, Elmira F. 292
  James T. 241
  Julia Ann 71
  Mary A. 165
  Susan 350
Ramsey, Baldy 43

Ramsey (cont.)
  John 360
  Woodson J. 276
Randsome, Elizabeth 16
Raney, Annie 276
  E. Harriett 37
  Henry 276
  Lucy 86
  Mary A. 87
  Petta 355
Rankin, Jesse 213
Ransom, Henry 217
  Henry W. 53
  Mary 176
Rany, Thos. H. 5
Ratin, Evan 272
Ratley, Nancey 6
Raven, John 8
Ravens, Sarah 162
Rawlings, Augusta J. 319
Ray, Martha 30
  Priscilla 14
Read, Barshabe 5
  Christian 290
  E. A. 24
  Edwin G. 178
  Emily 290
  Jane E. 81
  Jno. 307
  Polly 106
  Ransom 290
  Robt. H. 96, 125, 165, 235
  Sarah J. 196
Reade, Pattie (Mrs.) 168
Reames, Alexander 172
  D. C. 238
Reams, G. A. 100
  J. R. 105
Rear, Margarett 317
Reardon(?), Dennis 347
Reaves, Caroline 202
  Elisabeth 252
  Hardy 169
  Patient 8
  Salley 238
  Thos. 238
  William H. 248
  Wm. W. 241
Reavis, Addie S. 316
  Anadella 143
  Ann E. 60
  Betsy 146
  Dilly 334
  Dilly H. 252
  Elisn 278
  Elizabeth J. 197
  Elizabeth T. 334
  Ella 262
  Emily J. 75
  Geo. B. 25, 259, 334
  Harriett 171
  Jack 171
  Lewis 334
  Lucy 151
  Lucy W. 364
  Martha 107, 278
  Martha J. 334
  Mary 334
  Mary H. 192
  Mary L. 334
  Mary W. 49
  Nancy 151, 171
  Nancy H. 356
  P. D. 92
  Peter 277
  Rebecca J. 42
  Rebeccah 141

Reavis (cont.)
  Rosa 35
  Sally 324
  Sally T. 365
  Saml. 151
  Samuel J. 141
  Samuel J., Jr. 143
  W. W. 32
  Warren 278
  William 207
  Wm. W. 80
Red, Ann 142
  Emma 62
Redd, Mary J. 32
Reddick, Joseph K. 250
Reddy, Joseph 222
Redford, James 271
Redman, Jane C. 362
  Permelia 271
Redwine, Christan 324
  Michael 324
Reece, Margaret L. 15
  Rebeckah 241
  Richard 322
  Sarah 194
Reed, Frances Maria 261
  Mary 231
  Peggy 261
  Polly 230
Reeks, Elizabeth N. 231
Reeks(?), Frances 180
Reeks, John 263, 314
  Mary An 273
  Sally 329
  Thos. 235
Reeves, Abner 278
  Frederick 160
Reeves(?), George J. 169
  H. 145
Reeves, John 345
  Mary 323
  Salley 71
  William 213
  Willie 252
  Wm. 109
Regans, Peter F. 111
Reid, Jas. L. 245, 263
  Robert 129, 312
  Thos. J. 99
  W. B. 226
Renals, John 113
Renn, W. Z. 363
Revis, Nancy 35, 36
Reynolds, William 63, 205
Rhea, Andw. 244
  Matilda 14
Rhinshaw, Charles Fredrick 276
Ricards, Sabrina 151
Rice, Betsey 211
  David 70, 74, 134, 279
  Eliza 312
  Harris 14
  Jesse 369
  John W. 159
  L. W. 317
  Lewellen 308
  Lucy 260
  Margarett 315
  Mary 70, 78
  Nancey 161
  Patsey 195
  Polly A. 333
  Presly 28
  Susan 74

Rice (cont.)
  Tho. 111
  Thomas 70, 218
  Thos. 70
  W. T. 43
  William 112, 249
  Wm. T. 279
  Zadock 297
Rich, Agness 328
  Shadrach 328
Richard, Milly 45
Richards, John H. 326
  Mary F. 31
  Polly 362
  Rebeckah 292
  Sally 75
Richardson, John T. 136
  Lucinda 230
  Nancy 280
  Olive 20
  Salley P. 152
  Sam. 280
  Susan 334
Richerson, Eliza 67, 229
  George 145
  Martha 105
  Nancy 9
  Sally 316
Richmond, Obra 207
  Peter 207
  Susan 207
Ricks, Jno. 351
  John 244, 270, 357
  Thomas 161, 323
  Thomas, Jr. 195, 308
Rideout, Catherine 281
  Martha A. 281
  Mary A. 259
Ridley, Amelia M. 165
  B. 216
  Elizabeth 48
  Eveline 70
  Frances 123
  Francis 308
  James 90, 138, 300
  Mary 281, 282, 309
  Mary R. 319
  Milley 4
  Polly 138
  Robt. M. 73
  Sally D. 28
  Thomas D. 255
  Thos. D. 83
  Thos. L. 28
  Tisha 281
  Virginia L. 300, 364
  Will M. S. 171
  Willis 206
Ridly, Sarah C. 202
Ridout, D. T. 281
Riggan, Eliza J. 24
  Moses T. 241
Riggans, Emily B. 342
Riggin, Emeline 252
Riggins, Polly 195
Riggs, Hennessee 148
Right, Jordan 100
Riley, James 282
  John 279
Rittaylander, Mary 31
Rivers, Lucy A. R. 141
Roach, Robert 266
Robards, Ann 347
  Celia 257
  Elizabeth 225, 284
  Fanny 309
  Fanny A. 47

Robards (cont.)
  G. Y. 207
  George 103, 282
  H. G. 349
  H. J. 66, 295
  H. L. 281, 301, 320, 340
  Isabellah 237
  Jane E. 291
  Jenny 188
  Mack 287
  Mary 282
  Mary Ann 194
  Mary Jane 226, 284
  Nathaniel 41, 305
  Nathl. 246, 254
  Polley 196, 318
  Prudence W. 48
  Syrus 237
  Telitha J. 211
  Temperance 214
  Thom. 301
  William 234, 364
  William N. 35
  Willie 218
Robarts, George 257, 282
Roberds, Anna 235
  Betsy 319
  Martha Jane 283
Roberson, Adnah 300
  Dolley 210
  Feraby 107
  Geo. 154
  India 57
  Jincy 144
  Lemuel 284
  Martha 26
  Martha A. E. 35
  N. C. 283
  Nathl. 74
  Parthena 76
  R. Hobgood 362
  Robert 284
  Sally 89
  Sally T. 107
  Sarah W. 283
  Susan 40
  Susanna 53
  Tabatha 109
  Tabbitha 107
  Thomas 286
  William 98
  Winney 307
Roberts, Amelia 199
  Candis 86
  Caroline 246
  Charity W. 115
  Charlotte 257
  Edney 143
  Elisha 284
  Elizabeth 142
  Fanny 126
  Francis 190
  Gaston 217
  George P. 231
  Jacob 284
  Jane 231, 291
  Jane R. 127
  Jeremiah 262
  Lewis 284
  Lively 285
  Lucy 7
  Lucy Ann 212
  M. P. 127, 142, 184, 284
  Magga 200
  Martha 237, 347
  Mary 190

Roberts (cont.)
　Moses 234, 291
　Moses H. 257
　Muel 291
　Nancy 188, 363
　Polly 184
　Rebecca 62, 142, 284
　Salina 32
　Sally 64, 257
　Selva 284
　Temp. 326
　Thomas 233
　Tyresa 38
　W. P. 346
　William 140, 284
　Willis 84, 199, 358
Robertson, Amelia Ann 65
　Damsel 153
　Elisabeth 57
　Eliza 54
　Elizabeth 346
　Frances 94
　Francis 346
　Frankey 370
　Indiana 286
　Jane 285
　John 113
　Martha R. 359
　Mary 3, 285
　Nancey 67
　Nancy 107
　Peter 65
　Riney 299
　William 183
Robey, Martha 121
Robinson, Adnah 357
　Jacob 87
　Robert 125
Robison, Judith 297
　Wm. 297
Rochel, Precilah 111
Rochelle, Martha 259
　William 24
Rodes(?), M(?) 16
Rodgers, Dicey 234
　Mary 286
　Matilda 286
　Nancy 278
Rodgers(?), Sarah 278
Rodman, John T. 271
Roe, Ransom 286
　Willis 140
Roffe, Elizabeth 36
　Judy W. 255
　Nancey 335
　Rachael D. 170
　Sally L. 142
　Woodson 142, 255
Rogers, Ann Eliza 141
　Bettie A. 187
　David 189
　Delila 6
　Dessie 6
　Dilliard 287
　Elinor 121
　Elisabeth 152
　Frances 193
　Frank 251
　H. 288
　Horace 287
　John 193, 237, 287
　John W. 182
　Joseph 269
　Josiah C. 50
　Lively 209
　Lucretia 287
　Martha 112

Rogers (cont.)
　Mary 23, 252, 287
　Mary H. 189
　Milia 251
　Nancey 113, 213
　Obedience 304
　Rachal 267
　Rachel 113
　Rebecca F. 71
　Sarah 253
　Susan 112
　W. 167
　William 267
　Williamson 297
Roges, Virginia L. 210
Rogester, Elesh 268
Roland, Salley 273
Rooker, John 138
Rose, Amey 93
　Catey 228
　Howel 166
　William P. 360
　Winnefred 225
Ross, Atha Ann 50
　Anna M. V. 185
　Charles 288, 291
　Cinthy 50
　Elizabeth Ann 259
　Francis 314
　Hixy 214
　James 17, 89, 182
　Judith 274
　Mary 4
　Nancy 288
　Patrick 89, 90
　Patsey 2
　Sarah 230
　Susan 4
Routon, W. B. 154, 171
Rowland, Amey 18
　Catharine 238
　Detrion T. 75
　Edna 311
　Elizabeth W. 169
　Frances 172
　Geo. J. 211, 231, 332
　George J. 56
　H. H. 129, 146, 279, 323
　Happy 56
　Henry 122, 289, 359
　Henry N. 310
　Horace H. 343
　Lillie 102
　Lucy 343
　Martha A. 216
　Milley 289
　Nancey 24
　Nancy 295
　Phoebe 289
　Presley 24, 158
　Robert 289
　Robert R. 360
　Susan 260
　W. H. 126, 277, 279, 365
　Windsor 102
Rowlett, J. M. 341
Royal, Josiah C. 151
Roycraft, Polly 349
Roycroft, Kinchen T. 289
Royrs, Willis 219
Royster, A. M. 366
　Amanda H. 275
　Ann 361
　Ann W. 269
　Bannester 323
　Betsey 298

Royster (cont.)
　Bettie Lyle 241
　Caroline 290, 322
　Charles M. 366
　D. 146
　E. P. 291
　Edity 290
　Elizabeth 79, 249, 366
　Ellen 29
　Emerly 306
　Emily 289, 300
　Emily F. 146
　F. A. 291
　Frances H. 107
　Francis 157, 160
Royster(?), George W. 301
　Henrietta 56
　Henry 290
　Horace 289
　James 93, 150, 155
　Jennie E. 361
Royster(?), John G. 212
Royster, John H. 107, 152, 351
　Juda 291
　Julia Ann 234
　Lethy Jane 22
　Letuce 244
　Louisa 13, 46
　Lucy A. 182
　M. D. 57, 132
　Maria 291
　Mariller 366
　Marquis 290
　Martha 290
　Martha A. 4
　Martha Jane 81
　Mary 232, 312
　Mary A. 280
　Mary Ann 350
　Mary B. 370
　Mary E. 290
　Mary J. 142
　Mary Jane 309
　Nancey 36
　Nancy C. 352
　Palla 45
　Panthea B. 57
　Patsy 292
　Raleigh 290
　Rebecca P. 316
　Richard 27, 244
　Robert 22
　Sarah E. 74
　Sarah A. M. 22
　Stellah 22
　Susan 27
　Susan A. 298
　Susan R. 92
　Tabern 234
Royster(?), Thomas 291
Royster, William 8, 196, 210, 361
　William H. 28
　William J. 316
　Willie 184
　Willis A. 199, 249, 312, 370
　Wm. H. 64
Rucks, Thomas E. 44
Rudd, Emily 55
　Field 94
　John D. 172
　Lucrecia 234
Ruseteim, Anne 42
Russ, Chas. E. 355
　Mary F. 312

Russell, Betty 185
  Catharine L. 65
  Elisa W. 113
  Emily H. 21
  Fannie 267
  Grandison 292, 296
  Hannah 230
  Harriet S. 27
  Ibby 2
  James H. N. 247
  Jas. 75, 366
  Jas. A. 187, 213, 259
  Jno. 65
  Joe 267
  John C. 288
  John G. 292
  Josephine 88
  Lovelace 212
  Lucy P. 201
  Martha 24
  Martha Ann 296
  Patsy 267
  Res. 5
  Rose 292, 296
  Sarah 166
  Susan P. 350
  W. F. 98
  William 184
Russill, Anney 292
Rust, Ann 14
  Benjamin 14
  Eliza Ann 14
  Emily S. 227
  Jeremiah 69, 293
  Jerh. 148
  John 69, 170, 293
  Polley 240
  Prissilla 271
  Sally 138
  Saml. 287
  Sarah 287
  Sarah H. 34
Rustel, Annah 9
Sadler, A-(?) 205
  Archer C. 233
  Eliza A. 253
  Elizabeth 178
  Mary E. 233
Salmon, Elizabeth T. 213
  Wm. 280
Salter, Patsey 199
Sam, Margaret 169
Sampel, James 127
Sample, Alexander 30
  Mary 337
  William P. 188
  Wm. 127
Samuel, Winny 358
Sandefer, Henry 43
Sanderford, Elizabeth 115
  Lucy 51
Sanders, Jesse 294
  Mary 50
Sandford, Ellen 146
  Epps 146
  Fanny 244
  Frances 123
  James 225
  John F. 270
  Louisa 352
  Lucy 66
  Lucy P. 328
  Mary 66
  Nancy J. 298
  Sylvia 146

Sandifer, Green 294
  Jane 294
Sandiferd, Priscilla 354
Sandler, Sarah E. 69
Sandlin, William 181
Sandling, Caswel H. 181
  Nancy 362
Sands, Henry 114
Sandys, Mary R. 76
Sanford, Elisabeth 248
  Eliza 329
  Henry 294, 351
  Louisa A. 322
  Mary A. E. 276
  Nancy A. 148
  Sarah 351
Saterwhite, Amey M. 175
  Ann 175
  Francis 17
  Silva 312
  Ursle 351
Satterfield, Wm. 64
Satterwhite, (?) 161
  A. 306
  Amelia 325
  Amy 279
  Ann 19, 333
  Ann K. 282
  Becky 312
  Betsey 289
  Catharine 160, 226
  David 162, 183, 307, 315
  Drury 125
  E. 156
  Edney 307
  Elijah 24, 76, 134, 136, 327
  Elisabeth 279
  Elizabeth 75, 82, 306
  Elizabeth M. 330
  Emily 290
  Eveline 5
  F. 338
  Frances 70, 85
  Frances A. E. 244
  Franklin 12, 235, 265, 301
  Harry 59
  Howel 359
  Howell 351
  J. M. 22
  Jacob 362
  James 295
  Jas. M. 116
  John 251, 257
  Liza 294
  Louisa 310
  Lucy 201
  Lucy A. 51
  M. 211
  Martha 244
  Mary 244
  Michael 227
  Mitchel 78
  Nathan 296
  Norsisa G. 92
  Patsey 266, 368
  Polly 295
  Rebecca 75
  Robt. 294
  S. 295
  Sarah 48
  Smith 7, 227, 266, 319
  Solomon 254
  Stephen 47, 77, 128, 169, 223, 245, 252,

Satterwhite, Stephen (cont.)
  267, 295, 296, 329, 351
  Stepn. 341
  Susan A. 295
  Susan Ann 295
  Susanna 251
  T. 52
  Thomas 48
  Thos. 177
  Tolivar 310
  Ursula 356
  William S. 35
Sauls, Celia M. 227
Saulter, Susanna 109
Saunders, Peggy 184
Scales, A. M. 296
Schoht, Prissilia 296
Scot, Emily 179
Scot(?), Mary R. 151
Scot, Prior 46
  Pyer 317
  Rutha F. 311
  Sarah 313
  Susan 296
Scott, Alonzo 276
  Anne 301
  Bettie R. 8
  Elisabeth Griggs 327
  Emily 106
  John L. 29
  Lizzie 276
  Lucy 296
  Martha 204
  Martha Ann 13
  Mary 125, 150, 306
  Peggey 210
  Rebecah 192
  Richd. 128
  Rowan 276
Scott(?), Susan A. 295
Scott, Theodorick 125
Scrugg, Lottey 301
Scrutcher, Martin 154
Scurry, Frances 125
Seaborn, Mary 271
Searcey, Polley 111
Searcy, Abner 169
  Bennet 36, 276, 301, 325, 356
  James 300
  John 63, 84, 206
  John, Jr. 152, 271
  John, Sr. 47, 163
  Martha 330
  Reuben 120, 125, 156, 228
  Richd. 330
  Reuben 296
  Salley 174
  Saml. 26
  Wm. 207
  Wm. H. 47, 308
Searcy(?), Wm. R. 339
Sears, Abner 135
  Anderson 163, 295, 297
  Anny 18
  Beverly 350
  Elizabeth 368
  Lucy 70
  Nancy 163
  Parthena A. 359
  Sally 297
  Sarah 160
  Temperence 297
  Washington 163
  William 279

Sears (cont.)
  Wm. 286, 297
Seat, Drury 102
  Dury 200
  Izabella J. 102
  Martha 102, 200
Seats, Elizabeth 147
  Mary 48, 134
  Rebecca 329
Semple, Ann 85
  Elizabeth 356
  Jane 293
  Janet 169
Sercey, Elisabeth 172
Sethey(?), Henry H. 156
Sevesey, Thos. 200
Shackelford, Mary 170
Shadrach, Paschall 136
  Ruthy 216
  Sarah 137
Shadrick, Mary 259
  Nancy 115
Shadwick, Elizabeth 89
  John 221
  Phereby 221
Shamwell, Mary 252
  Nelley 197
  Zachariah 94
  Zacheriah 252
Shanks, Elizabeth R. 268
  Lucy Ann 352
  Mary 161, 298
  Mary E. 232
  Robert 272
  Susan 128
  Virginia E. 290
Shapard, Thos. 321
Sharpe, Robert H. 298
Shaver, Fanny 15
  Polly 345
Shaw, John 298
  R. J. 114
Shearman, Anna 239
  Dinecy 258
  Elizabeth 262
  John 258, 262, 273
  Polley 258
Shemán, A. 356
Shemwell, Ellender 254
  Isaac 254
  Samuel 197
Shepard, Elizabeth 290
Sherman, A. 355
  Elizabeth 239
  John 306
Sherrin, Candis 336
  Drury 317
  Eliza 299
  Harriett 360
  Jehu 340
  Lucy C. 353, 359
Short, Elizabeth 285
  Ellender 14
  Fannie 210
  James 107
  Lucy Ann 205
  Susan 357
  Thos. W. 312
  Vines 113
  Wm. H. 5
  Wyatt 205, 300
Shotwell, Alfred 124
  James D. 291
  Julia 124
  Sarah A. F. 273
  Sarah F. 124

Shearin, Mary 103
  Nancy 202
  Sally 103
Shearing, Agitha 137
  Joseph 324
Shearman, J. 115
  John 321
  Mary 37
  Sarah 329
  Squire 173
  Rowan 28
Shemwell, Samuel 197
Shepard, Wm., Jr. 309
Sheppard, Anne 19
Sherin, Jehu 61
Shering, Jesse 27
Sherman, Lucinda R. 87
Sherrin, Harriet 126
  John 40
  Polly Ann 193
  Susan J. 59
Shert, James A. 153
Short, Ellen 142
  Julia Ann 33
  Lucey Ann 205
  Margaret 85
  Mary A. 58
  Sarah 100
  Thos. 107
  Vines 153
Shotwel, Mary (Mrs.) 273
Shotwell, Bettie T. 147
Shuno, Jos. L. 82
Sigue(?), Jane 122
Sikes, Harriet S. 37
Simmons, Mary J. 44
  Molley 90
  Nancy 336
  Rebeccah 324
  Tabitha 272
Simon, Temperance 69
Sims, Allin 300
  Harbert 195
  Hollis E. 310
  James 110
  Lennard 360
  Mary 360
  Nancy 115
  William 286
Simpson, Mary 144
  Matthew 349
Singleton, Martha J. 43
Sisemore, Eddy 156
  Elisabeth 301
Sitgraves, Standfield H. 181
Sizemore, Bird 301
  Elizabeth J. 41
Skelton, William 271, 347
  Wm. 53
Skinner, C. M. 301
  Sallie C. 285
  William C. 301
Slaughter, A. 105
  A. R. B. 302
  Abraham 115, 302
  Affie L. 87
  Alice G. 302
  Barbara 179
  Catharine 70
  Charity S. 301
  David 325
  Elizabeth 12, 94
  Ellen 162
  Franky 94
  Isaac 301
  Jacob 201

Slaughter (cont.)
  Jacob L. 180, 302, 326
  John 301
  John B. 91
  Juba 325
  Laner 301
  Martha C. 163
  Mary 95
  Masten 302
  Nancy 6, 275
  Polly 95
  Rufus R. 352
  Sarah 248
  Solomon 301
  Susan 95
  Susanna 321
  W. P. B. 94
  W. P. S. 262
  William N. 302
Slotter, Laner 301
Slucer, Margaret 376
Small, John 328
  Nancy 328
Smiley, Agnes 239
  Hester 241
  Maria E. 278, 281
Smith, A. C. 306
  Agness 26, 193
  Alexander 83, 290, 306
  Alexr. 22, 250
  Allan 200, 285
  Allis 321
  Amy W. 304
  Anderson 104, 111, 186, 293
  Ann B. 183
  Ann D. (Mrs.) 213
  Ann H. 344
  Ann R. 65
  Anne 305
  Arabell 35
  Barbara 159
  Barbary A. 260
  Beedy 26
  Bella 227
  Betsey 3, 59, 62, 257
  Bettie 362
  Betty 261
  Brety 151
  Celia 62, 302
  Charity 169
  Charles 305
  Ciller 59
  Cornela 169
  David 303
  Dianna 297
  Dicey 176
  Edmond 305, 310
  Elisabeth 56, 186, 310
  Elisabeth H. 320
  Eliza 26, 324
  Elizabeth 1, 92, 160, 178, 197, 228, 237, 321, 351
  Elizabeth C. 303
  Elizabeth P. 40
  Emily 151
  Fanney H. 220
  Fanny 154
  Frances 220, 306
  Geo. C. 240
  Goodman 175
  Guy 25, 228, 303
  Hardy 104, 105
  Hawkins 169
  Henery 193
  Henrietta 325

Smith (cont.)
  Henry 26, 173
  Isabella 65, 336
  Isom 66
  J. C. 249
  J. L. 293
  J. W. 270
  James 80, 93, 269
  Jane 5, 322
  Jas. 314
  Jas. W. 92
  Jenney 239
  Jno. P. 146, 206
  Jno. Y. 259
  Jo. 159
  Joel 178
  John 26, 34, 101, 203, 269, 288, 289, 304
  John P. 92, 308
  John Y. 177, 238
  Joseph 81, 130, 201, 370
  Joseph L. 51
  Joseph M. 303
  Kizia 250
  L. C. 168
  Lemuel C. 46
  Leonard 138
  Leroy 169, 229
  Leroy E. 303
  Levina 40
  Lewis 17
  Louis 304
  Louisa 193
  Lucey 288, 302
  Lucy 59
  Lucy Jane 315
  Lucy W. 323
  Lun 302
  M. A. 153, 172, 339, 354
  M. S. 153
  M. T. 344
  Mahala 304
  Mahaly G. 306
  Maria L. 25
  Martha 153, 300
  Martha A. 44
  Martha Ann 313
  Martha P. 344
  Martha W. 152
  Mary 157, 258, 319, 358
  Mary A. C. 306
  Mary E. 246, 304
  Mary G. 58
  Mary Jane 300
  Mary W. 356
  Maurace 188
  Maurice 70, 228, 239, 302, 304, 306, 309
  Mead 28
  Mead A. 356
  Metilda 244
  Mima 244
  Morris 358
  Nancey 47, 192, 305
  Nancy 34, 153, 205, 272, 293
  Peggey 98
  Peggy 305, 325
  Phebe 26
  Polley 152
  Polly 37, 91
  Rachel 26
  Radaan 77
  Ransom 172, 349

Smith (cont.)
  Ransome 193
  Rebecca 364
  Rebekah 272
  Reubin 102
  Riley 149
  Rosella 303
  Rosey 105
  Roxanna 227
  Ruthy 256
  S. W. 344
  Salley 192
  Sally 352
  Sally Ann 220
  Sally P. 92
  Saml. 118, 306
  Samuel 73, 197, 303, 344
  Samuel W. 65, 140
  Sarah 66, 80, 187, 199, 349
  Sarah P. 354
  Sarah W. 85
  Sherwood 33
  Sihon 97
  Sophronia Ann 293
  Squire 244
  Stephen 303
  Susan B. 148
  Susan J. 190
  T. H. 303
  Tabithey 365
  Thomas 278, 310
  Vincent 5
  W. H. 310
  Wiatt 98
  Wiley 303
  Will. F. 304
  William H. 306
  William P. 40, 57
  Willie 149, 302
  Willie, Jr. 185
  Winney 174
  Wm. 368
Smithwick, Louisa 307
  Robt. 304
Sneed, Albert 219, 317
  Amanda 206
  Archibald H. 10, 208
  E. D. 132
  Elizabeth 177, 340
  Hannah 356
  Henry 194
  Isabella 307
  Jas. 282, 355
  Joseph P. 201
  Julea J. 131
  Junius 48, 202, 316
  Lewis 206
  Lucy 194
  Moses 307
  Nancey 126
  Rd. 229, 353
  Rebecer 341
  Richard 167
  Richd. 115, 243, 258, 275
  S. 48
  Sallie G. 277
  Sally W. 132
  Step. 7, 83, 124, 181, 208
  Step. K. 59, 186, 195, 258, 270, 299, 330, 333, 340, 352, 358
  Steph. 295
  Vilet 354

Sneed (cont.)
  W. M. 23, 24, 107, 167, 185, 234, 252, 279, 296, 297, 357
  William M. 19, 188, 198, 224, 281, 320
Snelling, Ann. 308
  Frances 155
  Hugh 130
  Kattey 130
  Lucey 130
  Tabathy 21
Snipes, Frances 197
  James 308
  Jesse 88
  John 264
  Mathew 75
  Nancy 308
  Nathaniel 116
  Thos. 184
  Willis 275
Soakeley(?), Jane 87
Sockwell, James 190
Soloman, Abby 20
  Birchett 318
  Jemima 301
  Polly Ann 283
  W. H. 301
  William 130
Somerhill, Elijah 81
  Norma(?) 346
Somerin, Jacob 272
Somervill, Susannah 98
Somerville, Ann 30
  Jno, Jr. 185
  John, Jr. 320
  Mary 355
Sommerhill, Horace 39
Southall, Elizabeth M. 367
  Mary E. 175
  Rebecca J. 365
Southerland, Jane O. 167
  Jno. 109
  Laura A. 95
  Sabat 308
  Senia 120
Sowell, Mary Ann 209
Spaigg, Jane 256
Spaight, Richard D. 140
Spain, Green 104
Spait, Richd. D. (Gov.) 357
Sparks, Richard 190
Spear, Nancey 133
Spears, Abbigal K. 53
  Catharine 347
Spears(?), Frances 261
Spears, John 285
  Martha 49
  Penny 154
  Polly 31
Speed, Jennie E. 33
  John J. 187
  Julia 328
  Louisa 365
  Louisa Y. 325
  Peter 328
  Rosalia 320
  Sallie J. 265
  Tho. 130
  Virginia F. 130
Speer, Nathaniel 321
Speers, Susannah 269
Speller, Wm. H. 316
Spencer, A. F. 142
  Eliza C. 260
  James 39, 115

Spencer (cont.)
  Mary A. 260
  Tilda G. 152
  Virginia B. 26
Spivey, Anne 362
Spivy, Repsey 366
Springer(?), Elisabeth 216
Springfield(?), Aaron 158
Stacey, Jane 137
Stacy, Matilda 312
Stalings, Lenney 261
Stamper, William 309
Stanback, Martha 290
  Nicholas 111
Stanley, Ezekiel 310
Stanton, G. 16, 174, 278, 292, 304, 310
  Mariah L. 349
  Martha Sarah 7
  Mary 147
  Mary A. 363
  Robert T. 238
  W. H. D. 284
  William 287
Stark, Dionetia S. 195
  Dolley 349
  Julia 310
  Kizah J. 260
  Kyzer J. 17, 195, 310, 358
  Lucretia 331
  Polly 5, 185
  Priscilla 360
  Susan F. 195
Starke, Lydia 158
Starks, Messa 257
  Sarah 88
Staunton, J. G. 55
Steagall, Jas. 192
Steed, Lucy Ann 155
Stegall, Ann 362
  Francis 200
  Leonard 311
  Margarett J. 264
Stem, Ann 183
  Asa 311
  Jacob 2
  L. B. 13
  Martha 127
  Nancey 336
Stemper, Betsey 192
Sten, Robert T. 126
Stephens, Deborah 53
  Frances 250
  Sally 136
Stephenson, Jane 191
  Jno. 311
  John 284
  Lucy 67
  Nancey 168
Stevalo, Matilda 312
Stevens, Arthur 109
  Sarah D. 149
Stevens(?), William 345
Steward, Elizabeth 118
  Ellen 274
  James 204
  Mary Ann 333
  Nancy 100
  Pitsey 234
  Sally 204
Stewart, Catharine 341
  James 107
  Manson 343
  Mary 22

Stewart (cont.)
  Mary E. 172
  Sallie A. 111
  Sally 107
  T. A. 37, 93
  Thomas A. 12
  W. J. 370
Stewert, Anne 18, 96
Stigall, Bedford 362
Stirk, Susan F. 64
Stokes, Alfred 310
  Hester 312
  Parthena 195
Stone, Benj. 57, 100
  Claborn 363
  Claiborn 293
  D. A. 28
  David A. 198, 250
  Eli 312
  Elizabeth H. 263
  Emily H. 143
  Fanny 305
  H. W. 62
  Harriett E. 17
  Helly 156
  J. A. 155
  James 225
  Jordan 313
  L. B. 58, 313
  Lucy 35
  Malissa 78
  Martha 170, 280
  Mary 121, 134
  Mary Ann 57
  Mary P. 336
  Minerva Ann 341
  Parker A. 74
  Parker F. 261
  Part. F. 123
  Sallie 164
  Sarah A. 300
  Susan M. 242
Stonum, Bryon 262
Stovall, Armon 169
  Bartholomew 313
  Barthw. 309
  Easter 205
  Eliza 260
  Elizabeth 160, 270, 312
  Ellen 295
  Esta A. 290
  John 31, 212, 313
  Lavina 220
  Margaret 7, 313
  Martha 312
  Mary Jane 142
  Parthena 140
  Phanny 212
  Pheby 290
  Rebecca 27
  Rebecca 157
  Sarah 366
  Sarah A. 327
  Sarah Ann 174
  Susan 57
  Susanna 249
  Tabitha 158
  William 312
Stover, David 124
Stowvall, Mary 21
Straider, Henry 170
Strand(?), Joella 187
Strange, Elizabeth 199
Strater, Caty 137
  Mary 313
Strator, Adam 204
Street, Peter W. 13

Strem, Nancey 304
Strickling, Quincy 270
Stringfellow, Richard 273, 343
Strong, Elizabeth A. 165
  Joysa 314
  Lizzie 154
  Lucy 237
  Nicy 314
  Unis R. 165
Strother, Jas. L. 50
  Louisa 204
  Minerva 177
Stroud, Adeline 94
  Elizabeth 208, 234
  John 314
  John L. 208
  Mildred 272
  Ruth 134
  Ruthy 179
  Susan 43
  Wm. 314
Strowd, Jane 146
Strum, Bartholomew 314
  Dorcas 161
  Elizabeth 201, 360
  Frances 178
  Ginna 328
  Hezekiah 35, 47
Strum(?), J. H. 326
Strum, Jas. A. 328
  Lucy 52
  M. H. 145
  Martha 110
  Martha Ann 350
  Mary Ann E. 296
  Mary Jane 185
  Nancy G. 279
  Rachel 38
  Sarah T. 310
  Sary 47
  Thos. 213
  William 68
  William H. 128
  Wm. 161
Strung, Betsey 70
Struno, James H. 201
Stuart, John 193
  Manson 30
  Tabby 59
Stumper, David 325
Sturdavant, Nancy 85
Sturdavent, Martha 49
Sturdivant, Mary 178
Sturm, Bartholomew 186
Style, Martha 324
Suit, Ann 240
  Barbery 299
  Edith R. 65
  Elisabeth 207, 256
  Harriett 252
  James R. 299
  Lucina 24
  Lucinda C. 24
  Margeret 125
  Mary 298, 315
  Nancy 62
  Polley 337
  Riley 18, 19, 183, 284, 342
  Robert L. 213
  Salley 63
  Susan 247
  William 40, 54, 257
Summerhill, Eliza 275
  Horace 275
  William 354

Summerhill(?), William
  Henry 370
Sumner, Chlora 281
Susanah, Brack 306
Sute, John 207
Suttan, John 335
Sutton, Alexander 88
  Julia 263
  Mary 1, 263
  Sandy 115
  Stephen 315
Swain, Amelia F. 315
  Elizabeth 97
Sweaney, Robt. R. 285
Sweat, Elisabeth 265
Sydner, Mary A. 96
Sykes, Eliza 104
  Mary 38, 321
  Wm. M. 35
Sythe, Anne 98
Tabern, Arthur 266
  Bettie 349
  Burton 151
  Eliza 144, 151
  Jane 86
  John 316
  Littleton 141
  Lotty 141
  Lucy Amy 141
  Minerva 316
  Nancy 59
  Robert 10
  Sallie 60
  Sally Ann 153
  Susan 136
Tabon, Bitha Ann 149
  Littleton 8
  Lottie 8
  Nellie 8
  Robi. 246
Taborm, Littleton 79
Taborn, Dunk 256
  Elizabeth 286
  Harriot 189
  Littleton 10, 229
  Martha 105
  Mary 20
  Sophia Jane 227
  Thomas 20
  Till 20
Tabour, Rufus 87
Tabourn, Armenta 87
  Jincey 330
  William 210
Taburn, Littleton 229
  Mary 10
  Sally E. 296
  Sarah 20
  Wm. 11
Talley, Elisabeth 255
  Elizabeth 253
  Emily 352
  John 234
  Martha 349
  Matilda 165
  Polley 184
  Reuben 157
  Salley 349
  William L. 352
Tally, Beverly B. 101
  Elizabeth 79
  Emaly 101
  Martha 62
  Rebecca M. 101
  Samuel A. 92
  Stephen 165
Tancey, Tryon 201
Tanner, Betsey 3

Tanner (cont.)
  Chloe 76
  Cynthia 294
  Eliza 240
  Esther Ann 318
  Leonora Ellen 313
  Lucinda 58
  Moses 54, 89
  Susan 358
  Teakle 3
Tarreys, Louisa 237
Tarry, Isabella 319
  Samuel, Jr. 125
Tarver, Sally 264
Tate, Thos. A. 133
Tatom, Abner 175, 176
  Elisabeth 188
  John 87, 188
  Jusiah 128
  Wm. 216
Tatum, Elisabeth Ann
  163
  Frances 103
Taybourn, Elilia 155
Tayloe, Fanny 6
  Jas. P. 65
  Mary 340
  Mills 107, 115, 156,
    169
Taylor, Adabyron 329
  Agnes B. 308
  Agness B. 44
  Alice 278
  Anderson 56, 109
  Ann G. 29
  Ann L. 367
  Anna 318
  Arch. 325
  Archd. 82, 252
  Archibald 40
  Ava 74, 319
  Betsey 176
  Betsy 320
  Burwell 300
  Caroline 48
  Cary Ann 259
  Cornelia 176
  David 318
  Dolly 319
  Edm. 291
  Edmund 39, 319
  Elisabeth 177
  Elizabeth 138, 291
  Elizabeth A. 322
  Elizabeth J. 122
  Fanny Anderson 299
  Fletcher 192
  Frances 209
  Francis 124
  Francis A. 308
  H. A. 180
  Horace 319
  Isabella 124
  Isabella A. 270
  Jack 319
  James 105
  James T. 257
  Jane 194, 321
  Jina 258
  John 91, 155, 318
  John R. 25
  Jno. C. 67
  Joseph 9, 39, 173,
    194, 210, 320
  Keronhappuck 91
  Leathy 319
  Lucey 138
  Lucy 105

Taylor (cont.)
  Luvenia 74
  Margarate 237
  Martha A. 120
  Mary 9, 39, 73
  Mary Ann 75, 206
  Mary E. 74, 322
  Mary F. 120
  Mary S. 177
  Nancy 135, 318, 319
  Nathl. M. 183
  Peter 74
  Philip 265, 336
  Philis 161
  Pinkey 318
  Polley 245
  Richard 16, 54, 133,
    340, 347, 357
  Richd. 65
  Richd. B. 332
  Richd. D. 352
  Richd. P. 324
  Robt. 321
  Salley 183
  Sally S. 206
  Sarah 138
  Sarah Jane 277
  Scipio 320
  Stephen 352
  Susan C. 39
  Susannah Martin 355
  Thomas 85, 128, 209,
    270, 327
  Thos. B. 112
  Warner 320
  William 308, 348
  William A. 74
  Wm. 279, 304
  Wm. V. 167
Tazwell, Mary 201
Teal, John 36
Teasley, Sarah 155
Tergury(?), Wm. 105
Terrell, Agnis 340
  John 65, 320
  W. Thomas 341
Terry, (?) 87
  Benjamin 327
  Betsey 3, 61
  Candis 323
  Elizabeth 65
  Fanny W. 247
  J. 362
  James 126, 321
  James T. 95
  John H. 227
  Mary 186
  Nancey 362
  Nancy D. 18
  Polly Ann 323
  Rowland 3, 126
  S. 247
  Sarah 126, 321
  Sarah E. 166
  Sarrat 247
  Stephen 50, 61, 301
  Sy. 19
  Thomas 3, 18, 227
  William 3, 52, 362,
    367
  Wm. 65, 87
Thacker, Mary 21
  Sally Ann 272
Thammel, Rebecca 225
Tharington, John E. 230
  Nancy W. 120
  Samuel H. 120
Tharp, Patsey 171

Tharrington, Fenner 37
  Harriet 321
  Thos. 321
Themwell, Samuel 235
Thomas, Ann 322
  Athansius 361
  Bettie 360
  Caroline 322
  Elisabeth 46
  Eliza 61, 96, 321
  Elizabeth 269, 322
  Elizebeth 357
  Emily Jane 181
  Frances 138
  George 160
  Haywood 265, 322
  J. W. 322
  James 322
  James J. 7, 72, 234
  Joana 265
  John 53
  John W. 285
  Judith 22
  Lucinda 181
  Maria 22, 46
  Martha 265
  Mary 268
  Mary Jones 344
  Molley 182
  Nancy M. 46
  Rebecah 245
  Richard 322
  Robert W. 46
  Salisbury 31
  Sallie F. 127
  Sally 105, 245, 358
  Seny 322
  Serry 265
  Susan 127
  W. H. 322
  William 358
  William G. 127
  Winefred 217
Thomason, Anne 174
  Elizabeth 232
  James 232, 323
  John 308
  Martha 104
  Nathaniel 280
  Salley 313
Thomasson, Ann 283
  Benjamin 99, 209, 224, 323
  Calvin 53
  Euphemia C. 37
  Geo. 74, 124, 136, 184, 199
  George, Jr. 42
  George P. 113, 120, 147
  Gleming 323
  Harriet 270
  John 323
  Louisa 227
  Lucy 167
  Lucy Ann 101
  Martha 190, 314
  Mary 207, 310
  Mary D. 74
  Nannie G. 224
  Nathaniel 70
  Nelson 64
  Parthena 31
  Polly 224, 323
  Richard 283
  Richd. 119
  Sippy 37
  Sothoron H. 254

Thomasson (cont.)
  Susan 63
  Thomas 185
  Virginia 320
  William 83, 293, 309, 313
  Wm. 199, 201
Thomerson, Elisabeth 185, 210
Thompson, Elisabeth 278
  Elizabeth B. 153
  Francis 188
  Geo., Jr. 5
  Henderson 329
  Henry 198
  James 6
  John 84
  John G. 192
  Jonothan 180
  Louisa Ella 101
  Lucey 188
  Mary 318
  Peter 188
  Sally A. 324
  Sarah 312
  Wm. 232
Thomson, Ann 175
  Benjamin 210
  Rebeka 278
  Rhoda 253
Thornton, Anna 204
  Harry 204
  Mary 204
  Patsey 99
  William 240
Thorp, Abbie 324
  Benjamin P., Jr. 344
  Charlotte 80
  Elizabeth 40
  Elizer 222
  Ella A. 132
  Happy Pete 324
  James 80
  John, Jr. 362
  Kizzie 325
  Lucinda 324
  Martha 206
  Millie Ann 136
  Nancy 131
  Parthenia 325
  Peggy 80
  Peterson 273
  Rowena 48
  Sabrina 246
  Sallie Ann Pete 324
  Sarah 321
  Terry 321
  Thos. 48
Thrift, David 215, 306
Throckmorton, Emily C. 68
  Mollie H. 58
Thrush, Guilford 342
  Leitha 342
Thurm, Anney 54
Thurman, Landey L. A. 366
Thweat, Mary 176
Tillerson, Mary 126
Tilletson, Allen 267
  Elizabeth F. 307
  H. 174
  Henry 174
  Rufus 174
  W. R. 238, 293
  Woody 30
Tilley, Dennis 299, 326
  F. J. 59, 218, 326, 335

Tilley (cont.)
  Francis J. 145, 256, 262
  Henry 284, 326
  Lucinda 102
  Margaret 127
  Mary 184
  Mildred 211
  R. C. 331
Tilliam, Delilah 324
Tillison, James 82
  John 211
  William 98
Tillotson, Adeline 357
  Mary 239
  Mary C. 244
  William 239
Tillottson, Amelia 245
  Henry 334, 366
  Julia 326
  Susan Ann 70
  William 326
Tilly, Henry 38
Tilman, David 149
Timberlake, Francis 307
  Peter 316
  Sophronia 316
  Tempy 316
Tindall, Sally 224
Tingel, Jacob S. 163
Tingen, John D. 162
Tinsley, Eliza D. 278
Tippet, Bethiah 115
  Jincy 255
  Ruthy 166
  Sarah 342
Tippett, Frances 320
  Harriet L. 314
  Jane 153
  John H. 218
  Jonathan H. 306
  Mary 193, 218
  Mary F. 135
  Sarah J. 90
  Simeon 135
  Thos. 166
  William T. 224
Tippit, John H. 143
  Luke 187
Tippitt, Orpha 224
Tisdale, Polley 183
To-(?), John 68
Toler, Eliza 328
Tolley, W. S. 308
Tomlinson, Albert G. 202
Tompkins, Henry, Jr. 136
Tompson(?), Esther 271
Toom, William F. 281
Toon, Eliza 360
Toone, Virginia Ann 360
Torean, Isabellah 309
Torenton, Wm. 341
Toter, Eliza J. 129
Totten, Joseph 306
Townes, Elizabeth T. 360
  Henry 60
Trailor, Wm. 181
Trairer, Charity 102
Traylor, Elizabeth 247
  Holly 239
  John 97
  Mary M. 255
  Salley 97
  Wills B. 263
Tredway, Moses 24
Trevain, Franky 274
Trevan, Montgomery 8
Trevan(?), Prudence 96

Trevelle, J. C. 299
Trewolla, J. C. 273
Trimmon, Ann 213
Trisdal, Nancy 328
  Wm. 328
Troler, Ann 171
Trotter, Henry 30
  Julia P. 14
Trowler, William 71
Truman, Lucy 21
  Susan 105
Trumore(?), Eliza 59
Trusty, Agness 202
  Geney 347
  John 347
Tuck, Abby W. 328
  Agness 253
  Almond 160
  Drana A. 329
  E. A. 329
  Jane 97
  John 329
  Jos. P. 123
  Martha 351
  Mary C. 328
  Mary C. V. 36
  Matilda 329
  Nancy 113
  Nathan F. 329, 352
  Nimrod 80
  Paul 328
  Powel 200
  Powell 329
  R. B. 329
  S. A. M. 67
  Sarah 124, 216
  Susan A. 274
  William R. 249
Tucker, Daniel 108
  Elizabeth 108, 199
  Glafrey H. 337
  Leathey 97
  Littlebery 329
  Martha 323
  Mary 97
  Rebecca 104
  Susan 116
  Tho. 179
  Thomas 171, 196
  William R. 240, 249, 329
Tudar, Henry 88
Tuder, John 231
  Tabitha 349
Tudor, Beckey 232
  Henry 330, 349
  Sarah 140
Tuen(?), Susanna 139
Tuill, James 328
Tunstall, Harriot B. 12
  Jerome 297
  Maggie E. 297
  R. A. 330
  Virginia E. 139
Turner, A. A. 331
  Amelia W. 310
  Archibald 153
  Betsey 31
  Christian 319
  Christiana E. 360
  Elisabeth 39
  Elizabeth 250
  Elizabeth C. 237
  H. H. 263
  Harriet 59
  India F. 263
  James 20
  James E. 225

Turner (cont.)
  Jas. A. 61
  John 19, 282, 347, 354
  Judy 17
  Lewis 319
  Lucy Ann 364
  Lucy R. 94, 156
  Maria 319
  Mark C. 31
  Martha 282
  Mary A. 331
  Mary A. (Mrs.) 263
  Mary P. 138
  Mildred 174
  Nancey 100
  Nancy 367
  Nancy B. 156
  O. W. 76
  Patsey 213
  Rebeca W. (Mrs.) 48
  Reeves 277
  Rhodey 76
  Richard H. 101, 182
  Sarah 81, 245
  Stephen R. 282
  Susannah 195
  Talitha 330
  Thos. 174
  Winnefred 346
Twisdal, Ann 128
Twisdale, Frances 276
  Letta 293
  Nancy 128
  Polly Ann 357
Twisdel, Elizabeth 222
Tyler, Betsy Ann 172
  Fanny 79
  Frances 79, 193, 280
  Leml. 10
  Lemuel 9, 331
  Lucy 105
  Margaret 79
  Mary 11, 229
  Mary Jane 79
  Wm. 185
Tylor, Ann 266
  Bartlet 308
Tyner, Arthur 331
  John 228
  Jonathan 266
  Patsey 266
  Uriah 331
Tynor, Anna 316
Ullerson(?), Mary 127, 128
Umphstead, Mary 130
Umstead, Abraham 204
Umstead, Isabella 339
  L. W. 339
  Lucy 285
  Margaret F. 335
  Richd. H. 256
Umsted, Ann 214
  William 214
Underwood, Lucy 57
Upchurch, Archd. H. 269
  Catey 173
  Elizabeth 185
  John 14
  John G. 338
  Martha 134
  Mary A. W. 253
  Mary Ann 257
  Priscilla M. 203
  W. H. 283
  Wm. A. 283
Usry, Adeline 361

Usry (cont.)
  Arabella C. 177
  Emily 231
  Frances 345
  Jane 231, 332
  Martha 215
  Thomas E. 229
  Thos. H. 168
  William 231, 332
Ussery, Kitty 168
  Lucy 65
  Nancy 120
  Salley 143
  Sarah W. 75
  Temperance 205, 358
Valentine, Abel 333
  Austin 21
  Bob 79
  Chesley James 333
  Elijah 190, 265
  John 332
  Judith 153
  Nancey 219
  P. 354
  Pleasant 333
  Ruthy 269
  Selina Ann 20
Vandyck, Jno. 131
  John 49
Vandyke, Anne Bullock 219
  Mary 131
Vane(?), Wm. D. E. 122
Vass, Benaham 333
  Elennor 304
  Elizabeth 73, 261
  John 241
  Margaret 117
  Martha 295
  Mary 116
  Nancy 149
  Ooney 333
  Parthenia P. 176
  Polly Ann 27
  Polly T. 22
  Robert H. 295, 300
  Rodah 303
  Salley 160
  Thomas, Jr. 27
  Thos. 116
  Thos., Jr. 77
  W. W. 313
Vasser, Levy 251
Vaughan, Brewer 195, 196
  Caroline 40
  Caswell 194
  Catharine 196
  Celestia A. 330
  Dinecy 310
  Elizabeth H. 40, 338
  Emily 161
  Fanny 99
  Frances 93, 272
  Isabella 280
  J. 277
  Jackson 40
  James 76, 174, 219, 254, 303
  James M. 262
  Jane 31, 271
  Jas. 50
  John 99, 176
  John J. 35
  Lumaga 330
  Martha 99, 271, 272
  Mary 31
  Mary E. 35, 41

Vaughan (cont.)
  Orsborn 334
  Patsey 94
  Peter G. 110, 303
  Polly 334
  Rebecah 143
  Rebecca 277
  Robt. 141
  Sarah 237
  Stephen 191
  Woodard 99
Vaughn, Asa 81
  David 62
  Frances 272
  James 334
  Jane 272
  Lettie 62
  Mary A. 62
  Polly 334
Veasey, William 157
Veazey, Abner 368
  Alfred M. 335
  Elijah 278, 332
  Elizabeth 29, 174, 307
  Emily J. 245
  Ezekiel 282
  Fielding 335
  Jemima 218
  John C. 218
  M. W. B. 339
  Margaret F. 335
  Mary 339
  Mary A. W. 257
  Milly 181
  Narcissa 295
  Rebecca 282
  Tiny 335
Veazy, Elijah 347
  Mark 67
Venable, A. H. 196
  Catharine 92
  Frances 44
  Geo. H. 237
  Isabella Brown 220
  Jane 176
  Martha E. 237
  Mary G. 82
  Mary Susan 176
  T. Brown 132
  Viney 259
Vilet, Lewis 309
Vincent, Amy 73
  Elizabeth 257
  Henry H. 56, 335
  Isaac 38
  Ishman 92
  Jacob, Jr. 315
  John M. 215
  John Merrit 219
  Louisa 311
  Margaret 65
  Mary 204, 327, 329
  Peter 314
  Rachel 335
  William 335
Volentine, Eligh 336
  Mary 106, 292
  Peggy 256
  Susan B. 316
  Wm. 292
  Wm. P. 20
Voluntine, Austin 193
  Elizabeth 171
Vowel, Mathew 336
Waddey, Elisabeth 25
  James 25
Waddle, Nancy L. 61

Wade, Benjamin 336
  Charity 195
  Elizabeth 272
  Margaret 92
  Mary 327
  Nancy 74
  Priscilla 272
  Rebecah 201
  Robt. 327
  Sary 16
  William H. 181
  Wm. H. 38
Wadford, Alexander 348
  William 115
Wadkins, John 193
Waggoner, George 292
  Henry 292
Waggstaff, Nancey 228
Wagoner, (?) 336
  John 336
  Mahala 93
  Viney 103
Wagstaff, Britania 304
  Elizabeth 268
  Frances 336
  John S. 336
  Jos. J. 360
  L. B. 305
  Louisa 263
  Salinea 77
  Sarah Alice 51
  Sophia 259
Wainwright, Rosabella B. 331
Walace, Sarah 250
Waldo, Catherine 337
  J. 70, 132
  Jos. 337
Waldon, Matilda 93
Walker, A. A. 92
  A. H. 183
  A. N. 190
  Amanda J. 296
  Ambrillas 222
  Ann 338, 356
  Ann V. 25
  Anthony 321
  B. 271
  Betsey 323
  Betsy 53
  C. W. 211, 332
  Caroline 93
  Coley 337
  Daniel 21
  Eless 337, 367
  Elis 109
  Elisabeth 72
  Elizabeth 166, 184, 206, 315
  Ellen 131
  Elless 180
  Emily 337
  George 338
  Glafrey H. 293
  Hannah 292
  Henry 293
  J. 155
  James 184, 337
  Jane Ellen 315
  Jarrat 338
  Jarret 338
  Jarrot 338
  Jno. 66
  John 54, 217, 339, 340
  John J. 54
  Joseph 285, 337
  Leanah 184

Walker (cont.)
  Lorenzo 54
  Lucy 165, 204, 261, 317, 337, 340
  Ludie W. 225
  Martha 24, 252
  Mary 121, 127, 134, 337
  Milly 46, 185
  Nancy Adeline 53
  Nathan 338
  Nathaniel 338
  Nelley 54
  Paul 310
  Polly 54
  R. H. 110
  Ransom 263
  Reany 338
  Rebecca 162
  Rebecker 211
  Rena 339
  Sallie 54
  Sallie J. 126
  Samuel 356
  Sarah 312, 339
  Solo. 86, 227
  Solomon 233, 317, 365
  Susan 326
  Susanna 233
  Susannah 270
  William 54, 131, 312
  William M. 283
  Willis 53
  Wm. 45, 61, 337
Wall, (?) (Major) 91
  Burgess 370
  Elizabeth 370
  Julia 2
  Mary 161
  Miles S. 2
  Permelia J. 133
  Rebecca Ann 334
  Virginia 51
Wallace, Mary 93
Waller, Adeline 365
  Allen 129
  Ann O. 326
  Barbary 129
  Betsey 188
  Caroline F. 127
  Critty 325
  Eliza 191
  Elizabeth 335
  Fannie 225
  Felice 299
  Frances 112
  Francis 203
  Frankey 331
  Harriet 204
  Jas. 38
  Job 339
  John 204, 339
  Joseph, Jr. 181
  Louisa G. 331
  Lucy 127
  Martha 331
  Mary 212
  Mary O. 212
  Mildred 12
  Mildred E. 326
  Nancy 114
  Patience 339
  Peggey 293
  Saluda 338
  Suffia 272
  Thos. 52
  Virginia 262
  Zeph. 12

Waller (cont.)
  Zephaniah 350
  Ziby Ann 212
Walls, Sally 179
Walsh, Jo. 123
Walters, Mary 244
  Pheba 169
Walthall, T. S. 307
Walton, Ann H. C. 29
  Barbary 200
  Henry C. 304
  Pamelia S. 108
Ward, George 193
  Mary 55, 119
  Patsey 27
  Peyton 29
  Polley 7
  Sarah 119
  Susannah 186
  William 26
Ware, Polley 237
  Sally E. (Mrs.) 246
  Thomas T. 273
Warf, Polley 72
Warmuth, William 180
Warren, Catarine 129
  Isham H. 124
  James 266
Washington, (?) 364
  Alexander 55, 340
  Aley 218
  Barbara Ann 55
  Catharine 315
  Demeris 55
  Emmit 123
  Jas. 340
  Jennie 212
  John 250
  Martha 192
  Mary Ann 370
  Millington 192
  Rebecca 129
  Rowan 285
  Salley 232
  Saml. P. 346
  Wm. G. 116, 166
  Woodson 114, 285
Watkins, Arreny N. 99
  Barbara 342
  Bettie 11
  Chana 11
  Christianna 170
  Delila M. 349
  Delphia 180
  Demcy 341
  Emily 81
  Emma 63
  Fannie 341
  Geo. 132
  H. T. 44
  Hanah 138
  James 342
  Jane 102
  Judith C. 46
  Lawson 138
  Lucy 128
  Luvenia 341
  Martha Ann 99
  Mary 262
  Mary A. 149
  Mary E. 341
  Mildred W. B. 341
  Sallie 128
  Sallie A. 99, 244
  William 11
Watson, (?) 139
  Charity 9
  John 9

Watson (cont.)
  John G. 343
  Mary Ann R. 121
  Mary M. 207
  Mathew 191
  S. R. 289
Watters, Jacob 73
  Jno. 1
Watterwhite, Solomon 245
Weak, Charles H. 118
Weather, Penelope P. 135
  Prudence 80
Weathers, Catharine 206
  Charity 238
  Charles H. 123
  Edward 154, 235, 361
  Elisabeth 43
  Emma A. 219
  James 342
  Jane 294
  Lucy 117
  Math. 260
  Nancy 154, 342
  Nathaniel H. 180
  Penney 118
  Piety 235
  Polly 154, 181, 361
  Robert 119
  Temperancy 187
Weaver, Absolem 343
  Amey 35, 343
  Ann Eliza 57
  Anne 136
  Dudley 300
  Elisabeth 72, 248
  Elizabeth 94
  Emily 12
  Isaac 148
  Jane 62
  Jas. 60
  Jemima 125
  John 17
  John W. 107
  Leuvinia 18
  Lucy 136
  Manus 12, 18
  Maria 269
  Martha 263
  Mary 359
  Mary A. 141
  Matilday 308
  Nancy 178
  Sally 1
  Susan 343
  Susannah 196
  William 62, 124, 178
  William G. 343
  William H. 57
Weazey, Elijah 42, 316
Webb, Amey 305
  Ann 260
  Dinah 208
  Edmund 344
  Elisabeth 251
  Frances 234, 291
  Isaac 90
  Isabella 145
  J. H. 148
  Jinnie 208
  Jas. L. 147
  John H. 71, 75
  Lewis 350
  Lucy 324
  Lucy A. 364
  Margaret C. 66
  Martha 44

Webb (cont.)
  Martha Ann 344
  Martha Y. 90
  Mary 83, 304
  Mary E. 143
  Mimcock 208
  Nancy 227, 324, 344
  Nelson 227, 324, 344
  Polly 344
  Rachael 171
  Sarah F. 4
  Thomas 89
  William 251
Webster, Jas. B. 44, 150, 311
Welch, Hilliard 264, 340
  Martha 144
  Nancey 345
  Nancy 34
  Rebecca 137
Weldon, Candess 259
  Danl. 207
  Harriet 5
  Priscilla 179
Wells, Elisha 221
  Elizabeth 79
  George H. 128
  Jas. H. 205
  Prissilla 221
  Tassa 230
Welsh, Martha 17
Wembish, Betsey 207
Wesley, Joseph 327
West, (?)-ry 221
  A. S. 255
  Alee 38
  Alex. 346
  B. H. 345
  Caroline 132
  Elisabeth 64
  Elizabeth 292
  Elizabeth J. 293
  Elizabeth Jane 345
  Elizabeth S. 248
  Ellis 262
  Faithy 294
  Hardemon 97, 345
  Hardiman 345
  Isabella 97
  James 346
  Jane 238, 351
  Jas. R. 346
  John 101
  Joseph 346
  Lizzie 324
  Lucinda 196, 346
  Margaret B. 345
  Martha 119, 210
  Mary 346
  Mary A. 97
  Nancy 132, 243
  Peter 345
  Peyton 81, 264
  Sally Ann 346
  Sarah 38
  Stella 191
  Susan 345, 346
  Susannah 116
  Thos. 77
  William 345
  Willis 97
Western, Sarah Elliott 357
Wever, Edney 328
Wethers, Prissilla 55
Wharf, George 65
Whatley, Michl. 96
Wheelar, Sarah 97

Wheeler, Betsey 12
  Celiah 346
  Dicey 190
  Edna 190
  Eliza 344
  Eliza J. 307
  Elizabeth 23, 127,
    224, 354
  Elvira 310
  Emeline 150
  Ezekiel 84, 191, 347
  Hannah 75
  Harriston 240
  Henry 12, 55, 114,
    225
  James 299
  Jane 109
  Jesse 311
  John G. 2
  Larcena 310
  Levina 331
  Line 187
  Lotty 130
  Louisa J. 63
  Martin 112, 188, 192
  Milly 125
  Moses 285, 310
  Murry 38
Wheeler(?), Paul H.
    311
  Polly 347
  Pricilla 130
  Rebecca 225
  Seley M. 256
  Silvia 187
  Susan 150
  Winneford 40
Wheelor, Winneford 247
Wheler, Benjamin 97
  Edy 40
Whicker, Benjamin, Jr.
    135
Whitacer, M. J. 44
Whitaker, Wm. H. 126
White, Abigal 70
  Alley 297
  Ann 8
  Buck 64
  Bulky 75
  Caroline N. 176
  Catharine 44
  Celia 212
  Coleman 348
  D. C. 148
  Elisabeth 260
  Elizabeth 7
  Elizabeth R. 297
  Emeline R. 170
  Emily 57
  Frances A. 238
  Frank 146
  George 348
  Gertrude E. 283, 285
  Hasky Ann 183
  Henry 17
  Hixey 361
  Holly D. 229
  Jacksey 300
  James 219
  James A. 135
  James H. 233
  Jemima 348, 350
  Jno. 215
  John 194, 359
  Joseph 122, 318, 332
  Joshua 6, 42, 168,
    347, 348, 359
  Kinelm 163

White (cont.)
  Larken 41
  Louisa G. 295
  Lucy C. 367
  Manerva G. 295
  Mark 16, 203, 213,
    214, 347
  Martha 296
  Mary 193, 324
  Mary Ann 29
  Mary Jane 192
  Mary R. 38
  Mary S. 112
  Miles 6
  Nancy 6
  Panola 64
  Philoe 197
  Polley 335
  Rhody 146
  Robert 29, 348
  Sally 295
  Seth 107
  Sison W. 337
  Susanna 215
  Tabitha 2, 64
  Thomas 258
  Valentine 293, 332
  W. P. 122
  William H. 28
  Wm. L. 242
  Wm. S. 134
  Wm. W. 311
Whitefeild, Patsey 158
Whiten, Nancy 278
Whitfield, Ann E. 233
  D. H. 16, 103, 215
  Elizabeth 272
  Emily N. 6
  J. E. 214
  M. Z. 294
  Margarette E. 330
  Martha C. 155
  Martha H. 44
  Mary 158
  Milly 7
  N. G. 237, 357
  Nancy K. 30
  Patsey 158
  Sarah 368
  Wesly 30
Whithead, Levi 167
Whitler, Elizabeth Susan
    133
Whitloe, Ann Hicks 349
Whitlow, Jesse 254
  Polley 72
Whitt, Samuel F. 100
  Susan A. 334
Whitted, Levi 167
Whobery, John 87
Wicker, Marey 358
  Mary 75
Wier, W. T. 18
Wiggins, Anderson 243
  Asjain(?) 81
  Bettie 213
  Edney H. 289
  Elizabeth 278
  Francis 133
  Fredk., Sr. 349
  G. C. 31, 104, 115,
    147, 148, 216, 257,
    365
  Jas. M. 65, 80, 85,
    122, 124, 131, 196,
    216, 234, 258, 363
  Jno. 81
  John 96, 143, 330, 334

Wiggins (cont.)
  Joseph 299
  July 243
  Lucy A. 101
  Martha A. 350
  Martha Ann 337
  Mary Eliza 77
  Molley 228
  Nancey 31
  Sealah 88
  W. R. 230
Wilbon, Frances 225
Wilborn, George 211
  Martha 71
Wilbourn, Jane 207
  R. P. 270
Wilburn, John 225
Wiles, Habun 143
  Jas. 366
  Overton 158
Wiley, C. H. 269
Wilkerson, Amelia 283
  Amey 43, 295
  Ann 352
  Ann J. 346
  Catharine 1
  Charles 352
  Correna H. 232
  D. S. 291
  David 294, 346, 351
  Elijah 222
  Elizabeth 32, 111
  Elizabeth J. 351
  Ella 222
  Emaly D. 351
  Emily K. 28
  Fanny 247
  Frances 273
  Franklin 351
  Franky 297
  George 325
  George W. 351
  Harriett 108
  Harris 350
  Henney W. 94
  Howel T. 117
  Isabella 107
  James 100
  James H. 351
  Jane 97
  Jane O. 329
  Jno. D. 351
  John 22, 231
  Joseph A. 82
  Judy 291
  Letty 267
  Levi 114
  Loney 128
  Louisa 51
  Lucy A. 82
  Margaret 226, 352
  Martha 218, 275, 329,
    338, 350
  Mary 152, 303
  Mary Ann 112
  Mary F. 353
  Nancy 196, 351
  Patsy 325
  Rebecca 325
  Rhoda 98
  Royal 352
  Salley 98, 297
  Sallie E. 24
  Sarah 82, 100, 217
  Sarah Ann 47
  Sarah F. 82
  Solomon 291
  Sophia 283

Wilkerson (cont.)
  Spencer 329
  Spencer G. 351
  Susan 45, 351
  Tabby B. 351
  Tabitha 329
  Wiat 37
  Wilmuth 72
Wilkes, John S. 188
Wilkins, Adaline 33
  Amanda F. 28
  Ann 188
  Caroline V. 353
  Clement 75, 355, 361
  Elisabeth 142
  L. S. 33
  Leroy 235
  Leroy P. 242
  Mary 201
  Mary S. 13
  Nancy 221
  Pocaman 334
  Polley 87
  Rebecca 147
Wilkinson, A. J. 82
  Francis M. 221
  Lucy 255
  Stephen 190
  Wm. E. 193
Willburn, Martha 279
Willeford, (?) (Squire) 87
  Lunsford 79
  Susan 353
  Tilly 282
Willey, Thomas 254
Williams, Agatha 48
  Agey 275
  Agness 80
  Airy Ann 147
  Alfred 88, 307
  Annie 312
  Austan 316
  Benjamin 280
  Bettie 174
  Charles 72
  Charlotte 222
  Crecy 307
  David L. 150
  E. A. 138
  Eliza 98, 215
  Eliza Ann 22, 153
  Elizabeth 93, 243, 271
  Elizabeth A. 305
  Elizabeth N. 226
  Elleanor 137
  Fanny 170
  Frances 299, 357
  Gideon 266, 272, 328
  Gilly 34
  H. 132
  Harriet 322
  Harriss 329
  Henry 354
  J. 356
  J. H. 51
  James 250
  Jane 32
  John 113, 129, 156, 172, 315, 355
  John J. 157
  John, Jr. 45
  Johnathan 354
  Joseph 354
  Joseph, Jr. 342
  Joseph G. 183
  Judith 113

Williams (cont.)
  Julia 307
  Julia Ann 13
  Latitia 98
  Leonard 179, 195, 355
  Lettey 331
  Lolly 19
  Lucy 143, 196, 261, 355
  Martha 55, 119, 121, 264, 303
  Mary 210, 307, 323, 354
  Mary Ann 342
  Mary E. 55
  Miles 88
  Nancy 32, 342
  Nathaniel 5, 209
  P. 355
  Patience 287
  Penny 312
  Person 167, 305
  Peter 312
  Phillis 228
  Phoebe 324
  Polley 72
  Polly 330, 335
  Presley 3
  Priscilla 233
  Prissillah 31
  Rebecah 127
  Rebecca 221
  Robert 354, 356
  Robt. 309
  Rowan P. 72
  Ralph 233
  Sally 306
  Sam. F. 322
  Saml. A. 98, 100, 123, 136, 146, 212, 215, 220, 305, 307
  Saml. S. 11
  Samuel F. 71
  Sarah 167, 356
  Sarah T. 137
  Sary 209
  Solo. 72
  Solomon 166, 357
  Susan D. 210
  Susannah 311
  Thomas 85, 91, 169, 208, 293, 354, 355
  Thos. L. 311
  Ursula 277
  William 23, 137, 236
  William, Jr. 357
  William G. 356
  Willie 80, 195, 353
  Wm. 56
  Wm. D. 356
Williamson, Amanda 366
  B. F. 212, 340
  B. R. 242
  James 239
  Jas. R. 358
  Julia 62
  Lonia 366
  Melinda 358
  Roselia 13
  Wm. 293
Willie, Jesse 252
  L. K. 37, 42, 148, 164, 197, 269
  Lewis K. 246
  Tho. H. 144
Williford, Mary 365
  Squire 32
  Susan 365

Willis, Elisabeth 65
  Mary 288
  Wm. 25
Willowford, Rebecca 248
Wilmoth, James 273
Wilson, Alexander 9
  Amanda O. 58
  Amy 134
  Armistead 17
  Benja. 228
  Benjamin 158
  Bolden 278
  Bowlin W. 298
  Dionysthea T. 310
  Edney J. 241
  Elija J. 200
  Elizabeth 134, 289
  Elizabeth A. 4
  Elvira S. 255
  Emily 251
  Fanny 63, 240
  Frances 167
  Francis 76, 267, 320
  Frank 167, 359
  Henrietta 68
  Henry 158, 359
  Henry B. 178
  Jane 191
  Jemima P. 17
  Jno. 178
  John 31, 240, 269, 309, 343, 358, 360
  John R. 200
  L. 267
  Lethe 358
  Lindy B. 199
  Linsey M. 178
  Malisa A. 211
  Margaret 221
  Marinda 183
  Marinun 245
  Martha 167, 181, 359
  Martha A. 359
  Mary 158, 206, 263
  Masey 134
  Mildred 205
  Nancy 17
  Polly 289
  Priccilla 359
  Rachel 209
  Rebeca 343
  Robert 125, 358, 359, 360
  S. P. 359
  Sabilla 128
  Sally 209
  Samuel P. 209, 216, 358
  Sarah 125, 321
  Sarah A. 150
  Sarah C. 293
  Sarah F. 340
  Sherard 4
  Solomon 359
  Solomon G. 17
  Stacy 4
  Susan 197, 295
  Susan A. 267
  Susannah 295
  Tempey 332
  Thos. 59
  Virginia H. 103
  William 251, 312
  Wm. H. 58
Wimbish, Caroline 138
  Henrietta 13
Wimbush, Caroline 360
  Peter 360

Winbush, Gabe 366
  Lucy 366
  Martha An 366
Winfield, Henderson 71, 180
  Mary 180
  Sallie 98
  Susan 71
Winfree, Collins 267
  Edney 308
  Nancy 249
  Sarah 241
Winfrey, Ann 241
  Anna 267
Winkfield, Nancy 8
Winn, Harriet C. 361
Winningham, Delilah 91
  Lucy 50
  Massey 133
  Sherwood 133
Winston, Ann 180
  C. 127
  Candis 203
  Catharine 263
  Charity 261
  D. 26
  E. 361
  Eady 261
  Elijah 203, 342
  Frances 369
  Isaac 356
  James 340
  James A. 312
  Martha J. 184
  Mary 137, 322
  Mary A. 203
  Nancy 248
  Nancy D. 340
  Priety 180
  Prudence 147
  Sarah 164
  Sidney 220
Winters, Bailey 57
Wirt, Wm. A. 51
Wise, Roxanna 194
Witehill, W. B. 305
Witherspon, Nannie 361
  Hyram 361
Wolff, Wm. B. 210
Womack, Cordelia L. 227
Wood, A. F. 94
  Alex. 2
  Anthony 247
  Anthony B. 52, 247
  Benjamin 124
  Catharine 16, 212, 247
  Charlotte 156
  Elisabeth 225
  Elizabeth 212
  Emily F. (Mrs.) 247
  James M. 221
  Jane 60, 69, 360
  Joanna 247
  Joannah 23
  John 24, 46, 196, 353
  Lucy 52
  Martha 148, 200
  Mary 163
  Mary D. 73
  Michael 327
  N. 261
  Nancy 92, 165
  Patsey 247
  Penuel 200
  Permellah 287
  Peyton 69, 108, 127, 315

Wood (cont.)
  Polley 32
  Rebecca B. 162
  Richard 163, 247, 348
  Richd. S. 83
  Robert T. 148
  Sally 52
  Sally Ann 251
  Sarah 258
  Sarah E. 329
  Tabitha 198
  Thomas B. 278
  William C. 362
Woodall, Absalom 147
  Judith 147
Woodfork, Lucy 175
Wooding, Alfred 205
Woodleff, John B. 124
Woodley, Polley 214
Woodlief, Martha 362
Woodlieff, Johnathan 256
Woodliff, Ann 363
  Ann Eliza J. 37
  Celestia 341
  Cornelius 363
  Elizabeth 341
  J. B. 363
  John 363
  Martha 238, 308, 340, 363
  Mary 267, 363
  Priscilla 88
  Thos. 164
Woodlock, Rhoda 237
Woodmon, Susanna 208
Woodward, W. 207
Wooten, Dinna 173
  James 364
  Martha 2
  Mary 32
Wooton, Edmund 225
  Spivey 18
Wotten, Martha A. 12
Worel, Martha Ann 211
Worham, William 82
Worls, Sally 139
Wormath, Mourning 225
Wornal, Nancy Ann 327
Worp, George 83
Worrel, Thos. 58
Worrell, Lindy 102
  Maria T. 355
Worsham, Francis H. 257
  P. H. 67
Wortham, Benjamin H. 81
  Cams. 133
  E. W. 141
  Geo. 84
  Henry 64
  J. J. 180
  James 18
  Martha 18
  Mary E. 27, 122
  Mary J. 122
  Polley 242
  Susannah 85
  Susanna A. 180
Worthan, Leonard 363
Worthington, Margaret M. 174
  Sallie 70
  Saml. 235
  William 174
  Willie 174
Worworth, Wm. W. 180
Wren, Clarissa 159
  Lily 16

Wrenn, Caroline 17
  Mary Ann 89
  Mary R. 363
Wright, Bartlet 278
  Benjamin 33
  Charlott 21
  D. 30
  Delsey 151
  Elizabeth 216
  Erasmus 23
  Frances 365
  Harriett 44
  Irana 274
  James 233
  Jno. H. 159
  John H. 365
  John L. 364
  Jordan 255
  Judith 192
  Lucy 99
  Lucy Ann 257
  Margret 317
  Martha 13
  Mary 25, 98, 100
  Mary Ann 184
  Mary E. 167
  Mary Pirdon 65
  Newton 156
  Pencie M. 344
  Phebah 255
  Rebecca 219
  Rhoda 139
  Sarah 110, 233
  Sophia C. 365
  Sophia H. 51
  Thomas 209
  Wealthy 79
  Woodson 365
Write, Mary 317
Wrothill, Elizabeth 112
Wyars, Peggy 68
Wyche, Anna 365
  Charlotte 12
  Elizabeth 325
  George 365
  Louisa 309
  Robert H. 325
Wyers, Elisabeth 193
Wynn, Ann 109
  Sarah Ann 363
Wynne, Jos. 248
  Joshua 99
  Williamson 268
Yance, Mollie E. 137
Yancey, Absolem 366
  Absalom 33, 133, 205
  Allen 248
  Amanda 326
  Annis 294
  Bartlett 22, 270
  Benj. W. 352
  Betty 233
  Calvin 352
  Charles 274, 361
  Chas. 317
  Dolley 205
  E. B. 102
  Eliza 250
  Henry 48
  Indianer 366
  James 33, 187, 294
  James, Jr. 251, 366
  James E. 137
  Jane 294
  Jenny 317
  Jinsey 61
  Mary 209
  Mary C. 28, 29

Yancey (cont.)
  Mary V. C. 348
  Nancy 309, 352
  P. H. 249
  Perlona 352
  Philip, Jr. 249
  Richard E. 241
  Robt., Jr. 161
  Roxy Ann 277
  Ruffin 67
  Sam 366
  Sena 366
  Sterling 58, 73, 137, 219, 317, 366
  Thomas 350
  Thornton 187
  Tryon 278
  Virginia C. 259
  William 366
  Wm. 366
  Wm. C. 13
Yancy, Allin 231
  C. A. 124
  Hezekiah 326
  John H. 366
  Joseph 358
  Lucy 366
  Martha 283
  Martha E. 206
  Sarah 189
  Thornton 56
Yarbrough, Thos. 158
Yates, Ann B. 329
Yearborough, Clora 208
  Jacob 208
  Nellie 208
Yeargan, James 367
  Susan 367
Yeargin, Dorris 367
Yoakley, Salley 54
Yokely, Mark 54
  Nancy 54
  Prudence 55
York, Caroline 233
  Clinthy 189
  Dilly 336
  Elisabeth 270
  Fanney 121
  Frances H. 300
  John 367
  John W. 29, 75, 316
  John W., Jr. 329
  Lucy Ann 189
  Margerite 367
  Margret 203
  Martha 104
  Mary 23
  Mary R. 298
  Narcissa H. 112
  Polley 119
  Sarah Jane 29
  Susan A. 29
  Thomas, Jr. 270
  William 367
  William C. 111
Young, (?) 95, 324
  Ab 368
  Angelin 278
  Ann Eliza 368
  Ann T. 309
  Arabella 325
  Bella 290
  B. F. 313
  D. E. 8, 78, 80, 206, 290, 304, 306
  D. J. 9, 180, 182, 360
  David J. 264, 294

Young (cont.)
  Elisabeth 314
  Ellen 253
  Frances 344
  Francis 368
  Francis E. 309
  George 290
  Harriet J. 69
  James 367
  Jane 318
  Jas. 280
  Joe 309
  John 27, 143, 368, 369
  John, Jr. 318
  John George 368
  Louisa 368
  Lucy A. 316
  Madison 149, 220, 295
  Mary 177
  Mary A. 309
  Mary C. 316
  Millicent(?) 109
  Millicent 275
  Milly B. 53
  Richd. 325
  Sally D. 20
  Saml. 158
  Samuel D. 368
  Sarah 27
  Stephen 278, 325
  Susan 368
  W. W., Jr. 260
  Wesley W. 213, 361
  Wm. W. 368

ADDITIONS

Avarett, Nancy P. 353
  Wyatt 353
Brinkley, Clony 277
  Eady E. 87
  Edna 64
Eliott, Mary 102
Farrah, Rebecca 305

Gressom, Eugene 342
Hillyard, Wm. 182
Jenkins, Priestly 170
Jones, Robert 266
Kenaday, Lucina 143
Lewis, Riah 324
McKissack, Jonathon 269

Miner, William 235
Norman, John 344
Ragland, James M. 311
Rowland, Fanny 37
  Henry 101
Stanton, Rody 90
  Salley 140
Williams, (?) H. 276

www.ingramcontent.com/pod-product-compliance
Lightning Source LLC
Chambersburg PA
CBHW071225290426
44108CB00013B/1299